THE ART OF TEACHING SCIENCE

THE ART OF TEACHING SCIENCE

Inquiry and Innovation in Middle School and High School

Jack Hassard

Georgia State University

New York   Oxford
OXFORD UNIVERSITY PRESS
2005

Oxford University Press

Oxford   New York

Auckland   Bangkok   Buenos Aires   Cape Town   Chennai
Dar es Salaam   Delhi   Hong Kong   Istanbul   Karachi   Kolkata
Kuala Lumpur   Madrid   Melbourne   Mexico City   Mumbai   Nairobi
São Paulo   Shanghai   Taipei   Tokyo   Toronto

Copyright © 2005 by Oxford University Press, Inc.

Published by Oxford University Press, Inc.
198 Madison Avenue, New York, New York, 10016
http://www.oup.com

Oxford is a registered trademark of Oxford University Press

Library of Congress Cataloging-in-Publication Data

Hassard, Jack.
The art of teaching science : inquiry and innovation in Middle School and High School/Jack Hassard.
       p.   cm.
    Includes bibliographical references and index.
    ISBN 0-19-515533-5 (pbk. : alk. paper)
      1. Science teachers—Training of—Handbooks, manuals, etc.   2. Science—Study and teaching
    (Secondary)—Handbooks, manuals, etc.   I. Title.
Q181.H156 2004
507′.11—dc22   2003020864

Text design by Cathleen Elliott

Printing number: 9 8 7 6 5 4 3 2 1

Printed in the United States of America
on acid-free paper

BRIEF CONTENTS

CONTENTS

PART 3 CONNECTING THEORY AND PRACTICE IN SCIENCE TEACHING

CHAPTER 8 Assessing Active Science
Learning • **299**

PART 4 STRATEGIES OF SCIENCE TEACHING

CHAPTER 9 Strategies Fostering Thinking in the Science Classroom • 331

CHAPTER 10 Facilitating Learning in the Science Classroom • 369

PREFACE

Science teachers and researchers have shown that all students are capable of learning science. *The Art of Teaching Science* is designed to help you achieve this vision and important goal of science teaching. The vision of all students learning science is highly dependent upon the beliefs we have about science, pedagogy, and students. Students learn when they are provided the opportunity to experience the richness of science through active inquiry and collaboration with peers and adults, as well as the tools to promote learning. The context of learning in this vision is humanistic through creative and imaginative encounters with teachers.

The Art of Teaching Science is rooted in the philosophy and structure of an earlier work, *Minds on Science*. *The Art of Teaching Science* extends this earlier work by providing a new organization of the context and focusing the preparation of science teachers on professional artistry. In this view, the *learning to teach process* involves encounters with peers, professional teachers, and science teacher educators. To help readers of this book achieve this goal, a number of pedagogical learning tools have been integrated into the text. These tools involve inquiry and experimentation and reflection through writing and discussion, as well as experiences with students, science curriculum, and pedagogy. Becoming a science teacher is a creative process. In the view espoused here, you will be encouraged to "invent" and "construct" ideas about science teaching through your interaction with your peers, teachers, and your instructors.

The Art of Teaching Science is a science teaching handbook/methods textbook designed for the professional development of middle and high school science teachers. The experiential tools in the book allow for its use in pre- and in-service teacher education environments. Science education in the early part of the twenty-first century will be characterized by profound changes in our understanding of the goals of science teaching, as well as the establishment of a new cadre of educators. I have written *The Art of Teaching Science* to provide meaningful learning experiences and connections with the most recent research and understanding of science teaching for this new cadre of science teachers.

The Art of Teaching Science is organized into four parts:

- Part 1: The Art of Teaching Science (a reconnaissance and view of science for all)
- Part 2: The Goals and Curriculum of School Science
- Part 3: Connecting Theory and Practice in Science Teaching
- Part 4: Strategies of Science Teaching

I invite you to explore the book experientially. In fact, I have included brief introductory comments in each chapter under the heading How to Read This Chapter, which I hope will help you decide how and what to read in the book.

Each chapter is divided into two sections: the first focuses on the content of the major theme of the chapter; the second is a newspaper-like feature called the *Science Teacher Gazette*, which contains a variety of strategies to help you extend your science teaching learning experience.

Throughout the book you will find a variety of what I call "pedagogical learning tools" that are based on the belief that we construct our intellectual knowledge of science teaching and that learning to teach is accelerated by:

- hands-on, experiential activity
- minds-on, high-level cognitive engagement
- socially arranged small-group learning
- reflective thinking

I have developed eleven pedagogical learning tools for the book, and you can view them in Table P.1. Perhaps one of the most important tools is the first, *inquiry activities*. I have designed forty-two inquiry activities that will give you the opportunity to creatively explore the dimensions of science teaching to help you construct and extend your professional expertise. I have begun each chapter with a *case study*, a problem-solving dilemma based on actual events about science teaching. You will also find reflective tools, including *think pieces* and *problems and extensions*. These tools should help you think, write, and share your developing ideas with others.

The Art of Teaching Science will bring you into contact with a worldwide community of science educators. I had the privilege of interviewing science teachers from Australia, Botswana, Canada, Chile, Ghana, Japan, Russia, and the United States. I have included some of their views and insights in chapter sections called *Science Teachers Talk*, which contain powerful insights and experiences for you to reflect upon and compare to your own views of teaching. I hope this feature will help you understand the kind of people that are your colleagues and what *they* think about science teaching.

Science teaching also has a very active and influential research community, and I wanted you to be able to connect with some of the research and learn how it affects the teaching of science. Much of the research about science teaching takes place in collaboration with practicing science teachers. Teams of researchers from universities and science education development centers work with colleagues in the K–12 school environment to ask questions about the nature of science teaching. I hope you find these "reports," called *Research Matters*, interesting and informative.

Finally, you will find discussions about science teaching written by educators from Australia, Chile, China, Ghana, Japan, and Russia (Chapter 4). Science education is a global community and the science educators from these countries have given us insight into science teaching in their nation.

Welcome to *The Art of Teaching Science*. I hope you find it an enjoyable experience as you begin or continue your professional development.

Table P.1 Pedagogical Learning Tools

Pedagogical Learning Tool	Purpose	Location in *The Art of Teaching Science*
Inquiry Activities	Science teaching investigations that enable you to reflect on the important concepts of teaching science using hands-on and minds-on processes.	There are forty-two Inquiry Activities located in the first section of each chapter of *The Art of Teaching Science*.
Think Pieces	Short essays (generally no more than two pages) or posters (no larger than one poster board) that reflect your views on some topic or subject in science education.	The *Science Teacher Gazette* of each chapter contains three or more Think Pieces.
Case Studies	Brief case study scenarios that engage you in reflective thinking, role playing, and discussion of science teaching problems pertinent to concepts of the chapter.	Each chapter begins with one, and you'll find more in the the *Science Teacher Gazettes*.
Science Teachers Talk	Craft-talk interviews with several practicing science teachers.	Located in most of the *Science Teacher Gazettes*. The concept is introduced in Chapter 1.
Research Matters	Consumer-type reports of research from the National Association for Research in Science Teaching (NARST) on selected topics on science teaching.	Located in most of the *Science Teacher Gazettes*.
Science-Teaching Literature	Brief essays and articles from journals of science education.	Located in the *Science Teacher Gazette* of most chapters.
Problems and Extensions	Hands-on and minds-on problems designed to engage individuals or cooperative groups in solving problems about science teaching.	Five to seven problems and extensions are located in each of the *Science Teacher Gazettes*.
On the Web	A collection of Internet resources related to the content of the chapter.	Located in the *Science Teacher Gazette* of each chapter.
Readings	Resources from the science-teaching literature pertinent to science teaching.	Located in the *Science Teacher Gazette* of each chapter.
Reflective Teaching	A laboratory encounter with teaching in which lessons are presented to develop a reflective approach to science teaching.	Inquiry Activity 6.1. Sample reflective teaching lessons are located in the *Science Teacher Gazette* of Chapter 6.
Microteaching	A scaled down version of teaching in which teachers present 5–10 minute lessons that are video-taped. Teachers practice models and strategies of teaching.	Inquiry Activity 9.1.

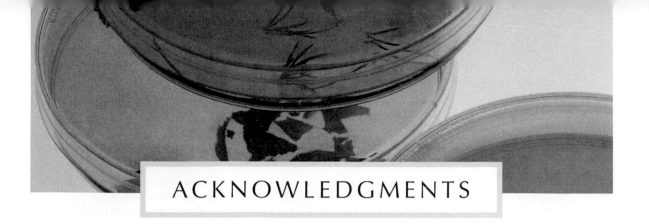

ACKNOWLEDGMENTS

The Art of Teaching Science was a collaboration among many people. I could not have written this book without their help and encouragement. First I wish to thank Karita dos Santos, who when we met was the education editor of Oxford University Press and encouraged me to submit a proposal to write this book. Several science educators reviewed the initial proposal, and I wish to thank them for their critique and recommendations for *The Art of Teaching Science*. First, I wish to thank Mike Dias, professor of science education at the University of Georgia, Athens, for all of his contributions. He has been an active researcher and practitioner for a constructivist approach to science teacher education for many years. His feedback on the proposal and the initial draft of the entire book was extremely important because he represents a new cadre of science teacher educators, and his opinions were extremely valuable. His detailed review provided specific and powerful recommendations that I have included in the final version. I also wish to thank Elaine J. Anderson, professor of science education at Shippensburg University, Shippensburg, Pennsylvania. She was a user of my earlier text, *Minds on Science*, and provided valuable recommendations for changes in the proposal and final draft for this book. Julie Weisberg, formerly a professor of science education at Agnes Scott College, Decatur, Georgia, and now with the Georgia Professional Standards Commission, has continuously given me feedback about the book and provided insight into making changes for a new publication. Lynn A. Bryan, a professor of science education at the University of Georgia, provided generous suggestions for change in my original proposal, especially in the way chapters are organized. I wish to thank each of these outstanding science educators for their expertise and care in providing critiques of my work.

Science educators from various countries wrote responses to interview questions that I used to create the *Science Teachers Talk* sections of the book. These wisdom-of-practice discussions provide brief, yet candid snapshots of teaching from the practitioner's point of view. Some of the interviews were carried over from *Minds on Science* and I wish to thank those educaters: Ginny Almeder, a former biology teacher from Georgia; Bob Miller, a biology teacher from Texas; Jerry Pelletier, a junior high teacher from California; John Ricciardi, a physics and astronomy teacher from Nevada; Dale Rosene, a middle school teacher from Michigan; and Mary Wilde, a middle school teacher from Georgia. To extend the *Science Teachers Talk* sections for this book, I interviewed two different groups of teachers, one with ten to fifteen years of teaching experience and the other comprising first-year teachers. The experienced teachers included Anita Bergman; a middle school teacher from Clayton County, Georgia; Ludmila Bolshakova, a chemistry teacher from

St. Petersburg, Russia; Ben Boza, a science teacher from Gaborone, Botswana; Tom Brown, a former high school science teacher and now professor of science education at Kennesaw State University; Virginia Cheek, a biology teacher from Cobb County, Georgia; Marina Goryunova, computer science teacher and teacher educator from St. Petersburg, Russia; Anna Morton, a middle school teacher from Fulton County, Georgia; Carol Myronuk, a science teacher from Vancouver, Canada; and Barry Plant, a science teacher from Melbourne, Australia.

The first-year teachers I interviewed graduated from a constructivist-based science teacher education program at Georgia State University (TEEMS) and were in their first year of teaching. I wish to thank Ann Gunn, a physics teacher in Futon County, Georgia; Michael O'Brien, a physics teacher in Cobb County, Georgia; and Rachel Zgonc, a middle and high school science teacher at the Westminster School, Atlanta, Georgia.

The Art of Teaching Science includes a global perspective. Science education should be for all students in each nation. To gain insight into science education in other nations, I asked science educators from six countries if they would prepare a short description of the current state of science education in their nation. These educators provided powerful descriptions of science education in their country, and I hope you will find these valuable as you develop your view of education. I wish to thank Roger T. Cross, of Burra, for his piece on Australia; Claudia Rose for writing about science education in Chile; Charles Hutchison for writing about the art of teaching science in Ghana; Ronald F. Price of Melbourne for his discussion of science education in China; Sergei Tolstikov of Moscow for his insights into Russian science education; and Shigehiko Tsaukahara for his article on Japanese science education. Each of these outstanding educators has provided us with an understanding of science teaching in another nation, thereby giving us further insight into our own.

From 1994 until 2003 I worked with the TEEMS science teacher education program at Georgia State University. During that period of time 145 men and women became middle and high school science teachers through a program based on the philosophy and pedagogy that forms the foundation for *The Art of Teaching Science*. Their brilliance and creativity, shown in their internship work and from reports we received of their work in school science, fostered the development of a TEEMS philosophy and provided enormous encouragement and support for the work of the faculty in the program. I wish to thank each of them for what they gave to us and for what they are now giving to their students.

I also wish to thank my colleagues in the field of science education for pursuing their passions and conducting research projects on science education that provide a knowledge base for all of us. I thank them for this work and for being able to include some of their ideas in *The Art of Teaching Science*.

There are several people at Oxford University Press whom I wish to thank, and they include Maura Roessner, assistant editor, Christine D'Antonio, production editor, and Terri O'Prey, copyeditor. Their contributions were professional and engaging and led to the creation of the final manuscript and book.

PART 1

THE ART OF TEACHING SCIENCE

The Art of Teaching Science
A Reconnaissance

"The most important discovery made by scientists was science itself," said Jacob Bronowski, a mathematician, philosopher of science, and teacher. What about science teaching? Have science educators made a comparable discovery about science teaching? Perhaps the discovery approach to learning itself is one candidate. Another candidate could be the discovery that students don't learn science through direct instruction, and instead construct their own knowledge from formal and informal experiences on their own. Maybe the discovery is that science teaching is form of *artistry*. There are many candidates for important "discoveries" that have been made by science educators. If you are interested in finding out about the world of science teaching and fascinating discoveries made by science teachers and researchers about learning, curriculum, and instruction, then this book is for you.

We'll start our exploration of the art of science teaching with a reconnaissance of the field. Just as a scout goes out ahead and looks around to get a view of the scene, so it is with this chapter. You'll look ahead by examining and comparing some of your ideas about science teaching with those of other science teachers. Before you know it, you'll be teaching and participating in science lessons prepared by you and taught to your peers. Next, you'll investigate some conceptions about the nature and philosophy of science and relate this information to approaches to science teaching such as inquiry, cooperative learning, and constructivism. We'll then introduce you to some students via brief vignettes designed to capture the intensity, personal dimensions, and holistic character of the students you'll teach.

Before you get too far into this chapter, I'd like to involve you in a case study, a vignette about an aspect of science teaching. Each chapter of the book will begin with a case study designed to pique your curiosity and involve you in some of the key ideas of the chapter

through reflection and discussion. Let's begin with the case "Kids Are Just Like Scientists."

 Case Study: Kids Are Just Like Scientists

The Case

Northside High School is a mathematics and science magnet school (grades 9–12) in a large metropolitan community. The science department comprises fifteen teachers, three of whom are first-year teachers. Each of the three first-year teachers has been assigned to teach two sections of introductory physical science and three sections of introductory biology. The veteran faculty in the science department are very committed to an inquiry approach to science teaching. Mrs. Thomas, the science department head, at the opening science department meeting reaffirms this by saying that instruction should be based on the assumption that "kids are just like scientists." She points out that students should be taught to think like scientists, that the laboratory experiments should reinforce the way scientists do their work, thereby developing in students the same skills that scientists use. One of the first-year teachers (Ms. Jameson), in a private conversation with the other two first-year teachers, disagrees with this philosophy. She claims that some kids simply don't think the way the scientific community thinks and shouldn't be penalized because of it. She says that other approaches should be considered in formulating the underlying philosophy of instruction. One of her ideas is that science instruction should be more application oriented; that science instruction should show students how science relates to their own lives. She wants to discuss these ideas with Mrs. Thomas. One of the other beginning teachers suggests that she bring it up at the next department meeting in a week.

At the next meeting Mrs. Thomas reacts negatively to Ms. Jameson's ideas. She insists that the kids she teaches are quite capable of scientific thinking, and therefore she can't understand why students in Ms. Jameson's classes wouldn't be capable as well.

The Problem

If you were Ms. Jameson, what would you do in this situation? How would you respond to Mrs. Thomas? What could you do to help Mrs.Thomas understand your view?

How to Read This Chapter

This chapter is a reconnaissance of the profession of science teaching and also a place to begin the learning-to-teach process. Some activities are designed to help you explore some of your prior conceptions about science teaching (e.g., Inquiry Activity 1.1); others are designed to have you investigate the ideas that experienced teachers hold about teaching and that students hold about science. All activities are here to help build on your prior knowledge and help in the construction of your ideas about teaching. You might get the most out of this chapter by skimming the main sections and then coming back to deliberately move though the chapter.

SECTION 1: A RECONNAISSANCE

Invitations to Inquiry

- What are your current views about science teaching? How do these compare with the views of professional science teachers?
- In what ways might science teaching be an art? Do you think that there is artistry to teaching?
- What are some major conceptual ideas about science teaching?
- Why do you want to be a science teacher?
- What do science teachers like most about teaching?
- What are some of the important characteristics of science?
- Is inquiry teaching a valid method in the secondary science classroom? What fosters inquiry? Are there other valid approaches?
- Do scientists and students represent two cultures? If so, how can these cultures be bridged?
- Who are the students we teach? What are they like?
- What characterizes an effective science teacher?

The Artistry of Teaching

Teaching is professional artistry. *The Art of Teaching Science* has been designed to provide encounters in various contexts focused on learning about teaching through reflection and discussion. I've included a number of pedagogical tools that I hope will help you build on and further develop your professional artistry. These tools involve inquiry and experimentation, reflection through writing and discussion, as well as experiences with science curriculum and pedagogy. It is my hope that these tools will assist you in making explicit, confronting, and enhancing your personal theories about teaching science.[1] You'll find case studies, inquiry activities, interviews with professional teachers, readings from the literature, think pieces, problems and extensions, and experiences on the Web. Professional artistry is contextualized and knowledge about science teaching is just as tentative as scientific knowledge.

Professional artistry is inherently related to human *imagination* and *creativity* and one's willingness to *experiment* and *play*. Bronowski uses these four concepts to draw similarities between art and science. According to Bronowski, "science uses images, and experiments with imaginary situations, exactly as art does."[2] For the teacher, Bronowski offers this pedagogical suggestion:

> Many people believe that reasoning, and therefore science, is a different activity from imagining. But this is a fallacy, and you must root it out of your mind. The child that discovers, sometime before the age of ten, that he can make images and move them around in his head has entered a gateway to imagination and to reason. Reasoning is constructed with movable images just as certainly as poetry is. You may have been told, you may still have the feeling that $E = mc^2$ is not an imaginative statement. If so, you are mistaken.[3]

Developing professional artistry suggests that teachers need to develop their own knowledge claims about teaching and learning rather than simply adopting the knowledge claims of others. Inquiry activities are a key aspect of *The Art of Teaching Science*. Embedded throughout the text, these experiences are designed to facilitate the construction of knowledge claims about science teaching. You will find that pedagogical knowledge is tentative, and by developing an understanding that teaching knowledge emerges as does knowledge in art and science, you also will cultivate professional artistry.

Teachers exhibit professional artistry in encounters with their students. When you see them teaching, you witness their imagination and creativity at play unfolding in the classroom. And, if you return a few days later, you see again the process at work, but this time with a different context and activity. The courage to be creative in a teacher's encounters with students is important in our understanding of professional artistry. May notes that a creative act is an encounter.[4] Thus, a teacher's professional artistry is exhibited as a creative act in the classroom. According to May, creative courage is the most important kind of courage in that it results in new patterns upon which a society or a profession is built. He says, "In our day, technology and engineering, diplomacy, business, and certainly teaching, all of these professions and scores of others are in the midst of radical changes and require courageous persons to appreciate and direct this change. The need for creative courage is in direct proportion to the degree of change the profession is undergoing."[5]

There is one other dimension of professional artistry. Tom Brown, one of the teachers interviewed for *The Art of Teaching Science*, believes caring is one of the most important aspects of teaching. He put it this way: "This may sound too warm and fuzzy but I honestly believe that my most important role as a teacher is to care for my students as individuals. As we all know, high schools can be very impersonal places and many students have a difficult time finding a way to fit in comfortably. It is our job as educators to reach out to our kids and be empathetic and encouraging."[6]

Becoming a teacher is a creative and artistic process. As you work with peers, your instructors, students, and mentors, let these encounters be the way you learn how to teach.

Unifying Themes of Science Teaching

What knowledge do you need to become a science teacher and how should you acquire it? To help you in this quest the content in the book has been organized around a set of unifying themes of science teaching that, taken as a whole, constitute a partial answer to the question. Furthermore, there are a number of learning tools spread throughout the book that are focused on helping you develop knowledge not only by reading, but by actively engaging in inquiry activities, case studies, think pieces, and other learning devices.

What does a person need to know to be a science teacher? Some science educators refer to unifying themes as conceptual themes. A conceptual theme is a big idea, a unifying notion, an organizational structure. However, simply "learning about" these themes will not necessarily result in learning how to teach. The artistry of teaching involves experiencing these themes, reflecting on your experiences, and moving forward into the realm of experimenting and risk taking as you learn to teach.

The conceptual themes selected for this book are well documented in the literature and they make sense to the practicing science teacher. The themes are clustered into three categories: the nature of science, the nature of teaching, and nature of learning and the learner (Figure 1.1).

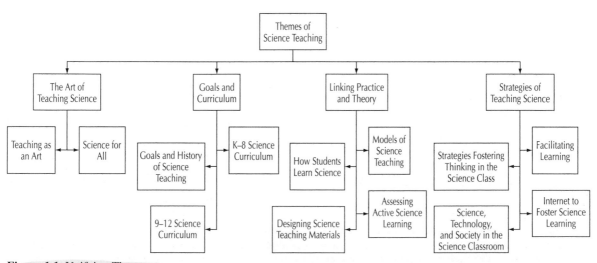

Figure 1.1 Unifying Themes.

INQUIRY ACTIVITY 1.1

Exploring Your Initial Ideas about Science Teaching

Later in this book, you will discover that secondary students come to science class with existing ideas about the science content that you will teach. Novices in a field of study, like students in your future science classes, possess initial conceptions of fields such as earth science or physics. Many of these ideas or initial conceptions are actually misconceptions or naive ideas. Indeed, we might call them "alternative frameworks." Nevertheless, these initial ideas represent a good place to begin instruction. Thus, this activity is designed to help you think about and *explore your existing ideas or your frameworks about science teaching*. It is not a pre-test, but rather an opportunity to discuss your initial ideas about science teaching from a problem-oriented vantage point.

Materials

- Index cards
- Information in Table 1.1

Table 1.1 Exploring Your Initial Conceptions of Science Teaching

Unifying Theme of Science Teaching	Problem Situation	Assessing Your Initial Conception
Nature of Science	Carl Sagan says, "science is a way of thinking, much more than it is a body of knowledge."	What is your view of science? Do your agree or disagree with Sagan? What are the implications of Sagan's definition for science teaching?
Inclusion: Science for All	A number of schools around the country with large numbers of at-risk students have adopted an approach called "integrative learning." This holistic approach appears to be successful with students who are disinterested in school and normally end up dropping out.	How would you teach the at-risk student, the student who has had a continuous record of failure in school, and clearly is prone to drop out of school? Can all students learn science?
Goals	According to a report on science teaching written by a prestigious group, the main goal of science teaching is to produce a scientifically literate society.	Do you agree with this? Are there other goals that are worthy and should be an integral part of science teaching?
Curriculum	The title of a keynote address at a major conference on science teaching is "The Science Curriculum: A Nonchanging Phenomenon!"	What is the science curriculum anyway? Is it nonchanging, or has the curriculum changed over the years? Should it?
Learning	You overhear a science teacher explaining to her eighth-grade earth science class that intelligence is incremental, not fixed. She believes that this will encourage students to try harder, especially when learning new and difficult ideas and concepts.	What is your view of intelligence? Do you think teaching students about human intelligence might help them learn science?
Models	A first-year teacher uses a nontraditional teaching model during the first week of school. It is a small group activity with hands-on materials. Students were asked to use meter sticks to measure various heights and lengths. Students were confused. How could they measure something bigger than the meter stick? One pair of students carved symbols and words in the meter stick and another group couldn't decide whether the smallest marks were centimeters or millimeters.	Are nontraditional models of teaching prone to problems and the unexpected? Should first-year teachers avoid them until they get their feet wet?

Table 1.1 *(cont'd)*

Unifying Theme of Science Teaching	Problem Situation	Assessing Your Initial Conception
Planning	At a conference between a student science teacher and her college supervisor, the student expresses anger that the students didn't enjoy the lesson that she had spent three hours planning. She just cannot believe they were rude during a lesson she worked so hard to plan.	How important is planning for lessons? Does this student teacher have expectations that are too high? How would you react in such a situation?
Assessing	A teacher announces that he is going to let students work in small teams on three quizzes each term. The students will turn in one paper, and each will receive the group's grade.	Do you think this is a good idea? Why? Would you employ such an assessment plan in your class?
Strategies	The most common strategy used in high school science teaching is lecture and discussion. Many science teachers claim that this is an inadequate strategy for most students, and suggest other strategies.	What do you think? Isn't lecture an efficient way to teach science? Are there other strategies that might reach more students? What are they?
Management and Facilitation	A fellow student returns from observing high school science classes with two maps drawn of the classrooms visited.	What can you infer about the teachers' view of classroom management? How does their view of facilitating learning compare?
Science, Technology, Society (STS)	A science teacher announces at a departmental meeting that she is going to include the following topics in her survey biology class: ethics and animal rights, birth control methods, abortion, and AIDS counseling. One teacher objects, saying, "these are too controversial, we'll have half the parents in here."	What do you think? Should topics like these be part of the science curriculum? Why?
Technology	At an urban high school, the mathematics and science departments have decided to offer online versions of their courses. Students at the high school can choose either the fact-to-face course or the online course.	What do you think of this idea? Do you think that offering science courses online would be a better alternative to courses offered in a classroom?

Procedures

1. Read each of the situations given for the conceptual themes listed in Table 1.1.
2. Write the themes on individual index cards. Shuffle the cards and place them face down on a table around which four to six students are sitting.
3. Select one person to start. The person selects an index card from the top of the pile to identify the unifying theme. Read the problem situation associated with the theme aloud to your group. Use the questions listed in the third column to guide your exploration of the theme. To explore the theme, you can:
   a. Give your initial point of view and share it with the group. You can ask other group members if they agree or disagree.
   b. Ask each group member to write a brief statement and then read them aloud to the group.
   c. If the problem situation merits it, role play the situation with other members of your group. The person drawing the card and selecting the method asks for volunteers and directs the role-playing scene. The enactment should take no more than two or three minutes. Follow the role play with a discussion session.

Minds-On Strategies

1. How do your initial ideas compare with other students in your class?
2. What is a framework? How do frameworks develop? How can they change?
3. In what ways do you think your initial ideas or frameworks about science teaching reflect the most recent research and practice of science teaching?

The conceptual themes should be recognizable to you and, furthermore, you come to this course with knowledge and ideas about these conceptual themes. I suggest that the place to begin your study of science teaching is to evaluate your present views about teaching, learning, students, and the curriculum. In short, what do you bring to this course in terms of knowledge, attitudes, and appreciation about science teaching?

Science Teaching: Your Career Choice

For a variety of reasons, you've chosen to be a secondary science teacher. In studies to find out why people choose a career in science teaching, interest in the subject-matter field is rated as the most important factor.[7] Is this true for you? Other reasons for choosing a career in science teaching include the following factors:

- a belief that personal abilities are well suited to teaching;
- desire for opportunities to work with young people;
- faith that teaching contributes to the betterment of society; and
- a longing to change careers and become a teacher.

You may also have made a choice between teaching middle school/junior high and high school.[8] Perhaps you are interested in working with early adolescent students in either a middle school or a junior high school. Maybe, you've decided that you want to work with older students and have focused your preparation on high school science teaching. In either case, being a science teacher will require you to blend knowledge of science, pedagogy, and how students learn. How can this be done so that students learn and develop an appreciation for science and you perceive science as a rewarding career? What will it entail?

As you begin your study of science teaching, keep in mind that these conceptual themes will be helpful organizational ideas for you, but, nonetheless, you should also acknowledge that having a theoretical base for these notions would not ensure your success in the classroom. Teaching requires an integration of practice (meaning experiences with students, teachers, and schools) and theory. I have purposely written "practice" first because we will advocate in *The Art of Teaching Science* an experiential approach to learning about

Figure 1.2 Science teaching is a challenging career choice. Students learn science in environments that foster active learning, problem solving, and discovery. *Source: Photodisc Collection/Getty Images.*

teaching, and thus practical, experiential activities in classrooms and schools will provide a base for theory building. There is a good chance that the course you are taking will also involve some practical work in a middle school/junior high or a high school. These opportunities during your teacher preparation experience are important as you develop a professional outlook on science teaching. So, you will find in this book a number of practical, "laboratory"-oriented experiences designed to help you integrate experience and theory.

To gain more insight into your career choice, we will hear from practicing science teachers and learn what they have to say about the rewards of science teaching.

Wisdom of Practice

In preparation for this book, I interviewed a number of practicing middle and high school science teachers because I wanted to include their ideas—their wisdom of practice, if you will—as we explored science teaching. (A copy of the interview questions is in the *Science Teacher Gazette* in this chapter.) I wanted these teachers to report how they deal with the main concepts and ideas of science teaching. In this chapter I will introduce you to these teachers, all of whom are real practicing science teachers:

- Ginny Almeder, a biology teacher from Georgia
- Anita Bergman, a science teacher in Georgia
- Ludmila Bolshakova, a chemistry teacher from Russia
- Ben Boza, a science teacher from Botswana
- Tom Brown, a physical science and biology teacher in Georgia
- Virginia Cheek, a biology teacher in Georgia
- Marina Goryunova, a computer science teacher and teacher educator from Russia
- Anne Gunn, a physics teacher from Georgia
- Bob Miller, a biology teacher from Texas
- Anna Morton, a science teacher from Georgia

- Carol Myronuk, a science teacher from Canada
- Michael O'Brien, a science teacher from Georgia
- Jerry Pelletier, a junior high science teacher from California
- Barry Plant, a science teacher from Australia
- John Ricciardi, a physics and astronomy teacher from Nevada
- Dale Rosene, a middle school science and computer teacher from Michigan
- Mary Wilde, a middle school science teacher from Georgia
- Rachel Zgonc, a middle and high school science teacher in Georgia

In subsequent chapters, these wisdom-of-practice interviews will be found in the *Science Teacher Gazette* under the section entitled "Science Teachers Talk." The comments made by the teachers are brief, but candid, and are presented to give you insight into teaching from a practitioner's point of view.

Many teachers report that science teaching can be a very rewarding career. What do science teachers like most about teaching? Surely this will give us some insight into the profession of science teaching and help you formulate goals and strategies for making your choice of science teaching a successful, fulfilling, and meaningful one.

Science Teachers Talk

"What do you like most about teaching?"

JOHN RICCIARDI: What I like most about science is that I can be myself, which is being part of a body of teenagers. Their spirit, ambience, and energy can become the self that is more and who I am becomes naturally part of them. For me, teaching science is becoming myself by becoming one with all that "sciencing" is in my students.

GINNY ALMEDER: Science is my way of questioning the universe, a pursuit we appear compelled to follow by our human nature. Teaching high school provides me with an opportunity to share my love of science with young people. Students are generally enthusiastic and open-minded about their world. It is a good time to introduce them to the joys of science. I appreciate having the opportunity to help young people realize their potential, especially in the area of science. It is gratifying to observe students

improving their skills, becoming more questioning, and developing a healthy self-concept.

JERRY PELLETIER: I am fascinated by science. It encompasses a myriad of subjects and experiences and is an ever-changing and developing field. Some ideas have remained unchanged for hundreds of years, while others have changed many times through the centuries. I find that my excitement for the subject of science can easily be transmitted to students. I enjoy observing students interacting while trying to understand and solve scientific concepts. Science lends itself to the inductive method of teaching. Students are constantly questioning themselves and their observations. In essence, science is fun for students as well as me.

MARY WILDE: What I like most about teaching science is the variety of ways and techniques one can use to teach a particular concept. You can prevent yourself from becoming "burned out" because there are always new demonstrations, activities, and experiments to incorporate in your curriculum that can explain old concepts. It is very exciting to be part of the new discoveries, new theories, and new conceptual ideas that take place in the scientific world. What is even more "thrilling" is the sharing of these new theories and discoveries with our young people. The teaching of new scientific principles or old scientific principles in new ways stimulates a curiosity and creative desire within the student. Thus, for me, science is a very successful tool to help the student develop creative skills, thought process skills, and problem solving skills while learning factual content and conceptual theories that explain how this world "ticks." Science is the "why" and "how," and isn't that what everyone wants to know?

These teachers believe that science can be fun for students, that they enjoy interacting with students, that it provides an opportunity to introduce students to the joys of science. Let's begin our study of science teaching by visiting a high school classroom where science content, pedagogy, students, and teachers meet—a glimpse into the *art of teaching science*.

On the Nature of Science Teaching

"What are these?"
"Where did they come from?"
"How old are they?"
"Where did you get them?"
"Are they all the same?"
"What are they used for?"

Questions asked by the teacher? No! These are questions asked by students in a ninth-grade teacher's physical science class at a metro-Atlanta High School. The teacher, one of thousands of new science teachers in the United States, began the first day of school with a very brief activity. She distributed fossil crinoid stems, placing one in each student's hand and telling him or her not to look at the object until she gave that instruction. The students were asked to explore the object without looking, write observations of the object, and make a small drawing of it. The teacher then asked the students to call out some of their observations of the unseen object (e.g., hard, breaks easily, gritty, grainy, cylindrical, about 2 cm in diameter, grooves along the side, a hole in the center). Next, the teacher provided the students with Play-Doh, and asked them to make a replica of the crinoid (still without looking). Finally, the teacher asked the students to guess what the object was (e.g., rock, bone, dog biscuit, pottery) and then to look at the object. Without telling the students very much, she asked them if they had any questions about the object. Curiosity led to several questions, as listed at the start of this section, and then to a discussion of the 400-million-year-old fossils from Silurian rock beds of North Georgia.[9] The next day, the teacher divided her students into groups and assigned a different task to each group. Later in the lesson, a student from each group reported its results to the class.[10]

The teacher began her class by actively engaging her students with natural materials, having them work in groups, and encouraging them to use their observation skills and creative abilities to solve problems and participate in interesting tasks. However, this lesson and the way these students felt about science is in stark contrast with what is known about science teaching in the United States and other countries around the world. In general, students see science class as dull, no fun, and a place where they do not wish to be. Students do not like the typical or traditional science classroom.[11] Although studies about science teaching reveal that many factors seem to make science teaching more interesting and result in high achievement (these will be discussed Chapter 6), one factor that seems to be very important is engagement, the active involvement of students in the learning process. Active involement occurs when students are engaged in handling, operating, or practicing on or with physical objects as part of the lesson.[12]

Perhaps the one metaphor about science teaching that has become a password for "good science teaching" is that science teaching should be *hands-on*. In recent years, however, this metaphor has been enriched and expanded with the use of the phrase "minds on."[13] These metaphors seems like simple and logical steps in the teaching process, but the evidence from science education research studies is quite to the contrary.[14]

1. The predominant method of teaching in science is recitation (discussion), with the teacher in control. Approximately 33 to 37 percent of each class period is spent on this form of instruction. We will call this the delivery mode of teaching, contrasting it from the engagement mode.
2. The secondary science curriculum is usually organized with the textbook at the core and the main goal of the teacher is to cover (or deliver) all the content in the book.
3. The science demonstration ranks second as the most frequently observed science "activity." Two out of five classes perform demonstrations once a week. It is important to note that in most demonstrations, students are typically passive observers.

4. Student reports and projects are used about once a month or more in half of all classes.
5. The focus on covering the text results in sparing, if any, use of inquiry techniques. Instead, activities are generally workbook exercises in following directions and verifying information given by the textbook or teacher.

A great controversy exists in the field of science education surrounding the issue of engagement versus delivery. Which model is more effective? Which is more efficient? How do students react to these models?

Which model helps most students understand science? Which model do you prefer?

Let's explore the differences between the delivery and engagement models of science teaching in order to develop a better notion of the nature of science teaching. To do this, you will plan and teach two lessons using a microteaching format. Microteaching is a scaled down version of teaching in which you present a short lesson (usually five to fifteen minutes in length) to small group of peers or secondary students (five to seven people), videotape the episode, evaluate the lesson, and make recommendations for possible changes. You will find more details on microteaching in Chapter 10.

INQUIRY ACTIVITY 1.2

 The Fossil and the Nature of Science Teaching

To explore the nature of science teaching, plan at least two microteaching lessons based on the following ideas and carry them out with a group of peers or a group of secondary students. Using Table 1.2, select one of the microteaching lessons from the list entitled engagement mode and select the other microteaching lesson from the list entitled delivery mode.

Materials

- Collection of fossils of the same species (e.g., Trilobites, Crinoid stems, Brachiopods)
- Metric rulers
- Crayons or marking pens
- Newsprint
- Bell caps
- String and glue
- Other materials and equipment to carry out the microteaching lesson

Procedure

1. Divide into groups and select a task from either the engagement or delivery mode of teaching. Your group is to prepare a ten-minute microteaching lesson based on the task you selected. You can teach the lesson to either a peer group or a group of secondary students. You may want to videotape the lesson so that you can replay it.
2. When groups are finished, one member should present the group's results to the whole class.

Minds-On Strategies

1. Evaluate the lesson by comparing the engagement mode to the delivery mode of instruction by considering the following questions: Was there evidence of curiosity on the part of the students during the lesson? Did the students show their creativity? Did they ask questions? Was there an aesthetic dimension in the lesson? Which lesson model did the students (learners) prefer? Which lesson did the teachers prefer?
2. Which approach do you think is more motivational? Why?

Table 1.2 Engagement versus Delivery Modes of Teaching

Task	Engagement Mode Tasks	Delivery Mode Tasks
1. Scientists	a. You are a group of scientists. Make as long a list of observations of the Trilobites as possible. When your group has completed the list, go onto the second part. (*Note:* be sure to write your lists on large sheets of chart paper, and remember that you can use more than words.) b. Classify each of the observations your group made according to the human sense used for each observation, for example, F = feel; T = taste; S = smell; E = sight, eyes; H = hearing, sound; O = other senses.	Lecture and carry out a discussion on the physical characteristics of the fossil. Be sure to include observations that require the use of the five senses.
2. Mathematicians	You are a group of mathematicians. Measure the lengths and/or widths of at least fifteen Trilobites. (You will have to visit other groups and use their Trilobites to make your measurements.) Make a population graph of the Trilobites you measured. Draw your graph on a piece of chart paper; make it large and colorful. Seek out another group that did this task and compare your graphs.	Make a presentation and discuss the population characteristics of the fossil. Focus attention on one characteristic, such as length or width. Explain the terms fossil, population graph, and species characteristics to your class.
3. Historians, anthropologists, geologists	Use your imaginative side and draw a complete picture of the trilobite. When you complete your drawing, put the trilobite in the context of the environment in which it might have lived. Ask questions of your group: Where does this animal live? Does it live alone, or are there others about? What does it eat? How does it get its food? Who are its predators? Prey?	Introduce your students to the concept of environment. Use the Trilobites as the species to study. Use diagrams and pictures so that the students will be able to describe the ecological characteristics of the trilobite environment.
4. Poets	You're a group of writers. Poets! Your task is to prepare several poems about the Trilobite that your team will read to a group of peers. Write several poems, called syntus, using the following strategy: Line 1: Single word or concept such as fossil, Trilobite, age, or time. Line 2: An observation of line 1 using your senses. Line 3: An inference about line 1. Line 4: A feeling you have about the fossil. Line 5: A synonym for line 1. (*Notes:* Brainstorm observations, inferences, and feelings about the Trilobite. Try to think about being the trilobite, living during the Paleozoic era in a marine environment. Use the results to help construct your poems. Write your final poems on sheets of chart paper. Make them colorful and easy to read.)	Give a brief lecture on Trilobites so that students will be able to describe what Trilobites are, how they are formed, and they tell us about the earth. The students should be able to write short stories or poems based on your presentation.
5. Artists	You are a group of artists. Your task is to make pendants or some form of art using the Trilobite. To make pendants, you might want to obtain bell caps, gold or silver string, and glue. Other materials should be gathered related to the art form you create.	Make a presentation on the artistic and practical aspects of fossils. How are fossils used in arts and crafts? What people in the community would have a use for fossils?

The Nature of Science

You are entering the science teaching profession at a time when many science educators, scientists, and the general public are calling for new directions in science education. The growing impact of science and technology on societal and individual affairs has resulted in a call from many sectors of society to reappraise science education and chart a new direction for advancing study. Paul DeHart Hurd suggests that the science curriculum of the future be based on interrelationships between human beings, natural phenomena, advancements in science and technology, and the quality of life.[15] He suggests that science teachers examine closely the nature of science, especially the multidimensional changes in science, technology, and society. Hurd and other educators criticize the content of the present science curricula as being remote from human needs and social benefits, reflecting the concern that science is alien and separate from individual and public interests. To make science understandable and useful to people, it is essential that the nature of science be communicated to students in the science curriculum. Yet, in a recent survey of science and mathematics educators, the objectives least likely to be heavily emphasized are learning about the history and nature of science and learning about the applications of science to society.[16] Let's explore the nature of science to learn how it could be more heavily emphasized in science teaching.

What Is Science?

One scientist who had an effect not only on the scientific community, but on the nonscience community as well, was Richard Feynman, a theoretical physicist and popularizer of science. In his book *Surely You're Joking, Mr. Feynman*, he said, "Before I was born, my father told my mother, 'If it's a boy, he's going to be a scientist.'" Not only did Feynman become a scientist, he also won the Nobel Prize.[17] Feynman saw science as an attempt to understand the world. To him, understanding the world was analogous to understanding the rules of a game like chess:

> We can imagine that this complicated array of moving things which constitutes "the world" is something like a great chess game being played by the gods, and we are observers of the game. We do not know what the rules of the game are; all we are allowed to do is to *watch* the playing. Of course, if we watch long enough, we may eventually catch on to a few of the rules. *The rules of the game* are what we mean by *fundamental physics*. Even if we know every rule, however . . . what we really can explain

in terms of those rules is very limited, because almost all situations are so enormously complicated that we cannot follow the plays of the game using the rules, much less tell what is going to happen next. We must, therefore, limit ourselves to the more basic question of the rules of the game. If we know the rules, we consider that we "understand" the world.[18]

Another scientist, a chemist named Michael Polanyi, explored the nature of science and described a "republic of science," a community of independent men and women freely cooperating, collaborating, and exchanging ideas and information. This community cut across national borders and brought scientists together from all over the globe as a cooperative global community. Polanyi also claimed that to be a scientist, one had to be inducted into the profession by working with a master as an apprentice. Interestingly, he also believed that the practice of science was not a science, but rather an art to passed from one scientist to another.[19]

If you look up science in a dictionary, the usual definition is "knowledge, especially of facts or principles, gained by systematic study; a particular branch of knowledge dealing with a body of facts or truths systematically arranged."[20] Yet prominent scientists, like Carl Sagan, define science as a way of thinking much more than it is a body of knowledge. Sagan says this about science:

> Its goal is to find out how the world works, to seek what regularities there may be, to penetrate the connections of things—from sub-nuclear particles which may be the constituents of all matter, to living organisms, the human social community, and thence to the cosmos as a whole. Our perceptions may be distorted by training and prejudice or merely because of the limitations of our sense organs, which of course perceive directly but a small fraction of phenomena of the world . . . Science is based on experiment, on a willingness to challenge old dogma, on an openness to see the universe as it really is. Accordingly science sometimes requires courage—at the very least the courage to question the conventional wisdom.[21]

Exploring the nature of science a little further, and relating it to the views of Feynman, Polanyi, and Sagan, we might consider several relationships, as described next.

Science and Courage

One important human quality in science is courage. If we put this in terms of willingness, as Sagan said, to question conventional wisdom, then we are led to an important notion: Questioning all things is a fundamental value underlying thinking in science. For example, Nicholas Copernicus, the sixteenth-century Polish scientist, questioned the conventional wisdom of the Ptolemaic, earth-centered universe. His questioning of an old idea led to a new one—that the sun was the center of the solar system and the planets revolved around the sun rather than the earth. About a hundred years after the publication of Copernicus's book, Galileo narrowly escaped the rack of the Holy Inquisition by recanting his support for the Copernican concept of the universe.

Questioning well-established ideas or proposing a radically different hypothesis to explain data are courageous acts. Quite often, people who propose such ideas are shunned, considered crazy, or rejected by the "establishment." For example, in 1920, Alfred Wegener, a German meteorologist, proposed that the continents were not stationary masses but were moving platforms of rock that had drifted apart over millions of years of geologic time. At the time, Wegener's idea was considered far-fetched and crazy. Physicists and geologists pointed out that there were no forces within the earth to move billions of kilograms of rock. Fifty years later, most geologists supported the theory of plate tectonics, that the earth's crust is composed of large plates that drift about, colliding, spreading apart, and sliding past each other.

A more recent example of courage is the case involving Dr. Frances Oldham Kelsey. In a book entitled *Women of Courage*, Frances Kelsey is referred to as "the doctor who said no."[22] After earning a Ph.D. in pharmacology (an infant field of science at the time) and then a medical degree from the University of Chicago, Kelsey moved with her husband and two children to Washington, D.C., and took a job with the Food and Drug Administration (FDA). Her job was to evaluate applications for licenses to market new drugs. In the fall of 1960, shortly after Kelsey arrived at the FDA, the William S. Merrell Company applied for a license to market a new sleeping pill called Kevadon. It had been used all over the world, was effective in relieving pregnant women from morning sickness, and was very profitable. Truman describes how Kelsey showed great courage as a scientist in the case of Kevadon:

> While Kelsey at the FDA was reviewing Merrell's application, they were distributing 2,000 kilograms of the drug. At the time this was a legal practice as long as the drug company labeled the drug "experimental." Merrell, in their advertising and marketing materials, informed their salespeople that they had firmly established the safety, dosage and usefulness

of the drug by both foreign and U.S. laboratory clinical studies. They had not.

At the FDA, Merrell's application was being reviewed. Dr. Kelsey and her research team were not satisfied with the information Merrell provided as part of their application. For example, the drug when administered to animals showed no sign of toxicity but did not make the animals sleepy. The drug was being distributed to humans as a sleeping pill. Two days before the sixty-day approval period was up, Dr. Kelsey told the Merrell Company that its application was not approved and the company would have to submit further information.

This initial rejection (November 10, 1960) of Merrell's application to distribute the drug was followed by a series of episodes between Dr. Kelsey and the Merrell Company. There were attempts by the Merrell Company to go over Kelsey's head and in so doing try to embarrass her in front of her superiors. This did not work. Merrell even supplied research reports supposedly documenting the safety of the drug. Upon investigation it was discovered that the researcher's name that appeared on the report did not even write it. And Merrell threatened Kelsey with a lawsuit, saying that one of her letters to the company was libelous. Through all this Kelsey stood firm and boldly held her ground. It culminated with the banning of the drug in December 1961, when thalidomide had been traced to an outbreak of deformities in newborn babies by the thousands in Europe. Then, in 1963, the American public was stunned when they read stories and saw the horrible pictures in their newspapers that one gallant woman doctor had stood between them and a repetition of this disaster in the United States.

On August 7, 1963, President Kennedy presented Dr. Kelsey the Distinguished Federal Civilian Service Medal. Kennedy applauded Dr. Kelsey's work, saying she had defended the hopes that all of us have for our children. The courageous behavior of Frances Kelsey also led to an increase in the FDA's staff and a change in the laws regulating the distribution and sale of drugs to humans.[23]

Science, Problem Solving, and the Human Mind

Thinking in science is often associated with creativity and problem solving. These are important aspects of the nature of science and should be essential goals of the science curriculum.[24] In his book *How Creative Are You?*, Eugene Raudsepp identifies a long list of human qualities that are characteristic of people who think creatively: innovative, risk taker, mold breaker, willing to ask questions, fearless adventurer, unpredictable, persistent, highly motivated, ability to think in images, ability to toy with ideas, tolerance of ambiguity, anticipates productive periods. The social implication of creative thinking is that we live in an ever-changing world, affected no less than by science and technological innovations. Many popularizers of science and creative thinking believe that all people are creative and are able to deal with change. Science courses have traditionally focused only on helping students learn scientific facts and concepts and then instruction stopped. Rarely were students encouraged to tackle real problems, thereby putting to use the facts and concepts they learned. But as educators like Hurd warn, the future science curriculum should present problems to solve that are desirable to students; that is, ones in which students have a stake in the solution, such as nutrition, chemical safety, space exploration, human ecosystems, drugs, population growth, eco-crises, quality of life, and so on.

To solve problems and deal with situations creatively requires the use of imagination. Historians of scientific discovery often point out that imagery and imagination have played important roles in intellectual discoveries and breakthroughs. This fact is nicely conveyed in the title of a book by June Goodfield, *An Imagined World: A Story of Scientific Discovery*. Goodfield describes the drama of scientific discovery and sheds light on role of creativity and imagination in this endeavor.[25] The world of imagery is safe harbor for thoughts and images and for the mind's participation in problem solving. For example, Einstein's famous thought experiments and images led him to many of his concepts of space and time. Indeed, Einstein used imagery to experience what he thought it would be like to ride a beam of light.

Jacob Bronowski believed that imagination was one of the important qualities of the mind. In *A Sense of the Future*, he said this about imagination, the human mind, and science:

> All great scientists have used their imagination freely, and let it ride them to outrageous conclusions without crying "Halt." Albert Einstein fiddled with imaginary experiments from boyhood, and was wonderfully ignorant of the facts that they were supposed to bear on. When he wrote the first of his beautiful papers on the random movement of atoms, he did not know that the Brownian motion, which it predicted, could be seen in any laboratory. He was sixteen when he invented the paradox that he resolved ten years later, in 1905, in the theory of relativity, and it bulked much larger in his mind than the experiment of Albert Michelson and Edward Morley which had upset every other physicist since 1881. All his life Einstein loved to make up teasing puzzles like Galileo's, about falling lifts and the detection of gravity; and they carry the nub of the problems of general relativity on which he was working.[26]

Science and Human Values

When society acknowledges the importance of qualities of the mind such as independence in thinking, originality, freedom to think, or dissidence, it is elevating them to social values. And, as social values, they are given special protection through laws governing society's behavior. Because science is an activity of women and men, certain values must guide their work. Bronowski claims that, because of this, science is not value free and the work of science is based on a search for truth. In his book *A Sense of the Future*, Bronowski discusses the human values that are indeed the values that guide science:

> If truth is to be found, and if it is to be verified in action, what other conditions are necessary, and what other values grow of themselves from this?
>
> First, of course, comes independence, in observation and thence in thought. The mark of independence is originality, and one of its expressions is dissent. Dissent in turn is the mark of freedom. That is, originality and independence are private needs of the truthful man, and dissent and freedom are public means to protect them. This is why society ought to offer the safeguard of free thought, free speech, free inquiry, and tolerance; for these are needs which follow logically when men are committed to explore the truth. They have, of course, never been granted, and none of the values, which I have advanced, have been prized in a dogmatic society.[27]

Sometimes the values that motivate scientists result in behavior that wouldn't hold up to Bronowski's ideas. For instance, in the 1950s the race was on to discover the structure of the DNA molecule. Horace Freeland Judson, in his book, *The Eighth Day of Creation*, said, "DNA, you know, is Midas' gold. Everyone who touches it goes mad."[28] In this case we ask: What part do ambition, achievement, and success play in the practice of science? How does a scientist's gender affect relationships? Are female scientists left behind their male counterparts? Is it possible for a scientist to literally "go mad" in the pursuit of what would be an astonishing discovery? Are scientists sometimes motivated by blind ambition? The story that follows will enable you to consider these questions.

The setting for this tale is in England about a hundred years after Charles Darwin and Alfred Russell Wallace co-discovered a theory of evolution. In the 1950s, a race was on among researchers to be the first to discover and unlock the secret that would reveal the basis for life. That secret was locked away in the structure of the DNA molecule—the substance of life. Two people emerge at first: James B. Watson, a twenty-four-year-old American-born scientist fresh out of graduate school with a new Ph.D., and Francis Crick, a thirty-eight-year-old graduate student at Cambridge University, England, still working on his Ph.D. Watson and Crick teamed up and decided to go all out to discover the structure of DNA. Their reward, if they could unlock the secret before the famous American chemist Linus Pauling, would be the Nobel Prize.

The process of discovering the structure of the DNA molecule was multifaceted. For Watson and Crick, driving force was their motivation to discover and report their findings before Pauling did. Pauling, 6,000 miles away in Pasadena, California, was working diligently on the DNA problem as well. Watson and Crick, but especially Watson, were worried that news would break from Pasadena. Watson wrote:

> No further news emerged from Pasadena before Christmas. Our spirits slowly went up, for if Pauling had found a really exciting answer, the secret could not be kept for long.[29]

The research process also involved collaboration with Maurice Wilkins and Rosalind Franklin, both of whom were researchers at King's College, England. Wilkins was trained in physics but became interested in the structure of the DNA and had been pursuing its structure for years.

When Watson and Crick entered the DNA search, Wilkins was the only researcher in England giving serious attention to the DNA problem. Rosalind Franklin, however, was also conducting important research. Trained in the study of crystals and how they were arranged, Franklin used X-rays to study the structure of crystals and was probably one of the most competent researchers in the field. Wilkins thought of her as his assistant. Franklin thought of herself, not as Wilkins assistant, but as a bona fide researcher pursuing the DNA structure as her main line of research. She was, in fact, hired to work in the same laboratory as head of a research group, a position equal to that of Wilkins.[30]

Vivian Gornick writes that the relationship between Watson and Crick "was its own double helix: all attracting opposites and catalytic joinings. These two ate, drank, slept, and breathed DNA."[31] Franklin did not have this kind of relationship with anyone. "If she had someone to talk to, chances are she would have gotten to DNA first, it was all there in her notes and photographs, she just didn't know what to make of what she had."[32]

Gornick, in the introduction of her book *Women in Science*, raises questions about the work of women in science: What was it like to be a female scientist? What if a woman working in science feels that success is not so accessible to her? What if a woman in science feels she must prove herself many times more often than a man does, that her work is more often challenged and less often supported?[33]

Was Franklin, as a woman, not privy to the discussions among Watson, Crick, and Wilkins? In James Watson's book *The Double Helix*, some insight on this assertion is revealed:

> Clearly Rosy had to go or be put in her place. The former was obviously preferable because, given belligerent moods, it would be difficult for Maurice [Wilkins] to maintain a dominant position that would allow him to think unhindered about DNA . . . Unfortunately, Maurice could not see any decent way to give Rosy the boot. To which, she had been given to think that she had a position for several years. Also, there was no denying she had a good brain. If she could only keep her emotions under control, there would be a good chance she could really help him. . . . The real problem, then, was Rosy. The thought could not be avoided that the best home for a feminist was in another person's lab.[34]

Anne Sayre, author of *Rosalind Franklin and DNA*, finds Watson's description of Rosalind quite different than her own view. In her biography of Franklin, Sayre questions the accuracy of some of Watson's facts:

> A question arose concerning the accuracy of some of Watson's facts, simply because he presented in *The Double Helix* a character named "Rosy" who represented, but did not really coincide, with a woman named Rosalind Franklin. . . . The technique used to change Rosalind Franklin into "Rosy" was subtle, but really not unfamiliar, part of it, at the simplest level, was the device of the nickname itself, one that was never used by any friend of Rosalind's, and certainly not to her face. . . . For we are presented with a picture of a deplorable situation. The progress of science is being impeded, and by what? Why, by a woman, to begin with, one labeled as subordinate, meant—or even destined—to occupy that inferior position in which presumably all women belong, even those with good brains. . . . But perhaps the progress of science is also being impeded somewhat by a man as well, one too inhibited by decency to be properly ruthless with female upstarts, and so to get on with the job.[35]

Rosalind Franklin's work on the DNA problem was brilliant. Had she lived until 1962 (she died of cancer in 1958 at the age of 37), she no doubt would have shared the Nobel Prize awarded to Watson, Crick, and Wilkins.

Since these events, the nature of science has been influenced by the increased participation of women in the field of science. However, the participation of women and minorities in science has been exacerbated by the nature of school science and by the negative effect school science has had in attracting women to careers in science. In the next chapter, we will explore this issue in more depth. Beginning in the 1970s, there has been a movement in the fields of science and science education to support an approach to science teaching based on women's studies, methods and theories to attract women to science courses during middle school and high school, and encourage women to pursue careers in mathematics, science, and engineering.[36]

Science and Democracy

When science is examined as an enterprise that involves the values of independence, freedom, the right to dissent, and tolerance, it is clear that as a social activity science cannot flourish in an authoritarian climate. Some philosophers of science such as Bronowski claim that science cannot be practiced in authoritarian regimes. In a democratic environment, old ideas can be challenged and rigorously criticized, albeit, with some difficulty because of the human desire to hold onto old ideas, especially by the original proposers. Yet it is the essence of scientific thinking to propose alternative ideas and then to test them against existing concepts. As pointed out in an American Association for the Advancement of Science report, *Science for All Americans*, "indeed, challenges to new ideas are the legitimate business of science in building valid knowledge."[37] The principles upon which democracy is built are the very concepts that describe the scientific enterprise. Recall that Polanyi felt science was organized as a republic of science in which independent people freely cooperated to explore and solve problems about the natural world. The values of a democratic society are the values that undergird Polanyi's concept of a republic of science.

The Scientific Enterprise and Teaching

The concepts presented here about the nature of science have implications for science teaching. There should be consistency between discussions about the nature of science and the nature of *teaching* science. If we are trying to convey to students not only the facts and information of science, but the process of science as well, then we are obliged to establish environments in classrooms that presume the same values that guide the practice of science. Questions we can raise about our classrooms in this regard are as follows:

- To what extent are students given the opportunity to challenge ideas?
- Are activities planned in which there are alternative methods, answers, and solutions?
- Are students encouraged to identify and then try to solve problems relevant to their lives?
- Is it acceptable for students to disagree with ideas and propose new ones?
- Do the problems that students work on have any consequence in their lives now?

Science is defined as much by what is done and how it is done as it is by the results of science. To understand science as a way of thinking and doing, as much as "bodies of knowledge," requires that science teaching emphasize the thought processes and activities of scientists. Thus, we are led to explore one of the fundamental thought processes in science, namely, *inquiry*.

Science Teaching and Inquiry

Imagine science classrooms in which:

- The teacher pushes a steel needle through a balloon and the balloon does not burst. The teacher asks the students to find out why the balloon didn't burst.
- Students are dropping objects into jars containing liquids with different densities and recording the time it takes each object to reach the bottom of the jar. They are trying to find out about viscosity.
- Students are using probes connected to a microcomputer to measure the heart rates of students before and after five minutes of exercise. They are investigating the effect of exercise on pulse rate.
- Students are reading newspaper articles on the topic toxic waste dumps in order to form opinions about a proposed dump being established in their community.

In each case, students are actively involved in measuring, recording data, and proposing alternative ideas to solve problems, find meaning, and acquire information. In these situations, students were involved in the process of *inquiry*. The greatest challenge to those who advocate inquiry teaching is the threat to the traditional and dominant role of the teacher in secondary education. It is worthwhile to explore inquiry teaching first because of its relationship to the essence of science and because of the philosophical implications of siding with an inquiry approach. By taking a stand in favor of inquiry teaching, the teacher is saying, "I believe students are capable of learning how to learn; they have within their

INQUIRY ACTIVITY 1.3

 Surveying Students' Views of Science

Knowing what your students think of science can play an important role in influencing your day-to-day lesson plans. This activity is designed to help you detect and describe secondary students' views of science. Three methods are described in this activity: writing an essay, drawing a picture, and completing a survey.

Materials

- Drawing paper
- Pencils and crayons
- Copies of science survey instruments

Procedure

Choose one of the three methods and survey ten to fifteen students on their view of science. After you have surveyed the students, arrange a time where you can discuss the results of the survey with them. (*Note*: this activity can also be carried out with a group of your teacher training peers.)

Minds-On Strategies

1. Summarize the results of the your method of investigation by analyzing and drawing conclusions from the drawings, perhaps by creating a poster of the drawings or tabulating the results of the survey.
2. Compare the method you used with the other two methods. How do students view science? Do they have a positive view of science? What is their image of a scientist? How do students compare science and technology? What effect does science have on society? Society on science?

Method 1

The Essay. Have the students write an essay explaining what they think science is and how scientists do their work. To help the students, you might give them one of several sentence starters as a vehicle to begin:

> *Science is . . .*
> Scientists believe that . . .
> *The purpose of science is . . .*

Method 2

The Drawing. Have students make a drawing of a scientist. Ask the students to show the scientist at work. You might also have the students write a brief statement explaining their drawing. Use the "draw-a-scientist" assessment rubric to analyze your students' drawings (Figure 1.3).

Method 3

The Questionnaire. Survey the viewpoints that middle school and high school students hold on the items listed in Figure 1.4. The items are based on an instrument developed to survey Canadian high school students and has been modified for use here.[38] Have a group of students respond to the items. Mark a different item on each student's questionnaire with an asterisk. Ask each student to write reasons for his or her choice for that item. The purpose of each item is given in parentheses, which you do not need to include when you distribute the questionnaire to the students. The purpose of each item will be important, however, when you analyze the results.

Figure 1.3A This is a drawing made by a tenth-grade student. Use the rubric to "analyze" the drawing. What conclusions can you draw concerning the view this student has of scientists? *Source:* Drawing used with permission of Jesse Kent, Elm City, N.C.

Directions: Analyze the Draw-a-Scientist drawing using the following list of characteristics. For each characteristic observed, score 1 point and record it in the chart.

Characteristic	Prior to Instruction	After Instruction
Bald		
Eyeglasses		
Facial hair		
Frizzy hair		
Indoor scene		
Male		
Pencils and pens in pocket protector		
Signs of technology (such as computer, camera, probes)		
Signs or labels like "fire, danger, poison"		
Symbols of knowledge (such as books, filing cabinet)		
Symbols of research (such as test tubes, burners)		
Unkempt appearance		
Wearing a Labcoat		

Scoring: 1 point for any of the items above: lower score is a higher rating.

Figure 1.3B Draw-a-Scientist Rubric.

Instructions

Please check whether you agree or disagree with the following statements. If you cannot agree or disagree then check "can't tell" for the statement. For the item with an asterisk, please write the reasons for your choice.

1. Science and technology have little to do with each other. (relationship between science and technology)
   _____agree _____disagree _____can't tell

2. Technology gets ideas from science and science gets new processes and instruments from technology.
   _____agree _____disagree _____can't tell

3. In order to improve the quality of living, it would be better to invest money in technological research rather than scientific research. (science, technology, and quality of life)
   _____agree _____disagree _____can't tell

4. Although advances in science and technology may improve living conditions around the world, science and technology offer little help in resolving such social problems as poverty, crime, unemployment, overpopulation, and the threat of nuclear war. (science, technology, and social problems)
   _____agree _____disagree _____can't tell

5. Scientists and engineers should be given the authority to decide what types of energy to use in the future (e.g., nuclear, hydro, solar, coal burning, etc.) because scientists and engineers are the people who know the facts best. (technocratic and democratic decision-making postures)
   _____agree _____disagree _____can't tell

6. The government should give scientists research money only if the scientists can show that their research will improve the quality of living today. (mission-oriented perspective)
   _____agree _____disagree _____can't tell

7. The government should give scientists research money to explore the unknowns of nature and the universe. (the basic science perspective)
   _____agree _____disagree _____can't tell

8. Communities or government agencies should not tell scientists what problems to investigate because scientists themselves are the best judges of what needs to be investigated. (role of government and communities in the choice of research problems)
   _____agree _____disagree _____can't tell

9. Science would advance more efficiently if our government more closely controlled it. (government control of research)
   _____agree _____disagree _____can't tell

10. Science would advance more efficiently if it were independent of government influence.
    _____agree _____disagree _____can't tell

11. The political climate has little effect on scientists because they are pretty much isolated from society. (effect of political climate on scientists)
    _____agree _____disagree _____can't tell

Figure 1.4 Opinions about Science.

repertoire the abilities as well as the motivation to question, to find out about and seek knowledge; they are persons and therefore learners in their own right, not incomplete adults." The philosophy of inquiry implies that the teacher views the learner as a thinking, acting, responsible person.

Characteristics of Inquiry

Inquiry is a term used in science teaching that refers to a way of questioning, seeking knowledge or information, or finding out about phenomena. Many science educators have advocated that science teaching should emphasize inquiry. The vision of inquiry presented in the National Science Education Standards includes

the "processes of science" and requires that students combine processes and scientific knowledge as they use scientific reasoning and critical thinking to develop their "understanding of science."[39] According to the Standards, engaging students in inquiry helps them develop

- understanding of scientific concepts,
- an appreciation of "how we know" what we know in science,
- understanding of the nature of science,
- skills necessary to become independent inquirers about the natural world,
- the dispositions to use the skills, abilities, and attitudes associated with science.

Wayne Welch, a science educator at the University of Minnesota, argues the techniques needed for effective science teaching are the same as those used for effective scientific investigation.[40] Thus, the methods used by scientists should be an integral part of the methods used in science classrooms. We might think of the method of scientific investigation as the inquiry process. Welch identifies five characteristics of the inquiry process:

1. *Observation:* Science begins with the observation of matter or phenomena. It is the starting place for inquiry. However, as Welch points out, asking the right questions that will guide the observer is a crucial aspect of the process of observation.
2. *Measurement:* Quantitative description of objects and phenomena is an accepted practice of science and is desirable because of the value placed in science on precision and accurate description.
3. *Experimentation:* Experiments are designed to test questions and ideas and, as such, are the cornerstone of science. Experiments involve questions, observations, and measurements.
4. *Communication:* Communicating results to the scientific community and the public is an obligation of the scientist and is an essential part of the inquiry process. The values of independent thinking and truthfulness in reporting the results of observations and measurements are essential in this regard. As pointed out earlier (in the section on the nature of science), the "republic of science" is dependent on the communication of all its members. Generally, articles published in journals and discussions at professional meetings and seminars facilitate this.
5. *Mental Processes:* Welch describes several thinking processes that are integral to scientific inquiry: inductive reasoning, formulating hypotheses and theories, deductive reasoning, as well as analogy, extrapolation, synthesis, and evaluation. The mental processes of scientific inquiry may also include other processes, such as the use of imagination and intuition.

In the Standards approach to inquiry, we find a high degree of agreement with Welch's earlier ideas. In the Standards, the following abilities have been identified as crucial for high school students:

- identify questions and concepts that guide scientific investigations,
- design and conduct scientific investigations,
- use technology and mathematics to improve investigations and communications,
- formulate and revise scientific explanations and models using logic and evidence,
- recognize and analyze alternative explanations and models,
- communicate and defend a scientific argument.

As we will see, and as pointed out in the Standards, inquiry refers to the abilities students should develop to be able to design and conduct scientific investigations. It also refers to the teaching and learning strategies that teachers use to enable students to understand scientific concepts through active learning methods.[41]

Inquiry teaching can be considered a method of instruction, yet it is not the only method that secondary science teachers employ. However, because of the philosophical orientation of this book toward an inquiry approach to teaching and the strong emphasis seen in the Standards, I will explore it first, but also highlight three other methods (direct/interactive teaching, cooperative learning, and constructivist teaching) that contemporary science teachers use in the classroom.

Inquiry in the Science Classroom

Secondary science classrooms should involve students in a wide range of inquiry activities. The description "scientific inquiry" is a general description of the inquiry model of teaching. The inquiry model of teaching presented in this book includes guided and unguided inductive inquiry, deductive inquiry, and problem solving.[42] Students engaged in a variety of inquiry activities will be able to apply the general model of inquiry to a wide range of problems. Thus, the biology teacher who takes the students outside and asks them to determine where the greatest number of wildflowers grow in a field is engaging the students in guided inquiry. The students would be encouraged to make observations, record measurements of the flowers and the field, perhaps create a map of the field, and then draw conclusions based on these observations. In an earth science class, a teacher who has used inductive inquiry to help students learn about how rocks are formed may then ask the students to devise their own projects and phenomena to study about rocks. Inductive inquiry is a teacher-centered form of instruction.

On the other hand, unguided inductive inquiry is student-centered inquiry in that the student, not the teacher, will select the phenomena and the method of investigation. However, this does not mean that the teacher is not involved. The teacher may gather the class for a brainstorming session to discuss potential phenomena to explore and study, based on the classwork to date. Small teams of students may then be organized. The teams discuss the list of topics and phenomena generated in the brainstorming session and proceed to devise a project of their own.

In both forms of inductive inquiry, students are engaged in learning about concepts and phenomena by using observations, measurements, and data to develop conclusions. We might say the student is moving from specific cases to the general concept. In deductive inquiry the student starts with the big idea, conclusion, or general concept and moves to specific cases. For instance, in a classroom situation, a physics teacher may want the class to test the principle that light is refracted when it passes from one medium to another. The students perform a laboratory exercise in which they make observations of light as it passes through water, glycerin, and glass. The lab is designed to help students confirm the concept. Many of the laboratory activities embedded in secondary science textbooks are deductive inquiry exercises. Is deductive inquiry teacher centered or student centered? Why do you think so?

Learning how to solve problems is another form of inquiry teaching. Secondary students can investigate challenging problems such as:

- How did life originate on earth?
- What will the consequences if earth's average temperature continues to rise?
- How can AIDS be prevented?
- What is the effect of diet and exercise on the circulatory system?
- What solid waste products are the most environmentally hazardous?
- What resources are most critically in short supply?

Posing problems such as these brings real-world problems into the science classroom and furthers students' appreciation for the process of inquiry. Teachers who use problem solving are providing a perspective for students in which they will propose solutions to problems and make recommendations about what should be done to change, improve, correct, prevent, or better the situation. Involving students in solving problems that are important to the culture and themselves is an important goal of science teaching. Paul DeHart Hurd comments "a problem-oriented societal context for science courses provides the framework essential for the development of such intellectual skills as problem solving, decision making, and the synthesis of knowledge."[43]

Environments That Foster Inquiry

The classroom environment has psychological, sociological, philosophical, and physical dimensions affected by the curriculum, students, teachers, school, community, and the nation. Yet, in much of the research investigating classroom environments, the teacher's role is often seen as a powerful determinant of the classroom climate. In his book *Teaching Science as Inquiry*, Steven Rakow points out that behaviors and attitudes of the teacher play an essential role in inquiry teaching, and he identifies the following as characteristic of successful inquiry teachers:

1. They model scientific attitudes.
2. They are creative.
3. They are flexible.
4. They use effective questioning strategies.
5. They are concerned both with thinking skills and with science content.

Unfortunately, the overriding characteristic of the environments that foster inquiry is the attitude of the teacher toward the nature of students and the nature of science knowledge. Departing from the traditional role as a primary giver of information, the science teacher who "takes-on" the inquiry philosophy is more of a facilitator of learning and manager of the learning environment. The student is placed in the center of the inquiry teacher's approach to teaching, thereby fostering the student's self-concept and development. Such teachers bring to the classroom an assortment of approaches designed to meet the needs of the array of students that fill their classrooms. Although inquiry centralizes these teachers' philosophy, they also incorporate other methods of teaching.

Life beyond Inquiry

Just as there are more ways than one to skin a cat, there are many approaches to help students understand science. There is more than one way to learn; there is more than one way to teach. Students will come to your classroom with different learning styles and, more importantly, you will develop a your own artistry that should not only be congruent with contemporary research on teaching, but should be equally based on your personality, experience, values, and goals. We will explore a spectrum of approaches in Chapter 6 to help you develop a repertoire of methods and strategies. Here, we briefly describe a few of these methods.

Table 1.3 Direct/Interactive Instructional Behaviors

Daily Review of Homework	Teachers review the key concepts and skills associated with homework; go over the homework; ask key questions to check for student understanding.
Development	Teachers focus on prerequisite skills and concepts; introduce new ideas and concepts using an interactive approach including examples, concrete materials, process explanations, questioning strategies; check student understanding by using a highly interactive process utilizing questions and designing a controlled practice activity for individual or group participation; teachers also use a lot of repetition.
Guided Practice	Teachers provide specific time during the lesson for uninterrupted successful practice; teachers use a sustained pace with a lot of momentum; students know that their work will be checked by the end of the period; teacher circulates about the room, checking student work and asking questions as needed.
Independent Practice	Teachers assign on a regular basis a homework assignment that is not lengthy, and can be successfully completed by the students.
Special Reviews	Effective teachers conduct reviews once a week, preferably at the beginning of week. Focus is on the skills and concepts developed during the previous week; monthly reviews are conducted to review important skills and concepts.

Source: Based on Good, T. L., and Brophy, J. E. *Looking into Classrooms.* New York: Harper & Row, 1987, pp. 459–95.

Direct/Interactive Teaching

Think for a moment about the roles and interactions among students and teachers in most secondary science classrooms. You probably can envision the teacher working directly with the whole class, perhaps presenting a brief lecture and then engaging the students by asking questions. The students might also be observed doing desk work, sometimes on their own, other times with a partner or a small group. Homework is assigned near the end of the class period, and students might get a head start on the assignment before class ends. Various models, sometimes referred to as direct/interactive instruction, have emerged over the past few years based on the relationship between observing teacher behavior and relating the behavior to student learning. A significant number of studies have supported a general pattern of key instructional behaviors (see Table 1.3).

Cooperative Learning

Cooperative learning is an approach to teaching in which groups of students work together to solve problems and complete learning assignments.[44] One of the most common teaching strategies among science teachers, cooperative learning is a deliberate attempt to influence the culture of the classroom by encouraging cooperative actions among students.[45] Cooperative learning is a strategy easily integrated with an inquiry approach to teaching. Furthermore, science teachers have typically had students work in at least pairs, if not larger small groups during lab. Cooperative learning strategies have been shown to be effective in enhancing

problem solving and high-level thinking goals. In Chapters 6 and 7, we will explore a variety of cooperative learning models that are easily put into practice.

Constructivist Teaching: Learning as Making Meaning

A growing number of science education practitioners and researchers have developed an approach to science teaching that focuses on the problem of conceptual change. According to these science educators, students come to the science class with naive conceptions or misconceptions about science concepts and phenomena. Further, these science educators suggest that concepts students hold are constructed; they are neither discovered nor received directly from another person. To help students overcome their naive theories, some educators suggest that teaching be organized into a series of stages of learning called a learning cycle. In most learning cycles, the first stage helps students detect and articulate their initial conceptions through exploratory activities, stage two focuses on comparing initial and "scientific views" to develop alternative conceptions, and the third stage provides experiences to encourage students to apply the concepts to new situations.[46] We will learn that this approach integrates inquiry, direct/interactive teaching, and cooperative learning, and indeed it might be the "discovery" alluded to at the beginning of the chapter.

We will explore other approaches to science teaching. For now, however, inquiry, direct/interactive instruction, cooperative learning, and constructivist teaching should get you started.

The Scientist and the Student: Two Cultures?

One idea that prevailed during the curriculum reform movement of the 1960s and 1970s was that students were like little scientists: curious, imaginative, interested, and inventive. An idea that has emerged in recent years, however, is that students are quite different from scientists, and indeed come to science classes with their own theories and explanations for science concepts and phenomena. The assumption made by many science educators that scientists and students are very much alike is questionable and perhaps has contributed to many instructional problems such as motivation, success on standardized tests, and overall performance in science.

Students in middle schools and high schools are not scientists, and we shouldn't be anxious to make them into scientists. They are adolescents, some of whom may choose to be scientists later in life, but most of whom will not. Let's look at some of the differences between scientists and adolescent students and consider some of the implications of these differences.

Some Differences

For starters, most people will not become scientists or engineers. In a typical school with a thousand students in the ninth grade, only thirty-nine would earn baccalaureate degrees in science and engineering, five would earn master's degrees in those fields, and only two would complete a science or engineering doctoral degree.[47] A more important difference, however, is apparent when we examine scientist and student thinking.

Adolescents are limited in the extent to which they can reason in the abstract, whereas scientists deal with abstractions as commonly as students deal with concrete ideas. As we will discuss in the next chapter, formal or abstract thinking elludes the majority of middle school and high school students. As some science education researchers point out, scientists work with concepts that have no directly observable circumstances (such as atoms, electric fields) and concepts that have no physical reality (such as potential energy).[48] Students, on the other hand, tend to consider only those concepts and ideas that result from everyday experience. As a result, many students will enter your classroom with misconceptions about scientific ideas, ideas that are firmly held and very difficult to alter.

Another difference between students and scientists has to do with what we might call "explanations" of concepts and phenomena. According to Osborne and Freyberg, students are not too concerned if some of their "explanations" are self-contradictory, and they do not seem to distinguish between scientific (testable, disprovable) and nonscientific explanations. Scientists, on the other hand, are "almost preoccupied with the business of coherence between theories."[49] Osborne and Freyberg also point out that while scientists search for patterns in nature, for predictability, and the reduction of the unexpected, students are often interested in the opposite (in looking for the irregular, unpredictable, and the surprise).

Students' interests, thinking processes, and the way they construct meaning are also limited by their prior knowledge, experiences, cognitive level, use of language, and knowledge and appreciation of the experiences and ideas of others. Scientists' interests, Osborne and Freyberg argue, follow from their participation in the scientific community. Scientists also have access to a wide range of technical supports enabling them to extend their knowledge base by means of computer networks and databases, telescopes, electron microscopes, and a common language.

Students and scientists have very different attitudes about science. It appears that the more school science students experience, the less is their interest in science. For example, in one study, nearly two thirds of nine-year-olds, 40 percent of thirteen-year-olds, and only 25 percent of seventeen-year-olds reported science class to be fun. This pattern persisted when students were asked whether science classes were fun and whether science classes made them feel curious, successful, and uncomfortable.[50]

Bridging the Gap

How can science education be sensitive to the differences between students and scientists? How can we create science programs that nullify the negative trends in attitudes and achievement that have persisted for the past decade?

One place to begin is pedagogy. Research study after research study has described a picture of the science classroom as a pedagogical monotone. In most classrooms, a teach, text, test model prevails. For the majority of students, this model leads to disastrous results. What is needed is greater variety in pedagogy. There are many pedagogical models of teaching that place the student in an active role as opposed to the widespread practice of students being passive receptors of information. Chapter 6 presents a number of pedagogical varieties for the science teacher, including inquiry, conceptual change, direct/interactive, small group, and individualized models of teaching.

Science educators need to reconsider the goals of science teaching and take a careful look at the objectives and concepts that secondary school students are expected to learn. Many science educators suggest that the humanistic and societal aspects of science should be emphasized in the science curriculum. Some suggest that science teaching—and the resulting curriculum—should help students generate ideas about the science–society interface. The interaction between science and society can lead to topics in science teaching that focus on student interests in contemporary scientific, social, and planetary issues, and can help students use science concepts and methods in the investigation of these problems.

The emphasis in science teaching is on the teaching of facts and concepts. Little emphasis is placed on the application of science knowledge to societal problems, the consequences of scientific discoveries, or the values undergirding science. Mary Budd Rowe's proposal (Figure 1.5) for a shift in science education incorporates each of these components in a holistic paradigm of a science education program.[51] Unfortunately, even with most of the attention given to this goal, American students have not done very well on standardized tests, especially when compared to their counterparts in other information-age societies.

As you examine Figure 1.5, keep in mind that Rowe suggests that, for the most part, teachers and texts concentrate on the question "What do I know?" under the

Table 1.4 Percentage of Classes with Heavy Emphasis on Various Objectives

Science Content Objectives Composite	Nature of Science Objectives Composite
Learn basic science concepts (78%)	Learn to evaluate arguments based on scientific evidence (25%)
Learn important terms and facts of science (48%)	Learn about the history and nature of science (11%)
Learn science process/ inquiry skills (64%)	Learn how to communicate ideas in science effectively (39%)
Prepare for further study in science (43%)	Learn about the application of science in business and industry (15%)
	Learn about the relationship between science, technology, and society (26%)

Source: Weiss, Iris R. *Report of the 2000 National Survey of Mathematics and Science Teaching.* Chapel Hill, N.C.: Horizon Research, Inc., 2001, p. 62.

Ways of Knowing component. In fact, she points out that a typical high school science text averages between seven and ten new concepts, terms, or symbols per page. Making assumptions about the number of pages in the text, she estimates that students need to learn between 2,400 to 3,000 terms and symbols per science course. This translates to about twenty concepts per fifty-five minute period![52]

To underscore Rowe's analysis, a recent survey of science and mathematics educators, indicated that science teachers emphasize more heavily science content objectives as compared to nature of science objectives (Table 1.4). As can be seen by both Rowe's earlier descriptions on the data from this more recent survey, the heavy emphasis on learning concepts and facts overshadows learning about the history and nature of science and on the applications of science to society. The implication of this data is that science lesson plans need to incorporate a wider spectrum of objectives.

Giving students a broader perspective of science will help bridge the gap separating them from the world of scientists. Most students will not become scientists, but they will become consumers of scientific discoveries and technological inventions as well as decision makers at the polling booths.

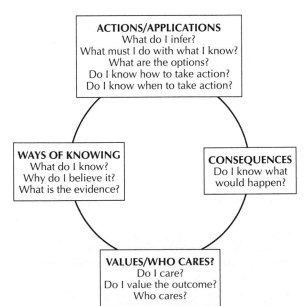

Figure 1.5 Mary Budd Rowe's Model of Science Education. *Source:* Used with permission of the National Science Teachers Association.

The Students We Teach: Who Are They?

Our students are adolescents. According to the dictionary, *adolescence* is derived from the Latin word *adolescere*, which means "to grow up." Students in middle school, junior high school, or senior high school range in age from twelve to eighteen, the typical age span for adolescence. According to psychologists, adolescence is the period of life that marks a transition from childhood and maturity. In your pedagogical training, you most likely have explored, in courses on human growth and development and educational psychology, a variety of theories to explain cognitive, psychosocial, physical, sexual, and emotional development of adolescents. In the next chapter, we explore some aspects of these theories, especially as they impinge on how adolescent students learn, what motivates them, and how to get them interested in learning science. It is important to realize, however, that each of the 100 to 175 students you will teach each day is a whole person integrating a constellation of feelings, attitudes, abilities, motivations, physical attributes, and ambitions. It goes without saying that each student is unique. At the secondary education level, however, these students are taking on new roles, are influenced by peer pressure, wonder who they are, and imagine what they will become. As

a science teacher, love of science and commitment to teaching make it easy to put subject matter first and forget that you are teaching individuals. If you consider science as the vehicle that brings you and your students together, you will see an opportunity to explore such questions as: How can science teaching contribute to the development of our students? How can science teaching foster the development of healthy young aduts with positive self-concepts? How can I inspire students to experience the same joy I feel about science?

You will come to know your students in the context of a particular school, which may be a large urban high school with 5,000 students or a small rural school with only a hundred students in each grade. The context of school is important because the school itself plays a role in the daily life of the student. Inquiry Activity 1.4 presents a sample of students you teach and the kinds of environments they encounter so as to introduce the notion that "students are first" in any discussion of learning, science education, and the profession of teaching.[53]

INQUIRY ACTIVITY 1.4

The Student Is First

This activity is designed to engage you in an exploration of secondary school students based on several student vignettes. Your role is to participate with a team of peers to devise some strategies to spark interest among students in the vignettes.

Materials

- Student vignettes (included)
- Newsprint or chart paper
- Marking pens

Procedure

1. Working with a small team of peers, read each vignette to discover some of the student's characteristics. Your role in the team is to

   a. List as many characteristics of the student as possible;
   b. Identify potential activities, events, and procedures you think the student will enjoy participating in;
   c. Identify potential problem areas for the student. Are there aspects of science class this student may not like? What can be done to mitigate this circumstance?

2. Prepare a profile on each student by summarizing the major characteristics, potential positive activities, and problem areas on a large sheet of newsprint or similar paper.

Minds-On Strategies

1. Examine the analyses of other teams in your class. How do the analyses compare to your team's results?
2. Are there any at-risk students in this group (i.e., students who you think might drop out of school)? As a teacher, how could you make science be a positive influence in a high-risk student's life?

Student Vignettes

Chris

Chris attends a large urban high school. He has an academic curriculum and works after school three days a week and on weekends. Chris comes to school by car, usually picking up three or four friends on the way. After the half-hour ride to school, Chris goes to his locker, talks with a few friends, and gets to his first class by 8:00 A.M. His girlfriend, Monica, is in his first class, so he usually makes it there on time to talk briefly with her. Chris's first class is an ESL class, which he likes because the teacher treats all the students with great respect. The teacher has told the students that he is available after school to help with language problems.

During math class, which Chris does not like, he feels frustrated because he loved math last year. This year, he finds that a lot of time is wasted because a group of troublemakers constantly misbehaves, which diverts the teacher's attention. In English class, currently being taught by a student teacher, Chris is asked to read aloud a poem he wrote. After reading the poem, Chris is embarrassed and just shrugs his shoulders when asked to explain the meaning. In biology, the teacher has just begun a unit on amphibians. She announces to the class that, in lab this week, lab teams will dissect a frog. Chris is not thrilled about this activity.

Mary

Mary is thirteen years old and her family has just moved from New York City to a small town outside a large southern city. She rides the bus to school each morning, getting up at 6:00 A.M. and riding for an hour to reach school by 7:30 A.M. The school, a regional middle school, is in its second year of operation. Mary is a student in one of three eighth-grade teams, each of which comprises about 115 students and four teachers. When she arrives at school, she goes to the cafeteria to eat breakfast before going to her homeroom. Mary starts the day with a bowl of cereal, a biscuit, and a carton of orange juice. A first-year teacher who has a lot of energy, and sometimes surprises the students with a mysterious demonstration, teaches Mary's first class, prechemistry. Although she doesn't like the subject, Mary loves coming to prechemistry because the teacher encourages all the students to learn and enjoy science. Her next class is math. All the students in Mary's prechemistry class move en masse to math across the hall. Mary hates this class. The teacher, who is also on the job for the first time, embarrasses students by pointing out their mistakes, especially when they are sent to the board to "work" problems. In interrelated arts, the teacher has invited a well-known potter to come in and show the students some of his work and how he makes pots. Mary is excited and looks forward to interrelated arts today. Mary's class eats at the early first lunch period, which causes her to be hungry every day around 2:00 P.M. Mary's science teacher has asked for volunteers to form a science club and she is not sure whether she will join. Mary learns that two of her friends plan to join.

Thomas

Thomas is the oldest sibling in a family with five children. Both of his parents work, his mother during the day and his father at night. Thomas usually leaves home without breakfast, but stops at the "Quick Mart" for a sweet roll and a soft drink. Thomas is a very quiet student and tends to keep to himself, except for two friends who he sees each day at lunch and briefly after school while he walks to the bus station to go to work. Thomas reads at the sixth-grade level and is having a great deal of difficulty with homework assignments in English and in U.S. history. He goes to his homeroom for attendance, and then to his first class, general chemistry. His teacher has explained that they are using a new textbook this year, that the emphasis is on chemistry in the community, and that chemistry applies to everyday life. In chemistry class, the teacher is explaining the chemistry of digestion as Thomas's stomach is rumbling. When it rumbles very loudly, a student in the next seat starts to giggle, and pretty soon the back of the class is giggling. Thomas likes school, but he would rather be at work. He is assistant manager of the evening shift of a pizza joint, and he feels very important in this role. Thomas often wishes he had already graduated from high school and he gives a great deal of thought to dropping out, something his younger brother did.

Joseph

Joseph, a fifteen-year-old in seventh grade of a junior high school, is overweight and towers over other students. He was retained twice in the third grade, and he can't wait until next year when he will be able to drop out. Joseph goes to bed late each night. He lives with his mother and two older sisters in a high rise apartment. Joseph belongs to a gang, and most of the members live in his apartment building or adjacent ones. His gang has not been involved in any violence, but the regularly meet and smoke dope. Joseph knows that his teachers and especially the assistant principal keep an eye on him and his friends. Still, Joseph has smoked in the boy's room and has come to class many times stoned. His first class is life science and, as for all classes, Joseph never shows up with his textbook, a pencil, or paper. Joseph comes to school an average of three or four days a week and is forever behind in his work. Joseph shows some interest when the science teacher does a hands-on activity, but otherwise disdains reading the text or doing worksheet exercises. The teacher, however, rarely does a hands-on activity because some of Joseph's friends misbehave and cannot be trusted with the teaching materials.

Alice

Alice is a senior at a small high school in a mid-sized city in a western state. She, like most of the students attending the school, rides the bus. She would like to have her own car, but she can't afford one, and her parents refuse to get her one. Alice is fond of art and language, especially French, and is a member of the drama club. This year she decided to try out for one of the lead roles in *Romeo and Juliet*. In art class, the teacher has agreed to help the drama coach build the set for the play. Alice offers to make some quick sketches so they can get an idea of how the different plans would look. Derek sits next to Alice and starts talking about how bad he is going to feel when they leave school in a few months. After class, they go to the student lounge and talk for a while longer. Alice suddenly feels sad, too, and is happy to share her feelings with Derek. The conversation becomes more personal. Derek tells Alice that he has liked her for a very long time, but has been afraid to say anything because Alice was dating another boy. The bell rings and Alice and Derek go to separate classes. Alice goes to advanced biology, where the students are giving reports. Her mind wanders to the conversation with Derek. At lunch, she does her best to avoid looking at Derek. Derek finds her after school, and they talk again. He has tears in his eyes when tells Alice how much he likes her. She tries to comfort him, but nothing helps. She goes home sad, angry, and flattered.

These are only a few of countless scenarios of students in secondary schools. You can add to it from your own memory. As you progress in the process of becoming a science teacher, I hope these scenarios will help you remember that students in your class experience a life "outside of science" that will have a significant effect their learning, just as significant as the theories and models of learning and teaching that will be presented in this book.

The Effective Science Teacher: Who Are You?

As a science teacher, you will have a special role in bridging the gap between the world of science and scientists and the world of students in middle/junior and high schools. Are there characteristics common to teachers who do this effectively? The following characteristics are the result of effective teaching research over the past twenty-five years.

Effective Teachers

In recent years, researchers have investigated the relationship between teacher behavior (strategies and methods of instruction) and student performance (conceptual learning, attitudes). Through a technique in which a large number of research studies are synthesized, researchers have found clusters of instructional strategies and methods that are related to increased cognitive outcomes.[54] At this stage in your study of science teaching, I assume that you have not mastered these behaviors. Instead, these characteristics will be viewed as advance organizers for our study of effective science teaching. The list that follows has been paraphrased from Borich.[55]

Individual teachers will vary considerably in their style and in the specific strategies they use to help students come to enjoy and learn science. However, there appears to be a clustering of broad patterns of behaviors that effective teachers employ. Here is a set of behaviors that characterize secondary teachers in general and secondary science teachers.

- *Clarity.* Presentation to the class is clear and understandable. Initial explanations are clear, logical, and easy to follow.
- *Variety.* These teachers use a variety of behaviors to reinforce students, ask many and diverse questions, use an assortment of learning materials, equipment, and displays—in short, hands-on materials.
- *Task orientation.* These teachers spend more time on intellectual content than on procedures or classroom rules and tend to have higher rates of achievement.
- *On-task behavior.* This trait refers to the amount of time that students actually spend on tasks, engaged with learning materials and activities. On-task behavior is closely related to the classroom management behaviors of the teacher.
- *Success rate.* This characteristic is closely related to student self-esteem. Naturally, if students are succeeding at moderate to high rates, then students are going to feel good about themselves as science learners and have positive attitudes about science. A key behavior here is the teacher's ability to design learning tasks that lead to high success rates but are not dull, repetitive, or viewed as a waste of time
- *Using student ideas.* Acknowledging, modifying, applying, comparing, and summarizing students' comments can contribute to a positive learning environment. Teachers who use student ideas are genuinely interacting with students, thereby positively affecting student self-esteem.
- *Instructional set.* This strategy refers to teacher statements made at the beginning of a lesson or at transition points in the lesson to help students organize what is to come or what has happened before.
- *Questioning.* Teachers can and do ask a variety of questions. Knowing the kinds and times to ask questions seems to be important to student learning. Related to questioning is the behavior of "wait time," which refers to the amount of time teachers wait after asking students a question before providing the answer.
- *Enthusiasm.* This humanistic behavior refers to the teacher's vigor, power, involvement, excitement, and interest during a class presentation. Enthusiasm manifests itself by the teacher's use of eye contact, gesturing, movement, use of supportive and approval behaviors, variety of teaching techniques, and love of science.

As you continue your study of science teaching, come back to these characteristics—those resulting from the science of research and the wisdom of practice.

SECTION 2: SCIENCE TEACHER GAZETTE

Volume 1: The Art of Teaching Science: A Reconnaissance

Think Pieces

Think pieces are short essays (generally no more than two pages) or posters (no more than one large poster board) that reflect your views (appropriately supported by references) on some topic or subject in science education. Throughout the book, a few think pieces will be suggested for consideration, reflection, and action. Here are a few for this chapter:

1. Write an essay on the artistry of teaching, making use of your prior experiences with teachers in your K–12 schooling and college education.
2. In what ways should the teaching of science reflect the nature of science?
3. Why do you want to be a science teacher?
4. What are the best qualities of a science teacher?

Case Study: The Student Who Just Can't Relate to This "Physics Stuff"

The Case

A high school physics teacher typically asks students an open-ended evaluation question on each unit exam. On the first exam, the teacher receives this comment from a student: "Last year I related to biology so well. I saw things all around me. I just can't relate to this physics stuff. Pushes and pulls; how objects bounce off each other. So it does! So what?"

The Problem

Is this student's "complaint" about physics legitimate? Is relevancy to the student's everyday world something the science teacher should be concerned about? If you were the physics teacher how would you handle this situation? What would you say to the student?

SCIENCE-TEACHING LITERATURE

SCIENCE IS NOT WORDS

Richard P. Feynman

I would like to say a word or two about words and definitions, because it is necessary to learn the words.[56] It is not science. That doesn't mean just because it is not science that we don't have to teach the words. We are not talking about what to teach; we are talking about what science is. It is not science to know how to change degrees Celsius to Fahrenheit. It's necessary, but it is not exactly science. In the same sense, if you were discussing what art is, you wouldn't say art is the knowledge of the fact that a 3B pencil is softer than a 2H pencil. It's a distinct difference. That doesn't mean an artist gets along very well if he doesn't know that. (Actually, you can find out in a minute by testing the pencils, but that's a scientific way that art teachers may not think of explaining.)

In order to talk to each other, we have to have words and that's all right. It's a good idea to try to see the difference, and it's a good idea to know when we are teaching the tools of science, such as words, and when are teaching science itself.

To make my point still clearer, I shall pick out a certain science book to criticize unfavorably, which is unfair, because I am sure that with little ingenuity, I can find equally unfavorable things to say about others.

There is a first-grade science book that, in the first lesson of the first grade, begins in an unfortunate manner to teach science because it starts off with the wrong idea of what science is. The book shows a picture of a wind-up dog a hand reaching for the winder, and then the dog having the ability to move. Under the last picture, the text says, "What makes it move?" Later, there is a picture of a real dog and the question "What makes it move?" Then there is a picture of a motor bike (and so on) and the question "What makes it move?"

I thought at first that the authors were getting ready to tell what science was going to be about: physics, biology, and chemistry. But that wasn't it. The answer was in the teacher edition of the book; the answer I was trying to learn is that "energy makes it move."

Now, energy is a subtle concept. It is very, very difficult to get right. What I mean by that is that it is not easy to understand energy well enough to use it right, so that you can deduce something correctly using the energy idea. It is beyond the first grade. It would be equally well to say that "God makes it move," or "spirit makes it move," or "movability makes it move." (In fact, one could equally well say "energy makes it stop.")

Look at it this way. That's only the definition of energy. It should be reversed. We might say when something can move that it has energy in it, but not "what makes it move is energy." This is a very subtle difference. It's the same with this inertia proposition. Perhaps I can make the difference a little clearer: If you ask a child what makes the toy dog move, you should think about what an ordinary human being would answer. The answer is that you wind up the spring, which tries to unwind and pushes the gear around. What a good way to begin a science course. Take apart the toy; see how it works. See the cleverness of the gears; see the ratchets. Learn something about the toy, the way the toy is put together, the ingenuity of the people devising the ratchets, and other things. That's good. The question is fine. The answer is a little unfortunate, because what the authors were trying to do is teach a definition of energy. But nothing whatsoever is learned. Suppose a student says, "I don't think energy makes it move." Where does the discussion go from there?

I finally figured out a way to test whether you have taught an idea or you have only taught a definition. Test it this way: You say, "Without using the new word that you have just learned, try to rephrase what you have just learned in your own language." Without using the word "energy," tell me what you know now about the dog's motion." In our energy case, you cannot. So you learned nothing about science. That may be all right. You may not want to learn something about science right away. You have to learn definitions. But for the very first lesson is that not possibly destructive?

I think, for lesson number one, to learn a mystic formula for answering questions is very bad. The book has more examples: "gravity makes it fall," "the soles of your shoes wear out because of friction." Shoe leather wears out because it rubs against the sidewalk and the little notches and bumps on the sidewalk grab pieces of leather and pull it off. To simply say it is because of friction is sad because it's not science.

I went to MIT. I went to Princeton. I came home, and he (my father) said, "Now you've got a science education. I have always wanted to know something that I have never understood; and so my son, I want you to explain to me." I said yes.

He said, "I understand that they say that light is emitted from an atom when it goes from one state to another, from an excited state to a state of lower energy."

I said, "That's right."

"And light is a kind of particle, a photon, I think they call it."

"Yes."

"So if the photon comes out of the atom when it goes from the exited to the lower state, the photon must have been in the atom in the excited state."

I said, "Well, no."

He said, "Well, how do you look at it so you can think of a particle photon coming out without it having been in there in the excited state?"

I thought a few minutes, and I said, "I'm sorry, I don't know. I can't explain it to you."

He was very disappointed that so many years of schooling had produced such poor results.

What science is, I think, may be something like this: There was on this planet an evolution of life in a stage when there were evolved animals, which are intelligent. I don't mean just human beings, but animals that play and can learn something from experience (like cats). But at this stage each animal would have to learn from its own experience. They gradually developed until some animal could learn from experience more rapidly and could even learn from another's experience by watching. Perhaps one could show the other or say what the other one did. There came a possibility that all might learn from the experience, but the transmission was inefficient and they animals would die, and maybe the one who learned it died, too, before passing the information to others.

The world looks different after learning science. For example, trees are made of air, primarily. When they are burned, they go back to air, in the flaming heat is released the flaming heat of the sun, which was bound in to convert the air into tree, and in the ash is the small remnant of the part that did not come from air, but that came from the solid earth instead.

These are beautiful concepts, and the content of science is wonderfully full of such ideas. They are very inspiring and can be used to inspire others.

Another of the qualities of science is that it teaches the value of rational thought as well as the importance of freedom of thought; the positive results that come from doubting that the lessons are all true. You must here distinguish—especially in teaching—the science from the forms or procedures that are sometimes used in developing science. It is easy to say, "We write, experiment, and observe, and do this or that." You can copy that form exactly. But great religions are dissipated by following form without remembering the direct content of the teaching of the great leaders. In the same way, it is possible to follow from and call it science, but that is pseudoscience. In this way, we all suffer from the kind of tyranny we have today in the many institutions that have come under the influence of pseudoscientific advisors.

When someone says, "Science teaches such and such," he or she is using the word incorrectly.

Science doesn't teach anything; experience teaches it. If you hear, "Science has shown such and such," you might ask, "How does science show it? How did the scientists find out? How? What? Where?" It should not be "science has shown," but "this experiment, this effect, has shown." And you have as much right as anyone else, upon hearing about the experiments (but be patient and listen to all the evidence) to judge whether a sensible conclusion has been reached.

It is necessary to teach students to accept *and* to reject the past with a kind of balance that takes considerable skill. Science, alone of all the subjects, contains within itself the lesson of the danger of belief in the infallibility of the greatest teachers of the preceding generation. So, carry on.

Interview a Science Teacher

These are the questions I used to interview teachers in preparation for the Science Teacher Talk sections of future issues of the *Science Teacher Gazette*. You might want to use some or all of the questions to design and carry out a study assessing local science teachers' views on teaching.

1. If you were to describe to prospective science teachers what you like most about science teaching, what would you say?
2. How do you accommodate students with different learning styles in your classroom?
3. Do you have a philosophy and set of goals that guide your instructional actions with your students? How do you communicate these to your students?
4. Is the inquiry model of teaching important in your approach to science teaching? Why?
5. What strategy of teaching do you find to be most effective with your students?
6. Try to describe your normal teaching method by ranking the following techniques in terms of the frequency with which you use them (e.g., 1 means, "I use this technique most frequently of all," 2 means, "I use this next most often," etc.). Leave blank those you almost never use at all. You may give several items the same number, indicating yoiu use them with equal frequency.

__ Lectures that deviate widely from specific text material.
__ Lectures that are based closely on the text material.
__ Exercises taken from the text and performed by students in class.
__ Exercises taken from the text and assigned as homework.
__ Exercises I make up myself (or find in non-text sources) and have the students perform them in class.
__ Exercises I make up myself (or find in nontext sources) and assign for homework.
__ Class discussions, normally of the question-and-answer variety, based closely on text material.
__ Open, wide-ranging class discussions that deviate widely from the text and the normal question-and-answer format.
__ Lab periods (for hands-on, scientific experimentation).
__ Students working in small groups on research or projects that will be shared with the rest of the class.
__ Students working independently on research or projects that will be shared with the rest of the class.
__ Students working independently with self-directed study materials other than texts (self-graded workbooks, prepared audiovisual materials, etc.).
__ Field trips.
__ Class activities and projects that will be shared with an audience outside the classroom (exhibits, publications, plays, debates, etc.).
__ In-class visitors from the community.
__ Students working independently (or in small teams) on projects specifically designed, with student input, to link real-world experiences in the community with the subject material being studied.
__ Other:

7. How do you accommodate students with special needs, such as those with learning or behavior disorders? What have you found to be effective with these students?
8. Do you deal with controversial issues in your classroom? If so, which ones, and how?
9. What tips would you give beginning teachers about planning and preparing lessons?
10. How do you manage your classroom? What is the most important piece of advice you would give a prospective teacher concerning classroom management?

11. How do you evaluate the progress of your students? If you were to evaluate your colleagues, what criteria would you use to judge their teaching?

12. Do you have a favorite science lesson or activity? What is its essence? Why is it your favorite?

13. How do you use technology (including the Internet) in your science lessons? Why do you use it and what do you see as the benefits for your students?

Problems and Extensions

1. What are your current conceptions about science teaching? What, in your opinion, does a person need to know in order to be a good science teacher?

2. Interview several science teachers to find out what they like most and least about teaching. What are they doing to improve or change those aspects they like least? Do teachers seem to agree on what they like most about teaching?

3. How important is imagination in science? In what ways can imagination be part of the secondary science classroom?

4. What has your experience in the science been like? Do you see science in the ways Bronowski, Feynman, Polyani, or Sagan see it? What is you notion of science?

5. Think back to your high school and college experience as a science student. Did you have any teachers that you admired or considered to be outstanding science teachers? What characterized their teaching?

Lousy teachers, too!

Notes

1. Michael Dias, "Pedagogical Perspectives and Implicit Theories of Teaching: First Year Teachers Emerging from a Constructivist Science Education Program" (Ph.D. diss., Georgia State University, 2000).

2. J. Bronowski, *The Visionary Eye* (Cambridge: MIT Press, 1978), p. 20.

3. Ibid. p. 21.

4. Rollo May, *The Courage to Create* (New York: W. W. Norton, 1975), p. 41.

5. Ibid. pp. 21–22.

6. Thomas Brown, "What Students Are Saying about Science: Student Perspectives of Meaningful, Effective, and Ineffective Experiences in Science" (Ph.D. diss., Georgia State University, 2000).

7. Linda Darling-Hammond, Lisa Hudson, and Sheila Nataraj Kirby, *Redesigning Teacher Education: Opening the Door for New Recruits to Science and Mathematics Teaching* (Santa Monica, Calif.: The RAND Corporation, 1995) p. 56.

8. It should be noted at this point that there are clear differences between middle schools and junior high schools in terms of philosophy, curriculum organization, and instruction. These differences, and differences between middle school/junior high and high schools, will be discussed later in the book.

9. For the next day's lesson, the teacher divided the students into groups. Each group was involved in a different activity and shared the results with whole class. See Inquiry Activity 1.2 and try these tasks with a group of students.

10. See Inquiry Activity 1.2 for a description of the tasks.

11. Iris R. Weiss, *Report of the 2000 National Survey of Mathematics and Science Teaching* (Chapel Hill, N.C.: Horizon Research, Inc., 2001).

12. K. C. Wise and J. R. Okey, "A Meta-Analysis of the Effects of Various Science Teaching Strategies on Achievement," *Journal of Research in Science Teaching* 20 (1983): 419–35.

13. Jack Hassard, *Minds on Science* (New York: HarperCollins Publishers, 1992).

14. See Weiss, *Report of the 2000 National Survey.*

15. Paul DeHart Hurd, "New Directions in Science Education," in *Third Sourcebook for Science Supervisors*, ed. LaMoine L. Motz and Gerry M. Madrazo (Washington, D.C.: National Science Teachers Association, 1988), pp. 3–7.

16. See Weiss, *Report of the 2000 National Survey*, pp. 61–62.

17. Richard P. Feynman, *Surely You're Joking, Mr. Feynman* (New York: W.W. Norton, 1985), p. 21. Feynman was a member of the Rogers Commission, which investigated and reported on the cause of the space shuttle *Challenger* explosion. In the sequel to *Surely You're Joking, Mr. Feynman*, entitled *What Do You Care What Other People Think?* (New York: W.W. Norton, 2001), Feynman writes about about his experiences as a member of the commission. It would be an understatement to say that his actions and thoughts were always welcomed by the commission chair, but through the eyes of this scientist we witness the inner workings of the commission and get an insight into the confusion and misjudgment that characterized the management of NASA leading up to the *Challenger* disaster. Perhaps most vivid of all is the scenario where Americans observed Feynman using his knowledge to reveal the cause of the disaster by dropping a ring of rubber into a glass of cold water and then pulling it out, now misshapen.

18. Richard P. Feynman et al., *The Feynman Lectures on Physics*, vol. I (Menlo Park: Addison-Wesley, 1963), p. 2–1.

19. Michael Polanyi, *The Republic of Science* (Roosevelt University, 1962), p. 5.

20. *The International Webster New Encyclopaedia Dictionary*, 1975, s.v. "science."

21. Carl Sagan, *Broca's Brain: Reflections on the Romance of Science* (New York: Random House, 1979), p. 13.

22. Margaret Truman, *Women of Courage* (New York: Bantam, 1976).

23. Ibid., pp. 178–96.

24. Eugene Raudsepp, *How Creative Are You?* (New York: Perigee, 1981).

25. See June Goodfield, *An Imagined World: A Story of Scientific Discovery* (New York: Harper and Row, 1981).

26. Jacob Bronowski, *A Sense of the Future: Essays in Natural Philosophy* (Cambridge, Mass.: The MIT Press, 1977), p. 28.

27. Ibid., p. 209.

28. Horace Freeland Judson, *The Eighth Day of Creation* (New York: Simon & Schuster, 1979), p. 70.

29. James Watson, *The Double Helix* (New York: Atheneum, 1968), pp. 17–18.

30. Anne Sayre, *Rosalind Franklin and DNA* (New York: W.W. Norton, 1975), p. 17.

31. Vivian Gornick, *Women in Science* (New York: Simon & Schuster, 1990), p. 12.

32. Ibid., p. 12.

33. Ibid., p. 13.

34. Watson, *The Double Helix*, pp. 17–18.

35. Sayre, *Rosalind Franklin and DNA*, pp. 18–19.

36. There is a large body of literature on women in science. See, for example, Sue V. Rosser, *Female-Friendly Science* (New York: Pergamon Press, 1990). Also refer to the readings presented in Chapter 2.

37. F. James Rutherford and Andrew Ahlgren, *Science for All Americans* (Washington, D.C.: American Association for the Advancement of Science, 1989).

38. Based on R. W. Fleming, "High-School Graduates' Beliefs about Science-Technology-Society. II. The Interaction Among Science, Technology, and Society," *Science Education* 71, no. 2 (1987): 163–86.

39. National Research Council, *National Science Education Standards* (Washington, D.C.: National Academy Press, 1995), see chap. 6.

40. Wayne Welch, "A Science-Based Approach to Science Learning," in *Research within Reach: Science Education*, ed. David Holdzkom and Pamela B. Lutz (Washington, D.C.: National Science Teachers Association, 1986), pp. 161–70.

41. National Research Council, *Inquiry and the National Science Education Standards* (Washington, D.C.: National Academy Press, 2000), p. xv.

42. See Donald C. Orlich, "Science Inquiry and the Commonplace," *Science and Children* (March 1989), 22–24; and Donald Orlich et al., *Teaching Strategies: A Guide to Better Instruction*, 2d ed. (Lexington, Mass.: D.C. Heath, 1985), see, especially, chap. 8.

43. Hurd, "New Directions in Science Education," p. 6.

44. David Johnson and Roger Johnson, *Circles of Learning* (Alexandria, Va.: Association for Supervision and Curriculum Development, 1990).

45. Jack Hassard, *Science as Inquiry*. (Parsippany, N.Y.: Goodyear Books, 2000).

46. See R. Osborne and P. Freyberg, *Learning in Science: The Implications of Children's Science* (Auckland: Heinemann, 1985); or J. D. Novak and D. B. Gowin, *Learning How to Learn* (Cambridge, England: Cambridge University Press, 1984), and Jack Hassard, *Increasing Your Students' Science Achievement* (Bellevue, Wash.: Bureau of Education and Research, 2000).

47. B. G. Aldridge and K. L. Johnston, "Trends and Issues in Science Education," in *Redesigning Science and Technology Education*, ed. R. W. Bybee, J. Carlson, and A. J. McCormack (Washington, D.C.: National Science Teachers Association, 1984).

48. Osborne and Freyberg, *Learning in Science*, pp. 55–56.

49. Ibid., p. 56.

50. R. E. Yager and J. E. Penick, "Perceptions of Four Age Groups Toward Science Classes, Teachers, and the Value of Science," *Science Education* 70, no. 4 (1986): 355–63.

51. M. B. Rowe, "Science Education: A Framework for Decision-Makers," in *Third Sourcebook for Science Supervisors*, ed. L. L. Motz and G. M. Madrazo, Jr. (Washington, D.C.: National Science Teachers Association, 1988), pp. 23–34.

52. Ibid., p. 25.

53. These scenarios were developed after B. M. Newman and P. R. Newman, *Adolescent Development* (Columbus, Ohio: Merrill, 1986), pp. 330–32.

54. See C. A. Hofwolt, "Instructional Strategies in the Science Classroom," in *Research within Reach: Science Education*, ed. D. Holdzkom and P. B. Lutz (Washington, D.C.: The National Science Teachers Association, 1985), pp. 43–57; and G. Borich, *Effective Teaching Methods* (Columbus, Ohio: Merrill, 1998), especially pp. 1–17.

55. Borich, *Effective Teaching Methods*, pp. 1–17.

56. Based on R. P. Feynman, "What Is Science?" *The Physics Teacher* (September 1969): 313–20. Used with permission.

Readings

Alic, Margaret. *Hypatia's Heritage: A History of Women in Science from Antiquity through the Nineteenth Century*. Boston: Beacon Press, 1986.

Barman, Charles R. "Completing the Study: High School Students' Views of Scientists and Science." *Science and Children* 36, no. 7 (April 1999): 16–21.

Berliner, David C., and Rosenshine, Barak V., eds. *Talks to Teachers*. New York: Random House, 1987.

Bronowski, Jacob. *Science and Human Values*. New York: Harper and Row Publishers, 1956.

Bronowski, Jacob. *A Sense of the Future: Essays in Natural Philosophy*. Cambridge, Mass.: The MIT Press, 1978.

Bybee, Rodger W. *National Standards and the Science Curriculum: Challenges, Opportunities and Recommendations*. Dubuque, Iowa: Kendall/Hunt, 1996.

Goodfield, June. *An Imagined World: A Story of Scientific Discovery*. New York: Harper and Row, 1981.

Gornick, Vivian, *Women in Science*. New York: Simon & Schuster, 1990.

Hurd, Paul DeHart. *Inventing Science Education for the New Millennium*. New York: Teachers College Press, 1997.

Hurd, Paul DeHart. *Transforming Middle School Science Education*. New York: Teachers College Press, 2000.

Lowery, Lawrence, ed. *NSTA Pathways to the Science Standards*. Arlington, Va.: National Science Teachers Association, 1997.

National Research Council, Inquiry and the National Science Education Standards. Washington, D.C.: 2000.

Sagan, Carl. *Broca's Brain: Reflections on the Romance of Science*. New York: Random House, 1979.

On the Web

Adolescents and Teens: http://www.cdc.gov/health/adolescent.htm. A CDC site that outlines a number of links dealing with health issues related to teenagers.

Eisenhower National Clearing House: http://www.enc.org/. This site, at Ohio State University, provides up-to-date information on science teaching, including lesson plans, curriculum development projects, and technology.

The Science Learning Network: http://www.sln.org/. The Science Learning Network is an online community of educators, students, schools, and science museums that demonstrates a new model for inquiry science.

2 Science for All

"Science for all" implies there's something in it (science) for everyone. It means that nearly every child can learn and experience the essence of science. Science for all acknowledges that science education in the past has *not* been science for all, that large numbers of persons have indeed been failed or passed over by the science curriculum. Science for *all* means including everyone.

The science for all theme implies that science education should be based on several fundamental characteristics of learners and what school science should be:

1. Each learner is unique.
2. All students can learn.
3. There is enormous diversity among learners, and this diversity should be respected and accepted.
4. School science should be designed to meet the needs of all students, not just the science prone or those who will pursue careers in science.
5. School science should be inclusive, not exclusive. Those who have been traditionally turned away from science should be encouraged to study it.

In this chapter, we will explore the theme science for all from four interrelated perspectives: global thinking, multicultural education, feminist perspectives, and exceptional children and youth. Each of these perspectives requires teachers to incorporate the notion of uniqueness and diversity at the same time; in so doing, the teacher approaches science teaching from a holistic point of view. Mary M. Atwater, writing about multicultural education in science education, says:

> Multicultural science education is a field of inquiry with constructs, methodologies, and processes aimed at providing equitable opportunities for *all* students to learn *quality* science. Multicultural science education research continues to be influenced by class, culture, disability, ethnicity, gender, and different lifestyles;

however, another appropriate epistemology for this area of research is social constructivism.[1]

This chapter is designed to heighten your awareness, provide background information on global, multicultural, and gender perspectives of science teaching, and help you explore the range of the exceptional types of students who will be part of all of your science courses.

Case Study: A New Buzz Word?

The Case

Eric Hannapool has just returned from a summer institute on strategies to enhance the course and career options for women and minorities in middle and high school science programs. He is prepared to give a report to the rest of his science department at a special meeting for this purpose. The department is composed of fifteen faculty members, five women and ten men. During Eric's report, one of the male teachers interrupts to ask, "What is this multicultural stuff? Is this just another buzz word?" Eric responds with, "You're joking!" The teacher replies, "Absolutely not!" Two or three other teachers appear to support this buzzword position. Eric flashes back to what the principal told him last spring: "I want a multicultural policy and program implemented in all departments, and since you're the science department chair, I want you to lead the effort."

The Problem

How should Eric respond to the three or four teachers who don't seem to see much value in multicultural education? How can he get them on his side?

How to Read This Chapter

The chapter comprises four sections, including global thinking, multicultural education, gender issues in science teaching, and exceptional children and youth. You can focus on any one of these themes individually, but as you begin to explore the science for all concept, you will see that these ideas are interrelated. The issues discussed in this chapter will play a pivotal role in your development as a teacher. You will want to return to this chapter from time to time to review some of the ideas and follow up on some of the Web sites found in the *Science Teacher Gazette* section.

SECTION 1: SCIENCE FOR ALL

Invitations to Inquiry

- What is the implication of the theme "science for all"? Is this a reality in today's schools? What needs to be done to make it a reality?
- Should global thinking be incorporated into the philosophy and objectives of school science? How should this be accomplished?
- What are some specific strategies science teachers might use to infuse global thinking into the science curriculum?
- How can science be made understandable and accessible to all students? How can schools overcome barriers to equitable educational opportunities and outcomes?
- What are some approaches that science educators can use to infuse equity and multiculturalism into the science program?
- What is the nature of a feminist perspective on science education?
- What are some strategies to encourage females in science courses and careers?
- What should the nature of science teaching be for exceptional students?
- How does the concept of the at-risk student compare to the concept of the at-promise student?
- How would you approach teaching science to physically impaired, learning disabled, gifted and talented, and at-risk students?

Global Thinking

Should science teachers incorporate global thinking in the goals and objectives of science courses? If they should, what is the rationale for doing so? Why should science educators become involved? How can global thinking be of service to the science for all theme? (Note that there is a section in Chapter 4 on science teaching in other countries that was written by science educators from Australia, Chile, China, Ghana, Japan, and Russia. You might want to look ahead to these discussions and learn what colleagues from other nations think about science teaching.)

Global Events Fostering Global Thinking

Science and science education have had a global reach for centuries. Over the past decade, science educators from around the world have reached across their borders to provide global experiences for their students:

- From 1994 to the present, more than 10,000 American and Russian secondary students and teachers participated in the Youth Exchange Program between U.S. and Russian students and teachers. Funded by the United States Information Agency, this program made it possible for American and Russian youth to live in each other's homes and participate in science, mathematics, social studies, and cultural projects.[2]
- In the summer of 1991, 1,000 American and Soviet teachers met in Moscow to exchange ideas about science education. At the conference, teachers from these two nations presented workshops, engaged in panel discussions, and heard presentations by distinguished teachers and scientists. But beneath all of this was something more profound: The teachers in attendance were drawn together by the deep human bond of wanting to understand and find out about each other.
- Since 1983, a group of science educators focused in Atlanta, and involving teachers from various parts of the United States, has developed a global/Web-based project (Global Thinking Project, www.gsu.edu/~www.gtp) with teachers from Russia, Spain, Australia, and the Czech Republic. The project has supported the exchange of over 500 youths and 200 teachers. The project currently supports two major Web-based inquiries, including the International Clean Air Project and the International Water Watch Project, involving participants from most of the continents.
- The GLOBE Program has created teaching materials and a Web site (www.globe.gov) that enables students and teachers from more than 200 countries to work together gathering data on environmental issues.

These and other projects that will be highlighted in chapters ahead are the tip of an iceberg reflecting profound changes in the possibilities for intercultural and global activities for teachers and students around the world.

Rationale for Global Thinking

In recent years, there has been an effort to globalize education. This effort is being made in a variety of ways and it is worthwhile to discuss the underlying reasons.

Let's start with Albert Einstein. In May 1946, in a fund-raising letter for the Emergency Committee of Atomic Scientists, Einstein wrote, "The unleashed power of the atom has changed everything save our modes of thinking, and thus we drift toward unparalleled catastrophe."[3] With the advent of war science and technology, whose consequences could be as dire for the victor as for the vanquished, Einstein realized the increasing importance of thinking from a global as well as a local perspective and of considering the long-term consequences of political or military decisions on the fragile ecosystem of earth. We could infer that what Einstein was calling for was a move toward "systems thinking"; that is, toward an ability to predict the consequences of altering any subpart of a system on the functioning of the whole. This kind of thinking about complex issues implies an ability to view a problem from multiple perspectives and to predict the consequences.

Education for global thinking is not unlike education for "global citizenship" or education for a "global perspective," two other ideas that have been widely written about over the past two decades. All three concepts (global thinking, global citizenship, and global perspective) emphasize the importance of perspective taking, which might be viewed as learning to see problems and issues through the eyes and minds of others. Perspective taking incorporates elements of both empathy (ability to put oneself in another's shoes) and intercultural competence, and ability to function within the norms and expectations of another culture. Global citizenship also includes recognition of the interdependence of global systems and the responsibility of individuals as well as nation-states to be actors on the world stage. These elements have formed the basis for the contemporary global education movement, which seeks to prepare students to participate on the world stage by developing their knowledge about different parts of the world, increasing their empathy, and teaching them skills for participating in the civic life of their communities.[4]

Robert Hanvey, discussing a rationale for a global perspective, suggested that it

involves learning about those problems and issues that cut across national boundaries, and about the interconnectedness of systems—ecological, cultural, economic, political, and technological. Global education involves perspective taking—seeing things through the eyes and minds of others—and it means the realization that while individuals and groups may view life differently, they also have common needs and wants.[5]

Hanvey makes an important point about perspective taking—seeing things through the eyes and minds of others. To create learning environments for all students requires this philosophical position. Not only is this position supported by global education activities such as international business, the Peace Corps, foreign student exchange programs, and international activities, but by changes in the social structure of the world and the globalization of America. Let's examine how these affect the perspective of science teachers as they think about the goals and objectives of the science education in global terms.

GLOBAL THINKING ACTIVITIES Teachers and students in today's classes are already involved in global activities. Many teachers have traveled to other countries and share their experience with their students. In some classrooms, a number of students were born in a foreign country and bring with them the perspective of their native country. Students may belong to clubs, churches, and civic groups that are involved in international activities. All of these activities are examples of global education activities. In the past few years, a number of technology-related projects have brought distance learning into the classrooms of teachers in many parts of the world. Over the past twenty years, educators in many countries have worked together to design inquiry-based projects in which students work together at remote locations in the context of global cooperation.[6]

CHANGING STRUCTURE OF THE WORLD Another factor supporting global education is the way in which the social structure of the world has changed. The first, and perhaps most obvious change, is the accelerating growth of global interdependence. This is evident in fields such as economics, politics, geography, ecology, and culture, to name a few. For example, in the realm of economics, world markets dominate many companies and, indeed, the emergence of the multinational corporation (MNC) is an indicator of the social changes in the economic arena. A product produced by an MNC might be assembled in the United States, but it may consist of parts from as many as fifteen different countries. Changes in transportation and communication have lessened people's isolation. This flow of people and electronic traffic has affected money, information, ideas, goods and services, technology, diseases, and weapons.

The science teacher can easily help students understand the ecological implications of changes in the social fabric of the world. Diseases spread rapidly from one continent to another: The AIDS epidemic is a good example of this as is the annual fear of viruses being spread around the world. Environmental problems, which twenty years ago were examined as if they were national in scope have now taken on a global perspective given concerns over the depletion of the ozone, global warming, thermonuclear war, toxic and nuclear waste disposal, deforestation, and the extinction of animal and plant species.

GLOBALIZATION Perhaps one of the most powerful rationales for a global perspective is the fact that the world has become globalized. This change can be seen in terms of world economy, political life, and culture, as well as growth in global consciousness.[7] For instance, according to Anderson, American workers make products in which more than one in five is exported, and more than 50 percent of the most important industrial raw materials are imported.[8] Many U.S. firms have branches abroad and an increasing number of U.S. firms are foreign owned. Anderson makes a powerful point when he reminds us to think about the products we use every day. What do they have in common? (*Answer*: All the following products were made by companies that are foreign owned: Pillsbury flour, Hills Brothers coffee, Carnation creamer, Friskies cat food, Bic pens, Foster Grant sunglasses, the Burger King Whopper, Michelin tires, and Shell gasoline.)

Using America's political life as an example, it obviously has become globalized as well. Anderson writes, "Thus, it is not surprising that the accelerating globalization of the American economy is paralleled by an increasing internationalizing of American government and politics."[9] America's politicians look beyond their own constituents and many travel abroad. The action is at the state level. In recent years, nearly all the governors traveled abroad to seek markets for their states' products and recruit foreign firms to their cities. Other signs show how American politics has become globalized. Lobbying groups representing multinational firms now exist in Washington to influence politicians. These and other reasons acknowledge the globalization of U.S. governments and politics.

GLOBAL CONSCIOUSNESS Because of the business opportunities at a global level, the awareness or consciousness, especially in the business community, has become increasingly global.[10] The scientific community has also influenced the global consciousness of Americans. International conferences, reports by science panels and institutions, and even science curriculum efforts have raised the awareness level of people so that terms like global warming, ozone depletion, and acid rain are familiar to the average person.

Youth exchanges have also affected global consciousness. In recent years, educators from different nations have worked with each other to provide exchange opportunities for their students in which youths from collaborating nations live and participate in activities in the host country.[11]

Goals of Global Thinking: Implications for Science Teaching

There is a strong support base for including global thinking in science teaching. Global thinking is an underlying basis for an interdisciplinary and multicultural approach to science teaching. This can imply that individual courses—say, chemistry—can involve students in interdisciplinary and multicultural thinking as well as school districts developing individual science courses. Some potential goals of global thinking include:[12]

1. *Perspective consciousness:* An awareness of an appreciation for other images of the world. Students can learn to understand how people in Eastern, as well as in developing nations, conceptualize the world. Global thinking will enrich the activities of students by involving them with a world that is multicultural.
2. *State of planet awareness:* An in-depth understanding of global issues and events, including the identification of the important global problems facing the planet and what it will take to achieve solutions.
3. *Cross-cultural awareness:* A general understanding of the defining characteristics of world cultures, with an emphasis on understanding similarities and differences.
4. *Systemic awareness:* A familiarity with the nature of systems and an introduction to the complex international system in which state and nonstate actors are linked in patterns of interdependence and dependence in a variety of issue areas.
5. *Options for participation:* A review of strategies for participating in issue areas in local, national,

Table 2.1 Elements of Global Thinking

Global Thinking Element	Description	Implications/Examples
Perspective consciousness	Recognition that one's own view of the world may not be universally shared. Represents a worldview that influences how individuals respond to issues or situations.	Involving students in cross-cultural activities to help them discover that people in other cultures may have their own way of looking at things.
State of awareness of the planet	Knowing about the conditions outside of one's own community.	Using media and cross-cultural experiences to involve students in seeing differences between their environment and environments in distant locations.
Cross-cultural awareness	Awareness of the diversity of ideas and practices that exists in the world. Helping people see that all humans are members of the same species, despite differences in customs and beliefs.	Using the media, such the Internet, to enable students from different cultures to see each other, to discuss important issues, and accept differences in views.
Knowledge about global dynamics	An understanding of the planet as comprising interconnected systems, a change in any one of which affects them all.	Participation in global projects (see the Web resources) in which students exchange information about a system (air or water) and use it to compare and contrast local and distant information.
Awareness of human choices	An awareness of the ability to make choices and recognition that different choices have different long-term consequences.	Involving students in projects in which they can assess the impact of changing (making a choice) some aspect of a system.
The citizen–scientist	One who combines the processes and habits of mind of science with public decision making.	Bring activities to the science classroom that enable students to be activists who are motivated to apply their knowledge and skills to improve a situation. See Chapter 12 for examples of such activities and projects.

Source: Based on Hanvey, Robert G. *An Attainable Global Perspective*. Denver, Colo.: Center for Teaching International Relations, 1976; and Hassard, Jack, and Weisberg, Julie. "The Emergence of Global Thinking among American and Russian Youth as a Contribution to Public Understanding." *International Journal of Science Education* 21 (1999): 1–13.

and international settings. Technology-related systems of communication enable all students to communicate with people in remote places.

6. *Thinking as a citizen–scientist:* An ability to integrate the habits of mind of science with public decision making.

Table 2.1 provides a closer look at the elements of global thinking.

There are a number of ways that the global perspective can be applied to science teaching: infusing global education into the science curriculum, integrating it into planning, using technology, and developing curriculum models. Individual science teachers can implement the first three implications, whereas the fourth implication will require the collaboration of state science curriculum planners or district level science coordinators.

Infusing Global Thinking into the Science Curriculum

Aspects of global education can easily be infused into individual science courses from grades K–12, thereby helping students make connections between their study of science (biology, chemistry, earth science, physics) and global issues and problems. To some science educators, global education is important enough that it should be a theme or strand running throughout the curriculum. Mayer, describing a rationale for teaching science from a global view, says:

Thus, global education should be a thread running through science curriculum. Our future leaders and voters (today's students) must understand our interrelationships with peoples around the work and how our daily activities affect our planet and its resources.[13]

Table 2.2 Curriculum Strategy for Infusing Global Education into Science Teaching

Grade Level	Global Topic/Unit	Purpose/Goals
Sixth Grade	Windows on the World: Student Perceptions	1. Focus activities on value systems—individual, group, societal, cultural, or planetary. 2. Involve all students in simulation studies centering on the global way of life from the viewpoint of various topic areas.
Seventh Grade	Stewardship of the Spaceship Earth	1. Focus activities on environmental issues at a local and/or state level and examine how they contrast with national and/or global issues. 2. Develop activities centering on the types of alternatives that are available with regard to environmental issues.
Eighth Grade	Citizen Responsibilities Concerning the Environment	1. Focus investigations and activities on local, state, and national channels of government and the techniques they use to respond to environmental needs and/or issues. 2. Investigate and compare the U.S. system of government with that of a foreign government. In addition, develop activities exploring the United Nations and other international efforts to respond to global environmental concerns.
Ninth Grade	Understanding Human Choices	1. Focus activities on the problems confronting individuals, nations, continents, and the human species as global concerns expand. 2. Focus activities on students' abilities to understand difference between pre-global and global perspectives.
Tenth Grade	Opinion and Perspective	1. Focus activities on awareness of varying perspectives with regard to the individual and the world, followed by investigative research about the different perspectives. 2. Focus activities on discovering and recognizing global perspectives that differ profoundly from those of this country.
Eleventh Grade	The World in Dynamic Change	1. Focus on research and investigative activities revealing present key traits, mechanisms, or technologies that assist in the operation of global dynamics. 2. Conduct activities on awareness of theories and related concepts regarding current global change.
Twelfth Grade	State of Planet Earth	1. Focus activities on the most recent worldwide environmental conditions—migration, political change, war and peace, economic conditions, and so forth. 2. Develop activities on awareness of students' roles and their responsibility to become involved in one or more of these world conditions and to work toward a resolution.

Source: Based on Rosengren, Frank H., Crofts Wiley, Marylee, and Wiley, David S. *Internationalizing Your School.* New York: National Council on Foreign Language and International Studies, 1983, pp. 17–18.

An example of the infusion of a thread of global education running through the science curriculum is the Pennsylvania Department of Education's strategy of providing supplementary curriculum or study units in global education (Table 2.2).

Integrating Global Science Education Activities into Planning

Another strategy is to integrate global science activities, such as the Global Food Web,[14] into chapters of textbooks and units of study. The Global Food Web is a science program focusing on environment, food supply, and human nutrition. It consists of activities designed to expose Georgia students to issues of both national and international relevance, especially in the interrelated areas of environment. The challenge is to relate science concepts and units of study to global themes such as environment, pollution, natural resources, energy, food, population, war technology, and human health and disease. There is a wealth of sourcebooks and curriculum projects that teachers use to develop ideas and lesson plans (see Chapter 11 on STS for specific curriculum projects).

Using the Internet to Globalize the Classroom

By means of online communication via the Internet, a classroom in Decatur, Georgia, can be connected to a classroom in Botswana, and classrooms anywhere can tap into large databases available via the Internet. The globalization of the science classroom enables students in one culture to communicate with students in another. Students can use the Internet to send e-mail to students in distant lands. Students can investigate problems together (such as comparing the levels of pollution in streams and rivers), share information on acid levels in rivers, or conduct a joint study to analyze trash removal systems in different cities.

Many schools around the globe have turned some of their rooms into global Internet hubs by joining Web-based projects that enable them to collaborate with teachers and students in other countries. A good example is the KidsNet Project, created by the National Geographic Society. In this system, students share information and explore an environmental problem (e.g., acid rain) by conducting research experiments locally. Classes in one region compare their measurements and data with students in different parts of the world. KidsNet also has the provision of providing an expert—a scientist to whom the students can communicate and ask questions.

Another program that uses technology to help geographically diverse students interact is the GLOBE Program (www.globe.gov), a collaborative effort among scientists, teachers, and students around the world in more than 200 countries. The GLOBE Program enables students to share information about phenomena unique to their local environment with students in the other countries.

A team of teachers and science educators at Georgia State University has collaborated with teachers and researchers in Australia, the Czech Republic, Russia, Spain, and other countries to develop the Global Thinking Project. The project links classrooms to study common environmental problems and is designed to foster global thinking.

These and other efforts have made the notion of a global science classroom a reality and therefore a powerful tool in helping students connect with peers in other countries and develop an awareness of other people.

Recent research has suggested that networking activity, not network connections, should be the driving force in the creation of global classrooms. The technical connections need to be used by creative teachers to provide another vehicle for human communication. In this case, human communication is among students from diverse cultures, continents, and ethnic groups.

World (Global) Core Curriculum

In response to the question, "Is Global Educated Needed?" Robert Muller, Assistant Secretary-General of the United Nations, responded with a proposal that became known as the "world core curriculum." Muller's curriculum is based on his thirty-three years of experience in the United Nations and knowledge of the state of the planet's educational system. He says:

Let me tell you how I would educate the children of this planet in the light of my thirty-three years of experience at the United Nations and offer you a world core curriculum which should underlie all grades, levels and forms of education including adult education.

Alas, many newly born will never reach school age. One out of ten will die before the age of one and another 4 percent will die before the age of five. This we must try to prevent by all means. We must also try to prevent that children reach school age with handicaps. It is estimated that 10 percent of all the world's children reach school age with a handicap of a physical, sensory or mental nature. In the developing countries, an unforgivable major cause is still malnutrition.

Thirdly, an ideal world curriculum presupposes that there are schools in all parts of the world. Alas, this is not the case. There are still 814 million illiterates on this planet. Humanity has done wonders in educating its people: we have reduced the percentage of illiterates of the world's adult population from 32.4 percent to 28.9 percent between 1970 and 1980, a period of phenomenal population growth. But between now and the year 2000, 1.6 billion more people will be added to this planet and we are likely to reach a total of 6.1 billion people in that year. Ninety percent of the increase will be in the developing countries where the problem of education is more severe. As a result, the total number of illiterates could climb to 950 million by the Bimillennium.

Education for all [italics mine] remains, therefore, a first priority on this planet. This is why UNESCO has rightly adopted a World Literacy Plan 2000. With all these miseries and limitations still with us, it remains important, nevertheless, to lift our sights and to begin thinking of a world core curriculum.

As I do it in the United Nations, where all human knowledge, concerns, efforts, and aspirations converge, I would organize such a curriculum, that is, the fundamental life-long objectives of education, around the following categories:

I.   Our Planetary Home and Place in the Universe
II. Our Human Family
III. Our Place in Time
IV. The Miracle of Individual Human Life[15]

A world core curriculum, as Muller envisions it, would enable all students to understand the planet upon which they were born and to know their relationship to human groups all over the planet. Ethnic and cultural understanding is an important aspect of Muller's core curriculum. He also suggests that students need to understand their place in time—where humanity came from and where it is going. Finally, the Muller proposal suggests that "individual human life is the highest form of universal consciousness on the planet," and that the curriculum should be based on a holistic integration of physical well-being, mental development, moral development, and spiritual development.

The Muller world core curriculum is distinctly interdisciplinary and multicultural. The global perspective for education, as envisioned by Muller, is organized around four harmonies. Although traditional topics are part of the plan (students study our relationship to the sun, the atmosphere, biosphere, mountains, minerals, nutrition, etc.), they are viewed in relationship to a larger consciousness—the global perspective.[16]

INQUIRY ACTIVITY 2.1

 Exploring Global Thinking

This activity is designed to engage you in a global science activity and inspire you to consider some applications of the global perspective to science courses of study.

Materials

- One set of "global problem" cards for each team
- Sheet of newsprint
- Marking pens

Procedure

1. You should join with several class members to do this activity to create several "global" teams, each of which should represent a different country. Form your groups and then as a large group decide which country each team will represent.
2. Take a few minutes and make a list of information about the country you represent. You may need reference books to provide the teams with background information about the countries for each team.
3. Each team should have a set of global problem cards (Figure 2.1). These problems represent some of the most important environmental problems facing the earth today.[17] Your team should investigate these problems from the point of view of citizens of the country you represent.
4. To prepare for a cross-cultural discussion, your team should engage in the following activities:
   a. Rank order the cards from most important or significant problem to least important or significant. Make a record of your team's decision.
   b. Select the most pressing problem, and then arrange the other problems in a "web" or "map," and indicate how the global problems interrelate. Make a record of your team's work on a sheet of newsprint.
5. Bring all the teams together to simulate an international conference on global environmental problems. Choose a moderator from the group and then have each team prepare a short (no more than five minutes) report.
6. The moderator should use the questions in the following section to facilitate a group discussion.

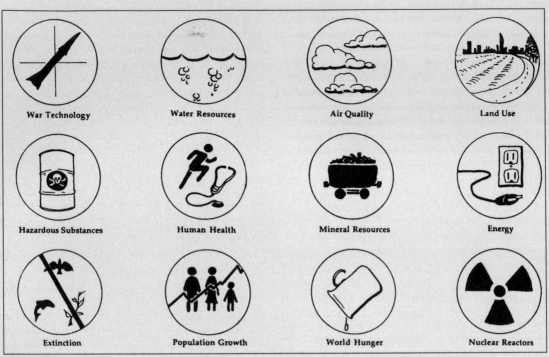

Figure 2.1 Global Problem Cards. *Note:* Copy this page and cut into twelve global problem cards to be used for Inquiry Activity 2.1.

Minds-On Strategies

1. In what school science context would you use this activity? What would be the goals and purpose of using this activity? Suggest appropriate follow-up activities that this activity would stimulate for students.[18]
2. To what extent did you feel competent understanding global problems from the point of view of a citizen from another country? Does this understanding influence decision making and deciding upon the significance of a problem? In what way?
3. Try this activity with a group of secondary students. Evaluate their performance in light of your own.
4. How does an activity like this help develop a global perspective for students? For teachers?

Multicultural Perspective

As a historical note, the Association for Multicultural Science Education (AMSE) was founded in April 1989 and held its first meeting at the National Science Teachers Association conference in Atlanta. In the bylaws of the AMSE, the following statement defines its purpose and objectives:

The purposes for which this Association is organized are to stimulate and promote science teaching to students of culturally diverse backgrounds and to motivate such students to consider science-related careers; to explore and promote the improvement of science curriculums, educational systems and teaching methods in schools to assist such stimulation; to recruit and involve teachers of all minorities in science education and to initiate and engage in activities and programs in furtherance of improving the science education of culturally diverse students.[19]

In this section we will explore multicultural education and indicate the central place that multicultural science education should play in planning science lessons, choosing content, selecting teaching materials, and teacher behavior in the classroom. Recent work by science education researchers is helping us understand issues in secondary schools, especially those in urban settings. Multicultural education is a movement that began in the 1970s, but as James Banks points out, it has expectedly suffered from some confusion:

> Since multicultural education . . . deals with highly controversial and politicized issues such as racism and inequality (it) is likely to be harshly criticized during its formative stages because it deals with serious problems in society and appears to many individuals and groups to challenge established institutions, norms and values. It is also likely to evoke strong emotions, feelings and highly polarized opinions. As it searches for its raison d'etre, there are bound to be suspicions and criticisms.[20]

What Is Multicultural Education?

According to Fred Rodriguez, the acknowledgment of the importance of multicultural education was reflected in a statement by the American Association for Colleges of Teacher Education (AACTE), "No One Model American." The statement has become the basis for most other definitions of multicultural education. Multicultural education, according to the AACTE statement, involves the following:

- Multicultural education is education, which values cultural pluralism.
- Multicultural education rejects the view that schools should seek to melt away cultural differences or the view that schools should merely "tolerate" cultural pluralism.
- Multicultural education programs for teachers are more than "special courses" or "special learning experiences," grafted onto the standard program.
- The commitment to cultural pluralism must permeate all areas of educational experience.[21]

Another organization, the National Council for the Accreditation of Teacher Education (NCATE), advocated that multicultural education should be part of all teacher-training programs. The NCATE definition of multicultural education is as follows:

Multicultural education is preparation for the social, political and economic realities that individuals experience in culturally diverse and complex human encounters . . . this preparation provides a process by which an individual develops competencies for perceiving, believing, evaluating and behaving in different cultural settings.[22]

Multicultural education is seen not as a course of study or a subject, nor as a unit of study, nor for just minority students. It is, rather, a way of teaching and learning, thereby offering a perspective on education.[23] The teacher who embodies a multicultural approach creates a classroom environment that respects cultural diversity and presents lessons that draw upon the cultural diversity implicit in the content being presented.

Status and Goals

In a report entitled *Education That Works: An Action Plan for the Education of Minorities*, by the Quality Education for Minorities Project (QEMP) at the Massachusetts Institute of Technology, the authors propose a national effort to create a new kind of learning system that recognizes the value and potential of all students. They set forth the following goals for the twenty-first century:[24]

- Goal 1: Ensure that minority students start school prepared to learn.
- Goal 2: Ensure that the academic achievement of minority youth is at a level that will enable them, upon graduation from high school, to enter the workforce or college fully prepared to be successful and not in need of remediation.

The QEMP authors pointed out that goal 1 will be achieved when it is ensured that tracking does not occur at any point along the educational pipeline; any performance gap is bridged between nonminority and minority students by the fourth grade; minority students leave elementary school with the language, mathematics skills, and self-esteem that will enable them to succeed; by eighth grade minority youth are excelling in core academic courses (science, math, history, language) that keep their college and career options open; and schools achieve, at a minimum, the same high school graduation rates for minority and nonminority students.

- Goal 3: Significantly increase the participation of minority students in higher education, with a special emphasis on the study of mathematics, science, and engineering.

- Goal 4: Strengthen and increase the number of teachers of minority students.
- Goal 5: Strengthen the school-to-work transition so that minority students who do not choose college leave high school prepared with the skills necessary to participate productively in the world of work and with the foundation required to upgrade their skills and advance their careers.
- Goal 6: Provide quality out-of-school educational experiences and opportunities to supplement the schooling of minority youth and adults.

As pointed out in the QEMP report, the school population in the United States is changing such that the term "minority" will, if it hasn't already, lose its meaning. About 20 percent of the U.S. population is Alaska Native, American Indian, black, or Hispanic, and, by 2020, over a third of the nation will be "minority." Some states (New Mexico and Mississippi) have "minority-majority" enrollments in schools, and California and Texas will soon be in the same category.

One of the points that the authors of the report make is that many minority and low-income students not only begin school without the skills required to succeed in the present school system, but teacher expectations of students abilities are often low, thereby resulting in poor performance and low levels of success.[25] The high drop-out rate among minority students can be traced to factors such as being behind in school, low teacher expectations, having to work, becoming teenage parents, being involved in gangs, and boredom.[26]

In order to ensure a quality education for minority youth, the QEMP focused on a number of strategies and suggestions for middle and high school curriculum and instruction. It is important to take note of these recommendations because, although the QEMP authors are moving toward a national focus and agenda, individual schools and teachers can implement their strategies as part of a multicultural approach. Here are some of the the recommendations, especially those that relate to the teaching of science:

1. Focus on team learning by establishing "schools-within-schools," families of learning, and, indeed, implement cooperative learning strategies in the science classroom.
2. Implement science curriculum reforms, including Project 2061, the NSTA scope and sequence, and curriculum efforts such as the BSCS Human Biology Project. (Of special note, the report emphasized a *science for all theme* in the sense that it favored a science education program that

was hands on and that made an explicit connection between science and familiar events.) The committee also supported National Council of Teachers in Mathematics (NCTM) standards, which recommend an emphasis on problem solving, the understanding of underlying concepts, tools such as calculators and computers, and the application of mathematics disciplines to real life.

3. Replace the tracking curriculum in high school and replace it with a core academic curriculum to prepare students for college and the workplace. The committee puts strong emphasis on making sure that all students arrive at high school with a course in algebra and that all students take mathematics and science in high school as part of the core.
4. Provide on-site health services and strengthen health education. Schools should work with students to deal with drug and alcohol dependency and help reduce the number of teenage pregnancies. Drug and sex education programs should be part of the school curriculum.
5. To increase the number of minority students in higher education, especially in the study of mathematics, science, and engineering, high schools and colleges should work together to provide programs to not only encourage, but also provide academic programs to support, this goal. Examples include offering six-week summer science residential programs for high school juniors and seniors on college campuses to study mathematics, science, and engineering. The project also recommended expanding funds available for recruitment.

Although these were not the only recommendations of the QEMP, they do provide insight into the directions that science education should move. Let's explore multicultural education as it specifically pertains to science education.

Talent Development Approach

Researchers at Howard University and Johns Hopkins University have developed an approach to working with students who have traditionally been underachievers. The approach, called the Talent Development Approach, is based on the philosophy that "all students can learn to high standards when there is a supportive environment, when high expectations are held by all stakeholders, and when there is a clear accountability on the part of students, staff, families, and the community."[27]

Jagers and Carroll, advocates of the Talent Development Approach, state that they do not subscribe to the concept of "at-risk" children and youth. Their argument is that this term is a euphemism for a "cultural deprivation and deficit model approach." They show, for example, that African American youth are placed at risk for underachievement and potential for dropping out of school by a variety of environmental factors. According to Jagers and Carroll, the solution is to identify and put into practice multiple-based strategies and supports to place students at promise for intellectual and social growth and development.[28]

The Talent Development Approach is based on four principles:

1. *Overdetermination of success:* Multiple activity approach is put into place, any one of which may lead to enhanced student outcomes. Differentiating instructional practices lead to opportunities to learn for a wide range of students.
2. *Promotion of multiple outcomes:* Academic success must be placed in the context of economically and personally valued skills, broad-range intellectual competence, social/emotional proficiency, community and social responsibility, cultural empowerment, and positive life transformations.
3. *Integrity-based social ethos:* This mandates that educational stakeholders hold high expectations for themselves and others; take responsibility for and ownership of educational process and outcomes, emphasize voice and choice among participants in the process; and draw on existing knowledge, competencies, and understandings to encourage students' optimal development.
4. *Co-construction:* The co-construction process entails respecting the social and cultural dynamics of students, families, teachers, and other school personnel that affect learning to ensure that these stakeholders have authentic input in the learning process.

At the Center for Research on the Education of Students Placed at Risk (CRESPAR), work is being guided by three central themes (ensuring the success of all students at key development points, building on students' personal and cultural assets, and scaling up effective programs) and conducted through research and development programs in the areas of early and elementary studies; middle and high school studies; school, family, and community partnerships; and systemic supports for school reform, as well as a program of institutional activities.

Two particularly significant programs are the Talent Development Middle Schools and the Talent Development High Schools. According to the high school Web site (www.csos.jhu.edu/tdhs/index.htm), the Talent Development High School with career academies is a comprehensive reform model for large high schools that face serious problems with student attendance, discipline, achievement scores, and dropout rates. The model consists of specific changes in school organization and management to establish a strong, positive school climate for learning; curricular and instructional innovations to transition all students into advanced high school work in English and mathematics; parent and community involvement activities to encourage college awareness; and professional development systems to support the implementation of the recommended reforms.[29]

Multicultural Science Teaching

According to Mary M. Atwater, multicultural science education should be considered an integral part of the discipline of science education. She points out that a body of knowledge about multicultural science education exists and that this knowledge includes understandings of group identification, culture, and science. Atwater goes on to say that multicultural science education relates to science learning and achievement, science instruction and the involvement of different human beings in the science.[30]

Steven J. Rakow and Andrea B. Bermudez suggest that meeting the needs of Hispanic students in science teaching requires that teachers go beyond the simplistic view of the group differing only in language. They outline a holistic approach in which communication is only one factor that may influence science learning. Their broader approach considers the influence on learning of learning style, family, and historical culture.[31] Using Banks's six elements, which can be used to understand the needs of various ethnic groups, they suggest examining multicultural science education in terms of values and behavioral styles, language and dialects, cultural cognitiveness, identification, nonverbal communication, and perspectives, worldviews, and frames of reference.

What should science teachers do to implement a multicultural approach in their own school and classroom? Three levels of decision making and action taking are presented. As a beginning science teacher, you should find the science department and classroom recommendations to be pertinent.

SCHOOL LEVEL Effective change should involve the entire school. Too often, teachers who act as individual trailblazers get discouraged by lack of support and assistance. To increase the chances of a successful multicultural approach in the classroom, teachers should implement the following processes:[32]

1. Establish a whole-school multicultural policy and then ensuring that the science department, or members of interdisciplinary teams in middle schools, reflect this policy.
2. Use all appropriate opportunities to challenge prejudice when it arises in the school community.
3. Ensure a consistent approach to dealing with racist incidents in the school.
4. Provide, whenever possible, opportunities for teachers to gain some experience of different cultures.

SCIENCE DEPARTMENT/TEAM LEVEL Members of a department or a team should engage in discussion and agreement on a policy of multicultural science education. Some steps, strategies, and ways to accomplish this are as follows:[33]

1. Develop a policy for the teaching of science from a multicultural perspective in a way that will seek to counter the causes of inequality and prejudice.
2. Ensure that all members of the department or team are provided with in-service training to aid them in implementing this policy.
3. Review the approaches to language in science to take into account the role of science education in language development. In this regard, it is important to use the research on the ways students learn. You have learned that teachers should start with the ideas students themselves have and then to use a variety of ways to help students express their ideas: talking, writing, reading, and listening. In Chapter 8, a number of strategies were developed to aid in student learning. The strategies we use in the science classrooms need to reflect our attempt to create a multicultural environment. By respecting students' ideas in both monolingual and bilingual settings, we will encourage students to express themselves, thereby helping them understand science concepts.
4. Collaborate with ESL (English as a second language) teachers to share expertise.
5. Discuss the values underlying assessment schemes being used. In Chapter 9, a broad-based model of assessment is presented that places value on a wide variety of student work and encourages the use of performance test procedures as well as small-group problem-solving assessments.
6. Ensure that resources do not contribute to stereotypical views or carry racist implications (see Inquiry Activity 2.2).

7. Use and develop links with parents and other members of the local community in order to gain a better understanding of different customs, diets, and religious beliefs.

IN THE SCIENCE Classroom Science teachers can enrich their approach to teaching by taking a multicultural perspective in the preparation and carrying out of lessons, units, and courses of study. The suggestions that follow will influence the way you view science and, combined with the next section on gender issues in science education, give you a broader view of the field.[34]

1. Adopt the view that sees cultural diversity as a positive advantage. Students from different cultural backgrounds will bring varied experiences to the classroom. Valuing this diversity can enrich the examples that will come forth during class discussions of concepts and phenomena.
2. Make use of science topics and concepts for teaching in a multicultural context. Choosing content topics such as genetics, evolution, foods, and communication, for example, can provide a rich starting point in the multicultural context.
3. Science teachers can challenge notions that ethnic origin places limitations on individual potential. Activities can be developed that show students that stereotyping of individuals is an inaccurate view of the world, and they can explore this via case studies, field trips, and guest speakers. As is the case in the research on women in science, people of color have been forgotten in the science. The history of science is full of examples of contributions to the field by ethnic minorities, and this historical perspective can be important in this regard.
4. Demonstrate the validity of technology in particular cultural contexts. Viewing technology as a response to human need means investigating the notion of appropriate technology. Teachers can provide opportunities for students to study the positive and negative implications of particular technologies. This content area can result in powerful discussions and topics for research. For instance, in the British report, science teachers suggest that at one level there is the issue of technological change and the proposition that such changes, introduced to enrich the lives of some, may also impovish the lives of others. An example might be the construction of a highway, which might bring some the benefits of travel but for others create havoc in their environment.

5. Illustrate that science has different implications for individuals in different parts of the world.

6. Set Western science in a historical context to illustrate that it is relatively young in terms of the history of science. (Western science emerged in the sixteenth century and can be compared to older science practiced in China and the Arab world.)

7. Develop an awareness and knowledge of student learning styles and plan lessons that provide a variety approaches. Within any group of students there will be a range of learning styles (e.g., field dependent versus field independent; visual, auditory, kinesthetic, tactile; left brain, right brain; active, reflective; concrete, abstract). Using a variety of learning activities will meet the learning style needs of students and provide the experiences students need to develop concepts and an interest in science.

8. Arrange the classroom physical environment in a way that clearly communicates to students that you value and respect cultural diversity. Involve students in the development of bulletin boards that recognize the contributions of ethnic and female scientists in the development of science. Provide books and magazine articles for students to read about the diversity of scientists and careers in science.

Effective Teaching Practices

In their work with Hispanic students, Padron, Waxman, and Rivera maintain that the educational success for Hispanic students needs to include research-based teaching strategies and specifically address concerns of Hispanic students who come from a different culture and are quite often trying to learn a new language.[35] They identified five such research-based teaching, which are included to help you form a foundation for thinking about multicultural teaching strategies. The teaching practices include culturally responsive teaching, cooperative learning, instructional conversation, cognitively guided instruction, and technology-enriched instruction.[36]

CULTURALLY RESPONSIVE TEACHING Culturally responsive teaching emphasizes everyday concerns of students, such as critical family and community issues, and tries to incorporate these concerns into curriculum. Developing learning activities based on familiar concepts helps facilitate literacy and content learning and helps students feel more confident and comfortable about their work.

COOPERATIVE LEARNING Cooperative learning (which is developed more fully later in the book) stimulates learning and helps students come to complex understanding by discussing and defending their ideas with others in small groups. According to Padron, Waxman, and Rivera, cooperative learning is particularly effective with Hispanic students in a number of ways: (a) it provides opportunities for students to communicate with each other; (b) it enhances instructional conversations; (c) it decreases anxiety; (d) it develops social, academic, and communication skills; and (e) it enhances self-confidence and self-esteem through individual contributions and achievement of group goals.

INQUIRY ACTIVITY 2.2

 Investigating Images Portrayed in Science Teaching Materials

This activity is designed to help you detect the extent to which materials are biased in terms of ethnicity. It has been estimated that 90 percent of all science teachers use textbooks and that the textbook is what school districts use—by and large—to determine the science curriculum. For students, the textbook is the main contact with science and the image it portrays of science will have a powerful impact on them.

Materials

- Science textbooks
- Multicultural Textbook Evaluation Checklist (Figure 2.2)

Section A. The Image of Science	Yes	No
1. Is the application of science illustrated with examples from all over the world? Comments:	____	____
2. Is up-to-date technology only illustrated by Western examples? Comments:	____	____
3. Is science set in a context that relates to people? Comments:	____	____
4. Does the way in which the material is presented suggest that only Western ways are valid? Comments:	____	____
Section B. Images of People		
5. Are the people featured in the material from more than one cultural background? Comments:	____	____
6. Does the material present a positive view of people from different cultural backgrounds? For example, are they shown performing tasks of equal esteem? Comments:	____	____
7. Are negative images confined only to people from a particular cultural background? Comments:	____	____
8. Are people who are considered eminent scientists from different parts of the world represented? Comments:	____	____
9. Does the material present equal images of women and men? Comments:	____	____
Section C. General		
10. Is the material presented in such a way as to eliminate damaging feelings of superiority, based on race, in the European person? Comments:	____	____
11. Are the customs, lifestyles, and scientific traditions of people presented in a way that helps to explain the value meaning and role of customs in their lives? Comments:	____	____

Figure 2.2 Multicultural Textbook Evaluation Checklist. *Source:* The items in the checklist are based on Ditchfield, Cristine. *Better Science: Working for a Multicultural Society.* London: Heinemann Educational Books/ Association for Science Education, 1987, p. 40.

Procedures

1. Work with a team (or individually) to evaluate the images of science and people as portrayed in more than one secondary science textbook. You might want to compare a contemporary book in a field with one published twenty to thirty years ago.
2. Use the checklist in Figure 2.2 to determine the multicultural character of the books.

Minds-On Strategies

1. How valid are the images that are portrayed in the books?
2. What affect do you think the images portrayed will have on secondary students?
3. If you were assigned one of these books to use as the text for a course, how could you compensate for a deficiency in the materials?

INSTRUCTIONAL CONVERSATION Instructional conversation is a teaching practice that provides students with opportunities for extended dialogue in areas that are rich in content value as well as relevance for students. Teachers using this strategy provide extended discourse between themselves and students.

COGNITIVELY GUIDED INSTRUCTION Cognitively guided instruction emphasizes the development of learning strategies and teaches techniques and approaches that foster students' metacognitive and cognitive monitoring of their own learning.

TECHNOLOGY-ENRICHED INSTRUCTION The use of technology such as multimedia is effective because it connects school learning with the real world. Using the Web to create telecommunication networks is effective in that students can communicate with peers and adults through the Internet. Linking Hispanic students with peers who speak their native language is motivational and again links schooling to students' interests.

Gender Issues

- In the United States women comprise approximately 50 percent of the workforce; yet only 9 percent are employed as scientists and engineers.
- Only 12 percent of students enrolled in high school technology programs are female.
- In the recent National Assessment of Educational Progress science study, girls continue to score below the national mean on all science achievement items and express negative attitudes toward science.[37]
- Many more females are less interested than males in fields with a significant mathematical component, such as physics, chemistry, and engineering.[38]
- Research studies suggest that teaching styles and other school-related factors are important in encouraging girls (as well as boys) to continue courses and careers in science.[39]

The issue of gender is a real one in the mathematics and science classroom and in this section we will investigate the research that has been done to discover ways to improve the participation of girls in middle school and high school science and to increase the career participation of women in science. A number of researchers and teachers, not only in the United States but also in many countries around the world, have

- conducted research to document and explore the problem of gender differences in the classroom,

- compiled teacher training courses and in-service programs to improve teachers' ability to create environments conducive to "female-friendly" science,[40]
- developed curricular and instructional materials designed to increase equity and encourage girls and minorities in science courses and careers.[41]

Participation of Women in Science

"I wonder whether the tiny atoms and nuclei or the mathematical symbols or the DNA molecules have any preference for either masculine or feminine treatment."[42] As Anne Haley-Oliphant points out, it is doubtful that inanimate objects have a preference for being studied by males or females, but the statistics on the participation of women in science is much less than the percentage of women in the population.[43]

The history of scientific ideas reads like the history of male scientists even though women have participated in science since antiquity. Women's status and role were always in the shadows of men and much of their work was unrecognized by the scientific community, stolen, or lost because it was never published.[44]

In her book *Hypatia's Heritage*, Margaret Alic provides a historical glimpse of the accomplishments of women in science from antiquity through the nineteenth century. She describes the research, theories, and observations made by a long list of female contributors to the field of science. Alic sounds an important challenge to science teachers by documenting the contributions of women in science and asserting that in school science, women's discoveries, theories, and writings are left out of the pages of most school textbooks. She says:

Science is that body of knowledge that describes, defines, and, where possible, explains the universe— the matter that constitutes it, the organisms that inhabit it, the physical laws that govern it. This knowledge accumulates by a slow, arduous process of speculation, experimentation, and discovery that has been an integral part of human activity since the dawn of the race. Women have always played an essential role in this process.

Yet we think of the history of science as a history of men. More than that, we think of the history of science as the story of very few men—Aristotle, Copernicus, Newton, and Einstein—men who drastically altered our view of the universe. But the history of science is much more than that. It is the story of the thousands of people who contributed to the knowledge and theories that constituted the science of their eras and made the "great leaps" possible. Many of these people were women. Yet their story remains virtually unknown.[45]

The impact of keeping this aspect of the history of science from science courses is to convey a sexist character of science. Although blatant racism and sexism have been eliminated from textbooks, there is evidence to suggest that women and people of color are absent from the written content of the textbooks.[46] Stories, anecdotes, and accomplishments about women and minorities are missing, in general, from textbooks. Providing vignettes and involving students in an exploration of the contributions of a wide range of scientists— not just Western white males—can have a positive impact on students' perceptions of science.

The current status of women in medicine and engineering in Western, Eastern, and some developing nations reveals a pattern that provides the basis for an analysis of the status of women in science and engineering. The comparison between Western countries, such as the United States and Britain, reveals differences in participation compared to some Eastern and developing countries (see Table 2.3). To help eliminate this disparity in the participation of women in science, a number of Western nations have developed intervention programs. The programs are quite varied. For example, in Britain, several programs have been developed. One program, Girls into Science and Technology (GIST), focused on

1. raising teachers' awareness of girls' underachievement and helping them realize that they can do something about it,

Table 2.3 Percentage of Female Physicians and Engineers in Nine Countries

	Physicians	Engineers
Western Countries		
Britain	17	0.5
Canada	33	8.2
France	15	2.0
United States	10	1.0
West Germany	30.6	7.8
Eastern Countries		
Hungary	42	no data
Poland	44	2
Soviet Union	75	44
Developing Countries		
Burma	50	15
Mexico	34.7	6.7

Source: Based on Haley-Oliphant, Anne E. "International Perspectives on the Status and Role of Women in Science." In *Women in Science*, edited by Jane Butler Kahle. Philadelpha: The Falmer Press, 1985, p. 170.

2. testing children's entering attitudes and knowledge in science and technology for comparison with later performance and choice, and
3. arranging a series of visits to schools by women working in scientific and technological jobs who could act as role models for girls.[47]

GIST followed a cohort of approximately 2,000 students from the time they entered secondary school until they made their option choices at the end of the third year. The purpose of GIST was to alter girls' attitudes toward physical science and technical subjects by the end of year three so that in years four and five they would choose those courses of study. Although the results were not clear cut, the project had an impact on students' and teachers' attitudes toward science and helped create a climate of discussion, debate, and investigation of issues surrounding gender in the science classroom in Britain.

The programs that were designed to improve the status of women and minorities in science careers as well as participation in science courses of study in secondary schools investigated the reasons for the gender disparity phenomenon. For instance, Joan Skolnick, Carol Langbort, and Lucille Day indicate that gender socialization negatively affects girls attitudes toward mathematics and science. They point out that female socialization promotes fears about competence, reliance on the judgment of others, an interpersonal and verbal orientation, and unfamiliarity with toys, games, and activities, that stimulate learning of spatial relationships and basic mathematics concepts.[48] According to Skolnick and colleagues, the strategies used to teach mathematics and science don't favor confidence building, rely on abstract knowledge, and are generally devoid of activities and group work. They suggest a problem-solving strategy in which students' confidence and competence in problem solving are built through active, hands-on experiences.

In addition, Alison Kelly, in investigating why girls don't study physical science, suggests that girls' lack of confidence may be a factor, but that the masculine image of science and the impersonal approach of science also contribute to the problem. In studies of students' attitudes about science, Kelly found that a large number of boys but very few girls agree with statements like "a woman could never be a great scientist" or "girls don't need to learn about electricity or light." She points out that, if boys believe that science is a man's world and this attitude carries over to the science classroom, boys will dominate the lab, discussions, and other activities.[49]

Teacher classroom behavior may also contribute to the low percentage of girls pursuing science in secondary school. Kahle reports one particular example in a study of gender issues in the science classroom. In two in-depth investigations of science classrooms, Kahle found that the grades students received influenced their science options. This is not surprising because grades contribute to students' self-confidence. In the cases that Kahle studied, however, one teacher gave twice as many high grades to boys as girls; the other teacher gave equal numbers of girls and boys the highest grades. In the case of the teacher who gave more boys the highest grade, the percentage of females taking courses in physics, chemistry, and physical science ranged from 14 percent to 33 percent, whereas 45 percent and 50 percent of the other teacher's female students took physics and chemistry, respectively.[50]

The way in which teachers interact with students in the classroom can affect students' attitudes about science and future career choices. Kahle suspects that the role or metaphor the teacher uses to describe his or her teaching style may be a factor. For example, the teacher who sees himself or herself as a facilitator of learning provides a classroom climate more conducive to non-sexist teaching. Taking on a facilitative role as teacher may be a result of prior educational experiences. In Kahle's research, this teacher was perceived as a facilitator of learning:

> Sandra, on the other hand, clearly saw her role as change agent. She felt that she had experienced discrimination and she consistently endeavored to be a transformer, not reproducer, of sex-role stereotypes which promulgated gender differences.[51]

It is interesting to note that Kahle's other teacher described the role of the teacher as a dispenser of knowledge and information. In this role, perhaps science is perceived as impersonal and perhaps the teacher sees the role as one of passing on information rather than helping students find out and use their own resources to learn.

What can science teachers do to reduce bias in teaching? What strategies can be employed in the classroom to reduce sex stereotyping and encourage girls to participate in science courses and careers?

Strategies to Encourage Females in Science Courses and Careers

One of the characteristics of successful strategies to increase the participation of females in science courses and careers has been to focus on the skills identified in research that might cause the disparity. Thus, there is a strong emphasis on developing spatial ability, problem-solving ability, and mechanical skills. Another trend in successful strategies is an emphasis on mathematics. Researchers realized that students needed to take mathematics in secondary school in order to pursue science courses of study in college. This focus on math became known as the "critical-filter" idea. Science teachers can play an important role by counseling students into math as well as integrating math in an appealing way into science classes. Let's take a closer look at the strategies and characteristics of successful programs that are applicable to the science classroom.

SUCCESSFUL PROGRAM CHARACTERISTICS In summarizing a report published by the American Association for the Advancement of Science on programs that increased access and achievement of females and minorities, Cole and Griffin pointed out that results are hopeful in producing positive outcomes. They listed the following as characteristics of programs that raised the achievement level and increased science career choices of females and minorities:

- strong academic component in mathematics, science, and communications, focused on enrichment rather than remediation;
- academic subjects taught by teachers who are highly competent in the subject matter and believe that students can learn the material;
- heavy emphasis on the applications of science and mathematics and careers in these fields;
- integrative approach to teaching that incorporates all subject areas, hands-on opportunities, and computers;
- multiyear involvement with students;
- strong director and committed and stable staff who share program goals;
- stable long-term funding based on multiple funding sources;
- recruitments of participants from all relevant target populations;
- university, industry, school cooperative program;
- opportunities for in-school and out-of-school learning experiences;
- parental involvement and development of base of community support;
- specific attention to removing educational inequities related to gender and race;
- involvement of professionals and staff who look like the target population;
- development of peer support systems;

Table 2.4 Characteristics of Students and
Science Teaching

Analytical/Instrumental	Nutritive
Interest in rules	Interest in relationships
Interest in machines	Interest in people
Interest in fairness and justice	Pragmatism
Views world as hierarchy of relationships (competitive)	Views world as network of relationships (cooperative)
Emphasis on analytical thought	Emphasis on aesthetic appreciation
Interest in controlling inanimate objects	Interest in nurturing living objects

* evaluation, long-term follow-up data collection;
* "mainstreaming," integration of program elements supportive of women and minorities into the institutional program.[52]

SUCCESSFUL TEACHING STRATEGIES A number of strategies have proven to be successful in influencing female attitudes and achievement in science and mathematics. In general, these strategies support a hands-on approach in which students work in small learning teams and have opportunities for "academic discussions." But there is a great deal more than this general approach involved in enhancing female participation in science. Let's look at some specific strategies.

Content and Activities Barbara Smail has suggested that science classes need to provide more experiences that she calls "nutritive" to provide a balance to the "analytical/instrumental" activities that she suggests characterize most school science (Table 2.4).[53] The comparisons of analytical/instrumental with nutritive characteristics are similar to left-brain to right-brain dichotomy, which we discuss in Chapter 5. Proponents of left-brain and right-brain thinking, such as McCarthy,[54] suggest an integration resolution to this dichotomy, as Smail recommends. Students should be exposed to a variety teaching activities. A balanced selection of content and activities would result in an array of creative activities.

For example, one school Smail worked with suggested changing writing assignments and examinations to reflect the following:

* instructions on how to make something, such as an electric motor;

* descriptions of solutions to problems in unusual situations (e.g., building a distillation apparatus from bits and pieces available on a desert island);
* letters to friends describing experiments or concepts;
* letters to newspapers expressing ideas on social implications of science (e.g., dumping of nuclear wastes, seal-culling, vivisection);
* newspaper reports (e.g., of acid tanker accident, hazards, and clean-up);
* advertisements (e.g., for Bunsen burners and other laboratory equipment);
* imaginative accounts (e.g., carbon or nitrogen cycle from the point of view of an atom involved, expeditions into ears, bloodstream);
* diaries;
* script for TV interviews of inventors;
* poems on scientific phenomena.[55]

Social Arrangements Another strategy that appears to enhance females' interest in science and contributes positively to academic performance is altering the work arrangements in the classroom. There is considerable evidence that cooperative, mixed-ability group processes enhance learning and cognitive development in some circumstances.[56] However, there is a potential problem in the use of student-led small groups, as has been pointed out by Cohen. Although learning content in a small peer group is positively related to frequency of interaction, frequency of interaction is correlated with social status in the classroom.[57] There is a danger that high-status students will dominate peer groups, leaving out low-status students, who oftentimes are students with low socioeconomic status and low ability.[58]

Proponents of cooperative learning have devised management practices in which leadership roles in peer groups are rotated, thereby giving students of varying status the opportunity to play out leadership roles.

Confidence Building Skolnick, Langbort, and Day have described strategies that teachers can implement to build confidence in the ability to solve science and mathematics problems. As they point out, expert problem solvers *believe they can do it*. It is crucial that middle and junior high school science teachers employ these methods because this is a critical time for students (boys and girls) to be influenced into or out of mathematics and science courses at the high school level. Skolnick and colleagues suggest five strategies to build the confidence of girls in solving science and mathematics problems:

1. Success for each student
2. Tasks with many approaches
3. Tasks with many right answers
4. Guessing and testing
5. Estimating[59]

Sex-Role Awareness One way of discovering that students perceive science roles as masculine is to have students draw pictures of scientists (see Inquiry Activity 1.3). In her research, Kahle reported that only 10 percent of rural American boys and 28 percent of girls drew female scientists.[60] Males and females think that science is a male profession. In order to help students see new possibilities, the teacher must take an active role in a number of awareness activities to multiply the options for students. Skolnick, Langbort, and Day suggest two categories of strategies:

1. Content relevance
2. Modeling new options[61]

Content relevance means choosing and using science content to help students see the relevance of science in their lives now as well as a potential career option later. For instance, Smail reports that science programs should capitalize on the fact that girls who have a positive view of the effects of science on the environment and humans were more likely to choose courses in the physical sciences. She points out that, in Britain, new curriculum goals emphasize:

• Study of those aspects of science that are essential to understanding oneself and one's personal well-being. The renewed emphasis on "human biology" for the middle school science curriculum is an example of putting this goal into practice.
• Study of key concepts that are essential to understanding the part science and technology play in the post-industrial and technological society.
• Appreciation that technologies are expressions of the desire to understand and control the environment and that technologies evolve in response to changing social needs. This goal and the previous goal underscore the importance of emphasizing the science-technology-society theme (Chapter 11) in science education.[62]

Content relevance and modeling new options can be directly tied to career awareness. Connecting science courses to careers in science and engineering is an important content dimension of all science courses.

Skolnick, Langbort, and Day suggest how the content in a science or mathematics course can do this:

> The content of math and science problems can provide a fundamental kind of career education. It can develop new perspectives on work and on the abilities of both sexes. Word problems can inform children about occupations unfamiliar to them and provide information about the labor market, such as jobs and salaries, women's position in the work force, and math and science courses they will need for particular careers. Illustrating many kinds of content relevance, creative math and science problems encourage girls' pursuit of nontraditional occupations.[63]

Although there are a number of excellent resources to help plan activities, in the final analysis the teacher is the most important resource. The teacher's day-to-day modeling will overshadow any "special" program that is provided by the school or science department.

Science for All Exceptional Students

The science teacher can have a powerful impact on the exceptional student, whether physically disabled, behaviorally disordered, at-risk, or gifted and talented. Understanding, indeed empathizing with people with disabilities, is the first step in expanding the theme that science is for all. For instance, read what Barbara Mendius, who has poliomyelitis, said about her experiences in school science.

> I acquired my entire formal education while in a wheelchair. Since sixth grade my major academic interest has been science; this culminated with an M.S. of Biology from the University of Illinois in October 1977.
>
> In considering my own education, I firmly believe that my laboratory experience was most important in shaping my scientific ability. The first major obstacle for the handicapped student of science is getting the hands-on laboratory experience so important to engender scientific expertise.
>
> I feel lucky indeed as I recall the variety of lab work which I performed in school. I have thought carefully about the factors which contributed to my successful scientific education; it all comes down to people—parents, administrators, and teachers— willing to cooperate on my behalf. Realizing the value of scholarship, my parents took an active interest in my education. Active, but not pushy. Beginning in fourth grade, I attended the local public school. For class field trips, mom would drive one of the groups to the museum or to the nature

center—for laboratories are not only found in schools. Dad went to the entire parents' nights, talked with my teachers, and came home glowing about my progress. Impressed with my parents' interest and my ability, school administrators were wonderfully cooperative. For some of the administrators, I was their first and only handicapped student.

That all changed in high school. There, all of my parents' interest and all of the administrators' cooperation would have been wasted were it not for enthusiastic science teachers who gave me the freedom to do as much as I could of what everyone else was doing. Sometimes it only meant putting the microscope or analytic balance on a low table. Sometimes it meant rearranging the greenhouse so I could get down the overgrown aisles. In one case it meant encouraging this shy student to enter the state science fair and helping me choose an appropriate experiment which I could carry out myself. My teachers were the ones who ultimately placed science within my reach.

But we worked together, so my stubbornness and perseverance deserve some credit also. Science had piqued my brain; I was determined to learn as much as I could, actually doing as much as I could. I realized that if I wanted to do the acid/base experiments I would have to show that I could carry solutions around in my lap without spilling. If I wanted to fire-polish my own glassware I had to show I could use a Bunsen burner without setting myself aflame. If I needed to move a microscope to a lower table, I had to show that I could do that without smashing it to smithereens. I had to prove myself all along the way, but my teachers accepted my physical abilities and, although I often caught a watchful eye on me, they did not stifle my enthusiastic investigations.

In summary, my major recommendation for science education is to involve the orthopedically disabled student in laboratory experiments. Visual, auditory, tactile, olfactory, and gustatory clues can elucidate scientific principles; ingenuity and perhaps some extra work are all that are required.[64]

Exceptional Students in the Regular Science Classroom

Public Law 94-142, the Education for All Handicapped Children Act, was enacted in 1975. It is the law that most school districts use as the legal requirements for mainstreaming disabled students into the regular classroom. Although this law was preceded by Public Law 93-380 (which safeguards for the rights of handicapped individuals) and Public Law 93-22 (the Rehabilitation Act of 1973, which maintained that handicapped individuals must not be excluded from benefits of any organization receiving federal funds), Public Law

94-142 is of most importance in this discussion of exceptional students in science education. The law was enacted to ensure that:

> all handicapped children have available to them . . . a free appropriate public education which emphasizes special education and related services designed to meet their unique needs, to assure that the rights of handicapped children and their parents or guardians are protected, to assist states and localities to provide for the education of all handicapped children, and to assess and assure the effectiveness of efforts to educate handicapped children.[65]

The federal regulations for disabled students require that all disabled students be provided the most appropriate education in the least restrictive environment. There are a number of principles that you should be aware of when dealing with exceptional students in the science classroom.

RIGHT TO DUE PROCESS OF LAW All students have a right to a least restrictive learning environment, and the federal laws protect students and parents by insisting on a specific procedure that must be followed in all cases. This procedure includes notification in writing before evaluation begins, parental consultation, right to an interpreter or translator if needed, the right of the parent to inspect all educational records, and a procedure for appeals.

PROTECTION IN EVALUATION PROCEDURES Each state and school district must ensure that a nonbiased, meaningful evaluation procedure is in place. For instance, tests and other evaluation materials must be administered in the student's native language, unless it is clearly not feasible to do so.

EDUCATION IN THE LEAST RESTRICTIVE ENVIRON-MENT According to Public Law 94-142, it is required "that special classes, separate school, or other removal of handicapped children from the regular educational environment occurs only when the nature or severity of the handicap is such that education in regular classes . . . cannot be achieved satisfactorily."[66] The concept of least restrictive environment must be determined for each student on an individual basis.

INDIVIDUALIZED EDUCATIONAL PROGRAM (IEP) The requirement for an IEP is a way of ensuring that each exceptional student is considered as an individual and is not simply placed in a class and not treated in accordance with his or her needs. The IEP is regulated by the following procedures:

1. A statement of the present levels of educational performance.
2. A statement of annual goals, including short-term instructional objectives.
3. A statement of the specific educational services to be provided to this handicapped student and the extent to which such student will be able to participate in regular educational programs.
4. The projected date for initiation and anticipated duration of such services.
5. Appropriate, objective criteria and evaluation procedures and schedules for determining, on at least an annual basis, whether instructional objectives are being achieved.[67]

PARENTAL INVOLVEMENT AND CONSULTATION According to the laws surrounding the exceptional student, parents should play an important and integral part in the education of their children. The law makes it necessary for schools to involve parents in planning educational programs for students with special needs and to become aware of and be sensitive to the value of parental involvement.[68]

COOPERATION AND JOINT PLANNING WITH SPECIAL EDUCATORS The "least restrictive" environment for students with special needs usually means the regular classroom. Joint planning between the regular classroom teacher and the special educator is an intent of the law, which is evident in requiring both educators to be involved in the development of the student's IEP.

The Exceptional Student in the Science Classroom

All students who enter the science classroom should be accepted, should be included, and should be allowed to participate as fully as everyone else. One of the most significant factors mitigating against full participation of disabled students in the mainstream is lowered expectations. Lowered expectations of teachers, combined with lowered expectations of parents, can contribute to the problem. Stefanich put it this way:

> Parents of the severely disabled support this lowered expectations of teachers for two basic reasons: (1) a lack of confidence that their handicapped child may someday be able to find employment and become a useful part of society and (2) a hesitancy to place increased demands on the child because they perceive that the hard work and time necessary for adequate academic functioning would deprive the child of leisure time activities or physical therapy.[69]

In a report by the Task Force on Women, Minorities, and the Handicapped in Science and Technology, it was estimated that 22 million Americans of working age have some physical disability, yet only 7.2 million of these people are employed. The National Science Foundation found only 94,000 disabled scientists and engineers working in 1986. The reports stressed that people with disabilities live longer and are able to pursue careers because of improving medical technology. People with disabilities are a large and growing segment of the population. In fact, in 1987, over 1.3 million of the 12.5 million students (or 10.5 percent) enrolled in postsecondary education institutions reported having at least one disability, which makes them the largest "minority."[70]

The report also pointed out that low expectations and lack of encouragement are keeping students with disabilities from participating fully in mathematics and science, particularly in science laboratory courses. Parents, science and mathematics teachers, and counselors must encourage students with disabilities to pursue the study of and careers in science and engineering.

What can the science teacher do to provide for the special needs of exceptional students? How can students with handicaps be encouraged to pursue science courses and careers? What can the science teacher do to build the self-esteem of students? There are a number of broad guidelines that the science teacher can follow. These include:

- Obtain and read all relevant information and health background information available on the student.
- Educate yourself on the physical and/or psychological nature of the handicap and how it affects the student's potential for learning.
- Contact the special education expert in your school to determine the source of help available.
- Determine the special equipment needed by the student (see Keller et al.[71] for specifics on types of equipment available).
- Talk with the student about limitations due to his or her handicap and about particular needs in the science class.
- Establish a team of fellow teachers (including resource teachers and aids) to share information and ideas about the special students.
- Be aware of barriers, both physical and psychological, to the fullest possible functioning of the disabled student.
- Consider how to modify or adapt curriculum materials and teaching strategies for the disabled student without sacrificing content.

• Encourage the disabled student. Teachers' perceptions of student's abilities can become self-fulfilling prophecies.

• Educate other students about handicaps in general, as well as the specific handicaps of students in their class. It is wise to confer with the disabled student before making a decision to take this action.[72]

Exceptional students should be encouraged to participate fully in science experiences and the science teacher must make special provisions for this to happen. If one of the important goals of school science is develop scientific thinking skills to inquire about natural phenomena, then the exceptional student, like other students, must be included in inquiry and laboratory activities.

In the sections to follow, we will explore physically impaired students (motor/orthopedic, visual, and hearing disabilities), speech impaired students, learning disabled students, gifted and talented, and at-risk or low achieving students.

Physically Impaired Students

Physical impairments represent a broad categorization of conditions including nervous system disorders (e.g., cerebral palsy), mental disorders (mental retardation), muscular-skeletal disorders (e.g., rheumatoid arthritis), cardiovascular disorders (e.g., coronary heart disease), respiratory disorders (e.g., emphysema), digestive disorders (e.g., cancer of the colon), urogenital disorders (e.g., kidney disease), endocrine-metabolic disorders (e.g., diabetes mellitus), and sense organ disorders (e.g., hearing and visual impairment). Only three of the impairments will be discussed here: motor/orthopedically impaired, visually impaired, and hearing impaired.

MOTOR/ORTHOPEDIC IMPAIRED STUDENTS The orthopedically disabled student is one who has an impairment that interferes with the normal functioning of the skeletal system, the joints, the connective tissue, and muscles.

An assessment technique that allows the science teacher to determine an appropriate mitigative strategy for a particular student is the "life function impairment assessment," which interrelates general disability areas (motor/orthopedic, behavior, chronic disease, auditory, and visual) with five categories of functional impairment (health, mobility, communication, social/attitudinal, and cognitive/intellectual). Each block of the table is used to indicate the degree of impairment for the individual student being assessed. Table 2.5 shows a life function impairment assessment for a male student with spina bifida. The student is wheelchair bound, but he can use crutches for short distances and can transfer to a chair or bench from the wheelchair. The chart shows a problem in the communication life function. In this case it is observed that he has trouble keeping friends. A urine bag is necessary for his functioning and this has contributed to an odor problem. The student tends to use

Table 2.5 Life Function Impairment Assessment for a Male Student with Spina Bifida

Life Function	General Disability Area				
	Motor/Orthopedic	Behavior	Chronic Disease	Auditory	Visual
Health	Some Problem[a]				
Mobility	Some Problem[b]				
Social/Attitudinal	No Problem				
Communication	Significant Problems[c]				
Cognitive/Intellectual	Some Problems[d]				

[a] Use of urine bag is necessary. Time must scheduled for emptying.

[b] Most of the time is wheelchair bound. Can use crutches for short distances and can transfer to chair or bench from wheelchair.

[c] Has great difficulty making and keeping friends. Part of the problem is that urine odor causes avoidance by peers. Uses wheelchair aggressively, makes inappropriate use of vulgar language. Disrupts class with outbursts and unrelated information. General lack of self-discipline and respect for authority.

[d] Problem of depressed grades, despite average IQ. No indication that this problem is directly due to disability, but he was a home-bound student through the fourth grade.

Source: Based on an assessment of student in a marine science summer program, from Keller, E. C. et al. *Teaching the Physically Disabled in the Mainstream Science Class at the Secondary and College Levels.* Morgantown, W.Va.: Printech, 1983, p. 41.

the wheelchair aggressively. In terms of cognitive/intellectual life function, he has lowered grades, despite an average IQ.

Some strategies that teachers can use to help physically disabled students in the science class include:

1. Provide for assistance (if necessary) from other people for such activities as pushing a wheelchair or taking notes for the disabled student.
2. Be aware of and use mechanical devices as needed, such as a wheelchair lapboard, tape recorder, voice synthesizer, electric hot plates instead of Bunsen burners, or pencil holders.
3. Employ teaching strategies such allowing more time to complete assignments, nonmanual types of teaching techniques, breaks for stretching, storing materials so as to be accessible to all.
4. Evaluate the architectural facilities of the classroom. Consider access to wheelchairs, lowering chalkboards, altering the height of desks and lab tables, use of nonskid flooring for students with crutches.
5. Use a variety of student presentations, including oral and written. Use nonverbal signals such as blinking, head nodding, or a pointer.

VISUALLY IMPAIRED STUDENTS In working with students with visual impairments, Kenneth Ricker points out that the emphasis should be on the student, not the visual impairment. Ricker believes that we should place the emphasis on teaching science to students who happen to have some sort of visual impairment.[73]

Visually impaired students include both students with limited vision and the totally blind. Ricker suggests that science teachers will find it helpful to know how the student functions effectively in learning situations that involve four different levels of tasks:

1. Close-up tasks such as reading a book, drawing a diagram, or using a microscope.
2. Nearby tasks at arm's length, such as manipulating objects or handling lab equipment.
3. Distance tasks such as reading what is on the chalkboard or viewing what is on the screen.
4. Mobility tasks such as moving to different places in a lab or going on field trips.[74]

One important aspect of working with students who are visually impaired is ensuring that they get to perform hands-on science activities. Science teachers and researchers have developed a variety of strategies to encourage hands-on science teaching for the visually impaired. Here are some ideas that science teachers can use to help visually disabled students become science learners:

- Keep materials, supplies, and equipment in the same place, whether it is on a laboratory table or in a field kit.
- Describe and tactually/spatially familiarize the student to all equipment.
- Describe and tactually/spatially familiarize the student to the classroom and laboratory.
- Have the student do a trial run before the activity.
- Enforce safety rules rigidly because the visually impaired student is more apt to work closer to the activity and laboratory table.
- Use simple adaptive procedures on equipment.
- Use tactile models to show visually impaired students what you visually show nonimpaired students.
- Convert color change indicators in chemistry laboratories to tactile indicators by filtering the precipitate and having the student touch the precipitate on filter paper.
- Use a thermoform machine to make multiple, reproducible tactile diagrams.
- Make arrangements for tactile examination if touch is not normally permitted.
- Present examinations in a form that will be unbiased to visually impaired students.
- Use various mechanical devices such as tape recorders, overhead projectors, slide previewers, raised-line drawings, and so forth.
- Nondominant laboratory partners can facilitate the work of the visually impaired during hands-on activities and while working in the lab.[75]

HEARING IMPAIRED STUDENTS Hearing impaired students may have either partial or total hearing loss. Hearing loss results in varied implications for students who are not able to hear, either completely or partially, human voices and environmental sounds. Hearing loss can also affect the individual's language development, depending on the age of onset of the hearing loss. Speech and voice quality may also be affected by hearing loss. Therefore, the teacher should be aware that cognitive, personal, and social development might also be affected by a hearing impairment.

The teacher can help the hearing impaired student in science class by being aware of the following:

- In considering the physical environment, place the student within 15 feet of the teacher. The student should also be placed with his or her better ear toward the class. Try to avoid placing the student near congested areas or where there are excessive vibrations and noise.

- To help the student with communication, ensure the presence of an interpreter where needed. Communicate directly with the student, and use note-writing and the chalkboard for one-to-one discussion. Speak clearly, at a moderate pace, and without exaggeration or overenunciation while making eye contact.
- Teaching strategies such as providing an outline of the lesson or activity as well as step-by-step directions prior to a lab activity are helpful. Use multiple sensory activities, especially visual techniques, to reinforce vocabulary and science concepts.
- Encourage students to ask questions, make use of glossaries, and take notes on major points of a lesson or activity.
- Arrange for a nondominant lab partner for helping with communication.[76]

Learning Disabled Students

A specific learning disability means a disorder in one or more of the basic psychological processes involved in understanding or in using language (spoken or written), which may manifest itself in an imperfect ability to listen, think, speak, read, write, spell, or do mathematical calculations. It is estimated that 2 percent of adolescents have some type of learning disability, making this the most common type of handicap. Learning disabilities also include perceptual handicaps, brain injury, minimal brain dysfunction, and dyslexia. The term does not include students who have learning problems that are fundamentally caused by visual, hearing, or motor handicaps, of mental retardation, of emotional disturbance, or of environmental, cultural, or economic disadvantage.[77]

However, a controversy exists around the identification of learning disabled students. Some specialists claim that at least half the students labeled as learning disabled could be more accurately labeled as slow learners, as students with second-language backgrounds, as students who misbehave in class, as those that are absent often or move from school, or as average learners in above-average school districts.[78]

Another controversy exists surrounding what type of intervention program should be used to help learning disabled students. One concern that specialists at the secondary level have is the emphasis recent reforms have placed on academic goals. Secondary teachers

working with learning disabled students will have to work harder to help these students keep up with the demands of the curriculum. One remedy is to balance the curriculum for learning disabled student with what is called a "functional" approach, in which students are taught life or living skills that will aid them in employment opportunities beyond high school.

What can be done in the science classroom to help learning disabled students? Charles Coble and colleagues suggest that focusing on structure in the science classroom will benefit the learning disabled student. They suggest that structure is important because of the perceptual and cognitive difficulties that the learning disabled student has in being unable to mask out extraneous stimuli to deal with the task at hand. These researchers suggest a number of ways to promote structure:[79]

1. Establish a routine.
2. Limit choices.
3. Ensure that the student is attending.
4. Give the student clues to facilitate remembering.
5. Sequence instruction.
6. Be specific in criticism and praise.
7. Provide visible time clues.
8. Confer with the LD teacher.
9. Develop empathy.

Science education has much to offer the learning disabled student. Providing a hands-on curriculum within the structured environment can help meet the twin needs of the learning disabled: structure and motivation. For example, Coble and colleagues outline ways to modify science instruction for some learning disabled characteristics[80] (see Table 2.6).

The Gifted and Talented in Science (Advanced Learners)

Although the term "gifted" has been used to describe a subgroup of students, a more powerful term suggested by Tomlinson is "advanced." Tomlinson uses this term (advanced learner) instead of gifted, high-end, or academically talented because it is less controversial and is not limited by labeling.[81] Advanced students, like students with learning disabilities or students with physical disabilities, have unique learning needs that require a special education. "Giftedness" has to do with people who have special gifts that are in some way superior to others of the same age. In science education, gifted education has been known variously as gifted in science, science talented, science prone, or students with high ability in science. The Westinghouse

Table 2.6 Modifying Science Instruction for Learning Disabled Students

LD Student Characteristic	Modification in Science Classroom
1. The LD student may lack coordination (e.g., drop equipment, cut self while using strippers).	Use plastic containers; teach use of wire strippers
2. Equipment and material may distract the impulsive student.	Clear desk of extraneous equipment. Use one item at a time and collect each after use. Package materials for activities that reduce distractions.
3. Impressed with the end-product, the LD student misses the scientific concept.	Ask questions that emphasize cause-effect relationships. Ask a series of sequential questions.
4. LD student generalizations may be incorrect.	Anticipate possible misconceptions and discuss differences before errors are made.
5. The LD student may have difficulty comprehending abstract terms and concepts.	Begin at the concrete level and move step by step to the abstract level. Use demonstrations, models, and pictures.
6. LD student may have a reading disability.	"Rewrite" the text using a highlighter to emphasize important information. Teach "mapping" strategies to give students an alternative way of "reading" text material. Have volunteers tape the textbook.
7. The LD student may lack exploratory drive.	Use forced/interesting choice strategies. Give students structured options.
8. The LD student may explore in a random, purposeless manner.	Use the direct teaching model.

Source: Based on Coble, Charles R., Levey, Betty, and Matheis, Floyd. "Science for Learning Disabled Students," February 1985, p. 20. ERIC, ED 258803.

Talent Search, science fairs, and Advanced Placement courses in science are examples of the emphasis on giftedness in science education. However, as Tomlinson points out, using the concept of the "advanced learner" will be much more productive in preparing lessons and engaging these students.

There are a lot of myths, as well as a low level of tolerance for giftedness in society. These myths and problems are similar to the kinds of myths and problems surrounding students with disabilities. First, let's examine what giftedness is and the myths surrounding giftedness, then move on to characteristics of giftedness in science and examples of ways of working with gifted students in science education. It will be helpful to begin by examining some of the earlier work done on the concept of giftedness. First, though, what is giftedness or the notion of an advanced learner?

There are a number of definitions that focus on the notion of performance. One of the earliest definitions states that gifted and talented or advanced students are those identified by professionally qualified persons who are capable of high performance. Students capable of high performance include those with demonstrated achievement and/or potential ability in any of the following areas:

1. General intellectual ability
2. Specific academic aptitude
3. Creative or productive thinking
4. Leadership ability
5. Visual and performing arts[82]

A more recent definition (by Renzulli, Reis, and Smith), and one that is widely accepted, suggests that gifted or advanced students are those who have demonstrated or shown potential for:

1. High ability (including high intelligence)
2. High creativity (the ability to formulate new ideas and apply them to the solution of problems)
3. High task commitment (a high level of motivation and the ability to see a project through to its conclusion)[83]

One of the strengths of using a multiple criterion definition is that it expands the potential pool of gifted and advanced students (and multiple abilities seem to be characteristics of gifted people in practice). Hallahan and Kaufman point out that if one were only to use IQ as a determinant then most "gifted" would come from high socioeconomic status families, have fewer siblings, and have better educated parents.[84] Furthermore, the notion of intelligence has changed dramatically in recent years. Work by Gardner at Harvard has suggested evidence of multiple intelligences rather than a single general intelligence. Gardner suggests eight intelligences, including the following (refer to Chapter 6 for more details about multiple intelligences):[85]

1. Logical-mathematical
2. Linguistic
3. Musical
4. Spatial
5. Bodily-kinesthetic
6. Interpersonal
7. Intrapersonal
8. Ecological

The point of recent work in intelligence and reformulation of the definition of giftedness suggests that giftedness is identifiable only in terms of an interaction among ability, creativity, and task commitment.

Two additional aspects of the definition of giftedness need to be considered. The first is gifted minority and the second is gifted handicapped.

Gifted minority students typically have been left out of gifted programs, although some strides have been made in recent years.[86] Selection criteria for inclusion of students in gifted programs needs to take into consideration cultural diversity, language, and parental involvement. Recent suggestions for expanding the talent pool of gifted students includes the following practices:

1. Seeking nominations from a variety of persons, professional and nonprofessional, inside and outside school;
2. Applying knowledge of the behavioral indicators by which children from different cultures dynamically exhibit giftedness in the development of nomination forms;
3. Collecting data from multiple sources, objective and subjective, including performances and products;
4. Delaying decision making until all pertinent data can be collected in a case study.

As Hallahan and Kaufman point out, "different cultural and ethnic groups place different values on academic achievement and areas of performance. Stereotypes can easily lead us to overlook intellectual giftedness or to over- or underrate children on any characteristic because they do not conform to our expectations based on their identity or socioeconomic status."[87]

It is estimated that 2 to 3 percent of disabled students are gifted, and it should be a goal to identify these students and make a gifted education available to them. One only needs to look to the field of science to identify a number of eminent scientists who had a severe disability (e.g., Charles Steinmetz, Stephen Hawking). Phyllis Stearner has described the lives of scientists who were disabled, but who successfully pursued careers in science and engineering.[88] These vignettes provide role models and support for the science teacher who encourages the identification of gifted handicapped students.

CHARACTERISTICS OF ADVANCED STUDENTS
There are many characteristics of advanced students, and it is this constellation of characteristics that helps describe gifted young in the broadest sense. Myths such as gifted persons are physically weak, socially inept, narrow in interests, and prone to emotional instability and early decline need to be offset with more accurate characterizations of gifted students.[89]

Gifted or advanced students show the following characteristics:

- academically superior
- apply systems approaches
- apply abstract principles to concrete situations
- careless in handwriting and similar routine tasks
- courteous
- deliberately underachieve under certain conditions
- difficulty conversing with age mates
- emotionally stable
- extraordinarily verbal
- generally curious
- give uncommon responses
- have a high energy level, especially in mental and intellectual tasks
- have a high vocabulary level
- imaginative
- intellectually curious
- intellectually superior
- inquisitive
- superior in logical ability
- make individualistic interpretations of new subject matter
- obnoxious or rebellious when asked to do repetitive tasks
- original
- outspokenly critical of themselves and others
- perceive and identifie significant factors in complex situations
- persistent in achieving goals

- have good physical ability
- take pleasure in intellectual pursuits
- have good power of concentration
- recognize and are uncomfortable with unresolved ambiguity
- rebel against conformity
- scientifically oriented
- seek older companions
- have sense of humor
- sensitive to problems of others
- skip steps in normal thinking sequence
- socially aware
- have strong sense of responsibility
- superior in ability to remember details
- superior in ability to see relationships
- unhappy with most group-participation projects (with normal peers)
- unaccepting of routine classroom rules
- have an unusually good memory
- verbally facile
- verbally flexible

WHY ADVANCED STUDENTS DON'T REACH THEIR POTENTIAL Although advanced students have been described as possessing a constellation of skills and abilities, the evidence in practice is that many do not reach their potential. There are many reasons for this. Some students, according to Tomlinson, become mentally lazy, even though they do well in school.[90] Other students become "hooked" on the trappings of success. This often leads to the unwillingness to take risks and to focus on being "right" rather than "thinking or moving out-of-the-box." Too often advanced students become perfectionists, Because they are praised so often for doing well, their self-worth is tied to the rewards of schooling and, as a result, these students tend to avoid failure at all costs. This possibly leads students to becoming "less productive" and schooling becoming less satisfying.

Another factor contributing to advanced students not reaching their potential is that they fail to develop a sense of self-efficacy. Some students may fear the world finding out that they are not so capable after all. The overabundance of praise may become a goal for students rather than stretching their abilities and fostering the development of new skills. Because many advanced students "coast" through school, they fail to develop important skills such as persistence, hard work, and taking risks.

SCIENCE LEARNING ENVIRONMENTS FOR ADVANCED LEARNERS Schools have developed a variety of programs for the advanced student. Generally, the programs are designed to provide enrichment (providing additional experiences without early advancement to higher grades) or acceleration (moving students ahead of their age peers). The following list presents the range of program opportunities for advanced students:

1. Enrichment in the regular classroom
2. Consultation teacher program in which a differentiated program is provided in the regular classroom with the advice of a specialty teacher
3. Resource room/pullout program
4. Community mentor program
5. Independent study programs
6. Special class
7. Special school[91]

There are a number of strategies that the science teacher can use to work with gifted students in science classes. Both individual and cooperative learning strategies are recommended, as is the opportunity for the gifted student to engage in science inquiry and problem-solving activities.

- Self-directed learning: provide the student the opportunity to assume responsibility for defining and choosing the direction for solving problems and studying topics.
- Cooperative learning: Although there is controversy surrounding placing gifted students in cooperative teams with "normal" students, Johnson and Johnson provide evidence to support teachers engaging gifted students in cooperative learning activities in the regular classroom.[92]
- Engage the students in high-level problem-solving activities.
- Encourage students to get involved in science fair and olympiad projects.
- Modify the curriculum (curriculum compaction) for gifted students so that they may pursue some topics in more depth or seek a breadth of topics.
- Use learning contracts (either individually or in pairs) enabling gifted students to break away from the regular content of the course. Students can be encouraged to report back to entire class.

At-Risk Students in Science (Struggling Learners)

Just as Tomlinson suggested using the concept of advanced learner to describe gifted learners, she suggests the use of the term "struggling learner" instead of the term at-risk, disadvantaged, culturally deprived, underachiever, nonachiever, low ability, slow learner, less able, low socioeconomic status, language-impaired, dropout-prone, alienated, marginal, disenfranchised, impoverished, underprivileged, low-performing, or remedial.[93]

We might think of struggling learners as low-achieving students whose poor performance hinders subsequent success and frequently leads to withdrawal from school. Struggling learners typically have low self-esteem and for school-related and academic performance the situation is only exacerbated with continued failure and difficulties. Students who are struggling in science class will typically show the following characteristics: academic difficulty, lack of structure, inattentiveness, easily distracted, short attention span, excessive absenteeism, dependence, discipline problems, lack of social skills, inability to face pressure, fear of failure, and apparent lack of motivation.[94] How can students with these kinds of problems be helped? What can science teachers do to motivate these students to succeed in science?

There is a great deal of controversy surrounding what kinds of interventions are effective with at-risk students. The controversy focuses remedial instruction versus instruction aimed at high-order thinking. Most educational programs for at-risk students stress "small mechanical skills and rote memory and regurgitation."[95] The reason for this emphasis is the psychological theory that many educators use to explain the "nature" of at-risk students. The prevailing theory suggests that at-risk students fail in school because of cognitive deficits and because, by and large, many of these students come

INQUIRY ACTIVITY 2.3

 Finding Out about Science Programs for the Exceptional Student

One of the most important steps the "regular" classroom teacher can take regarding education in school science for the exceptional student is to find out about interventions and programs that will help exceptional students in the science classroom. In this inquiry activity, you will join a team of peers to investigate one or more areas of exceptional students and make a presentation to your class. This activity will also focus on helping you become aware of ways to encourage students with disabilities to achieve in science.

Materials

- List of exemplary programs/resources for exceptional students (included)
- Web site: Special Education Resources on the Internet (SERI): http://seriweb.com/

Procedures

1. Your team is to select an exceptionality from the list below and imagine that it applies to one or more students in your classes.

   a. Hearing impaired
   b. Visually impaired
   c. Orthopedically/health impaired
   d. Learning disabled
   e. Mentally retarded
   f. Advanced learner
   g. Struggling learner

   Speech and Language challenged
   assign each student one exceptionality
   Emotionally challenged

2. Your team's role is to prepare a set of recommendations to the class that include answers to the following questions:

   a. What are the characteristics of students who have this exceptionality?
   b. What is the cause of the exceptionality?
   c. What teaching strategies should be used with students having this exceptionality?
   d. What changes or modifications should be made to the physical arrangement of the classroom?

Minds-On Strategies

1. What are some general principles concerning how the science teacher can facilitate learning for exceptional students in the regular classroom?
2. In what ways do you think exceptional students and the teacher's implementation of mitigating strategies can benefit the "normal" student in the regular classroom?

Exemplary Programs/Resources for Exceptional Students

American Foundation for the Blind
   15 West 16th Street
   New York, NY 10011
   http://www.afb.org/

American Printing House for the Blind, Inc.
   1839 Frankfort Ave.
   P.O. Box 6085
   Louisville, KY 40206
   http://www.aph.org/

Gallaudet College Press
   Distribution Office
   7th Street & Florida Avenue, NE
   Washington, DC 20002
   http://www.gallaudet.edu/
   (Resources on/for the deaf student)

Information Center for Individuals with Disabilities
   20 Park Plaza
   Boston, MA 02116
   http://www.disability.net/

National Association for Visually Handicapped
   305 East 24th Street, 17-C
   New York, NY 10010
   http://www.navh.org/

National Federation for the Blind
   1800 Johnson Street
   Baltimore, MD 21230
   http://www.nfb.org/

National Science Teachers Association
   1742 Connecticut Avenue, NW
   Washington, DC 20009
   http://www.nsta.org

National Technical Institute for the Deaf
   Rochester Institute of Technology
   1 Lomb Memorial Drive
   Rochester, NY 14623
   http://ntidweb.rit.edu/

Recording for the Blind and Dyslexic
   20 Roszel Road
   Princeton, NJ 08540
   http://www.rfbd.org/

from disadvantaged environments. This framework suggests that education should make up for these deficits by providing an educational program that remediates cognition and environment. An alternative view suggests that the cognitive deficit theory is biased or misguided, that these students are capable of learning and thinking at quite high levels, and that the educational programs that have been provided fail to take into account cultural pluralism.[96]

Recent models for working with struggling students go well beyond the three views just mentioned. New models emphasize "accelerated learning," teaching high-order thinking skills, focusing on student learning styles, and using enrichment programs rather than remedial programs.

Here are some suggestions that science teachers can use to help struggling learners:

1. Look for students' positives. Focus on each student's learning style and provide opportunities for students to make choices in their assignments and tasks.

2. Plan activities that are relevant. The struggling learner can be helped by participating in activities that are not so "school-like." Activities that focus on real-world applications, community-based actions, and focus on self and society can help students see the relevance of science in their day-to-day life.

3. Teach up. Create activities that are a bit more difficult for the struggling learner. By focusing on student's learning style, one can teach for success: encouraging, giving support, guiding their work, and helping students become convinced that their hard work will lead to success.

4. Involve at-risk students in hands-on activities using concrete materials. These students, perhaps more than any other group of students, need to be given the opportunities to work with real materials. Too many "activities" for the at-risk student involve the use of worksheets, which is counterproductive vis-à-vis student learning styles.

5. Struggling learners benefit from being members of heterogeneous groups. Cooperative learning is a crucial learning format for at-risk students. Typical remedial programs, which tend to isolate at-risk students and involve them in individual learning activities (usually worksheets), counter the student's real needs. These needs include being able to talk with able learners; working alongside students who are successful; cooperating with other members of the class; learning social skills; learning how to ask questions—in short, learning how to learn. Cooperative learning strategies have been shown to raise the academic performance of at-risk students in heterogeneous classes.

6. Teaching students metacognitive strategies. In this approach, students are taught how to learn by teaching them planning strategies: mind mapping, brainstorming, questioning skills.

7. Science teachers can help at-risk students by assessing their learning style and then planning activities accordingly. For example, consideration should be made for students who prefer kinesthetic learning or tactile activities. See the discussion of learning styles and science teaching in Chapter 5.

SECTION 2: SCIENCE TEACHER GAZETTE

Volume 2: Science for All

Think Pieces

1. Why should multicultural education be an integral part of science education? Support this position with at least three references from the literature.

2. What steps should be taken to ensure that girls are provided equity in terms of science courses and careers in science and engineering?

3. What are the major issues regarding multicultural education?

4. How can science teachers counteract the effects of racism and sexism in the science classroom?

5. What philosophy should guide the actions that science teachers take with regard to exceptional students in the regular science classroom?

Case Study: The Experiment

The Case

A university professor has gained permission to plant genetically engineered seeds in a small farming town. The population of this rural town is composed of three main groups: a small, highly educated white middle class; a large, poorly educated white population of low socioeconomic status; and a large ethnic minority population of low socioeconomic status, most of whom have a high school education.

The Problem

How do you think the different groups that live in the town will respond to the planting of the genetically engineered seeds? Do you think democratic standards and attitudes will be employed when dealing with the ethnic minority and low-income populations?[97]

Science Teachers Talk

How do you accommodate students with exceptional needs, such as the gifted and talented, hearing impaired, visually impaired, mentally retarded, students with learning disabilities, students with behavioral disorders, or potential dropouts? What have you found to be effective in working with these students?"

JOHN RICCIARDI: On the high school level, I believe the present system of public education is critically limited in its ability to provide effective and meaningful instruction for its "high-risk" population of potential dropouts and students with behavioral abnormalities. This is a frightening problem in America's schools today. Rather than trying to understand and identify the specific educational needs and learning styles within this population group, too many schools are resorting to solutions that essentially segregate, isolate, and intimidate the individual. It's dehumanizing and psychologically counterproductive.

My basic astronomy course (a section offered in our high school, four of which I teach) attracts a fair number of "behavioral disordered" students and potential dropouts. I don't treat these kids any differently other than yielding more to their "scatter braininess." I have virtually no discipline problems in my classes because, I believe, I first show a sense of trust and respect for the individual's integrity and self-worth. When you allow yourself to do this, when you honor the individual, you just keep moving . . . facilitating, and soon you watch your instructional objectives flow into place.

GINNY ALMEDER: I have worked primarily with physically handicapped, learning disabled, and behaviorally disordered students. For the physically handicapped students, I have made appropriate room arrangements to accommodate at least one wheelchair. I integrate the student into a regular lab group and make arrangements for one member of the group to make a carbon copy of notes and lab data. On occasion in the past, the special education department has provided an aide for additional assistance during lab activities.

With learning disabled students, I identify their learning problem with the assistance of the resource teacher and then work with them in developing skills. This approach involves a combination of individual attention and peer support from their group. I have found that increasing their participation in class discussions enhances successful learning.

The behaviorally disordered students are the most challenging. Typically, I work with them individually in developing appropriate classroom behavior. A firm but friendly approach usually works. I have found that most students will respond if they believe that I am concerned about their success.

JERRY PELLETIER: At the present time I am working mainly with gifted and talented students. I have found that these students need to be challenged with high-quality thinking materials and strategies. Besides accumulating knowledge and comprehending it, these students must learn to analyze and evaluate this knowledge. In order to meet these special needs, I use many different types of materials besides the text in our basic science program. These students are asked to do special science projects, research papers, and read literature that is associated with various fields of science. It is my feeling that this will enrich their backgrounds and challenge their analytic thinking. It is not my purpose to demand more of these students in the sense of quantity but to demand more in the sense of quality.

BOB MILLER: We have been somewhat successful with student involvement in raising animals for classroom use. Students seem to take pride in raising the animal and telling other students about their experience. The approach seems to fit a variety of students with varying disabilities, physical or emotional.

MARY WILDE: I would first like to focus on how to work with the gifted child in the classroom. I am very much opposed to pulling that gifted child out of the classroom for instruction, particularly at the middle school level. Isolating those students only creates attitude problems, social problems, and morale problems among teachers who do not have those "sparks" in the classroom. I gear my instruction to those students by providing greater course content and problem-solving activities. I then do a lot of small-group work so that these students apply what they have learned by helping others learn the same information. Therefore, more students have benefited by an "enrichment" program. It is really neat to see the interaction among gifted students and those who want to learn but need a little more time and a little more instruction. I do use the advanced child to set my instructional goals, however, I allow for learning rate differences among individual students.

The behavioral problem students always create a difficult situation in the classroom. When a teacher has these students, the reaction is to pull back the reins, take away all freedom, and develop a very structured classroom so that the students have fewer opportunities to cause havoc. However, this treatment usually makes me miserable, and the learning that takes place in the classroom is minimal. It is very difficult, but I find I have better success when I provide more hands-on activities and a less structured classroom setting. I must spend more time organizing and planning, for it is important that all directions and expectations are very clear. However, the real key to working with the discipline problem student is that you show real interest in that person. You go out of your way to know everything about that child, so that you can comment and ask that child questions that communicate a caring concern for that person. This helps create positive attitudes and respect for the teacher, thus diminishing disrespectful behavior in the classroom. There are times when you don't think your effort is successful, but with a little patience, the rewards will come.

SCIENCE-TEACHING LITERATURE

SCIENCE FOR ALL

Peter J. Fensham

After a decade of stagnation, science education in many countries is seeing renewed interest and nationally supported curriculum efforts.[98] In 1983 new funds in the United States initiated a number of projects. In Britain, the first major project since the 1960s, the Secondary Science Curriculum Review, was established in 1982. Even earlier, New Zealand set up the Learning in Science Project in 1979 and, in 1982, a corresponding elementary school project. This new activity extends beyond developed or industrialized countries. In 1984 the Asia region of UNESCO, which ranges from Iran to Japan, endorsed a science education program as one of its few priorities for the rest of the 1980s.

In both rhetoric and rationale, these programs share in common a strong emphasis on Science for All. This slogan is a compelling and attractive one in societies where applied science and technology are evident in new products and new forms of communications. New jobs emerge and old, familiar ones disappear. There is a cry for new skills and expertise and a chronic toll of unemployed persons who lack technical skills.

This sort of analysis of the curriculum movement of the 1960s and 1970s and hence of the present state of science in our schools can be used to begin to define characteristics that may be essential if science education is to be effective as Science for All and other characteristics that are at least worth trying.

First, elite or traditional science education must be confined to and contained within an upper level of schooling. It needs to be identified for what it is: a form of vocational preparation. Containment is not achieved by offering alternatives at the levels of schooling where Science for All is to be achieved. It is no good having a proper science for the few and science for the rest.

Second, science must be reexamined and recognized as a variegated source of human knowledge and endeavor. A wider range of appropriate aspects of science needs to be selected for converting into the pedagogical forms of a science curriculum that will have a chance of contributing to effective learning for the great majority of students.

I have argued that present science curriculums are really an induction into science. The ones that might provide Science for All must involve much more learning about and from science.

These curriculum processes are quite fundamentally different. For instance, in the first we use teachers who have themselves been inducted into an acquaintance with some of the basic conceptual knowledge of an area of science to repeat the first steps of this process with their students. Since the teachers usually have little experience of the exciting practical applications of their knowledge or of the process of trying to extend the knowledge of a science, the induction they offer into the corpus of science is through the same abstract route they followed as part of a former elite who could tolerate it and cope with its learning. Few of their students are interested enough to follow.

In the alternative that I envisage for Science for All, students would stay firmly rooted outside the corpus in their society with its myriad examples of technology and its possibilities for science education. Science teachers, as persons with some familiarity and confidence with the corpus of science, will need to be helped to be not inductors but couriers between the rich corpus and their students in society.

Third, some clear criteria must be established for selecting the science that is to be the learning of worth . . .

Such criteria should include, for example, (1) aspects of science that students will very likely use in a relatively short time in their daily lives outside of school and (2) aspects of natural phenomena that exemplify easily and well to the students the excitement, novelty, and power of scientific knowledge and explanation.

At a recent international curriculum workshop in Cyprus these two criteria were used to spell out a skeletal content for a quite new sort of science curriculum. They were found to be logically applicable in a range of broad topic areas such as senses and measurement; the human body; health, nutrition, and sanitation; food; ecology; resources; population; pollution; and use of energy.

A fundamental difference between the sort of science education (and hence curriculums) that we have had hitherto and what may be needed for a genuine Science for All is the fact that the "All" must be thought of as existing outside of science. In other words, science is an institutionalized part of all our societies in very definite and varied ways. On the other hand, even in the most highly technical, scientifically advanced societies no more than 20 percent of the population could be even remotely identified with the institutionalized part. The remaining 80 percent are, and for their lives will be, outside of science in this sense.

It is this sense of "outside of science" that I think we must understand and translate into curriculum terms if Science for All is to succeed from our present opportunities.

SCIENCE-TEACHING LITERATURE

OUR APARTHEID: THE IMPERATIVE OF MULTICULTURALISM IN SCIENCE EDUCATION

Randy Moore

Despite decades-long proclamations about the importance of "science for all," our educational system has produced a scientific apartheid.[99] For example, although African Americans and Hispanics comprise almost 25 percent of the U.S. population, they earn only 13 percent of the U.S. science and engineering bachelor degrees and only 7 percent of the doctorates.[100] Only one third of the minority students who begin in the sciences graduate with a degree in science or engineering.[101]

Similarly, black and Hispanic scientists and engineers are less likely than white faculty to be full professors, and they earn lower salaries than white scientists and engineers. And, of the more than 1,800 living scientists elected to the National Academies of Sciences, only two are African American.

The most common strategy in recent years for increasing minority representation in science has been recruiting more minorities into science classes. This approach is based on the popular assumption that we best serve students from underrepresented groups by helping them "fit in"

and adapt to existing curricula and teaching methods. However, these compensatory "add-minorities-and-stir" programs have often failed because they have placed the responsibility of reform on those already marginalized by science.

Marginalized students are not the problem; the system that marginalizes them is the problem. As a result, most minorities continue to feel implicitly inferior and unwelcome in the neighborhood of science. Because science education has not accommodated the different learning styles and cultural backgrounds of most of these students, many longstanding obstacles remain.

We should all be concerned about the lack of diversity in science. In addition to the moral and ethical problems associated with the exclusion of minorities, there is a pragmatic reward for involving them: Diversified viewpoints enhance science. For example, before 1993, when President Bill Clinton signed legislation requiring the National Institutes of Health to include women and minorities in all of their clinical health studies, there was no federal policy to adequately enforce the representation of these two groups in public health research. As a result, scientists and science teachers often lacked data for a variety of important phenomena that affect women and minorities (for example, the contraction of AIDS by women and minorities). Similarly, important new theories and ideas have been discovered when traditionally excluded groups have been given opportunities to excel in science.

We must rededicate ourselves to making our courses, curricula, and classrooms more accessible and friendly to minority students, students with disabilities, and students from poor socioeconomic backgrounds. This demands hard work.

But there is good news. We already know what to do. We must:

- Consider the terms upon which students are included in (and excluded from) science;
- Help students see themselves reflected in the curriculum;
- Value courses that function as "pumps" to help students succeed instead of sieves that "weed out" students;
- Understand our students' demographic diversity and the social construction of group differences;

- Emphasize process and discovery over "facts";
- Stress knowledge as something that is constructed by students rather than a commodity imparted by teachers;
- Recognize the unequal academic opportunities that characterize different socioeconomic backgrounds;
- Discuss the biases of science; and
- Acknowledge how factually neutral tests and knowledge can in practice reinforce the power and influence of dominant groups.

If "science for all" is to be achieved, science educators must respond to educational inequalities. Similarly, if we are to enhance science education, we must remove the structural, institutional, and pedagogical barriers that impede or block the success of minorities. It's up to each of us to help students feel invested in and capable of succeeding in science. "Science for all" begins with access for all.

RESEARCH MATTERS

ENCOURAGING GIRLS IN SCIENCE COURSES AND CAREERS

Jane Butler Kahle

In the United States women comprise approximately 50 percent of the workforce, yet only 9 percent are employed as scientists and engineers.[102] Factors contributing to this situation have been analyzed in research studies. Explanations have ranged from differences in spatial ability related to a sex-linked gene to differences in early childhood toys and games. One study reported a dramatic decline in positive attitudes toward science as girls mature. The authors attribute this decline to startling inequities in the number of science activities experienced by males and females in elementary and secondary classrooms. In addition, the analysis of the results from the National Assessment of Educational Progress science study indicate that girls continue to score below the national mean on all science achievement items and to express negative attitudes toward science. Although societal, educational,

and personal factors are all involved, differences within the science classroom may be a contributing factor to low interest of women in science and scientific careers.

However, some girls like science and continue to study science. In order to determine what motivates these girls to pursue science courses and careers, a group of researchers conducted nationwide surveys to identify teachers who have motivated high school girls to continue in science. In addition to assessing instructional techniques, classroom climate, and teacher-student interactions, a selected sample of students (former and current) responded to questionnaires that assessed attitudes, intellectual and socio-cultural variables.

Two types of research, observational and survey, were used to gather data for this project. The case studies, which were the observational parts of this project, provided information about the student-teacher and student-student interactions. Case studies are limited in the extent to which they may produce generalizations applicable to other situations. Therefore, they were supplemented with survey data, describing the abilities, activities, and aspirations of the involved students and teachers. These research efforts led to the following conclusions:

Teachers who successfully *encourage* girls in science:

- Maintain well-equipped, organized, and perceptually stimulating classrooms.
- Are supported in their teaching activities by the parents of their students and are respected by current and former students.
- Use nonsexist language and examples and include information on women scientists.
- Use laboratories, discussions, and weekly quizzes as their primary modes of instruction and supplement those activities with field trips and guest speakers.
- Stress creativity and basic skills and provide career information.

Factors that discourage girls in science:

- High school counselors who do not encourage further courses in science and mathematics.

- Lack of information about science-related career opportunities and their prerequisites.
- Sex-stereotyped views of science and scientists, which are projected by texts, media, and many adults.
- Lack of development of spatial ability skills (which could be fostered in shop and mechanical drawing classes).
- Fewer experiences with science activities and equipment, which are stereotyped as masculine (mechanics, electricity, astronomy).

The teachers, both male and female, who were successful in motivating girls to continue to study science practiced "directed intervention." That is, girls were asked to assist with demonstrations; were required to perform, not merely record, in the laboratories; and were encouraged to participate in science-related field trips. In addition, teachers stressed the utility of math and science for future careers.

Both male and female students in the schools identified as "positive toward girls in science" were questioned about their attitudes toward science and science careers. When compared with a national sample, the students in these schools had a much more positive outlook. This difference was especially pronounced among girls. When asked how frequently they like to attend science class, 67 percent of the girls responded "often," compared with 32 percent of the girls in the national sample. And when asked if they would like to pursue a science-related job, 65 percent of the girls said "yes," compared with 32 percent of the girls in the national sample.

This research suggests that teaching styles and other school-related factors are important in encouraging girls as well as boys to continue in science courses and careers. The path to a scientific career begins in high school and requires skilled and sensitive teachers. This research identified the following "dos" and "don'ts" for teachers who want to foster equity in science classrooms.

Do

- use laboratory and discussion activities
- provide career information
- directly involve girls in science activities
- provide informal academic counseling
- demonstrate unisex treatment in science classrooms

Don't

- use sexist humor
- use sex-stereotyped examples
- distribute sexist classroom materials
- allow boys to dominate discussions or activities
- allow girls to passively resist

Problems and Extensions

1. Working in a small group, discuss each of the following statements in terms of (a) What are the values and assumptions implicitly in the statement? (b) What kinds of power relations are at work here? and (c) What are the implications for practice?

   a. It is absolutely natural for boys to behave in aggressive, "macho" ways and for girls to be quiet and passive. Men and women are supposed to complement one another and we should not try to change that fact. It is all down to our genes!

   b. If female teachers have trouble with disciplining boys that is their problem!

   c. Don't misunderstand me. I'm against sexism like the next person. But I think discussion about sexism in school takes time away from the really important thing—and that's getting kids through the course to take exams, isn't it?[103]

2. Find out who the following scientists were and what their contributions were to science. Design a science lesson using one, a few, or all of these scientists.

   a. Benjamin Banneker
   b. Vilhelm Bjerknes
   c. Elizabeth Blackwell
   d. Sofie Brahe
   e. Charles Richard Drew
   f. Caroline Herschel
   g. Charles Steinmetz

3. Write to several organizations serving disabled and exceptional students and report on their services and publications.

4. What actions would you take if a student placed in your class was wheelchair bound?

5. If you were a school board member, what actions would you recommend the school district take to ensure that all females, minorities, and disabled who attend school in the district aspire to excellence in science, mathematics, and engineering?

Notes

1. Mary M. Atwater, "Social Constructivism: Infusion into the Multicultural Science Education Research Agenda," *Journal of Research in Science Teaching* 33, no. 8 (1996): 821–37.

2. Jack Hassard and Julie Weisberg, "The Emergence of Global Thinking Among American and Russian Youth as a Contribution to Public Understanding," *International Journal of Science Education* 21 (1999): 1–13.

3. Cited in R. D. Holt, "Can Psychology Meet Einstein's Challenge?" *Political Psychology* 5 (1984): 199–225.

4. Based on Robert G. Hanvey, *An Attainable Global Perspective* (Denver, Colo.: Center for Teaching International Relations, 1976).

5. Ibid., p. 22.

6. A. Feldman, C. Konold, and B. Coulter, *Network Science a Decade Later: The Internet and Classroom Learning* (Mahwah, N.J.: Lawrence Erlbaum Associates, 2000).

7. Lee F. Anderson, "A Rationale for Global Education," in *Global Education: From Thought to Action*, ed. Kenneth A. Tye (Alexandria, Va.: Association for Supervision and Curriculum Development, 1990), pp. 13–34.

8. Ibid., p. 21.

9. Ibid., p. 27.

10. Ibid., p. 31.

11. Hassard and Weisberg, "The Emergence of Global Thinking Among American and Russian Youth."

12. Steven L. Lamy, "Global Education: A Conflict of Images," in *Global Education: From Thought to Action*, ed. Kenneth A. Tie (Alexandria, Va.: Association for Supervision and Curriculum Development, 1990), p. 53.

13. Victor J. Mayer, "Teaching from a Global Point of View," *The Science Teacher* 14 (January 1990): 47–51.

14. *Global Food Web* (Athens, Ga.: The University of Georgia, Cooperative Extension Service, 1990).

15. Robert Muller, "A World Core Curriculum," *New Era* (January 1982)

16. *The Robert Muller School: World Core Curriculum Manual* (Arlington, Tex.: Robert Muller School, 1986), p. 10.

17. From Rodger W. Bybee, "Global Problems and Science Education Policy," in *Redesigning Science and Technology Education*, ed. Rodger W. Bybee, Janet Carlson, and Alan J. McCormack (Washington, D.C.: National Science Teachers Association, 1984), pp. 60–75.

18. For a source of global science activities, see Betty A. Reardon, *Educating for Global Responsibility* (New York: Teachers College Press, 1988).

19. Bylaws of the Association for Multicultural Science Education (Washington, D.C.: AMSE, 1989), p. 1.

20. James A. Banks, "Multicultural Education and Its Critics: Britain and the United States," in *Multicutural Education: The Interminable Debate*, ed. Sohan Modgil, Gajendra Verma, Kanka Mallick, and Celia Modgil (London: The Falmer Press, 1986), p. 222.

21. Fred Rodrigues, *Mainstreaming a Multicultural Concept into Teacher Education* (Saratoga, Calif.: R & E Publishers, 1983), p. 12.

22. Ibid., pp. 13–14.

23. Ibid., p. 15.

24. Quality Education for Minorities Project, *Education That Works: An Action Plan for the Education of Minorities* (Cambridge, Mass.: Massachusetts Institute of Technology, 1990), pp. 7–9.

25. Ibid., p. 17.

26. Ibid., p. 18.

27. Boyken, (2000), as cited in R. J. Jagers and G. Carroll, "Issues in Educating African American Children and Youth," in *Educating At-Risk Students*, ed. S. Stringfield and D. Land (Chicago: University of Chicago Press, 2002), p. 49.

28. Ibid., pp. 50–51.

29. Talent Development High School, information available online: www.csos.jhu.edu/tdhs/index.htm.

30. Mary M. Atwater, "Multicultural Science Education: Definitions and Research Agenda for the 1990s and Beyond" (paper presented at the annual meeting of the National Association for Research in Science Teaching, Atlanta April 1990), p. 4.

31. Steven J. Rakow and Andrea B. Bermudez, "Science Is *Sciencia*: Meeting the Needs of Hispanic American Students." *Science Education*, no. 77, 6 (1995), 669–83.

32. Based on Cristine Ditchfield, *Better Science: Working for a Multicultural Society* (London: Heinemann Educational Books/Association for Science Education, 1987), p. 38.

33. Ibid., p. 38.

34. Items 1 through 6: Ibid., pp. 12–38.

35. Y. N. Padron, H. C. Waxman, and H. H. Rivera, "Issues in Educating Hispanic Students," in *Educating At-Risk Students*, ed. S. Stringfield and D. Land (Chicago: University of Chicago Press, 2002), pp. 66–88.

36. Ibid., pp. 72–76.

37. Ina V. S. Mullis and Lynn B. Jenkins, *The Science Report Card: Elements of Risk and Recovery* (Princeton, N.J.: Educational Testing Service, 1988), pp. 23–30.

38. Daryl E. Chubin, *Elementary and Secondary Education for Science and Engineering* (New York: Hemisphere Publishing Company, 1990), p. 17.

39. Jane Butler Kahle, "Retention of Girls in Science: Case Studies of Secondary Teachers," in *Women in Science: A Report from the Field*, ed. Jane Butler Kahle (Philadelphia: The Falmer Press, 1985), pp. 49–76.

40. See Sue V. Rosser, *Female-Friendly Science* (New York: Pergamon Press, 1990).

41. Kathleen S. Davis, "Advocating for Equitable Science-Learning Opportunities for Girls in an Urban City Youth Club and the Roadblocks Faced by Women Science Educators" *Journal of Research in Science Teaching* 39, no. 2 (2002): 151–63.

42. Wu Chien-Shiung, "The Commitment Required of a Woman Entering a Scienfic Profession (Panel Discussion)," in *Women and the Scientific Profession*, ed. J. A. Mattfeld and C. G. Van Aken (Cambridge, Mass.: MIT Press), cited in Kahle, *Women in Science*, p. 169.

43. Anne E. Haley-Oliphant, "International Perspectives on the Status and Role of Women in Science," in Kahle, *Women in Science*, p. 169.

44. Margaret Alic, *Hypatia's Heritage: A History of Women in Science from Antiquity through the Nineteenth Century* (Boston: Beacon Press, 1986).

45. Ibid., p. 1.

46. Sue V. Rosser, *Female-Friendly Science* (New York: Pergamon Press, 1990), p. 74. Especially refer to Chapter 6, "Sexism in Textbooks."

47. See Alison Kelly, Judith Whyte, and Barbara Smail, "Girls into Science and Technology: Final Report," in *Science for Girls*? ed. Alison Kelly (Milton Keynes, England: Open University Press, 1987), pp. 100–122.

48. Joan Skolnick, Carol Langbort, and Lucille Day, *How to Encourage Girls in Math and Science* (Englewood Cliffs, N.J.: Prentice-Hall, 1982), p. 47.

49. Kelly, *Science for Girls?* p. 15.

50. Jane Butler Kahle, "Real Students Take Chemistry and Physics: Gender Issues," in *Windows into Science Classrooms: Problems Associated with Higher-Level Cognitive Learning*, ed. Kenneth Tobin, Jane Butler Kahle, and Barry J. Fraser (London: The Falmer Press, 1990), pp. 92–134.

51. Ibid., p. 127.

52. Michael Cole and Peg Griffin, *Contextual Factors in Education: Improving Science and Mathematics Education for Minorities and Women* (Madison, Wisc.: Wisconsin Center for Educational Research, 1987), pp. 12–13.

53. Barbara Small, "Organizing the Curriculum to Fit Girls' Interests," in *Science for Girls?*, ed. Alison Kelly (Milton Keynes, England: Open University Press, 1987), p. 83.

54. McCarthy, *About Teaching—4MAT in the Classroom* (Wauconda, Ill.: About Learning, Inc., 2000).

55. Small, "Organizing the Curriculum," p. 83.

56. Cole and Griffin, *Contextual Factors*, p. 33.

57. Elizabeth Cohen, *Designing Groupwork* (New York: Teachers College Press, 1988).

58. See Cole and Griffin, *Contextual Factors*, pp. 24–42.

59. Skolnick, Langbort, and Day, *How to Encourage Girls in Math and Science*, pp. 49–50.

60. Kahle, "Real Students Take Chemistry and Physics," p. 131.

61. Skolinick, Langbort, and Day, *How to Encourage Girls in Math and Science*, p. 56.

62. Smail, "Organizing the Curriculum in Girls Interests." p. 84.

63. Skolnick, Langbort, and Day, *How to Encourage Girls in Math and Science*, p. 56.

64. Greg P. Stefanich et al., "Addressing Orthopedic Handicaps in the Science Classroom," ERIC, ED 258802. 1985, pp. 13–15.

65. Public Law 94-142, *Federal Register* 42 (23 August 1977), Education for all Handicapped Children Act of 1975.

66. Bill R. Gearheart, Mel W. Weishahn, and Carol J. Gearheart, *The Exceptional Student in the Regular Classroom* (Columbus, Ohio: Merrill, 1988), p. 27.

67. Ibid., p. 29.

68. Ibid., p. 33.

69. Stefanich et al., pp. 1–2.

70. Task Force on Women, Minorities, and the Handicapped in Science and Technology, "Changing America: The New Face of Science and Engineering, Final Report" (1989), p. 24, ERIC, ED 317386.

71. E. C. Keller, T. Pauley, M. Ellsworth, E. Starcher, and B. Proctor, *Teaching the Physically Disabled in the Mainstream Science Class at the Secondary and College Levels* (Morgantown, W.Va.: Printech, 1983), pp. 19–20.

72. Based on Rodger Bybee, "Helping the Special Student to Fit In," *Science Teacher* (October, 1979): 23–24.

73. Kenneth S. Ricker, "Science for Students with Visual Impairments," ERIC, ED 258800. 1985.

74. Ibid., p. 2.

75. Keller et al., *Teaching the Physically Disabled*, pp. 19–20.

76. Ibid., pp. 38–39.

77. Gearheart, Weishahn, and Gearheart, *The Exceptional Student in the Regular Classroom*, p. 271.

78. John O'Neil, "How 'Special' Should the Special Ed Curriculum Be?" *ASCD Curriculum Update* (September 1988): 1–3.

79. Charles R. Coble, Betty Levey, and Floyd Matheis, "Science for Learning Disabled Students," February 1985, pp. 7–10, ERIC, ED 258803.

80. Ibid., p. 20.

81. Carol Ann Tomlinson, *How to Differentiate Instruction in Mixed-Ability Classrooms* (Alexandria, Va.: Association for Supervision and Curriculum Development, 2001).

82. Gearheart, Weishahn, and Gearheart, *The Exceptional Student in the Regular Classroom*, p. 356.

83. J. S. Renzulli, S. M. Reis, and L. H. Smith, *The Revolving Door Identification Model* (Mansfield Center, Conn.: Creative Learning Press, 1981).

84. Daniel P. Hallahan and James M. Kaufman, *Exceptional Children* (Englewood Cliffs, N.J.: Prentice Hall, 1991), p. 424.

85. Howard Gardner, *Frames of Mind: The Theory of Multiple Intelligences* (New York: Basic Books, 1985).

86. Mary M. Frasier, "Poor and Minority Students Can Be Gifted, Too!," *Educational Leadership* (March 1989): 16–18.

87. Hallahan and Kaufman, *Exceptional Children*, p. 424.

88. Phyllis Stearner, *Able Scientists—Disabled Persons: Careers in the Sciences* (Oakbrook, Ill.: John Racila Associates, 1984).

89. Gearheart, Weishahn, and Gearheart, *The Exceptional Student in the Regular Classroom*, p. 359.

90. Tomlinson, *How to Differentiate Instruction*, pp. 9–11.

91. Hallahan and Kaufman, *Exceptional Children*, pp. 426–27.

92. Roger T. Johnson and David W. Johnson, "Cooperative Learning and the Gifted Science Student," in *Gifted Young in Science: Potential Through Performance*, ed. Paul F. Brandwein and A. Harry Passow (Washington, D.C.: National Science Teachers Association, 1988), pp. 321–29.

93. Tomlinson, *How to Differentiate Instruction*.

94. Judy Brown Lehr and Hazel Wiggins Harris, *At-Risk, Low-Achieving Students in the Classroom* (Washington, D.C.: National Education Association, 1988), p. 2.

95. Daniel U. Levine, "Teaching Thinking to At-Risk Students: Generalizations and Speculations," in *At-Risk Students and Thinking: Perspectives from Research*, ed. Barbara Z. Presseisen (Washington, D.C.: National Education Association, 1988), p. 28.

96. Barbara Z. Presseisen, "Teaching Thinking and At-Risk Students: Defining a Population," in *At-Risk Students and Thinking: Perspectives from Research*, ed. Barbara Z. Presseisen (Washington, D.C.: National Education Association, 1988), pp. 19–37.

97. Based on Mary M. Atwater, "Including Multicultural Education in Science Education: Definitions, Competencies, and Activities," *Journal of Science Teacher Education* 1, no. 1 (Spring 1989): 17–20.

98. Excerpted from Peter J. Fensham, "Science for All," *Educational Leadership* (January 1987): 18–23. Used with permission.

99. Randy Moore, "Our Apartheid: The Imperatives of Multiculturalism in Science Education," *The Science Teacher* 69, no. 3 (March 2002): 10. Used with permission of the National Science Teachers Association.

100. C. M. Rey, "Making Room for Diversity Makes Sense," *Science* 293: 1611–12.

101. Ibid.

102. Jane Butler Kahle, *Encouraging Girls in Science Courses and Careers*, Research Matters . . . to the Science Teacher Monograph Series (National Association for Research in Science Teaching, 1985). http://www.educ.sfu.ca/narstsite/publications/research/encourage.htm. Used with permission.

103. Based on Sue Askew and Carol Ross, *Boys Don't Cry* (Milton Keynes, England: Open University Press, 1988), pp. 98–99.

Readings

Alexakos, Konstantinos. "Inclusive Classrooms." *The Science Teacher*, 24 (March 2001): 40–43.

Alic, Margaret. *Hypatia's Heritage: A History of Women in Science from Antiquity through the Nineteenth Century*. Boston: Beacon Press, 1986.

Banks, James A, and McGhee, Cherry A. *Multicultural Education: Issues and Perspectives*. 4th ed. New York: John Wiley & Sons, 2002.

Calabrese Barton, Angela. *Feminist Science Education*. New York: Teachers College Press, 1998.

Gornick, Vivian. *Women in Science*. New York: Simon & Schuster, 1990.

Hademenos, George, Heires, Nancy, and Young, Rose. "Teaching Science to New Comers." *The Science Teacher*, 71, no. 2 (2004): 27–31.

Kahle, Jane Butler. *Women in Science: A Report from the Field*. Philadelphia: The Falmer Press, 1985.

Kelly, Alison, ed. *Science for Girls?* Milton Keynes, England: Open University Press, 1987.

Lynch, Sharon J. *Equity and Science Education Reform*. Mahwah, N.J.: Lawrence Erlbaum Associates, 2000.

Miles, Rheq, and Matkius, Juanita Jo. "Science Enrichment for African-American Students." *The Science Teacher*, 71, no. 2 (2004): 36–41.

Nix, Maria. "Stellar Women." *The Science Teacher* 65, no. 3 (March 1998): 28–31.

Ramsey, Patricia G, Vold, Edwina Battle, and Williams, Leslie R. *Multicultural Education: A Source Book*. New York: Garland, 1989.

Rosser, Sue V. *Female-Friendly Science: Applying Women's Studies Methods and Theories to Attract Students.* New York: Pergamon Press, 1990.

Rosser, Sue V. *Re-Engineering Female Friendly Science.* New York: Teachers College Press, 1997.

Songer, Nancy Butler, Lee, Hee-Sun, and Kam, Rosalind. "Technology-Rich Inquiry Science in Urban Classrooms: What Are the Barriers to Inquiry Pedagogy?" *Journal of Research in Science Teaching* 39, no. 2 (2002): 128–50.

Stringfield, S., and Land, D., eds. *Educating At-Risk Students.* Chicago: The University of Chicago Press, 2002.

Tomlinson, Carol Ann. *How to Differentiate Instruction in Mixed-Ability Classrooms.* Alexandria, Va.: Association for Supervision and Curriculum Development, 2001.

On the Web

The American Forum for Global Education: http://www.globaled.org/. For over thirty years, the American Forum has been nationally recognized for providing leadership and assistance to school systems, state departments of education, and colleges and universities by initiating hundreds of programs and developing educational materials, teacher training seminars, and publications to guide and implement these programs. Its goal is to promote the education of our nation's youth for responsible citizenship in an increasingly interconnected and rapidly changing world.

Center for Research on the Education of Students Placed At Risk: http://www.csos.jhu.edu/crespar/. The Center, at Johns Hopkins and Howard University, conducts research and promotes programs to transform schooling for students placed at risk.

Center for Talent Development: http://www.ctd.northwestern.edu/. Located at Northwestern University, the Center for Talent Development serves gifted students and their families through a program of research and programming.

Federal Resource Center (FRC) for Special Education: http://www.dssc.org/frc/. The FRC supports a nationwide technical assistance network to respond to the needs of students with disabilities, especially students from underrepresented populations. Through its work with the RRCs and the technical assistance networks, the FRC provides a national perspective for establishing technical assistance activities within and across regions by identifying and synthesizing emerging issues and trends.

All Kinds of Minds: http://www.allkindsofminds.org/. All Kinds of Minds provides programs, tools, and a common language for parents, educators, and clinicians to help students with differences in learning achieve success in the classroom and in life. Founded in 1995, All Kinds of Minds is a private nonprofit institute, affiliated with the University of North Carolina at Chapel Hill, that offers a powerful system of programs for helping kids succeed.

Urban Education Web: http://iume.tc.columbia.edu/. This Web site is dedicated to urban students, their families, and the educators who serve them.

Office of Special Education (OSEP): http://www.ed.gov/about/offices/list/osers/osep/index.html. OSEP is dedicated to improving results for infants, toddlers, children, and youth with disabilities ages birth through 21 by providing leadership and financial support to assist states and local districts.

Special Education Resources on the Internet (SERI): http://seriweb.com/. SERI is a collection of Internet accessible information resources of interest to those involved in the fields related to special education. This collection exists in order to make online special education resources more easily and readily available in one location.

PART 2

THE GOALS AND THE CURRICULUM OF SCHOOL SCIENCE

The Goals and History of Science Education

Educators in the last century used the year 2000 as a reference point to evaluate then-current practices; warn people of ecological, population, and economic disasters; and make suggestions for what education should be. Now that we have passed the year 2000, it is even more evident that we need to evaluate the goals of science curriculum, reflect on the past emphases in science education, and—some would say—make bold recommendations for change in the teaching of science.

For example, in the 1980s, a number of studies compared the academic performance of U.S. students in science to their counterparts in Japan, Germany, Sweden, the Soviet Union, and some other countries. In every comparative study, the United States ranked as one of the lowest in science performance. In studies comparing science students' performance over the period between 1968 and 1986, the general trend was a lowering of student cognitive achievement and diminished attitudes toward science.

In the 1980s, the scientific community and governments around the world began to recognize the importance of developing a global perspective for the solution of ecological-environmental problems, the reduction of nuclear arms, the ethics involved in the use of high technology, and the drug epidemic that has especially ravaged North and South American societies. These and other global problems signaled the advent of a new and imperative way to think, namely globally or holistically.

Another significant event in the 1990s was the democratization of Eastern Europe and the former states of the Soviet Union. No one could have predicted these events, but the implications of these dramatic changes provide a new alliance of democratic thinking.

Global interdependence in a variety of areas (including the economy, politics, science and technology, individual and societal security, and the environment) dominated the world of the 1990s. Many observers predicted that acts of environmental destruction and terrorism posed a greater threat to national security than the military aggressiveness of other nations. This became monstrously evident on September 11, 2001.

Economic security will depend on each nation's ability to compete in the global marketplace. Technological and scientific changes and advances will continue at breathtaking leaps, posing greater problems for individuals, societies, and governments and, at the same time, inspiring hope for alleviation of some of the world's pressing problems.[1] Yet, more than competition is at stake. The twenty-first century must be based on agreement and cooperation if we are to solve the real problems facing the planet today, such as alleviation of world hunger, reducing environmental threats, and creating a sustainable world society. The world of science education—in this country and around the world—will have to grapple with how it can contribute to the perceived needs of individuals, societies, and the planet as a whole.

The focus in this chapter is on the goals of the science curriculum. We will explore changes in the goals of science education during the past century, but will pay particular attention to the contemporary nature of the science curriculum and reports and recommendations issued by a number of groups, commissions, and professional societies in the latter part of the twentieth century (including their implications for science education in the years ahead). As you will learn, the new science curriculum should be focused on the utilization of science technology for public welfare and human benefit.[2]

Case Study: Divine Intervention

The Case

Mr. John Moore is a biology teacher in a small community about 50 miles from a large metropolitan area in the midwestern region of the country. He has been teaching biology to ninth and tenth graders for seven years in this school district. The state he teaches in adopts new science textbooks every five years, and this year it is time to review and make final selections for secondary science books. Mr. Moore was asked by the district science supervisor to chair the six-member biology textbook adoption committee. The district procedures include placing the textbooks in all the district school libraries and three of the public library branches so that parents and interested citizens can review the books being considered for adoption.

During the review process, Mr. Moore receives a letter for an irate parent who objects to some of the content in the biology books, especially the treatment of evolution. The parent, Mr. Alan Hockett, an engineer with a Ph.D. in chemical engineering from a prestigious university in California, claims that creation theory is as likely a scientific hypothesis as evolution. He points out in his letter that neither theory can be supported by observable events, neither can be tested scientifically to predict future events, and neither is capable of falsification. He claims that denying students opposing "scientific views" is indoctrination. He says that "equal time" should be given to creation science if evolution is taught in the biology curriculum. Mr. Hockett demands to meet with the committee and ends his letter by saying that he will go to the school board if he is not satisfied with the committee's responses to his claims.

The Problem

Should the committee meet with Mr. Hockett? What should the committee do to prepare for the meeting? How will this complaint affect the adoption process? What position should the biology committee take? What is the position of organizations such as the National Association of Biology Teachers (www.nabt.org) and the National Science Teachers Association (www.nsta.org) on this issue?

How to Read This Chapter

There are two sections to this chapter. In the first you will find a discussion of key reports and recommendations that have influenced science education. The second part of the chapter focuses on the history of ideas in science education, including how researchers have documented the field of science teaching. You might want to start with the history of science. You'll find a Web site developed by Annette Parrott, a science teacher in Atlanta who traced the field of science teaching (science and technology as well), thousands of years into the past. She has also focused on the contributions of different ethnic groups to science education.

SECTION 1: GOALS AND PHILOSOPHY OF SCIENCE

Invitations to Inquiry

- What are goals and how are they formulated?
- What factors or forces affected the goals of science education for the 1990s?
- How and why have the goals of the science curriculum changed in this century?
- What are the origins of modern science education?
- What was the progressive education movement and how did it influence the science curriculum?
- What were the characteristics of the science curriculum reform during the golden age of science education and how do they compare with the standards-based reforms of the 1990s?
- What are the contemporary trends in science education?
- What will science education emphasize in the early part of the twenty-first century?

The Philosophy and Goals of Science Education

What are the goals of science teaching? Is it possible to agree on goals for science teaching? Who determines the goals of science teaching? Did the goals of science teaching change during the twentieth century and how did they affect the current emphases in science education? These are a few of questions that we'll explore in this section to gain insight into an important aspect of science education; namely, the goals of science teaching.

Goals are ends toward which we direct our attention. They tend to be reflective statements expressing an individual's or a group's philosophic perspective on the broad aims or objectives of education. For example, consider this goal: *Science education should help students in making personal decisions.* This broad aim or goal, which reflects a recent emphasis in science education and one that many recommend for the years ahead, highlights how science education should contribute to the personal needs of individuals as well how to use science to make everyday decisions. Goals should have relevance to student's lives.

When we speak about goals of science education (or, for that matter, the goals of education in general) it is important to keep in mind that the United States is the only highly technical, industrialized country that does not have a national science curriculum. Education is set in a decentralized system, with individual states and school districts determining the goals and the curriculum for its students. However, during the latter part of the twentieth century, the National Research Council published the *National Science Education Standards* and these, as you will see, have greatly influenced the goals of science teaching at the state and local level.

Goals represent the desired or the hoped for directions for science teaching. What are desired directions of science education? To answer this question, we will examine the recommendations of a number of commissions, professional organizations, and convened groups. The science education community has been and will be influenced by these reports and recommendations. This influence will affect, among other things, the nature of textbooks, curriculum development efforts at the national and local levels, and teaching practices.

The goals of science education in the future will be very different than the goals of the 1960s, which shaped science education curriculum, instructional practices, and textbooks into the 1990s, in that the new goals will encompass science competence for all students, regardless of sex, race, and economic status. There will be disagreement among science teachers as to which goals are of most worth. For example, some science educators ask, "Why should all students be taught to think like scientists?" Some science educators claim that instead of valuing only the mode of thinking practiced by the scientific community, science education should value

INQUIRY ACTIVITY 3.1

 The Goals of the Science Curriculum

What do you think teachers emphasize in their courses? What do you think should be emphasized? This activity will give you an opportunity to find out and compare your opinions with practicing science teachers' opinions.

Materials

- Goals of the science curriculum questionnaire (Figure 3.1).

1. Learn basic science concepts
2. Increase students' interest in science
3. Learn important terms and facts of science
4. Learn science process/inquiry skills
5. Prepare for further study in science
6. Learn how to communicate ideas in science effectively
7. Prepare for standardized tests
8. Learn about the relationship between science, technology, and society
9. Learn to evaluate arguments based on scientific evidence
10. Learn about the history and nature of science
11. Learn about the applications of science, business, and industry

Figure 3.1 Goals of the Science Curriculum.

Procedures

1. Write the questionnaire goals on individual index cards and use the cards while you go through some decision-making procedures.
2. First consider what you think. If you were teaching a science course in grades 7 through 9, which goal would you emphasize the most? Rank order the remainder of the goals from most emphasized to least emphasized. Write your sequence on a sheet of paper.
3. Shift your attention to a high school course. Rank order the goals from most emphasized to least emphasized at the high school level.
4. Finally, group the goals into clusters or categories. What criteria did you use? Is it easier to consider the clusters of goals rather than the entire list of goals?

Minds-On Strategies

1. The results of the survey reported by Weiss show that secondary science teachers consider the most important goals to be: learn basic science concepts, increase students' interest in science, learn important terms and facts of science, and learn science process/inquiry skills. How do these results compare with yours?[3]
2. Are there differences between middle/junior high science goals and high school science goals? Should there be?

the abilities and cultural relevance of diverse modes of thinking that can contribute to the solution of problems.[4]

Some science educators have pointed out that if the science curriculum is to become truly responsive and responsible to citizens in a scientifically and technologically oriented world, then the concerns of all citizens need to be elevated to top priority. The science curriculum that was designed for aspiring scientists and engineers, with its heavy emphasis on the scientific process, may have to give way to new forms of science curriculum that advocate a variety of ways and methods of getting involved in science education. This orientation toward citizenship has its roots in reports issued in the later part of the nineteenth century, but the direction was most notably developed in the 1930s, when science educators insisted that science education should be an integral part of general education in a democratic society.

Champagne and Hornig report that many goals have been proposed for the science curriculum of the future, including:[5]

- The development of a productive workforce that will maintain economic prosperity and security (a nationalistic, economic goal).
- The development of a literate citizenry that is knowledgeable about scientific and technological issues and able to make informed decisions in public and private life (scientific literacy goal).
- The widespread adoption of the intellectual style of scientists, which is equated with better thinking ability (an academic or discipline-centered goal).
- The development of the ability to apply social, ethical, and political perspectives to interpretations of scientific information (an application goal).

These and other goals will be proposed. However, the tide has turned in favor of developing science curriculum programs based on goals that are solidly rooted in interaction of science and its citizens. Gone are the days (at least for now) where science is viewed as a pristine discipline with underlying assumptions and tacit way of knowing, to be learned by all schoolchildren as if they were little scientists.

What do you think should be the goals of the science curriculum? Read ahead and participate in Inquiry Activity 3.1.

Science Education Reports Influencing the Future

During the 1980s, science educators reflected on the philosophy and goals that should guide science programs and curriculum into the twenty-first century. It was a period marked by numerous reports and proposals (over 300) by convened committees funded by various public and private granting agencies as well as by a number of scientific organizations. This period of reflection was brought on by what some citizens in the United States perceived as a crisis in (science) education. One report claimed that the nation was at risk because of the "rising tide of mediocrity that threatens our very future as a nation and a people."[6] The report continued, "If an unfriendly foreign power had attempted to impose on America the mediocre educational performance that exists today, we might well have viewed it as an act of war."[7] Strong statements, indeed. Yet a host of reports appeared that made similar charges. Later in the chapter we'll examine these reports in more detail.

Most of the organizations within the community of science education issued reports making recommendations for science teaching in general and, depending on the organization, recommendations for one aspect of science education (e.g., biology, chemistry, earth science). Organizations typically do this from time to time, especially during periods of crisis. For example, one report issued by the National Science Teachers Association called *Scope, Sequence, and Coordination Project*[8] proposed a new organization of the science curriculum in which science courses should be integrated from grades 7 through 10 (teaching biology, chemistry, earth science, and physics as an integrated course each year). The Committee on High School Biology Education of the National Research Council issued a report in 1990 entitled *Fulfilling the Promise: Biology Education in the Nations Schools*.[9] The American Geological Institute developed a report on the teaching of earth science entitled *Earth Science Education for the 21st Century*.[10] Another report, *Professional Standards for Teaching Mathematics*, issued by the National Council of Teachers of Mathematics, stresses the connection between mathematics, science, and computers.[11]

For now, let's focus our attention on three reports that have and will continue to have a powerful impact on the direction of science education. We will briefly examine the following reports, their recommendations, and implications for goals of the science curriculum. You can also view these reports on the Web, along with some of the supporting documents each created.

- Project 2061, by the American Association for the Advancement of Science (AAAS) (www.project2061.org)
- The *Scope, Sequence, and Coordination Project*, by the National Science Teachers Association (www.nsta.org)

- The *National Science Education Standards*, by the National Research Council (www.nap.edu/readingroom/books/nses/html/)

Project 2061: Science for All Americans

Project 2061 (2061 is the year of the next arrival of Halley's Comet and the period of the next human life span) is a massive project to examine the goals of science education, develop experimental programs in selected school districts around the nation, and eventually use the results of the project to transform the face of science education. Quite a challenge.

Project 2061 has issued three major reports: *Science for All Americans* (1989), *Benchmarks for Scientific Literacy* (1995), and *Blueprints for Reform* (1998). All of these reports can be viewed online at the Project 2061 Web site (http://www.project2061.org/default.htm).

Science for All Americans (*SFAA*) was a report written by Project 2061 staff of the AAAS. According to the AAAS project staff, the "terms and circumstances of human existence can be expected to change radically during the next human lifespan. Science, mathematics, and technology will be at the center of that change— causing it, shaping it, responding to it. Therefore, they will be essential to the education of today's children for tomorrow's world."[12]

Benchmarks for Scientific Literacy issued statements of what all students should know or be able to do in science, mathematics, and technology by the end of grades 2, 5, 8, and 12. The grade demarcations suggest reasonable checkpoints for estimating student progress toward the science literacy goals outlined in *SFAA*. The benchmarks are a tool to be used by educators in designing a curriculum that makes sense to them and meets the standards for science literacy recommended in *SFAA*. Moreover, *Benchmarks* does not advocate any particular curriculum design. Far from pressing for one way of organizing instruction, Project 2061 pursues a reform strategy that will lead eventually to greater curriculum diversity than is common today. Here are some of the key principles that the authors of *Benchmarks* outlined that shaped the way they are used by science educators:

- *Benchmarks* is different from a curriculum, a curriculum framework, a curriculum design, or a plan for a curriculum.
- *Benchmarks* is a compendium of specific science literacy goals that can be organized however one chooses.
- *Benchmarks* specify thresholds rather than average or advanced performance.

• *Benchmarks* concentrates on the *common core* of learning that contributes to the science literacy of all students.

There are twelve benchmarks in Project 2061:

1. The nature of science
2. The nature of mathematics
3. The nature of technology
4. The physical setting
5. The living environment
6. The human organism
7. Human society
8. The designed world
9. The mathematical world
10. Human perspectives
11. Common themes
12. Habits of mind

Blueprints for Reform and the companion *Blueprints Online* provide science educators, administrators, researchers, and parents with tools to help understand science education in the schools from a systems point of view. *Blueprints* is an analysis and a set of recommendations for school science reform. The topics that emerged from many conferences and discussions are organized into three groupings:

• The Foundation: Equity, Policy, Finance, and Research
• The School Context: School Organization, Curriculum Connections, Materials and Technology, and Assessment
• The Support Structure: Teacher Education, Higher Education, Family and Community, and Business and Industry

PHILOSOPHY OF PROJECT 2061 Project 2061 is based on the idea that science for all Americans is about scientific literacy. To Project 2061, a scientifically literate person is one who[13]

• is aware that science, mathematics, and technology are interdependent human enterprises with strengths and limitations;
• understands key concepts and principles of science;
• is familiar with the natural world and recognizes both its diversity and unity;
• uses scientific knowledge and scientific ways of thinking for individual and social purposes.

Although the report points out that most Americans do not understand science, they take a point of view that goes beyond individual self-fulfillment and the national interests of the United States. As the authors point out, more is at stake. The serious problems that humanity faces are global: unchecked population growth, acid rain, the shrinking of tropical forests, the pollution of the environment, disease, social strife, extreme inequities in the distribution of the earth's wealth, the threat of nuclear holocaust, and many others. In this context, scientific literacy takes on a global perspective. The scientifically literate citizen in a global world would realize the potential of science in the following ways:[14]

• Science can provide humanity with the knowledge of the biophysical environment and of social behavior to effectively solve global and local problems.
• Science can foster the kind of intelligent respect for nature that should inform decisions on the uses of technology.
• Scientific habits of mind can be of value to people in every walk of life to solve problems that involve evidence, quantitative considerations, logical arguments, and uncertainty.
• The knowledge of principles related to the nature of systems; for example, such understanding can give people a sound basis for assessing the use of new technologies and their implications for the environment and culture.
• Knowledge of technology, especially continuous development and creative uses, can help humanity deal with survival and work toward a world in which humanity is at peace with itself and its environment.

Project 2061 is divided into three phases, each with specific actions and goals: (I) content identification, (II) educational formulation, and (III) educational transformation.

The purpose of phase I is to build a rationale for science education and develop an outline of what science, mathematics, and technology content ought to be included in an education for elementary and secondary curriculum. *SFAA* included recommendations on the nature of science, mathematics and technology, the physical setting, the living environment, the human organism, human society, the designed world, the mathematical world, historical perspectives, common themes, and the habits of mind.

Five panels were organized, and each developed reports outlining the subject matter that should constitute the essence of literacy in science, mathematics, and technology. The panel reports that are of most interest to science teachers include biological and health sciences, physical and information sciences and engineering, and technology.

PHYSICAL SCIENCE The panel on the physical and information sciences and engineering recommended that focusing on key unifying concepts could facilitate the task of teaching the physical and information sciences and engineering in elementary and secondary schools. They identified four key unifying concepts—materials, energy, information, and systems—and several other unifying concepts, including equilibrium, time rate, conservation, efficiency, uncertainty, risk, cost effectiveness, and benefit analysis. The panel then identified key specific concepts in physics; chemistry; and earth, planetary, and astronomical sciences; information science and computer science; and engineering.[15] Table 3.1 shows the key unifying concepts for physics and chemistry, earth science, information science, and engineering.

BIOLOGY The biological and health sciences panel suggested that each citizen should come to know biology in order to understand himself or herself as a product of evolution and as a single individual in an ecological scheme. Second, the panel felt that biology "teaches rules to live by." The topics the panel included in the report show the recommended emphasis for biology in elementary and secondary curriculum: human biology, the evolution of diverse life forms, environmental biology, and human ecology. The panel posed a number of questions that they hoped eighteen-year-olds would be able to answer. Some of these questions include: How does the human organism work and what does it take to keep it healthy? How are humans like and unlike other living organisms? What determines the productivity of an ecosystem? How does accumulating pollution affect humankind's future?[16]

TECHNOLOGY The technology panel defined technology as the application of knowledge, tools, and skills to solve practical problems and extend human capabilities. The panel highlighted the notion that technology is part of social progress as well as a technical process. Technology education should emphasize the interface between technology and society. The panel pointed out that citizens must be able to develop, articulate, and illustrate how technology affects society and how society affects technology.[17]

The technology group identified several fields of technology that should provide the framework for technology education: materials, energy, manufacturing, agriculture and food, biotechnology and medical technology, environment, communications, electronics, computer technology, transportation, and space. The panel report outlined the nature of each of these technology fields and identified suggested experiences for students. For example, suggested activities in the communications area included having students make simple devices that can be used in communications, from historical gadgets (such as a carbon microphone or simple telegraph) to modern electronic circuits. Students should also be encouraged to undertake imaginative projects, such as inventing ways of communicating with people in remote lands or searching for information from outer space that might reveal life there.[18]

The second phase of the project is an extension of phase I of Project 2061. In the second phase, the focus of attention will be to develop, in five school districts across the nation, alternative K–12 curriculum models for education in science, mathematics, and technology.[19] Development teams will design curriculum plans for science, mathematics, and technology and then field-test and evaluate the results. The second phase will also include creating a set of blueprints for reforming the other components of education that complement curriculum reform, increasing the pool of educators and scientists able to serve as experts in the school curriculum reform, and fostering public awareness of the need for reform in science, mathematics, and technology education.

Phase III of Project 2061, referred to as the educational transformation phase, will be a "highly cooperative, nationwide effort which will mobilize resources, monitor progress, and, in general, provide direction and continuity of the effort."[20] The goal of the third phase is to use the products of phases I and II to broaden the scope and raise the quality of education in science, mathematics, and technology.

The overall and general direction of Project 2061 is multifaceted, but includes the following goals:[21]

- To ensure scientific literacy, curricula must be changed to reduce the sheer amount of materials.
- Weaken or eliminate the rigid subject-matter boundaries.
- Pay more attention to connections among science, mathematics, and technology.

Table 3.1 Unifying Concepts in Science, Technology, and Engineering

	Key Concepts		
Physics and Chemistry	**Earth, Planetary, and Astronomical Sciences**	**Information Science and Computer Science**	**Engineering**
• All physical and chemical phenomena are governed by a few basic interactions. • The quantum principle: on a microscopic-length scale, many physical quantities—such as electric charge, mass, and energy—are found in tiny fixed units called quanta; atoms gain and lose energy in fixed quantum units. • The behavior of simple static and moving systems can be explained using the laws first laid out by Isaac Newton. • Intuitive ideas of space, time, energy, and mass fail at great distances and when speeds approach the speed of light. • Electromagnetic radiation, of which light is an example, occurs in a very large range of wavelengths; such radiation is emitted and absorbed as particles or bundles of energy. • Electrical phenomena can be understood in terms of the behavior of the electric charge. • For many purposes, matter can be viewed as being composed of atoms and molecules that have well-defined sizes, shapes, structures, compositions, and energy contents. • Atomic nuclei undergo changes.	• Our universe has an enormous number of galaxies. • The sun is one of the many stars within the Milky Way Galaxy; the earth is one of the planets of the sun. • The earth is a nearly spherical rotating body; its dimensions, motion, and position relative to the sun govern our lives. • Forces deep within the earth, acting over geologic time, have caused continents to move, rupture, and collide. • Life on the earth arose through natural processes several billion years ago. • The oceans and atmosphere are very large, buffered chemical, biological and geological systems. • Climate is the long-term expression of the movements of masses of fluids in the ocean and atmosphere. • Waves, wind, water and ice are agents of erosion and deposition that sculpt the Earth's surface to produce distinctive landforms. • Humans need and use many substances found naturally on the Earth's surface and in its interior. • All places on Earth have characteristics that give them meaning and character and that distinguish them from each other.	• Information is the meaning attributed to data. • Different kinds of information can be derived from the same data. • Information can be expressed in many forms and can be represented in analog (continuous) or digital (discrete) formats. • Information generally degrades during transmission or storage. • All systems, both natural and human-made, are internally coordinated by processes that convey information. • Information is more useful when it is represented by orderly collections of symbols called data structures. • Procedures can be formalized as algorithms. • Computing machines are constructed from simple components. • All general-purpose computing machines are fundamentally equivalent. • To ensure that an information system will be successful in the real world, the design must include both logical rigor and an understanding of social forces, cultural beliefs and economic realities.	• A key ingredient of the engineering process is the ability to plan and manage a project. • Modeling conceptualizes the problem to be solved and the solution itself, formulating them as much as possible in quantitative terms. • Every design or system has constraints that must be identified and taken into account. • Optimization endeavors to determine the best possible solution to a problem under its relevant constraints. • The design is the core of the engineering process. • Each design has its side effects. • The artifacts created by design cannot be allowed to perform unassisted; they require operation supervision, maintenance and repair. • We must constantly be alert to the possibility of engineering failure; most failures occur at the interface between systems; failures can occur in all systems, even well-maintained and supervised ones.

Source: Based on Bugliarello, G. *Physical and Information Sciences and Engineering: Report of the Project 2061 Phase I Physical and Information Sciences and Engineering Panel.* Washington, D.C.: American Association for the Advancement of Science, 1989.

- Present the scientific endeavor as a social enterprise that strongly influences and is influenced by human thought and action.
- Foster scientific ways of thinking.
- Teaching related to scientific literacy needs to be consistent with the spirit and character of scientific inquiry and with scientific ideas.
- Teaching should begin with questions about phenomena rather than with answers to be learned.
- Engage students actively in the use of hypotheses, collection and use of evidence, and the design of investigations and processes.

The Scope, Sequence, and Coordination Project

The Project on Scope, Sequence, and Coordination (SS&C) was initiated by the National Science Teachers Association (NSTA) as a major reform effort to restructure secondary science teaching.[22] One major feature of the SS&C was the proposal to eliminate the tracking of students (survey, general, and advanced courses, for example) and replace it with a science program in which all students study science in a well-coordinated science curriculum including each year physics, chemistry, biology, and earth and space science. An outcome of the proposal was a school curriculum that provides for "spacing" the study of sciences over grades 6 though 12.

SS&C also integrated the outcomes of Project 2061 as the goals for the science curriculum. Although separate projects, each having its own staff, infrastructure, and dissemination centers, each project "contends that less content taught more effectively over successive years will result in greater scientific literacy of the general public."[23]

SS&C CURRICULUM MODELS The SS&C project experimented with several models of curriculum development. Curriculum sites were established in Texas, California, North Carolina, Iowa, and Puerto Rico. For example, in the Houston, Texas, models a "block" approach (a sequenced collection of laboratories focusing on a series of coordinated concepts from biology, chemistry, earth and space science, and physics) has been adopted. An example of a block, "Floating and Sinking," will help illustrate the Houston approach to curriculum: What is density and how can it be experienced directly? How is the density of a solid or a liquid measured? Why do some things float which others sink? Before the block was over, students discussed density (physics), solutions (chemistry), oceans (earth science), and marine organisms (biology). These and other topics lead students to experience the effect of density on

familiar objects for themselves and they more easily learned the concepts involved.

In the Iowa project of the SS&C, the emphasis was on STS (science, technology, and society; see Chapter 11). In California, individual schools and districts applied for grants through the California Department of Education. In this model, a school could propose to realign its secondary science curriculum, implement the change, and research the impact on student learning and teacher participation. According to the California developers, one aim was to create a challenging, nontracked science program, especially for schools with high minority populations. In Puerto Rico, the emphasis was on integrated blocks; that is, blocks not only in English and Spanish but integrating mathematics and science.

SS&C PRINCIPLES The SS&C project was based on principles of curriculum that described its approach to science curriculum reform. Examine the list of principles on the list and think about the implications of these statements on the development of science lessons and units of teaching.[24]

1. The four basic subject areas (biology, chemistry, earth and space science, and physics) are addressed each year, and the connections between them are emphasized.
2. The coordinating themes identified by Project 2061 are used as unifying threads between disciplines: systems, models, constancy, and patterns of change, evolution, and scale.
3. Science is shown to be open to inquiry and skepticism and free of dogmatism or unsupported assertion by those in authority. The science curriculum promotes student understanding of how we come to know, why we believe, and how we test and revise our thinking.
4. Science should be presented in connection with its applications to technology and its personal and societal implications.
5. Students should have the opportunity to construct the important ideas of science, which are then developed in depth through inquiry and investigation.
6. Vocabulary is used to facilitate understanding rather than as an end in itself. Terms are presented after students experience the phenomena.
7. Texts are not the source of the curriculum but serve as references. Everyday materials, laboratory equipment, video, software, and other printed materials such as reference books and outside reading provide a substantial part of the student learning experience.

8. Lessons provide opportunities for skill building in data collection, graphing, record keeping, and the use of language in verbal and written assignments.
9. Of particular importance is that instruction enhances skepticism, critical thinking, and logical reasoning skills. Thinking and reasoning skills such as controlling variables and drawing inferences need to be fostered.

The National Science Education Standards

The *National Science Education Standards*, published in 1995, grew out of the reform that began with Project 2061 and the SS&C project. By 1992, there was a growing consensus that the United States needed a set of content standards in science. The NSTA took the leadership in this endeavor and urged the National Academy of Sciences and the National Research Council (NRC) to lead the effort to develop K–12 science standards. With funding from many federal agencies, the NRC convened a National Committee on Science Education Standards and Assessment. Three working groups—content standards, teaching standards, and assessment standards—began work in 1992 and for the next eighteen months developed a pre-draft document for input from selected focus groups. In 1994, a draft version of the *Science Standards* was published and distributed to individuals and groups for feedback. The final version of the *Standards* was published in December 1995. The *Standards* can be viewed online at the NSES Web site (http://books.nap.edu//readingroom/books/nses/html/). Throughout this book, I will refer to the *Standards* and relate them to various aspects of science teaching.

A prominent feature of the *Standards* is the emphasis on inquiry. In the *Standards*, the term "inquiry" is used in two ways, and it might be helpful to think about these now:[25]

- It refers to the abilities students should develop to be able to design and conduct scientific investigations and to the understandings they should gain about the nature of scientific inquiry.
- It also refers to the teaching and learning strategies that teachers use to enable scientific concepts to be learned through investigations. Thus, there is a link or connection between learning science, learning to do science, and learning about science.

Thus, a second publication that we should use in understanding science teaching is *Inquiry and the National Science Education Standards*.[26] We'll examine the role of inquiry in the next section of the book.

Influence of Research on the Goals of Science Teaching

You will discover that the science education community is increasingly interested in correlating the results of research with the practice of science teaching. For example, the National Science Teachers Association has published a series of monographs entitled *What Research Says to the Science Teacher*. One of the reasons for this series is the difficulty that has existed in trying to connect research to practice. It is fitting that the last volume of the 1980s published in this series was subtitled *Problem Solving*. The monograph contained a series of papers designed to help the science teacher focus on the important goal of helping students solve problems in the disciplines of biology, chemistry, earth science and physics.[27]

The National Association for Research in Science Teaching has published a series of documents entitled *Peers Matter* (view them online at www2.educ.sfu.ca/narstsite/) on a range of topics. These two-to three-page papers are like consumer reports in which researchers translate the results of studies into practical, consumer-friendly reports. Some of these, such as "Pupil Behavior and Motivation in Eighth Grade Science," and "Encouraging Girls in Science Courses and Careers," are found in a column of the *Science Teacher Gazette*.

Based on their work, researchers in the cognitive science tradition have also suggested some directions for the future science curriculum. Here are several directions that cognitive researchers feel are direct implications of their research.[28]

1. The goals of the science curriculum should be redefined and broadened to reflect technological advances and societal needs. Science education should focus on creating environments that foster science for all citizens, rather than science for future careers in science.
2. The goals of the middle grades curriculum (grades 4 through 8) should focus on students' concerns about the impact of science on society. For example, science programs at this level that involve students in environmental education activities where they explore on the local level connections between science and society would capitalize on students' interest in these topics. Having students investigate pollution, recycling, causes of disease, waste disposal, and the impact of power plants on the environment are examples of promising topics. The middle years are significant and influential to students. It is the time when

students lose interest in science, and it is imperative that science programs be designed to capitalize on their interests and motivations.

3. Less is better. Researchers think science courses should cover less topics and go into the topics that are included in more depth. Through in-depth treatment of selected topics, teachers would be able to plan comprehensive problem-solving activities. Currently, teachers must skip quickly from one topic to another, giving very little attention to real understanding of science concepts and problem solving.

4. The content of the science disciplines should be integrated. Project 2061 and the *National Science Education Standards* reports recommended an interdisciplinary approach to the science curriculum. Students should be helped to make connections among the fields of science by being engaged in activities that require them to link one discipline to another. Except for elementary science, the science curriculum in the United States is organized in such a way that students study only one science discipline each year, reinforcing the separateness of science fields. As we will see in the next chapter, students in a number of other countries are introduced to physics, biology, and chemistry early in their secondary education and continue to study *each* of these subjects for as many as five years.

INQUIRY ACTIVITY 3.2

Icons of Science Education: How Do They Tell the Story of Science Education?

The famous photograph of Clarence Darrow and William Jennings Bryan at the 1925 trial of John T. Scopes (the science teacher accused of breaking the state law against teaching evolution) is surely one of the icons of the history of science education. What are some other icons of the history of science education? In this activity you will work with a collaborative group to explore one of the phases of science education (as identified in this chapter) in order to identify the icons of that phase.

Materials

- Text material
- Reference materials on science education history (see the Readings section at the end of this chapter)
- Poster board, art supplies

Procedures

1. The class will inquire into the various phases of the history of science education. The questions in Table 3.2 are designed for use in exploring any phase in the history of science education.

Table 3.2 Inquiry into the History of Science Education

Phases of Science Education History	Inquiry Questions
I. Roots of Modern Science Education, 1900–1930	What social forces influenced science education?
II. Progressive Education and Science, 1930–1950	What reports or commissions affected the goals of science teaching?
III. The Golden Age of Science Education, 1950–1975	
IV. Textbook Controversies and the Back-to-Basics Movement, 1975–1983	What were the desired goals of science teaching?
V. A Nation At Risk and the 1980s, 1983–1990	What was the focus of the science curriculum?
VI. Reform Efforts of the 1990s	
VII. Science Education for All and the New Millennium	

2. Each team should choose a different period in science education history to investigate. The team's task is to assemble icons—images, representations, artifacts, and pictures—of the period under investigation. The icons can be presented on a large poster or as a series of individual exhibits.

Minds-On Strategies

1. What are some icons of science education? Compare the icons from the different periods of science education history. How has science education changed?
2. What are the important issues in science education today?
3. What are some of your *predictions* for science education in the year 2061?

There are many other implications for science teaching based on the work of science education researchers. I have identified a number of implications that have direct bearing on the goals and nature of the curriculum. In Chapter 6, a number of implications will be identified related to cognitive development, student learning styles, and metacognitive strategies. As you continue your study of science teaching, it's important to make connections between research and science teaching practice.

Science Education: A Historical Perspective

Have you ever wondered what science teaching was like a hundred years ago? What did teachers emphasize in their lessons? What did educators believe science could contribute to the education of students? How is teaching today related to the past? What can we learn about contemporary teaching by reaching into the past?

The historical perspective is important from the standpoint of trying to understand contemporary trends and changes in science teaching. A great many events, developments, and reports have contributed to shaping the goals and nature of the K–12 science curriculum during the twentieth century.

An Inquiry into the Historical Nature of Science Education

In this section we will go back in time and examine the history of science education. Dividing the history of science education into time units is an arbitrary process; therefore, for convenience I have identified the following phases:

- Phase I: The Roots of Modern Science Education, Pre-1900–1930

- Phase II: Progressive Education and Science Education, 1930–1950
- Phase III: The Golden Age of Science Education, 1950–1977
- Phase IV: Textbook Controversies and Back to Basics, 1977–1983
- Phase V: A Nation at Risk, the 1980s
- Phase VI: The Reform Efforts of the 1990s
- Phase VII: Science for All and the New Millennium

Phase I: The Roots of Modern Science Education, Pre-1900–1930

The roots of what we might call modern science education can be traced to the latter part of the nineteenth century; many of the recommendations and philosophies proposed in these early years have continued to influence science education to this day. Several important ideas that form the foundation for modern science education had their origins during this period. These include the organization of the science curriculum, the methodology of inquiry, nature study, elementary science, and the social goals of science teaching.

In 1895, the National Education Association appointed a committee of twelve university scientists and an equal number of high school teachers. Four years later the committee recommended a K–8 and 9–12 science program as follows:[29]

- *Elementary School* (K–8; two lessons per week)
  Nature study
- *High School* (9–12; four lessons per week)
  Grade 9: Physical geography
  Grade 10: Biology; botany and zoology; or botany or zoology
  Grade 11: Physics
  Grade 12: Chemistry

The main purposes of teaching science during this early period was:

- Formal discipline
- Teaching of facts and principles
- College preparation
- Some, but limited, emphasis on skills and methods of science
- Very little emphasis on scientific method, scientific attitudes, appreciations, or social implication of science

At the elementary school level, two contrasting approaches to science education dominated the curriculum, namely nature study and elementary science. Nature study was a child-centered approach to teaching that focused on helping students develop a love of nature. The content focused primarily on the study of plants, animals, and ecology, with teachers emphasizing the study of the local environment. Many of the progressive schools in America adopted the nature study approach. Study guides, teachers' resource books, and lesson plans were written and distributed describing the approach of the nature study advocates. Because of its progressive nature, the nature study movement was associated with an educational concept known as "teaching the whole child." Nature study was an interdisciplinary approach, and science was seen as an integral part of art, language, and literature. Lawrence Cremin, in his book *The Transformation of the School*, says this about the nature study movement:

> Science was begun in the form of nature study, and under the brilliant leadership of Wilbur Jackman, the children conducted trips through neighboring fields and along the lakeshore. They made observations, drawings, and descriptions, thus correlating their work in science with their studies in language and art.[30]

Nature study was the dominant approach to science in the elementary school, and its program reached its peak in the period 1900–1910. Elements of the nature study movement persist today. But as a movement it faded away in the 1930s. Individual "nature study units" were integrated into the dominant approach to science in the elementary school, and as a "movement" nature study reappeared in late sixties and seventies. In the language of the 1990s, nature study is analogous to the environmental education movement, which we will discuss in Chapter 11. Elementary science, however, moved into the classroom, and the content was broadened to include physical science.

The alternative approach to science in the elementary school was the elementary science movement, which was defined and outlined by Jerrold Craig.[31] In a study on the curriculum for elementary science, Craig recommended a science program that was broad in scope, including the life and physical sciences. He devised a continuous program, K–8, emphasizing an articulated unified program aimed at developing an understanding of significant ideas in science. Panels of parents developed the content of elementary science and educators identified important ideas and generalizations that should be emphasized grade by grade. This method, and indeed the results of study, dominate the content of elementary science textbooks and state science curriculum guides—even today! Craig's recommendations became the basis of elementary science text programs around the country. Science readers were developed for each grade and, consequently, elementary science became more abstract in comparison to the nature study approach, which valued first-hand student experiences in nature. For all practical purposes, science teaching remained the same until the development of the elementary science reform projects of the 1960s and 1970s.

The secondary science curriculum during the period up to 1920 consisted of one-semester courses in many different subjects, such as astronomy, geology, physical geography, botany, zoology, and physiology in the first two years of high school. Later during this period, the organization of the science curriculum (9–12) evolved to the general science, biology, chemistry, and physics as one-year courses. This pattern, for all practical purposes, has persisted to the present.

High school teachers, near the later part of this phase, shifted their goals to include process, attitudes, and application. Some major goals proposed during this period included scientific thinking and understanding of the scientific method, development of attitudes toward science, and increased emphasis on the practical application of scientific knowledge.

A phenomenon that had an impact of the science curriculum was the junior high movement. To provide a transition from the elementary to high school environment, a 6-3-3 organization of schools was proposed. Elementary science was limited to grades K–6. General science had replaced physical science as the "terminal" course for students not completing high school. With the advent of the junior high school, general science was "pushed down" to the seventh and eighth grades and became the dominant science offering at this level for many years. Although the junior high school was designed to provide a transition from elementary to high school, its curriculum took on the appearance and character of high school. Teachers were organized into subject matter departments and the course offerings reflected the high school curriculum.

Now, let's shift our attention away from the content of the early science and take a look at the nature of inquiry in science teaching. What were its roots? When did it emerge in science teaching?

According to Carlton Steadman, until the mid-1800s, most practicing scientists, for philosophical reasons as are currently understood and practiced, resisted inquiry and experimentation.[32] Integrating them into science teaching has taken even longer. In 1842, the American Association for the Advancement of Science was organized as a result of a conference in Boston of the American Association of Geologists and Naturalists. The geology group essentially was transformed into the AAAS. AAAS joined forces with the forerunner of the National Education Association and the groups proposed the idea of a national university and a school for advanced training in science. However, because they were concerned with basic research and more uniform curricula, the academic climate was still not receptive for inquiry.[33]

Much of the early innovation in science education had its beginnings at the university level, especially in the work of several college teachers. Stedman highlights the work of three early scientists who influenced science teaching.

Benjamin Silliman (1779–1864) developed Yale's first chemistry lab and is credited with teaching the first course in geology in the United States. He believed in using visual aids in teaching, and illustrated his lectures with a 5-foot square pictures.[34]

Louis Agassiz, whose claim to fame as a scientist was his early work on glacial theory, was also an outstanding educator who blended Pastalozzi's object lessons (having the student experience objects using the senses), discovery learning, and active involvement. As a teacher, Agassiz had students work in his lab to observe specimens firsthand, thereby gaining knowledge experientially. Steadman reports that Agassiz gave students over 1,000 specimens and had them separate the specimens into species. Upon examining their work he praised their accomplishments and discoveries.[35]

Asa Gray, a colleague of Agassiz's at Harvard, was a biologist who, according to Stedman, was the "first citizen of Darwin." Gray, through public speaking and writing, tried to reduce the conflict between evolution and religious views, a conflict that is still with us. As a teacher, Gray tried to help students perceive his subject (botany) as a whole related system.[36]

Silliman and Agassiz attempted to make learning meaningful (at a time when the classics flourished and mental discipline was stressed) by encouraging laboratory experiences and practical experience. It is here that the roots of inquiry teaching lie. It took many years for the roots of inquiry to grow into a dominant philosophy in science teaching. This occurred in the late 1950s and 1960s with the development of the science reform projects.

Phase II: Progressive Education and Science, 1930–1950

Several reports influenced science teaching during this period. In 1932, *A Program for Teaching Science* was published by the National Society for the Study of Education, which emphasized a continuous twelve-year curriculum, the organization of science courses around general principles, generalizations or "big ideas" in science, and the inclusion of the method of science as an integral part of science.[37] Although the term "inquiry" was not used, the implication was that science teaching should constitute more than the teaching of facts and should involve students in the methods of science through observing, experimenting, and hypothesizing.

The authors of *A Program for Teaching Science* proposed that science education should contribute to the major aim of education, namely "life enrichment through participation in a democratic social order."[38] In fact, the report suggested that the utility of subject matter would be measured by the degree to which it reached the interests and related to the well-being of students.[39]

The authors also recommended a K–12 science curriculum based on the major generalizations of science. They advised the addition of more physical science to the elementary program and suggested general science for grades 7 through 9. They suggested that content should include problems that are related to the student's world and would enable students to use the methods of science.[40]

A second report of this period was *Science in General Education*, published by the Progressive Education Association in 1938. This report focused attention on the needs of students and recommended a program that looked at the psychology of the learner. The report also recommended a greater correlation between science and everyday living. The main aims of science, according to this report, included:[41]

1. To acquire understanding in science as distinguished from information.
2. To develop the ability to think.

3. To develop particular skills or abilities related to problem solving.
4. To develop certain attitudes and dispositions useful in problem solving.

The progressive education movement was a movement that provided an alternative approach to the traditional school. Dewey suggested that the progressive education movement appealed to many educators because it was more closely aligned with America's democratic ideals. Dewey put it this way:

> One may safely assume, I suppose, that one thing which has recommended the progressive movement is that it seems more in accord with the democratic ideal to which our people is committed than do the procedures of the traditional school, since the latter have so much of the autocratic about them. Another thing which has contributed to its favorable reception is that its methods are humane in comparison with the harshness so often attending the policies of the traditional school.[42]

Two aspects of the progressive education movement that affected all of education, but perhaps appealed to science teachers, were the movement's notion of the child-centered curriculum and the project method. Both ideas have survived, even to this day, and over the years were given different degrees of emphasis. For example, in the late 1960s and 1970s, the child-centered curriculum was represented in the humanistic education movement (sometimes known as affective education). The humanistic ideas of the present day were similar to the progressive ideals of the 1930s.

The child- or student-centered approach is a major paradigm implying beliefs about the nature of learning, the goals of education, and the organization of the curriculum. Emphasis on student-centeredness has waxed and waned in American education to the present day. The progressive education movement represents one of the first and most important advocates of student-centeredness.

The progressive education movement sparked the development of a number of experimental schools that embodied the philosophy of progressive educators. Science in progressive schools was an opportunity to involve students directly with nature, or with hands-on experiences with science phenomena, and to relate science to not only the emotional and physical well-being of the child, but to the curriculum as a whole. There is a rich literature on this movement that describes innovative child-centered programs such the organic school, Dewey's Schools of To-Morrow, the Gary (Indiana) plan, the Lincoln School, and the Parker School.[43]

The project method, which had not been a foreign idea to science teachers, was given great impetus during the progressive education movement. William Kilpatrick, a professor at Teachers College of Columbia University, described the project method. Glatthorn summarizes Kilpatrick's approach as follows:

> Any meaningful experience—intellectual, physical, or aesthetic—could serve as the organizing center of the project, as long as it was characterized by purpose. And, for every project, there were four steps: purposing, planning, executing, and judging. While it might be necessary from time to time for the teacher to make suggestions about each of these four stages, it was preferable, from Kilpatrick's viewpoint, for the child to initiate and determine each stage. And this project, strung together, became the curriculum.[44]

Near the end of this period, there was an increasing emphasis on the importance of science in general education. The report *Science Education in American Schools* (1947) by the National Society for the Study of Education, summarized the Educational Policies Commission report and the Harvard Committee on General Education with the following statements:[45]

- Science instruction should begin early in the experience of the child.
- All education in science at the elementary and secondary levels should be general. Even for students going to college, general courses in biological science and in physical science (according to the Harvard report) "should make a greater contribution to the student's general education and his preparation for future study than a separate one-year course in physics and chemistry." The document of the Educational Policies Commission goes even further in its recommendations for reorganization of high school science courses.
- The development of competence in use of the scientific method of problem solving and the inculcation of scientific attitudes transcend in importance other objectives in science instruction.

Phase III: The Golden Age of Science Education, 1950–1977

During the period 1950–1977 science education witnessed a massive curriculum movement (the course content curriculum project movement) that no other period has witnessed. It was a period of federal intervention in education and the expenditure of huge sums of money on curriculum development and teacher training. It was, as many coined it, the "golden age of science education." What brought about such change? What were the forces influencing this movement?

Paul DeHart Hurd made an interesting point when he said that "at some point an awareness emerges: the present curriculum is no longer serving the needs of either student or society."[46] And at that point something needs to be done. Such was the climate in phase III, where the desire was to *reform, not revise* the nation's science and mathematics curriculum.

After World War II, the advances in science and technology increased at an enormous rate. These advances were described in a series of stages: first the atomic age, then the age of automation, then the space age, and the computer age. These changes occurred at a very rapid pace and there was a growing concern that America was not producing enough scientists and engineers to meet this need.[47]

The early 1950s has been characterized as a period in which American anxiety often bordered on hysteria. America was in the midst of the cold war with the Soviet bloc nations. The McCarthy hearings were in full swing and there was a "massive retaliation" against communist aggression abroad. England points out that many Americans of "normally placid temperament became convinced that Moscow was directing a conspiracy, reaching around the globe, to bury Western democracy, and their fears were intensified by the speed of the Russian development of nuclear weapons. Belief in a substantial margin of American superiority began to crumble."[48]

The National Science Foundation (NSF), created in 1950, took the leadership in addressing the problem of manpower shortages in science and engineering, the concern that high school science courses were inadequate in light of the rapid changes in science and technology, and the recognition that many science teachers needed more training in science and improved methods of teaching and that the textbooks being used were outmoded and needed to be updated.

Even with the growing concern for science education in the schools, NSF showed reluctance at first to support high school science. Instead, support would be directed at colleges and universities.[49] Partly due to limited funds, NSF didn't think it could make a dent in the nation's schools. However, in 1953, the first two "NSF Summer Institutes" were held at the University of Colorado for college mathematics and at the University of Minnesota for college physics and a companion group of high school physics teachers. Deeming the institute a success, NSF moved into the institute business and sponsored eleven in 1954 and twenty-seven in

1955 (two of these were year-long institutes for high school mathematics and science teachers).[50]

In 1956, NSF funded a group of physicists at the Massachusetts Institute of Technology under the direction of Professor Jerrold R. Zacharias. Known as the Physical Science Study Committee (PSSC), the physicists outlined in 1956–57 ideas for a new high school physics course and, in the summer of 1957, assembled sixty physicists, teachers, apparatus designers, writers, artists, and other specialists to produce a pilot version of the PSSC physics course (text, teacher's guide, lab manual, equipment, and, later, films and books written by scientists).[51]

Oddly enough, as late as fall 1957, NSF was thinking of reducing its institutes for science teachers. NSF-sponsored teacher institutes had come under attack. Some people were concerned that the Academic Year Institutes were aggravating the shortage of teachers by taking science and mathematics teachers (often the best) out of the classroom. It was also known that many high school teachers showed little interest in applying for refresher courses in science (even with tuition paid and a stipend).[52]

Then, on October 17, 1957, everything changed.

THE SPUTNIK WATERSHED The Soviet launch of Sputnik into orbit around the earth was a shot that had reverberating effects on American science and mathematics education like no other event in the twentieth century. According to England, "the launching of Sputnik changed the outlook dramatically. It brought another big boost in the institute budget and a chance to try out a variety of other projects, some of them reaching down into the elementary school."[53]

Sputnik "created an intellectual climate" that fostered the adoption of new courses of study by the nation's schools and spurred Congress to ensure funding for course improvement projects and summer institutes to train teachers in the new courses of study in science and mathematics.

The golden age of science education came about as a response to the apparent superiority of Soviet science and technology, yet it is rooted beyond Sputnik to the perceived crisis in the quality of secondary science teachers, courses, textbooks, and teaching materials.

REFORM PROJECTS More than $117 million was spent on over fifty-three separate course improvement projects during the years 1954–1975.[54] Table 3.3 details the literal explosion of course content improvement projects.

The curriculum projects developed during the golden age of science education were characterized as follows.

Table 3.3 Selected Science Content Improvement Projects of the Golden Age of Science Education

Course Content Improvement Project	Charter Year	Grades	Content Focus
High School Projects			
PSSC Physics	1956	12	Physics
Project Physics	1962	12	Physics
Chemical Bond Approach Chemistry (CBA)	1957	11	Chemistry
CHEM Study	1959	11	Chemistry
Biological Sciences Curriculum Study (BSC)	1958	9, 10	Blue Version: physiological-biochemical emphasis Yellow Version: classical emphasis Green Version: ecological-evolutionary emphasis
Engineering Concepts Curriculum Project (ECCP)	1965	11, 12	The Man Made World (title of ECCP book) focuses on logic, computers, models, and energy
Individualized Science Instructional System (ISIS)	1972	9–12	Over thirty minicourses in applied physics, chemistry, biology, health, and earth-space science
Junior High/Middle School Projects			
Introductory Physical Science (IPS)	1965	8, 9	Matter and energy
Earth Science Curriculum Project (ESCP)	1962	8, 9	Interdisciplinary approach to geology, astronomy, meteorology, and oceanography
Intermediate Science Curriculum Study (ISCS)	1965	7, 8, 9	Individualized science. Grades 7 and 8 focus on physical science, grade consists of eight books, each focusing on earth-space, biology, or environmental science
Elementary Science Projects			
Science Curriculum Improvement Study (SCIS)	1961	K–6	Physical and life science
Science—A Process Approach (SAPA)	1963	K–8	Processes of science (e.g., observing, measuring, classifying, inferring, controlling variables)
Elementary Science Study (ESS)	1963	K–8	Self-contained units on a wide range of science topics

1. The reformers were typically scientists, specialists in physics, chemistry, biology, or earth science. Their research interests and the nature of science colored their views of what elementary and secondary science should be.[55] The reformers criticized contemporary science programs by stating that, although "biology, chemistry and physics is taught, there is very little evidence of the science of these subjects presented."[56]

2. The criteria for the selection of content came from the discipline (as opposed to earlier criteria, such as meeting the needs of the child). Thus the "content of science, with its concepts, theories, laws and modes of inquiry is given."[57] The new science curricula were also based on the assumption that science was a way of knowing. The learning activities in the new curricula were designed to help students experience science as a way of knowing and therefore were engaged in "experimenting, observing, comparing, inferring, inventing, evaluating, and many other *ways* of knowing."[58]

3. According to the developers of the projects, students would be motivated intrinsically. The interesting nature of the science activities would themselves motivate students. This idea was fully developed by Bruner in his book *The Process of Education*, which was a report of a conference among scientists and educators at Woods Hole in 1959.[59]

4. The goals of science teaching as they developed with these reform projects was very different from science teaching goals in the past, and they were in stark contrast to what science educators are advocating for the 1990s and beyond. Hurd describes the goals of the curriculum reform projects in this way:

What is expressed is more a point of view or rationale for the teaching of science. This point of view lacks the societal orientation usually found in statements of educational goals. The "new" goals of science teaching are drawn entirely from the disciplines of science. Social problems, individual needs, life problems and other means used in the past are not differentiated for local schools or for individuals. If the discipline of science is to be the source of educational goals, then differences are not possible without violating the structure of science. To do otherwise would be teaching un-science, a major criticism of the traditional curriculum. Thus we find the reformers define educational goals within the framework of science as they are reflected in the separate disciplines. Their logic is simple and straightforward: this is what we know with some degree of reliability; this is how we find out about what we know; and this is how it all fits into the big picture—*conceptual schemes* [italics mine]. Now then, whatever personal or social problems involving science are to be solved must begin with authentic concepts and with fruitful processes of inquiry.[60]

Phase IV: Textbook Controversies and Back to Basics, 1977–1983

Nothing lasts forever! The course content improvement projects, which were propelled by the nation's desire to improve science and mathematics, came under attack in the mid-1970s. Two ideas surfaced during this time that an impact on science education. One was a movement that became know as the back-to-basics movement and the other had to do with the questioning of science textbooks by individual citizens, textbook watchers, and religious groups (especially Fundamental Christians).

The back-to-basics movement was a reaction to the current wave of course content improvement projects and also was spurred by antagonism toward the progressive movement in education (which surfaced in the late 1960s and 1970s as the humanistic education movement). The conservative movement "labeled progressive schools 'anti-intellectual playhouses' and 'crime breeders,' run by a 'liberal establishment.'"[61] One of the projects funded by NSF came under furious scrutiny by certain conservative congressmen, but most notably Representative John Conlan of Arizona. According to Nelkin, citizen groups in Arizona complained to Conlan (then, a state senator) about *Man—A Course of Study* (MACOS). Conlan's staff investigated the complaints and, eventually, Conlan took steps to stop appropriations for MACOS "on the grounds of its 'abhorrent,

repugnant, vulgar, morally sick content.' "[62] Others also criticized MACOS. Nelkin claims that the Council for Basic Education objected to MACOS for its emphasis on cultural relativism and its lack of emphasis on skills and facts. Even liberal congressmen got on the anti-MACOS bandwagon because of their desire to limit executive bureaucracies like NSF and "their resentment of scientists, who often tended to disdain congressional politics; and above all, the concern with secrecy and confidentiality that followed the Watergate affair."[63]

The MACOS controversy brought the issue of censorship into the public arena. However, in order to avoid the claim of censorship, which probably would not have been acceptable to many in Congress, Conlan focused on the federal government's role in implementing MACOS as well as all other NSF-funded curriculum projects. One issue that surfaced was "the marketing issue—the concern that the NSF used taxpayers' money to interfere with private enterprise."[64] Along with this was the position that conservative writers, such as James Kilpatrick, who attacked NSF science programs as "an ominous echo of the Soviet Union's promulgation of official scientific theory."[65] The temper of the times was quite clear: "resentment of the 'elitism' of science reinforced concern that NSF was naively promulgating the liberal values of the scientific community to a reluctant public."[66] The result: On April 9, 1975, Congress terminated funds for MACOS, further support of science curriculum projects was suspended, and the entire NSF educational program came under review.

The federal funds that would have been used to support the NSF curriculum projects were used for research and college science programs. The NSF did, however, fund three large studies to answer the charges that science and mathematics education had not improved as a result of the course content curriculum projects.[67] The three studies, which were mentioned earlier in this chapter, were: (1) a review of the science education research between 1954 and 1974;[68] (2) a demographic study that assessed factors important to science educators such as enrollments, offerings, teachers, and instructional materials;[69] and (3) case studies of science teaching.[70]

In response to the volume of data provided by the three status studies, NSF funded a fourth study, called Project Synthesis. Project Synthesis recommended expanding the goals of science education to include not only content (science as preparation for further study), but also science for meeting personal needs, resolving societal problems, and for career awareness.

To recoup its position as an active force in science education, NSF prepared a report in 1980 entitled

Science and Engineering Education for the 1980s and Beyond to the Carter administration. Unfortunately for NSF, Carter was defeated, and the new president, Ronald Reagan, rejected the report's recommendations and tried to eliminate the science education section of NSF. During the early 1980s, the influence of NSF in science education was limited to college faculty improvement and graduate student fellowships in the basic sciences.[71]

Another wave of controversy occurred during this period over the teaching of evolution in the public schools and other science concepts and ideas that touched on beliefs, religion, values, and morals (e.g., teaching human sexuality, human reproduction, and birth control in biology classes). But it was Darwin's evolutionary theory that resulted in court cases and laws being passed to regulate the teaching of evolution (such as giving equal time to "creation science" if "evolution science" was presented in a science class).

A phenomenon that reached its pinnacle during this time was the general scrutiny of textbooks, especially in biology, earth science, social studies, and literature. In the 1960s, when the Biological Science Study Committee (BSCS), whose textbooks emphasized Darwin's theory of evolution (in contrast to many high school biology texts at the time), submitted books for state adoption in the lucrative market of Texas, serious trouble surfaced. The Reverend Ruel Lemmons led a protest (which reached the Texas governor's office) to the get the BSCS textbooks banned, claiming the books were pure evolution, completely materialistic, and atheistic.[72] The books were not banned, but changes were made to lighten their evolutionary emphasis. Nelkin reports that BSCS had to specify that evolution theory was a *theory*, not a fact, and that it had been modified, not strengthened, by recent research.[73]

This was just the tip of the iceberg. A group of fundamentalists began to develop a worldview of creation based on the story in Genesis in the Holy Bible. The creationists rejected the notion of a five-billion-year-old earth, instead claiming that biological life began approximately five to six thousand years ago. One of the forceful voices in the creation science movement was John Morris, representing the Institute for Creation Research's point of view (see IRC Web site at http://www.icr.org/). In an article published in the *American Biology Teacher*, Morris set out the differences, from his point of view, between the creation model and the evolution model.[74] Essentially the creationists "theorized" that all living things were brought about by the acts of a Creator. The evolutionary model proposed that naturalistic processes due to properties inherent in inanimate matter brought about all living things. The creationists, in their literature, set the creation model alongside the evolutionary model and insisted that good science education would provide alternative views on the same topic and would let students evaluate them to form their own position.

In 1969, the California board of education modified the *Science Framework on Science for California Schools* so that the theory of creation would be included in textbooks. The *Science Framework on Science for California Schools* sets forth the guidelines for the adoption of science textbooks (currently over $40 million are spent on science books in California during the science adoption year). Vernon Grose, an aerospace engineer, wrote and presented a document arguing that evolutionary theory was biased and should be taught only if alternative views were presented. He convinced the board of education to modify its position on the teaching of evolution and the board inserted the following statement into the framework:

> All scientific evidence to date concerning the origin of life implies at least a dualism or the necessity to use several theories to fully explain relationships . . . While the Bible and other philosophical treatises also mention creation, science has independently postulated the various theories of creation. Therefore, creation in scientific terms is not a religious or philosophical belief. Also note that creation and evolutionary theories are not necessarily mutual exclusives. Some of the scientific data (e.g., the regular absence of transitional forms) may be best explained by a creation theory, while other data (e.g., transmutation of species) substantiate a process of evolution.[75]

The "evolutionists were incredulous that creationists could have any influence."[76] A number of individuals and groups, such as National Association of Biology Teachers (NABT), the National Academy of Science, and the Academic Senate of the University of California, protested and lobbied against the state board's ruling. The solution to the creation–evolution issue resulted only after the state board had received numerous complaints about the earlier decision. In 1972 the California Board of Education decided to approve a statement prepared by its curriculum committee by proposing neutrality in science textbooks. Dogmatic statements in science books would be removed and replaced with conditional statements. Textbooks dealing with evolution would have printed in them a statement indicating that science cannot answer all questions about origins and that evolution is a theory, not a fact. Some textbooks, even today, contain statements to this effect, usually printed on the inside cover. The effect of this policy change prevented textbook publishers from having to include in science books a section on "creation science." The board's decision, which was called the Antidogmatism Statement, caused publishers to rethink the way they were presenting science information in textbooks.

The controversy has continued to be an issue at the state district and district levels. In 1999, the Kansas State Board of Education removed Darwin's theory of evolution from the state standards. The 1999 vote never banned the teaching of evolution or required the teaching of the biblical story of creation. But it dropped Darwin's theory from standardized tests taken by Kansas students. In February 2001, the board reversed its 1999 decision by restoring evolution to the state standards.

In the Cobb County school district, Georgia's second largest school system, the board of education ordered that all biology texts include the following insert (starting with the 2002–2003 school year): "This textbook contains material on evolution. Evolution is a theory, not a fact, regarding the origin of living things. This material should be approached with an open mind, studied carefully, and critically considered."

Although the disclaimer has not affected the curriculum per se, the statement could cause confusion among students about the meaning of the word theory. Theory in science is the best explanation of a set of observations and facts. On the other hand, the disclaimer also provides an opportunity to discuss with students their view of "theory" and to help them develop a sense of how science develops theories and how a theory is different than a religious view.

By the late 1970s, the emphasis in education had focused on the "basics" and the literature was replete with the so-called back-to-basics slogans (e.g., schools need to attend to basic skills). The place of science in the curriculum lost the priority it had had in the 1960s. The interest now was in teaching the basic skills of reading, mathematics, and communication.

Phase V: A Nation at Risk, the 1980s

Some point to the year 1983 as being similar in some respects to the Sputnik year, 1957. Two reports were issued by very prestigious commissions, which marked another turning point in the nation's perception of education (Actually, over 300 reports were issued during the mid-1980s calling for reforms in education). In 1957, the perceived concern was the nation's inability to prepare scientists and engineers to meet the challenge of the space age. In 1983, the perceived concern was

America's ability to compete economically in the world. In the report by the National Commission on Excellence in Education (*A Nation at Risk*), established by the secretary of education to report to the American people on the quality of America's education, the authors (only one of fourteen a teacher) made this statement on the first page:

> If an unfriendly foreign power had attempted to impose on America the mediocre educational performance that exists today, we might well have viewed it as an act of war. As it stands, we have allowed this to happen to ourselves. We have even squandered the gains in student achievement made in the wake of the Sputnik challenge. Moreover, we have dismantled essential support systems, which helped make those gains possible. We have, in effect, been committing an act of unthinking, unilateral educational disarmament.[77]

The report goes on to say that the United States is being taken over as the leader in science, technology, commerce, industry, and innovation by Japan, as well as some other nations, and this is most likely due to the "rising tide of mediocrity in our schools."[78]

The commission supported its statement of risk by citing scores on various achievement tests. For example, the commission reported that international comparisons of student achievement completed a decade earlier revealed that on nineteen academic tests American students were never first or second and, in comparison with other industrialized nations, were last several times. The commission also cited falling scores on standardized tests such as on the College Boards and SATs.[79] It is important to note that some took issue with the commission for citing the poor performance of American students based on international comparisons. The director of the report of the International Project for the Evaluation of Educational Achievement warned against using the data to make generalizations about individual countries' educational systems. He also stated that "the best American students are comparable in achievement to those of other advanced nations." He went on to say that the comprehensive systems, such as in the United States, result in bringing more people into the talent pool.[80]

The report nevertheless had an effect on education in general and on science education specifically. Using the language of the back-to-basics movement, the commission recommended that all students seeking a diploma from high school be required to complete a curriculum, called the Five New Basics, consisting of: (a) four years of English; (b) three years of mathematics; (c) three years of science; (d) three years of social studies; and (e) a half year of computer science (college-bound students should take two years of a foreign language). With regard to high school science, the commission recommended a curriculum to provide all graduates with the following:[81]

1. The concepts, laws, and processes of the physical and biological sciences.
2. The methods of scientific inquiry and reasoning.
3. The application of scientific knowledge to everyday life.
4. The social and environmental implications of scientific and technological development.

The report also specified that science courses must be revised and updated for both college-bound students and students with other plans. With regard to computer science, students should (a) understand the computer as an information, computation, and communication device; (b) use the computer in the study of the other basics and for personal and work-related purposes; and (c) understand the world of computers, electronics, and related technologies.[82] Among the other recommendations, the commission suggested raising college entrance requirements, administering standardized achievement tests at major points in students' careers, upgrading textbooks by having states evaluate texts on the basis of their ability to present rigorous and challenging material clearly. The report also recommended that American students stay is school longer each day (from a six- to a seven-hour day), and to extend the school year to at least 200 days per year (then 180), but preferably to 240 days.

The report did give state and local district science educators the "rationale" to require more science and, indeed, many states passed laws requiring more science for graduation. There was also an increased effort to require more time-on-task, and some states required science teachers to log the number of hours students were engaged in science laboratory activities. (Georgia, for example, requires that 25 percent of instructional time be spent doing laboratory activities.)

Another report, perhaps more significant for science education, was *Educating Americans for the 21st Century*. Issued by the National Science Board, the report is very clear about the main goal for improving science, mathematics, and technology education. The authors of the report state the following as the one basic objective:

The improvement and support of elementary and secondary school systems throughout America so that, by the year 1995, they will provide all the nation's youth with a level of education in mathematics, science, and technology, as measured by achievement scores and participation levels, that is not only the highest quality attained anywhere in the world but also reflects the particular and peculiar needs of our nation.[83]

Some critics have charged that the report is overly nationalistic and is reminiscent of the era of the cold war and space race.[84] The report also uses the language of the back-to-basics movement, stating that education must return to the basics for the twenty-first century, including not only reading, writing, and arithmetic, but also communication, higher order problem-solving skills, and scientific and technological literacy.[85] The report also has been criticized for its failure to address the social implications of science and importance of science education in general education. Further critics have charged that the board ignored the shortcomings of the course content curriculum projects of the 1960s and 1970s and instead recommended that the National Science Foundation be the leader in curriculum development efforts by promoting the development of new curricula.[86]

Even with these criticisms, the report had an impact and has been used by a number of groups as a rationale for charting "new" curricula and for seeking funding. *Educating Americans for the 21st Century* suggested that the K–12 science curriculum should be revamped, and that science and technology education at the elementary and secondary levels should result in the following outcomes:[87]

- Ability to formulate questions about nature and seek answers from observation and interpretation of natural phenomena.
- Development of students' capacities for problem solving and critical thinking in all areas of learning.
- Development of particular talents for innovative and creative thinking.
- Awareness of the nature and scope of a wide variety of science- and technology-related careers open to students of varying aptitudes and interests.
- The basic academic knowledge necessary for advanced study by students who are likely to pursue science professionally.
- Scientific and technical knowledge needed to fulfill civic responsibilities, improve the student's own health and life, and ability to cope with an increasingly technological world.
- Means for judging the worth of articles presenting scientific conclusions.

The report also recommended a K–12 curriculum plan as follows:[88]

- *K–6:* Emphasis should be on phenomena in the natural environment, with a balance between biological and physical phenomena. The curriculum should be integrated with other subjects and should be implemented with hands-on activities.
- *Grades 7–8:* The focus in middle school should be on the biological, chemical, and physical aspects related to the personal needs of adolescents. The curriculum should also focus on the development of qualitative analytical skills. Experimentation, science texts, and community resources should be used in instruction.
- *Grades 9–12:* Biology should be presented in a social/ecological context. Topics should include health, nutrition, environmental management, and human adaptation. The biology curriculum should be inquiry oriented and problems should be selected in a biosocial context involving value or ethical considerations. Chemistry should emphasize the social and human relevance of chemistry and should include topics from descriptive and theoretical chemistry. Physics courses should be designed for a wide variety of students and should be built upon students' earlier experiences in physics. The emphasis in grades 9–11 should be on the application of science and technology. Schools should offer discipline-oriented career preparation courses in grades 11–12, in which several disciplines would be taken in each year.

Because of these and other reports, action to modify and change school programs was set into motion at the national, state, and local levels.[89] At the national level, the National Science Foundation received appropriations from Congress to once again develop curriculum materials for the schools. During the 1980s and continuing into the 1990s, NSF funded a number of curriculum projects, especially at the elementary and middle school levels. Many of these funded projects were joint efforts involving the public and private sectors. In nearly all of these projects, a publisher or a commercial enterprise teamed up with a university group or science education center (such as the BSCS) to develop science curriculum materials. Some of these projects will be discussed later in the chapter.

Science education in the 1980s was also a time of reflection and recommendations for science education toward the year 2000. Earlier in the chapter, I described the work and recommendations of Project Synthesis.

Project Synthesis represents the most comprehensive approach to the analysis of science education and science curriculum goals.

In 1982, the National Science Teachers Association began its Search for Excellence in Science Education program. This program, begun by then NSTA President Robert Yager, was designed to identify exemplary programs in science education. The criteria used to identify exemplary programs were the desired states identified by the Project Synthesis subgroups (elementary science, biology, physical science, science/technology/society, and inquiry). Several volumes in the Search for Excellence Series have been published by NSTA as follows:

Volume 1 (1982)	Volume 2 (1983)	Volume 3 (1984)
Science as Inquiry	Physics	Energy Education
Elementary Science	Middle School/	Chemistry
Biology	Junior	Earth Science
Physical Science	Non-School Settings	

Phase VI: The Reform Efforts of the 1990s: A Contrast with the Golden Age

In the 1990s science and technology, as well as the development of major reform efforts, influenced the nature of science education, and the impact will be of utmost significance to you as you enter or continue in the science education profession.

Four movements or developments merged in the 1990s that resulted in a new ways of thinking about science education. These ideas included:

- Science for the social responsibility and a scientifically literate citizenry
- The *National Science Education Standards*
- A constructivist view of learning
- The emergence of the Internet

The goals of science education shifted in the 1990s such that for curriculum developers and science teachers the central goal was to "develop scientifically literate individuals who understood how science, technology, and society influenced each other."[90] This central goal merged with new ways of thinking about how students learn science, as well as with the emphasis that the National Research Council's *National Science Education Standards* placed on inquiry. In the *Standards*, the authors noted that the following outcomes should characterize science curriculum and teaching:[91]

- Understanding of scientific concepts and developing abilities to do inquiry
- Learning subject matter disciplines in the context of inquiry, science and technology, science from personal and social perspectives, and the history and nature of science
- Integrating all aspects of science content (life science, physical science, and earth science)
- Studying a few fundamental concepts
- Implementing inquiry as an instructional strategy

The movements the 1990s regarding how students acquired and learned science affected the development of curriculum projects (see Chapter 4 for a detailed discussion). As Krajcik, Mamlok, and Hug point out,

Current theory holds that understanding does not result from memorization, but from an individual's construction of meaning based upon his or her experiences and interactions in the world. In a sense learners make their understanding; understanding does not occur by passively taking in information transmitted from a teacher. Building understanding is a continuous process that requires new experiences where students construct and reconstruct what they know.[92]

What emerged during the 1990s were new curricula that embodied the new learning theory and goals and resulted in fresh approaches to science curriculum. Several characteristics defined the nature of these projects (some of which are described later).

1. Students, with the help of their teachers, engaged in authentic tasks (e.g., monitoring ozone, analyz-

ing the quality of the water in a local stream, comparing and contrasting soils across regions, etc.)
2. Learning in context, such as at an environmental site in students' community
3. Engaging students in research investigations
4. Collaborating with other students and teachers across the Internet
5. Using cognitive tools such as computer software programs
6. Meeting the *Standards*

The projects that emerged were quite different than projects developed in the 1960s or 1970s. Students were more actively engaged in "real problems," as opposed to "learning concepts" described in text material and reinforced in laboratory investigations.

THE GLOBAL LAB (GL) One of the first Internet-based projects, the GL developed by TERC created a curriculum in which students used tools to investigate the local environment and used the Internet to share information, stories, and images.

COMPUTER AS LEARNING PARTNER (CLP) Developed at the University of California, Berkeley, the CLP applied the conceptual change model and used computer technology tools to enable students to explore their ideas.

KIDS NETWORK One of the first of the new generation projects, Kids Network was developed by TERC and published by the National Geographic Society. In the project, students in elementary grades engaged in authentic problem solving by investigating environmental

---

INQUIRY ACTIVITY 3.3

How Were Course Improvement Projects of the 1960s Different from the Reform Projects of the 1990s?

In this inquiry you will compare and contrast a course improvement project developed in the 1960s with a reform project developed in the 1990s.

Materials

- Course improvement project textbook (e.g., *PSSC Physics*, *ChemStudy*, *BSCS Biology*, *ESCP*, *IPS*)
- Access to one or more of these projects via the Internet: Global Lab (www.terc.edu), GLOBE (www.globe.gov), Computers As Learning Partners (http://clp.berkeley.edu/).

Table 3.4 Comparison of Curriculum Projects Developed in the 1960s and Projects of the 1990s

Criteria for Comparison	1960s	1990s
Purpose/Role of Inquiry	Student inquiry was centered on exploring regularities and patterns in science concepts. Typically, student labs were designed to explore specific concepts such as inertia, chemical equilibrium, and so on.	Student inquiry is focused on applying concepts and principles to explore meaningful questions. For example, in Global Lab and the Global Thinking Project, students explore the quality of the water in a local stream and in so doing are introduced to a variety of science concepts.
Instructional Differences	Focused on exploring science concepts with little or no application to society. Collaboration was not part of these projects. Students were assessed using paper-and-pencil tests. The projects used little or no technologies other than cleverly designed "laboratory" apparatus.	Focus is on interesting questions that students can relate to their lives and community. Often, students collaborate with students in other schools in other nations. Student assessment uses a variety of methods, including performance assessment. New technologies permeate these projects, including computers and hand-held portable devices, all connected to the Internet.
Intended Outcomes	Purpose was to prepare students who would pursue careers in science and technology.	Projects focus on scientific literacy for all students.

Procedures

1. Working with a team, select one text or science program from the list of course improvement projects of the 1960s, and a reform project of the 1990s (see Table 3.4).
2. Make a chart using your own criteria to compare and contrast the projects from these two eras. You might consider the following questions for your criteria:
   - What was the role of inquiry in each of the projects?
   - What were the goals or intended outcomes of the project and course?
   - What was the context of learning science concepts and principles in each project?
   - What was the role of the laboratory in each program?
   - To what extent was the application of science to society emphasized?
   - How were students assessed in each program?

Minds-On Strategies

1. What are the fundamental differences between the course improvement project programs of the 1960s and the 1990s?
2. Jerome Bruner was one of the psychologists associated with the early course improvement projects. How were his theories manifested in these programs? (Refer to Chapter 5 for Bruner's ideas.) How do Bruner's theories compare with the learning theory (constructivism) that underscored the programs of the 1990s?
3. What do you think were some of the problems associated with implementing the course improvement project programs and how can this knowledge be used to prevent implementation problems for the 1990s projects?

phenonomena (e.g., acid rain) and using technology to share results with other schools around the world.

THE GLOBAL THINKING PROJECT (GTP) Developed by science educators from Georgia (U.S.) and Russia, the developers created one of the first telecommunications systems between schools in the United States and Russia. The GTP used a series of environmental projects (clean air, water watch, solid waste) to engage students in authentic problem solving. Using the Internet and related cognitive tools, students and teachers collaborated with each other and also participated in exchange programs enabling students from these two cultures to live and conduct environmental research in each others' communities.

Phase VII: Science for All and the New Millennium

This chapter began with an examination of goals and objectives for the science curriculum with an eye to the future. We surveyed the results of Project 2061, the *Scope, Sequence, and Coordination Project*, the *National Science Education Standards*, and cognitive research, and identified some of the implications for the science curriculum goals.

As we move forward, the goals of the science education will be influenced not only by the items I just mentioned, but also by several other factors. Here very briefly are some of those factors that will affect science education in the new millennium. Although recent research has shown that the science curriculum has not changed very much in the last twenty-five years, these issues will be debated, described, and put into practice in individual classrooms, school districts, and states.

EQUITY In the Project 2061 report *Blueprints for Reform*, equity was identified as one of the central problems for reformers to deal with and "to make science understandable, accessible, and perhaps even enjoyable to all K–12 students."[93] Key questions for educators to consider as outlined in *Blueprints* include:[94]

- Is it possible to reconcile a commitment to equity as equal opportunity with that of equity as equal outcomes?
- What characteristics of the American educational system are the greatest barriers to equal opportunity or outcome? Which of these are most amenable to improvement?
- Can science literacy for all be achieved given the current unequal distribution of financial resources?
- Which groups of students are most in need of help in science and mathematics?

- How can a common set of learning goals be achieved while honoring individual and cultural differences?

GLOBAL ENVIRONMENTAL ISSUES AND PROBLEMS The major conferences held during in recent years focused on the environment and the economic impact environmental problems have on all nations. Science education programs will have to attend to a number of global environmental issues, such as air pollution, global warming, ozone depletion, and deforestation. Science education will have to address the global environmental problem head on beyond the nineties. Earth Day 2000 (April 27) marked the thirtieth anniversary of the environmental education movement and represented a call for action among governments, action groups, and citizens to deal with the fate of the earth's environment. The environmental theme will permeate science curriculum development at the local, state, national, and international levels—in short, globally. Many of the Web-based science projects that have recently been developed chose environmental science to formulate themes and projects for students around the world to work on collaboratively. This collaboration will continue into the future.

SCIENCE-TECHNOLOGY-SOCIETY (STS) INTERFACE This interface (developed more fully in Chapter 11) is the bridge that science teachers will use to connect the ideas of science with their utility in society. It will be the vehicle to humanize science teaching and make the content of science relevant to students in middle and high schools. The STS theme makes sense as an organizing principle for science teaching, especially in light of recent history of science curriculum development. If you recall, the curriculum reform of the 1950s and 1960s was discipline centered, and this approach was found to be ineffective with most students. The STS theme forces us to ask such questions as: How does science relate to the world of the student? How can science contribute to the fulfillment of healthy life and environment? What is the relationship between humans and the environment? How can science be in the service of people?

The STS theme has the intrinsic appeal of having us to stay current and relate science to the student's world of today and dreams of tomorrow. It also has the structure of incorporating some of the other major forces that are influencing education today; namely multicultural programs, interdisciplinary thinking, conceptual themes, and global environmental issues.

STANDARDS-BASED TEACHING If you recall, the notion of big ideas was put forward in the 1930s and was an important construct during the curriculum reform era of the late 1950s and 1960s. The major themes of science have been called in addition to big ideas, "overarching truths," and "unifying constructs." Project 2061 and the *National Science Education Standards* recommend that science content be organized around conceptual themes. Combining the publication of *Benchmarks for Scientific Literacy* by Project 2061 with the *National Science Education Standards*, specific content goals and big ideas have been outlined for each grade level and in each content area.

Conceptual themes, however, have support in the recent research in cognitive science. One of the recommendations that has been made is to reduce the amount of content in science courses. Organizing courses around a reduced list of conceptual themes is right on target. The themes identified in *Benchmarks for Scientific Literacy* include:[95]

- Energy
- Evolution
- Patterns of Change
- Stability
- Systems and Interactions
- Scale and Structure

Accordingly, the main criterion of a good theme is its ability to integrate facts and concepts into overarching constructs. Themes have the characteristic of linking content between the disciplines, therefore being transdisciplinary. But they also have the quality of helping students link science with other disciplines in the curriculum, such as mathematics, history, economics, political science, language arts, and literature.

INTERDISCIPLINARY THINKING AND PLANNING Key concepts and conceptual themes are the structures needed to link thinking across the disciplines (e.g., biology and physics or geology and economics). Interdisciplinary thinking is a strategy that will enable students to see the relevance of science content, especially when science is linked with issues of the day. For example, the field of sports physiology is a way of linking biology, health, and physics, but also a way to connect science with economics, management, and sports.

Middle schools are organized to put interdisciplinary thinking and planning into action more so than junior high schools or senior high schools because of the organization of teachers into multidiscipline teams and because in many middle schools, these teams have time allotted in the school day for planning. In many middle schools, the mathematics, science, social studies, and language arts team develops interdisciplinary units of study. In some high schools, the science teacher plans with the social studies teacher to investigate the historical aspects of a particular environment or community. In other settings, the mathematics and science teacher team up to help students integrate topics in mathematics with topics in biology, earth science, chemistry, and physics.

ROLE OF THE INTERNET AND TELECOMMUNICATIONS TECHNOLOGIES Computer technology tools and the Internet will continue to provide the impetus for a variety of science education experiences for students and teachers. Students can collaborate with peers around the world and come in contact with "experts" in a variety of fields that relate to the kind of learning experiences provided by their teachers. Students and teachers no longer need to be isolated. The new technologies also enable students to investigate phenomena locally and participate in project-based learning on topics relevant to their own communities. With the Internet they can share their insights and understandings with other students thereby, comparing and contrasting their work.

THE CITIZEN SCIENTIST: A NEW CONCEPTION OF THE STUDENT LEARNER The goals of science teaching are shifting toward getting students involved in solving authentic problems related to themselves and their communities. The term "community of practice" has emerged recently and it means that students in a class in one school can join with students in another school to forge a "community of practice" to solve problems of mutual concern. Students become activists in this role, not only applying science concepts and gaining a deeper understanding of some community problem (e.g., why asthma cases have increased in recent years), but also using social science skills in taking positions on important issues and learning how to communicate their ideas to entire community. Thus, the concept of "citizen scientist" has emerged, defining a role for the active student learner.[96]

SECTION 2: SCIENCE TEACHER GAZETTE

Volume 3: Goals and History of Science Teaching

Think Pieces

1. How have the goals of the science curriculum changed over the past twenty-five years?

2. How do the recommendations of the *National Science Education Standards* and Project 2061 compare? What are the similarities and differences?
3. Write an article for the newspaper using one of the following headlines:

- Science Educators Create New Goals for Teaching: New Hope for the Future
- Science Teacher Designs New Course: Career Awareness Biology
- New Standards in Science Approved by the School Board
- Multicultural Science Curriculum Implemented

 Case Study: Rehashing the Sixties

The Case

The report *Science for All Americans*, published by the American Association for the Advancement of Science, outlines recommendations for the improvement of science in the nation's schools. Newsome Wave, a former high school science teacher but now a school superintendent, is a sharp critic of the report. He asserts that the AAAS has created a warmed-over version of recommendations that are similar to the reform proposals of the 1950s and 1960s. In an article published in a major Los Angeles newspaper, Wave said, "this report [*Science for All Americans*] reinforces the elitism of the scientific establishment and fails to deal with the needs of all students who pass through our schools. How can a report that has scientists, who for the most part are remote from and outside the school environment, identify what should be taught in the schools and be taken seriously? One of the lessons we learned from the curriculum reform projects of the 1960s was they addressed the needs of a very small part of the school population. The AAAS seems headed the same direction that cursed the 1960s science reform project. Haven't we learned that national curriculum projects simply cannot meet the needs of the diverse population of school students, let alone the diversity of the science teaching force?"

Reginald Regis, the coordinator of science of a highly populated western state and an advocate of AAAS's effort at science curriculum reform, wrote a blistering rebuttal to Wave in the journal *New Science*. Regis pointed out that Wave failed to men-

tion that the AAAS has developed a broad program that includes the involvement of cooperating school districts. He also pointed out that, although panels comprising scientists and university officials did write the unifying concepts, educators reviewed the panel's recommendations.

Wave and Regis have agreed to appear together at the annual conference of the National Science Teachers Association to debate the issues surrounding each educator's point of view.

The Problem

First consider your position in this case. Is the AAAS report a rehash of the wishes of the 1960s? What do others in your class think? Take the position of either Wave or Regis. What are the facts that support your position? What are your arguments? Prepare for a debate with your opponent.

 Case Study: New Science Goals— Just Another Fad

The Case

Miss Jennifer Harris is the chair of the science department of Block High School in an urban school district in the northeast part of the country. It is her first year as chair, but her tenth year of teaching at Block. The science department has agreed to implement in all courses a new emphasis by incorporating the goals proposed by Project Synthesis. At a meeting of the science department, Miss Harris explains that in each science course, content will be emphasized in terms of:

- personal needs
- societal issues
- academic knowledge
- career education

The teachers agree that all course syllabi should reflect these new "goal clusters," and they agree to rewrite them to show this change.

About a month into the term, Miss Harris's receives a parent note from a student in her first period class. The parent is furious about the new science goals. He is "sick and tired" of these "new education fads," which seem to come and go and never produce any positive results. He wants to know why time is being spent in science classes on

Table 3.5 Excerpts from the Parrott Timeline Comparing Science, Science Education, and Technology Innovations and Developments from 2000 B.C. to the 1990s

	2000 B.C.	400 B.C.	A.D. 1700	1920	1990
Science	Contraceptives in Kemet First zoo in China Physicians form professional groups in Babylon and Syria Preshet, female physician	350 B.C. Aristotle classified animals into 500 species and 8 classes, named father of zoology	1711 Luigi Marsigli corals animals not plants 1735 Carolus Linnaeus system for classification of organisms (rejects notion of evolution in 1751) 1748 John Needham and Buffon "prove" spontaneous generation Charles Boonet first uses term "evolution" 1785 Lazzaro Spallanzani artificial insemination in dogs 1796 Smallpox vaccination by Edward Jenner	1924 *Australopithecine* skull found 1928 penicillin's discovery (later use in 1939) George Washington Carver worked with agricultural products developed industrial applications from farm products, called chemurgy	1990 Mary Claire King found the location of the breast cancer predisposition gene 1992 *Sachromyces cervisiae* genome identified 1998 James Thomson successfully isolated and cultured human embryonic stem cells 1998 Viagra approved by FDA
Science Education	Rhind papyrus shows use of mathematical formula including (2000 years before the birth of Pythagoras)	"Advanced schools" attributed to Plato 387 B.C. called "Academy"	1750 Start of American academies over European educational theory with Ben Franklin's Philadelphia Academy. Curriculum including surveying, navigation, agriculture and accounting	"Progressive era"/"Progressive education movement" in American Education: child centered, real-world application, social importance of knowledge, learning enjoyable and meaningful: 1917–1957, 1890–1930, 1930–1950 1925 Scopes Monkey Trial (TN) on teaching of evolution in the classroom, later revisited in Kansas and other states	1993 Project 2061 had gone on to develop *Benchmarks for Scientific Literacy National Science Education Standards* Published
Technology	Quadratic equation in Mesopotamia Arithmetic in Babylonia	450 Kushite settlers in Kenya develop astronomical observatory Abacus by Herodotus	1716 Edmund Halley diving bell with air refreshment system 1749 Electricity by Ben Franklin	1920 U.S. Army officer John T. Thompson patents submachine "Tommy" gun 1921 cultured pearls 1926 *The Jazz Singer*, first talking motion picture 1928 FM radio introduced, W.A. Morrison and quartz-crystal clock	1990 President Bush funded "Decade of the Brain" 1991 World Wide Web (WWW) released by CERN

Source: Used with permission of the author, Annette Parrott.

personal needs and career education. Can't the school counselor do that?

The Problem

What should Miss Harris do? How should she respond to her student's parent? Are these goals simply a new education fad or are they grounded in defensible educational practice?

The Parrott Timeline

To give you a broader perspective on the historical markers affecting not only science education, but also technology and science, I present a timeline developed by Annette Parrott, a science educator at Lakeside High School in Decatur, Georgia. She has traced developments in science education, technology, and science back thousands of years and has paid close attention to contributions to these fields by people from many different ethnic groups and affiliations. Her findings presented in an abbreviated time line in Table 3.5. You can explore Parrott's more complete time line at http://scied.gsu.edu/Hassard/parrott_timeline.html.

SCIENCE-TEACHING LITERATURE

BACK TO THE FUTURE WITH SCIENCE EDUCATION

Larry Loeppke

Twenty-five years ago the context for changing educational materials and practices was clear.[97] Our country's goal was to secure peace and national prosperity through global political and economic dominance. As a technological society in full bloom, we were developing new nuclear submarines, new B–52 bombers, lunar landing modules, and an interstate highway system. Classroom pedagogy reflected the scientific foundation of our technology. The application of scientific inquiry began to be used as a teaching technique in the public schools, thanks to new curricula developed with National Science Foundation funds by such groups as the Biological Sciences Curriculum Study (BSCS), the Earth Science Curriculum Project, the Physical Science Study Committee, and the American Chemical Society (ACS).

For the young people of the early 1960s, the relevance of science was fairly clear. New scientific miracles, such as CorningWare, were in use in the family kitchen and discussed at the dinner table. Entertainment shows, such as *Star Trek*, convinced us that ionic bonding, plasma physics, and other such mysteries were going to be a part of our daily lives. Students were fascinated by the impact science would have on their careers; someday, as members of the workforce, they too would be bringing us such new and exciting technological miracles as remote control television and microwave ovens.

Over the years, however, we became accustomed to miracles. Science became simply another part of our economic enterprise. We described rock bands as "awesome"—not laser beams at the grocery checkout. We came to attention when a space shuttle exploded—not when it flew. We became wired to the rest of the world through new global communications technology, and then suffered the fate of novices on the global economic stage. As we lost interest in the mystery and novelty of scientific inquiry and technological innovation, we lost our sense of their immediate relevance and importance. And then we lost our memory of scientific facts. Educators who deal in study skills and learning theory would put it this way: without a "significant context" there is no long-term memory of content.

When scientific literacy began to drop in the 1970s, the "education industry"—public and private entities that develop, publish, and teach our science curricula—attempted to tackle the problem by increasing the number of facts students were expected to learn. Most of the textbooks that have been used in classrooms ever since exemplify this "content" solution. They are fact-filled because market research shows that educators want them to be. And educators want textbooks full of facts because student assessments measure how many facts students know, not how much knowledge they can apply. Textbooks now not only include a growing number of facts, but they are also written at oversimplified reading levels, come with ancillary materials that have the effect of reducing the teacher's individualized input, and generally have the effect of replacing scientific inquiry with memorization. Meanwhile, students have been left to fend for themselves when it comes to figuring out why what they are memorizing is personally relevant and applicable to their lives.

Fortunately, as we approach the new century, educators are involved in a great "rethink" about the process of education. And it seems that science educators have now developed a fairly clear—though still very general—consensus on two broad areas of change: (1) Science teaching should be the guided but direct application of scientific inquiry by the student in a hands-on fashion; (2) Science teaching should be carried out in a context that is personally and socially relevant to the student in order to fan the spark of curiosity generated by scientific inquiry.

With this foundational agreement, it is simply unnecessary for us to enter the twenty-first century with the kind of mediocre textbooks, ineffective pedagogy, and ill-prepared graduates we have tolerated over the past fifteen years. Our schools, our universities, and our educational businesses know where we need to go. Now we must manage our resources wisely and cooperatively to get there.

The trends that will shape science education for the twenty-first century are increasingly evident. To some degree, the question of where we are going has already been answered. We are moving toward the teaching of science as a thinking process—a way of "knowing and reknowing" our world as it changes before us. The question of how this teaching can be done is also in the process of being answered. New curricula, new textbooks, and teacher training are all in the works. How widespread will these changes be? How lasting? These are the questions we must ask ourselves now. And the answers depend largely on the willingness of those of us engaged in science education to rediscover that science is the channeling of wonder into a learned process of real-world investigation.

Problems and Extensions

1. Design a K–12 scope and sequence of science goals. The scope and sequence should delineate elementary, middle, and high school, and show the connection and articulation of goals across the three grade groupings.
2. Find two textbooks in your field (e.g., biology, chemistry, earth science, or physics) and examine them in light of the *National Science Education Standards*. To what extent are the *Standards* used as a framework for the text? What is the role of inquiry in the texts? What is overall assessment of the two books with respect to their integration of the *Standards*? Which book would you use?
3. Design a time line of events in the history of science teaching in the last two centuries. Consider three concurrent historical timelines: science, technology, and science education. Plot the events on adding machine tape or some other material. Line the separate timelines up so that you can compare and contrast them across content areas.

Notes

1. See Lee F. Anderson, "A Rationale for Global Education," in *Global Education: From Thought to Action*, ed. Kenneth A. Tye (Alexandria, Va.: Association for Supervision and Curriculum Development, 1990).

2. Paul Dehart Hurd, "Modernizing Science Education," *Journal of Research in Science Teaching* 39, no. 1 (2002): 3–9.

3. For further details, see Iris R. Weiss, *Report of the 2000 National Survey of Science and Mathematics Instruction* (Chapel Hill, N.C.: Horizon Research, Inc., 2001).

4. See R. A. Cohen, "A Match or Not a Match: A Study of Intermediate Science Teaching Materials," in *The Science Curriculum*, ed. A. B. Champagne and L. E. Hornig (Washington, D.C.: American Association for the Advancement of Science, 1987), pp. 35–60.

5. Audrey B. Champagne and Leslie E. Hornig, *The Science Curriculum* (Washington, D.C.: American Association for the Advancement of Science, 1987), pp. 1–12.

6. National Commission on Excellence in Education, *A Nation at Risk* (Washington, D.C.: U.S. Department of Education, 1983), p. 1.

7. Ibid., p. 1.

8. National Science Teachers Association, *Scope, Sequence, and Coordination Project* (Washington, D.C.: NSTA, 1990).

9. National Research Council, *Fulfilling the Promise: Biology Education in the Nation's Schools* (Washington, D.C.: National Academy Press, 1990).

10. *Earth Science Education for the 21st Century* (Alexandria, Va.: American Geological Institute, 1990).

11. National Council of Teachers of Mathematics, *Professional Standards for Teaching Mathematics* (Preston, Va.: 1991).

12. F. James Rutherford, *Science for All Americans: A Project 2061* (New York: Oxford University Press, 1991).

13. Ibid., p. 20.

14. Ibid., pp. 12–13.

15. G. Bugliarello, *Physical and Information Sciences and Engineering: Report of the Project 2061 Phase I Physical and Information Sciences and Engineering Panel* (Washington, D.C.: American Association for the Advancement of Science, 1989).

16. *Biological and Health Sciences, A Project 2061 Panel Report* (Washington, D.C.: American Association for the Advancement of Science, 1989).

17. *Technology, A Project 2061 Panel Report* (Washington, D.C.: American Association for the Advancement of Science, 1989).

18. Ibid., p. 23.

19. *Science for All Americans*, p. 161.

20. F. J. Rutherford, A. Ahlgren, and J. Merz, "Project 2061: Education for a Changing Future," in *The Science Curriculum*, ed. A. B. Champangne and L. E. Hornig (Washington, D.C.: American Association for the Advancement of Science, 1987), pp. 61–65.

21. *Project 2061: Science for All Americans* (Washington, D.C.: American Association for the Advancement of Science, 1989).

22. *Scope, Sequence, and Coordination of Secondary Science: A Rationale* (Washington, D.C.: National Science Teachers Association, 1990).

23. Ibid., p. 1.

24. Ibid., pp. 8–9.

25. *Inquiry and the National Science Education Standards* (Washington, D.C.: National Academy Press, 2000), p. xv.

26. Ibid.

27. *What Research Says to the Science Teacher: Problem Solving*, vol. 5 (Washington, D.C.: National Science Teachers Association, 1989).

28. The implications are based on a paper describing a planning conference on research and science teaching held at and sponsored by the Lawrence Hall of Science, Berkeley, California, and the National Science Foundation. See M. C. Linn, "Establishing a Research Base for Science Education: Challenges, Trends and Recommendations," *Journal of Research in Science Teaching* 24, no. 3 (1987): 191–216.

29. P. D. Hurd, *Biological Education in American Schools, 1890–1960* (Washington, D.C.: American Institute of Biological Sciences, 1961), pp. 16–17.

30. Lawrence A. Cremin, *The Transformation of the School* (New York: Vintage Books, 1964), p. 133.

31. G. S. Craig, *Certain Techniques Used in Developing a Course of Study in Science for the Horance Mann Elementary School* (New York: Columbia University Press, Teachers College, 1927).

32. Carlton H. Stedman, "Fortuitous Strategies on Inquiry in the 'Good Ole Days,' " *Science Education* 71, no. 5: 657–65.

33. Ibid.

34. Ibid.

35. Ibid.

36. Ibid.

37. Gerald S. Craig et al., *A Program for Teaching Science* (Chicago: National Society for the Study of Education, 1932).

38. Ibid.

39. Hurd, *Biological Education in American Secondary Schools*, pp. 57–58.

40. Ibid.

41. Commission on Secondary School Curriculum, *Science in General Education* (New York: Appleton-Century, 1938).

42. J. Dewey, *Experience and Education* (New York: Collier Books, 1938), pp. 33–34.

43. See Cremin, *The Transformation of the School*.

44. A. A. Glatthorn, *Curriculum Leadership* (Glenview, Ill.: Scott, Foresman and Company, 1987), p. 39.

45. National Society for the Study of Education, *Forty-Sixth Yearbook of the National Society: Science Education in American Schools* (Chicago: University of Chicago Press, 1947).

46. P. D. Hurd, *New Directions in Teaching Secondary School Science* (Chicago: Rand McNally and Company, 1970), pp. 1–2.

47. Ibid., p. 2.

48. J. M. England, *A Patron for Pure Science: The National Science Foundation's Formative Years, 1945–57* (Washington, D.C.: National Science Foundation, 1982), p. 248.

49. Ibid., P. 238.

50. Ibid., p. 238.

51. *Physical Science Study Committee Physics* (Boston: D.C. Heath, 1960), p. 627.

52. England, *A Patron for Pure Science*, p. 237.

53. Ibid., pp. 247–48.

54. J. Sealy, "Curriculum Development Projects of the Sixties," *R & D Interpretation Service Bulletin, Science* (Charleston, W.Va.: Appalachia Educational Laboratory, 1985).

55. Hurd, *New Directions in Teaching Secondary School Science*, p. 15.

56. Ibid., p. 27.

57. Ibid., p. 31.

58. Ibid., p. 31.

59. See J. Bruner, *The Process of Education* (Cambridge, MA: Harvard University Press, 1963), Chapter 6.

60. Hurd, *New Directions in Teaching Secondary School Science*, p. 34.

61. D. Nelkin, *Science Textbook Controversies and the Politics of Equal Time* (Cambridge, Mass.: The MIT Press, 1977), p. 41.

62. Ibid., p. 112.

63. Ibid., p. 112.

64. Ibid., p. 114.

65. Ibid., p. 114.

66. Ibid., p. 114.

67. R. E. Yager, "Fifty Years of Science Education, 1950–2000," in *Third Sourcebook for Science Supervisors*, ed. L. L. Motz and G. M. Madrazo, Jr. (Washington, D.C.: National Science Teachers Association, 1988), pp. 15–21.

68. S. L. Helgeson, P. E. Blosser, and R. W. Howe, *The Status of Pre-College Science, Mathematics, and Social Science Education: 1955–75* (Columbus, Ohio: Center for Science and Mathematics Education, Ohio State University, 1977).

69. I. R. Weiss, *Report of the 1977 National Survey of Science, Mathematics, and Social Studies Education: Center for Educational Research and Evaluation* (Washington, D.C.: U.S. Government Printing Office, 1978).

70. R. E. Stake and J. Easley, *Case Studies in Science Education* (Urbana, Ill.: Center for Instructional Research and Curriculum Evaluation, University of Illinois, 1978).

71. Yager, *Fifty Years of Science Education*, p. 18.

72. Nelkin, *Science Textbook Controversies*, p. 29.

73. Ibid., p. 29.

74. H. Morris, "Creation and Evolution," *American Biology Teacher* (March 1973).

75. Nelkin, *Science Textbook Controversies*, p. 83.

76. Ibid., p. 85.

77. National Commission on Excellence in Education, *A Nation at Risk* (Washington, D.C.: U.S. Department of Education, 1983), p. 5.

78. Ibid., p. 5.

79. Ibid., pp. 8–9.

80. For a full analysis and critique of various commission reports of 1983, see D. Tanner, "The American High School at the Crossroads," *Educational Leadership* (March 1984): 4–13.

81. National Commission on Excellence in Education, *A Nation at Risk*, p. 25.

82. Ibid., p. 26.

83. National Science Board, *Educating Americans for the 21st Century* (Washington, D.C.: National Science Foundation, 1983), p. 5.

84. Tanner, "The American High School at the Crossroads," p. 8.

85. National Science Board, *Educating Americans*, p. v.

86. Tanner, "The American High School at the Crossroads," p. 8.

87. National Science Board, *Educating Americans* (Washington, D.C.: National Science Foundation, 1983), p. 5.

88. Ibid., p. v.

89. Additional reports issued from 1982 through 1984 included: (1) Task Force on Education for Economic Growth, *Action for Excellence: A Comprehensive Plan to Improve Our Nation's Schools* (Denver, Colo.: Education Commission of the States, 1983); (2) J. I. Goodlad, *A Place Called School* (New York: McGraw-Hill, 1984); (3) E. L. Boyer, *High School: A Report on Secondary Education in America* (New York: Harper & Row, 1982); (4) M. Adler, *The Paideia Proposal* (New York: Macmillan Publishing Company, 1982); (5) College Examination Board, *Academic Preparation for College: What Students Need to Know and Be Able to Do* (New York: The College Board, 1983).

90. J. Krajcik, R. Mamlok, and B. Hug, "Modern Content of the Enterprise of Science: Science Education in the Twentieth Century," in *Education across a Century* (Chicago: University of Chicago Press, 2000), pp. 205–37.

91. National Research Council, *National Science Education Standards* (Washington, D.C.: National Academy Press, 1995), pp. 4–5.

92. Krajcik, Mamlok, and Hug, "Modern Content of the Enterprise," p. 220.

93. Project 2061, *Blueprints for Reform* (New York: Oxford University Press, 1998), p. 7.

94. Ibid., p. 3.

95. Project 2061, *Benchmarks for Scientific Literacy* (New York: Oxford University Press, 1994), pp. 1–5.

96. Jack Hassard and Julie Weisberg, "The Emergence of Global Thinking Among American and Russian Youth as a Contribution to Public Understanding," *International Journal of Science Education* (1999): 1–13.

97. Based on L. Loeppke, "Back to the Future with Science Education," *Science Books and Films* 24, no. 4 (March/April 1989): 194, 262. Used with permission.

Readings

Archambault, Reginald D. *John Dewey on Education*. New York: The Modern Library, 1964.

DeBoer, George E. *A History of Ideas in Science Education: Implications for Practice*. New York: Teachers College Press, 1991.

Duschl, Richard A. *Restructuring Science Education*. New York: Teachers College Press, 1990.

Eich, Charles J. "The Democratic Classroom." *Science Scope*, 24 (November 2001): 27–31.

Hurd, Paul DeHart. *Inventing Science Education for the New Millennium*. New York: Teachers College Press, 1997.

Leonard, William, Penick, John, and Douglas, Rowena. "What Does It Mean to Be Standards-Based?" *The Science Teacher*, 26 (April 2002): 36–39.

Llewellyn, Douglas. *Inquire Within: Implementing Inquiry-Based Science Standards*. Arlington, Va.: National Science Teachers Association, 2001.

National Research Council. *National Science Education Standards*. Washington, D.C.: National Academy Press, 1995.

National Research Council. *Inquiry and the National Science Education Standards*. Washington, D.C.: National Academy Press, 2000.

Project 2061. *Blueprints for Reform*. New York: Oxford University Press, 1998.

Lawery, Lawrence, Texley, Juliana, and Wild, Ann, eds. *Pathways to the Science Standards—Elementary Grades K–8*. Arlington, Va.: NSTA Press, 2000.

Rakow, Stephen, Texley, Juliana, Reynold, Karen, and Lawery, Lawrence. *Pathways to the Science Standards—Middle Level, Grades 5–12*. Arlington, Va.: NSTA Press, 2000.

Texley, Juliana, and Wild, Ann, eds. *Pathways to the Science Standards—High School, Grades 9–12*. Arlington, Va.: NSTA Press, 1996.

On the Web

Parrott's Science Education Time Line: http://scied.gsu.edu/Hassard/parrott_timeline.html. Annette Parrott has developed a timeline comparing the developments in science, technology, and science education from antiquity to the present. Her emphasis on multicultural contributions makes this a very interesting site to visit.

Project 2061: http://www.project2061.org/default.htm. Visit the home page of Project 2061 and connect to links that allow you to read their publications online, including *Science for All Americans*, *Benchmarks*, and *Blueprints for Reform*.

The *National Science Education Standards* Online: http://books.nap.edu/html/nses/html/index.html. This site will enable you to have access to the complete published version of the *Standards*.

Scope, Sequence, and Coordination Project: http://www.nsta.org. At this site you will find teaching and learning resources that emerged as a result of the project. You will find detailed lesson plans, investigations, and student handouts for activities in life and physical science.

Thinkers in Education: http://www.ibe.unesco.org/International/Publications/Thinkers/thinhome.htm. A series of profiles of 100 famous educators (philosophers, statesmen, politicians, journalists, psychologists, poets, and men and women of religion) drawn from many parts of the world.

Gallery of Educational Theorists: http://www.newfoundations.com/GALLERY/Gallery.html. This gallery of profiles on educational thinkers will provide you with insight on theorists including Adler, Confucius, Dewey, Gardner, Piaget, Plato, Sartre, and Vygotsky.

Science in the School Curriculum

In this chapter we will explore the K–12 science curriculum by focusing first on the curriculum of elementary schools, middle schools, and high schools. Then we'll turn our attention to the science curriculum perspectives in several countries. You have discovered from the last chapter that the science curriculum evolved over the twentieth century as a result of social, political, economic, and educational forces. Focusing on the science curriculum early in your study of science teaching will give you the big picture—a holistic view, if you will—of science in the school curriculum. From this vantage point, the methods, strategies, and development of lesson plans and management techniques can be viewed in the context of this larger framework.

 Case Study: A National Science Curriculum

The Case

James Goldrich is a prominent science educator who is the chief education officer of the prestigious American Science Commission on Education. In a recent international study it was concluded that Japan, China, and the Russia had a strong national commitment to science and mathematics education. Goldrich, an advocate of a rigorous, compulsory national science curriculum for American youth, said the following in a major American newspaper:

> The United States has no comparable commitment to science and mathematics education. To ignore the fact that these countries (Japan, China, and Russia), whose history,

resources, politics, economics, and culture are so different, have made strong national commitments to science and mathematics, is to be left behind. To assume our ways are better is to be arrogant.

Goldrich went on to say that science education in the United States should involve national leadership, national planning, and national policy making.

The Problem

Should the United States have a national science curriculum? Do you agree or disagree with Goldrich? Why? Is the American decentralized system of education an ineffective model? Should the United States move toward a more centralized system? Do the *National Science Education Standards* represent a "national curriculum"?

How to Read This Chapter

The chapter is divided into sections on science standards and curriculum as well as separate sections on elementary, middle, and high school science, and then a section on science education in Australia, Chile, China, Ghana, Japan, and Russia. You can focus on each section separately, depending on your interests. You might, for example, take a look at a description of science education in a country of your interest and compare it to your knowledge of science education in the United States. Several inquiry activities are presented to help you investigate various curriculum projects and curricula at the elementary, middle, and high school levels. Complete one of the inquiries and then go back and re-read the sections on your area of expertise.

SECTION 1: THE SCIENCE CURRICULUM

Invitations to Inquiry

- What is meant by the term *curriculum*?
- What should be the nature of the elementary, middle, and high school science curriculum as outlined by the *National Science Education Standards*?
- What was the influence of school science curriculum reform projects of the 1960s and how did they differ from the programs of the 1990s?
- What are the characteristics of exemplary elementary, middle, and high school science programs?
- What is the nature of the contemporary high school science curriculum?
- What were the characteristics of the high school science curriculum reform projects of the twentieth century and how have they influenced curriculum today?
- What are the characteristics of exemplary high school science programs?
- What are the science curriculum patterns in other nations?
- How does the science curriculum of the United States compare with the science curriculum in other nations?

The Curriculum: What Is It?

First, what is the curriculum? The curriculum is more than a textbook, a series of textbooks, or a curriculum guide. The curriculum includes the goals, objectives, conceptual themes, day-to-day learning activities, ancillary materials (e.g., films, videos, computer programs), and evaluation. You might think of the curriculum from three vantage points: the experience of the student, of the teacher, and of an observer. It is quite possible for the curriculum to be perceived one way by the teacher, experienced quite differently by the student, and reported in a third manner by an observer. Curriculum takes place in an environment—(formally in schools or in informal settings such as zoos (see Figure 4.1) or planetariums—and, no matter what the environment is, it will influence the curriculum in a variety of ways. For the sake of communication, we will use the following definition of curriculum:

The curriculum is the plans made for guiding learning in schools, usually described in documents (textbooks, curriculum guides, course syllabi, lesson plans) of several levels of generality, and the execution of those plans in the classroom, as experienced by learners; those experiences take place in a learning environment (classroom, laboratory, outdoors) which also influences what is learned.[1]

As you read about and discuss the science curriculum, realize that the science curriculum can only be fully appreciated in the context of real schools, teachers, and students.

In the study of the science curriculum, the impact of the teacher cannot be overlooked. Even with descriptions of course outlines for yearlong courses or school system curriculum guides for K–12 programs, curriculum is in actuality a dynamic concept involving interaction patterns among teachers, students, and learning experiences. I have divided this chapter into three major sections, each dealing with a part of the K–12 science curriculum as follows: the elementary science curriculum, the middle school science curriculum, and the high school science curriculum. Within each section you find a connection to the *National Science Education Standards* as well as a discussion of the curriculum and examples of curriculum projects. As you explore this chapter you might consider: How does the teacher influence the curriculum? How will you influence the curriculum? How do the students influence the curriculum? How does your philosophy of education influence the curriculum? What kind of science curriculum will you create in your classroom? What evidence is there that the science standards (state or national) are having an impact on the curriculum? We'll start our exploration of the science curriculum by briefly introducing the standards.

The Science Standards and the School Science Curriculum

According to the developers of the *National Science Education Standards*, the standards were designed to provide guidance to educators to create a scientifically literate society. In essence the *standards* describes a vision of the "scientifically literate" person and presents criteria for science education that will allow that vision to become a reality.

In each of the discussions of elementary, middle and high school science that follows you will find the standards that relate to the teaching of science at that level. This should be practical for you, and you will be able to make use of these ideas as you develop your own lesson plans and units of teaching.

The content standards have been divided into the following grade level categories: K–4, 5–8 and 9–12. In

Figure 4.1 The science curriculum can be part of informal environments such as a zoo. Zoos and other informal environments provide opportunities for students to gain understanding and experience with science in a natural setting. *Source:* Photodisc.

the sections that follow, the K–4 standards will appear in the section on elementary science, the 5–8 standards will define middle school science, and the 9–12 standards will describe high school science outcomes.

Goals Underlying the Standards

The standards are based on a set of overarching goals that we should keep in mind as we explore the science curriculum. Basically, the goal is to educate students who

- Are able to experience the richness and excitement of knowing about and understanding the natural world;
- Use appropriate scientific processes and principles in making personal decisions;
- Engage intelligently in public discourse and debate about matters of scientific and technological concern; and
- Increase their economic productivity through the use of the knowledge, understanding, and skills of the scientifically literate person in their careers.

Organization of the Content Standards

The content standards, K–12, are organized into the following areas:

1. Unifying Concepts and Processes Standard
2. Science as Inquiry Standards
3. Physical Science,
4. Life Science, and
5. Earth and Space Science Standards
6. Science and Technology Standards
7. Science in Personal and Social Perspectives Standards
8. History and Nature of Science Standards

UNIFYING CONCEPTS AND PROCESSES STANDARD
This standard unifies the disciplines and describes processes that students learn across grade levels. The unifying concepts and processes include:

- Systems, order, and organization
- Evidence, models, and explanation

Table 4.1 Science as Inquiry Standards

Levels K–4	Levels 5–8	Levels 9–12
Abilities necessary to do scientific inquiry	Abilities necessary to do scientific inquiry	Abilities necessary to do scientific inquiry
Understanding about scientific inquiry	Understanding about scientific inquiry	Understanding about scientific inquiry

Source: National Science Education Standards.

Table 4.2 Life Science Standards across Grade Levels

Levels K–4	Levels 5–8	Levels 9–12
Characteristics of organisms	Structure and function in living systems	The cell
Life cycles of organisms	Reproduction and heredity	Molecular basis of heredity
Organisms and environments	Regulation and behavior	Biological evolution
	Population and ecosystems	Interdependence of organisms
	Diversity and adaptations of organisms	Matter, energy, and organization in living systems
		Behavior of organisms

Source: National Science Education Standards.

Table 4.3 Science and Technology Standards

Levels K–4	Levels 5–8	Levels 9–12
Abilities to distinquish between natural objects and objects made by humans	Abilities of technological design	Abilities of technological design
Abilities of technological design	Understanding about science and technology	Understanding about science and technology
Understanding about science and technology		

Source: National Science Education Standards.

- Change, constancy, and measurement
- Evolution and equilibrium
- Form and function

SCIENCE AS INQUIRY STANDARD Science as inquiry is the fundamental concept in the science standards and highlights the idea that students should learn how to do science inquiry and develop an understanding about scientific inquiry.[2] Students at all grade levels (see Table 4.1) should have opportunities to use inquiry and develop the ability to think in ways that are inquiry oriented, such as asking questions about science phenomena, planning and carrying out experiments, gathering and analyzing data, and communicating what they have learned.

PHYSICAL, LIFE, AND EARTH SPACE SCIENCE STANDARDS These standards define the subject matter of science using three widely accepted divisions of science. Science subject matter focuses on the science facts, concepts, principles, theories, and models that are important for all students to know, understand, and use. These subject matter areas begin in K–4 science curriculum and extend through grades 9–12. Table 4.2 shows the progression of life science content throughout the K–12 curriculum.

SCIENCE AND TECHNOLOGY These standards focus on students' abilities to develop decision-making abilities. These are not standards for technology, but rather for the process of design and how students can use science to solve problems (Table 4.3).

SCIENCE IN PERSONAL AND SOCIAL PERSPECTIVES These standards emphasize personal and social responsibility on important issues that affect students and their community. Table 4.4 identifies key personal and social issues across the grade level.

HISTORY AND NATURE OF SCIENCE This standard emphasizes the history of science and its role in the development and understanding of science.

Table 4.4 Personal and Social Issues

Levels K–4	Levels 5–8	Levels 9–12
Personal health	Personal health	Personal and community health
Characteristics and changes in populations	Populations, resources, and environments	Population growth
Types of resources	Natural hazards	Naturual resources
Changes in environments	Risks and benefits	Environmental quality
Science and technology in local challenges	Science and technology in society	Natural and human-induced hazards
		Science and technology in local, national, and global challenges

Source: National Science Education Standards.

The Elementary Science Curriculum

Although you are going to be a secondary science teacher, knowing about the elementary science curriculum will be important in that each of your students will have experienced an elementary science curriculum. In the elementary school, science is taught about twenty-seven minutes per day in grades K–3 and thirty-seven minutes per day in grades 4–6.[3] As can be seen in Table 4.5, elementary teachers engage their students in a variety of activities. However, only one activity was reported by more than half of the teachers in the study, an indication that science is not taught on a daily basis in most elementary schools.

However, some activities, including doing hands-on/laboratory science and following specific instructions in an activity, were reported more frequently than other activities. Also significant in this report are the least frequently used activities, which were common across all of the grade levels. These included:

- work on extended science investigations or projects;
- design or implement their *own* investigation;
- use computers as a tool;
- participate in field work;
- take field trips; and
- make formal presentations to the rest of the class

Elementary science teaching has been influenced by the value that schools place on teaching science at this level. Over the years, science at the elementary level has often been taught in the afternoon on alternate days (with social studies). In most elementary schools major emphasis is given to reading, language arts, and mathematics.

Influential Elementary Science Projects

However, elementary science has also been influenced by national reports such as the *Standards* and *Benchmarks*

Table 4.5 Science Classes Where Teachers (K–4) Reported That Students Take Part in Various Instructional Activities at Least Once a Week

Activity	Percentage of Classes
Work in groups	64
Do hands-on/laboratory science activities or investigations	50
Follow specific instructions in an activity or investigation	46
Read other (nontextbook) science-related materials in class	44
Read from a science textbook in class	31
Watch a science demonstration	30
Record, represent, and/or analyze data	29
Answer textbook or worksheet questions	28
Use mathematics as a tool in problem solving	24
Write reflections (e.g., in a journal)	22
Watch audiovisual presentations (e.g., videotapes, CD-ROMs, videodiscs, television programs, films, or filmstrips)	18
Listen and take notes during presentation by teacher	15
Work on extended science investigations or projects (a week or more in duration)	9
Design or implement their *own* investigation	8
Use computers as a tool (e.g., spreadsheets, data analysis)	6
Participate in field work	5
Take field trips	5
Prepare written science reports	4
Make formal presentations to the rest of the class	3

Source: Based on Weiss, I. R. *Report of the 2000 National Survey of Science and Mathematics Education.* Chapel Hill, N.C.: Horizon Research, Inc., pp. 47–48.

for Scientific Literacy, and by the development of elementary science curriculum projects since the early 1960s. Three projects that have influenced current curriculum project efforts at the elementary school level are explored next.

SCIENCE—A PROCESS APPROACH (SAPA) SAPA emphasized an elementary science program (K–6) that developed process skills of science, including observing, classifying, using space/time relations, using numbers, communicating, measuring, predicting, and inferring. At the upper grade levels, additional process skills included formulating hypotheses, controlling variables, experimenting, defining operationally, formulating models, and interpreting data. SAPA had an elaborate scheme for its curriculum and each lesson was based on a set of behavioral objectives and very specific activities for teachers to carry out with their students. The program had no textbooks. All of the materials and lesson plans (booklet sized) were contained using the "science kit" approach.

ELEMENTARY SCIENCE STUDY (ESS) ESS comprised fifty-six units in a nonsequential organization, each containing activities and explorations that could be infused into an ongoing elementary science curriculum or be used as the science curriculum. The ESS teaching materials had an "open-ended and creative flair" and were used by educators that supported a "discovery approach" to teaching and learning. The ESS materials were organized as science kits (with a teacher's guide and hands-on materials), or as booklets (with no hands-on materials provided). The titles of some of the ESS units will give you an idea of the scope of the materials: Batteries and Bulbs, Gases and Airs, Kitchen Physics, Sink and Float, Daytime Astronomy, Mystery Powders, and Pond Water.

SCIENCE CURRICULUM IMPROVEMENT STUDY (SCIS) SCIS was a K–6 program that integrated the process approach of SAPA with the content of science. The program built around twelve instructional units based on a major concept. The program was organized into two content themes: physical/earth science and life/earth science sequence. The teaching of lessons in SCIS was based on a three-stage learning cycle, including the "exploration" phase, followed by the "invention" phase, and concluding with the "discovery" phase. SCIS materials were organized into science kits by grade level as follows: Grade 1, Materials Objects and Organisms; Grade 2, Interactions and Systems, and Life Cycles; Grade 3, Subsystems and Variables, and

Populations; Grade 4, Relative Position and Motion, and Environments; Grade 5, Energy Sources and Communities; Grade 6, Scientific Theories and Ecosystems.

Standards for Elementary Science

During the 1990s, the reform movements influenced elementary science as in middle and high school science. What should the curriculum be in the elementary school? According to the *Standards*, elementary science should be inquiry oriented and include content drawn from the standards for physical science, life science, and earth and space science (Table 4.6).

Physical science at the elementary level should include physics and chemistry. The *Standards* puts emphasis on properties of objects and materials; position and motion of objects; and light, heat, electricity, and magnetism.

Life science would include topics including health, botany, zoology, and environmental/ecology. The *Standards* emphasize the characteristics of organisms, life cycles of organisms, and organisms and environments.

Earth and space science at the elementary level includes geology, meteorology, oceanography, and astronomy. The *Standards* for earth and space science focus on properties of earth materials, objects in the sky, and changes in earth and sky.

Another area of emphasis in elementary science is STS (science-technology-society, see Chapter 11). Topics in STS focus on personal and social responsibility and include personal health, characteristics and changes in populations, types of resources, changes in environments, and science and technology in local challenges.

Exemplary Elementary Science Curriculum Projects

MARINE SCIENCE PROJECT: FOR SEA Focusing on the development of basic science skills and knowledge, FOR SEA provides interdisciplinary, activity-oriented marine education curriculum and teacher training.[4] The magic draw of water provides incentive to teach and learn science. FOR SEA has been used successfully as a core curriculum and has likewise proven effective in a thematic/unit teaching strategy. Close proximity to seawater is not necessary to implement this curriculum in the classroom. Curriculum guides are available for grades 1–2, 3–4, and 5–6. Each guide contains teacher background for each activity, student activity and text pages, answer keys for student materials, and a listing of vocabulary words. FOR SEA is designed to be implemented in classrooms at a room, grade, school, or

Table 4.6 Content Standards for Elementary Science

Content Standard Categories	Standard: As a result of activities in K–4, all students should:	Examples
Unifying Concept and Processes	Develop abilities aligned with the following concepts and processes: 1. Systems, order, and organization 2. Evidence, models, and explanation 3. Change, constancy, and measurement 4. Evolution and equilibrium, form and function	To develop conceptual and process knowledge about models, students can design and construct schemes or structures that correspond to real objects, events, or classes of events and use them to explain the scheme. Examples could include the construction of bridges with plastic straws, constructing volcanoes with various materials, and building a cell and its structures with food items.
Science as Inquiry: Content Standard A	1. Abilities necessary to do scientific inquiry 2. Understanding about scientific inquiry	Asking a question about objects, organisms, and events in the environment.
Physical Science: Content Standard B	1. Properties of objects and materials 2. Position and motion of objects 3. Light, heat, electricity, and magnetism	Asking students to describe and manipulate objects by pushing, pulling, throwing, dropping, and rolling. They also begin to focus on the position and movement of objects.
Life Science: Content Standard C	1. Characteristics of organisms 2. Life cycles of organisms 3. Organisms and environments	Designing activities that result in students asking questions such as: How do plants get food? How many different animals are there? Why do some animals eat other animals? What is the largest plant? Where did the dinosaurs go?
Earth and Space Sciences: Content Standard D	1. Properties of earth materials 2. Objects in the sky 3. Changes in earth and sky	By taking students to playgrounds and areas close to the school (parks), activities can be designed for them to observe a variety of earth materials; they can collect and observe rocks and vegetation and in so doing begin to see differences in soil from one area to another.
Science and Technology: Content Standard E	1. Abilities of technological design 2. Understanding about science and technology 3. Ability to distinguish between natural objects and objects made by humans	Having student construct a collection of weather instruments (rain gauge, anemometer, barometer) and use them to collect data are ways to show them how technological ideas are related to science inquiry.
Science in Personal and Social Perspectives: Content Standard F	Develop an understanding of: 1. Personal health 2. Characteristics and changes in populations 3. Types of resources 4. Changes in environments 5. Science and technology in local challenges	Activities can be designed to help students understand how the body uses food and how various foods contribute to health. Students can create daily menus of the food they ate and compare it to standards they are learning.
History and Nature of Science: Content Standard G	Develop an understanding of: 1. Science as a human endeavor	Teachers can use books, videos, and the Web to bring to the students "stories" of historical women and men (including minorities and people with disabilities) who have made contributions to science.

Source: National Science Education Standards.

district-wide level. In-service training provides implementing teachers with an overview of the program, implementation procedures, and hands-on activity sessions to familiarize participants with activities appropriate for their specific grade levels. Curriculum units are also available for grades 6–8 and 9–12.[5]

GREAT EXPLORATIONS IN MATH AND SCIENCE (GEMS) The Lawrence Hall of Science, University of California, Berkeley, has produced a series of more than seventy curriculum units based on successful programs conducted at the Hall. GEMS is packaged as a series of teacher's guides that detail the lessons for each unit.

Each unit focuses on a main topic, such as paper towel testing, and then develops skills and themes around the topic. For example in the Unit Paper Towel Testing, students are involved in designing controlled experiments, measuring, recording, calculating and interpreting data, while as the same time finding out about consumer science, absorbency, wet strength, unit pricing, cost-benefit analysis, and decision making.

Some of the units in the GEMS program include:

- Paper Towel Testing
- Chemical Reactions
- Discovering Density
- Animals in Action
- Ocean Currents
- Only One Ocean
- The Moons of Jupiter
- Acid Rain
- Global Warming and the Greenhouse Effect

Each of the GEMS units uses unique materials and activities to involve students in discovery activities. For example, in the Chemical Reactions unit, students observe chemical changes (bubbles, changes in color and heat) in a Ziploc bag. Students observe changes and design experiments to explain their observations.

The GEMS units are excellent models for infusion into the ongoing science curriculum. The developers have also alighted the GEMS materials to the *National Science Education Standards* as well many state-level standards.[6]

SCIENCE FOR LIFE AND LIVING: INTEGRATING SCIENCE, TECHNOLOGY, AND HEALTH (SFLL)
SFLL is a K–6 curriculum that integrates science as a way of knowing, technology as a way of doing, and health as a way of behaving into a full-year, activity-based elementary school science program. The program is organized around major concepts and skills that connect the hands-on activities in science, technology, and health. The program promotes the development of important concepts in science, technology, and health; encourages personal application of the concepts and skills; and fosters life-long learning through conceptual understanding and skill development.

Using an integrated approach, SFLL helps students and teachers understand and relate the broad themes of science (also referred to as "unifying concepts and processes" in the *National Science Education Standards*), such as order and organization, change and measurement, patterns and predictions, systems and analysis, energy and investigation, and balance and decisions,

Table 4.7 The SFLL Five-Stage Learning Cycle

Stage of Learning	Function and Nature of Student Activity
One: Engage	These activities mentally engage the student with an event or a question. Engagement activities help the students make connections with what they already know and can do.
Two: Explore	Students work with each other and explore ideas together, usually through hands-on activities. Under the guidance of the teacher, students clarify their understanding of major concepts and skills.
Three: Explain	Students explain their understanding of the concepts and processes they are learning. Teachers clarify their understanding and introduce and define new concepts and skills.
Four: Elaborate	During these activities, students apply what they have learned to new situations and build on their understanding of concepts. Students use these new experiences to extend their knowledge and skills.
Five: Evaluate	Students assess their own knowledge, skills, and abilities. These activities also focus on outcomes that a teacher can use to evaluate student progress.

Source: Based on *New Designs for Elementary School Science and Health, Biological Sciences Curriculum Study.* Dubuque, Iowa: Kendall/Hunt, 1989, pp. 36–39.

through motivating "hands-on, minds-on" activities. The SFLL emphasizes cooperative learning, a five-stage learning cycle (Table 4.7), and major concepts in science, student-centered approach and constructivist learning.[7]

The Middle School Science Curriculum

Up until the late 1960s, the dominant attendance pattern for early adolescent students (ages 11–14) was the junior high school, typically grouped in grades 7, 8, and 9. The first middle school opened in Bay City, Michigan, in 1950.[8] Middle schools didn't emerge on the American school scene until the 1960s, and then grew rapidly in the 1970s and 1980s. Middle schools dominate the educational organization of early adolescents today and, in most cases, schools comprise grades 6, 7, and 8 (some arrangements of middle schools also include 7–8 or 7–9).

As discussed earlier, the junior high school emerged in the period 1910–1920. For many years, the science curriculum of the junior high school consisted of three years of general science. General science programs generally included units at each grade level in physics, chemistry, biology, geology, meteorology, and astronomy.

Influential Middle School Projects

In the 1960s, several curriculum reform projects were developed that influenced the junior high science curriculum. Because the junior high was the typical pattern in American school systems for the early adolescent, these reform projects were geared for junior high schools, not middle schools. Let's look very briefly at three projects that had a powerful impact on middle and junior high science for many years.

INTRODUCTORY PHYSICAL SCIENCE (IPS) The typical junior high science course in the 1960s was general science in which students studied a variety of topics: chemistry, climate, geology, and physics. A new course proposed by developers at Educational Services Incorporated in Watertown, Massachusetts, represented a radical departure from the "general science" approach (see Table 4.8). Instead, with funding from NSF, the developers created the IPS course around a central theme: the development of evidence for an atomic model of matter. All content in the IPS course was selected and organized to help students build the concept and then use the atomic model of matter to predict ideas about heat and molecular motion. In the IPS course students performed more than fifty experiments. The experiments were integrated into the text and were designed to involve the student in gathering data and testing hypotheses about the physical world.

Table 4.8 Comparison of General Science and IPS

General Science Curriculum	IPS
Grade 7	**Grade 7, 8, or 9**
Unit 1. Water (suggested time six weeks)	Chapter 1. Introduction
2. Rocks and Soil (six weeks)	2. Quantity of Matter
3. Air (seven weeks)	3. Characteristic Properties
4. Fire (six weeks)	4. Solubility and Solvents
5. Trees (six weeks)	5. The Separation of Substances
6. The Human Machine (five weeks)	6. Compounds and Elements
Grade 8	7. Radioactivity
1. Earth and Its Neighbors (four weeks)	8. The Atomic Model of Matter
2. Weather and Climate (five weeks)	9. Sizes and Masses of Atoms and Molecules
3. Water, Its Effects, and Its Uses (four weeks)	10. Molecular Motion
4. Gardening (seven weeks)	11. Heat
5. Safety and First Aid (nine weeks)	
Grade 9	Experiments (IPS contained over fifty experiments integrated into the chapters) Examples (chapter numbers are shown in parentheses):
1. Environment (two weeks)	• Distillation of Wood (1)
2. Air and Its Work (five weeks)	• Measuring Volume by Displacement of Water (2)
3. Water and Its Work (two weeks)	• Density of Solids (3)
4. Heat and Its Work (two weeks)	• Solubility of Ammonia Gas (4)
5. Light, Its Use, and Control (three weeks)	• Paper Chromatography (5)
6. Study of Industry (four weeks)	• Flame Test of Some Elements (6)
7. Use and Control of Energy in Transportation (two weeks)	• Effect of Some Substances on a Photographic Plate and on a Geiger Counter (7)
8. Use of Food by the Human Body (six weeks)	• A Black Box (8)
9. Nervous System (three weeks)	• Size and Mass of an Oleic Acid Molecule (9)
10. Safeguarding and Improving Life of Individual and Community (five weeks)	• Growing Small Crystals (10)
	• Heating Different Substances (11)

The course was also built on the assumption that students would need to utilize the skills of inquiry to develop the main concept. The hands-on experiments developed such inquiry skills as observing, predicting, and analyzing data. Student-obtained data were used to develop ideas about the matter and energy. The authors also believed that students would develop a better understanding of inquiry and science through in-depth study of a topic, as opposed to skipping from one topic to another.

THE EARTH SCIENCE CURRICULUM PROJECT (ESCP) This course was a radical departure from the contemporary earth science course, which was offered in either the eighth or ninth grade. At the time (1962), earth science was not a major curriculum offering in the junior high school. Some states, such as New York, Connecticut, and Massachusetts, had strong earth science programs and relied on textbooks that divided the earth science into geology, astronomy, and meteorology. Oceanography was not a major topic in these early earth science programs.

ESCP was developed by scientists (geologists, oceanographers, astronomers, meteorologists, paleontologists), high school teachers, and science educators. The project produced a student textbook, teacher's guide, film series, field guides, and a specialized equipment package. The ESCP approach to curriculum was designed to give students an understanding of earth processes, the methods of science, and what earth scientists do. The ESCP emphasized inquiry, discovery, and interpretation of student-obtained data. The laboratory activities, which during the field-testing phases appeared in a separate laboratory manual, were integrated into the ESCP textbook (*Investigating the Earth*). ESCP was organized around ten overarching themes (see Table 4.9).

A significant contribution of the ESCP course was the organization the content of the earth sciences. Typically, content is organized into traditional subject matter divisions (geology, meteorology, oceanography, and astronomy). Instead, the ESCP course was organized into four interdisciplinary units:

Unit I. The Dynamic Earth

- Chapters: The Changing Earth, Earth Materials, Earth Measurement, Earth Motions, Fields and Forces, Energy Flow

Unit II. Earth Cycles

- Chapters: Energy and Air Motions, Water in the Air, Waters of the Land, Water in Sea, Energy, Moisture and Climate, The Land Wears Away,

Table 4.9 ESCP Organizing Themes

Behavioral	Conceptual	Historical
Science as inquiry	Universality of change	Historical development and presentation
Comprehension of scale	Flow of energy in the universe	
Prediction	Adjustment to environmental change	
	Conservation of mass and energy in the universe	
	Earth systems in space and time	
	Uniformity of process: a key to interpreting the past	

Sediments and the Sea, Mountains from the Sea, Rocks Within Mountains, Interior of the Earth

Unit III. Earth's Biography

- Chapters: Time and Its Measurement, The Record in Rocks, Life—Present and Past, Development of a Continent, Evolution of Landscapes

Unit IV. Earth's Environment in Space

- Chapters: The Moon: A Natural Satellite, The Solar System, Stars As Other Suns, Stellar Evolution and Galaxies, The Universe and Its Origin

ESCP had a positive effect on the teaching of earth science in the United States. Interest in the earth sciences increased during the 1960s and 1970s and, as a result, earth science is an integral part of the middle school curriculum today.

INTERMEDIATE SCIENCE CURRICULUM STUDY (ISCS) Developed at Florida State University, ISCS was a three-year individualized science curriculum project for grades 7, 8, and 9. ISCS was designed to help junior high students develop an understanding of physical and biological principles of science, an understanding of science and the scientific process, and the ability to use the processes of science.

The ISCS program was an individualized curriculum. The text materials were written to guide students along at their own pace. In practice, most teachers organized students into small teams and each team moved along at its own pace. The students were led through the materials by being actively involved in hands-on experiments, answering questions posed in the text materials, and solving problems.

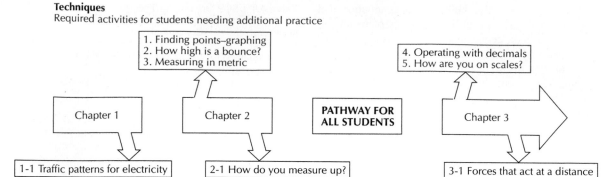

Figure 4.2 The ISCS was designed as an individualized science program in which students worked through the curriculum as depicted here.

Using material organized into core chapters and excursion activities (Figure 4.2), students were instructed to proceed through the text, completing activities and answering questions (in a separate science record book). Excursions, special activities referenced in the core chapters, were found in the back of the book. Theoretically, the student was invited to stop and do the excursion if it looked interesting or if it would help with the current chapter. In practice, teachers usually helped the students by suggesting which excursions were required and which were optional. The ISCS program offered junior high school a complete three-year science curriculum as follows:

Grade 7: Probing the Natural World (Volume 1)

- This grade focused on the development of the concept of energy and development of an operational definition of energy. The focus was on physics.

Grade 8: Probing the Natural World (Volume 2)

- This grade focused on chemistry, and students developed a particulate model for the nature of matter.

Grade 9: Eight Separate Books

- Why You're You (genetics)
- Environmental Problems (environmental science)
- Investigating Variation (biology)
- In Orbit (space science)
- What's Up? (astronomy)
- Crusty Problems (geology)
- Winds and Weather (meteorology)
- Well-Being (health science)

These programs, and other NSF curriculum projected aimed at the junior high school, influenced the nature of the curriculum for early adolescent students. The NSF reform projects tended to be discipline oriented (e.g., physics, physical science, earth science), whereas the typical junior high science program was three years of general science. By the late 1970s, general science was still the typical curriculum sequence (in 70 percent of schools), with 21 percent life science, 20 percent earth science, and 13 percent physical science. By 1986, the pattern was more evenly distributed across the content areas, with about 30 percent biology and life science, 22 percent earth science, 22 percent general science, and 21 percent physical science.

The results of studies that compared the effects of new junior high science curricula on student performance versus traditional science programs tended to favor the new science programs.[9] Physical science curricula produced positive effects on student performance in achievement and perceptions of science. Overall, the junior high programs produced positive effects in achievement (although not in each curriculum case), perceptions, and process skills. These programs did not do as well in analytic and related skills areas, however.

The Middle School Movement

The odds are that, if you are asked to observe or teach early adolescent students in your teacher education program, you will do so in a middle school. The middle school movement began with experimental or reform-minded junior high schools in the 1960s. Some of the early innovations included team teaching, modular and flexible scheduling, and interdisciplinary teaching practices. Wiles and Bondi point out that overenrollment and desegregation had as great an effect on the spread of the middle school movement as did curriculum theory or organizational planning.[10] By the mid-1970s, a number of national organizations began to focus on the educational problems and issues of the middle school learner. During this period, the National Middle School Association was formed, and, at annual meetings of organizations such as the National Science Teachers Association, an increasing number of workshops, seminars, and speeches were given on teaching middle school science. The literature on the middle school and the middle school learner exploded, and researchers began to pay attention to the special needs of the preadolescent. The National Science Teachers Association created a journal specific to middle school science called *Science Scope* and, in 1991, the National Science Middle School Teachers Association was formed.

Although junior high had been developed in the period 1910–1920 to respond to the special needs of the preadolescent student, the original child-centered focus was lost and junior high schools tended to resemble the high school in curriculum and organization of staff. The focus was on the content, not the child.[11]

The middle school educators of the 1970s and 1980s developed schools with a philosophy that responds to the needs of the preadolescent learner. This philosophy includes physical development, intellectual development, social-emotional development, and moral development. The middle school learner is an emerging adolescent, experiencing changes in each of these realms. The middle school philosophy establishes the rationale for creating a school environment that addresses these needs and changes. For example, this sample philosophy and goal statement, typical of contemporary middle schools, incorporates the needs of emerging adolescents to create a school that is flexible and exploratory, as well as designed to help students understand the content of the major disciplines, mature personally, and develop basic thinking skills.

> We believe that students who are making the transition from childhood to adolescence need a special learning environment. This environment should emphasize experiences that foster growth from dependent learners to independent learners. The middle school bridges the gap from elemntary school to the specialized subject-field approach of the high school with a progam that challenges all students intellectually while meeting the students' physical, emotional, social, and academic needs.
>
> - Provide an environment which combines for students a sense of security with the motiv-

ation to grow and become independent life-long learners.
- Vary instructional procedures to meet the student's changing needs caused by her/his developmental needs.
- Help students to work with others, and learn to appreciate and respect others as well as themselves.
- Provide opportunities for students of all abilities, interests, and backgrounds to develop fully as learners.
- Provide opportunities to explore new areas and to develop creativity.
- Provide experiences which will contribute to the development of values, standards, and self-esteem.
- Help students understand themselves and make good decisions.[12]

The organization of the middle school provides for the transition from the self-contained classroom of the elementary school to the departmentalization of the high school. Briefly, here are some of the organization trends that you will find in most middle schools in terms of teacher grouping, student grouping, and time.[13]

Teachers are organized into interdisciplinary teams to provide instruction in the core subjects of science, mathematics, reading, language arts, and social studies. The interdisciplinary teams work with a common group of students and control a block of time. Teachers in a team usually have their rooms in close proximity to one another. Members of a team often have a common planning block, with one of the teachers assigned team leader. The facilities of the modern middle schools, in which team members are located in close proximity, facilitate close working relationships among teachers.

Students are ordered by grade level. Each grade level is typically organized into teams of about 85–135 students. Provision is made to deal with individual differences by providing instruction for varying ability levels, skills levels, and differences in interest.

In the middle school, teachers of each interdisciplinary team normally have a ninety-minute common planning time. Provision is made for a flexible, modular schedule. Typically, a block of time equal to five 45-minute time segments is assigned to each interdisciplinary team for instruction. Students also have a 90-minute block of time for exploration activities and physical education.

Middle School Science Curriculum Patterns

Science curriculum offerings in the middle school can be viewed as traditional or integrated and applied. These two groupings were used in a study of U.S. curriculum and are a convenient way to examine courses of study.[14] According to the results of this earlier study (which focused on grades 5, 9, and 12), the most emphasized of the traditional sciences in grades 5 and 9 was earth science. The most emphasized topics were the solar system and meteorology. Biology, although not emphasized as much as earth science, scored higher ratings than physics and chemistry. Chemistry is the least emphasized traditional science subject in the middle school.

In the survey results for applied and integrated science, environmental science content is the most common in the science offerings in grades 5 and 9. The only subject that is emphasized more is earth science. Health was rated fairly high compared to physics and chemistry.

Since this earlier study, there have been changes in middle school curriculum patterns. In a recent survey of science teachers in the United States, Weiss found that life science is the most commonly taught science course in grades 7 and 8 (63 percent of the schools). Forty-eight percent of the schools reported teaching earth science, and 43 percent reported teaching a course in physical science. Sixty-five percent of the schools reported offering a general, coordinated, or integrated science course.[15]

Instructional activities that take place as part of the science curriculum in the middle school are shown in Table 4.10. The activities that dominate the middle school science curriculum (reported by more than 50 percent of the sample) include:

- work in groups
- do hands-on/laboratory science activities or investigations
- follow specific instructions in an activity or investigation
- record, represent, and/or analyze data
- listen and take notes during presentation by teacher
- answer textbook or worksheet questions

When teachers were asked to identify those activities that never occurred, the most commonly identified activities were very similar at the middle and high school levels. Teachers reported that the following activities rarely were used:

- work on an extended science investigation
- design their *own* investigation
- use computers as a tool
- participate in field work
- take field trips
- make formal presentations to the rest of the class

Table 4.10 Science Classes Where Teachers (middle school) Reported That Students Take Part in Various Instructional Activities at Least Once a Week

Activity	Percentage of Classes
Work in groups	80
Do hands-on/laboratory science activities or investigations	65
Follow specific instructions in an activity or investigation	70
Read other (nontextbook) science-related materials in class	32
Read from a science textbook in class	46
Watch a science demonstration	42
Record, represent, and/or analyze data	51
Answer textbook or worksheet questions	56
Use mathematics as a tool in problemsolving	36
Write reflections (e.g., in a journal)	32
Watch audiovisual presentations (e.g., videotapes, CD-ROMs, videodiscs, television programs, films, or filmstrips)	19
Listen and take notes during presentation by teacher	54
Work on extended science investigations or projects (a week or more in duration)	10
Design or implement their *own* investigation	13
Use computers as a tool (e.g., spreadsheets, data analysis)	11
Participate in field work	7
Take field trips	3
Prepare written science reports	16
Make formal presentations to the rest of the class	9

Source: Weiss, I. R. *Report on the 2000 National Survey of Science and Mathematics Education.* Chapel Hill, N.C.: Horizon Research, Inc., p. 65.

The reports for the late 1980s and the most recent survey show a pattern that might be defined as a traditional approach to science teaching. Yet, during the 1990s, a large-scale effort to reform science education was launched through AAAS efforts in Project 2061 and the publication of the *National Science Education Standards.* What do the *Standards* recommend? What should be the nature of the middle school science curriculum? What should be emphasized?

Hurd, however, criticizes recent efforts to reform middle school science. One of his major concerns is that "nowhere do we find the early adolescent at the center of science curricula in the middle years."[16] He goes on to say that developers have yet to create a middle grades science curriculum that is focused on the "biological, social, psychological, emotional, and cultural needs of the early adolescent."[17]

Hurd outlines a recommended curriculum pattern for the middle school, which he calls "Preparing for Life: A Science of Ourselves." He suggests that the curriculum should be viewed as a "human life science" and should be integrative in nature drawing upon a vast domain of studies including anthropology, biology, biogeography, medical sciences, psychology, sociology, and technology.[18] As you look ahead at the standards for middle school science, think about the recommendations made by Hurd and the current curriculum patterns in the middle school.

Standards for Middle School Science

The authors of the *Standards* strongly recommend an inquiry-oriented program at the middle school level. Unifying concepts and processes should provide a thread linking the traditional content areas of physical, life, and earth science in an activity-based curriculum. The *Standards* also support a strong movement toward STS curricula and suggest that students engage in investigations of personal health, populations, resources, environments, natural hazards, risks and benefits, changes in environments, and science and technology in society. Table 4.11 identifies the eight categories of content standards and indicates the specific concepts and ideas that should underscore the curriculum for early adolescent students. I have also included examples of how the standards might be applied for each category.

Exemplary Middle School Science Programs

In the following pages you will find descriptions of a number of middle school science programs that support the intent of the *Standards* and represent inquiry-oriented programs that have been successfully implemented in middle schools.

MIDDLE SCHOOL SCIENCE AND TECHNOLOGY This program was developed especially to match the unique characteristics of middle school students and, more importantly, to meet their educational needs in science. This multilevel thematic program integrates life, earth-space, and physical sciences in the context of themes and issues that have meaning for middle school students. Using hands-on activities and an explicit 5-E learning cycle in a cooperative learning environment, Middle School Science and Technology encourages an inquiry approach to science and aligns with the *National Science Education Standards*.

Middle School Science and Technology creates opportunities for students to learn skills, develop concepts, and acquire attitudes in many areas of science and technology. In this curriculum, students develop a conceptual understanding of the foundations of science and technology while they study specific concepts, such as the theory of plate tectonics, the particle theory of matter, the chromosome theory of inheritance, the theory of evolution, principles of design, cost-and-benefit analysis, and systems analysis. The program also introduces students to scientific and technological attitudes, such as accepting ambiguity, searching for evidence, working to support and justify answers, recognizing inferences, and not always expecting right and wrong answers or simplistic solutions for complex scientific questions or for technological problems.[19]

Key characteristics of the program include:

- a focus on the development of the early adolescent
- strategies to encourage the participation of female, minority, and handicapped students
- an emphasis on reasoning and critical thinking
- cooperative learning as a key instructional strategy
- an instructional model that enhances student learning
- a conceptual approach to science and technology fields
- inclusion of STS themes

GEOLOGY IS This program provides geosciences learning activities based on an interdisciplinary approach.[20] It includes a broad range of materials and media-delivery instruments that promote variety in teaching and learning. The program emphasizes the content of geology, as well as the social implications in the wise use of earth resources. The content of the program is designed to help students become more responsible consumers of earth resources and make more informed decisions for the future regarding energy, geologic hazards, and land use. The program is organized around five units:

- Introduction to Geology
- Earth Materials
- Observing the Earth
- Internal Processes
- External Processes

Table 4.11 Middle School Science Standards

Content Standard Categories	Standard: As a result of activities in grades 5–8, all students should develop:	Examples
Unifying Concepts and Processes	Abilities aligned with the following concepts and processes: 1. Systems, order, and organization 2. Evidence, models, and explanation 3. Change, constancy, and measurement 4. Evolution and equilibrium, form and function	Students should be engaged in a variety of activities in which they use a microscope to interpret accurately what they see, enhancing their study of systems and order (of cells).
Science as Inquiry: Content Standard A	1. Abilities necessary to do scientific inquiry 2. Understandings about scientific inquiry	Students should be involved in authentic activities in which they collect data on a natural phenomenon (air pollutants) and then engaged in questions such as: How should we organize the data to present the clearest answer to our question? How should we organize the evidence to present the strongest explanation?
Physical Science: Content Standard B	1. Properties and changes of properties in matter 2. Motion and forces 3. Transfer of energy	Teachers can design activities in which students observe and measure properties of materials such as boiling points, melting points, solubility, and simple chemical changes.
Life Science: Content Standard C	1. Structure and function in living systems 2. Reproduction and heredity 3. Regulation and behavior 4. Population and ecosystems 5. Diversity and adaptations of organisms	Students can visit a community (a wooded area, a park, or even the school grounds, and investigate the kinds of organisms that live in the environment and study how they compete with other organisms in the community. They might construct a scheme that represents a model of the community.
Earth and Space Sciences: Content Standard D	1. Structure of the earth system 2. Earth's history 3. Earth in the solar system	Students can plot the location of the epicenters of earthquakes and the sites of active volcanoes and use this data to draw inferences about the structure of the lithosphere.
Science and Technology: Content Standard E	1. Abilities of technological design 2. Understanding about science and technology	Students work in small teams to design a "container" that will enable an uncooked egg to survive a crash landing from a height of 5 meters. The students should evaluate elements of the design of the container and the materials used.
Science in Personal and Social Perspectives: Content Standard F	1. Personal health 2. Populations, resources, and environments 3. Natural hazards 4. Risks and benefits 5. Changes in environments 6. Science and technology in society	Students can be involved in the investigation of environmental issues such as those related to air pollution or water pollution. By participating in "online" project such as GLOBE (www.globe.gov), students can do an authentic project and learn how to contribute to their community's understanding of an environmental problem.
History and Nature of Science: Content Standard G	1. Science as a human endeavor 2. Nature of science 3. History of science	Many people from different cultures and ethnic groups have contributed to science. Working in small groups, students can investigate the life of a scientist by reading, viewing videos, or researching on the Web. Students can report to the class via poster or digital presentation.

Source: Based on the *National Science Education Standards.*

Each unit contains multiple chapters, with the five units comprising a full-year course. Each unit contains text material, laboratory exercises, and activities, as well as objective and subjective tests. Slide-tapes, films, and videotapes are provided as well. Instruction encourages small-group and individual exploration. Because of the importance of outdoor applications, off- and on-campus field experiences are outlined.[21]

INVESTIGATING EARTH SYSTEMS This program is a modular earth science curriculum component for middle school. It includes nine activity-based modules designed for grades 5–8. Modules are grouped into three grade levels: grades 5–6, 6–7, and 7–8. Modules introduce concepts through a series of investigations (six to seven per unit), which are presented within a standard format that includes both the skills and the content students are expected to learn. Every investigation follows a learning cycle including a problem or a question, a series of activities that lead students through finding possible answers to the challenge, content notes for students' background information, and a review-and-reflect section that encourages students to reflect on what they have done and summarize what they have learned in their journals. A section on thinking about scientific inquiry guides students on a process for thinking back on the use of the inquiry processes.[22]

WILDLIFE INQUIRY THROUGH ZOO EDUCATION (WIZE) This grade 7–9 program, developed at the Bronx Zoo, New York, explores issues related to wildlife survival in the twenty-first century. The program uses a nontraditional, multidisciplinary approach to help students understand concepts related to population ecology, wildlife conservation, and species survival. The program consists of two modules: Module I (Diversity of Lifestyles) and Module II (Survival Strategies). The program, which involves about fifteen weeks of instruction, is a hands-on approach in which students learn that animals are members of populations that interact with one another and that the ecological processes the affect animals also affect humans.

The instructional materials include student resource books, photo cards, discovery cards, worksheets, teacher's manual, audiocassettes, filmstrips, and wildlife games. The program is activity oriented, and includes zoo visits. The two modules form a continuum in the study of wildlife ecology, although either could be used separately in a life science or general science program.[23]

SCI-MATH This program is designed to help students apply mathematics to introductory science. The course can be used as a physical science course for eighth- or ninth-grade students. The NDN suggests that it can be used for high achievers at the seventh-grade level, and slow learners at the eighth- or ninth-grade levels.

The program consists of two modules. Module One focuses on the mathematics involved in pre-algebra dealing with arithmetic and logic of operations. Module Two explores how algebraic equations express proportions and studies the graphical representation of proportions. There are twenty-three hands-on activities in the program. The problems and activities deal with variables that are familiar to the student, and materials used in the investigations are readily available and inexpensive items such as rulers, string, pennies, spoons, jars, and masking tape.[24]

INFORMAL SCIENCE STUDY (ISS) This program offers an alternative and supplement to the physical science course. The ISS materials presents several mini-units based on the student's involvement with popular park rides, sports, and playground experiences to develop physical science concepts. The program topics include motion, acceleration, relativity, forces, gravity, time, graphing, conservation of energy, and frames of reference. Each mini-unit is designed to involve the students in dialogue through an introduction and review/application of the physical science concepts in a low-key, nontechnical language. Terms are kept to a minimum and are introduced only after instruction. Some of the units include laboratory activities using toys and playground equipment. The developers have shown that students significantly increase their knowledge and comprehension of science concepts after as few as three weeks of instruction.[25]

The High School Science Curriculum

The high school science and mathematics curriculum is under a great deal of pressure to produce the most academically talented group of high school students in the world. Most of this pressure is from politicians in the White House to governor's houses. In the 1990 State of the Union Address, the President George H. W. Bush indicated that the improvement of mathematics and science was of the highest priority in his administration. A few days later, Bush appointed a commission to advise him on mathematics and science. Since that time, *Benchmarks for Scientific Literacy*, by the American Association for the Advancement of Science, and the *Standards*, by the National Research Council, were published.

Yet, with all this rhetoric, which is not new to the high school mathematics and science scene, life goes on in American high schools. In this section, we will examine the high school science curriculum, swinging briefly into the past to examine some of the curriculum reform programs, then we'll take a look at the *Standards* for high school science, and finally examine exemplary programs as clues to the possible future of the high school science curriculum.

Contemporary High School Curriculum Patterns

If you were able to create an image of the science curriculum in American high schools today, you would find the following:[26]

* Ninety-five percent offer a course in Biology I, introductory biology, general biology, or college preparation biology; 28 percent would offer AP biology; and 48 percent would offer a course in second-year biology.
* Ninety-one percent offer a course in Chemistry I or general chemistry; 24 percent offer AP chemistry, and 17 percent offer a course in second-year chemistry.
* Eighty-one percent offer a course in Physics I, conceptual physics, or introductory physics; 15 percent offer AP physics; and 6 percent offer an advanced physics or second-year physics.
* Thirty-four percent offer a course in earth and space science.

It's quite clear that biology, chemistry, and physics are the most common course offerings in the science curriculum; a few schools offer a course in earth and space science, typically as a course in geology or a course in astronomy. Courses in marine science and oceanography are less likely to be found in the science curriculum.

When we look at the activities that science teachers use in the science curriculum (Table 4.12) we find that the following experiences dominate high school science (reported by more than 50 percent of surveyed science teachers):

* listen and take notes during presentation by teacher
* work in groups
* do hands-on/laboratory science activities or investigations
* follow specific instructions in an activity or investigation
* record, represent, and/or analyze data
* use mathematics as a tool in problem solving

Table 4.12 Science Classes Where Teachers (High School) Reported That Students Take Part in Various Instructional Activities at Least Once a Week

Activity	Percentage of Classes
Work in groups	80
Do hands-on/laboratory science activities or investigations	71
Follow specific instructions in an activity or investigation	71
Read other (nontextbook) science-related materials in class	20
Read from a science textbook in class	28
Watch a science demonstration	43
Record, represent, and/or analyze data	54
Answer textbook or worksheet questions	72
Use mathematics as a tool in problem solving	52
Write reflections (e.g., in a journal)	15
Watch audiovisual presentations (e.g., videotapes, CD-ROMs, videodiscs, television programs, films, or filmstrips)	21
Listen and take notes during presentation by teacher	86
Work on extended science investigations or projects (a week or more in duration)	7
Design or implement their *own* investigation	9
Use computers as a tool (e.g., spreadsheets, data analysis)	16
Participate in field work	4
Take field trips	2
Prepare written science reports	24
Make formal presentations to the rest of the class	6

Source: Based on Weiss, I. R. *Report on the 2000 National Survey of Science and Mathematics Education.* Chapel Hill, N.C.: Horizon Research, Inc., p. 65.

In high school science the dominant teaching strategy is lecture with students recording notes; however, high school science teachers also involve their students in group work and hands-on/laboratory work. Although it is difficult to create a model that defines the teaching approach of high school science teachers, later you will encounter several teaching models, including the Direct/Interactive Teaching Model, Cooperative Learning Teaching Model, and Inquiry Teaching Model. High school teachers use a variety of approaches.

These facts describe the picture of the traditional science curriculum. Although the United States does not have a national curriculum, the evidence from survey research studies shows that the American secondary science curriculum can be described in terms of a few science textbooks, about five or six different kinds of courses, and with a limited variety of instructional techniques.

Weiss reports that lecture and discussion are the mainstays of the high school science curriculum. In 1977, lecture and discussion were considerably more common than laboratory activities and in another study (1986) the same was found, only the difference was even greater.[27] As we've seen, lecture and discussion still dominate the high school curriculum.[28]

When a randomly selected sample of high school science teachers was asked about a recent lesson, three out of four in 1977 said it was a lecture/discussion lesson and slightly more than half said it *included* hands-on activity. In 1986, more than 80 percent of teachers reported lecturing as their most recent lesson and only 40 percent said they used a hands-on lesson.[29] In 2000, 80 percent indicated having students take notes from presentations.[30]

The science curriculum in American schools has been described as a layer cake model. In the layer cake model (Figure 4.3), a different science course is offered each year as the student progresses through the science curriculum. This stacking of one science course on top of another is the pattern that was established in the early

part of the twentieth century. However, the model is actually complicated.

The National Science Teachers Association recommended a radical change in the science curriculum model employed in most school systems in the United States. Borrowing on the models of other countries, especially Russia, the NSTA Scope and Sequence proposed offering four strands (biology, chemistry, earth science, and physics) that would run through the science curriculum from grades 7 through 12. Each year, students would be exposed to each strand; that is, they would have experiences in biology, chemistry, earth science, and physics starting in grade 7.

Although not all school systems track students, the evidence suggests that less than 50 percent of all science classes are heterogeneous. Survey courses are designed for students who are either struggling or have not performed very well academically. General courses are for the large population of secondary students: the average student who is college bound, but not necessarily focusing on science. Accelerated and advanced placement courses are designed for high school students who are contemplating a career in science or mathematics in college and who have been successful in previous mathematics and science courses. Weiss found that 40 percent of high school students are assigned to their high school science curriculum by ability level, as is seen in Table 4.13. Furthermore, Weiss found that classes labeled low ability were more likely to have a high proportion of minority students.[31]

Table 4.14 shows the science curriculum for typical urban school systems in the Southeast. Notice that for each subject except life science there is survey, general, and accelerated (or advanced) courses. For juniors and seniors, many school systems offer advanced placement courses in which the student can earn college credit for a high school science experience. Also note that at the eleventh- and twelfth-grade levels, there are elective courses in marine biology, biology II, and anatomy and physiology.

| Physics: Grade 12 |
| Chemistry: Grade 11 |
| Biology: Grade 10 |
| Physical Science: Grade 9 |

| Earth Science: Grade 8 |
| Life Science: Grade 7 |
| General or Physical Science: Grade 6 |

| Elementary Science: K–5 |

Figure 4.3 The Layer Cake Model of the Science Curriculum. In this depiction, the science course offerings are layered, one on top of the other, starting with elementary science, then middle school science, and finally the high school curriculum.

Table 4.13 Ability Grouping in High School Science

Grouping	Percentage of Students
Fairly homogeneous and low ability	7
Fairly homogeneous and average ability	29
Fairly homogeneous and high ability	27
Heterogeneous, with a mix of two or more abilities	37

Source: Weiss, I. R. *Report of the 2000 National Survey of Science and Mathematics Education*. Chapel Hill, N.C.: Horizon Research, Inc., 2001, p. 57.

Table 4.14 Typical Secondary Science Curriculum

Grade	Course	Textbook	Grade	Course	Textbook
7	Life Science	*Life Science* (Prentice Hall)	11	Chemistry:	
8	Earth Science:			Survey	*ChemCom: Chemistry in the Community* (Kendall/Hunt)
	Survey	*Earth Science* (Prentice Hall)		General	*Chemistry: A Study of Matter* (Prentice Hall)
	General	*Earth Science* (Prentice Hall)			
	Accelerated	*Earth Science* (Silver Burdett)		Accelerated	*Chemistry* (Addison Wesley)
9	Physical Science:			Advanced Placement	*Chemistry* (Random House)
	Survey	*Physical Science* (D.C. Heath)		Biology:	
	General	*Physical Science* (Prentice Hall)		Biology II	*Biology* (Addison Wesley)
	Jr/Sr	*Physical Science* (Addison Wesley)		Marine Biology	*Marine Biology* (Benjamin/ Cummings)
	Biology:			Anatomy and Physiology	*Essentials of Human Anatomy and Physiology* (William C. Brown)
	Accelerated	*Modern Biology* (Holt)			
10	Biology:		12	Physics:	
	Survey	*Biology: An Everyday Experience* (Merrill)		Physics I	*Modern Physics* (Holt)
				Conceptual Physics	*Conceptual Physics* (Addison Wesley)
	General	*Biology* (HBJ)			
	Accelerated	*Modern Biology* (Holt)		Physics II	*College Physics* (HBJ)
				Advanced Placement	*College Physics* (HBJ)

INQUIRY ACTIVITY 4.1

Science Curriculum Patterns

Curriculum patterns in science vary from state to state and within school districts in the states. In this activity, your task is to compare curriculum patterns of two school districts in your state. To do this, you will have to obtain copies of the science curriculum guide from two school districts. You can obtain these by browsing the district's Web site.

Materials

- Curriculum guides from two school districts
- Curriculum patterns chart (Figure 4.4)

Procedures

1. List the overall goals of the science curriculum of the districts you are investigating.
2. Identify the curriculum for the elementary, middle/junior high, and high school grades by completing the chart in Figure 4.4.

Level	Course	Textbook
Elementary School		
Middle/Junior High School		
High School		

Figure 4.4 Curriculum Patterns.

Minds-On Strategies

1. How do the patterns compare? Are there similarities between the two districts? What are the differences?
2. Are there any differences in the stated goals that give you insight into each district's philosophy of science education?
3. To what extent is the layer cake model of science curriculum implemented in these districts?
4. To what extent are the *Standards* implemented?

High School Reform Projects

PHYSICS Prior to 1956, the content and organization of physics at the high school level was highly influenced by the Harvard Descriptive List of Experiments or by the periodic emphasis on the application of physics (e.g., toy physics, household physics, consumer physics, atomic age physics). In 1956, Jerrold R. Zacharias, a professor of physics, held a conference at Massachusetts Institute of Technology. The state of high school physics teaching was discussed and the seeds were planted for the development and implementation of a new high school course for physics.

PSSC Physics During the period 1956–1960, several hundred physicists, high school teachers, apparatus designers, writers, and editors developed PSSC Physics. The result was a course that contained a student textbook, teacher's guide, laboratory experiments, tests, films, and a series of paperback books on selected topics in science.

PSSC Physics departed from the traditional course in physics, which emphasized facts and description of physics concepts; the PSSC course was designed to help students "do physics," by engaging the students in activities and thought processes of the physicist. The goals of this new program included helping students:[32]

- understand the place of science in society
- understand physics as a human activity and a product of human thought and imagination
- appreciate the intellectual, aesthetic, and historical background of physics
- appreciate the limitations of knowledge about the physical world
- understand that knowledge of physics comes about from observation and experimentation
- appreciate the spirit of inquiry
- appreciate the logical unity of physics and the way that physicists think about the world
- understand basic principles of physics that manifest themselves in astronomical as well as human and atomic scales

In the 1960s and 1970s there a number of studies were conducted by science educators to evaluate the effectiveness of PSSC Physics and other course improvement projects, and also to compare their effectiveness to the traditional courses in the respective disciplines. Studies showed that PSSC students did better on higher-level cognitive tasks than their peers in traditional physics courses.[33]

The PSSC course involved students in a series of unique laboratory activities. Over fifty experiments were designed to support and help develop the concepts in the textbook. The experiments were not designed to verify a concept that had been introduced by the teacher or the textbook. Instead, the laboratory experiments created a novel situation in which students had to think about a problem, gather relevant data, and analyze results. To accomplish this, the PSSC developers designed special laboratory equipment that was simple, easily assembled, and inexpensive. All other course improvement projects followed this pattern of designing special equipment. The PSSC equipment included roller-skate carts, doorbell timers, and ripple tanks.

Project Physics Another physics course developed during this period was Project Physics. It departed from the PSSC model, perhaps because the developers were science educators, involving high school teachers from the beginning. Project Physics set out to develop a general education physics course based on good physics, but designed for today's citizen.[34]

Project Physics developed a course along humanistic lines in that the developers were interested in emphasizing human values and meaning as opposed to PSSC physics, which focused more on the intrinsic structure of physics. The objectives in Project Physics were designed to help students understand and appreciate:[35]

- how the basic facts, principles, and ideas of modern physics developed
- who made the key contributions and accomplishments
- process of science as illustrated by physics
- how physics relates to the cultural and economic aspects of society
- the effect of physics on other sciences
- the relationship and interaction between physics and contemporary technology

Project Physics produced a vast array of teaching materials, including: (1) six student texts, called student guides (Concepts of Motion, Motion in the Heavens, Energy, Waves and Fields, Models of the Atom, and The Nucleus); (2) physics readers (articles and book passages related to the topics in the student guides); (3) a laboratory guide (student experiments); (4) laboratory equipment; (5) film loops; (6) films; and (7) a teacher's guide.

PSSC Physics and Project Physics were the two major physics curriculum projects developed with funds from NSF. Physics enrollments continued to decrease during the period of time when these courses were developed and thereafter. Research results showed that the courses were effective in improving student understanding of physics and ability to accomplish high-level cognitive tasks.

CHEMISTRY During the golden age of science education, three major chemistry curriculum projects were developed with support from NSF; namely, Chemical Education Materials Study (CHEM Study), Chemical Bond Approach (CBA), and Interdisciplinary Approaches to Chemistry (IAC). Table 4.15 compares some of the features of these three programs. These programs represent two very different approaches to chemistry. CHEM Study and CBA were innovative but were closely aligned to the traditional organization and approach to chemistry. IAC, on the other hand, was more socially relevant in that there was a closer connection to the real world of the student and the materials were interdisciplinary. Furthermore, IAC was designed as a series of modules, a forerunner of the Individualized Science Instructional System (ISIS), which designed over thirty minicourses in general science, earth science, biology, chemistry, and physics.

According to Shymansky, Kyle, and Alport, CHEM Study and CBA did not fare as well as the NSF projects in physics and biology. As these researchers put it, "of the three traditional secondary disciplines (biology, chemistry, and physics), it probably is safe to conclude on the basis of the data . . . that the new chemistry curricula produced the least impact in terms of enhanced student performances."[36] Student performances were low in achievement and process skills. The authors speculate that the small differences in achievement may have been due to the fact that CHEM Study and CBA were not too different than traditional chemistry courses.

BIOLOGY Biology education in the United States has been influenced to the greatest degree (aside from the socio-political-cultural issues of the evolution–creation science debate) by the Biological Sciences Curriculum Study (BSCS) than by any other force or group. The BSCS was organized in 1959 at the University of Colorado. It is still as active as a curriculum force in science education, with headquarters at Colorado College, Colorado Springs.

BSCS developed three approaches and separate curricula for the high school biology program. The three versions of BSCS were organized around levels and,

Table 4.15 Golden Age Chemistry Programs

Chemistry Course	Development Center	Approach	Curriculum
CHEM Study	Harvey Mudd College, Claremont, Calif.	Chemical concepts should be developed inductively by active student involvement. The laboratory experiments are designed for students to gather data, not verify concepts. Three commercial versions of CHEM were created after the original curriculum was designed.	Student text: *Chemistry: An Experimental Science* (W. H. Freeman) Laboratory manual Teacher's guide Tests Films Programmed materials
CBA	Reed College, Portland, Oregon	The course is organized around a conceptual theme: the chemical bond. Students are encouraged to use theoretical models to explain data. The lab is integrated with discussion and with the text.	Student text: *Chemical Systems* (McGraw-Hill) Laboratory manual Teacher's guide Teacher's laboratory guide
IAC	University of Maryland	IAC is an interdisciplinary approach to chemistry. After an introductory module, unifying themes connect students to various areas of chemistry, such as organic, nuclear, and environmental.	Student texts (Modules): • *Reactions and Reason* • *Diversity and Periodicity* (Inorganic) • *Form and Function* (Organic) • *Molecules in Living Systems* (Biochemistry) • *The Heart of the Matter* (Nuclear) • *The Delicate Balance* (Environmental) • *Communities of Molecules* (Physical)

according to Mayer, "in order not to prejudice prospective users for or against any one of the three approaches, there were no descriptive titles: rather, the three texts were designated by color."[37] The versions and each "level of organization" are as follows:

- *BSCS Blue Version:* (Molecular) Biological Science: Molecules to Man
- *BSCS Yellow Version:* (Cell) Biological Science: An Inquiry into Life
- *BSCS Green Version:* (World biome) Biological Science: An Ecological Approach

BSCS materials were also organized around a set of unifying themes: "the characteristics and concepts that provide the most comprehensive and reliable knowledge of living things known to modern science."[38] The unifying themes were identified as follows:[39]

1. Change of living things through time: evolution
2. Diversity of type and unity of pattern in living things
3. The genetic continuity of life
4. The complementarity of organism and environment
5. The biological roots of behavior
6. The complementarity of structure and function
7. Regulation and homeostasis: preservation of life in the face of change
8. Science as inquiry
9. The history of biological concepts

Hurd points out that the first five unifying themes were used to organize the content in each version, themes eight and nine refer to the internal structure of biology, and themes six and seven refer to content and structure.[40]

The three versions of BSCS (Table 4.16) affected high school biology enormously. Shymansky, Kyle, and Alport reported that there was more research data available on the BSCS programs than any other new curriculum project. BSCS programs compared very favorably against traditional biology courses. With the exception of physics, the new biology programs "showed the greatest gains across all criteria measured" (achievement, perceptions, process skills, analytic skills).[41]

Standards for High School Science

The *Standards* for high school science, like the *Standards* for elementary and middle school science strongly

Table 4.16 BSCS Yellow, Blue, and Green Curricula

Yellow Version Biological Science: An Inquiry into Life	Blue Version Biological Science: Molecules to Man	Green Version Biological Science: An Ecological Approach
• Unity: life from life, basic structure and functions, living chemistry, the physiology and reproduction of cells, and the heredity materials.	• Biology, the interaction of facts and ideas: science as inquiry, the variety of living things, conflicting views on the means of evolution, the origin of living things.	• The world of life: the web of life, individuals and populations, communities and ecosystems.
• Diversity: viruses, bacteria, important small organisms, molds, yeasts and mushrooms, the trend toward complexity, the land turns green, photosynthesis, stems and roots.	• Evolution of life processes: forerunners of life, chemical energy for life, light as energy for life, and life with oxygen.	• Diversity among living things: animals, plants, and protists.
	• The evolution of the cell: master molecules, the biological code, and the cell theory.	• Patterns in the biosphere: patterns of life in the microscopic world, on land, in the water, in the past.
• Continuity: patterns of heredity, the chromosome theory of heredity, Darwinian evolution, the mechanisms of evolution, and the cultural evolution of man.	• Multicellular organisms: new individuals: multicellular organism, reproduction, and development.	• Within the individual organism: the cell, bioenergetics, the functioning cell, the functioning animal, and behavior.
	• Multicellular organisms: genetic continuity: patterns of heredity, genes and chromosomes, the origin of species.	• Continuity of the biosphere: reproduction, heredity, and evolution.
• Interaction: a population out of balance, a perspective of time and life: molecules to man.	• Multicellular organisms: energy utilization: transport, respiratory, digestive, and excretory systems.	• Man and the biosphere: the human animal, man in the web of life.
	• Multicellular organisms: unifying systems: regulatory, nervous, skeletal, and muscular systems, the organism and behavior.	
	• Higher levels of organization: human species, populations, societies, and communities.	

emphasize an inquiry-oriented approach to the science curriculum. Inquiry involves developing the abilities to do science inquiry, and this means that students must be actively involved in investigations and use cognitive skills to do so. The *Standards* authors issue this challenge to science teachers:

One challenge to teachers of science and to curriculum developers is making science investigations meaningful. Investigations should derive from questions and issues that have meaning for students. Scientific topics that have been highlighted by current events provide one source, whereas actual science- and technology-related problems provide another source of meaningful investigations. Finally, teachers of science should remember that some experiences begin with little meaning for students but develop meaning through active involvement, continued exposure, and growing skill and understanding.[42]

As you look over Table 4.17, notice the emphasis in each of the three traditional content areas of science (physical science, life science, and earth space science). These content emphases do not differ from previous recommendations regarding the scope of the high school curriculum. In fact, if you compare this content

to the course titles of the high school science curriculum in Table 4.14, you find a strong match. The *Standards*, however, place science in a larger context and emphasize the content standards of science and technology, personal and social responsibility, and the history of science. The unifying concepts and process provide a thread linking the other content standards together.

Exemplary High School Science Curricula

A number of curriculum projects have been designed that either support the recommendations of the *Standards* or were *Standards*-developed projects.

BIOLOGY Biology is one of the most important courses in the American science curriculum because for many students it is their last experience with a formal course in science. More than half of all high course science courses are in the field of biology. This includes survey, general, and accelerated biology courses, biology II courses, marine biology, and human anatomy and physiology.

Biology teaching at the high school level has emphasized the vocabulary and very specific cognitive objectives, as opposed to focusing on more general goals such as understanding biological systems, how

Table 4.17 High School Science Content Standards

Content Standard Categories	Standard: As a result of activities in Grades 9–12, all students should develop:	Activity and Curriculum Examples
Unifying Concepts and Processes	Abilities aligned with the following concepts and processes: 1. Systems, order, and organization 2. Evidence, models, and explanation 3. Change, constancy, and measurement 4. Evolution and equilibrium, form and function	Students might be encouraged to become involved the school's science fair and design a project that focuses on an authentic study of a science topic. In the process, the student will realize that unifying concepts will be important as the project is designed and carried out.
Science as Inquiry: Content Standard A	1. Abilities necessary to do scientific inquiry 2. Understandings about scientific inquiry	Students should be involved in activities in which they analyze data collected as part of a science research project. They should be encouraged to examine their data in light of questions such as: What explanations did you expect to develop from the data? Were there any surprises in the data? Encouraging students to present their research to peers for review is an important step in the inquiry process.
Physical Science: Content Standard B	1. Structure of atoms 2. Structure and properties of matter 3. Chemical reactions 4. Motions and forces 5. Conservation of energy and increase in disorder 6. Interactions of energy and matter	Students can be involved in laboratory research projects to study the property of substances and their changes through a range of chemical reactions. This experience enables students to understand reaction types and how they apply to the real world, such as in extracting elements from ores, manipulating the structure of genes, and the synthesis of polymers.
Life Science: Content Standard C	1. The cell 2. Molecular basis of heredity 3. Biological evolution 4. Interdependence of organisms 5. Matter, energy, and organization in living systems 6. Behavior of organisms	Students can be given two different collections of fossil brachiopods. Students investigate the collections by making observations and measuring the widths and lengths of each individual fossil. Students summarize their data using graphs and tables and conclude that they may have two different species of brachiopods based on the population graphs.
Earth and Space Sciences: Content Standard D	1. Energy in the earth system 2. Geochemical cycles 3. Origin and evolution of the earth system 4. Origin and evolution of the universe	To explore the origin and evolution of the earth system, students might be asked to plot twenty-five significant events in the history of life and geology on a time line. Using 5 meters of adding machine tape and scale of 1 meter = 1 billion years, students can display the "history of earth/life" on the tape.
Science and Technology: Content Standard E	1. Abilities of technological design 2. Understanding about science and technology	Students might be challenged to assemble electronic components to control the sequence of operations or they might analyze the features of athletic shoes to see what criteria and the sport, human anatomy, and the materials might impose constraints.
Science in Personal and Social Perspectives: Content Standard F	1. Personal and community health 2. Population growth 3. Natural resources 4. Environmental quality 5. Natural and human–induced hazards 6. Science and technology in local, national, and global challenges	Teachers might engage students in a project-based activity in which they participate in a study that helps them understand the relationships among populations, environments, and resources.
History and Nature of Science: Content Standard G	1. Science as a human endeavor 2. Nature of scientific knowledge 3. Historical perspectives	Students might discuss controversial issues in any field of science and discuss the ethical implications of the issue and how this impinges on the ethical traditions of science.

Source: Based on National Research Council. *National Science Education Standards.* Washington, D.C.: National Academy Press, 1995.

biological knowledge is developed, and how biological information can benefit humans and society.

As pointed out by biology educators, the rapid changes in the biological sciences in the last forty years and the impact of these changes on the individual and society have been profound. Students leaving high school today are living in a "new biological world."

In a more recent report on the teaching of biology, the National Research Council recommended a biology program at the high school level that is leaner (in the number of terms and concepts introduced) and for the course "the scaffolding should include an understanding of basic concepts in cell and molecular biology, evolution, energy and metabolism, heredity, development and reproduction, and ecology. Concepts should be mastered through inquiry, not memorization of words."[43]

As pointed out in the report, the formula for change in the current teaching scheme of high school biology should be focused on teaching scientific concepts, reasoning, and learning through inquiry. The committee viewed the following as the scope of change needed to ensure a high school biology course that meets this criterion:[44]

1. In designing a course, we must identify the central concepts and principles that every high school student should know and pare from the curriculum everything that does not explicate and illuminate these relatively few concepts.
2. The concepts must be presented in such a manner that they are related to the world that students understand in a language that is familiar.
3. We must teach by a process that engages all students in examining why they believe what they believe. That requires building slowly, with ample time for discussion with peers and with

---

INQUIRY ACTIVITY 4.2

 Exploring Science Curriculum Materials

It is important to become familiar with science curriculum materials, the textbooks as well as the ancillary materials. In this activity you will investigate two textbooks representing the same curriculum field (e.g., earth science, biology, chemistry, or physics). You can examine two contemporary books or choose a contemporary book and compare it to one that was developed in the same discipline during the golden age of science education. Your investigation will be designed to identify and compare differences and similarities in the curriculum materials you explore.

Materials

- Two science textbooks
- Optional ancillary materials (tests, lab manuals, teacher's guide, audio-visual materials, computer software)

Procedures

Analyze each text using the chart shown Figure 4.5. A rating scale on a five-point spread will allow you to gather some data for comparative purposes. If other individuals or groups chose the same books, you will be able to compare your interpretations.

Minds-On Strategies

1. To what extend are the *Standards* met in the curriculum materials you investigated?
2. How are contemporary curriculum materials different than those produced during the golden age of science education? (You may have to collaborate with others who studied books in this era.)
3. Is the science-as-inquiry theme evident as an integral part of the curriculum materials? How is this accomplished?

| Evaluation Criteria | Textbook #1_____ | | | | | Textbook #2_____ | | | | |
| | Poor | | | Outstanding | | Poor | | | Outstanding | |
	1	2	3	4	5	1	2	3	4	5
Goals • Evidence is present to educate students who are able to experience the richness and excitement of knowing about and understanding the natural world. • Evidence is present that results in the use of appropriate scientific processes and principles in making personal decisions. • Evidence is present that students engage intelligently in public discourse and debate about matters of scientific and technological concern. • Evidence is present that students will increase their economic productivity through the use of the knowledge, understanding, and skills of the scientifically literate person in their careers.										
Content of Text 1. Accuracy 2. Depth 3. Breadth 4. Processes of science 5. Nature of science 6. Understandability 7. Other										
Laboratory Investigations 1. Process oriented 2. Integral part of curriculum 3. Other										
Features 1. Design of the book 2. Use of photography and graphics 3. Use of learning tools for students 4. Readability 5. Interest 6. Other										
Ancillaries 1. Laboratory manual 2. Study aids 3. Computer software 4. Films, videos, filmstrips 5. Other										
Summary 1. Overall point total 2. Strengths 3. Weaknesses 4. Comments										

Figure 4.5 Curriculum Evaluation Chart.

the teacher. In science, it also means observation and experiments, not as an exercise in following recipes, but to confront the essence of the material.

Hurd recommends that new science curricula be based on the recent reports (*Benchmarks* and the *Standards*), but suggests that new biology curricula must be viewed as a way of life, not a body of information.[45] The exemplary biology programs cited below reflect the goals and desired directions of this new view of biology education.

Biology: A Community Context This program is an inquiry-based biology curriculum. A text and support materials allow you to create a classroom in which students work both individually and in groups, learning the key concepts of biology in the context of their own lives and community. The unique instructional design encourages students to challenge their assumptions, dig deeply into science issues, and develop new ways of thinking and acting in response to their learning. The emphasis throughout the program is on active investigation. Students learn about the scientific process through hands-on inquiry into real-world problems. In fact, the seven-part instructional strategy is constructed to reflect the process of scientific inquiry and allows students to "do" science rather than just read about it.[46]

Insights in Biology An introductory biology course intended to develop conceptual understanding through investigations of socially and personally significant issues, this program is organized into five thematic modules, each with a student manual and a supporting teacher guide. Each module contains a "storyline" that encompasses the biology content, and the concepts introduced are connected within and among modules. The modules can be taught in any order, but the lessons within each module are intended to be taught sequentially. The modules require between thirty-five and sixty days to complete, with an average of fifty days per module. There are three components to the Insights in Biology curriculum:

- A teacher guide for each module,
- A student manual for each module, and
- An implementation guide for the entire program.

Each of the thematic units contains seven to fifteen learning experiences (LE). Each LE is structured so that new concepts build upon prior experiences. The experiences are based on society's need for a scientifically

literate citizenry, which has increased dramatically in the last few decades, and on the fact that a solid knowledge base in the biological sciences is critical for the health and well-being both of the individual and of our society. In addition, in order to succeed in the technology-based, information-intensive society of today individuals must possess certain process and critical thinking skills that will enable them to seek out the knowledge they need and apply it to new situations. To prepare for the challenges of this kind of society, students must acquire and practice these skills in their educational experiences. With this perspective in mind, the goals of Insights in Biology include:[47]

- Provide a core understanding of essential knowledge in biology by exploring specific concepts in depth and in a context relevant to the student.
- Present each concept in several different contexts to demonstrate the unifying themes in biology and to emphasize the connected nature of biology.
- Connect the understanding of biological principles with applications to day-to-day living with social, economic, and ethical issues, and with the responsibility for making decisions about one's own health and environment.
- Develop the skills to transfer the knowledge of these concepts to new situations and to apply them appropriately.
- Develop critical thinking and problem-solving skills through direct experience in the laboratory, in research investigations, in inquiry-based activities, in role-playing, and in case studies.
- Provide support to teachers in developing new instructional strategies and pedagogical approaches that are interactive, inquiry based, hands-on, and that develop science process and thinking skills.
- Foster in each student the willingness and skills required to engage in inquiry, the ability to address a problem, phenomenon, or issue and to reach an understanding, conclusion, or opinion using knowledge and critical thinking and problem-solving skills.
- Cultivate in students an appreciation for the aesthetic value of biology as well as for its roles in technological advances and in everyday decision making in the home, community, and workplace.

CHEMISTRY The *Standards* call for an inquiry-oriented approach to high school chemistry teaching. Approaches should involve students in high-interest projects and activities in which chemistry is used to solve community problems.

Active Chemistry Unlike traditional chemistry programs, Active Chemistry has qualitative analysis, quantitative analysis, electrochemistry, thermodynamics, and kinetics (as you would expect), but not where you would expect to find them. In a traditional chemistry course, dimension analysis is taught in fall, thermochemistry in winter, and electrochemistry in spring. In Active Chemistry, students are introduced to chemistry concepts on a need-to-know basis as they explore chapters like Sports Drinks, Cool Chemistry Show, Movie Special Effects, and The Periodic Table.

Each chapter is independent of the others, allowing teachers to begin the year with the chapter of their choice. For example, suppose the teacher chooses to begin with the Cool Chemistry Show chapter. On day one, students are introduced to the chapter challenge. For example, it could be that a local elementary school has asked the class to produce and present an entertaining and informative chemistry show to its fourth- and fifth-grade students. To meet their challenge, students must:

- understand a variety of different types of chemical reactions and what took place in each reaction;
- present their demonstrations in an exciting and informative manner;
- practice acceptable safety procedures throughout their demonstrations.

According to the developers, key ideas about Active Chemistry are as follows:[48]

- Flexible: Since each chapter is independent of one another, it provides a great deal of flexibility and multiple opportunities for students to be successful.
- Student-friendly chemistry: Students do not need high levels of math and reading to be successful. Students learn important chemistry concepts by doing chemistry. Students know that they have a real-life challenge and that the activities will help them achieve their goal.
- Engaging: Themes are relevant to students' lives. Students in Active Chemistry never ask, Why am I learning this? Teachers of Active Chemistry never have to respond, Because one day it will be useful to you. Active Chemistry is relevant chemistry.

PHYSICS Physics has the reputation as being the elitist of the high school science courses. A very small proportion of high school students enroll in physics. Exemplary physics programs, such as Physics for All described below, focus on how physics can be relevant

to all students. One of the problems physics teachers have had to come to grips with is the "mathematics" issue. Can students "understand" physics without a strong background in mathematics? It is conventional wisdom that many students avoid physics because they suffer from math phobia. The recommendations of groups like Project 2061 and physics teachers are that a multilevel approach to physics in the high school is in order. The course Conceptual Physics, offered in an increasing number of high schools, is an example of physics teaching in which the quantifiable approach to physics is downplayed in favor of a qualitative approach. Concepts in physics can be understood without a lot of mathematics. Exemplary programs in the area of physics follow.

Active Physics Active Physics is an introductory physics course organized into six thematic units, each with a student book and a supporting teacher's edition. Each unit contains three chapters that, although all related to the theme, are quite independent of each other. The chapters in the units can be taught in any order and sequenced with chapters from other units. Each chapter is designed to last about a month and contains an average of eight activities. The activities in each chapter build toward a "chapter challenge" project that is designed to have real-world application and appeal to teenagers.

Usual physics coursework over the year is very predictable: mechanics in fall, followed by waves in winter, then electricity and magnetism in spring. In contrast, Active Physics takes a whole new approach. Keeping the *National Science Education Standards* in mind, it includes thematic science units the students can relate to: communication, home, medicine, predictions, sports, and transportation.[49]

Conceptual Physics This nontraditional approach to traditional physics topics includes the following units of study:

- mechanics
- properties of matter
- heat
- sound
- electricity and magnetism
- light
- atomic and nuclear physics
- relativity

Conceptual Physics focuses on comprehension and understanding of physics concepts without the mathematics elegance that characterizes the traditional physics approach. Conceptual Physics does not downplay high-level thinking. On the contrary, the course is full of problem-solving exercises and activities that will challenge all students. Through some well-conceived review exercises, home projects, and in-class exercises, students are engaged in a wide range of intellectual activities.

Science Curriculum: A Global Perspective

The science education community extends beyond the boarders of the United States and is an active force throughout the world. We live on a planet that some describe as a global community. Computers, satellites, fax machines, telephones, and television bring educators together from countries as far apart as Australia and Russia. What is the education of students in other countries about? When do students begin studying science in other nations? What is the nature of the science curriculum in other countries?

I asked colleagues from other countries to write brief descriptions describing the curriculum and teaching issues in Australia, Chile, China, Ghana, Japan, and Russia. As science educators, we are members of a community of practice that is worldwide. What are the issues in other countries, and how do these help inform us about our own issues? The authors of these international pieces have based their writing on personal experiences with the culture. In most cases the authors were born, educated, and taught in the country they described.

The writers of these descriptions also share another common experience, and that is of being either an international teacher or international student. Charles Hutchison started his teaching career in his native Ghana and then immigrated to the United States and taught secondary school science for ten years. He is now a university professor. His dissertation research focused on pedagogical incongruencies facing international science teachers when they immigrate to teach in U.S. high schools.[50] In his study, Hutchison identified some of the differences in pedagogy and curriculum that international teachers had to face when they began a teaching career in a different country. The descriptions that follow will give us some insight into incongruences that exist among the various nations presented.

Sergei Tolstikov, a teacher in Moscow, Russia, has had many experiences teaching and consulting with schools in Georgia. He also has been involved for the past fifteen years in two Web-based projects that linked American and Russian teachers and students. Roger T.

Cross, born in England, has lived most of his adult life in Australia. He has taught secondary science in Australia, but has spent most of his professional career as a university professor at LaTrobe University and the University of Melbourne. He recently retired from the University of Melbourne. With his colleague Ronald F. Price, Cross has traveled several times to China and has been very involved in Chinese science education. Shigehiko Tsukahara taught science in Japan for more than fifteen years and then came to the United States to study science education at the graduate level. Claudia Rose, from Chile, earned a master's degree in the United States and is currently a secondary teacher in Chile.

Australia

Roger T. Cross   *Roger T. Cross, born in the United Kingdom, is an Australian citizen. He has a Ph.D. in physical organic chemistry from the University of Adelaide. After spending time in research and industry, Cross taught in schools for ten years before becoming a science education lecturer. He has published more than a hundred articles and seven books. Prior to his retirement in 2003, Cross was senior lecturer, Department of Science and Mathematics Education, University of Melbourne. He now researches science for citizenship. His latest book,* Fallout: Hedley Marston and the British Bomb Tests in Australia, *has created considerable media interest.*

The education system in each of the Australian states and territory has distinctive features. This resulted from the autonomy of the states from each other prior to Federation in 1901. There are six states and two territories (although both the Northern Territory and the Australian Capital Territory now have parliaments of their own and are no longer administered by the central government). Consequently, there are eight separate educational systems that contain many common features but also have particular characteristics of their own. This individuality makes it difficult to generalize, except to say that the Australian educational system owes much to the that of the United Kingdom, both in the structure of primary and secondary schooling and the mix of state schools and private schools.

One interesting feature is the strength of the Catholic segment of private schooling, which stems from the large, predominantly Catholic Irish and Italian immigration to Australia, particularly in the state of Victoria. The state educational authorities exercise different control over the curriculum in their schools to different extents, some very prescriptive and others giving control to the schools. It is this latter type that is perhaps the most interesting and is seen to the greatest extent in Victoria, the second most populous state. It should be noted that the federal government has been attempting to convince the states of the need for a common core curriculum. The rationale for this has been the difficulties children experience when they move from one state to another. This proposal has met with limited success because of the differing philosophical stances taken by states toward education.

The Example of Victoria

Approximately a third of all children are in private schools; of these Catholic religious-based schools predominate. Schools have total autonomy to set the curriculum for the first eleven years of schooling (called P–10); however, the Ministry of Education has, in the last two years, released framework documents for the key subject areas that can be viewed as a retreat from this position. It should be noted that the documents are in no way imposed on schools. The political and educational debate surrounding the battle for autonomy was, I believe, lively and initiated by reformists in education in the 1960s and early 1970s.

The schooling consists of:

1. Kindergarten: optional for four-year-olds
2. Primary School: seven years of schooling, classes preparatory to grade 6. Children enter at age five.
3. Secondary School (now called post-primary school): six years of school, of which grades 7–9 are compulsory.

The retention rate (percentage of students who graduate) to year 12 is rapidly increasing and is now approaching 70 percent. The retention rate has been steadily increasing from a rate of 45 percent and is expected to rise to 85 percent by the end of the decade. Students can leave school at the end of year 10 (at approximately sixteen years of age). Those students who complete post-primary school go on to year 12 and upon graduation receive the Victorian Certificate of Education (VCE). This new policy requires all students to take four units of mathematics/science/technology studies.

Australian Science Education: The Case of the State of Victoria

Primary school science (P–6) is quite variable. Students may or may not receive what can be described as a science education. Many schools run a completely thematic approach to teaching, although mathematics and language are separated for special attention. The amount of science may vary from grade to grade as much as it varies from school to school. A recent study by the federal government into maths and science has recommended an increase in the time devoted to science in preservice training. It is probably valid to say that few children receive what can be identified as science for primary children in a systematic way throughout their primary schooling.

Secondary school science is quite a different story. In the first four years of secondary school (years 7–10), science is a core part of the curriculum and is generally compulsory to year 10. The allocation varies, but is normally in the order of three to four 50-minute periods per week (150–200 minutes total). Although there is autonomy and a wide range of textbooks to choose from, the curriculum doesn't vary a great deal from school to school. Most often it is a topical approach, as shown in Table 4.18. Students are involved in laboratory activities and work in small teams to investigate phenomena related to the topic.

Some schools organize each year of science around a theme, such as Sun, or Earth. Refer to Figure 4.6 for a level-10 science course organized around the theme Earth. By the use of the theme Earth as a unifying concept, it is believed that students will better appreciate that compartmentalization of science is artificial and unnecessary, and come to know and understand a bit more about the "spaceship" that hurtles earthlings through space.

The science subjects for the last two years are part of the offerings of the VCE administered by the Victorian Curriculum and Assessment Board. The following subjects are available to students: biology, chemistry, geology, science, psychology, and physics. Each subject is divided into four parts and counts four units of the twenty-four-unit value VCE. Students are expected to complete at least two of the four units of a course. Some flexibility is built in, allowing students to enter the beginning of unit one, unit two, or unit three of each course.

One of the innovative attempts of the Victorian Curriculum and Assessment Board is the science syllabus for each subject. There is a strong attempt to give students a picture of the role of science in society, thereby emphasizing an STS approach. Central ideas or concepts are identified in the science syllabus, followed by very explicit contexts in which the ideas can be explored. The contexts involve the students in exploring science in everyday environments (e.g., household for electricity, car for electrical systems).

Table 4.18 Australian Science Curriculum, Years 7–10

Year	Core	Additional Units
7	Classification of Living Things	Forces
	Metric Measurement	Things and Places
	Mice and Men	Plants
	Introductory Chemistry	Sky Throughout the Year
		Crystals
8	The Changing Earth	Astronomy
	Heat Transfer	Energy and Change
	When Substances Are Heated	
	Cells	
9	Electricity	Coordination of the Body
	Reactions	Space Science
	Forces/Mechanics	Water
	Digging up Evidence	Consumer Science
	Human Physiology	Sound
10	Further Chemistry	Geological Mapping
	Geological Processes	Microorganisms
	Light	Human Sexuality
	Heredity	Drugs
	Forest Ecology/Conservation	Insight into Measurement

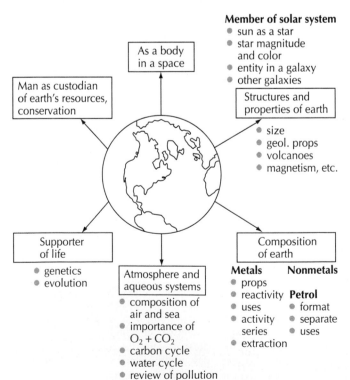

Figure 4.6 An Australian Level-10 Science Course Organized around the Theme Earth.

Chile

Claudia Rose *Claudia Rose, born in Mexico City D.F., Mexico, studied veterinary medicine at the University of Chile in Santiago. After working for ten years as a veterinarian in a government laboratory animal facility, she made a career change to teaching in 1997 and earned an M.A. in integrative education at TIES (The Institute for Educational Studies), associated with Vermont College. Rose has been teaching at the International School Nido de Aguilas in Santiago, Chile, for the past five years.*

The educational system in Chile has recently undergone significant and ambitious reform, leading to administrative decentralization and the implementation of a national standards-based curriculum developed during the 1990s through the cooperative effort of many educators throughout Chile. Historically, the Ministry of Education played a central role in Chilean education, defining everything from the specific curricula for each level to the number of hours assigned to each topic in every subject. Although the Ministry of Education has kept a regulatory role, as of 1990, schools by law have the freedom to prepare their own plans and study programs, as long as they demonstrate that these comply with the fundamental objectives and minimum contents established for each grade level by the ministry.

The Chilean Constitution of 1980 guarantees education and municipal public schools must provide free education to all students. Ninety-two percent of all students enrolled attend either municipal schools or strongly subsidized private schools, while the remainder attend private schools fully financed by parents. Enrollment is considered good, as 98.2 percent of all children six to thirteen years of age, and 85.9 percent of adolescents ages fourteen to seventeen, attend school regularly. Students first attend an obligatory common eight-year elementary program (Educación Básica) and then attend a four-year high school (Educación Media). Students are tracked either into high schools oriented toward the humanities and science (attended by most college-bound students) or into technical high schools where students also learn a trade and tend to enter the workforce directly, although they retain the possibility of applying to college.

The science curriculum stresses the understanding of the natural world, as well as the understanding of the nature of science and its relationship to society, and emphasizes the use of inquiry and hands-on activities to develop knowledge. Many topics are covered from a systems approach and stress the need for understanding environmental issues. The curriculum is of a spiral nature, as topics are covered repeatedly in increasing depth and complexity.

During the first four years of elementary school, science education forms part of a wider curricular unit, Understanding the Natural, Social, and Cultural Environment, that leads children to explore the natural world through diverse activities. Between grades 5 and 8, science education is considered a separate curricular unit, during which students study and gain further understanding of the workings of nature while touching on topics from the various disciplines of science (Table 4.19).

Between grades 9 and 12 (Primero medio to Cuarto medio), students cover topics in biology, chemistry, and physics each year. The new standards are academically demanding, but content is presented within the context of Chile's culture and economy. Societal and environmental issues have a major role in the standards, and the nature of scientific enterprise is also emphasized throughout all topics, as attaining a high level of scientific literacy is one of the main objectives of the reform to science curricula. Table 4.20 presents the minimum expected contents to be covered during each year of high school. Technical schools are also expected to complete these requirements through grade 10, after which technical preparation begins.

The implementation of the new curricula for science and all other subjects has led to a number of other changes in Chile's educational system. The lengthening of the school day from a half-day to a full-day schedule is still underway throughout the country, as funds are made available for the construction of more schools to accommodate the doubled load of students. Teachers will require support in terms of training and materials to carry out inquiry and hands-on activities, and work hours and pay scales will also need to be adjusted. The college-entry testing system is also being modified to reflect the changes in curriculum, creating considerable controversy among all sectors involved. In this sense, the main concern is equity, and the fear is that the new curricula and college-entry testing will tip the scales in favor of those few who can pay for private schools, where the cost of implementation is not a problem. At present, the majority of those who enter college belong to the 8 percent of students who attend private schools. The challenge, then, is implementation in the majority of schools, where resources are scarce, teachers are poorly paid, and students are unmotivated by the bleakness of their academic future.

Table 4.19 Chilean Science Standards, Grades 5–8

Grade 5	Grade 6	Grade 7	Grade 8
Forces and Motion • force and motion • trajectories • application of physical concepts to simple machines	Properties of Matter • quantification • particle theory of matter • substances	Atoms and Chemical Properties of Matter • atoms, elements, and molecules • general chemical properties of matter	Changes and Conservation in Physical Processes • phase changes • latent heat • conservation of energy in natural phenomena
The Human Body as a System • nervous system • senses • movement	Properties of Energy • transfers and transformations • energy flow in thermic reactions • energy flow in combustion	Particle Nature of Gases • properties of gases • relationships between temperature, pressure, and volume	Changes and Conservation in Chemical Processes • chemical reactions • acids and bases • combustion
Characteristics and Diversity of the Environment • diversity of living organisms • population dynamics • natural resources and conservation	Flows of Energy and Matter in Biological Systems • flows between organisms and environment • photosynthesis • flows of energy and matter in ecosystems	Sexuality • puberty and adolescence • male and female anatomy and physiology • embryonary and fetal development • responsible sexuality	Changes in the Earth and Universe • theories regarding formation of the universe and solar system • impact of technology on scientific exploration and vice versa • global warming • sustainable development
	Integrative Projects • flows of matter and energy in natural and social systems • environmental impact of human activity	Heterotrophic Nutrition • comparative anatomy • human nutrition (absorption, metabolism, and excretion) • basic characteristics of living organisms	Evolution of Life • origin of life • reproduction as a source of variability • inheritance • natural selection and speciation • validation of scientific knowledge
		Health as Equilibrium • communicable diseases • immune barriers to disease • personal and social responsibilities in health • tobacco, alcohol, and drugs	

Source: Ministry of Education of Chile (MINEDUC) 2000: Study Programs for Grades 5, 6, 7, and 8 (Santiago, Chile).

Table 4.20 Chilean High School Science Standards

Chemistry	Biology	Physics
	Grade 9	

Chemistry	Biology	Physics
Water	Cell Structure and Function	Sound
• electrolysis of water	• structure of plant and animal cells	• vibration and sound
• contamination and purification	• transport across membranes	• sound waves
Air	• organic molecules	• sound composition
• composition	• emergent properties of cells	Light
• compressibility and diffusion of gases	Vital Processes and Functions	• light transmission
• seasonal variations in quality and composition	• nutrition and balanced diets	• nature of light
• use of natural gas as energy source	• catabolic and anabolic metabolism	Electricity
Petroleum	• digestion and absorption of nutrients	• electric charge and current
• origin and commercialization	Circulation	• magnetism
• production, consumption, and reserves; substitutes	• circulatory system	• electricity
Soils	• blood	
• classification	• adaptations to training	
• conservation	Respiratory System	
• mineralogy	• comparative anatomy	
• copper exploitation	• oxygen availability and debt during exercise; relationship to aerobic and anaerobic respiration	
	Excretion	
	• Urinary system	

Chemistry	Biology	Physics
	Grade 10	

Chemistry	Biology	Physics
Atomic Theory	Cell Structure and Function	Motion
• structure and dimensions	• cell cycle	• describing motion
• periodic properties	• chromosome theory	• forces and motion
Chemical Bonds	• mitosis and meiosis	• mechanical energy
• VSPER theory	Vital Processes and Functions	Heat
• ionic, covalent, and metallic bonds	• hormonal control of reproduction and gametogenesis	• temperature
• bond angles and 3D representations	• hormonal control of growth and development	• thermal energy
Organic Chemistry	Human Biology and Health	
• functional groups	• mutagenesis	
• common organic compounds	• medical use of hormones	
• stoichiometry and energetics of the oxidation of sugars, proteins, and fats	• sexually transmitted diseases	
• distillation of an alcoholic beverage and estimation of alcohol content	• genetic disorders	
	Variability and Heredity	
	• definition and sources of genetic diversity	
	• animal breeds	
	• ethical issues surrounding cloning	

Table 4.20 *(continued)*

Chemistry	Biology	Physics
Grade 11		
Reactivity and Equilibrium	Cell Structure and Function	Mechanics
• energetics	• cellular adaptations	• circular motion
• stoichiometry	• relationship between structure and	• conservation of energy
• redox reactions	function	
Kinematics	Vital Processes and Functions	Fluids
• rates of reaction	• homeostasis	• hydrostatics
• catalysts	• nervous system	• hydrodynamics
Reactivity in Organic Chemistry	• muscular system and motor response	
• chemical reactions of organic compounds	Human Biology and Health	
• organic chemistry in food science	• psychoactive drugs and addiction	
	• stress	
Grade 12		
Natural and Synthetic Polymers	Cell Structure and Function	Electricity and Magnetism
• polymers	• genome, genes, and genetic engineering	• forces between charged particles
• protein structure	Vital Processes and Functions	• alternating current circuitry
• DNA structure and replication	• immune system (specific and nonspecific	• electromagnetic waves
Nuclear Phenomena	defenses)	Atomic Theory
• isotopes and nuclear instability	Human Biology and Health	• models
• nuclear fusion and fission	• blood groups	• uncertainty principle
• medical applications of isotopes	• immune disorders	• nuclear physics
Industrial Chemistry	• artificial immunization	
• mining and extraction techniques	Organism and Environment	
• glass, cement, and ceramics	• interspecific relationships	
• polyethylene, nylon, and silicone	• populations and communities	
	• biodiversity, human population growth, and	
	assessment of environmental impact	

Source: http://www.mineduc.cl/planesprog/index.htm#a2.

China

Ronald F. Price *Ronald F. Price, born in Wales (1926), was educated in England, obtaining an External London degree in botany and zoology, followed by teacher training at Exeter. Price taught biology in technical colleges in England and trained science teachers in Ghana and Australia. Also taught in Bulgaria and China. Following writing Education in Communist China (1970), Price obtained a Ph.D. in comparative education at London University and then taught comparative education and science method at La Trobe University, Melbourne, Australia, retiring in 1991. He continues to live and write in Melbourne.*

China has the largest educational system in the world, with more than 200 million students enrolled in public schools. Estimates, however, indicate that only 20 percent of the students who enter kindergarten complete the ten-year program of formal schooling. About 80 percent of the population of China lives in rural areas, and enrollment in school tends to be lower in the rural areas when compared with the Chinese cities.

Science education, like other subjects in the Chinese curriculum, has experienced change. During the Great Proletarian Cultural Revolution in China (1966–1976), schooling was given less emphasis, being shortened from twelve to ten years, as well as becoming less academic and more vocational. Cross and Price point out, however, that "this period in education in China is of undoubted interest for teachers in the West because of the way in which Chinese curriculum writers appear to have attempted to produce textbooks that stressed the relevance of science rather than its theoretical aspects."[51]

For example, an analysis of Chinese physics texts by Cross and Price revealed that there appeared to be a greater emphasis on "useful knowledge rather than understanding laws and principles."[52] Although the present Communist regime in Beijing has rejected the Great Cultural Revolution, Cross and Price point out that what might be lost is the attempt of Chinese educators during this period to "combine education with productive labor" in contrast to traditional "goose-stuffing" methods.

In 1978, two conferences were held to rebuild the science curriculum after the Great Cultural Revolution. These conferences, attended by thousands of scientists and educators, shaped the new emphasis on science in China, which, according to Hurd, is as follows: "In contrast with science education policies characteristic of the Cultural Revolution, the new science program was viewed as one emphasizing basic theories and stressing logical and abstract thinking. Problem solving, conceptualizing, and applying knowledge led to production were to be stressed."[53]

The new science program in China, which has resulted in new textbooks and curricula, is based on goals formulated by scientists and teachers as follows:

1. Mastery of key concepts and basic information;
2. Ability to conceptualize and make inferences;
3. Development of systematic and logical methods for analysis and synthesis in solving problems;
4. Appreciation of the importance of physical models in thinking;
5. Facilitation of the student's ability to apply knowledge to practical problems, especially in agriculture and production;
6. Appreciation of the evolution of science concepts to foster a dialectical-materialistic point of view and way of thinking;
7. Development of skills in experimental procedures and in the use of scientific instruments.[54]

Textbooks that are written by committees of scientists and teachers drive science education in China. According to Hurd, the first set of texts produced after the Cultural Revolution were criticized as being too theoretical and impractical for many Chinese students.

Following is a brief examination of the scope and sequence of the Chinese science curriculum, and some comments about science instruction in Chinese schools.

The Scope and Sequence of the Science Curriculum

Primary school science in grades 1 to 3 is not taught as a separate "subject" but is part of the physical education program. The texts use stories about science, inventions, animals, personal hygiene, and community sanitation to present science. In grades 4 and 5, science is taught twice a week throughout the school year. Grade 4 science emphasizes weather and the atmosphere and the biology of plants and animals. The course also emphasizes human physiology and diseases, physics topics (including simple machines, sound, electricity, heat, and light), and topics in earth and space science (including the earth's rocks and soils, the solar system, stars, and the universe).

Secondary level science is divided into three years each at the junior and senior levels. Science courses make up slightly more than 20 percent of the Chinese student's curriculum in most of the nation's schools. The curriculum is arranged as shown in Table 4.21.

Although there are different arrangements of Chinese schools (five-year versus six-year schools, priority versus nonpriority), the science curriculum is generally as shown in Table 4.22.

As in many of the other countries discussed in this section, science is given high priority in the Chinese curriculum. One question that we might raise given the priority of science in China's schools is how is science taught?

In an analysis of science textbooks in Chinese schools, Cross, Henze, and Price concluded, after an exhaustive analysis of topics and questions at the end of each chapter, that the aim was to produce specialists and the textbooks did not appear to provide training skills that would be useful in a variety of situations. They also concluded that the following goals were not emphasized: problem solving, the application of principles to novel situations, and interpreting and predicting.[55] Although it is difficult to generalize on the actual nature of classroom instruction in the Chinese classroom, Cross, Henze, and Price make the following observations:[56]

- Class sizes are very large, often ranging from fifty to seventy students per class.

Table 4.21 Timetable of the Chinese Curriculum

	Junior Level			Senior Level				
Course	I	II	III	I	II	III	Hours	Percent of Curriculum
Biology	2	2				2	198	3.5
Chemistry			3	3	3	3	372	6.7
Physics		2	3	4	3	4	500	9.0
Math	5	6	6	5	5	5	1,026	18.5
Total Hours/Week	31	31	31	29	26	26	——	——

Table 4.22 Chinese Secondary Science Curriculum

Junior Level	Senior Level
Physics: The physics course begins in the second year of the junior school with the study of mechanics. Topics include measurement, weight, force, pressure in liquids and gases, buoyancy, force and movement, simple machines, work and energy, change of state, heat energy, and heat engines. In the third year, the course includes current electricity, electrical work, transmission in liquids and gases, electromagnetism, and an introduction to light.	Physics: Three years of physics are offered. Topics include mechanics, concepts of equilibrium and motion including Newton's laws; mechanical vibration and wave motion and the gas equations; electric and magnetic fields, static electricity, alternating current electricity, the nature of light, and elementary concepts of atomic structure.
Chemistry: The chemistry course begins in the third year of the junior level with topics including oxygen, hydrogen, solutions, moles and heats of reaction, the structure of matter, nitrogen subgroup, speeds of reaction and equilibrium, the carbon group, and organic compounds.	Chemistry: Senior level chemistry begins in year one with sodium and sulfuric acid, heats of reaction, the periodic table of the elements, the nitrogen group, the carbon group, and colloids. In year two topics include electrolysis, magnetism and aluminum, transitional elements, hydrocarbons, sugars and proteins, and high polymer compounds.
Biology: The biology course begins in the first year of the primary school and continues into the second year. The course begins with a consideration of the structure of living things, including cells, tissues, and organs. The organs of flowering plants, seeds, roots, stems and leaves, flowers, and fruit follow this. Students then study the structure and functions of the major groups.	Biology: Senior level biology begins with the structure and function of the cell and then considers the origin of life, assimilation and metabolism, reproduction and development, regulation and control, heredity and variation.

- Only in a few schools within each province is equipment comparable to what one finds in schools in the advanced industrial countries, though in the best-equipped schools it is excellent, both in quality and quantity.
- Probably for reasons of class size and availability of equipment, class experiments are confined to the few student experiments listed in the textbooks or may even be totally absent.
- Teacher demonstration is common, often involving special apparatus.
- Lessons are formal, closely following the textbook.

- Students memorize a great deal of material and work through exercises, regularly being brought to the blackboard to answer questions orally.

Ghana

Charles Hutchison *Charles Hutchison was born in Ghana, where he earned a B.S. at the University of Cape Coast and taught general science and biology. He then studied immunogenetics in Hungary, worked at Georgetown University, and then got an M.A. at*

Oklahoma Christian University of Science and Arts. Hutchison taught science (7–12) in Atlanta for nine years. He earned his Ph.D. in science education at Georgia State University. He is a professor of science education at the University of North Carolina, Charlotte.

Ghana is a West African nation with a population of about 18 million, a gross domestic product (GDP) of about $462.8 (1993), and a land mass comparable to the state of Oregon (238,537 sq. km. or 92,000 sq. mi.). It lies just north of the equator, and on the Greenwich meridian. It was colonized by the British, and was granted independence in 1957.

Science education has always been a part of the Ghanaian (and Sub-Saharan) cultural phenomenon. Prior to the advent of modern education in Ghana, there were both "formal" and "informal" forms of education. Both forms generally took after the apprenticeship model, although direct instruction was prevalent in specific situations. "Informal education" involved working with a close relative to learn a family trade, in a relatively casual climate. In "formal education," a child would generally be sent to learn a trade from a master craftsman, with some type of specific arrangement. This arrangement would then be formalized with a symbolic seal, such as a drink. On completing the apprenticeship, there were formal graduation rites and celebrations.

Modern education in Ghana came with the advent of European missionary and mercantile enterprises and has largely become the vehicle for social upward mobility. Education in general, and science education in particular, for that matter, are serious issues for all Ghanaians.

Educational Administration in Ghana

Education in Ghana is centrally administered under the purview of the Ministry of Education, which is responsible for the formulation of the national educational objectives. This ministry oversees the Ghana Education Service (GES), which is responsible for pretertiary levels of education, and the National Council for Tertiary Education (NCTE), which is responsible for tertiary education (more information is available at http://www.ghana.edu.gh/).

The GES organizes its constituencies into a 6:3:3 format: Six years of primary education, three years of junior secondary school (JSS), and three years of senior secondary school (SSS). All children in Ghana are compulsorily expected to enroll in school at the age of six

for a free, nine-year basic education (primary and JSS). Those who enter the SSS generally pursue their education with their economic future in mind.

The Science Curriculum and Delivery

The Ghanaian science curriculum follows the spiral approach, treating the same themes at different times and in greater depths within each educational level. At the primary and JSS levels are environmental studies and integrated science. The curriculum is the modern replacement of what used to be called nature study. This is a generalist, survey course that exposes the child to the universe. At this level, the students would get the basic exposure to scientific ideas and learn about the history of science. They also learn the basic scientific vocabulary at this level.

At the JSS level, the science curriculum comprises integrated science. At this level, the students are exposed to the rudiments of physics, chemistry, and biology. Following the "Ghana Science Series" for three years, the students spiral through the following topics:

1. The Nature of Things around Us: Some properties of matter, measurement, the nature of matter
2. Some Effects of Energy: Energy, some effects of heat on matter, movements of living and non-living things, making work easy (machines)
3. Life Activities: New life from old life, seeding in plants and animals, uses of food in living things, getting rid of waste materials from the body
4. Humans and Their Environment: Crop production, raising animals, food processing, a balanced diet, hygiene and health

At this stage, students are prepared for one of five GES-endorsed programs at the SSS level. Science education is held in the highest regard in Ghana and only the best students are admitted into the SSS program with the science concentration option.

At the SSS level, all students take, at minimum, integrated science (comprising general science, agriculture, and environmental studies). For those who qualify to enter the SSS science option, the science curriculum includes the individual disciplines of physics, chemistry, biology, and physical education. The agricultural science option curriculum includes general agriculture, crop husbandry, animal husbandry, physics, and chemistry. The SSS integrated science curriculum guide employs the "SSS Science," authored to seamlessly follow the JSS science book series. The curriculum outline is as follows:

Year One: Introducing Science
- Diversity of living and nonliving things; the cell; matter and energy (I); air and water; matter and energy (II); acids, bases, and salts

Year Two: Interactions in Nature
- Life activities in man; matter and energy (III); change and equilibrium

Year Three: Variation
- Inheritance and evolution; matter and energy (IV); some elements and their compounds; compounds of carbon; science and society; science and technology

At the university level, students enter the science departments corresponding to their SSS program. The science curriculum is further delineated into zoology, botany, physics, and mathematics. The agricultural option is also delineated into animal and crop sciences, agricultural economics and extension, agricultural engineering, and soil science. Students have the option to major (concentrate) in any of the more specific areas toward the final year of their program.

The Art of Pedagogy in Ghana: How and Why

Ghana, despite its colonial past, still cherishes its cultural heritage. A part of this cultural heritage is respect for the elderly—naturally including teachers. For this reason, the cultural tradition strongly influences the classroom environment. In this tradition, elders are deemed as the custodians of knowledge. Consequently, the teacher embodies the proverbial "sage on stage." The result is that children generally are less apt to ask questions in class and the teacher is the final authority of knowledge. The concomitant method of instruction for the majority of teachers is the lecture approach; delivering knowledge, as it were, into "empty, but willing vessels." This teaching method, although a somewhat expected spillover of the general cultural climate, shares a European heritage: Since the modern Ghanaian educational system began with the missionaries, there was a basic evangelic-ecclesiastical orientation. Obedi-

ence, memorization of material, and the "direct delivery" approach were all a part of the ecclesiastical scholasticism Ghana inherited in the early missionary days of education—and such went to buttress the cultural tendency to do the same.

It must be mentioned, however, that science teaching and learning inherently resist the all-lecture approach, and readily lend themselves to practical work. For this reason, it is common practice to find the Ghanaian science teacher doing demonstrations or lab work, where facilities are available, and employing the guided-discovery approach in instruction. One would readily find a science teacher taking students to the school farm to learn agriculture by practice or going to a nearby stream to collect live specimen for dissection.

In light of the relatively lecture-heavy method of science instruction in Ghana, it must be noted that, granted the Ghanaian cultural environment, a good instructor could masterfully execute a science lesson by incorporating analogies, anecdotes, and personal narratives and by employing the inherently rich, colorful language forms of Africa. As opposed to a cultural environment where students may be less apt to sit and listen for longer time periods, the typical Ghanaian student would listen longer as a result of motivation. In the Ghanaian cultural milieu, therefore, the science teacher has the additional cherished facility: the student's "cognitive presence" for a longer period of time—and he or she takes advantage of it.

Educational Reforms and Science Teaching in Ghana

During the 1970s and the early 1980s, Ghana experienced serious economic problems that created a brain drain; many teachers left the country to work in neighboring countries. There was also a general feeling that the educational system was not responding to the realistic economic future needs of the students and the nation. There was, therefore, a reorganization of the educational system into the current result (see http://www.ghana.edu.gh/past/eightiesReforms.html for more information). Interestingly, there was also a sense of failure of the prevalent educational processes and methodologies to create an understanding of the information taught. This brought about a new movement in methodologies, whereby "best practices" are being viewed as the provision of more hands-on, minds-on experiences. This is a new phenomenon in the Ghanaian scene, and may bear some counter-culture implications. Granted that it will take time for the teacher-sages to step down from their "stages," and the students to move from their relatively "passive-assimilators-of-knowledge" roles to engage their teachers in science discussions, this new movement is a step in the right direction.

Japan

Shigehiko Tsukahara *Shigehiko Tsukahara, born in Shiga, Japan, earned a B.S. in applied chemistry from Okayama University of Science. After ten years of teaching science (7–12) in public schools in Shiga prefecture, Tsukahara came to the United States to attend graduate school, earned an M.A.E. (chemistry education) from Northern Michigan University, and currently is attending Georgia State University.*

Since 1947, the Course of Study, a national guideline, has ruled Japanese education K–12. It is referred to as "6-3-3 system" of the years of elementary, junior high, and senior high schools, with first nine years compulsory. The Course of Study has been revised about every ten years and the latest revision was done in 1998 and 1999. It became effective for all students in grades 1–9 in 2002, and high school freshmen beginning in 2003.

Textbooks used in grades 1–12 are written based on the national guideline and Monbusho's (Ministry of Education, Science, Sports, and Culture) authorizations are required. Several publishers are providing textbooks for each grade and subject. Selection of the textbooks is done by the intermediate school district at public elementary and junior high schools. The expense of the textbooks at 1–9 is paid by the government, but other supplies, such as workbooks, are charged to parents. At high schools, each school selects textbooks. Because the textbooks are the possessions of students, they are soft-covered, relatively inexpensive, and lightweight compared to those in the United States.

Currently, Japanese children start to study science in the third grade. In 1992, the first and second grade science and social studies were abolished and a new subject, Life Environmental Studies, was born. The elementary science covers three areas: (1) living things and their lives, (2) matter and energy, and (3) the earth and universe.[57] These three areas first appeared in the Course of Study in 1968, when Japan had been influenced from several science projects developed in the United States.

The 7–9 science curriculum is organized into two fields: Field I corresponds to physics and chemistry and Field II is for biology and earth science (Table 4.23). This basic concept has not changed since it was introduced in 1958. Today, the junior high school science curriculum has seven main items in each field. It is required to be taught in this order during three years, but it is not specified at which grade.[58]

Approximately 70 percent of Japanese students advance to college-bound high schools and the other 30 percent go to schools that are providing vocational courses.[59] Students are required to take at least two science courses among the selective courses provided at their school (Table 4.24).[60]

If you are visiting science laboratories in Japanese schools, you will notice the commonality of each lab, all of which are equipped by similar number of devices. The similarity is due to the science education promotion law, which regulates the standards of teaching aids and supports its expense by national treasury and was promulgated as early as 1953 to assure the opportunities of science education for every student. All science teachers keep their labs neat, comfortable, and rich in equipment.

One characteristic of elementary science is a school science garden, which is necessary for pursuing the scope of Living Things and Their Lives and The Earth and Universe (most of which cannot be done in the classroom). Each grade of students grows and observes annual plants in this garden for science class. Because the Japanese school year starts in early April and ends in late March, students can experience seeding to fruition seamlessly. Science gardens especially play important role in urban areas where children seldom come in direct contact with nature.

Because their ordinal teaching licenses never expire, Japanese teachers do not have to go back to college to maintain their certificates. Instead, in-service training courses are provided by each prefecture's board of education. Some training is mandatory, but many science teachers participate in the optional study groups offered by boards of education or private organizations. For example, a chemistry teacher proposed that his study group to make a periodic table display with real element samples (originally found in the national science museum in Tokyo) for each school lab. Although there are some missing elements, due to prohibitions for general usage by law, the home-brew displays are very impressive and attract students' attention at participating high school labs in Shiga prefecture. One regretful aspect is that this kind of practice sharing is usually only at the local level and is rarely introduced nationwide.

Table 4.23 Main Structure in the Japanese Junior High School Science Curriculum

Field I	Field II
(1) Familiar Physical Phenomena A. Light and sound B. Forces and pressures	(1) Kinds of Plants and Their Lives A. Observations B. Constructions of plant body C. Groups of plants
(2) Substances Found in Our Surroundings A. Aspect of substance B. Aqueous solutions	(2) The Earth's Crust and Its Changes A. Strata and past appearance B. Volcanoes and earthquakes
(3) Electric Current and Its Utilization A. Electric current B. Utilization of electric current	(3) Kinds of Animals and Their Lives A. Constructions of animal body B. Groups of animals
(4) Chemical Change and Atoms, Molecules A. Formations of substances B. Chemical change and mass of substances	(4) Weather and Its Changes A. Weather observations B. Weather changes
(5) Regularity of Motions A. Regularity of motions	(5) Cells of Living Things and Reproduction A. Living things and cells B. Reproduction of living things
(6) Substances and Utilization of Chemical Reactions A. Substances and utilization of chemical reactions	(6) The Earth and Universe A. The earth's rotation and revolution B. The solar system and stars
(7) Science and Technology and Human Beings A. Energy resources B. Science and technology and human beings*	(7) Nature and Human Beings A. Nature and environment B. Nature and human beings*

* Selective.

Table 4.24 High School Science Subjects

Basic Science*
General Science I*
General Science II*
Physics I*
Physics II
Chemistry I*
Chemistry II
Biology I*
Biology II
Earth Science I*
Earth Science II

* Required two subjects, with at least one from Basic Science, General Science I, and General Science II

Russia

Sergei Tolstikov *Sergei Tolstikov is a graduate teacher of EFL from Moscow, Russia. He is a well-known educator having taught English at Moscow Gymnasium school 710 and currently is doing research work at the Russian Academy of Education and is an editor of the Foreign Languages at School Journal. An active participant of the Global Thinking Project for more than ten years, Tolstikov has worked with science educators from several nations, and continues to collaborate with American science educators.*

The Russian education system is now being fundamentally renewed, undergoing diversification and decentralization. Included in the reform is also the transition to twelve-year school (by the year 2008) and such controversial issues as the state school standards, a unified state examination, and a voucher system.

The legislative basis of the Russian education system is organized on three levels: federal, ethnic–regional, and institutional. Strategic decisions and state requirements are formulated at the federal and regional levels, but they find their specific implementation at the institutional (school) level.

The Russian education system overall organization is 4-5-2 (primary school, basic school, senior school) and will be 4-6-2 under twelve-year schooling. Under the existing eleven-year schooling, the basic school curriculum consists of three components: federal, regional, and school. The federal component is invariable and determines the compulsory minimum of educational program content, the maximum amount of teaching periods for students, and the required student achievement. The regional and school components give schools and regions significant autonomy in curriculum content decisions, allowing schools to add extra study hours for in-depth study of different subjects of their choice, providing they meet the state requirement. (In the planned twelve-year school the basic school curriculum will consist of the federal, ethnic–regional, school, and student components, where the first and the second will be invariable.)

The compulsory curriculum for science is shown in Table 4.25. All students are introduced to science at the junior level (classes 1–4) and then begin their study of science in earnest in the fifth level.

Junior Level Science

The Russian science curriculum begins with a two-year experience called The World Around in classes 1 through 4. The focus of this experience is the exploration of the natural environment, including gardens, parks, the countryside, changing seasons, and caring for pets and indoor plants.

This experience is followed by Nature Study in class 5. Nature study involves students in developing skills in observation, inquisitiveness, and love of nature. The aims of the nature study include:

- Observing the weather, plants, behavior of wild creatures, and consequences for human health and agriculture.
- Focusing on natural surroundings in the Russian Federation, the human body, health and fitness, and the concern for the health of the people.
- Developing a holistic picture of the natural world.
- Emphasizing the processes of science, including observing natural objects, comparing and contrasting, deduction, and generalizing.

The content of nature study also includes earth and other bodies, air and the water cycle, conservation, rocks and soil, living organisms and their environment, the effect of human activity on the living world, and ecology.

Senior Level Science

The Russian science curriculum from classes 6–12 is described as a spiral curriculum. In the curriculum, each science is taught over a period of several years. For example, in class 6, students begin their study of biology, which continues for the next five years (Table 4.25). Notice that in each of the next two years students study first physics, then chemistry, and continue studying these subjects each year. Let's look at each subject.

Table 4.25 Russian Science Curriculum: The Compulsory Minimum of Hours per Week by Subject: Subjects and Grades

Course	Grade Level										
	1	2	3	4	5	6	7	8	9	10	11
The World Around	1	1	2	2							
Nature Study					2						
Biology						2	2	2	2	2	2
Physics							2	2	2	2	2
Chemistry								2	2	2	2
Total hours per week	1	1	2	2	2	2	4	6	6	6	6

The biology curriculum in level 6 is botany, and students meet for two periods of instruction per week. Zoology is introduced in level 7 and continues into level 8. Human anatomy and physiology are taught in level 9, and general biology is offered in the levels 10 and 11.

The content of physics in level 7 includes physics phenomena, the structure of matter, interaction of bodies, pressure, work, power, and energy. In level 8 students study thermal, electrical, electromagnetic, and light phenomena. In level 9 students study kinematics, conservation laws, and waves. In level 10 they study molecular physics and electrodynamics, followed in level 11 with a continuation of electrodynamics, as well as electromagnetic waves and quantum physics. As a part of the physics curriculum, in the last year of school, students also take a course in astronomy, which introduces a contemporary view of the universe focusing on the practical use of astronomy.

The chemistry curriculum begins in level 8. The chemistry curriculum is focused on exploring two basic systems of knowledge; namely, substances and processes. The content in levels 8 and 9 is the study of inorganic chemistry, while in levels 10 and 11 the focus is on organic chemistry.

The reform opens way to the increasing number of specialized secondary schools, lyceums, and gymnasiums, where a variety of elective subjects are taught and students can acquire a thorough knowledge in some field of study. Sometimes specialized classes with an intensive study of certain subjects, such as physics and mathematics, biology, and chemistry, are organized inside the general secondary school. An example of specialized science class's curriculum is shown in Table 4.26.

Table 4.26 Specialized Science Classes: Subjects and Grades

Course	Physics and Math Class			Chemistry and Biology Class		
	9	10	11	9	10	11
Biology	2	2	2	3	4	4
Chemistry	2	2	2	4	4	4
Physics	5	6	6	3	4	4
Total hours per week	9	10	10	10	12	12

SECTION 2: THE SCIENCE TEACHER GAZETTE

Volume 4: The Science Curriculum

Think Pieces

1. What are the advantages and disadvantages of the present American science curriculum model (layer cake)? What are the advantages and disadvantages of the NSTA scope and sequence curriculum model?

2. What should characterize a high school biology, chemistry, or physics course in light of recent reports, especially Project 2061?

3. Find and locate literature to support the development of a science course that is conceptually oriented and that is designed to develop scientific thinking skills to inquire about natural phenomena and develop scientific explanation.

4. What are the science education programs like in some other countries, in addition to the ones described here? You might want to investigate science education in Mexico, France, Great Britain, Hungary, or the Philippines. Prepare a brief report by creating a poster presentation for the country you choose.

5. What are some of the differences and similarities between U.S. science education and science education in Australia, Japan, and Russia? Make a chart identifying the variables that you will use to make comparisons, and show how each country fared on the variable.

6. What do you think should be the main goals of the science curriculum for middle schools? What differences in goals, if any, should exist between middle and high school science?

7. Should the United States adopt a national science curriculum or should it maintain the emphasis on a decentralized system of science education? Find and locate in the literature information about NSTA's scope and sequence report.

8. What are the most important things a student should learn from earth science, life science, physical science, or general science? (Choose one area.)

9. Do you think requiring students to take a course in science in each year of high school a good idea? Why?

Case Study: Unified Science

The Case

Sarah Jenkins is the science department head in a large high school in an urban area. During the summer the new principal of the high school organized a two-day retreat for all the department heads to discuss plans for the year and curriculum changes. Jenkins, like the other department heads wonders what the principal means by "curriculum changes." At the meeting the principal, a middle-aged woman with a Ph.D. in curriculum and administration, leads the group in a discussion of how the curriculum could be changed to make it more interesting and relevant to students. When the discussion gets to the science curriculum, a proposal that emerges from the group is the possibility of integrating the separate subjects of biology, chemistry, and physics into a single, unified science program (e.g., Science I, Science II, Science III, Science IV). The principal grabs on to this idea and charges Jenkins to come up with a plan that might be implemented on a small scale starting this year.

The Problem

What should Sarah Jenkins do? Is this a valid approach to high school science? Is the principal justified in making this demand?

Case Study: The Science Proficiency Race

The Case

At a recent conference on science teaching it was reported that:

- U.S. fifth graders performed at about the average level of fifteen countries in an international study.
- U.S. grade 9 students and advanced science students (second-year biology, chemistry, and physics) had lower performance levels than their counterparts in most other countries.
- Only 42 percent of the U.S. thirteen-year-olds demonstrated an ability to use scientific procedures and analyze scientific data, compared

with more than 70 percent in Korea and British Columbia.

A professor from a very prestigious public university in Atlanta reported the results to an audience of about 500 science educators. To make the results more visual, the professor showed a number of graphs depicting the results among the thirty-eight countries that had participated in the most recent international test of science proficiency. One graphic compared the average mathematics and science achievement of eighth-grade students by nation. According to the data, the United States ranked eighteenth in science and nineteenth in mathematics out of the thirty-eight countries studied. A teacher from the audience disputed the professor's results, claiming that the other countries had different goals and commitments to science and that the comparison of test results wasn't fair.

A number of other teachers seemed to agree because they started nodding their heads affirmatively. The professor, who appeared unshaken by the response, went on to describe specific areas in science where U.S. students lagged behind their counterparts.

The Problem

If you were in the audience, how would you react to the professor's international test results? Are comparisons across cultures and countries "fair"? What do results like these suggest about the science curriculum?

RESEARCH MATTERS

USING TEXTBOOKS FOR MEANINGFUL LEARNING IN SCIENCE

Sarah L. Ulerick

Introduction

Much of science teaching is guided by and based upon the contents of science textbooks.[61] Gatherings of science educators frequently condemn this practice, as they recommend more and better hands-on science activities in the K–12 curriculum. If we look carefully at classroom practice and textbooks, however, we might ask,

"Is it the books themselves that are the problem or is it the manner in which students and teachers use them?" This [selection] presents a rationale and strategies for teachers to facilitate meaningful learning from science textbooks.

Constructing Meaning

Over the past twenty to thirty years, views of how learners acquire knowledge have shifted from behaviorist theories of the 1950s and 1960s to a "constructivist" view. The constructivist view of knowledge acquisition holds that learning is a process of connecting new knowledge to existing knowledge, involving active engagement of the learner's mind. What we learn from any experience, including the experience of reading, depends upon what we already know and how we choose to "connect" our knowledge with the sensory input we perceive. Said differently, we use what we already know to make sense of what we don't.

Reading researchers have acknowledged for some time that reading is a process of active construction of meaning; and the ideas supporting constructivism are well documented by research on comprehension of written text. A number of studies have shown how a reader's knowledge interacts with text to influence comprehension, recall, and usefulness of what is read. For example, in a study described in Bransford, readers were given the [following] passage to read and comprehend.[62] Read the passage and see if you think it is easy to understand.

The procedure is actually quite simple. First you arrange items into different groups. Of course one pile may be sufficient depending on how much there is to do. If you have to go somewhere else due to lack of facilities that is the next step; otherwise, you are pretty well set. It is important not to overdo things. That is, it is better to do too few things at once than too many. In the short run this may not seem important but complications can easily arise. A mistake can be expensive as well. At first, the whole procedure will seem complicated. Soon, however, it will become just another facet of life. It is difficult to foresee any end to the necessity for this task in the immediate future, but then, one can never tell. After the procedure is completed one arranges the materials into different groups again. Then they can be put into their appropriate places. Eventually they will be used once more and the whole cycle will then have to be repeated. However, that is a part of life.[63]

Most readers find this description of a procedure difficult to understand when read without a title. When the title was provided, readers had no difficulty following the paragraph. The title was "Doing the Laundry!"

Why is this nontechnical description of a familiar procedure so difficult to make sense of without its title? Most of us have prior knowledge to understand the paragraph, but are unable to use it without the "cue" or "context" that the title provides. If we are reasonably good readers, we probably tried to make sense of the sequence of sentences as we read along; we might have had one or two tentative hypotheses about the topic of the paragraph as we struggled to construct some coherent meaning for ourselves. If we are less persistent and resourceful readers, we might have given up halfway through the paragraph in frustration, concluding that it simply "made no sense."

Now read the following paragraph from a popular high school biology textbook:

Water enters the mouth, where it passes over the gills on either side of the head. The water is then forced out through separate pairs of gill slits. The gills are respiratory organs of the fish. The shark has large, well-developed eyes on either side of the head above the mouth. Paired nostrils on the ventral side if the head lead to olfactory sacs. These olfactory sacs sense odors in the water. As already mentioned, shark skeletons are made up of cartilage rather than bone.

Unless you have recently taught a unit on "Class Chondrichthyes," you might not have recognized this passage as a description of the respiratory system of the shark. Even when presented in the context of the printed textbook page, this passage is difficult to visualize in any concrete manner. Now, imagine you are a science-indifferent or science-phobic tenth grader with poor-to-average reading skills. How will you make sense of this passage? Even if you want to try, will you have the skills to do so? And why should you struggle to understand the passage to begin with?

Difficulties in Learning from Science Textbooks

The effort a reader puts into comprehending or making sense from text depends on several factors. The reader's purpose in reading is foremost among these. We tend to put more effort into figuring out things we really want to know. Our purpose also prescribes the context for the connections we will make between the information we are reading and what we already know. For example, readers who are told to compare and contrast ideas in a passage tend to read more slowly and to recall ideas in a compare/contrast structure. In many science classes, the traditional approach to using a textbook is to have students read a chapter and answer questions typically found at the end of the chapter. The questions tend to be low in cognitive level, inviting a search-and-find learning strategy.[64] Since answering these questions is their only purpose, students tend to engage at a very low cognitive level. Therefore, we should hardly be surprised that many students fail in the difficult task of making meaning from science prose.

The shallow purpose students are given for reading presents the first of several difficulties students have in learning from science textbooks. The low cognitive demands of such assignments discourage students from actively making meaningful connections to their existing knowledge and from actively monitoring their comprehension. When difficult passages are encountered, many students simply skip them, rather than undertake the effort to sort out a meaning for themselves.

Second, most science textbooks (particularly middle and secondary level books) are written in an impersonal, seemingly objective tone, which ignores the readers' needs. The style seldom offers invitations to the reader to access or "check-in-with" his or her prior knowledge about a topic. Textbook authors write as if the reader has as much prior knowledge as they do; and they assume that readers are familiar with the style and structure of expository writing.

A third problem in learning from science textbooks is that many do a poor job of making connections clear between ideas within the text. One of the unfortunate casualties of applying readability formulas to science writing is that many of the linking connections, such as "because," or "therefore," are removed in the interest of creating shorter sentences. Long, technical words are used only once to keep the word-length count down, when using them repeatedly might allow students to understand the terms through their contexts of usage. The abundance of technical words in science textbooks adds to the problem of identifying key ideas and their interconnections.

Last, successful comprehension also depends on the relevant prior knowledge a reader has. This includes knowledge about the topic of the text and about the conventions of writing. Good readers appear to utilize their knowledge of text and purpose and to monitor comprehension in an almost automatic fashion; poor readers are unaware or uninformed of the knowledge they need and often are lacking in metacognitive skills as well.

Alternate Ways to Use and Learn from Science Textbooks

Given the difficulties outlined [earlier], the reactionary stance has been "Don't use textbooks in science." This stance, however, seems to "throw the baby out with the bathwater." If we want our students to be scientifically literate, surely they should be able to learn about science issues through reading critically about them. Also, we should remember that the "standard" list of science process skills is only a partial list of what scientists actually do. Scientists read and learn from their reading. Like scientists, students can obtain useful knowledge from textbooks.

In order to get students to learn from their textbooks in more meaningful ways and to use their textbooks in more resourceful ways, we, as teachers, need to examine our beliefs about the role of the textbook in our teaching. Are we being overly dependent on the contents of the text in our science teaching? Or do we see the textbook as only one of many resources we can provide our students? Are we emphasizing learning about the products of science or does our teaching emphasize the processes of science and how science knowledge is created?

How we view the role of the textbook strongly affects the way our students will perceive the textbook and the nature of science. In using textbooks, we should assist our students to become more active and constructive readers of science prose.

Meaningful Purposes for Reading

The most powerful strategy we, as teachers, can implement is to provide our students more meaningful purposes for reading and more meaningful texts to read. If we reflect on the purposes scientists have for reading, we can discover other uses for textbooks to promote meaningful learning. Scientist read to (1) obtain background or explanatory information for a project; (2) obtain data that other scientists have already published; and (3) to challenge their own ideas with new viewpoints. In essence, they read because they have questions, which can be answered by reading. The questions tend to be purposeful and research or project related.

The key to providing meaningful purposes for reading is to have the students determine their own purpose for reading. Have students generate their own questions to answer using the textbook or other resources. Meaningful questions can arise when students conduct hands-on experiences prior to reading relevant portions of their textbook. During the hands-on activity, students are told to record all questions that arise. The questions are categorized into those that need more experimentation to answer and those that could be answered through reading. Students use their books to find answers to their own questions. In this way, the textbook becomes a resource, in the way that you, as a teacher, probably use your own books.

You can probably think of strategies in which one or more textbooks can be used as data resources. A useful practice is to have students use several texts to gather information. In doing so, they learn that authors present information differently; and even established "facts" will vary

from book to book. Learning can occur as students argue about and discuss variances they have found.

There are other opportunities for creating meaningful purposes in reading textbooks. For example, you can help students to identify a conclusion that the textbook author has drawn. Students are then directed to look back in the text and assemble the evidence the author has presented for the conclusion. Students can evaluate the conclusion both in terms of the evidence presented and the outcomes of hands-on performed in class. Similar conclusions in other textbooks can be analyzed for evidence presented there. Here, students have an analytical purpose in reading. The strategies given here can also be used in reading scientific articles. By using a number of text resources in your class, you demonstrate to students that science information does not "live" in one textbook, but can be gained from many different books and viewpoints.

Understanding Science Prose

Strategies to assist readers to understand expository prose involve identifying key topics or ideas and the relationships among them. Traditional outlining of a chapter generally fails to identify the nature of the relationships among ideas. Graphic strategies, such as networking, relational mapping, schematizing, and concept mapping assist the reader to show in a "web" or interconnected visual form how key ideas are related to one another. These techniques are easy to learn with practice and assist students in recognizing the connections among ideas in texts.

Students' personal "maps" of ideas can be related to text readings. Prior to reading, students can map their understanding of how concepts (preferably those they come up with) are related to a particular topic. As they read, they can add to their map or revise it in light of the information presented. Or they can make a map of the reading and compare it to their own.

Strategies for Metacognition

Metacognition refers to how we know or think about our thinking or comprehension processes. Good readers tend to know when they are having difficulty comprehending a text and they automatically put in extra time and effort to "untangle" the difficult prose. Readers who do not automatically monitor their comprehension can practice strategies to do so. Any process that involves checking one's understanding is a metacognitive strategy.

The graphic learning strategies described [here] are metacognitive strategies because they encourage students to assess their understanding. As students work to identify key ideas and relationships they are engaged in thinking about what they are reading. Another strategy is to read and summarize, paragraph-by-paragraph or section-by-section. Have pairs of students read together and discuss each section they read. The students would need to agree on their understanding of the section. Their consensus can be written out to create a summary of the reading. Students in pairs can also write questions for each other about particular sections, taking turns asking and answering the questions.

Still another metacognitive strategy is to give students a "checklist for comprehension" to accompany their reading assignments. The checklist might be as simple as a five-point "comprehension" rating scale, which is checked for each paragraph read. Paragraphs that are rated low in comprehensibility by an individual student can be involved in further class discussion or in individual assistance.

All of these suggested strategies are intended to assist students to pay attention to their comprehension. Learning to monitor breakdowns in comprehension is a necessary step toward the goal of learning more effectively from a textbook.

Summary and Conclusions

Textbooks have a role to play in science learning, although that role is vastly different from the traditional role. This point is critical. The traditional student-reads-textbook interactions, if left unchanged, will probably not result in meaningful learning. However, if teachers mediate the interaction of students and texts with strategies for meaningful learning, the interaction can be productive. As teachers, we can provide meaningful purposes for reading, we can assist our students to understand the complexities of science prose, and we can provide strategies for metacognition. All of these interventions call upon students to engage in learning from texts at a much higher cognition level than has been the case. We should not be surprised if students initially resist our "invitations to think." We should expect that they must think in order to learn meaningfully.

SCIENCE-TEACHING LITERATURE

THE MIDDLE SCHOOL STUDENT

Steven J. Rakow

While the phrase "middle school" is often used to refer to an administrative structure, it also refers to the particular age group of students that middle school serves—ten- to fourteen-year-olds.[65] What are the unique characteristics of these learners?

Physically, middle school students are developing at a rate faster than at any time in their lives except infancy. This rapid growth may bring with it clumsiness and poor coordination. Often the young compound their anxiety; growth rates among classmates might differ by several years, leading some children to wonder if they will ever catch up with their rapidly maturing classmates. Early adolescents tend, therefore, at times, to be very self-conscious and may become "behavior problems."

Socially, middle school children seek to establish their own identity and their own self-concept. As they seek to "fit in," their peers become increasingly important influences on their lives. Along with this newly established identity is the need to make their own decisions. Often, middle school students are reluctant to act in accordance with the demands of their parents or those of other adults. While this stage of development may bring a certain anxiety to parents and teachers, it is an indication that the early adolescent is developing a greater capacity to conceive of alternative approaches to solving personal problems.

Middle school classrooms contain a fascinating array of cognitive abilities. Barbel Inhelder and Jean Piaget provide one model that attempts to describe the intellectual development of the young.[66] They suggest that individuals progress through four states of intellectual development: sensory-motor (ages birth to two years), preoperational (ages two to seven), concrete operational (ages seven to eleven), and formal operational (ages eleven to fourteen). In brief, Inhelder and Piaget propose that, at different stages of cognitive development, people have a repertoire of patterns of reasoning—which individuals may apply to solving problems. The "concrete operational" student will be able to carry out logical thought process using concrete objects, while the "formal operational" student will be able to engage in the manipulation of purely mental constructs. Several other differences also distinguish these two categories, such as the ability of "formal operational" students to use proportional and probabilistic logic patterns, to consider the influence of many variables simultaneously, and to examine many possible combinations of a group of objects. Inhelder and Piaget's conclusions about patterns of reasoning could have implications for the kind of cognitive demands that we place upon students in science classrooms.

Subsequent research, however, has questioned Piaget's formulations, particularly as applied to specific age groups. It has been suggested that an individual's ability to approach a problem may be as much a factor of experience as of his or her generalized cognitive development.

In any case, successful middle/junior high school teachers need to be aware of and sensitive to the physical, emotional, affective, and cognitive characteristics of their middle school students. Because of the heterogeneity of abilities and physical characteristics, and because of the rapid rate at which these early adolescents are developing, the identification of special ability is particularly difficult.

Problems and Extensions

1. Suppose you are a member of curriculum selection team for your middle school. The task of the team is to make recommendations to the district curriculum department concerning the goals and curriculum for a middle school program, grades 6–8. What would your recommended curriculum look like?

2. Investigate one of the "exemplary middle school science programs." You should locate the materials of the program and write a brief report outlining the strengths and weaknesses of the program. What are the goals of the curriculum? How do the goals of the program compare to the recommendations for middle schools by the *Standards*?

3. Demonstrate at least one activity from one of the "exemplary middle school science programs" with a group of peers or middle school students.

4. Suppose you were asked to make recommendations to a school system on the content for the ideal course in biology, chemistry, physics, and earth science for high school students. What are the aims of the course? What are the major curriculum topics?

5. Evaluate one the biology, chemistry, or physics "exemplary science program" and provide evidence to support the program's effectiveness with high school students.

6. Find and locate one research study that comparesthe effectiveness of a golden age high school science course (e.g., biology, chemistry, and physics). What variables were used to make the comparisons?

7. Visit a high school science teacher and interview the teacher about his or her science course. What program or textbook does the teacher use? How effective is the course with the teacher's students?

Notes

1. Based on A. A. Glatthorn, *Curriculum Leadership* (Glenview, Ill.: Scott, Foresman and Company, 1987), p. 10.

2. For a deeper insight into science inquiry, you might want to refer to the publication *Inquiry and the National Science Education Standards: A Guide for Teaching and Learning* (Washington, D.C.: National Academy Press, 2000).

3. I. R. Weiss, *Report of the 2000 National Survey of Science and Mathematics Education* (Chapel Hill, N.C.: Horizon Research, Inc., 2001) pp. 47–48.

4. U.S. Department of Education, *Science Education Programs That Work* (Washington, D.C.: Office of Educational Research and Improvement, 1988), p. 9. You can write for this document: 555 New Jersey Avenue, NW, Washington, DC 20208.

5. For more information, contact FOR SEA Institute of Marine Science, PO Box 188, Indianola, WA 98342.

6. For more information, visit the GEMS Web site: http://www.lhgems.org.

7. Additional Information about SFLL can be obtained from Kendall/Hunt Publishing, Dubuque, Iowa, or from the Biological Science Study Committee (www.bscs.org).

8. K. T. Henson, *Methods and Strategies for Teaching in Secondary and Middle Schools* (New York: Longman, 1988) p. 371.

9. J. A. Shymansky, W. C. Jr. Kyle, and J. M. Alport, "The Effects of the New Science Curricula on Student Performance," *Journal of Research in Science Teaching* 20, no. 5 (1983): 387–404.

10. J. Wiles, and J. Bondi, *Making Middle Schools Work* (Alexandria, Va.: Association for Supervision and Curriculum Development, 1986), p. 1.

11. Ibid., pp. 3–5.

12. From the Great Falls Middle School, Massachusetts, philosophy statement, 2000. Available at http://k12s.phast.umass.edu/~szabko/GPHILO.html.

13. The discussion is based on Wiles and Bondi, *Making Middle Schools Work*, p. 26.

14. J. K. Miller, "An Analysis of Science Curricula in the United States" (Ph.D. Dissertation, Teachers College, Columbia University, 1985).

15. Weiss, *Report of the 2000 National Survey.*

16. Paul Dehart Hurd, *Transforming Middle School Science Education* (New York: Teachers College Press, 2000), p. xi.

17. Ibid., p. xii.

18. Ibid., p. 65.

19. For more information, contact Biological Sciences Curriculum Study (BSCS), Colorado College, Colorado Springs, CO, or www.bscs.org.

20. U.S. Department of Education, *Science Education Programs That Work*, p. 5.

21. For more information, contact Geology Is, O'Fallon Township High School, 600 South Smiley, O'Fallon, IL 62269. Kendall-Hunt, Dubuque, IA, publishes Geology Is.

22. For more information, contact the American Geological Institute at www.agiwb.org.

23. Program materials are available from Curator of Education, Bronx Zoo, New York Zoological Society, 185th Street and Southern Boulevard, Bronx, NY 10460.

24. Awareness materials are available from Sci-Math Director, Education and Technology Foundation, 4655 25th Street, San Francisco, CA 94114.

25. These materials are available from Informal Science Study, University of Houston, Room 450, Farish Hall, Houston, TX 77004.

26. Weiss, *Report of the 2000 National Survey*, p. 65

27. I. R. Weiss, "The 1985–86 National Survey of Science and Mathematics Education," in *The Science Curriculum*, ed. A. B. Champagne and L. E. Hornig, (Washington, 1987), pp. 230–31.

28. Weiss, *Report of the 2000 National Survey*, p. 65.

29. Weiss, "The 1985–86 National Survey," pp. 230–33.

30. Weiss, *Report of the 2000 National Survey*, p. 65.

31. Ibid.

32. P. D. Hurd, *New Directions in Teaching Secondary School Science* (Chicago: Rand McNally & Company, 1969), pp. 187–88.

33. Shymansky, Kyle, and Alport, "The Effects of New Science Curricula," pp. 387–404.

34. Hurd, *New Directions*, p. 194.

35. Ibid., p. 195.

36. Shymansky, Kyle, and Alport, "The Effects of New Science Curricula," pp. 387–404.

37. W. V. Mayer, ed., *Biology Teachers' Handbook* (New York: Wiley, 1978), p. 9.

38. Ibid., p. 9.

39. Ibid., pp. 11–14.

40. Hurd, *New Directions*, p. 154.

41. Shymansky, Kyle, and Alport, "The Effects of New Science Curricula," p. 395.

42. National Research Council, *National Science Education Standards* (Washington, D.C.: National Academy Press, 1995), p. 21.

43. Committee on High School Biology, *Fulfilling the Promise: Biology Education in the Nation's Schools* (Washington, D.C.: National Academy Press, 1990), p. 21.

44. Ibid., p. 25.

45. Paul Dehart Hurd, *Inventing Science Education for the New Millennium* (New York: Teachers College Press, 1997), p. 63.

46. For more information about Biology: A Community Context, contact the publisher, Everyday Learning Corporation.

47. For more information on Insights in Biology, contact Kendall/Hunt Publishing Company.

48. For further information about Active Chemistry, contact the publisher: It's About Time, 84 Business Park Drive, Armonk, NY 10504.

49. For additional information, contact the publisher: It's About Time, 84 Business Park Drive, Armonk, NY 10504.

50. Charles Hutchison, "Pedagogical Incongruences Facing International Science Teachers When They Immigrate to Teach in United States High Schools" (Ph.D. Dissertation, Georgia State University, 2001).

51. Roger Cross and Ronald Price, "School Physics as Technology in China during the Great Proletarian Cultural Revolution: Lessons for the West," *Research in Science Education* 17 (1987): 165–74.

52. Ibid., pp. 165–74.

53. Paul DeHart Hurd, "Precollege Science Education in the People's Republic of China," in *Science Education in Global Perspective: Lessons from Five Countries*, ed. Margrete Siebert Klein and F. James Rutherford (Washington D.C.: American Association for the Advancement of Science, 1985), p. 70.

54. Ibid., pp. 69–70.

55. Roger T. Cross, Juergen Henze, and Ronald F. Price, "Science Education for China's Priority Schools: The Example of Chemistry," *School Science and Mathematics* 92, no 6: 325–30.

56. Ibid.

57. Monbusho (Ministry of Education, Science, Sports, and Culture), *Shogakko—gakushu shido yoryo* (Tokyo: Okurasho Insatsu Kyoku, 1998).

58. Ibid.

59. Monbusho, *Statistical Abstract of Education, Science, Sports, and Culture*, 2000 edition (Tokyo: Okurasho Insatsu Kyoku, 2000), pp. 52–53.

60. Monbusho, *Kotogakko—gakushu shido yoryo* (Tokyo: Okurasho Insatsu Kyoku, 1999).

61. Sarah L. Ulerick, *Using Textbooks for Meaningful Learning in Science*, Research Matters to the Science Teacher Series (National Association for Research in Science Teaching). Used with permission.

62. J. D. Bransford, *Human Cognition* (Belmont, Calif.: Wadsworth, 1979).

63. Ibid., pp. 134–35. Originally study by J. D. Bransford and M. K. Johnson, "Contextual Prerequisites for Understanding: Some Investigations of Comprehension and Recall," *Journal of Verbal Learning and Verbal Behavior*, 11 (1972): 717–26.

64. See R. E. Stake and J. Easley, *Case Studies in Science Education, Vols. I and II* (Urbana: Center for Instruction Research and Curriculum Evaluation, University of Illinois at Urbana-Champaign, 1978), and K. Tobin and J. Gallagher, "The Role of Target Students in the Science Classroom," *Journal of Research in Science Teaching*, no. 24 (1978): 61–75.

65. Steven J. Rakow, "The Gifted in Middle School Science," in *Gifted Young in Science: Potential through Performance*, ed. Paul F. Brandwein and A. Harry Passow (Washington, D.C.: National Science Teachers Association, 1988), pp.143–44. Used with permission.

66. Jeannette McCarthy Gallagher and D. Kim Reid, *The Learning Theory of Piaget and Inhelder* (Monterey, Calif.: Brooks/Cole, 1981).

Readings

American Association for the Advancement of Science. *Benchmarks for Science Literacy*. New York: Oxford University Press, 1993.

American Association of Physics Teachers (AAPT). *Active Physics*. Armonk, N.Y.: It's About Time, 1997.

American Chemical Society. *ChemCom: Chemistry in the Community*. Dubuque, Iowa: Kendall/Hunt Publishing, 1998.

American Geological Association. *EarthComm*. Armonk, N.Y.: It's About Time, 2002.

Eick, Charles, and Samford, Kelly. "Techniques for New Teachers." *The Science Teacher* 23 (November 1999): 34–37.

Hurd, Paul DeHart. *Inventing Science Education for the New Millenium*. New York: Teachers College Press, 1997.

Hurd, Paul DeHart. *Transforming Middle School Science Education*. New York: Teachers College Press, 2000.

Leonard, William, Penick, John, and Douglas, Rowena. "What Does It Mean to Be Standards-Based?" *The Science Teacher* (April 2002): 36–39.

Loucks-Horsley, Susan, and Bybee, Rodger W. "Implementing the *National Science Education Standards*." *The Science Teacher* 23 (September 1998): 22–26.

Project 2061. *Blueprints for Reform: Science, Mathematics, and Technology Education*. Washington, D.C.: American Association for the Advancement of Science, 1998.

On the Web

Trends in International Mathematics and Science Study (TIMSS): http://nces.ed.gov/timss/. TIMSS and Trends in International Mathematics and Science Study-Repeat (TIMSS-R) are the result of the need in the American education community for reliable and timely data on the mathematics and science achievement of our students compared to that of students in other countries. Forty-two countries were involved in these studies.

High School Hub: http://highschoolhub.org/hub/hub.cfm. The High School Hub is a noncommercial portal to excellent free online academic resources for high school students. It features learning activities, an ongoing teen poetry contest, a reference collection, college information, and subject guides for English, mathematics, science, social studies, world languages, arts, health, music, and technology.

EDC K–12 Science Curriculum Center: http://www2.edc.org/cse/work/k12dissem/materials.asp. The curriculum center is a library of the featured K–12 science curricula. Each curriculum at the site is linked to a brief description; a longer, more substantial profile of the curriculum; and publication information. From this site you will come in contact with dozens of K–12 science curricula and be directed to the curriculum Web site.

National Science Education Standards: http://www.nap.edu/readingroom/books/nses/. You can access the *Standards* at this site and read them online.

Middle School Resources: http://www.nmsa.org. This page lists Internet sites that focus on (or have some section that focuses on) middle-level education or the development of adolescents.

PART 3

CONNECTING THEORY AND PRACTICE IN SCIENCE TEACHING

CHAPTER
5
How Students Learn Science

Our knowledge of how students learn has been and continues to be the foundation upon which the science curriculum and classroom instruction are based. Increasingly, science education researchers working with classroom teachers have made great strides in trying to explain how students learn and are encouraging others to implement the results in the classroom.

In this chapter you will explore some of the current theories that explain how students learn. There is no single theory that we can rely on to explain student learning. Rather, there are several theories that seem to compliment each other and, taken as a whole, provide the science teacher with the most recent ideas and research on how students learn science. Research on learning has moved from an emphasis on behaviorism and Piagetian views to constructivist and sociocultural views. The *Standards* discussed earlier in the book, as well as many of the exemplary science projects, use constructivist ideas as the basis of design. The students who appear in your classroom have unique ways of learning. Teachers have long recognized this and have devised ways to accommodate students with different learning styles. The chapter concludes with an investigation of this important dimension of learning; namely, student learning styles.

Case Study: A New Approach to Learning

The Case
Ruth Wilson, a second-year high school biology teacher in a community that has only one high school, took a graduate course in the summer at the local university. In the course, she became extremely interested in a theory of learning, called constructivism, proposed by several theorists.

Constructivism, as Wilson understood it, provided a framework to understand how students acquired knowledge. One of the basic notions underlying the theory was that students "constructed and made meaning" of their experiences. The theory provides more freedom for the students in terms of their own thinking processes. Wilson felt strongly that this "constructivist" framework supported her teaching philosophy better than the more structured approach she used during her first year of teaching. Prior to the opening of school, Wilson changed her curriculum plans to reflect the constructivist theory. She spent the first two weeks of school helping the students become skilled and familiar with hands-on learning. For many of her students, this was a new venture. Wilson planned activities where students had to make choices among objectives, activities, or content. Knowing that students like to work together, she decided to place students in small teams. After two weeks, Wilson instructed the teams to decide and select the activities and content in the first part of the text that would interest them. They should formulate a plan, and carry it out for the remainder of the grading period. A few weeks later, a rather irate parent called Mr. Brady, the principal of the school, complaining that her son was wasting his time in Wilson's class. The parent complained that her son was not learning anything and she demanded a parent–teacher conference.

The Problem
How would you deal with this situation? What would you say to the parent? Is Ms. Wilson on sound footing regarding her theory of teaching? How would you explain your teaching theory to the principal? What is your personal view on this approach to teaching and learning?

How to Read This Chapter

This chapter organizes ideas about learning into two key topics, theories of learning and learning styles. John Dewey wrote about science learning in the early part of the twentieth century and, from then on, science education researchers have worked with practicing science teachers to try to explain how students learn. You will find the learning theories divided into three categories: constructivist, sociocultural, and behavioral. You might want to look at any one of these three approaches to learning and see how they relate to your own ideas about learning. You also might be interested in exploring ideas on student learning styles and how these ideas influence science instruction. You will also find that Chapter 6, Models of Science Teaching, is correlated with the theories that are presented here. Although, this chapter is more theory-oriented and Chapter 6 is more practical, together they form an important link between theory and practice.

SECTION 1: HOW STUDENTS LEARN

Invitations to Inquiry

- How important is it to the secondary science teacher to know about learning theory?
- What is constructivism, and why has it emerged as one of the most significant explanations of student learning?
- How do cognitive psychologists explain student learning?
- How do social psychologists explain student learning?
- How do behavioral theories explain student learning in science?
- What were the contributions of theorists like Skinner, Bruner, Piaget, Vygotsky, and von Glasersfeld to secondary science teaching?
- What is meant by multiple intelligences and how do they affect student learning?

INQUIRY ACTIVITY 5.1

 How Do Students Learn Science?

In this chapter you are going to be introduced to a number of theories that are used to explain how students learn science. Before you begin your study of this important topic, you might want to interview practicing science teachers or some of your peers to find out how and under what circumstances they think students learn best.

Materials

- Tape recorder

Procedures

1. Working with a team of peers, put together a series of interview questions designed to pique the knowledge base of practicing science teachers or a group of your peers about the basic question posed in this chapter: How do students learn science? Some questions that you might consider for the interview are listed next. You should also refer to the questions that were used to interview the teachers for the Science Teachers Talk sections of the *Science Teacher Gazette*. (You can find these on page 32.)

Interview Questions about How Students Learn
- In your experience, what have you found to be successful ways to help students learn?
- Do you believe a particular theory is more effective than others in explaining how your students learn (e.g., behaviorist versus constructivist theories)?
- How do you motivate students to learn? What are some effective strategies?
- What do you think are some of the reasons students have difficulty learning science concepts?

- What do you do to help students that are struggling with science or have learning disabilities become interested in and understand science?

2. Once you have a set of questions, contact the teacher you wish to interview. Explain the purpose of the interview and how the information will be used. You should keep in the mind human rights issues with regard to interviewing or gathering data on human subjects. Although this is not a research project, you should maintain the confidentiality of the individual and respect the person's integrity. You should explain fully why you are conducting the interview and how you will use the results. You should explain that the person's identity will not be used in any discussions among other members of your class unless permission is granted.

3. Visit the school and conduct the interview. Make sure the teacher understands the purpose of the interview and grants you permission to tape record the interview, if you plan to do so.

Minds-On Strategies

1. What are the main concepts that teachers believe account for student learning? That is, how do practicing science teachers think students learn science?
2. What do science teachers think motivates students to learn science?
3. What are your opinions about how students learn science?

- How do learning styles of students influence learning in the classroom?
- What is metacognition and how can it help students learn science?

Students and Science Learning

Paradoxically, one of the significant turning points in the history of American science education was the launching of Sputnik by the Soviet Union in 1957. From that moment, the American public, especially the U.S. Congress, began to ask questions about the state of science education in the United States. Why were the Soviets the first nation to launch a satellite? Was American science and technology education inferior to Soviet science and technology education? Was the nature of secondary science education in jeopardy? The response of Congress was to increase funding to the National Science Foundation, which lead to a plethora of science curriculum projects in the late 1950s, 1960s, and 1970s. During this period of science education reform, scientists and science educators began a quest to find ways to improve science learning.

Another period of reform emerged in the 1990s and is affecting science education in the twenty-first century. This reform was energized by reports by commissions, professional organizations, and governments, and the publication of the *Standards* for science education. The

reforms have reached all levels of science education. The present reforms are focused on student learning and how schools can provide experiences for all students that will result in increased student learning.

Science learning has at least two dimensions; namely learning about science and how to do science. Champagne and Hornig outline the main elements in these categories and point out that these two views of science learning are quite different.[1] The two views and the subset of science learnings are outlined in Table 5.1. As you can see from Table 5.1, students can learn about the products of scientific inquiry, which includes facts, concepts, principles, and theories. The major emphasis in contemporary science programs is on this form of science learning. When newspapers report the proficiency of students in science, they are reporting what students know about this type of science learning. Yet there are many other things that students can learn about. They can learn about the nature of the scientific enterprise, values and attitudes, applications and risks of science and technology, and science careers.

Student learning also includes learning how to do science—to apply the process skills and inquiry skills that are typical of scientific thinking. One of the directions that science education took after Sputnik was to pay attention to the process of science and emphasize inquiry in the development of science teaching materials. The "how to" aspect of science learning is the

Table 5.1 What Students Can Learn in Science

They Can Learn About	They Can Learn How To	Processes They Undergo
• Knowledge products of scientific inquiry (facts, concepts, principles, theories) • Nature of the scientific enterprise (world view, methods, habits of thought, approaches to problems) • Values and attitudes (of the scientific community, society at large, local community, one's racial or cultural group, one's family) • Applications and risks of science and technology (societal context, personal context) • Science careers (what scientists do, who scientists are, how scientists get educated) • Themselves (interest in science, capacity to do science)	• Act upon or apply information (evaluate, manipulate, solve problems) • Learn (strategies to seek and acquire new information and to seek and acquire new skills) • Produce knowledge (question, test, evaluate)	• Internalize values (about the utility and risks of science and technology, habits of thought and conceptual skills, and who does science) • Assess self (interest in science, capacity to do science) • Make choices (about studying science, science careers, and applying science knowledge and skills to daily life)

Source: Based on information in Champagne, A. B., and Hornig, L. E. *Students and Science Learning.* Washington, D.C.: American Association for the Advancement of Science, 1987, pp. 3–5.

complement of the "learning about" side of science. Yet, even with the emphasis on process and inquiry within the science education community, student learning in science showed disappointing results. To counter this effort, the *Standards* have taken a strong position on the role of inquiry in science teaching. Fundamental to the *Standards* are these two abilities for science inquiry: At all grade levels, K–12, all students should develop:

- abilities necessary to do scientific inquiry
- understandings about scientific inquiry

During the last thirty years, a numbers of theories of learning have influenced the way science educators have looked at student learning in science. The early years of science education reform were dominated by the behavioral theories of learning. The behavioral psychologists, in particular B. F. Skinner, have influenced science education enormously, as evidenced by the use of behavioral objectives to define student learning and in the classroom management systems that dominate contemporary science teaching. However, as you will find out in this chapter, there are other theories and perspectives on learning that play a prominent role in science teaching, the development of science curriculum materials, and the preparation of science teachers. Developmental psychology, led by the work of Jean Piaget, influenced research in science education starting in the 1960s and 1970s and extending to today.[2] The impact of Piaget can be seen in the recommendations of science educators to encourage direct experience with learning materials and to be aware of the student's level

of cognitive development. Piaget laid the groundwork for the contemporary or "new learning theory," called constructivism.

In the section that follows, I examine several theories and perspectives on learning, starting with the most recent and compelling idea of how students learn (constructivism) and the implication for science teaching.

Theories of How Students Learn

You know from your own experience as a student of science that theory is an important aspect of science. Scientists try to unravel and explain the nature of the physical and biological world by developing theories to explain and predict events and phenomena. I think you will agree that two scientists can look at the same set of data and give quite different explanations. Educators, sociologists, historians, and psychologists attempt to explain the nature of student learning just as scientists attempt to explain the nature of the atom, earthquakes, biological change, and so on. And just as there are competing alternative theories in science, there are alternative ideas to explain student learning.

From Theory to Practice, or Practice to Theory?

What help can theory and associated science education research be to the beginning science teacher? Aren't theories too impractical for the real world of the everyday secondary science classroom? Perhaps. However, in this book an attempt will be made to show the value of being theoretically oriented and showing you that most theories emerge from practice. One issue to think about is how you will develop an understanding of the theories of learning and teaching. Should theory be taught to you first, so that with this "knowledge" you can apply it in your teaching experience? Or should you experience teaching and learning and use the "experience" to begin to construct and develop theories of learning and teaching? These questions form a key issue.

I prefer the "practice to theory" path to understanding, primarily because my own development as a teacher and a teacher educator was steeped in experience and reflection and because I think it is more natural and will be a powerful way for you to learn about teaching. However, I also realize that there are those that think that moving from "theory to practice" can be an effective way to learn to teach. Therefore, if you are oriented to the practice to theory path, then you might want to simply scan this chapter, working back and forth between it and the Chapter 6, and then come back to it later, after you have developed lessons and presented them to students in the context of a school. On the other hand, if you are following the path of theory to practice, then this chapter will be an important first step for you.

Many science teachers value the work being done by science education researchers. In fact, the National Science Teachers Association (NSTA) has published a multivolume series entitled *What Research Says to the Science Teacher*. These volumes describe the results of research on different topics and demonstrate practical applications that can be drawn from this work. Various journals, especially *Science Scope* (for middle school/junior high science teachers) and *The Science Teacher* (for secondary science teachers), include articles on science teaching that demonstrate the practical application of theory and research. And you will find a column in some of the *Science Teacher Gazette* sections of this book entitled: *Research Matters . . . to the Science Teacher*. This column is based on brief reviews of research published by the National Association for Research in Science Teaching (NARST). You can visit the NARST Web site and look over all of the *Research Matters* articles online (see the Web sites listed at the end of the chapter for more details).

The Idea of Theory

The word *theory* is derived from the Greek word *theoria*, which means vision. A theory of learning is a vision that educators have to explain the complexity of human learning. We'll explore several theories or perspectives on learning. I've organized the theories into three perspectives:

- constructivist perspectives
- sociocultural perspectives
- behavioral perspectives

Table 5.2 outlines some of the main elements of each of the theories and perspectives in terms of key ideas, the nature of the learner, and the context of learning. Study the table before you continue, noting the similarities and differences among these learning theories. Refer to the table as you continue with this chapter.

Constructivist Theories of Learning

Science educators, using the work of Jean Piaget as a foundation, have developed a number of theories to explain learning. In general, these researchers are interested in how information is taken into the organism, interpreted, represented, and acted upon. These science educators agree with Piaget that knowledge is constructed and theorize that students are builders of knowledge structures. These science educators have developed a number of alternative models that have direct implication for teaching science to secondary students. The models that are discussed next represent recent work being done by cognitive scientists. Although these models differ in some respects, they share the following characteristics.[3]

1. Importance of content knowledge: Cognitive scientists put a lot of emphasis on what they call "expert knowledge." They suggest that "experts," say in physics or geology, reason more powerfully about a topic in their respective fields than a novice. In fact, one of the things you will find common in the models that follow is an attempt by teachers to find out what the novice learners (students) know about a topic before teaching them new concepts. Another idea that cognitive scientists have put forth is that learning requires knowledge, yet knowledge cannot be given directly. Students must generate their own knowledge. For this to be achieved, the teacher must provide a learning environment where students can discuss and question what they are told, investigate new information, and build new knowledge structures. Further, teachers need to provide ways to ascertain what students know and then find ways to link this knowledge (which quite often is naive) to new knowledge structures.

2. Integration of skills and content: Because the cognitive approach places the student in the center of learning, the development of thinking skills must be integrated with content knowledge. This is, of course, an idea proposed by many other theorists, especially Piaget and Bruner. It is just as important for students to

Table 5.2 Comparison of Theories and Perspectives of Learning

Learning Theory or Perspective	Key Ideas	Nature of Learner	Context of Learning
Constructivist Perspectives			
Constructivism (von Glasersfeld, Vygotsky)	Construction of knowledge with individual mechanisms or social influences	Learners construct their own sets of meanings or understandings (psychological constructivism) or by means of language (social constructivism)	Learning is enhanced by providing activity-based instruction and promoting learning in collaborative groups
Cognitive theories Examples: Discovery Learning (Bruner), Cognitive development (Piaget)	Changes in the mental structures that contain information and procedures for operating on that information	Learner constructs knowledge and is actively seeking meaning	Interacting with the physical world is crucial. What the learner brings to the learning environment and developmental differences in reasoning affect science learning
Sociocultural Perspectives			
Sociocultural Theories (Vygotsky)	The social organization (classroom or culture at large) is the agent for change for the individual	Learners develop knowledge as a social activity in the context of institutional and cultural frameworks	Language and culture of the social group play the crucial role in helping students develop ideas and knowledge
Feminist Perspectives	Scientific knowledge is "gendered." Feminist perspective should account for ways in which gender shapes learning	Learning is the transformation of "identity-in-practice." Using situated cognition, teachers provide learners with experiences that transform	Students could be involved in authentic experiences whereby they take on identities like environmentalists or a "smart" health care consumer
Deweyan Theory of Experience	Engage learners in "an experience" that is whole and runs its course	Learner is active and participates in the context of educative experiences or projects that have a structure, flow, and energy	Inviting students to participate in compelling educative experiences whose consummation is energized by anticipation on the part of the learners
Behavioral Perspectives			
Behaviorism Example: Operant Conditioning (Skinner)	Changes in the overt behavior of the learner as a result of experience	The mind of the student is a black box. Focus is on the interaction between the environment and behavior	Learning is enhanced through operant conditioning as a result of reinforcement

observe, question, test, and hypothesize as it is to develop cognitive structures about gravity, electrons, plate tectonics, and carnivores. In fact, without observing, questioning, testing, and hypothesizing, the student has little chance of developing scientific conceptions about these or any other concepts.

3. Intrinsic nature of motivation: This is a major change in the emphasis for cognitive scientists. Typically, motivation has been the subject of social psychologists who are interested in attitudes, effort, and attention. Cognitive scientists have realized the importance of developing a learning environment in which

students will want to learn. Cognitive scientists, unlike behaviorists, focus their attention on the intrinsic nature of content and instruction as a means to motivate. Cognitive scientists are also learning that students' concept of self can be a contributing factor in motivation. Resnick and Klopfer report that social psychologists have found that motivation is closely related to students' conceptions of intelligence. In one study, if students were helped to understand that intelligence is an incremental ability rather than a fixed entity, the students who believe the former, when faced with challenging or difficult problems, stuck with the problem and tried to use what they have to solve the problem. The other students, according to the researchers, might in some cases give up, saying that they lacked the intelligence to find the solution.[4] Interesting, thought provoking, challenging, and stimulating approaches to instruction may motivate students more so than the positive reinforces suggested by behavioral psychologists.

4. Role of learning groups: Cognitive scientists believe that the social setting for learning is crucial. They have found that cooperative problem-solving groups have been effective with students of varying abilities. Reshick and Klopfer suggest that skilled thinkers (the instructor or high-ability students) can demonstrate desirable ways of solving problems, thereby helping students who lack these mental abilities or experiences.[5] The implication for the science teacher is to develop in the classroom open, positive communication patterns and to place students in small, mixed-ability cooperative groups where social interaction can occur. In either case, cognitive scientists are calling for the formulation of "social learning communities," environments where questioning, critical thinking, and problem solving are valued. According to cognitive scientists, these learning communities can be critical in helping the less able student learn thinking patterns that the more able student possesses.

The Constructivist Perspective

According to constructivist theory, a large number of students show up in science classes with lots of ideas about science concepts, many of which are "incorrect," naive, or are, as these researchers call them, alternative frameworks. The aim of science teaching is to "help students overcome naive conceptions or habits of thought and replace them with scientific concepts and principles."[6] First, let's consider the nature of some alternative frameworks in science and then describe a theory to improve students' understanding of science.

In a physics or physical science class, the coin toss problem will illustrate the problem of misconceptions. The problem, shown in Figure 5.1, is an application of Newton's laws of motion. A coin is tossed upward in the air, and the student is asked, "What are the forces on the coin at point B, when it is moving upward through the air?" The typical answer to this problem by students is, "While the coin is on the way up, the 'force from your hand' (F_h) pushes up on the coin. On the way up it must be greater than the force of gravity (F_g), otherwise the coin would be moving down." The expert or physicist answer is the only force acting on the coin at point B is the downward force due to gravity (and a small additional downward force due to air resistance).

What are the forces on the coin at point B, when it is moving upward through the air?

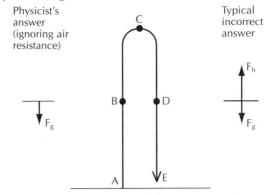

Typical incorrect explanation: While the coin is on the way up, the "force from your hand" (F_h) pushes up on the coin. On the way up it must be greater than F_g, otherwise the coin would be moving down.

Figure 5.1 The Coin Toss Problem. *Source:* Adapted from Clement, John. "Student Perceptions in Introductory Physics." *American Journal of Physics* 50 (1982): 66–71.

Anderson and Smith report that in one study of college engineering majors who had taken a course in high school physics, the percentage of students answering the question correctly after instruction rose from 12 percent to only 28 percent.[7]

In chemistry, an example of an alternative framework is illustrated when a student, four months into the course, is asked to explain what happens when a nail rusts. The explanation is that "the coldness reacts on it [the nail] . . . plastic doesn't rust because coldness doesn't cause the same reaction . . . rusting is a breakdown of the iron because it [coldness] brings out the rusting . . . it [coldness] almost draws it [rust] out, like a magnet . . . like an attractor it brings it out." Anderson and Smith report that this student consistently said he was satisfied with his explanation, that it made sense to him, and that scientists would explain the situation the same way.[8] Alternative frameworks (sometimes called "misconceptions") make sense to the student and they are firmly held to the learner as a mental structure. This makes things very difficult for the science teacher!

Students hold misconceptions in all areas of science. In a biology class, students were presented with the amputated finger problem: "If a little girl had an accident and her finger was amputated and she married someone with a similar amputation, what would you predict their children's fingers would look like at birth?" Even after instruction in a unit on genetics, students had the following misconceptions: "The finger was cut off too

Table 5.3 Alternative Frameworks in Earth Science

Earth in Space	Solid Earth	Biosphere	Atmosphere	Hydrosphere
The earth is sitting on something.	Mountains are created rapidly.	Dinosaurs and humans existed at the same time.	Rain comes from holes in clouds.	Most rivers flow "down" from north to south.
The earth is larger than the sun.	Rocks must be heavy.	Humans are responsible for the extinction of dinosaurs.	Rain comes from clouds sweating.	Groundwater "typically" occurs as basins, lakes, and fast flowing streams.
The earth is round like a pancake.	The earth is molten, except for the crust.	Evolution is goal directed.	The oxygen we breathe does not come from plants.	Salt added to water doesn't change the weight of the water.
Gravity increases with height.	Continents do not move.	Evolutionary changes are driven by need.	Gas makes things lighter.	Glaciers are rapidly created.
Rockets in space require a constant force.	The soil we see today has always existed.	Human beings did not evolve from earlier species of mammals.		
The sun goes around the earth.				
The universe is static, not expanding.				

Source: Excerpted from *Earth Science Education Connection* 1, no. 2 (Winter 1989): 3.

fast for the genes to change," "The child will probably have a finger missing because the traits of both parents are strong," and "The lost finger would be inherited from the parents."[9]

Let's look at some alternative frameworks that students bring to earth science classes. Table 5.3 lists earth science misconceptions in several conceptual areas. Even after instruction, misconceptions are still prevalent among students in science classes. Teachers who direct their attention at student misconceptions report that a student misconception is "knowledge spontaneously derived from extensive personal experience."[10] Because these misconceptions were derived by students and make sense to them, students often hold on to these ideas despite alternative (scientific) conceptions. Because it is assumed that knowledge cannot be given directly to the learner, the task of the teacher who focuses on misconception theory is as follows:

1. Help students become dissatisfied with their existing conception.
2. Help students achieve a minimal initial understanding of the scientific conception.
3. Make the scientific conception plausible to students.
4. Show the scientific conception as fruitful or useful in understanding a variety of situations.

Lawson and Thompson point out that the intellectual level of the students will affect their understanding in science and may prevent some students from understanding the scientific conception, especially if it is expressed as a theoretical conception. They suggest that the concrete student lacks reasoning patterns necessary to evaluate competing hypotheses (e.g., the hypothesis of the inheritance of acquired characteristics [the typical misconception] versus the natural selection of genetically acquired characteristics). The concrete student may be unable to reject the naive inheritance theory because he or she does not understand the concept of natural selection and gene transfer. The implication of this study is that teachers should provide students with opportunities to discuss their prior conceptions and carefully compare them with the scientific conceptions. Another, perhaps more important implication, is that we need to develop alternative ways of expressing concepts, as you will see in the section on Bruner.

One specific application of constructivist theory is the theory of conceptual-change teaching. Table 5.4, in which the students' prior conceptions are detected, time is provided for students to compare their misconceptions to the scientific conceptions and, finally, an opportunity to use the new conceptions in a variety of learning situations. The classroom implication of conceptual-change teaching will be discussed in Chapter 6.

Meaningful Learning Model

David Ausubel is a psychologist who advanced a theory that contrasted meaningful learning with rote learning (Table 5.5). In Ausubel's view, to learn meaningfully, students must relate new knowledge (concepts and propositions) to what they already know. He proposed the notion of an advanced organizer as a way to help students link their ideas with new material or concepts. Ausubel's theory of learning claims that new concepts to be learned can be incorporated into more inclusive concepts or ideas. These more inclusive concepts or ideas are advance organizers. Advance organizers can

Table 5.4 Theory of Conceptual-Change Teaching

Before Instruction	Instruction	After Instruction	End Product
Naive conceptions Identify student misconceptions by means of interviews, having students respond to a few problems based on the central concepts to be taught	Present information in light of students' misconceptions Focus on comparing new conceptions with student naive conceptions Provide opportunities for students to explore new conceptions through laboratory activities, demonstrations, audiovisual aids, and discussions of familiar phenomena Use questioning strategies and everyday phenomena to help students "test" their new conceptions	Evaluate the change in students' conceptions Use questions that were used to assess student misconceptions as base line for change Design questions that ask students to justify their ideas	Scientific conceptions

Table 5.5 Meaningful Learning Contrasted with Rote Learning

Type of Learning	Characteristics
Meaningful Learning	Nonarbitrary, nonverbatim, substantive incorporation of new knowledge into cognitive structure
	Deliberate effort to link new knowledge with higher order concepts in cognitive structure
	Learning related to experiences with events or objects
	Affective commitment to relate new knowledge to prior learning
Rote Learning	Arbitrary, verbatim, nonsubstantive incorporation of new knowledge into cognitive structure
	No effort to integrate new knowledge with existing concepts in cognitive structure
	Learning not related to experience with events or objects
	No affective commitment to relate new knowledge to prior learning

Table 5.6 Ausubel's Model of Learning

Phase 1: Presentation of Advance Organizer	Phase 2: Presentation of Learning Task or Material	Phase 3: Strengthening Cognitive Organization
Clarify aim of the lesson Present the organizer Relate organizer to students' knowledge	Make the organization of the new material explicit Make logical order of learning material explicit Present material and engage students in meaningful learning activities	Relate new information to advance organizer Promote active reception learning

be verbal phrases (e.g., "the paragraph you are about to read is about Albert Einstein") or a graphic. In any case, the advance organizer is designed to provide, what cognitive psychologists call "mental scaffolding: to learn new information."[11]

Ausubel believed that learning proceeds in a top-down or deductive manner. Ausubel's theory consists of three phases: presentation of an advance organizer, presentation of learning task or material, and strengthening the cognitive organization. The main elements of Ausubel's model are shown in Table 5.6.

Concept Mapping for Meaningful Learning

Novak and Gowin have developed a theory of instruction based on Ausubel's meaningful learning principles that incorporates "concept maps" to represent meaningful relationships between concepts and propositions.[12] A cognitive map is a "kind of visual road map showing some of the pathways we may take to connect meanings of concepts."[13] According to Novak and Gowin, concept maps should be hierarchical; the more general, more inclusive concepts should be at the top of the map and the more specific, less inclusive concepts at the bottom of the map. An example of this hierarchical principle of concept map is shown in the concept map of oceans, drawn by seventh graders (Figure 5.2).

The concept map is a tool that science teachers can use to determine the nature of students' existing ideas. The map can be used to make evident the key concepts to be learned and suggest linkages between the new information to be learned and what the student already knows. Concept maps can precede instruction and can be used by the teacher to generate a meaningful discussion of student ideas. Following the initial construction and discussion of concept maps, instructional activities can be designed to explore alternative frameworks, resulting in cognitive accommodation.

Cognitive Theories of Learning

Cognitive theories of learning had their roots in Gestalt psychology. During the period of time that behavioral theories were being developed, a competing and alternative group of theories was developed by Gestalt psychologists. Unlike behaviorism, Gestalt theory emphasized the importance of mental processes. In Gestalt psychology, the learner reacts to meaningful wholes. According to Gestalt psychologists, learning can take place by discovery or insight. The idea of insight learning was first developed by Wolfgang Kohler, who described experiments with apes in which the apes could use boxes and sticks as tools to solve problems. In the box problem, a banana is attached to the top a chimpanzee's cage. The banana is out of reach but can be reached by climbing upon and jumping from a box. Only one of Kohler's apes (Sultan) could solve this problem. Kohler introduced a much more difficult problem involving stacking boxes. This problem required the ape to stack one box on another, and master gravitational problems by building a stable stack. Kohler also gave the apes sticks that they used to rake food into the cage. Sultan, Kohler's very intelligent ape, was able to master a two-stick problem by inserting one stick into the end of the other in order to reach the food. In each of these problems, the important aspect of learning was not reinforcement, but the coordination of thinking to create new organizations (of materials). Kohler referred to this behavior as insight or discovery learning.[14]

Cognitive thinking and research got a boost from the launching of Sputnik. As mentioned earlier, Sputnik sparked a massively funded science and mathematics curriculum reform effort in the United States. The emphasis of the reform was to produce students who could think like scientists through discovery and inquiry learning and active student involvement. This emphasis

brought together scientists, teachers, and psychologists. One of the most influential psychologists during this period in science education was Jerome Bruner, Director of the Harvard Center for Cognitive Studies.

BRUNER AND DISCOVERY LEARNING Because of Bruner's connection with the NSF curriculum development projects of the 1960s and 1970s, his thinking had a powerful effect on approaches to science learning. Bruner believed that students learn best by discovery and that the learner is a problem solver who interacts with the environment, testing hypotheses and developing generalizations.[15] Bruner felt that the goal of education should be intellectual development and that the science curriculum should foster the development of problem-solving skills through inquiry and discovery.

Bruner said that knowing is a process rather than the accumulated wisdom of science as presented in textbooks. To learn science concepts and solve problems, students should be presented with perplexing (discrepant) situations. Guided by intrinsic motivation, the learner in this situation will want to figure out the solution. This simple notion provides the framework for creating discovery learning activities. Bruner described his theory as one of instruction rather than learning. His theory has four components, detailed next.[16]

Curiosity and Uncertainty Bruner believed that experiences should be designed to help the student be willing and able to learn. He called this the predisposition toward learning. According to Bruner, the desire to learn and to undertake problem solving could be activated by devising problem activities in which students would explore alternative solutions. The major condition for the exploration of alternatives was "the presence of some optimal level of uncertainty."[17] This level related directly to the student's curiosity to resolve uncertainty and ambiguity. According to this idea, the teacher would design discrepant event activities that would pique the students' curiosity. For example, the teacher might fill a glass with water and ask the students how many pennies they think can be put in the jar without any water spilling. Because most students think that only a few pennies can be put in the glass, their curiosity is aroused when the teacher is able to put between twenty-five and fifty pennies in before any water spills. This activity then leads to an exploration of displacement, surface tension, variables such as the size of the jar, how full the glass is, and so forth. In this activity, the students would be encouraged to explore various alternatives to the solution of the problem by conducting their own experiments with jars of water and pennies.

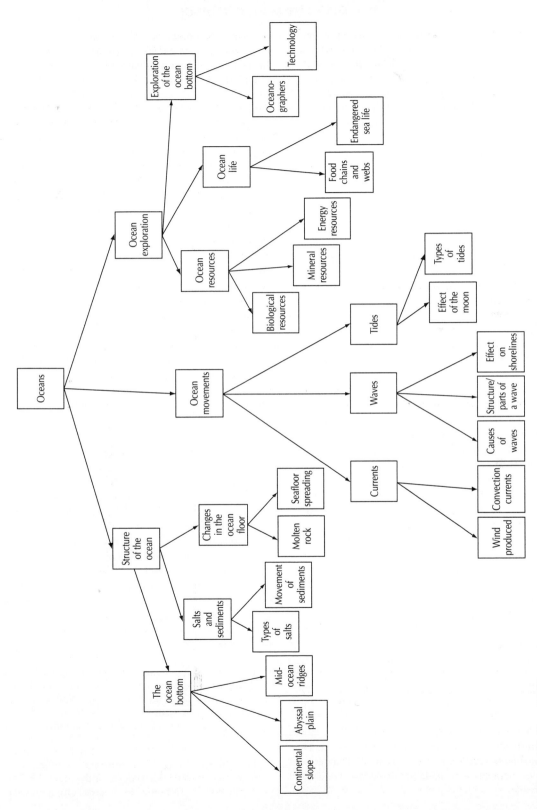

Figure 5.2 Concept Map.

Structure of Knowledge The second component of Bruner's theory refers to the structure of knowledge. Bruner expressed it by saying that the curriculum specialist and teacher "must specify the ways in which a body of knowledge should be structured so that it can be most readily grasped by the learner."[18] This idea became one of the important notions ascribed to Bruner. He explained it this way: "Any idea or problem or body of knowledge can be presented in a form simple enough so that any particular learner can understand it in a recognizable form."[19]

According to Bruner, any domain of knowledge (e.g., physics, chemistry, biology, earth science) or problem or concept within that domain (e.g., law of gravitation, atomic structure, homeostasis, earthquake waves) can be represented in three ways or modes: by a set of actions (enactive representation), by a set of images or graphics that stand for the concept (iconic representation), and by a set of symbolic or logical statements (symbolic representation). The distinction among these three modes of representation can be made concretely in terms of a balance beam, which could be used to teach students about quadratic equations.[20] A younger student can act on the principles of a balance beam and can demonstrate this knowledge by moving back and forth on a seesaw. An older student can make or draw a model of the balance beam, hanging rings and showing how the beam is balanced. Finally, the balance beam can be described verbally (orally or written) or described mathematically by reference to the law of moments (see Figure 5.3). The actions, images, and symbols would vary from one concept or problem to another, but, according to Bruner, knowledge can be represented in these three forms.

Sequencing Bruner's third principle is that the most effective sequences of instruction should be specified. According to Bruner, instruction should lead the learner

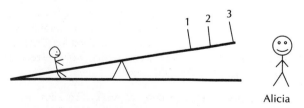

Figure 5.3 The Balance Beam Problem: Where should Alicia sit to balance the beam? Here, through an enactive representation (a set of actions), the student can understand the law of moments in a mode that is understandable and recognizable.

through the content in order to increase the student's ability to "grasp, transform, and transfer" what is learned.[21] In general, sequencing should move from enactive (hands-on, concrete), to iconic (visual), to symbolic (descriptions in words or mathematical symbols). However, this sequence will depend on the student's symbolic system and learning style. As we will see later, this principle of sequencing is common to theories developed by Piaget and other cognitive psychologists.

Motivation The last aspect of Bruner's theory is that the nature and pacing of rewards and punishments should be specified. Bruner suggests that movement from extrinsic rewards, such as teacher praise, toward intrinsic rewards inherent in solving problems or understanding the concepts is desirable. To Bruner, learning depends on knowledge of results when it can be used for correction. Feedback to the learner is critical to the development of knowledge. The teacher can provide a vital link to the learner in providing feedback at first, as well helping the learner develop techniques for obtaining feedback on his or her own.

PIAGET'S DEVELOPMENTAL THEORY Leaning theory has been influenced perhaps no more than by Swiss psychologist Jean Piaget. Although Piaget's work began in the early part of the twentieth century, it had little influence in the United States until the 1960s. Piaget's chief collaborator, Barbel Inhelder, attended the 1959 Woods Hole Conference chaired by Jerome Bruner. This conference precipitated interest in Piaget's ideas on cognitive development and led to a great deal of attention by educators (science educators, especially) and psychologists.[22]

Piaget's theory focuses on the development of thinking patterns from birth to adulthood. To Piaget learning is an active process and is related to the individual's interaction with the environment. According to Piaget, intellectual development is similar to the development of biological structures, such as those shown in mollusks. Margaret Bell-Gredler describes Piaget's thinking this way:

> He found that certain mollusks, transported from their calm-water habitat to turbulent wind-driven waters, developed shortened shells. This construction by the organism was essential for the mollusks to maintain a foothold on the rocks and thereby survive in rough water. Furthermore, these biological changes, which were constructed by the organism in response to an environmental change, were inherited by some descendents of the mollusks. The organism, in response to altered environmental

conditions, constructs the specific biological structures that it needs.[23]

To Piaget, this biological development describes the nature of intellectual development. Intelligence is the human form of adaptation to the environment. Piaget and other cognitive scientists theorize that cognitive structures (mental structures) grow and develop through a process of interaction with the environment. How do these mental structures develop?

Development of Mental Structures According to Anton Lawson and John Renner, both science educators, the most important idea in Piagetian theory is that mental structures (which they nicely describe as mental blueprints) are derived from the dynamic interaction of the organism and the environment by means of a process called self-regulation or equilibration.[24] Lawson and Renner also point out that the mental structure comes not from the organism or the environment alone, but from the organism's own actions within the environment. This idea that the individual constructs the mental structure is an underlying principle in all cognitive theories that we will explore in this chapter.

Let's look at an example of self-regulation in the classroom of a teacher who applies Piaget's theory. The teacher is presenting a unit on air pressure to junior high students. A demonstration is in progress. The teacher heats up a metal can containing a small amount of water. After a few minutes steam begins to rise out of the can. The teacher removes the can from the heat source (a hot plate) and caps it. Then the teacher waits. In a few moments the can begins to cave in, bends to the side, and falls over. The teacher then asks students to describe and explain what they observed. For many of the students this event is a contradiction or a discrepancy. Discrepancies produce a state of disequilibrium in which you are literally thrown off balance.

According to Lawson and Renner, the students' present mental structures are inadequate to explain the "crushed can" and they must be altered. By means of interaction with the environment (doing experiments and activities on the effects of pressure changes on material objects, for instance), the student can assimilate the new situation and build new structures. Later in this chapter, in the section that deals with conceptual change teaching, you will find out that it is not an easy matter to change students' current mental structures or conceptions.

According to cognitive scientists, there are three additional factors that influence the development of mental structures: experience with the environment, the social environment, and maturation.

Experience with the environment is essential because interaction with the environment is how new structures are made. Piaget distinguishes between two types of experiences; namely, concrete and abstract (logico-mathematical). It is important to remind ourselves that knowledge is constructed through experience, but the type of knowledge will be dependent on the type of experiences the individual is engaged in. Concrete experiences are physical experiences in which the student has a direct encounter with physical objects. Piaget suggested that interaction with material objects was essential to the development of thinking. Lawson and Renner suggest that science teachers should use the laboratory to precede the introduction of abstract ideas.[25]

Students need more than experiences with the environment, they also need to interact socially. Here the role of language and verbal interaction in the classroom environment will accelerate or retard cognitive development. The crucial aspect of this factor is that students be given the opportunity to examine and discuss their present beliefs and conceptions. The science teacher should not only provide concrete and abstract experiences with the environment, but must provide for social interaction via the use of language. Small- and large-group discussions are crucial to the development of cognitive structures.

The third factor facilitating the process of self-regulation is maturation. Piagetian theory is developmental, thereby placing importance on the maturation level of the student.

Cognitive development is a cyclic process involving interaction with new events, materials, properties, and abstractions. Science educators have developed a unique model of learning that is based on Piaget's theory of development.

COGNITIVE PROCESSES AND THE LEARNING CYCLE Piaget's ideas on the development of knowledge are the foundation for the constructivist view of learning. There were several aspects that Piaget considered fundamental to the development of knowledge. As teachers, it is important to understand Piaget's beginning point and that is by starting with the idea of an operation. He put it this way:

> Knowledge is not a copy of reality. To know an object, to know an event, is not simply to look at it and make a mental copy or image of it. To know an object is to act on it. To know is to modify, to transform the object, and to understand the process of this transformation, and as a consequence to understand the way the object is constructed.[26]

Piaget went on to formulate the idea that the development of new cognitive structures will be the result of three different mental processes: assimilation, accommodation, and equilibration.[27] Cognitive development is the result of the individual's interaction with the environment. The nature of the interaction is an adaptation involving these three mental processes.

Assimilation Assimilation is the integration of new information with existing internal mental structures. A student who identifies the rock sample of coarse-grained rock as granite is assimilating that rock into his or her schema of rocks. Piaget suggested that assimilation was dependent on the existence of an internal structure so that the new information could be integrated.

Accommodation Accommodation is the adjustment of internal structures to the particular characteristics of specific situations, events, or properties of new objects. Biological structures, for example, accommodate to the type and quantity of food at the same time that the food is being assimilated. Piaget theorized that in cognitive functioning, internal mental structures adjust to the unique properties of new objects and events.

Equilibration Equilibration, like assimilation and accommodation, has a biological parallel. The organism, in biological functioning, must maintain a steady state within itself at the same time remain open to the environment to deal with new events and for survival. In cognitive functioning, equilibration is the process that allows the individual to grow and develop mentally, but maintain stability. Piaget suggests, however, that equilibration is not an immobile state, but rather a dynamic process that continuously regulates behavior.[28]

This cycle of assimilation, accommodation, and equilibration has been used as a basis for the development of several science-teaching cycles called the learning cycle. One of these cycles is shown in Figure 5.4. Three teaching processes—exploration, concept introduction, and application (expansion of the idea)—are parallel processes to assimilation, accommodation, and equilibration.

Exploration is an active process involving students directly with objects and materials. The exploration phase can be open ended or can be structured by the teacher. The important element is the active engagement of the student for the sake of creating some

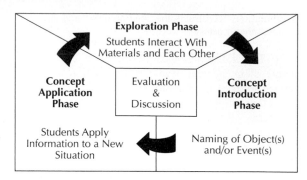

Figure 5.4 The learning cycle integrates the three phases of learning: exploration, conceptual invention, and discovery. *Source:* Charles R. Barman. Used with permission.

disequilibrium. During the exploration phase, students observe, gather data, and experience new phenomena.

Concept introduction is the phase in the learning cycle that is analogous to accommodation, when new structures are built to integrate new information. Renner and Marek calls this phase conceptual invention.[29] The invention process has a high degree of teacher direction. Using the language and experiences of the exploration phase, students invent new concepts with the aid of the teacher. The experiences students had during the exploration phase are used as data for a new structure that is proposed by the teacher. The invention phase is interpretive. Students process new information and modify current conceptions and frameworks to accommodate the new information.

The application phase is designed to provide students with active learning situations where they can apply, test, and extend the new ideas and concepts. The application phase is analogous to equilibration, but like equilibration, it is dynamic. Students, even at this phase, are still in a state of disequilibrium and require further exposure to active learning lessons. The application phase allows students to apply the new ideas to different situations, further reinforcing the development of new mental frameworks.

This is a brief introduction to the learning cycle. You will find more information on the learning cycle idea and application to science teaching strategies in Chapter 9 and in the section on lesson planning in Chapter 7.

PIAGET'S STAGES OF HOW STUDENTS THINK Piaget identified four stages or patterns of reasoning that characterize human cognitive development. Piaget viewed these as qualitative differences in the way

Table 5.7 Piaget's Stages of Development

Stage	Overview
Sensorimotor period (birth to 1–1½ years)	This period is characterized as presymbolic and preverbal. Intellectual development is dependent on action of the child's senses and response external stimuli. Child is engaged in action schemes, such as grasping and reaching for distant objects. Characteristics include reflex actions, play, imitation, object permanence, nonverbal.
Preoperational period (2–3 to 7–8 years)	Child's thought is based on perceptual cues and the child is unaware of contradictory statements. For example, the child would say that wood floats because it is small and a piece of steel sinks because it is thin. Characteristics include language development, egocentrism, and classification on single feature, irreversibility.
Concrete operational period (7–8 to 12–14 years)	Logical ways of thinking begin as long as it is linked to concrete objects. Characteristics include reversibility, seriation, classification, conservation (number, substance, area, weight, volume).
Formal operational period (over age 14)	Students are able to deal logically with multifaceted situations. They can reason from hypothetical situations to the concrete. Characteristics include theoretical reasoning, combinatorial reasoning, proportional reasoning, control of variables, probabilistic and correlational reasoning.

humans think from birth to adulthood. At each stage the individual is able to perform operations on the environment to develop cognitive structures. A summary of the four stages is shown in Table 5.7.

Sensorimotor Stage Beginning at birth to about two years, the first stage is characterized by perceptual and motor activities. The behavior of children during this stage can be described as nonverbal, reflex actions, play, imitating others, and object permanence. Early in this stage of development, if an object that the child has seen is removed from view, the object is forgotten (out of sight, out of mind). However, later in this stage, if a child is playing with an object and it is hidden from view, the child will look for the object.

The child from the beginning is an agent of his or her own cognitive development. Piaget described the young infant as taking control in procuring and organizing all experiences of the outside world. Young children follows with their eyes, explore things, and turn their heads. They explore with their hands by gripping, letting go, pulling, and pushing. We all recognize the exploration of children with their mouths. The child continues his or her exploration with body movements and extends this exploration by putting hands, eyes, and mouth into action at once. With these early life explorations, the child, according to Piaget, develops mental schemes or patterns based on these experiences. These experiences, particularly if they are satisfying, will be repeated by the child. Through the processes of assimilation and accommodation, the child builds internal

structures; the child adapts to the world.[30] Near the latter phase of this stage, the child's experiences are enriched by means of imaginative play, combined with greatly enhanced exploratory abilities; namely questioning, listening, and talking. These activities lead the child to the next stage of cognitive development, the preoperational stage.

Preoperational Stage During the preoperational stage (ages two to seven years), the child's intellectual abilities expand greatly. The child, during this stage, is able to go beyond direct experience with objects. The preoperational child is able to represent objects in their absence, thereby developing the ability to manipulate in the mind. Thus, the child can engage in activities such as symbolic play, drawing, mental imagery, and language.[31]

Table 5.8 compares how the child's mental abilities change from the beginning of the operational stage to the end of this stage. Note the differences in abilities at the beginning phase during which the child can classify only on the basis of one characteristic, as well as not being able to conserve compared to the latter phase of this stage in which the child can conserve mass, weight and volume.

Concrete Operational Stage The concrete operational stage begins around age seven and extends to ages twelve to fourteen. During this stage of development, individuals learn to order, classify, and perform number operations such as adding, subtracting, multiplying,

Table 5.8 Differences during Early and Late Phases of the Preoperational Stage

Preoperational Stage: Ages 2–4	Preoperational Stage: Ages 4–7 (Intuitive Phase)
Classify on the basis of single property	Able to form classes or categories of objects
Unable to see that objects alike in one property might differ in others	Able to understand logical relationships of increasing complexity
Able to collect things based on a criterion	Able to work with the idea of number
Can arrange objects in a series, but cannot draw inferences about things that are not adjacent to each other	Develops the ability to conserve (e.g., mass, weight, volume, continuous quantity, number)

and dividing. They also learn to conserve, develop the ability to determine the cause of events, and understand space/time relationships.

Concrete operations means that the child is able to perform various logical operations, but only with concrete objects. An operation is an action—a manipulation of objects. We might think of an operation as a reasoning pattern. Since most of the students that you will teach will be either at the concrete or formal stage of development (or in transition between these stages), we will explore these reasoning patterns in some detail. At the concrete stage there are several reasoning patterns that impinge on science teaching and some will affect students' performance in your classroom. These reasoning patterns include class inclusion, serial ordering, reversibility, and conservation (Table 5.9).

Class inclusion is an important pattern of reasoning in science courses. Class inclusion is a prerequisite for the development of concrete concepts such as animal, plant, rock, mineral, and planet. For example, suppose you show a student a picture of some plants (carrot, grass, oak tree, cabbage, dandelion). In this task the student is asked to identify which of the pictures is a plant. Most children will readily include the grass in the category of plant, but not tree, carrot, or dandelion. (The tree was a plant when it was little, but now it is big, and therefore a tree.) As students grow older, and their cognitive development gets more sophisticated and their experiences widen, they will develop the ability to include all these objects in the general class of plant.[32]

Students are conservers in the concrete stage. For example, they are able to understand that the quantity of a substance remains the same if nothing is added or taken away. To understand this, show a student a ball of clay the size of a tennis ball. After the student has observed the ball, roll it into a cylinder. Then ask the student if the cylinder (you can call it a snake or a dog) has more, less, or the same amount of clay as the ball. The student that can conserve mass will respond that the cylinder has the same amount of clay. Conservation abilities develop in different areas such as number, mass, weight, and volume.

Table 5.9 Concrete Reasoning Patterns

Concrete Reasoning Pattern (Operations)	Explanation and Examples
Class inclusion	Classifying and generalizing based on observable properties (e.g., distinguishing consistently between acids and bases according to the color of litmus paper; recognizing that all dogs are animals but that not all animals are dogs)
Serial ordering	Arranging a set of objects according to an observable property and possibly establishing a one-to-one correspondence between two observable sets (e.g., small animals have a fast heartbeat while large animals have a slow heartbeat)
Reversibility	Mentally inverting a sequence of steps to return from the final condition of a certain procedure to its initial condition (e.g., after being shown the way to walk from home to school, finding the way home without assistance)
Conservation	Realizing that a quantity remains the same if nothing is added or taken away, though it may appear different (e.g., when all the water in a beaker is poured into an empty graduated cylinder, the amount originally in the beaker is equal to the amount finally in the cylinder)

Source: Based on Karplus, R., et al. *Science Teaching and the Development of Reasoning*. Berkeley, Calif.: Lawrence Hall of Science, 1978, p. 53.

The reasoning patterns in the concrete operational stage can be explored by administering tasks to individual students. By administering Piagetian tasks, you can develop insights into the reasoning abilities of your students. You might want to complete Inquiry Activity 5.2: Piagetian Concrete Reasoning Patterns. To compare students' concrete and formal reasoning patterns, you might complete Inquiry Activity 5.3: The Mealworm and Mr. Short.

INQUIRY ACTIVITY 5.2

Piagetian Concrete Reasoning Patterns

Piaget developed a number of tasks designed to be administered to the individual student. This activity will enable you to administer several tasks to explore the nature of preoperational versus concrete thinking patterns.

Materials

- Piagetian tasks
- Clay
- 2 vials
- 2 candy bars

Procedures

1. Administer these tasks to two or three elementary or middle school age students. You will have to make special arrangements to do this by contacting the appropriate school officials. There are certain processes that you should keep in mind when administering these tasks: (a) Help the student relax by saying that you have a few activities or games to play and that all answers are acceptable. (b) Accept all answers. Remember that you are trying to understand the student's thinking pattern, and the tasks are a way to discover this. Help the student as much as you can to verbalize thinking by encouraging him or her to go on and tell you more. (c) Give the student time to think after you ask a question. (d) Always ask the student to justify answers to the tasks. Again, be patient with the student by helping him or her along, and even suggesting or paraphrasing what other students may have said and asking the student to agree or disagree.
2. Gather all the materials needed for each task. When you are administering the tasks, only have in sight the materials pertinent to the current task. You might have all the materials in a small box, removing and returning the materials as needed.
3. Administer the tasks following the procedures outlined in Figure 5.5.

Minds-On Strategies

1. Summarize the results using Figure 5.6.
2. How did the students do on the following concrete reasoning patterns: class inclusion, serial ordering, reversibility, and conservation?
3. How would you classify the student's intellectual level of thinking: preoperational, transitional, or concrete operational? What are your reasons?
4. What would the implications be for a teacher working with these students if these concepts were presented: Newton's first law of motion, classification of rocks, the concept of geological time?

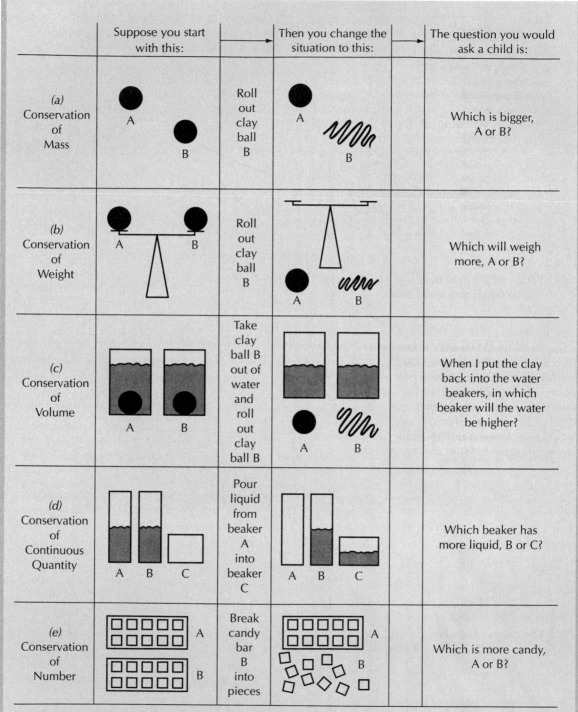

	Suppose you start with this:		Then you change the situation to this:		The question you would ask a child is:
(a) Conservation of Mass	A · B ·	Roll out clay ball B	A · B ~		Which is bigger, A or B?
(b) Conservation of Weight	A · B ·	Roll out clay ball B	A · B ~		Which will weigh more, A or B?
(c) Conservation of Volume	A B	Take clay ball B out of water and roll out clay ball B	A · B ~		When I put the clay back into the water beakers, in which beaker will the water be higher?
(d) Conservation of Continuous Quantity	A B C	Pour liquid from beaker A into beaker C	A B C		Which beaker has more liquid, B or C?
(e) Conservation of Number	A B	Break candy bar B into pieces	A B		Which is more candy, A or B?

Figure 5.5 Concrete Operational Science Tasks. *Source:* Based on Gage, N. L., and Berliner, D. *Educational Psychology. Source:* New York: Houghton-Mifflin, 1988. © 1988 by Houghton-Mifflin.

Task	Student Response	Justification	Intellectual Level: P: Preoperational Tr: Transitional C: Concrete
Conservation Mass Weight Volume Continuous **Quantity** Number			

Figure 5.6 Summary of Concrete Tasks.

Formal Operational Stage The formal operational stage (over age fourteen) is, in Piaget's theory, the stage where students can think scientifically. They are capable of mental operations such as drawing conclusions, constructing tests to evaluate hypotheses, and performing an expanded set of logical operations. The logical or formal operations, which we will call reasoning patterns, include theoretical reasoning, combinatorial reasoning, functionality and proportional reasoning, control of variables, and probabilistic reasoning. According to Piagetian theory, most students in high school should be able to exhibit these reasoning patterns. However, research studies have shown that many students have not developed them. The abilities may, in fact, be aspirations and goals of science education, rather than descriptions of student's cognitive functions.[33]

The scientific reasoning patterns at the formal operations level are shown in Table 5.10. At this stage of development, students are capable of organizing information and analyzing problems in ways that are impossible for a student at the concrete operations stage.

Table 5.10 Formal Reasoning Patterns

Formal Reasoning Patterns	Explanation and Examples
Theoretic Reasoning	Applying multiple classification, conservation logic, serial ordering, and other reasoning patterns to relationships and properties that are not directly observable. Examples: distinguishing between oxidation and reduction reactions, using the energy conservation principle, arranging lower and higher plants in an evolutionary sequence, making inferences from theory according to which the earth's crust consists of rigid plates, accepting a hypothesis for the sake of argument.
Combinatorial Reasoning	The student considers all conceivable combinations of tangible or abstract items. Examples: systematically enumerating the genotypes and phenotypes with respect to characteristics.
Proportional Reasoning	Stating and interpreting functional relationships in mathematical form. Examples: the rate of diffusion of a molecule is inversely proportional to the square root of its molecular weight; the rate of radioactive decay is directly proportional to its half-life.
Control of Variables	The student recognizes the necessity of an experimental design that controls all variables but the one being investigated. Examples: When designing experiments to find out what factors affect swing of a pendulum, students will hold one variable constant (e.g., if investigating mass, the length will remain the same).
Probabilistic and Correlational Reasoning	Interpreting observations that show unpredictable variability and recognizing relationships among variables in spite of random variations that mask them. Examples: In the mealworm puzzle (see Inquiry Activity 5.3), recognizing that a small number of specimens showing exceptional behavior need not invalidate the principle conclusion.

INQUIRY ACTIVITY 5.3

The Mealworm and Mr. Short

To help you understand the difference between concrete and formal reasoning patterns, two puzzles (Figures 5.7 and 5.8) are described in Table 5.11, followed by answers and explanations by secondary students (Table 5.12).

Materials

- Paperclips
- Copies of the puzzles

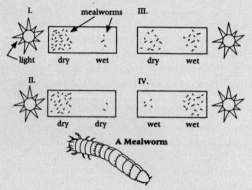

Figure 5.7 Mealworm Experimental Boxes.

Figure 5.8 Mr. Short.

Table 5.11 The Mealworm and Mr. Short Puzzles

The Mealworm Puzzle	The Mr. Short Puzzle
An experimenter wanted to test the response of mealworms to light and moisture. To do this, he set up four boxes as shown in Figure 5.7. He used lamps for light sources and constantly watered pieces of paper in the boxes for moisture. In the center of each box he placed twenty mealworms. One day he returned to count the number of mealworms that had crawled to the different ends of the boxes.	The drawing in Figure 5.8 is called Mr. Short. We used large round buttons laid side-by-side to measure Mr. Short's height, starting from the floor between his feet and going to the top of his head. His height was four buttons. Then we took a similar figure called Mr. Tall, and measured it in the same way with the same buttons. Mr. Tall was six buttons high.
The diagrams show that mealworms respond to (response means move toward or away):	Now please do these things:
A. light but not moisture	1. Measure the height of Mr. Short using paper clips in a chain. The height is _____.
B. moisture but not light	5. Predict the height of Mr. Tall if he were measured with the same paper clips. _____
C. both light and moisture	3. Explain how you figured out your prediction. (You may use diagrams, words, or calculations. Please explain your steps carefully.)
D. neither light nor moisture	
Please explain your choice.	

Table 5.12 Student Responses to the Mealworm and Mr. Short Puzzles

Student	Mealworm Puzzle Response	Mr. Short Puzzle Response
Student 1 (Norma, age 12)	Answer: D Explanation: "Because even though the light was moved in different places, the mealworms didn't do the same things."	Prediction for Mr. Tall: 8.5 paper clips Explanation: "Mr. Tall is 8.5 paper clips tall because when using buttons as a unit of measure he is 2 units taller. When Mr. Short is measured with paper clips as a unit of measurement he is 6.5 paper clips. Therefore, Mr. Tall is 2 units taller in comparison, which totals 8.5."
Student 2 (Jean, age 13)	Answer: B Explanation: "I, II, and III show that mealworms seem to like the light, but in III they seem to be equally spaced. This leads one to believe that mealworms like the dryness and the reason in pictures III and IV they are by the light is because of the heat that the light produces which gives a dryness effect."	Prediction for Mr. Tall: 9.2 paper clips Explanation: "The ratio using buttons of height of Mr. Short and Mr. Tall is 2:3. Figuring out algebraically and solving for x: $.75 = \dfrac{6.5}{x}$ gives you 9.2 as the height in paper clips."
Student 3 (David, age 14)	Answer: A Explanation: "They usually went to the end of the box with the light."	Prediction for Mr. Tall: 9 paper clips Explanation: "I figured out by figuring that Mr. Short is two thirds as tall as Mr. Tall."
Student 4 (John, age 16)	Answer: C Explanation: "Boxes I and II show they prefer dry and light to wet and dark. Box IV eliminates dryness as a factor, so they do respond to light only. Box III shows that wetness cancels the effect of the light, so it seems they prefer dry. It would be clearer if one of the boxes was wet-dry with no light."	Prediction for Mr. Tall: 9 clips (pencil marks along Mr. Short) Explanation: "I estimated the middle and then a fourth of Mr. Short. That's about the size of 1 button. I measured the button with my clips and found 1.5. So then I counted out 6 times 1.5 buttons and got 9."
Student 5 (Dolores, age 17)	Answer: C Explanation: "In the experiment, three mealworms split half wet, half dry. So it's safe to assume that light was not the only factor involved."	Prediction for Mr. Tall: 8 paper clips Explanation: "If Mr. Short measures 4 buttons or 6 paper clips (2 pieces more than buttons), then Mr. Tall should be 2 paper clips more than buttons."
Student 6 (Harold, age 18)	Answer: A Explanation: "Because there are seventeen worms by the light and there are only three by the moisture."	Prediction for Mr. Tall: 9–3/6 clips Explanation: "Figured it out by seeing that Mr. Tall is half again as tall as Mr. Short, so I took half of Mr. Short's height in clips and added it on to his present height in clips and came up with my prediction."

Source: Mealworm and Mr. Short Puzzles based on Karplus, R., et al. *Science Teaching and the Development of Reasoning*. Berkeley, Calif.: Lawrence Hall of Science, 1978, pp. 1–2, 1–6.

Procedure

1. First perform the puzzles yourself, writing your answers and explanations as the students did on separate sheets of paper.
2. If you are able to have secondary students complete the puzzles, you can use their responses to respond to the following questions, as well as the students responses included in Table 5.12.

Minds-On Strategies

When you have finished completing the puzzles, answer these questions.

1. What differences in reasoning did you find among the students' responses to
   a. The mealworm puzzle
   b. The Mr. Short puzzle
2. What similarities did you observe in the thinking patterns of Norma, David, and Dolores?
3. What similarities did you observe in the thinking patterns of Jean, John, and Harold?
4. Which students are using concrete reasoning patterns? Which are using formal reasoning patterns?
5. What are some characteristics of
   a. Concrete reasoning?
   b. Formal reasoning?

CONCRETE VERSUS FORMAL THINKING: IMPLICATIONS While reading through the responses to the two puzzles in Inquiry Activity 5.3, you should have noticed that some of the answers were more complete, more consistent, and more systematic than others. Each answer represents the reasoning of the student who wrote it. Yet, surprising as it may seem, inconsistent and incomplete answers were just as common as complete and consistent ones. The patterns of thinking that the students show as responses to these puzzle problems are integral aspects of Piaget's theory of cognitive development.

In the mealworm puzzle students using concrete reasoning tend to focus on one variable and exclude the others. The student cannot detect the logic of the experiment that allows one variable to be isolated and separated so that they can be dealt with as distinct causal agents. Formal reasoning patterns are shown when students realize that variables are held constant while only one is allowed to change, as in boxes II or IV, or comparing I with III. The formal thinker considers all possible causal factors to test the hypothesis that light or moisture is responsible for the distribution of mealworms.

In the Mr. Short puzzle, students who simply add the extra amount to the height of Mr. Tall recognize concrete reasoning. This type of thinking is a much more direct measure of qualitative difference than is the ratio, which the student makes only by making a correspondence between each individual button and paper clip. Formal thinkers understand that each button corresponds to a certain number of paper clips. Once the ratio is known, the answer is found by calculation.

Concrete thinkers need reference to familiar actions, objects, and observable properties. They use reasoning patterns that include conservation, class inclusion, reversibility, and serial ordering. Their thinking shows inconsistencies among various statements they make, and they often contradict themselves. Most of the students you will teach will be concrete thinkers, even though Piaget has suggested that the formal stage of development begins at about age fourteen. Studies have shown that many adolescents and adults do not develop formal thinking capacities.[34]

Formal or abstract thinkers reason with concepts ($F = ma$), indirect relationships, properties, and theories. They are able to use a wide range of thinking patterns, including combinatorial reasoning, proportional reasoning, control of variables, and probabilistic reasoning. Formal thinkers are able to plan out a course of action, manipulate ideas in their minds, and actively check the validity of their own ideas.

Sociocultural Theories of Learning

In the past, understanding learning was seen as a problem for psychologists to solve. Recently, it has become the purview of a wider group of professionals, including sociologists, anthropologists, historians, and linguists to grapple with the issue of how students learn. Lemke points out that teaching and learning should be viewed "as human social activities conducted within institutional and cultural frameworks." Lemke goes on to say that, according to this view, social interaction takes on a major role in student learning, and this interaction is "central and necessary to learning and not merely ancillary."[35]

The sociocultural perspective on science learning raises some interesting questions for us to ponder:

- What can science teachers expect students to learn about concepts such as electric currents, DNA research, and air pollution without considering the social and cultural backgrounds of their students?
- Is the masculine and rational view of science too narrow to accommodate students who might favor a more esthetic, spiritual, or pragmatic approach to learning?
- Must all students love all of the topics that are presented in the science curriculum or might there be room for a more wholistic and creative approach?

The sociocultural perspective raises the dilemma that we must take into consideration the sociocultural dispositions of the students and the community in which we practice science teaching, and that the view espoused by the constructivist theory of conceptual change might not be a simple as presented. As Lemke points out:

Changing your mind is not simply a matter of rational decision making. It is a social process with social consequences. It is not simply about what is right or what is true in the narrow rationalist sense: it is always also about who we are, whom we like, about who treats us with respect, about how we feel about others and ourselves. In a community, individuals are not simply free to change their minds. The practical reality is that we are dependent on one another for our survival, and all cultures reflect this fact by making the viability of beliefs contingent on their consequences for the community. This is no different in fact within the scientific research community than it is anywhere else. It is another falsification of science to pretend to students that anyone can or should live by extreme rationalist principles. It is often unrealistic even to pretend that classrooms themselves are closed communities, which are free to change their collective minds. Students and teachers need to understand how science and science education are always a part of larger communities and cultures, including the sense in which they take sides in social and cultural conflicts that extend beyond the classroom.[36]

One of the key implications of the sociocultural perspective on student learning is collaboration within groups in a classroom, as well as within larger networks using computers. Collaborative learning (also known as cooperative learning) is viewed as a promising practical application of sociocultural theory. Most teaching takes place in groups, and it is therefore imperative that science teachers closely examine the results of research on small-group learning. At one time or another, students in your classes will be involved with each other doing science laboratory activities, pairing off to answer questions or solve a problem, working in a small team to prepare a report or make a class presentation. Students interact with each other, and it is important to know how this interaction contributes to student learning. It is also important for the teacher to know how to apply sociocultural theory to improve student learning and instruction.

Over the past several years, a major educational innovation has emerged that is affecting classroom learning. Teachers are implementing programs in which students are organized into small groups to accomplish a task, solve a problem, complete an assignment, and study for a test through engagement in a hands-on activity.

Cooperative learning is based on the relationships among motivation, interpersonal relationships, and the accomplishment of specific goals. According to social psychology theorists, a state of tension within the individual motivates movement toward the attainment of desired goals. Thus, from this notion, it is the individual's drive to accomplish a desired goal that motivates behavior, whether it is individualistic, competitive, or cooperative.[37]

Cooperative learning theory posits that behavior among individuals in a group is synergic;[38] that is, the goals of the individuals in a group are linked together in such a way that cooperative goal attainment is correlated positively or is greater than the separate or individual performance of the group members.[39] This theoretical principle runs through a wide range of cooperative learning models, which will be discussed in detail in Chapter 6, but which are alluded to briefly next.

How does cooperative learning facilitate student learning? There are many points of view on this question. The behaviorist explanation goes like this: Students working in one group compete with other groups that the teacher has established. Students within a group work together to accomplish a task (e.g., complete a laboratory report, study together to prepare for a test, complete a science worksheet). Students are placed in a situation where their success is dependent on the behavior and performance of other students in their group. Success does not necessarily imply a grade, but simply doing well on a competitive task where one team's performance is rated against other teams' performances. Accordingly, team rewards and individual accountability are essential to achievement. In one of the most widely used models of cooperative learning (student teams—achievement divisions), student teams study together after being presented information by the teacher. After studying together, students take a test. Test scores are used, along with a system of improvement scores, to chart team recognition.

On the other hand, a cognitive perspective argues that the intrinsically interesting nature of learning tasks combined with the range of abilities and knowledge that students bring to the classroom promotes an environment of learning.[40] Learning tasks that require multiple abilities to accomplish appear to be effective in reducing the domination of group learning by high-ability students. Instead of relying heavily on reading ability, science teachers should design group-learning tasks that require reasoning, hypothesizing, predicting, and inductive thinking, the use of manipulative materials, and multimedia sources. According to social psychologists, such tasks "encourage students to modify their perceptions of their own and one another's competence."[41]

A number of social factors affect the success of cooperative learning. As Johnson and colleagues point out, cooperative learning is not having students sit together as they do individual assignments, not having high-ability students help slower students, and is not assigning a project wherein one person does all the work. Cooperative learning is instead based on positive interdependence, face-to-face communication, individual accountability, and interpersonal skills.[42]

Feminist Perspective

A feminist perspective on learning is the result of the contributions of women in science education over the past thirty years. Marjorie Gardner (former director of the Lawrence Hall of Science, University of California, Berkeley), Mary Bud Rowe (former professor of science education, Stanford University), and Jane Butler Kahle (professor of science education, Miami University, Ohio) were early leaders in changing the perception of the role of women in science and science education. In fact Gardner and Rowe were two of the first women to be employed by the NSF as program directors and decision makers in formulating NSF science education policy.

Although early contributions focused on increasing enrollments in science courses and careers, contemporary feminist research is focused on learning. Nancy Brickhouse put it this way:

> Theories of learning are important because of the resources they provide for solving problems. Theories of learning that split the person into thinking/feeling, mind/body too often diminish feminine-related attributes and reinforce dualism feminists are trying to overcome. Furthermore, they

limit our understanding of what learning is. A feminist perspective on learning should account for the ways in which gender shapes learning. The idea of learning as a transformation of identity-in-practice provides a way of thinking about learning that is gendered, but does not regard gender as a stable, uniform, single attribute. We are not born with gender. We do gender.[43]

Feminist perspectives on learning are compatible with sociocultural perspectives on learning. Feminists emphasize the importance of the social nature of learning and the transformative purpose of education. As you will see in the next section, these ideas are also compatible with the Deweyan perspective.

SITUATED COGNITION Situated cognition creates a learning environment in which learning activities can change students' identities by changing their ability to practice in the world.[44] Too often, most science activities are aimed at having students "consume" science concepts or develop the competence to "do science," in a very narrow way. This narrowness is defined as how well students do science in comparison with professional scientists.

From a feminist perspective, situated cognition would provide the framework to design learning activities in which the goal would be the transformation of student identities. According to Brickhouse, activities would be designed to help students reinvent themselves and the world around them. She goes on to say that the activities of the classroom community would be meaningful and would be connected to other communities of practice.[45]

COMMUNITIES OF PRACTICE In the feminist tradition, then, teachers would work toward designing activities enabling students to participate in authentic communities of practice. Within the community of practice, the goal would be the transformation of "identity-in-practice." Brickhouse supports the idea that "schools would better prepare students for life outside of school if communities in school better related to communities outside of school and if the scientific content of school played a more significant role in the construction of identities in practice."[46] She suggests that science activities would encourage students to take on roles such as the environmentalist, feminist, or smart health-care consumer.

Deweyan Theory of Experience

John Dewey wrote more than fifty books on education and philosophy and to try and summarize his ideas would be fruitless. However, I do want to discuss the implications of Dewey's philosophy for science teaching and demonstrate its relevance in a sociocultural context. The ideas that follow center around Dewey's conception of learning and his notion of experience.

CONCEPTION OF LEARNING Dewey believed that learning is embedded in experiences when the student clashes with the environment, which is when humans work to deal with the tensions between themselves and their surroundings. Dewey believed that learning is natural, not process limited. He would say that humans are always in motion trying to resolve or seek a goal, or working on something intently. To Dewey, the learner is active and, within science education, learners would be experimenting, analyzing an environment, and using tools like telescopes and a hand-lens to glimpse the world they are exploring.

To learn, Dewey insisted that we cannot "give" ideas directly to students, rather concepts have to be presented indirectly. For example, Fishman and McCarthy, when explaining this idea, put it this way:

> Dewey tells teachers that we cannot hand ideas to students as if they were bricks. Although Dewey does not develop this image, I believe he would say we are tempted to try and pass out ideas because, like bricks, they are separable. They can be isolated and decontextualized. But, according to Dewey, to understand aims, beliefs, and ideas we must, to extend his metaphor, see bricks as part of the building they support, as connected purposefully to other bricks as well as to timber and steel. Further, to even care about bricks, we must have the need to use them. We must have the desire to live in a building, construct a new one, or demolish an old one . . . this view of Dewey's—that learning is tied to use, to the drama of doubt, need and discovery—is central to his philosophy of education.[47]

Dewey believed that "nonschool learning" could be used to provide the kind of energy that learning in school would require to engage students. In science education today, educators are increasingly interested in "informal learning" opportunities, including field trips, museums, and community experiences. Dewey's concern is that learning in formal settings is presented in abstract and symbolic forms, whereas if educators reflected on the attributes of nonschool learning, greater emphasis would be placed on emotional and attitudinal aspects of learning. Thus, Dewey saw that "informal" and "incidental" learning was significant in that it would shed light on the shortcomings of "formal" and "intentional instruction."[48] One specific learning strategy that

has direct application here is "project-based teaching," which is discussed in greater detail the next chapter. In project-based teaching, students are involved in experiences that have elements of the informal and incidental, but within the context of the formal and intentional classroom.

EXPERIENCE AND IDEAS-BASED TEACHING The second idea that I would like to emphasize is Dewey's notion of experience and its implications for science learning. Wong and Pugh point out that Dewey's notion of experience is central to understanding the goals of education. They emphasize that it is the goal of education to "help students lead lives rich in worthwhile experiences." According to Wong and Pugh, for Dewey:

> We have *an* experience when the material experienced runs its course to fulfillment. Then and only then is it integrated within and demarcated in the general stream of experience from other experiences. A piece of work is finished in a way that is satisfactory; a problem receives its solution; a game is played through; a situation, whether that of eating a meal, playing a game of chess, carrying on a conversation, writing a book, or taking part in a political campaign, is so rounded out that its close is a consummation and not a cessation. Such an experience is a whole and carries with it its own individualizing quality and self-sufficiency. It is an experience.[49]

According to this view, our task as science teachers is to "provide students with transformative experiences: experiences that are valuable in themselves and valuable in their potential to lead to other worthwhile experiences."[50] According to this view, the goal is to create worthwhile experiences and, to do that, teachers have to set up experiences that create anticipation on the part of the students. One way to do that is to engage students in "big ideas." Wong and Pugh identify several characteristics of Dewey's "big ideas":

- Ideas need to be connected to the subject matter of science. Students need to anticipate the emotional qualities of an idea and, for example, "seized by the idea that plant seeds can be spread about by animals and begin to think about birds, dogs and cats differently, there is educative anticipation. There is an idea."[51]
- Ideas inspire action; only in action do ideas have meaning and value.
- Ideas have distinct emotional quality. Feelings are connected to anticipation—the seeking of

some future experience connected to the idea. And as Wong and Pugh point out, we are not talking about feelings of like or dislike of science. Students involved in experiences with emotional content are motivated and move on to experience the idea.

Elsewhere in this book we have discussed the *National Science Education Standards* and, in particular, the science content standards. If you look at these content standards (divided into categories such as life, earth and space, physical, science and technology), the statements are descriptions of concepts that students should learn. These concepts provide a framework to organize science courses or to write science textbooks for students. Wong and Pugh offer an alternative, and that is to organize science teaching around ideas rather than science concepts. Science concepts, as they point out, are the ways that people represent or think about the world. If you relate this to the *Standards*, concepts are what students learn. Also, if you look back at the section on conceptual change teaching, you will note that this constructivist model attempts to help students change their concepts and develop a "scientific view" of the concept.

Ideas, in the Deweyan sense, are quite different. According to Wong and Pugh, ideas are anticipations and are the basis for action and being. An idea is something that seizes students and transforms them. As Wong and Pugh point out, "the goal of ideas-based teaching is to help students be taken by an idea and to live with it, to be with it in their world."[52]

Ideas-based teaching starts with an examination of the concepts that a teacher would want to use to organize instruction. However, it is important that the teacher identify the "big ideas" in the domain that subsume the science concepts. For example, an earth science teacher presents students with the notion that, because of plate tectonics, the continents appear to be drifting. A rather static idea. The challenge is to "reanimate" the concept of "continental drift" so as to inspire action, thought, and feeling. Another example is in chemistry, where students learn how periodicity relates to the chemical elements and the pattern shown on the periodic table. Seldom is the story told of how Mendeleyev, an avid card player, was in a near-sleep state on a train trip from St. Petersburg to a country town when he was inspired to see a connection to his card playing and the chemical elements. On this particular Friday afternoon, once the train reached the distant town, Mendeleyev immediately boarded a train to return to St. Petersburg and his office at the university, where he wrote all he knew about each chemical element on small cards and then used his card playing experience to create the periodic table of the chemical elements. For students, learning about the chemical elements might take on a different power in this context.

To implement ideas-based teaching, Wong and Pugh suggest several metaphors. First, they find the arts—visual arts, music, literature, and drama—to be powerful sources of metaphors for science teaching. For example, if the teacher uses the story metaphor to present the "big idea," it provides a context for anticipation, as in the case of Mendeleyev. The teacher can embellish the story by creating characters, actions, and settings and then in a dramatic way tell the story. Video clips from movies can also provide a dramatic setting to lay out the stage for ideas. In Table 5.13, I've described several

Table 5.13 Concepts versus Ideas: An Experience

Science Concept	Corresponding Deweyan Idea
Science Concept and Corresponding Big Idea	
Newton's Laws of Motion Law of Inertia For every action there is an equal and opposite reaction.	For much of history, people had not been very successful at predicting and explaining motion. But Newton, with his three simple laws, figured out how to explain the motion of all observable objects. His laws gave him a vision into the very nature of the universe—which in his day was like seeing into the nature of God. And with that vision came a magnificent, but terrifying power—the power to explain, predict, and control the world. Since that day, the world has never been the same. Let's take a look at these ideas and see how they might also change ourselves and our world.
Photosynthesis: The process by which green plants are able to convert radiant energy into food.	Think about this. It is possible that plants are the only organisms in the universe that can convert the sun's energy to food energy—food that ultimately sustains every other life form.
Science Concept without a Big Idea *Select Concepts from the Standards and Generate Big Ideas*	

INQUIRY ACTIVITY 5.4

 Concepts versus Big Ideas: A Deweyan Experience

In this inquiry you will learn how to distinguish between scientific concepts and what Dewey referred to as a big idea. According to Deweyan theory, an educative experience is dependent on having a big idea and distinguishing an idea from a concept.

Materials

- Access to science textbooks
- State standards or the *National Science Education Standards*

Procedure

1. Examine the concepts and ideas in Table 5.13 to help you distinguish between a science concept and a big idea.
2. Try to construct a big idea that you might use with a group of students for the concepts that appears in the chart without a corresponding idea.
3. Think about the concepts you might teach in an earth science, life science, or physical science course. Select one content area (e.g., earth science) and identify several concepts that might be included in a course. You might want to consult the *National Science Education Standards* and simply identify the concepts from this reference.
4. Identify the big ideas that would correspond with the science concepts that you have selected.

Minds-On Strategies

1. How do concepts differ from ideas and what is the implication for you as you plan learning materials for your students?
2. To what extent do you think an idea is more motivational for students than concepts?
3. What are some of the big ideas in your field of expertise?

"big ideas" and juxtaposed them with the related science concepts. One of the roles of the teacher in ideas-based teaching is to identify the big ideas in an area of science, such as biology, and use them as the foundation for organizing the course.

Behavioral Theories of Learning

What do you think the following scenarios have in common?

- A teacher says to a student, "I'm proud of you. Your science fair project was outstanding."
- A teacher asks a question. A student answers. The teacher says, "Good answer."

- A biology teacher gives extra credit for students who bring in a newspaper clipping on bioethical issues.

All of these are applications of behavioral theories of learning. Behavioral theories emphasize overt or observable behaviors to influence and determine if learning has occurred. First, we will examine some of these behavioral theories and then identify some principles of behaviorism that can be applied to the classroom.

Conditioning

Conditioning, also referred to as classical conditioning, was one of the first theories of behaviorism. You are probably familiar with the famous experiments by the Russian scientist Ivan Petrovich Pavlov (1849–1936). He found out that dog behavior could be conditioned: A dog, when presented with a piece of meat, salivates. Pavlov called the meat an unconditioned stimulus resulting in an unconditioned response (salivation). To condition the response behavior, Pavlov rang a small bell the same time the meat was presented. After several practice sessions in which the bell and meat were presented simultaneously, the dog eventually learned to salivate when the bell was rung without the meat being presented. In this case, the bell is the conditioned stimulus.

According to Hilgard and Bower, Pavlov's contribution rested as much on his methodology as the results of his research.[53] His theorizing and the care with which he explored numerous relationships provided a foundation for further behaviorists.

Operant Conditioning

Of all the theories of behavioral learning, operant conditioning probably has had the greatest impact on the science teacher. B. F. Skinner (1904–1990) proposed a class of behavior that is controlled by stimulus events that immediately follow an action. Skinner labeled these operant behaviors because they operated on the environment to receive reinforcement. According to Skinner, once an operant behavior occurs, its future rate of occurrence depends on its consequences. According to Skinner and other modern behaviorists, operant behavior is to be distinguished from responding behavior. Responding behavior involves the reactions of the smooth muscles and glands and includes reflexive reactions such as salivating, secreting digestive juices, shivering, increased heart or respiratory rates, and so forth. Operant behavior, on the other hand, involves the striated muscular system (muscles under voluntary control), and results in behaviors such as talking, walking, eating, and problem solving.[54] Preceding stimuli, as shown in Figure 5.9, controls responding behavior. Operant behavior, on the other hand, is controlled by stimulus events that immediately follow the operant as shown in Figure 5.10.

Skinner designed a special apparatus (others called it the Skinner box) for use with white rats and later with pigeons. It consisted of a darkened sound-resistant

US   ⟶   UR
(Unconditioned Stimulus)   (Responding Behavior)
(Lemon juice in mouth)   (Salivation)

Figure 5.9 Classical Stimulus Response Psychology.

S ⟶ R ⟶ S
(Discriminant Stimulus)   (Operant Response)   (Consequent Stimulus)

Figure 5.10 Operant Conditioning.

box into which the rat (or pigeon) was placed. The box contained a small brass lever that, if pressed, delivered a pellet of food. Skinner connected the lever to a recording system that produced a graphical tracing of the rat's behavior. The pigeon box was slightly different; the pigeon "pecked" for its food at spot and received grain.[55]

Skinner's work resulted in the development of a number of principles of behavior that have direct bearing on science teaching. Two concepts stand out that have implications for the science teacher: consequences and reinforcement. In the sections that follow, we will explore these two concepts and then return to them again in Chapter 10 in discussion on classroom management.

Skinner found that pleasurable consequences "strengthen" behavior, while unpleasant consequences "weaken" it. Pleasurable consequences are referred to as reinforcers, while unpleasant consequences are called punishers. The teacher who says, "Alex, you did such a great job on your laboratory assignment that you can spend the remaining ten minutes working with one of the computer games" is making use of a reinforcer to strengthen classroom work. Let's examine reinforcers more carefully.

Behavioral psychologists differentiate between two types of reinforcers, primary and secondary. A primary reinforcer satisfies human needs for food, water, security, warmth, and sex. Secondary reinforcers are those that acquire their value by being related to primary reinforcers or to other secondary reinforcers. Secondary reinforcers are of greatest value to the science teacher. These reinforcers, which are also called conditioned reinforcers, can be divided into three categories: social, token, and activity.

SOCIAL REINFORCERS Teachers who want to strengthen desired classroom behavior and learning can use social reinforcers. Social reinforcers, especially praise, can be powerful tools for the science teacher. Although Brophy reports that praise is not used very frequently, he also reports that most students enjoy receiving some praise and teachers enjoy giving it.[56] To be effective, praise should be given only when a genuinely praiseworthy accomplishment has occurred. The teacher's praise should be informative, specifying some particulars about the noteworthy behavior or

Table 5.14 Examples of Social Reinforcers for the Science Classroom

Praising Words and Phrases	Facial Expressions	Nearness	Physical Contact
Good	Smiling	Walking among students	Touching
That's right	Winking	Sitting in student groups	Patting head
Excellent	Nodding	Joining the class at break	Shaking hand
That's clever	Looking interested	Eating with the students	Stroking arm
Fine answer	Laughing		
Good job			
Good thinking			
Great			
That shows a great deal of work			
You really pay attention			
I like that			
Show the class your model			
That's interesting			
Joan, you're doing so well with the microscope			
That was very kind of you			

performance, to help the student understand his or her successes. And, finally, praise should be genuine, sincere, and credible.

Social behaviors can be divided into four clusters: praising words and phrases, facial expressions, nearness, and physical contact (Table 5.14).[57] The use of these behaviors is common in many science classrooms.

TOKEN REINFORCERS Token reinforcers are things such as points, gold stars, or chips that can be earned and have a reinforcing effect by pairing with other reinforcers. Teachers have found the use of tokens very effective in managing student learning and classroom behavior. The use of a point system is especially effective in helping students learn how to manage their behavior, as well contributing their success as science learners. Many teachers set up their grading system using a point system (e.g., points can be earned for homework, laboratory assignments, projects, quizzes, and tests).

ACTIVITY REINFORCERS Activity reinforcers, also referred to as the Premack principle, are a third group of reinforcers that teachers have found effective in the classroom. According to psychologist David Premack, more-preferred activities can be used to reinforce less-preferred activities.[58] According to the Premack principle, any higher-frequency behavior that is contingent on a lower-frequency behavior is likely to increase the rate of lower-frequency behavior. Thus the

teacher would set up a situation in which students, when they complete the less-preferred activity, are permitted to participate in a more-preferred activity. In the science classroom, some examples of the Premack principle would be, "You may work in the computer game center when you finish cleaning the laboratory," "Those who score over 90 on today's quiz will not have to do homework tonight," or "If all students are in their seats when the bell rings, then the class may have three minutes of free time at the end of today's class." These examples will not necessarily work in each situation. The science teacher must determine the preferred activities and then use them to strengthen the less-preferred activities.

Theory into Practice

Behavioral theories of learning can be put into practice to the advantage of teachers and students alike. The underlying principle of behaviorism is "reinforce behaviors you wish to see repeated."[59] According to Robert Slavin, the main principles of the use of reinforcement to increase desired behavior changes in the classroom are as follows:

1. Determine the behaviors desired from the students and reinforce them when they occur.
2. Explain to students the behavior that is desired and, when they show the desired behavior, reinforce the students' behavior and explain why.

Table 5.15 Creating a Positive Classroom Environment by Means of Operant Conditioning

Step 1: Analyze the Environment	Step 2: Make a List of Positive Reinforcers	Step 3: Select Sequence of Behaviors to Be Implemented	Step 4: Implement Program, Maintain Records of Behavior, and Make Changes
Identify positive and undesirable student behaviors receiving reinforcement. What behaviors receive the punishment? What is the frequency of punishment? Have these behaviors been suppressed?	Determine students' preferred activities (students can contribute to this). Consider using punished behaviors as reinforcers. If talking with peers is a disruptive behavior consider using it (time to talk with peers) as a reinforcer.	Implement a positive reinforcement program. Instead of punishment for tardiness, reward students for being on time.	Make sure classroom rules are clear (see Chapter 10). Make sure students know how to earn reinforcement. Implement reinforcement schedule.

Science teachers deal with a complex classroom environment, often involving the handling of dangerous materials or doing experiments involving safety issues. Specifying the behaviors that you expect in the laboratory, or whenever students are handling materials, and reinforcing them when they occur will help students become independent and responsible science learners. Some science teachers post these behaviors in the science laboratory after spending time teaching and explaining these behaviors.

Skinner's concept of operant conditioning can be applied to the science classroom in many ways, but three seem clearly the most important: (1) the use of classroom questions and associated techniques, (2) developing a positive classroom climate, and (3) developing programmed teaching materials.

USE OF CLASSROOM QUESTIONS One of the most common teaching behaviors that you will employ is that of asking students questions. Questions can be directed at the whole class, small groups of students, or individuals. Mary Budd Rowe developed one of the most powerful applications of science education research.[60] Rowe investigated "wait time" (the time a teacher waits after asking a question and calling on a student). She found that wait times of three to five seconds changed a number of student behaviors including the length of response to a question, increased number of unsolicited responses, as well as the build-up of confidence. The technique (developed fully in Chapter 9) involves this sequence:

- Teacher asks a question
- Teacher pauses (wait time) from three to five seconds (to give students a chance to think of an answer)
- Teacher calls on a student

- Student responds
- Teacher responds to student (choices include praising the student, using the student idea)

CLASSROOM CLIMATE Although developed more fully in Chapter 10, here it is important to emphasize that Skinner's work can be applied to creating a positive classroom climate by having the teacher respond to student success rather than failure. For example, rather than pointing out what students are doing wrong, point out what they are doing right. When a student answers a teacher's question with a partially correct response, the teacher should pick up on the correct aspect of the answer to reinforce the student's contribution. Table 5.15 outlines the steps that can contribute to a positive learning environment based on Skinner's concept of operant conditioning.

PROGRAMMED TEACHING MATERIALS AND COMPUTER ASSISTED INSTRUCTION Skinner designed teaching machines that controlled the students' progress through a body of material. The teaching machine, usually by means of questions or fill-in-the-blank statements, provided reinforcement for right answers (by confirming them, allowing the student to move ahead). The teaching machine was a vehicle for programming instruction as well as providing an environment in which students could work at their own rate. Textbooks and workbooks were written to teach information about a variety of subjects, especially in science. The textbooks were equipped with a card that could be inserted in a page holder. As students worked through each statement or question, they would slide the card so that the correct answer would appear. Early machines and textbooks were limited in the types of reinforcements they could provide. However, with the development of the microcomputer, not only can a variety of reinforcements

INQUIRY ACTIVITY 5.5

 ### Meeting of the Minds

What would they talk about if they had the chance to be in the same room at the same time? In this activity, you are going to participate in role-playing activity in which four theorists come together in a "meeting of the minds." Imagine a constructivist, a behaviorist, a sociocultural theorist, and a feminist all in the same seminar room discussing how they think students learn and addressing other questions related to student understanding.

Materials

- Text material
- Web sites related to various theorists

Procedure

1. After being assigned a role from the selection of learning theorists, use the discussion in this chapter as well as other sources to identify the points of view of your "theorists" on how students learn. Gather enough material to play the role of your theorist in a discussion on the topic "How do students learn science?"
2. Participate in an enactment of the discussion that would occur if these theorists could be in the same seminar room at the same time. The discussion should be moderated by someone in your group or by your instructor. The person in charge might develop a few questions to guide the role-playing session: (a) What, in your view, is learning? (b) How would you go about teaching middle school students (age twelve or thirteen) about the value of science in society? (c) What are the most effective conditions under which learning takes place? (d) Why do some students not grasp a deep understanding of science? You should feel free to add questions. The moderator should capitalize on spontaneity and let the discussion move in the direction created by the "theorists."

Minds-On Strategies

1. Upon reflection, which theorists provided the most powerful argument explaining how students learn? What were their arguments?
2. How do the theorists' arguments compare to your own views of learning?
3. To what extent do you think the theorists dealt with the practical issues and problems that teachers face on a day-to-day basis?

be provided (a pleasant sound, a voice), but the software can be programmed to provide a variety of feedback for various responses. Drill and practice, tutorial, and some game software programs are based on the Skinnerian concept of programmed instruction.

Science teachers can make use of Skinner's concept of programmed instruction by providing students the opportunity to work in the microcomputer environment. Drill and practice and tutorial programs are available in most science content areas. Although not the most avant-garde use of the computer, such programs can help students learn science information efficiently and with little teacher effort.

Behaviorism has contributed greatly to the teaching of science, but, like any theory of learning, it has limitation and rivals. In the past twenty years, there has been an increase in the variety of learning theories to explain student learning in science.

Student Learning Styles: Implications for Teaching

Students learn in a variety of ways, and to accommodate these differences teachers have devised a variety of methods and strategies to correlate with student-learning styles. Various strategies have been researched and implemented in the classroom. For example, Rita and Kenneth Dunn have developed a comprehensive approach to learning styles and have found that learning styles are affected by students' (1) immediate environment, (2) emotionality, (3) sociological needs, (4) physical needs, and (5) psychological processes.[61] Other researchers explored the dichotomous way the left and right hemispheres of the brain process and interpret information. Some researchers have divided student learning styles into categories. For example, later in the chapter you will learn about Bernice McCarthy, who devised a system in which four learning styles are identified: innovative learners, analytic learners, common-sense learners, and dynamic learners. In this section we will explore these ideas and identify some implications for science teaching.

Students, Teachers, and Learning Styles

Learning style pertains to how we learn. To some educators, "one's learning style is a biologically and developmentally imposed set of characteristics that explains why the same lecture, readings, interactions, classroom settings, and teachers affect individuals so differently."[62] There are two crucial questions related to student learning styles: In what ways do students differ in their manner of learning? How do teachers accommodate students with different learning styles? In order to find out your ideas on these two questions, please complete the Inquiry Activity 5.6 before reading ahead.

INQUIRY ACTIVITY 5.6

 Ideas about Student Learning Styles

In this chapter, I have stressed the importance of helping students verbalize their existing ideas on concepts that the science teacher will introduce. One technique that can be used to ascertain one's ideas on a concept is a concept map. Using the concept map as a model, draw two concept maps, following the instructions described next.

Materials

- 2 large sheets of paper
- Writing instruments

Procedure

1. Draw a concept map about the topic: Factors Affecting Student Learning Styles
2. Draw a second concept map on the question: What are some ways to accommodate students with different learning styles?

Note: A concept map has a hierarchical structure to it, with the more general and inclusive concepts at the top and more exclusive and specific concepts further down.

Minds-On Strategies

1. Compare your concept maps to others in your class. What are the common factors affecting student learning styles based on these maps?
2. What is your class concept of student learning style?
3. Focus on ways to accommodate student learning styles. How do your methods compare to the ideas suggested by the teachers in the Science Teachers Talk section (p. 206)?

Now that you have explored your own ideas on student learning styles, compare them with the ideas suggested by teachers in the Science Teachers Talk section of this chapter's *Science Teacher Gazette*. As you read the teacher comments, note that they allude to a variety of methodologies in an attempt to increase student motivation and success in the science classroom. Let's explore the theory behind learning styles, and then apply learning style ideas to classroom science teaching.

The Psychology of Learning Styles

Some students in your class would rather look at pictures of plants than read about them. You might have a student who prefers to discuss questions in a small group rather than participate in a large-group discussion. Another student might prefer to learn chemical nomenclature by matching the chemical symbols printed on blue index cards with the names of the elements or compounds printed on green index cards. We all have preferences for the way we learn. What do we know about learning styles, and how can this information be helpful to you as a beginning science teacher?

DISCOVERING LEARNING STYLES Consider for a moment your own approach to learning. Here are some sample items from an instrument designed to diagnose student learning styles.[63] Do any of the following items describe your preferences when it comes to learning?

- I study best when it is quiet.
- I have to be reminded often to do something.
- I really like to draw, color, or trace things.
- I like to study by myself.

Rita and Kenneth Dunn have explored a universe of factors that affect the way students learn. The chart in Figure 5.11 summarizes the variety of elements that are organized into one of the following categories:

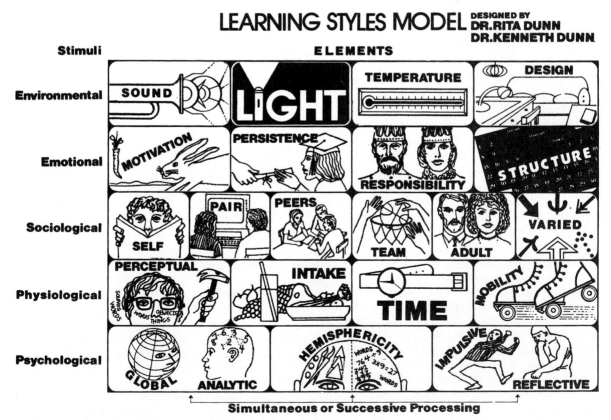

Figure 5.11 Learning Styles Model. *Source:* From Dunn, R., and Griggs, S. A. "A Quiet Revolution: Learning Styles and their Application to Secondary Schools," pp. 14–19. *Holistic Education Review* (Winter 1989). Reprinted with permission of Rita Dunn.

environmental, emotional, sociological, physical, and psychological. Using the Learning Styles Inventory—a comprehensive approach to assessing students' learning style—researchers have surveyed individuals' styles in each of the twenty-two areas. The instrument consists of over a hundred preference statements (like the four listed at the beginning of this section) that identify students' learning preferences.[64] Knowledge of these categories is helpful in understanding the differences in learning preferences of your students. Briefly, here are some comments on the five categories identified by the Dunns and their implications for science teaching.

Environmental Elements It shouldn't surprise us that sound, light, temperature, and design affect learning styles. According to Dunn and colleagues, 10 to 40 percent of students are affected by differences in sound (quiet versus sound), bright or soft lighting, warm or cool temperatures, and formal versus informal seating designs.[65] Science teachers have an opportunity to create a physical learning environment that is appealing to a wide range of students. One of the suggestions that the Dunns make is to "change the classroom box into a multifaceted learning environment."[66]

Emotional Elements Motivation, persistence on completing a task, degree of responsibility, and structure (specificity of rules governing work and assignments) constitute emotional elements that affect student learning style.

Physical Elements Several physical elements, including perceptual strengths, intake (of food or drink), time (of the day), and mobility influence learning. Perceptual strengths refer to learning through the different senses. At the secondary school level, greatest emphasis is given to auditory and visual learning. However, secondary teachers who have used electroboards, flips charts, task cards, and other manipulatives have reported increased achievement and interest for the tactile student. Secondary teachers who employed kinesthetic (whole body) activities such as field trips, dramatizing, interviewing, and role-playing, also reported increases in achievement and interest.[67] Many students also learn better if they are engaged in multisensory learning activities (e.g., combining tactile and kinesthetic or visual and auditory tasks).

Sociological Elements Do students like to learn alone, in pairs, with a small team, or with the whole class? The answer from the Dunn's research is that students respond to a variety of social groupings and appear to be "unresponsive to a consistent instructional routine."[68] The teacher who provides opportunities, not only throughout a science course but also within individual lessons, for variety in social groupings is paying attention to the sociological needs of the learner.

Psychological Elements A number of psychological factors that psychologists have examined are related to learning style. Two major ideas emerge in this regard; namely, how learners process information and how learners perceive. Processing information can be viewed as a global process or an analytical process. Global (processing in wholes) versus analytical (processing in parts) is analogous to right hemispheric thinking and left hemispheric thinking. Learners appear to perceive either actively or reflectively.

BRAIN HEMISPHERICITY AND LEARNING STYLE Considerable attention has been given to what is called brain hemisphericity and brain-based learning. According to neurosurgeon Joseph Bogan, brain hemisphericity is the reliance on one mode of processing over another by an individual.[69] Roger Sperry, a Nobel laureate in physiology for his work on hemisphericity, explained the nature of hemisphericity this way:

> Each hemisphere . . . has its own . . . private sensations, perceptions, thought, and ideas, all of which are cut off from the corresponding experience in the opposite hemisphere. Each left and right hemisphere has its own private chain of memories and learning experiences that are accessible to recall by the other hemisphere. In many respects each disconnected hemisphere appears to have a separate "mind of its own."[70]

These early brain researchers found that (1) the two halves of the brain, right and left hemispheres, process information differently; (2) in the split-brain patient, there seem to be two different people up there, each with his or her favorite ways of processing information, each with a different mode of thinking; and (3) both hemispheres are equally important.[71]

Left versus Right Brain Thinking Early findings on brain-based learning had direct and obvious implications for teaching, but especially for the growing field of student learning styles. Bernice McCarthy, who has applied the results of brain research to the 4MAT model of learning, sees the two hemispheres processing information and experiencing it differently. Table 5.16 presents some differences that McCarthy believes make a difference in helping to accommodate students with different learning styles.[72]

Table 5.16 Left and Right Hemisphere Information Processing

The Left Hemisphere	The Right Hemisphere
Does verbal things	Sees relationships
Likes sequence	Grabs for the whole
Sees the trees	Does visual-spatial things
Likes structure	Likes random patterns
Analyzes	Sees the forest
Is rational	Is fluid and spontaneous
Is theoretical	Is intuitive

One argument brain researchers make is that school learning emphasizes and favors "left" brain learning over "right" brain learning. If listening to lectures and relying on the science textbook are left brain activities, then there is evidence to support this argument.[73] For example, teachers who want to increase the number of right brain activities in their lesson plans, thereby giving right brain learners more of an opportunity for success, would include such approaches as mind-mapping, visualization experiences, imagery, analogies, use of paradox, role-playing, creative writing (yes, in science), demonstrations, experiments, intuitive activities, connecting ideas, and creative problem solving.[74]

Left/Right Brain: Implications from Research There is a tendency, as with any theory, to draw simplified interpretations, and so it is with brain functioning and student learning style. One of the major oversimplifications is that rationality is exclusively a left brain function and creativity a right brain function. Evidence supports the idea that both hemispheres play a part in rationality and creativity. There are, however, some results that have powerful implications for you as a teacher. A few follow.

Ann Howe and Poul Thompsen report that hemisphericity can play an important role in motivation and science teaching.[75] According to work being done in artificial intelligence, when a person is exposed to some new phenomenon the first thing that occurs is that in the deep part of the brain the person gives a preliminary value to the phenomenon: "Is it interesting or not?" If it isn't, the person doesn't give it any more attention. It is interesting, then after ten seconds or so the phenomenon enters the right hemisphere, which attempts to make holistic sense of it: "What's this all about?" If this succeeds, then the information is processed to the left hemisphere, where the brain tries to deal with it analytically. This notion supports the contention that we must pay close attention to the types of tasks that we present to students. Interest is an important aspect of science teaching, and the gatekeeper seems to be the deep recesses of the brain.

Another finding that has implications for teaching has to do with the role of emotion or feelings. The right hemisphere seems to play a special role in emotion. If students are emotionally involved in an activity, then both sides of the brain will participate in the activity, regardless of the subject matter or content.[76]

The two hemispheres are involved in thinking, logic, and reasoning, and in the creation and appreciation of art and music. This disputes earlier implications that the left brain was the logical side and the right brain the artistic side.

Applying Learning Style and Brain-Based Concepts to Science Teaching

There are many things you can do to help students learn in the science classroom and, certainly, applying what is known about learning styles is a place to begin. In this section I present some ideas on an approach to learning that incorporates brain research and student learning styles (the 4MAT system), offer specific suggestions for teaching students according to their own learning style, and introduce some tools to help students learn about their own learning (metacognition).

THE 4MAT SYSTEM 4MAT, devised by Bernice McCarthy, is a learning style system that identifies four types of learners:[77]

1. Imaginative learners
2. Analytic learners
3. Common sense learners
4. Dynamic learners

Imaginative learners (type 1) perceive information *concretely* and process it *reflectively*. They are sensory oriented as well as reflectors. They are imaginative thinkers and like to work with other people. Their favorite question is "Why?" Analytic learners (type 2) perceive information *abstractly* and process it *reflectively*. They are abstract thinkers who ponder their creations, which tend to be models and theories. They value sequential thinking. Their favorite question is "What?" Common sense learners (type 3) perceive information *abstractly* and process it *actively*. They are practical thinkers; they need to know how things work. They are skill oriented, experimenting and tinkering with things. Their favorite question is "How does this work?" Dynamic learners (type 4) perceive information *concretely* and process it *actively*. These learners

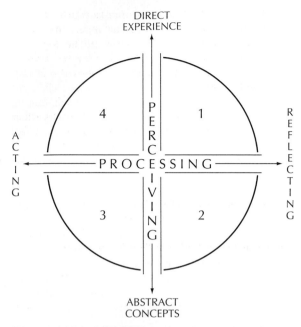

DIRECT
EXPERIENCE

ABSTRACT
CONCEPTS

Figure 5.12 Types of Learners in the 4MAT System. *Source:* McCarthy, B. *About Learning-4MAT in the Classroom.* Wauconda, IL: About Learning Inc, 2000, p. 31. Used with Perission of Bernice McCarthy.

integrate experience and application. They learn by trail and error, and are risk takers. Their favorite question is "What if?"[78]

How did McCarthy arrive at these four types of learners? McCarthy based her model on the work of David Kolb, who had studied learners and ways in which they perceive and process information.[79] Kolb theorized two continuums as follows:

- Perceiving: concrete (sensing/feeling) to abstract (thinking)
- Processing: active (acting/doing) to reflective (watching)

By combining these dualities, McCarthy developed a system in which four distinct learning styles emerged; each being defined as one of the quadrants in the model shown in Figure 5.12.

McCarthy's model is a cycle of learning. If you examine the model in Figure 5.12, imagine it as a clock. Learning begins at 12:00 with concrete experience. According to McCarthy, by moving clockwise around the circle, students then experience reflective observation; from this place they move to abstract conceptualization and finally to active experimentation. In

this way, all students are taught in all four ways. Each is comfortable some of the time, while at the same time being stretched to develop other learning abilities.

Another feature of 4MAT is that each of the four learning styles is integrated with left and right brain processing, giving teachers a comprehensive teaching model. Activities for each quadrant are equally divided between left and right brain modes. For example, a teacher would begin a learning sequence in Quadrant I (concrete/reflective) with a right brain activity to help the students explore by observing, questioning, visualizing, and imagining. Students would be helped to develop a reason for studying the material. The right brain activity would be followed by a left brain activity in which the students reflect on the active/concrete experience they began with. This pattern, alternating between right and left brain modalities, is continued around the remaining three quadrants of the 4MAT model.

TEACHING TO STUDENT'S INDIVIDUAL STYLES
According some researchers, students who do well in school tend to be the ones that learn either by listening or by reading. The focus on these two senses, especially at the high school level, tends to play havoc with the tactile and kinesthetic learners. Because so much of what happens in classrooms is focused on the auditory and visual modes, students who prefer tactile and kinesthetic modes are actually handicapped. In this section, a few suggestions are included to show how these other modalities can be included in science teaching, thereby creating a multisensory approach.

Keep in mind these characteristics: Visual learners learn by seeing and imagining; auditory learners learn by listening and verbalizing; kinesthetic learners learn by participating, moving, and talking; tactile learners learn by doing, touching, and manipulating. Also remember that these modes can be combined.

- Bring color into the science classroom with posters, bright bulletin boards, new paint. One technique that is effective is, instead of writing on the chalkboard, write your notes and make drawings with bright marking pens on a flip chart. If you use the overhead projector, write with a variety of colored pens.
- Make tactile learning aids. The Dunns describe a number of tactile aids that can be used repeatedly from class to class and year to year.[80] One example is the task card. This multisensory resource helps students review and check whether they understand material, allows students to work at their own pace or with someone else, and frees the

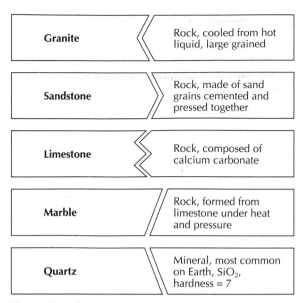

Granite	Rock, cooled from hot liquid, large grained
Sandstone	Rock, made of sand grains cemented and pressed together
Limestone	Rock, composed of calcium carbonate
Marble	Rock, formed from limestone under heat and pressure
Quartz	Mineral, most common on Earth, SiO_2, hardness = 7

Figure 5.13 Sample Geology Task Cards.

teacher to work with others. Suppose you want the students to review the meanings of important ideas and concepts. You would compile a set of questions with answers (or concepts with associated meanings) and prepare cards, as shown in Figure 5.13, by cutting stiff paper into strips, laminating the strips after writing the information on the cards, and then cutting each card in a unique fashion.

- Use the computer as a multisensory learning aid. Computers are powerful tools in their own right, but can be used to help tactile and kinesthetic learners. Establishing a computer center in the classroom and providing opportunities for individual or small groups of students to work in the center with games, tutorials, simulations, or problem-solving software allows tactile and kinesthetic learners opportunities for personal involvement, manipulation of the keyboard, and movement (to a different place in the classroom).
- Plan an occasional field trip, role-playing sessions, debates, and games in which the students move from one place in the classroom to another and manipulate objects. These activities favor the kinesthetic learner.
- Plan tabletop learning activities in which students handle and manipulate science materials, objects, and specimens. You do not have to wait to go into the lab to favor the tactile learner. Is it possible to teach every lesson wherein there is some tactile learning involved?

- Don't forget the auditory learner. Showing films, videos, listening to tapes, and hearing music (related to science) are activities that favor the auditory (and visual) learner. Discussion, debates, and question-and-answer sessions favor the auditory learner.

There are many other ways to create a multisensory classroom. For now, it is important to remember that providing a variety of sensory modes will ensure that each student's learning style is attended to at least some of the time.

METACOGNITIVE STRATEGIES Have you ever thought about your strengths (and weaknesses, too) as a learner? Do you know how you learn? Do you have strategies that you use to learn? These strategies are ways to help students learn about learning and learn about knowledge. Called metacognitive strategies, they play an increasingly important role in science teaching. I will briefly discuss them here, and will return to them again in Chapter 6.

There are several definitions of metacognition. One view is that it is our ability to know what we know and what we don't know. We might also think of metacognition as the ability to plan a strategy:[81]

1. for producing what information is needed;
2. to be conscious of our own steps and strategies during the act of problem solving;
3. to reflect on and evaluate the productivity of our own thinking.

Teaching metacognitive strategies is a potentially new goal for science teachers. Given that student learning styles influence the way students process and perceive, metacognitive strategies can be useful in helping students understand their unique learning patterns. What are some metacognitive strategies (skills) that students might learn to help them understand their own thinking, thereby increasing their ability to learn science?

Mind Mapping Introduced earlier as cognitive mapping, mind mapping is a powerful metacognitive tool. For example, Joseph Novak has reported high school biology students using concept maps were more on task in laboratory experiments and reported being very conscious of their own responsibility for learning. Novak also reported that some teachers are teaching "how to learn" short courses designed to teach students metacognitive strategies. Novak suggests that using cognitive maps as a metacognitive strategy increases meaningful learning over rote learning for students in a variety of science situations.[82]

Illustrating and Drawing Some learners are visually attuned to looking at things in pictures. There are many opportunities in which students could create an illustration or a drawing to explain their thinking or to show how they understand a concept.

Brainstorming List as many observations of this burning candle as you can. What are as many ways that one individual can differ from an other? What are as many hypotheses to explain the phenomenon? Brainstorming, a strategy used to help students creatively solve problems, can also be used a metacognitive strategy. Brainstorming should proceed without censorship. If students are working in a group, all ideas should be accepted. If the students are working alone, they should be told to consider all ideas that "bubble up." Teaching students not to censor their ideas at the beginning of a process is an important metacognitive tool.

Planning Strategies Students can be shown, prior to an activity (short term or long term) how to go about solving or completing it, special ways that might be helpful for attacking the problem, any rules and directions to follow (especially if working with equipment, chemicals, or other science materials). Asking students during a learning activity to share their progress or how they are proceeding with the activity or problem enables them to perceive their own thought processes.

Generating Questions and Other Inquiry Strategies Another metacognitive strategy is to teach students to pose questions regarding some material they will read in their science textbook, homework assignment, research project, or science laboratory investigation. The process of asking questions is the heart of scientific inquiry. Not only does questioning help focus thinking strategies, but the questions themselves show an understanding for the subject matter, and can, if students are asked to read information, help them with comprehension.[83] In the next chapter, we will explore other science inquiry strategies (processes of science), and it will be shown that these are indeed metacognitive strategies as well.

Evaluating Actions Some teachers ask students to evaluate what they liked or didn't like or what the pluses and minuses were of a science learning activity. This process enables students to reflect upon and evaluate their actions, and perhaps apply this learning to future actions.

Teaching Capability Some teachers have a rule in their class: "Outlawed: I can't do it!" Instead these teachers help students focus on what information, material, or skills are needed to do it. Earlier, I mentioned that teaching students that intelligence is not fixed, but is a developing ability based on experience. This position gives students a sense of personal power in that attempting a challenging problem or activity is indeed a way to improve their intelligence.

Communication Skills Communication skills are not only important to the teacher, but they are an integral metacognitive strategy. In the social learning theory section, I pointed out that teachers who adopt cooperative learning strategies would need to teach students new social norms and social learning skills. These skills (conciseness, listening, reflecting) are communication skills. An important metacognitive communication skill is reflection. Having students consider other students' ideas as well as their own, or having students rephrase what they just said, are ways of building upon and extending ideas.

Journal Keeping Keeping a diary or log of learning experiences is not new to the science education community. Many scientists have kept logs of their thinking, not only as a record, but also—and more importantly—as a haven for synthesizing and analyzing their thinking. The log is a place where the student can revisit ideas and review thinking processes used in an activity. Combining some of the other strategies, especially mind mapping, illustrating and drawing, and brainstorming can enhance the quality of logs.

Metacognitive strategies are tools for the science teacher to help students understand their own thinking. Throughout this book you will be introduced to many strategies. Teaching students about their own thinking might be as important as exposing them to the content of science.

SECTION 2: SCIENCE TEACHER GAZETTE

Volume 5: How Students Learn

Think Pieces

1. How do constructivists and sociocultural theorists explain student learning in science? What motivational strategies help students learn science concepts?

2. What is conceptual-change teaching?
3. In what ways do student learning styles influence learning?
4. What is the difference between right brain and left brain learning? What are the implications of these differences for science teaching?
5. What are some metacognitive learning strategies? In what ways can these strategies be helpful to students in a science class?

Case Study: Theory of Science Teaching

The Case

Sam Yarsborough, a graduate of the biology department of a small liberal arts college, always wanted to be a teacher. He decided, however, to complete a degree in biology and then try to find a teaching position in a school district near his college. In May, he signed a contract to teach introductory biology at Druid Lake High School, an urban school of 1,200 students. The district hired Yarsborough without certification and he was issued a provisional certificate to teach science, with the stipulation that he had to complete his requirements within three years. Yarsborough's department head told him about a teacher education program at a university close to his high school, designed for science teachers holding a provisional certificate. Yarsborough missed the summer institute phase of the program and began his teaching career without any science education preparation. After two weeks of teaching, he attended the first class session of a combined internship and science methods block, which met late in the afternoon at the university. There were twelve other teachers in the program, along with a professor and a veteran science teacher who was also a doctoral student interning in the TEEMS program. After brief introductions, everyone was paired off and asked to describe to their partner what the first two weeks of teaching were like and then to share a key idea with the whole class. Yarsborough's partner explained that she was trying to implement the "constructivist" theory they had focused on during the summer institute. Yarsborough was puzzled and asked how she could possibly be thinking about a theory of teaching when he was simply trying to survive the first two weeks of discipline problems, paperwork, and meetings. In the large group, Yarsborough asked how theory could be of help to him, when he was simply trying to teach his students one lesson at a time.

The Problem

How important to a beginning science teacher is theory? How should teachers learn about theories, assuming they might be helpful? Is Yarsborough's reaction typical of beginning teachers? What do you think?

Case Study: The Student Who Thought He Failed

The Case

Ashley Brinkley, a physics teacher in a large comprehensive high school, is known for her innovative approaches to teaching. After attending an in-depth conference and study group titled "Implementing Cognitive Theory into the Science Classroom," she decides that she is going to implement one of the ideas into her teaching approach. At the conference, Brinkley discovered that determining and helping the students detect their current ideas on the concepts to be taught is an important place to begin instruction. At the conference it was suggested that a simple activity or a demonstration presented to the students would enable them to demonstrate their ideas verbally and publicly. Brinkley planned a demonstration on falling objects. The idea was to let students identify the forces (by making a diagram and labeling it) on the falling object. After doing the activity and having the students make their diagrams, Brinkley carried on a discussion with the class. During the discussion she noticed one of the students was quite upset. The student was embarrassed that he didn't label the diagram "correctly," and felt inferior to the students sitting near him. Brinkley noticed that a couple of other students felt the same way.

The Problem

What should Brinkley do? What should she say to these students? To the whole class? Should she abandon this new approach?

Science Teachers Talk

"How do you accommodate students' varying learning styles in your classroom?"

ANNA MORTON: Accommodating students with different learning styles is a necessity. Students who are visual learners are provided with pictures, diagrams, charts, and graphs, and, when possible, students are asked to construct pictures, diagrams, charts, and graphs. Visual learners must be placed in front of the classroom, be given detailed notes or handouts, and like content or pictures on overhead transparencies. Visual learners must see the importance of a concept in order for it to have any relevancy; whereas auditory learners must hear the content. If a video or laser disc can be found for a particular subject, I find it helpful for both visual and auditory learners. I also find that auditory learners prefer lectures and class discussions. A class discussion linking the technology to the current content, followed by group work, adds clarity. Because class time is very limited, I find it necessary to pair auditory learners when they are conducting reading strategies like note taking. These learners help each other to read through the content and identify important details. Some learners require movement and touch. For these learners, hands-on activities are indispensable. Sitting in class without any movement is taxing for these students. The laboratory experience provides these students with an opportunity to explore and manipulate the physical world. I have found that matching my students' learning style to my teaching style helps to eliminate boredom and inattentiveness.

GINNY ALMEDER: I accommodate students with different learning styles in my classroom by using different modalities, which include auditory, visual, and tactile components. Each teaching unit is a composite of lecture, written work, large- and small-group discussion, audio-visual, and laboratory activities. I generally use activities, which involve all of the students one way or another. One other thing that I would add is this: There is some flexibility built into participation. For example, following group work students may do an oral presentation or a written presentation using the blackboard. For homework, they may elect to write out their objectives or cross-reference the objectives with the notes. This is a more efficient approach for those students who learn better by listening than by writing. Some students also benefit from reversing the teacher-student relationship by working in after-school study groups where they act as tutors. Some student mentors come to realize very quickly that teaching is a form of learning.

JOHN RICCIARDI: I try to plan and construct lesson activities that are constantly in a directional movement or "flow" from one particular learning style to another. Individual learning styles are not fixed, like still pools of water. Maximum brain-mind stimulus is more a style of learning that is symbolized by the water movement in a small country stream—the liquid patterns are observed to be in constant oscillating, pendulating motion. In the classroom, there are, say twenty-five different "stream" patterns of thought emanating and synergizing. The only real common denominator is that there is a pendulation or "back and forth" learning flow of focal attention. Like the bubbling brook, the brain-mind is constantly jumping here and there, picking and choosing between modalities of information, input (such as symbolic, visual, auditory, kinesthetic, and so forth). I try to juxtapose my lesson activities to this random mental movement, moving through at least three, and sometimes up to six, different instructional modalities within a fifty-minute period.

ANITA BERGMAN: I use a variety of materials and approaches in my classroom to help accommodate differences in learning style. I use visual aids when presenting orally to help both the visual and auditory learners. I also help my students understand their learning styles by teaching them about "colors"—personality and learning characteristics of blue, orange, gold, and green learners. This study helps them in group processing because it promotes understanding and appreciation of differences in style.

BARRY PLANT (AUSTRALIA): I choose a range of learning activities that can challenge the more gifted, excite the average, and allow the less capable some success. Each unit of work would encompass a range of tasks designed to offer students alternative pathways to learning.

Problems and Extensions

1. Suppose you could interview one of the following theorists: Ausubel, Bruner, Piaget, Skinner, or von Glassersfeld. How would the theorist you chose respond to the following: (a) Students learn best when they . . . (b) What is learning? (c) What is the best way to teach science? (d) How would you motivate reluctant learners?

2. Visit one or two secondary science classrooms to find out if there is any evidence of the following learning theories being put into practice: behavioral theories, cognitive theories, social learning theories. Cite examples of classroom practice that are related to the theories you observe.

3. Student attitudes in science have been slipping in recent years. What are some ways to turn this trend around? Collaborate with a small group and brainstorm as many ideas as possible. Rank order the ideas and then present them to the class. Ask members of the class if they have witnessed any of the recommendations your group made.

4. Select a chapter form a secondary science textbook. Examine the chapter in light of the theories of learning that you studied in this chapter. Is there any evidence of constructivist theory in the chapter? Cognitive learning theory? Social learning theory?

5. Design a model of learning using what you have learned in this chapter and from your previous courses and experiences. Your model should be a visual display and should reflect your beliefs and knowledge about student learning.

6. How do you suppose the following scientists would explain learning and what recommendations do you think they would make about contemporary science teaching? Albert Einstein, Rosalyn Franklin, Marie Curie, Linus Pauling, Stephen Jay Gould, Isaac Azimov, and Benjamin Banneker.

Notes

1. A. B. Champagne and L. E. Hornig, *Students and Science Learning* (Washington, D.C.: American Association for the Advancement of Science, 1987).

2. Jean Piaget, "Development and Learning," *Journal of Research in Science Teaching* 40 (2003): S8–S18. (Originally published in the *Journal of Research in Science Teaching* 2, no. 3 (1964): 176–86).

3. Based on L. B. Resnick and L. E. Klopfer, "Toward the Thinking Curriculum: An Overview," in *Toward the Thinking Curriculum: Current Cognitive Research*, ed.

L. B. Resnick and L. E. Klopfer (Alexandria, Va.: Association for Supervision and Curriculum Development, 1989).

4. Ibid., p. 8.

5. Ibid., p. 8.

6. C. W. Anderson and E. L. Smith, "Teaching Science," in *Educators' Handbook: A Research Perspective*, ed. V. Richardson-Koehler (New York: Longman, 1987).

7. Ibid., p. 87.

8. Ibid., p. 88.

9. A. E. Lawson and L. D. Thompson, "Formal Reasoning Ability and Misconceptions Concerning Genetics and Natural Selection," *Journal of Research in Science Teaching* 25, no. 9 (1988): 733–46.

10. Ibid., p. 733.

11. R. E. Slavin, *Educational Psychology* (Englewood Cliffs, N.J.: Prentice-Hall, 1988), p. 186.

12. J. D. Novak and D. B. Gowin, *Learning How to Learn* (Cambridge, England: Cambridge University Press, 1984), p. 15.

13. Ibid., p. 15.

14. Kohler discussion based on E. R. Hilgard and G. H. Bower, *Theories of Learning* (New York: Appleton-Century-Crofts, 1966), pp. 229–31.

15. J. Bruner, *Toward a Theory of Instruction* (Cambridge, Mass.: Harvard University Press, 1967); and M. E. Bell-Gredler, *Learning and Instruction* (New York: Macmillan, 1984).

16. Bruner, *Toward a Theory of Instruction*, pp. 40–45.

17. Ibid., p. 43.

18. Ibid., p. 41.

19. Ibid., p. 44.

20. This example was suggested by Bruner in *Toward a Theory of Instruction*, p. 45.

21. Ibid., p. 49.

22. Margaret Bell-Gredler, *Learning and Instruction* (New York: Macmillan, 1986), p. 221.

23. Ibid., pp. 193–94.

24. A. E. Lawson and J. W. Renner, "Piagetian Theory and Biology Teaching," *The American Biology Teacher* 37, no. 6: 336–43.

25. Ibid.

26. Piaget, "Development and Learning," p. S1.

27. Ibid., pp. S10–S11.

28. Bell-Gredler, *Learning and Instruction*, p. 200.

29. J. W. Renner and E. A. Marek, *The Learning Cycle and Elementary School Science Teaching* (Portsmouth, N.H.: Heinemann, 1988).

30. Based on Piaget, "Development and Learning," pp. S9–S12.

31. T. E. Gross, *Cognitive Development* (Monterey, Calif.: Brooks/Cole, 1985), p. 36.

32. The example is based on research reported by R. Osborne and P. Freyberg, *Learning in Science: Implications of Children's Science* (Aukland, New Zealand: Heineman, 1985), pp. 6–7.

33. R. Karplus, *Science Teaching and the Development of Reasoning*, Journal of Research in Science Teaching, 14, no. 2 (pp. 169–75, 1977, 1978), p. 55.

34. R. Good, *How Children Learn Science* (New York: Macmillan, 1977), p. 141.

35. J. L. Lemke, "Articulating Communities: Sociocultural Perspectives on Science Education," *Journal of Research in Science Teaching* 38, no. 3 (2001): 296–316.

36. Ibid., p. 301.

37. R. T. Johnson, D. W. Johnson, and E. J. Holubec, *The New Circles of Learning: Cooperation in the Classroom and School* (Alexandria, Va.: ASCD, 1994).

38. J. Hassard, *Science Experiences: Cooperative Learning and the Teaching of Science* (Menlo Park, Calif.: Addison Wesley, 1990), p. 18.

39. Definition is based on Johnson, Johnson, and Holubec, *The New Circles of Learning.*

40. E. G. Cohen, *Designing Groupwork: Strategies for the Heterogeneous Classroom*, 2d ed. (New York: Teachers College Press, 1995).

41. Ibid.

42. Johnson, Johnson, and Holubec, *New Circles of Learning.* Association for Supervision and Curriculum Development.

43. Nancy Brickhouse, "Embodying Science: A Feminist Perspective on Learning," *Journal of Research in Science Teaching* 38, no. 3 (2001): 290.

44. Ibid., p. 288.

45. Ibid.

46. Ibid., p. 289.

47. Stephen M. Fishman and Lucille McCarthy, *John Dewey and the Challenge of Classroom Practice* (New York: Teachers College Press, 1998), p. 20.

48. Ibid., p. 22.

49. J. Dewey, 1934, cited in David Wong, Kevin Pugh, and the Dewey Ideas Group at Michigan State University, "Learning Science: A Deweyan Perspective," *Journal of Research in Science Teaching* 38, no. 3 (2001): 320.

50. Ibid., p. 322.

51. Ibid., p. 323.

52. Ibid., p. 325.

53. E. R. Hilgard and G. H. Bower, *Theories of Learning* (New York: Appleton-Century-Crofts, 1966).

54. W. C. Becker, *Applied Psychology for Teachers: A Behavioral Cognitive Approach* (Chicago: Science Research Associates, Inc., 1986), p. 16.

55. Many of us dismiss the relevance of operant conditioning, yet many classrooms resemble the Skinner box in that student behavior (cognitive, affective, and social) is reinforced with grades, stars, and awards.

56. J. Brophy, "Teacher Praise: A Functional Analysis," *Review of Educational Research* 51, no. 1 (Spring 1981): 5–35.

57. Based on Becker, *Applied Psychology for Teachers*, pp. 24–25.

58. D. Premack, "Reinforcement Theory," in *Nebraska Symposium on Motivation*, ed. D. Levine (Lincoln: University of Nebraska Press, 1965).

59. Slavin, *Educational Psychology*, p. 116.

60. Mary Budd Rowe, "Wait-Time and Rewards As Instructional Variables, Their Influence on Language, Logic, and Fate Control: Part One—Wait-Time," *Journal of Research in Science Teaching* 40 (2003): S19–S32. Originally published in the *Journal of Research in Science Teaching* 11, no. 2 (1974): 81–94.

61. R. Dunn and K. Dunn, *Teaching Students Through Their Individual Learning Styles* (Reston, Va.: Reston Publishing Company, 1978).

62. R. Dunn and S. A. Griggs, A Quiet Revolution: Learning Styles and Their Application to Secondary Schools," *Holistic Education Review* (Winter 1989): 14–19.

63. Dunn and Dunn, Teaching Students.

64. Dunn and Griggs, "A Quiet Revolution."

65. R. Dunn, J. S. Beaudry, and A. Klavas, "Survey of Research on Learning Styles," *Educational Leadership* 2 (March 1989): 50–58.

66. Ibid., pp. 56–58.

67. Ibid.

68. Dunn and Griggs, "A Quiet Revolution," p. 18.

69. J. E. Bogen, "Some Educational Aspects of Hemispheric Specialization," *USCA Educator* 17 (1975): 24–35.

70. R. W. Sperry, "Lateral Specialization in the Surgically Separated Hemispheres," in *The Neuro-Sciences Third Study Program*, ed. F. O. Schmitt and F. G. Warden (Cambridge, Mass.: MIT Press, 1975), pp. 5–19.

71. B. McCarthy, *The 4MAT System: Teaching to Learning Styles with Right/Left Mode Techniques* (Barrington, Ill.: EXCEL, Inc, 1987), pp. 70–75.

72. Ibid., pp. 73–79.

73. J. Goodlad, *A Place Called School* (New York McGraw-Hill, 2004). Goodlad reports that the typical activity in secondary classrooms is lecture. Experiential types of learning activities were rarely, if ever, observed by Goodlad's researchers.

74. McCarthy, *The 4MAT System*, p. 79.

75. Ann Howe and Poul Thompsen, Raleigh, N.C.

76. J. Levy, "Research Synthesis on Right and Left Hemispheres: We Think With Both Sides of the Brain," in

Readings on Research, ed. R. S. Brandt (Alexandria, Va.: Association for Supervision and Curriculum Development, 1989), pp. 23–28.

77. McCarthy, *The 4MAT System*.

78. Ibid., pp. 37–43.

79. Ibid., pp. 20–26.

80. For suggestions on developing tactual and kinesthetic resources see Dunn and Dunn, *Teaching Students*, pp. 317–58.

81. A. L. Costa, "Mediating the Metacognitive," in *Teaching Thinking*, ed. R. S. Brandt (Alexandria, Va.: Association for Supervision and Curriculum Development, 1989), pp. 120–25.

82. J. Novak, "The Use of Metacognitive Tools to Facilitate Meaningful Learning," in *Adolescent Development and School Science*, ed. P. Adley (New York: The Falmer Press, 1989), pp. 227–38.

83. See Costa, "Mediating the Metacognitive."

Readings

Anderson, Charles W., Holland, J. David, and Palinscar, Annemarie S. "Canonical and Sociocultural Approaches to Research and Reform in Science Education: The Story of Juan and His Group." *The Elementary School Journal* 97, no. 4 (1997): 359–81.

Brickhouse, Nancy. "Embodying Science: A Feminist Perspective on Learning." *Journal of Research in Science Teaching* 38, no. 3 (2001): 282–95.

Bybee, Rodger W., and Sund, Robert B. *Piaget for Educators*, 2d ed. Prospect Heights, Ill.: Waveland Press, 1990.

Colburn, Alan. "Constructivism: Science Education's 'Grand Unifying Theory.'" *Clearing House* 74, no. 1 (2000): 9–13.

Duckworth, Eleanor. *The Having of Wonderful Ideas and Other Essays on Teaching and Learning*. New York: Teachers College Press, 1987.

Glaserfeld, Ernst von. "Cognition, Construction of Knowledge and Teaching." In *Constructivism in Science Education*, edited by Michael R. Mathews. Dordrecht: Kluwer Academic Publishers, pp. 11–30.

Jensen, Eric. *Teaching with the Brain in Mind*. Alexandria, Va.: ASCD, 1998.

Lemke, J. L. "Articulating Communities: Sociocultural Perspectives on Science Education." *Journal of Research in Science Teaching* 38, no. 3 (2001): 296–316.

Wong, David, Pugh, Kevin, and the Dewey Idea Group at Michigan State University. "Learning Science: A Deweyan Perspective." *Journal of Research in Science Teaching* 38, no. 3 (2001): 317–36.

On the Web

Apple Learning Interchange, K–12: http://ali.apple.com/. The Apple Learning Interchange (ALI) is an online resource for teaching, learning, research, and collaboration.

Learning Style Network: http://www.learningstyles.net/. The Learning Styles Network fosters life-long academic, intellectual, and personal success through the promotion and dissemination of research, information, publications, and other resources focusing on learning, teaching, and productivity styles.

Science Learning Network: http://www.sln.org/. The Science Learning Network (SLN) is an online community of educators, students, schools, science museums, and other institutions demonstrating a new model for inquiry science education.

What Research Says to the Science Teacher: http://www2.educ.sfu.ca/narstsite/publications/peers.html. A collection of articles written by science educators on a variety of topics, including multiculturalism, constructivism, female friendly classrooms, microcomputers, science literacy, and many more.

A chemistry teacher in a large school district in the southeastern part of the United States believes that excitement, enthusiasm, and inquisitiveness should reign in science class. She uses an approach to teach chemistry in which students work together in small teams on projects and activities that result in products that are presented to each other in forum-like sessions. To drop in and visit her classroom is to observe not only an exemplary teacher, but also one who puts into practice what science educators claim should characterize high school science teaching. Students are involved in watching minidemonstrations and then trying to figure out what happened, testing the acidity of rain (with cabbage juice as the indicator) in the Atlanta area over a long period of time, and then drawing conclusions based on their own data, conducting microchemistry experiments designed to help them learn chemistry concepts inductively. Furthermore, students in this classes are linked with students in Russia and other countries because of the teacher's participation in Web-based international projects that help students explore cooperatively environmental chemistry issues and problems from a global perspective. In short, her method of teaching gives the students the opportunity to inquire, question, and explore.

This teacher's approach to teaching is an integration of several models of teaching (inquiry-based teaching, project-based teaching, and cooperative learning) that science teachers employ in their classes. A model of teaching is a plan or pattern that organizes teaching in the classroom, and fashions the way instructional materials (books, videos, computers, science materials) are used and the curriculum is planned.[1] We will investigate several models of teaching in this chapter that will be important to you as you begin your career. The models are based on the learning theories and perspective described in Chapter 5. In addition, you will explore these other models of teaching: the direct/interactive teaching model, the learning cycle model of teaching, and several additional models, including synectics, person-centered learning, and the integrative model of learning.

We know from research and experience that practice makes perfect. A model of teaching, to be learned, must be practiced, practiced, and practiced. Unfortunately, some teachers will try a new idea, technique, or model once, not obtain very good results, and consequently abandon the notion. Some researchers report that teachers need to practice new approaches many times (perhaps as many as twenty) before the new model is integrated and part of the teacher's style of teaching. Thus, in this chapter and Chapter 9, you will be introduced to two laboratory strategies that are designed to help you "practice" new ideas about teaching. Reflective teaching will be used to help you implement the models of science teaching. By using another laboratory strategy called microteaching, you will learn how to implement specific teaching strategies and skills. These laboratory strategies have been developed to help you learn about teaching through teaching. It is a way to integrate theory and practice.

Case Study: Descent from Innocence

The Case

Michael A. Miller, who grew up in an upper middle-class community in upstate New York and graduated (cum laude) from the State University of New York at Buffalo, accepted a teaching position with the Los Angeles Unified School District. He was assigned to Orange High School, which has an enrollment of over 3,000 students (approximately 1,500 Hispanics, 1,000 blacks, 450 Asians, and about 300 other wise classified students).[2]

Miller reports his experience teaching with non-traditional activities:

It wasn't until I had been teaching for a few months that I fully understood the odd smile that appeared on the faces of other teachers when I told them of my class assignment: in addition to two periods of biology, I would be teaching three life science classes. Life science appears to be the dumping grounds for noncollege bound, nonacademic, potential dropouts. Now I realize that the smile meant, "Poor, naive, innocent soul—like a lamb to the slaughter and he doesn't even know it."

My descent from innocence was swift and brutal. I was given a temporary roll sheet, assigned a room—actually three different rooms—and with little other preparation was thrust into the world of teaching . . . I launched into my lessons.

One of the first units I covered was the metric system . . . I assumed that this unit would be a brief review for the students. Little did I suspect that, not only did the students have no knowledge of the metric system, they were also ignorant of measuring using the standard English system.

In order to teach this unit, I planned to conduct a brief lecture on metric prefixes and then have a laboratory exercise in which the students measured various objects and converted from one measurement unit to another. I typed up lab sheets explaining in detail what should be measured and in what units I wanted the measurements. The students were then assigned to lab tables, paired off, and provided with meter sticks. What next ensued can only be described as pandemonium.

My intention had been to visit with each group of students and answer any questions that they might have . . . The first group I visited with was made up of four girls. They were having a grand time chatting about local current events and had given up the lab as a futile exercise. It just wasn't possible to measure heights with a meter stick, since they were all taller than the stick. Unable to argue with such logic, I proceeded to the next lab group.

I arrived just in time to witness the finishing touches that a student was adding to his self-inspired metric project. He had beautifully carved his gang symbol into the meter stick with an 8-inch knife he had been carrying. He also asked me if, perchance, I would like to buy some "ludes" from him. I declined his offer, asked him to put away the knife, complimented him on his artwork, and proceeded to the third group.

At this lab table, two young men were having a dispute over a question on the lab handout which directed them to provide the width of their little finger in both centimeters and millimeters. They couldn't decide whether this measurement should be the long or short dimension of a finger. Peter was strongly emphasizing his point of view with well-placed punches on David's arm and chest region. I managed to separate them and clarify the meaning of the lab question. As I left them to visit with group number four, I overheard David say to Peter, "This side of the stick is meters," to which Peter replied, "No it isn't. That's the inches side." Two or three dull thuds punctuated Peter's response.

At table four, one student, who had just been released from jail the day before, was sharing with his lab partners the economics lesson he learned while incarcerated. Mercifully, the bell rang. "Well," I sighed hopefully to myself, "Only four more periods to go!"

This was just one of many labs conducted during my first year of teaching that didn't go quite as planned. Although none were as disastrous as the metric lab, each was as much an experiment for myself as it was for the students. Often, I half wished that I had taken my student up on his offer and purchased a healthy supply of central nervous system depressants. As they say, even the best laid plans sometimes go awry.

Now I am in my second year of teaching . . .

The Problem

Do you think Miller's expectations were too high for his students in doing lab activities? If you had watched this lab activity, what specific suggestions would you make to Miller to change the lesson in order to eliminate the pandemonium?

How to Read This Chapter

This chapter is correlated with Chapter 5, in which several theories of learning were presented. This chapter presents models of teaching based on those theories of learning. The models presented here are the scaffolding that you will find helpful as you begin to plan lessons and create an environment in your classroom that fosters active student involvement. Underlying all of the models presented here is the notion that students should be engaged. You can start anywhere in the chapter. The models presented here have their own protocols, and you should work with one model at a time. The best way to understand the models is to use them in the context of teaching. You might try to arrange opportunities to teach science to your peers (Inquiry Activity 6.1) or to a group of students in a school.

SECTION 1: MODELS OF SCIENCE TEACHING

Invitations to Inquiry

- What is a model of teaching?
- When and under what conditions should different models of teaching be used?
- What is the relationship between models of teaching and theories of learning?
- What are the direct/interactive teaching functions?
- What are some effective ways to organize content for direct/interactive teaching?
- How is inquiry teaching different than direct/interactive teaching?
- How do the models of inductive inquiry, deductive inquiry, discovery learning, and problem solving compare?
- What is the learning cycle? On what learning paradigm is the learning cycle based?
- What is conceptual-change teaching?
- What is the difference between peer tutoring and the conceptual and problem-solving models of cooperative/collaborative learning?
- What characterizes the following models of teaching: synectics, person-centered learning, integrative learning, and imagineering? How can they be used to help students understand science?

Models of Teaching: How Can They Be of Help to the Science Teacher?

Why is it important to know about models of teaching? Scientists use models to help them understand natural systems like rivers, atoms, and cells. Models describe a pattern or a phenomenon and are also like the scaffolding of a building: Scaffolding holds the building up and gives it shape and integrity. A model of teaching lays the foundation for actions and interactions between students and teachers. For example, a teacher-centered model would imply a set of actions and interactions different than a student-centered model of teaching. In the teacher-centered model, teachers would make most of the decisions about curriculum and learning, whereas in a student-centered model, students would be more involved in these decisions. What are some other obvious differences?

Models of teaching are designed to help students learn and, as you will see, they are prescriptive. Each model of teaching has its set of propositions and directions, enabling you to implement them in classrooms or in tutorial situations.

Bruce Joyce and Marsha Weil describe twenty models of teaching in their book *Models of Teaching*, and they point out that the many models of teaching used in schools are designed to give students the tools to grow.[3] The models that are described in this chapter are designed to help the beginning science teacher get started in the classroom, as well as provide the tools to help secondary students learn science.

Several models of science teaching are presented in this chapter. There is no intention on my part to claim that one model is better than another. Rather, each model has its inherent qualities and purposes for helping students learn. Many teachers use a combination of these models, integrating them into a personal model of teaching, while other teachers focus on one model and build their teaching repertoire around this favored approach.

Teaching to Learn

There is a substantial body of research supporting the models of teaching selected for inclusion in this chapter. Naturally, science educators make a strong claim on the inquiry approach to teaching, and rightfully so. Inquiry certainly is an integral aspect of the nature of science, as was discussed in Chapter 1. But, as science teachers, we must go beyond a singular view of teaching and incorporate a variety of models. Recent research and trends in practice support an integrative view for formulating instructional plans. For example, most of the recent curriculum development projects at the elementary and middle school level have described models of teaching that include not only inquiry (with hands-on activities), but cooperative learning as well. A further examination

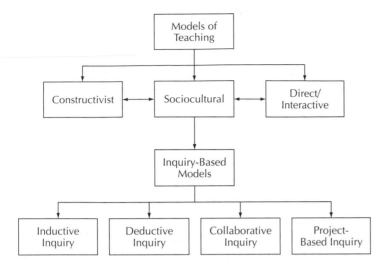

Figure 6.1 Concept Map Showing Relationships among the Models of Science Teaching.

of these projects also reveals that direct/interactive teaching strategies (especially teacher-directed activities and heavy reliance on teacher questioning) are an integral aspect of the approach.

What models should we explore? Using the learning theories presented in Chapter 5 as a conceptual rationale, we present eight models of teaching in this chapter (Table 6.1), thereby presenting a kaleidoscope for the science teacher. Figure 6.1 depicts the arrangement of the key models that are presented in this chapter. Please note that we will begin by looking constructivist models. Next, we will examine models of teaching based on sociocultural perspectives, and then examine

Table 6.1 Organization of Models of Teaching

Learning Theory Category	Model of Teaching
Constructivist Perspectives	Inquiry Teaching
	Learning Cycle
	Project-Based
	Synectics
Sociocultural Perspectives	Cooperative Learning
	Integrative
	Person-Centered
Behavioral Perspectives	Direct/Interactive Teaching

INQUIRY ACTIVITY 6.1

Teaching to Learn: Reflective Teaching

In this activity you will teach a science lesson to a small group of peers using any model of teaching you desire to accomplish a stated objective. This experience will provide you with the opportunity to find out why you were successful or unsuccessful in a teaching situation. In this activity you will have the opportunity to share teaching methods and become reflective about science teaching as well.[4]

Several members of your class will be given the same instructional objective. They will prepare a lesson based on the objective and then teach it to a group of peers concurrently. At the conclusion of the lesson they will assess the learners to find out how many of them can perform the objective. The "teachers" will conduct brief reflective teaching sessions in the small groups, and then all will assemble for a reflective discussion of the lessons.

Materials

- Reflective teaching lesson plans (Table 6.2)
- Teaching materials as required by each lesson (see pp. 248–50 for complete lesson plans)

Procedures

1. *Prepare.* Your class will be divided into small teams (of about five students); one person from each team will be selected as the first designated teacher (DT). Each DT will be assigned a reflective teaching plan by the professor. The DTs will have until the next class to prepare the lesson, which will be taught to a small group of peers. In preparing the lessons, the DTs should keep in mind that any materials and visual aids can be used to teach the lesson.

2. *Teach.* On the day that you are assigned, teach your lesson to your small group. You will have fifteen minutes to teach the lesson. Administer any test required for your lesson. Collect the tests, and then give each of your learners the learner satisfaction form to complete (Figure 6.2) Collect the learner satisfaction forms (give students about three minutes to complete them).

Table 6.2 Reflective Teaching Lessons

Lesson Topic	Focus
1. Creatures	Classification of a set of creatures
2. Shark's Teeth	Making observations and inferences
3. The Balloon Blower Upper	Making hypotheses
4. Mission to Mars	Evaluating NASA's mission to Mars

Learner Satisfaction Form

Name_____

1. During the lesson, how satisfied were you as a learner?

_____ very satisfied

_____ satisfied

_____ unsatisfied

_____ very unsatisfied

2. What could your teacher have done to increase your satisfaction?

Figure 6.2 Learner Satisfaction Form.

3. *Reflect.* Facilitate a reflective teaching session (about five minutes) with your learners using the following questions as a guide. Select only a few of these questions for your reflective teaching session.

- What knowledge, skills, or attitudes were you hoping to develop in your learners? To what extent do you believe you were successful in your effort? What do your learners think?
- In planning your lesson, which model of teaching influenced you most (e.g., direct/interactive teaching, inquiry, cooperative learning, the learning cycle)?
- What did you learn about teaching?
- How did your learners react to the model of teaching you used?
- What influenced you most in planning your lesson (e.g., your knowledge about the subject, your attitudes about teaching, materials available to you)?

4. *Whole Group Reflection.* When your reflective discussion is complete, join the whole class to discuss each of the reflective teaching lessons.

Minds-On Strategies

Use these questions to write a critique of your teaching session and the corresponding reflective discussion session.

1. What model of teaching was used by each DT? In what ways did the models vary?
2. How successful were learners in achieving the stated objectives for the lesson?
3. What was learned about effective teaching?

the direct interactive teaching model. We will then relate inquiry-based models to the three key models of teaching. Following these descriptions, we'll examine three additional models of teaching (synectics, person-centered teaching, and the integrative model).

Before reading and engaging in a study of the various models of teaching, we will participate as teachers and learners in a series of reflective teaching lessons. In this way, you will have a common experience and can examine the models in light of this laboratory encounter with teaching. One of the assumptions made here is that one way to learn about teaching is to teach.

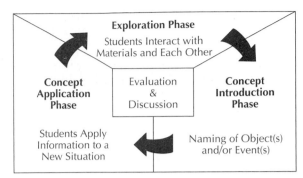

Figure 6.3 Learning Cycle Model: Early Constructivist. *Source:* Charles R. Barman. Used with permission.

Constructivist Models

Recent research (see Chapter 5) has suggested that students construct their own ideas about their world—including concepts—and any attempt to teach "new" concepts to students must take this into consideration. Researchers who have supported this view have been labeled "constructivists" because of their belief that students construct their own knowledge structures—concepts, beliefs, and theories. More often than not, the concept base that students bring to your class is naive and full of misconceptions. To understand science from the constructivist view means that students will have to change their concept, hence the term conceptual change.

The Learning Cycle: A Model of Conceptual Change

A number of conceptual change models have emerged over the last thirty years that suggest that teachers should sequence instruction into a series of teaching/learning phases.[5] The sequences have been described as learning cycles. For example, Chester Lawson, who described scientific invention as belief-expectation-test, suggested the earliest example of a learning cycle.[6] But Robert Karplus, Director of the Science Curriculum Improvement Study (SCIS) in 1970, proposed the first direct application of a learning cycle to science teaching: a three-phase cycle consisting of preliminary exploration, invention, and discovery. In essence, Karplus believed that students need to first explore the concept to be learned using concrete materials. The initial introduction of the concept was called invention. In this phase, the teacher assumed an active role in helping the students use their exploration experiences to invent the concept. To Karplus, the discovery phase provided the student with the opportunity to verify, apply or further extend knowledge of the "invented" concept.[7]

Research by Charles R. Barman and the team of Lawson, Abraham, and Renner, have proposed a learning cycle based on the work of Karplus, but have changed the terminology.[8] We shall use the updated terminology in this book when we refer to the learning cycle model.

Although most of the earlier constructivist models had only three phases to the learning cycle, in the model here, we shall use four stages: invitation, exploration, explanation, and taking action (see Table 6.3).

INVITATION PHASE During this phase the teacher invites students to learn about a new concept by linking their prior knowledge to a question, a demonstration, or a big idea.

EXPLORATION PHASE In this phase students explore a new concept or phenomenon with "minimal guidance." Students might make observations of and classify objects. They might be involved in "messing about" with batteries, bulbs, and wires to find out how the lightbulb works. Students might also perform experiments to gather data to test a hypothesis. In short, the exploration phase allows students to examine "new ideas" and test them against their own ideas. Students are actively engaged in interacting with ideas, as well with as their peers during the exploration phase. During this phase the teacher should facilitate the work of the students by establishing a reason for exploring new ideas. The use of discrepant events, followed by interesting science activities, is a way to get into the exploration phase. The teacher plays a facilitative role during this phase.

CONCEPT EXPLANATION PHASE During this phase (also called the concept introduction phase) the teacher assumes a more direct, active role and uses exploratory activities as a means of introducing the scientist's view of the concept or theory students investigated in the

Table 6.3 Conceptual Change Model (CCM) of Teaching

Invitation	Exploration	Explanation	Taking Action
Purpose: The CCM begins by engaging students with an invitation to learn. The invitation helps spark interest and expose initial ideas students have about the topic. Teacher establishes a context for learning and invites students to learn about a topic by: • Asking provocative questions. • Conducting a demonstration or an EEEP and asking students to ponder, think about the experience, and predict. • Asking students what they have heard about and questions they have about the topic.	Purpose: To provide an opportunity for students to explore phenomena or concepts through focused activities. • Teacher plans specific activities to enable students to test their predictions or initial ideas as well as engage in observation, data collection, and data interpretation experience. • Students work in cooperative groups to brainstorm, test ideas, discuss, and debate ideas.	Purpose: To enable students to propose explanations based on their own activity and to help them construct new views of the concepts. • Teacher plans activities that will enable students to communicate their ideas to each other as well as construct new explanations for concepts and phenomena. • Students work in small groups, but share ideas with the whole class through public displays of their work, poster reports, and class discussion.	Purpose: To take action on what they learned. • Teacher works with students to help them take personal and/or social action on issues related to the content of the concepts and phenomena. • Students apply knowledge and skills, share information about the topic, ask new questions, make decisions, develop products, and write letters.

exploratory phase. During this phase students express their ideas about the concepts and ideas and the teacher succinctly presents the meaning of the concepts and ideas from a scientific point of view. The teacher assumes the direct/interactive mode during this phase, planning lessons along the guidelines presented later in the direct/interactive section. The concept explanation phase is an intermediary step, and the teacher should move quickly to the next phase.

TAKING ACTION PHASE The taking action phase is a student-centered phase in which small teams of students engage in activities designed to apply and extend their knowledge of science concepts. The teacher should design activities that challenge the students to debate and defend their ideas. Activities in the concept application phase should be problem-oriented. The teacher resumes the facilitative role in the concept application phase.

LEARNING CYCLE LESSON 6.1

 What Can Be Learned from Skulls?

Overview

Students observe a variety of vertebrate skulls and attempt to identify the animal and what it eats. Concepts such as herbivore, omnivore, carnivore, nocturnal, diurnal, and niche are introduced.[9]

Invitation Phase

The teacher shows the students two or three vertebrate skulls and asks the students to predict what they could learn about the animal's behavior by studying skulls. Students work in small groups for about five minutes and then report their ideas to the class.

Exploration Phase

Skulls are placed at ten numbered stations. Students work in small teams and "visit" each numbered station, or the skulls are passed to each team. The teacher explains that the teams should be challenged to make inferences, like paleontologists do, about the lifestyle and habitat of vertebrates by observing their skulls. The teacher provides each group with one copy of the following questions:

- What type of food does this animal eat, and what is the evidence for your inference?
- Is this animal active during the day, night, or both? What is the evidence?
- Is the animal a predator or a prey? Why?

Concept Introduction

After the student teams have gathered data on each skull, conduct a session in which you ask different teams to describe each skull. Conduct a discussion focusing on the differences among the skulls. Students will focus on teeth. Write their descriptions on the board. Use the teeth to suggest function. Introduce the terms herbivore, carnivore, and omnivore. Ask the students to explain what these terms mean. You can clarify student concepts and misconceptions by explaining carefully; for example: "This animal has sharp teeth for tearing and no flat teeth for grinding. This implies that it eats only animals. An animal that eats other animals is called a carnivore."

Taking Action

Provide opportunities for students to investigate a variety of bones in addition to skulls. What inferences can they make from the structure about their function?

LEARNING CYCLE LESSON 6.2

 What Caused the Water to Rise?

Overview

Students invert a cylinder over a candle burning in a pan of water. They notice that the flame soon goes out and water rises into the cylinder. They engage in discussions to explain their observations. They then test their explanations, which lead to new explanations and understanding of combustion, air pressure, and scientific inquiry.

Materials

- Aluminum pie tins
- Birthday candles
- Matches
- Modeling clay
- Cylinders (open at one end)
- Jars (of various shapes and sizes)
- Syringes
- Rubber tubing

> **EEEP Data Sheet**
> **Exciting Examples of Everyday Phenomena**

Your prediction _____
_____
_____
_____

Data _____
_____
_____
_____

Drawing

[ ]

Explanation _____
_____
_____
_____

Figure 6.4 EEEP Data Sheet.

Invitation

The teacher begins the lesson by asking students to predict what they think would happen if a glass cylinder was put over a burning candle that was sitting upright in a pan of water. Students work in small teams to discuss their ideas and record them on the EEEP Data Sheet (Figure 6.4). The teacher then asks for group reports and records the students' initial ideas on chart paper.

Exploration

Give each team a student handout of instructions describing the inquiry procedure, as well as the materials listed above. Students should then be given the opportunity to explore the phenomenon by the following these procedures.

> **Instructions**
> 1. Pour some water into the pan. Stand a candle in the pan using the clay for support.
> 2. Light the candle and put a cylinder, jar, or beaker over the candle so that it covers the candle and sits in the water.
> 3. What happened?
> 4. What questions are raised?
> 5. What possible reasons can you suggest for what happened?
> 6. Repeat your experiment in a variety of ways to see if you obtain similar or different results. Do your results support or contradict your ideas in #5? Explain.

After thirty minutes of experimenting, stop the students for a discussion of their results. Focus the students on the questions "Why did the flame go out?" and "Why did the water rise?" The most likely explanation (misconception) to the second question is that because the oxygen was "burned up" the water rose to replace the oxygen, which was lost.

Lead the students to realize that hypothesis predicts that varying the number of burning candles will not affect the level of water rise. Four candles, for instance, would burn up the available oxygen faster and go out sooner than one candle, but they would not burn up more oxygen, hence the water should rise to the same level.

Have students do the experiment. The results will show that the water level is affected by the number of candles (the more candles, the higher the water level). Their ideas have been contradicted. Explain that an "alternative explanation" is needed and ask the students to propose one. As students propose alternative ideas do not tell them if they are correct. For example, the "correct" explanation (the heated air escaped out the bottom) should not be revealed even if students suggest it. Ask students to think of ways to test their hypotheses. If they propose the heated air hypothesis, this should lead to the prediction that bubbles should be seen escaping from the bottom of the cylinder. As alternative hypotheses are suggested, have the students test them and look for evidence to support predictions. If students do not suggest the "correct" explanation, suggest it yourself. You might say, "What do you think about this idea? The heat from the flame heats the air and forces it out the bottom of the cylinder." Encourage students to test your explanation rather than accepting as is.

Concept Introduction

After students have collected data testing various hypotheses, you should introduce the "correct" explanation again and introduce the term air pressure and a molecular model of gases that assumes air to be composed of moving particles that have weight and can bounce into objects (such as water) and push them out of the way.

Taking Action

Provide a number of problem-solving situations in which students must apply air pressure and the molecular model of matter.

1. Give students rubber tubing, a syringe, a beaker, and a pan of water. Tell them to invert the beaker of water in the pan of water. Challenge them to find a way to fill the beaker with water in that position (Figure 6.5). (The students will try forcing water in before discovering they must extract air from the beaker.

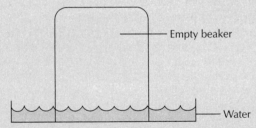

Figure 6.5 Fill the Beaker Challenge. How can you fill the beaker in this position?

2. Challenge the students to find a way to insert a peeled, hard-boiled egg into a bottle with an opening that is smaller in diameter than the egg. They cannot touch the egg after it is placed on the mouth of the jar. (After a small amount of water in the bottle has been heated, it is only necessary to place the smaller end of the egg over the opening of the bottle to form a seal. The egg will be forced into the bottle by the greater air pressure outside as the air cools inside.)

3. Pour a small amount of very hot water into a large (2 L) plastic soda bottle. Then screw the cap on tightly to form a seal. Place the bottle on a desk so that students can view it. The plastic bottle will begin to be crushed. Challenge the students to explain the result using the molecular model of gases and air pressure.

INQUIRY ACTIVITY 6.2

Constructivism in the Bag: Designing Constructivist Activities

Your textbook and the curriculum scope and sequence for your school district, as well as your state and national Standards will determine most of the concepts that you will teach. In this activity you will select a section from the textbook, and design lessons based on the learning cycle to teach the content in that section.

Materials

- Bags of science artifacts and learning materials
- Constructivist lesson sequence chart (Table 6.4)
- Science textbooks
- Access to your state or the *National Science Education Standards* (content)

Table 6.4 Constructivist Lesson Planning Template

Preliminary Decisions: Grade Level, Concepts (from Text or NSES), Objectives, Grouping of Students, Materials

Invitation: Inviting Student Ideas	**Exploration:** Students Explore Phenomena through Focused Activity	**Explanation:** Helping Students Propose and Compare Ideas	**Taking Action:** Application
Describe how you will find out about students' prior knowledge, ideas, and beliefs about the concepts in your sequence.	Describe at least one activity that you will use to assist your students in exploring the fundamental concepts.	Describe how the students will have the opportunity to hear differing views, to talk aloud about their ideas, to test ideas against "the scientist's" ideas.	Describe at least one activity that will assist students in taking personal and/or social action on issues related to the content of the concepts, or to assist them in applying the concepts to new situations.
Examples: <ul><li>Provocative questions</li><li>EEEP</li><li>Discrepant event</li><li>T-charts</li><li>Interview questions</li><li>Interesting challenge</li><li>Demonstration</li><li>Concept map</li></ul>	Examples: <ul><li>Inquiry activity</li><li>Writing to learn activity</li><li>Hands-on activity</li><li>Observation</li><li>Data collection</li><li>Data interpretation</li><li>Asking questions</li><li>Constructing explanations</li><li>Internet project</li><li>Communicating ideas</li></ul>	Examples: <ul><li>Small-group discussion</li><li>Debating alternative ideas</li><li>Large-group discussion</li><li>Displays of concepts on poster paper</li><li>Constructing models followed by presentations</li><li>Defending models</li><li>Journal/log writing</li><li>Active reading on the topic</li><li>Collaborative group questioning</li></ul>	Examples: <ul><li>Designing a long-term research project</li><li>Writing letters</li><li>Making posters about the topic</li><li>Hands-on activities</li><li>Seeking answers to their own questions</li><li>Sharing knowledge</li><li>Journal/log writing</li><li>Concept maps</li><li>Developing a Web page</li></ul>
Describe your activity or procedure:	Describe your activity: What are some questions you will be asking students to help them focus on the big ideas or concepts?	Describe how you will assist students to form explanations of the big ideas or concepts:	Describe the plan to assist students in taking action:

	Yes	No
I. Invitation Phase		
A. The lesson begins with an activity that provokes curiosity.	___	___
B. The invitation phase provides a way to access student prior knowledge, ideas, and beliefs about the concepts in the lesson.	___	___
II. Exploration Phase		
A. The lesson contains an exploration phase that is activity oriented.	___	___
B. Ample time is provided for the exploration phase.	___	___
C. The exploration activity provides student–student and student–teacher interaction.	___	___
III. Concept Explanation Phase		
A. The concepts are named or appropriate vocabulary is developed after an exploration activity.	___	___
B. The concepts and terms are an outgrowth of the exploration phase.	___	___
III. Taking Action Phase		
A. The students extend the concepts to a new situation.	___	___
B. Appropriate activities are used to apply the concepts.	___	___

Figure 6.6 Learning Cycle Checklist. *Source:* Based on Barman, Charles R. *An Expanded View of the Learning Cycle: New Ideas about an Effective Teaching Strategy.* Arlington, Va.: Council for Elementary Science International, 1990, p. 19.

Procedure

1. Working individually or as a member of small team, use the bag of science materials to identify one or more concepts or ideas that will form the nucleus for a constructivist lesson sequence. (Or select a chapter from the science textbook you have chosen; within the chapter, identify a section of content (content chunk) that you want to teach.)
2. Design a lesson sequence using the constructivist lesson sequence chart (Table 6.4), and similar in design to the examples given on pages 216–19.
3. When your lesson is complete, evaluate it using the learning cycle checklist shown in Figure 6.6 to make sure that you have developed a complete constructivist lesson.
4. If you have an opportunity, teach the lessons to a group of peers or secondary students.

Minds-On Strategies

1. What thinking skills did students have to use in your lessons? Differentiate among the four phases of the constructivist learning cycle. How do they compare?

Observation	Analyzing data
Classifying	Controlling variables
Predicting	Testing hypotheses
Inferring	Designing experiments

2. How would you classify your lessons based on the types of thinking skills (e.g., descriptive, empirical, hypothetical-deductive) in volved? Explain.

The Generative Learning Model

The generative learning model is a teaching sequence based on the view that the learner constructs knowledge. It is, therefore, a constructivist model. As James Minstrell, a high school physics teacher and cognitive researcher, says, "restructuring students" existing knowledge has become the principal goal of instruction."[10] Minstrell shows how he begins a unit of teaching based on the generative model with the following "preliminary phase" lesson:[11]

Teacher: Today we are going to explain some rather ordinary events that you might see almost any day. You will find that you already have many good ideas that will help explain those events. We will find that some of our ideas are similar to those of scientists, but in other cases our ideas might be different. When we are finished with this unit, I expect that we will have a much clearer idea of how scientists explain those events, and I know that you will feel more comfortable about your explanation.

Teacher: A key idea that we are going to use is the idea of force. What does the idea of force mean to you? [A discussion follows. My experience suggests that the teacher should allow this initial sharing of ideas to be very open.]

Teacher: You've mentioned words that represent many ideas. Most of them are closely related to the scientist's idea of force, but they also have meanings different from the scientist's ideas. Of the ones mentioned, probably the one that comes closest to the meaning the physicist has is the idea of push or pull, so we'll start with that. We'll probably find out that even that has a slightly different meaning to the physicist. [The teacher should allow the class to begin with this meaning for force rather than present an elaborate operational definition.]

Teacher: OK, let's begin [dropping a rock]: Here's a fairly ordinary event. We see something like this happening every day. How would you explain this event, using your present ideas about force? Instead of speaking right now, make drawings of the situation and show the major forces acting on the rock when it falls. Use arrows to represent the forces, and label each as to what exerts the force.

Students [naming the forces they have represented]:
Gravity by the earth
Weight of the rock
Both gravity and the weight
Air
Friction
The spin of the earth
Nuclear forces

Teacher: Which of these is the major force, or which are the major forces, acting on the rock while it is falling?

Students: Its weight. Gravity.

Teacher: Is the falling rock moving at a constant speed, or is it speeding up or slowing down? How do you know? [Teacher waits three to five seconds.]

Students: The same speed.
[More wait time]
No wait, if two things fall, they both fall equally fast.
I don't know.
I think the rocks speeds up.
[Students continue making suggestions. The teacher encourages as many students as possible to comment.]

Teacher: During the next several days we will look more closely at the idea we call force. Many of the ideas you've suggested today will be useful, but we may also find that we will want to change some of our notions about force to make them more consistent with the phenomena.

The "preliminary phase" of the generative model of learning is designed to identify existing student ideas. In the example cited here, the teacher, performing a simple demonstration, asked students to make a drawing of the event and then engaged the whole class in a discussion designed to identify the students' existing ideas. No attempt was made by the teacher to "correct" the student responses or label them "wrong" or give the scientific meaning of the concepts. Existing student ideas can also be determined by giving a diagnostic test at the beginning of a course or a short preinstruction quiz at beginning of a unit.

Osborne and Freyberg, advocates of the generative learning model, have identified three distinct phases to the model in addition to the preliminary phase: focus, challenge, and application.[12] The generative learning sequence is shown in Figure 6.7 and Table 6.5.

The focus phase is designed to help the teacher and student clarify the students' initial ideas.[13] Osborne and Freyberg suggest that the focusing phase is the time to involve the students in activities that focus on phenomena related to the concepts, to get the students thinking about these phenomena in their own words. The teacher's role is a motivational one, as well, during this phase. As I mentioned earlier, motivation to learn, in the cognitive view, is related to the intrinsic nature of learning. Providing interesting activities that focus attention on getting the students involved is suggested.

The challenge phase focuses attention on challenging student ideas. The teacher, through small-group discussion, or with the class as a whole, creates an

Preliminary ———► Focus ———► Challenge ———► Application

Figure 6.7 The Generative Learning Model Teaching Sequence.

Table 6.5 The Generative Learning Model

Phase	Teacher Activity	Pupil Activity
Preliminary	Ascertain students' views	Complete surveys, quizzes, or activities to ascertain existing ideas
Focus	Provide motivation experiences	Engage in activities to become familiar with phenomena related to "new concepts"
	Ask open-ended questions	
	Interpret student responses	Ask questions about phenomena and activities
	Interpret and elucidate students' views	Describe what they know about events and phenomena
		Clarify own views on concepts
		Present own view to small groups and whole class
Challenge	Facilitate exchange of views	Consider the view of another student, as well as all students in class
	Create an environment in which all views are considered	Compare the scientist's view with the class view
	Demonstrate procedures, phenomena, if necessary	
	Present evidence to support scientists ideas	
	Explore the tentative nature of students' reaction to new view	
Application	Design problems and activities that can be solved with the new idea or concept	Solve practical problems using the new concept as a basis
	Help students clarify views on the new ideas	Present solution to other students
		Discuss and debate the solutions
	Encourage an atmosphere whereby students verbally describe solutions to problems	Suggest further problems arising from the solutions presented

Source: Based on Osborne, R., and Freyberg, P. *Learning in Science: The Implications of Children's Science.* Auckland: Heinemann, 1985, pp. 109–10. Used with permission.

environment whereby students can articulate their ideas and hear other students' points of view. The students are challenged to compare their ideas to the scientist's view. The discussion during the challenge phase centers on the experiences students encountered during the focusing phase. In this phase, some degree of conceptual conflict will occur as students accommodate new ideas. It is, in the words of the cognitive psychologists, the tension or struggle that occurs mentally to accommodate new structures or modify existing ones.

The application phase is the instructional period in which students can practice using the new idea in differing situations. The teacher's role is one of creating problem situations for student application of the new ideas. Designing small-group activities and independent investigations that challenge students to apply the new concepts to different phenomena will facilitate the accommodation of the new idea and provide the time students need to reflect or think about their new knowledge.

By now you should have noted the high degree of similarity between the generative model of learning and the learning cycle model. Note that the major difference is the identification of a preliminary stage in the generative model; otherwise the phases correlate.

Collaborative Learning Models: Sociocultural Theory into Practice

A number of studies, as well as numerous practical applications, have led to a mountain of evidence that supports the use of small, mixed-ability cooperative groups in science classes. We are using the term collaborative in the heading of this section to emphasize the importance of verbal communication among students within small teams. Students need to talk about their observations, their ideas, and their theories in order to understand science. Students need to get along with each other.

As explained in Chapter 5, cooperative learning is a model of teaching in which students work together to achieve a particular goal or complete a task. A variety of cooperative learning models have been developed, field tested, and evaluated. Some delineate how tasks are structured and how groups are evaluated. In some models, students work together on a single task; in others, group members work independently on one aspect of a task, pooling their work when they finish. Regardless of the model, there appears to be essential components of cooperative learning that are integral to any model of cooperative learning. We'll examine these essential components first, then move on and look at several cooperative learning models.

Cooperative Learning

Cooperative learning brings students together to work on tasks: solving problems, reviewing for a quiz, doing a lab activity, completing a worksheet. In all cases it's the "working together" that is important. And this has presented a challenge to teachers, as well. When cooperative learning was introduced (in the early 1970s), American schools were faced with two important social changes. One was the mainstreaming of handicapped and disabled students into the regular classroom; the other was the integration of schools in which students from different cultural backgrounds were brought together in desegregated settings.[14] One of the solutions proposed to help students from different racial groups work together in the same school setting, and for many handicapped students who lacked many "social skills," was cooperative learning. David and Roger Johnson outlined the essential components of a teaching and learning strategy that would focus on bringing small groups of students together in teams to work "cooperatively" as opposed to individually or competitively.[15]

The Johnsons proposed a model in which five elements were essential for cooperative learning groups to be successful. That is, the lessons that teachers taught needed to be characterized by the following elements:

FACE-TO-FACE INTERACTION The physical arrangement of students in small, heterogeneous groups encourages students to help, share, and support each other's learning.

POSITIVE INTERDEPENDENCE The teacher must structure the lesson either through a common goal, group reward, or differentiated role assignments to achieve interdependence among students in a learning team. One way to achieve this is, instead of having each member of a lab team write up their own report, have each team complete *one* lab sheet and perhaps have all students sign off in agreement with its contents. A single grade is given based on the *team's* lab sheet. Assigning each person a role in the group is another way to achieve positive interdependence (e.g., members are assigned one of the following roles for an activity: chief scientist, researcher, observer/recorder, lab technician).

INDIVIDUAL ACCOUNTABILITY Each student in a learning team must be held accountable for learning and collaborating with other team members. Teachers can achieve individual accountability by focusing on (a) individual contributions of individuals (using roles, dividing the task, using experts, giving feedback) and (b) individual outcomes of individuals (using tests, quizzes, grading homework, giving group rewards for individual behavior, using random calling-on procedures).

COOPERATIVE SOCIAL SKILLS The Johnsons found that students needed to learn interpersonal skills such as active listening, staying on task, asking questions, making sure everyone contributed, using agreement, and so forth. Just as science teachers focus on scientific thinking skills (observing, inferring, hypothesizing, experimenting) and assume that students need to be taught these skills, cooperative learning experts have discovered that students need to be taught cooperative social skills.

GROUP PROCESSING The fifth essential element of cooperative learning is group processing. Students need to reflect on how well they worked together as a team to complete a task such as a laboratory activity. The teacher can structure this by simply asking the students to rate how well they did in the activity or how well they "practiced" the social skill that was central in the activity.

Cooperative Structures

A powerful technique for implementing cooperative learning into the classroom is to use a specific cooperative structure. Cooperative structures define how the social interaction within small groups will take place. Kagan and others have advocated this approach because the structure itself is "content-free," allowing the teacher to apply the structure in any content situation.[16] I have found that these structures are one of the most powerful and successful ways of implementing cooperative learning in the classroom, especially for beginning teachers. Here are some very popular cooperative structures that will expand your view of cooperative learning. Read through the structure descriptions and then refer to Table 6.6, which outlines various ways that the structures could be used in the science curriculum.

THINK-PAIR-SHARE Give students a question or a problem and have them think quietly of an answer or solution. Have them discuss their response with a student sitting nearby, and then have them share with the entire class. A time limit of one or two minutes should

Table 6.6 Using Collaborative Structures in Science Teaching

Teaching Function	Collaborative Structure
Pre-Lab	Numbered Heads Together
Laboratory Activity	Roundtable/Circle of Knowledge
Post-Lab	Roundtable, Pairs Check
Review Sessions	Numbered Heads Together, Think-Pair-Share, Pairs Check
Lecture	Think-Pair-Share, Pairs Check, Three-Step Interview, 10–2
Demonstrations	Think-Pair-Share, Pairs Check
Homework	Circle of Knowledge, Constructive Controversy
Small-Group Discussions	Talking Chips, Roundtable/Circle of Knowledge
Introducing a New Concept	10–2, Numbered Heads Together
Textbook Reading	STAD, Jigsaw
Researching and Debating Controversial Issues	Constructive Controversy

be used for the pair exchange. This is a good technique for breaking up a presentation, as well as an assessment of student understanding.

PAIRS CHECK Partners coach each other on a worksheet or text problem and/or check notes for completeness and accuracy. Time: two minutes.

THREE-STEP INTERVIEW Students form pairs and one partner interviews the other on a predetermined topic (e.g., significant health issues facing humankind today) for two or three minutes; partners then switch roles. Next, pairs combine to form groups of four. Each group member introduces his or her partner, sharing the information from the original interview. This is a great icebreaker activity and also fosters active listening.

STAD (STUDENT TEAMS-ACHIEVEMENT DIVISIONS) After a lecture, video, demonstration, or discussion of a chapter in the text, teams of three or four receive a worksheet to discuss and complete. When team members feel they have reached acceptable solutions, you can give a brief oral or written quiz to the group, representative, or each member of the team to assess mastery of the material.

JIGSAW Each member of a "base group" is assigned a minitopic to research. Students then meet in "expert groups" with others assigned the same minitopic to discuss and refine their understanding. Base groups reform, and members teach their minitopics to each other. You can give a brief oral or written quiz to the group, representative, or each member of the team to assess mastery of the material.

CONSTRUCTIVE CONTROVERSY Pairs in a group of four are assigned opposing sides of an issue. Each pair researches its assigned position and the group discusses the issue with the goal of exposing as much information as possible about the subject. Pairs can then switch sides and continue the discussion.[17]

NUMBERED HEAD TOGETHER Each member of a team of four is assigned a number. Pose a thought question, a problem, or present an Exciting Examples of Everyday Phenomena (EEEP), and allow a few minutes for discussion with the groups. Call out a number after randomly selecting a numbered card from a deck. The person whose number is called stands and represents the group. Call on selected students who are standing.

ROUNDTABLE/CIRCLE OF KNOWLEDGE Groups of three or more members brainstorm on an assigned topic, with each member taking turns writing one new idea on a single piece of paper. The process continues until members run out of ideas. When time is up, the group with the most number of independent ideas presents to the class.

TALKING CHIPS This is a method to ensure equal participation in discussion groups. Each member receives the same number of chips (or index cards, pencils, pens, etc.). Each time a member wishes to speak, he or she tosses a chip into the center of the table. Once individuals have used up their chips, they can no longer speak. The discussion proceeds until all members have exhausted their chips.

CO-OP CARDS Each partner in a pair prepares a set of flashcards with a question or a problem on the front and correct answer(s) on the back. One partner quizzes the other until the latter answers all the questions or problems in the set correctly. Then they switch roles and use the other set of flashcards. This is great technique to help students memorize information and review.

SEND A PROBLEM Similar to co-op cards, in this structure each member of a group writes a question or problem on a flashcard. The group reaches consensus on the correct answer or solution and writes it on the back. Each group then passes its cards to another group, which formulates its own answers or solutions and checks them against those written on the back by the sending group. Stacks of cards continue to rotate from group to group until they are returned to the original senders, who then examine and discuss any alternative answers or solutions by other groups.

10–2 In this structure, present information for ten minutes, then stop for two. During the "wait time" students in pairs or small groups share their notes, fill in the gaps, or answer a question.

THINK-ALOUD-PAIR-PROBLEM SOLVING Students are paired off, assigned a role of "problem solver (student A)," or "listener (student B)." Present a problem to be solved. Student A solves the problem by talking aloud, while student B encourages, supports, and asks questions (to help with the solution). Randomly select a group and ask them to present the solution to the class. Present a second problem, but this time ask the students in pairs to reverse roles.

Collaborative Models of Teaching

The models presented here fall into two broad categories: tutorial methods and problem-solving and conceptual methods. The tutorial methods tend to be structured and teacher centered, while problem-solving methods tend to be more open ended, and student centered. The tutorial methods posses many of the characteristics of direct instruction, while the problem-solving methods facilitate inquiry learning. Elements of both methods are useful in constructivist models.

TUTORIAL MODELS In tutorial models students work in small teams to rehearse and learn science information that has been identified by the teacher. Often the material is based on the science textbook and, because of this, tutorial models are easily applied to the secondary science classroom. These methods tend to be motivational because they often involve teams competing against each other for reward structures (e.g., points, prizes, free time). Three models are presented, STAD, Jigsaw II, and Two-Level Content Study Groups.

STAD Originated by Robert Slavin and colleagues at Johns Hopkins University, the STAD model underscores many of the attributes of direct instruction and is very easy to implement in the science classroom. As in the entire cooperative learning models to follow, STAD operates on the principle that students work together to learn and are responsible for their teammates' learning as well as their own.

There are four phases to the STAD model: teach (class presentation), team study, test, and team recognition. We will illustrate how STAD works by using an example for life science: food making (photosynthesis).

Phase I: Teach (Class Presentation) The class presentation is a teacher-directed presentation of the material—concepts, skills, and processes—that the students are to learn. Carefully written and planned objectives should be stated and used to determine the nature of the class presentation and for the team study to follow. Examples from a unit on food making would be:

- Students will identify the steps in the food-making process.
- Student will compare the light and dark phases of photosynthesis.

Key concepts should be identified as well. In this case the following concepts would be presented: ATP, chlorophyll, dark phase, energy, glucose, light phase, photosynthesis.

The presentation can be a lecture, lecture/demonstration, or audiovisual presentation. You also could follow the lesson plans in the your science textbook, including the laboratory activities, in this phase of STAD. Several lessons would be devoted to class presentations.

Phase II: Team Study In STAD, teams are composed of four students who represent a balance in terms of academic ability, gender, and ethnicity. The team is the most important feature of STAD, and it is important for the teacher to take the lead in identifying the members of each team. Slavin recommends rank ordering students in terms of performance.[18] Each team would be composed of a high- and low-ranking student and two students near the average. The goal is to attempt to achieve parity among the teams in the class. Teams should also be formed with sex and ethnicity in mind. Each team should be more or less an average composite of the class.

Team study consists of one or two periods in which each team masters material that you provide. Team members work together with prepared worksheets and make sure that each member of the team can answer all questions on the worksheet. Students should move their desks so that team members face each other. Give each team two worksheets and two answer sheets (not one for each student). For example, in the case of the food-making unit, the teacher would provide a diagram summarizing photosynthesis and construct a worksheet

1. The organ of the plant in which photosynthesis most often takes place is the
   a. stem
   b. root
   c. leaf
2. Plants need which of the following to carry on photosynthesis?
   a. O_2, CO_2, chlorophyll
   b. H_2O, CO_2, light energy, chlorophyll
   c. H_2O, O_2, light energy, sugar
3. The energy stored in plants comes form
   a. soil
   b. air
   c. sunlight
4. The first phase of photosynthesis is sometimes called the
   a. light phase
   b. dark phase
   c. chlorophyll phase

5. The oxygen released during photosynthesis comes from the
   a. chlorophyll
   b. carbon dioxide
   c. water
6. Photosynthesis takes place in the _____ of a plant cell.
   a. cell wall
   b. cytoplasm
   c. chloroplast
7. The energy from the sun is stored in a chemical compound called
   a. ATP
   b. CO_2
   c. H_2O
8. The second stage of photosynthesis is called the
   a. light phase
   b. dark phase
   c. chlorophyll phase

Figure 6.8 Sample Worksheet Questions (STAD).

consisting of about thirty questions related to food making (Figure 6.8).

In the STAD model the following team rules are explained and posted on the bulletin board:

1. Students have the responsibility to make sure that their teammates have learned the material.
2. No one is finished studying until all *teammates* have mastered the subject.
3. Ask all teammates for help before asking the teacher.
4. Teammates may talk to each other *softly*.

It is important to encourage team members to work together. They work in pairs within the teams (sharing one worksheet), and then the pairs can share their work. A principle that is integral, not only to STAD but to all cooperative learning models, is that students must talk with each other in team learning sessions. It is during these small-group sessions that students will teach each other and learn from each other. One of the ways to encourage deeper understanding is for students to explain to each other their answers to the questions. One way to facilitate this process is for the teacher to circulate from group to group, asking questions and encouraging students to explain their answers.

Phase III: Test After the team study is completed, the teacher administers a test to measure the knowledge that students have gained. Students take the individual

tests and are not permitted to help each other. To encourage students to work harder, STAD uses an "individual improvement score." Each student is assessed a base score, which is based on his or her previous performance on similar quizzes and tests. Improvement points, which are reported for each team on a team recognition chart on the bulletin board, are determined based on the percentage of improvement from the previous base score. Generally speaking, if the student gets more than 10 points below the base score, the improvement score is 0, 10 points below to 1 point below results in 10 improvement points, base score to 10 points above gives a score of 20, and more than 10 points above is worth 30 improvement points. (A perfect score, regardless of base score, earns 30 improvement points.)

Phase IV: Team Recognition Team averages are reported in the weekly recognition chart. Teachers can use special words to describe the teams' performance, such as *science stars*, *science geniuses*, or *Einsteins*. Recognition of the work of each team can occur by means of a newsletter, handout, or bulletin board that reports the ranking of each team within the class. Report outstanding individual performances, too. Sensitivity is required here. It is important to realize that praising students academically from low-status groups is an integral part of the effectiveness of cooperative learning. Elizabeth Cohen has found that it is important to be aware of students who you suspect have consistently low expectations for competence.[19] When such a student performs well (not just on the quiz), give immediate, specific, and public recognition for this competence.

One final note about STAD: There is another model developed by Slavin called Teams-Games-Tournaments (TGT) that is also recommended and is very similar to STAD. The same materials used in the team study are used in a series of games in a tournament-style class session.[20]

Jigsaw II This cooperative learning model, developed by Eliot Aronson, enables students to become experts on part of the instructional material about which they are learning.[21] By becoming an expert, and then teaching other members of their team, students become responsible for their own learning. The Jigsaw II model has the advantage of encouraging students of all abilities to be responsible to the same degree, although the depth and quality of their reports will vary.

In Jigsaw II students are grouped into teams of four members to study a chapter in a textbook. However, the content is broken into chunks, letting each team member become an expert on the one of the chunks and then responsible for teaching his or her team members that chunk. The phases of Jigsaw II are as follows.

Phase I: Text The first step in the use of Jigsaw II is to select a chapter that contains material for two or three days. Divide the chapter content into chunks based on the number of team members. For example, if you have four members in a team, then a chapter would be divided into four chunks (as shown next for a chapter on electronics in a physical science course):

- Chunk 1: How do early electronic devices work?
- Chunk 2: How are electronic devices used?
- Chunk 3: How is information processed in a computer?
- Chunk 4: What are some ethical issues concerning the use of electronic devices?

Each member of the team is assigned one of the topics and must read the chapter to find information about his or her assigned chunk. In the next phase, each team member will meet with experts from other groups in the class.

Phase II: Expert Group Discussion Expert groups should meet for about half of a class period to discuss their assigned topic. Each expert group should receive an expert sheet. (See Table 6.7 for sample expert sheets for the study of rocks.) The expert sheets should contain questions and activities (optional) to direct their discussion. Encourage diversity in learning methods. Groups might do hands-on activities, read from other source books, or use a computer for a game or simulation. The groups' goal is to learn about the subtopic and to prepare a brief presentation that group members will use to teach the material to members of their respective learning teams.

Phase III: Reports and Test In the next phase of Jigsaw II, each expert returns to his or her learning team and teaches the topic to the other members. Encourage members to use a variety of teaching methods. They can demonstrate an idea, read a report, use the computer, or illustrate their ideas with photographs or diagrams. Encourage team members to discuss the reports and ask questions, as each team member is responsible for learning about all of the subtopics.

After the experts are finished reporting, conduct a brief class discussion or a question-and-answer session. The test, which covers all the subtopics, should be administered immediately and should not take more than fifteen minutes for students to complete. Test design should include at least two questions per subtopic.

Team recognition should follow the same procedures used in STAD.

PROBLEM-SOLVING CONCEPTUAL MODELS The cooperative learning models presented to this point have stressed rehearsal for a quiz or placed emphasis on having students master a body of information. In each of the models, students tutor each other and then compete against other teams either through tests, tournaments, or games.

What cooperative learning models can be implemented if the science teacher's goals include problem solving and the development of higher order cognitive thinking skills? The cooperative learning models that follow emphasize a structure in which students share ideas, solve problems, discover new information, learn abstract concepts, and seek answers to their own questions.

Group Investigation Developed by Shlomo Sharan and Yael Sharan and their colleagues, the group investigation method is one of the most complex forms of cooperative learning.[22] The philosophy in this method is to cultivate democratic participation and an equitable distribution of speaking privileges. It also encourages students to study different topics within a group and to share what they learn with group members and with the whole class.

Table 6.7 Expert Sheets for Jigsaw II Unit on Rocks

Igneous Rock Expert Sheet	Sedimentary Rock Expert Sheet	Metamorphic Rock Expert Sheet	Home Sheet
Materials:	Materials:	Materials:	*Note:* This sheet is to be used in home groups after expert groups have met. Give this study sheet to each home team in preparation for a quiz on rocks.
Assortment of igneous rocks, dilute HCL acid, hand lenses, texts	Assortment of sedimentary rocks, mixed-sized sand, glass jar, water, HCL acid, and hand lenses	Assortment of metamorphic rocks, HCL acid, and hand lenses	

Activities:

1. How were these rocks formed?

2. Under what environmental conditions are these rocks formed? Try to illustrate your theory.

3. Observe each rock and collect observations on a chart that should include: name of rock or mineral, color (light or dark), shape and color of crystals, arrangement of crystals (even or banded), effect of acid, presence of fossils, and use of the rock.

4. What are some minerals in these rocks?

5. Where would you find these rocks in [your state]?

6. Would you find igneous rocks in, on, or under your school grounds?

7a. What would you predict about the size of crystals in igneous rocks if magma: (a) cooled slowly, (b) cooled rapidly, (c) cooled in water?

7b. Explain your prediction.

8. What is the difference between an intrusive and extrusive igneous rock? Give some examples.

9. If you wanted to demonstrate how an igneous rock is made, what would you do?

10. Do you think there are igneous rocks on Mars?

Activities:

1. How were these rocks formed?

2. Under what environmental conditions are these rocks formed? Try to illustrate your theory.

3. Observe each rock and collect observations on a chart that should include: name of rock or mineral, color (light or dark), shape and color of crystals, arrangement of crystals (even or banded), effect of acid, presence of fossils, and use of the rock.

4. What are some minerals in these rocks?

5. Where would you find these rocks in [your state]?

6. Would you find sedimentary rocks in, on, or under your school grounds?

7. Why might you expect to find fossils in sedimentary rocks?

8. Does shaking a jar of mixed sized sand and water and observing the results demonstrate part of the sedimentary process? Explain by using a diagram and words.

9. Do you think there are sedimentary rocks on Mars?

Activities:

1. How were these rocks formed?

2. Under what environmental conditions are these rocks formed? Try to illustrate your theory.

3. Observe each rock and collect observations on a chart that should include: name of rock or mineral, color (light or dark), shape and color of crystals, arrangement of crystals (even or banded), effect of acid, presence of fossils, and use of the rock.

4. What are some minerals in these rocks?

5. Where would you find these rocks in [your state]?

6. Would you find metamorphic rocks in, on, or under your school grounds?

7. If you wanted to demonstrate how a metamorphic rock is made, what would you do? Illustrate and explain.

Activities/Questions:

1. Consider the following rocks: sandstone, granite, and marble. (a) Under what environmental conditions is each formed? (b) Would they be found on Mars? (c) Where would you find these in [your state]?

2. What are the differences between igneous, sedimentary, and metamorphic rocks?

3. What are some rocks that can be identified by an acid test? What does this tell you about the composition of the rocks?

4. Complete these sentences:

   a. Metamorphic rocks form when . . .

   b. The southern part of [your state] contains rocks such as . . .

   c. In [a county next to yours], you'll find these rocks . . .

   d. Fossils can be found in . . .

Group investigation places maximum responsibility on the students, who identify what and how to learn, gather information, analyze and interpret knowledge, and share in each other's work. It is very similar to another method of cooperative learning developed by Spencer Kagan called Co-op Co-op,[23] and it has the greatest chance of success if students have experience with other forms of cooperative learning.

There are several phases to the method. Although group investigation places more responsibility on each group to make decisions about content and process, the teacher must stay in contact with the groups and facilitate their flow through the phases. The best topics for group investigations are ones that require problem solving on the part of each team. Topics can be fairly descriptive, but encouraging an investigative approach will reinforce inquiry learning in the science classroom.

Phase I: Topic and Problem Selection Students organize into groups of five or fewer members and choose specific topics or problems in a general subject area of science. Group investigation lends itself to a wide range of problem-solving strategies. Students can ask questions that require empirical research, survey or questionnaires, or historical reporting. Each group plans its own topic or subject of investigation and strategy for exploration. Then individuals or pairs within the group select subtopics or specific investigatory tasks and decide how they will carry them out.

Phase II: Cooperative Planning The teacher and the students in each learning team plan specific learning procedures, tasks, and goals consistent with the subtopics of the problem selected.

Phase III: Implementation Students carry out the plans formulated in the second step. Learning should involve a wide range of activities and skills and should lead students to different kinds of sources, both inside and outside of school. Students might work in small groups or individually to gather data and information.

Phase IV: Analysis and Synthesis Students meet to discuss the results of their subgroup or individual work. Meetings of this nature will naturally take place more than once during the implementation of group investigation. The information that has been gathered on the topic or problem is analyzed and each group member's piece is synthesized to prepare a report for the whole class.

Phase V: Class Presentation One of the attractive features of group investigation is that each team makes a presentation to the whole class. Students have to cooperate to prepare a presentation. Teams should be encouraged to prepare presentations that involve the audience, such as debates, demonstrations, hands-on activities, plays, or computer simulations.

During the presentation, the presenting team is responsible for setting up the room, gathering any equipment and materials, and preparing necessary handouts. Encourage the teams to allow at least five minutes for questions and comments from the class. In some cases, you should facilitate this aspect of the presentation.

Science Experiences John Dewey once said, "education must be conceived as a continuing reconstruction of experience; that the process and the goal of education are one and the same thing." Science experiences is a cooperative learning method that brings together the elements of discovery and inquiry methods.[24] Students are involved in scientific investigation, critical thinking, problem solving, and group participation.

The activity process for science experiences includes an orientation phase, an action phase, and a reporting phase. In the science experiences method, the teacher orients the students to the activity, most of which require multiple abilities to accomplish. The activities are designed not to rely on reading, but to emphasize reasoning, hypothesizing, predicting, inductive thinking, imaging, manipulating concrete materials, and using a variety of media sources. To show how science experiences can be implemented, the activity Intergalactic/Oceanographic Mission is described next.[25]

Phase I: Orientation The teacher sets the stage for the small-group activity by asking the students why humans have dreamed of traveling to the stars or sailing across vast oceans. Students can generate a lot of reasons, either as a whole class or as members of a small team. In the latter case, the lists are pooled. A general discussion follows based on these questions: What might it be like to go on a journey into space, or across the oceans? What would be some of the preparations necessary to take such a trip?

In this activity, students generate a list of survival needs necessary for long-term travel and create a blueprint for a spacecraft or an ark. They will also make value judgments and consider some ecological implications for long-term travel.

To heighten interest in the activity, the teacher should read each of the following scenarios with dramatic flair.

For the Space Trekkers

Scientists at NASA have discovered a new planet that seems almost identical to earth, but the new planet needs to be studied carefully before scientists know if it is safe to land spacecraft there. Your mission is to orbit the planet for one year in a sealed spacecraft and then return to earth. Draw the various rooms in the spacecraft and label the things in each room. Be sure to include everything the crew will need to stay alive and well for a whole year.

For the Ocean Anglers

The Cousteau Society and a local television station owner have hired you to explore a series of islands that have never been studied by scientists. Your mission is to study these islands for one year in an oceanographic vessel that you cannot leave. The ship will take you to the island area and return you to your homeport in a year. Draw the various rooms in the ship and label the things in each room. Be sure to include everything the crew will need to stay alive and well for the whole year.

Divide the class into teams of four and assign each either as a Space Trekker or an Ocean Angler.

Phase II: Action Give each team one instruction sheet that contains the following information and problems.

1. Draw and label the things that are most important to stay alive and complete the mission. Work together as a team to design either a spacecraft or an ocean arc. Decide within your group who will be the design engineer, spokesperson for the group, equipment and materials manager, and group facilitator.
2. Obtain a large roll (about 10 feet) of paper for your blueprint, crayons, rulers, and pens.
3. Construct the spacecraft or ocean arc.
4. When your blueprint is completed, make a list of the things that your team has brought on the voyage. Then rank the supplies into three categories:
   a. Things that are essential for life and without which you would die.
   b. Things that would be hard or uncomfortable to live without.
   c. Things that would be nice to have but are not necessary.
5. Discuss the following questions and problems:
   a. Will any of your supplies run out? Which ones?
   b. How could you make supplies last for 10, 50, 100, or 1,000 years?
   c. How would you get rid of waste materials?

Have the students post their blueprints on the walls of the classroom, and be prepared for reporting.

Phase III: Reporting Reporting is a whole-class activity, although it focuses on the work of the co-operative teams. In this case you should ask each spokesperson to explain their blueprint and the rationale for the items and rooms in their spacecraft or ship. Reporting to the whole class should encourage dialog between the teams. This can be done by conducting a small-group discussion among the spokespersons (with the rest of the class observing). Encourage critical thinking by asking students to explain and defend their team's work or results.

Direct/Interactive Teaching Model

An eighth-grade earth science teacher begins a lesson by showing students several slides depicting the moon at successive one-hour intervals. Then the teacher says, "Today we are going to discuss the sightings you made of the moon and stars in the western sky last night for homework, and then I will do a demonstration on how to measure the altitude and compass location of a star. You will use this information to practice making measurements of fictional stars in the classroom in small groups. Finally, I'll give you some problems to solve and then you'll use what you learned today to measure changes in star motion in tonight's sky for homework.

This opening statement by a middle school science teacher conveys some of the elements of the direct/interactive teaching (DIT) model. The DIT model is a good place to begin because it flourishes in many classrooms and calls on the teacher to direct students by assigning specific tasks that must be completed under direct teacher supervision. It is, however, a *dynamic* model in that the most effective form of direct teaching implies interaction between the teacher and the students.

The teaching of science information and skills can be accomplished quite effectively through the DIT model. In the science classroom, the material to be learned is subdivided into smaller chunks of information and is presented directly to the students. In this teacher-centered model, the teacher's role is very clear: to teach science information and skills in the most direct manner possible.

Research by a number of science educators shows that when direct instruction strategies are used a notable increase in achievement occurs. Research from several science education studies resulted in the following pattern. The science classroom that is based on the DIT model appears to be characterized by a number of factors as follows.[26]

1. Teachers gain attention at the start of each lesson by using focusing behaviors and strategies such as advanced organizers and set induction. These typically include asking questions, performing a short demonstration, or the use of an EEEP (see Chapter 9).
2. Students handle, operate on, or practice with science teaching materials. This includes the full range of manipulative materials, including the familiar science objects such as rocks, fossils, and plant specimens, pictorial stimuli, perhaps cardboard cutouts depicting science concepts such as crystal form, as well as the manipulation of paper products such as cards with the names and pictures of atoms, organisms, chemical equations, and the like.
3. Teachers alter instructional materials or classroom procedures to facilitate student learning.

4. Teachers integrate cooperative learning strategies to enable students to engage in peer–peer talk and activity.
5. Rewriting activity or experiment procedures from a textbook, making audiotapes of the science textbook, and giving students directions in writing are examples of how science teachers alter instructional procedures.
6. The science teacher focuses attention on the type and placement of questions asked during lessons.
7. In effective science classrooms, teachers provide immediate as well as explanatory feedback during the instructional process, rather than waiting until a quiz or major test.

The DIT model fosters a learning environment characterized by teacher-directed learning and high levels of teacher-student interaction. Rosenshine has identified six teaching functions that, taken together, constitute the essential principles of direct/interactive teaching.[27] These functions (Table 6.8) include checking previous

Table 6.8 Direct/Interactive Teaching Functions

Teaching Function	Specific Behaviors
1. Checking previous day's work and reteaching	• Check homework
	• Reteach areas where there are student errors
2. Presenting and/or demonstrating new content and skills	• Provide overview
	• Proceed in small steps, but at a rapid pace
	• If necessary, give detailed or redundant instructions and explanations
3. Leading initial student practice	• Provide a high frequency of questions and overt student practice
(*Note:* The key strategy here is to use cooperative learning breaks, in which students work in pairs or small groups to answer questions, solve a problem and do a miniactivity.)	• Provide prompts during initial learning
	• Give all students a chance to respond and receive feedback
	• Check for understanding by evaluating student responses
	• Continue practice until students are firm
	• Insure a success rate of 80 percent or higher during initial practice
4. Providing feedback and correctives (and recycling of instruction if necessary)	• Give specific feedback to students, particularly when they are correct but hesitant
	• Student errors provide feedback to the teacher that corrections and/or reteaching is necessary
	• Offer corrections by simplifying question, giving clues, explaining or reviewing steps, or reteaching last steps
	• When necessary, reteach using smaller steps
5. Providing practice so that students are firm and automatic	• Cooperative groupwork
	• Ensure unitization and automaticity (practice to overlearning)
	• Ensure student engagement through cooperative groupwork
6. Providing weekly and monthly reviews	• Reteaching, if necessary

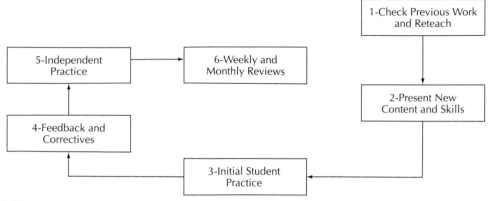

Figure 6.9 The Direct/Interactive Teaching Model.

day's homework, presenting and demonstrating new content and skills, leading the initial student practice session, providing feedback and correctives, providing independent practice, and conducting weekly and monthly reviews.

The DIT Model can be represented as a cycle of teaching. (Figure 6.9) As you implement this model of teaching it is important to note that four important aspects of the model stand out:

1. You will need to develop and implement a variety of learning tasks.
2. The learning tasks you develop should engage the learner at high levels.
3. You should strive for high levels of teacher-student and student-student interaction. You can achieve this by the use of teacher questions, hands-on activities, and small-group work.
4. Your students should perform at moderate-to-high rates of success.

Structuring Content for Direct/Interactive Teaching

Another important aspect of the DIT model is the presentation and structuring of science content. One of the key ingredients is to break content into manageable, teachable, and learnable chunks. Borich points out that most teachers "divide" content based on the content divisions in science textbooks. Borich explains that, this organization is often arranged to help students read the text, and therefore it may not be the best way to present content.[28] There are a number of ways to structure new science content. Following are four suggestions that you should find helpful in dividing science content for the DIT model. They include:

- Whole-to-part
- Sequential structuring
- Combinatorial organization
- Comparative relationships

WHOLE-TO-PART Organizing content in a whole-to-part format is useful in introducing science content in its most general form. For instance, if you were presenting information on rock types, you might start with the question What are the types of rocks? This would lead to natural subdivisions (sedimentary, igneous, and metamorphic) that can be easily learned by students (see Figure 6.10)

Whole-to-part structuring is a powerful way to organize information. Recent research using the technique of concept mapping (see Chapter 5) is based on the organization of knowledge from whole to part. Whole-to-part thinking gives students an organizational framework from which to operate. Big ideas can be used to "hook" subconcepts and subideas, rather than as isolated bits of information. In the previous chapter, I introduced the Deweyan notion of the "big idea." By identifying a big idea as a starting point in your plan, you provide students with a powerful tool to help them organize their learning and understanding of science content. For example, you might say, "there is evidence that all rocks in the universe, not only those found on earth, but rocks on the moon, Mars, and quite possibly all of the planets of our solar system and elsewhere in the universe, can be organized into three groups—and we can classify any rock into these groups. Let's see how this really works and if the rocks near our homes fit

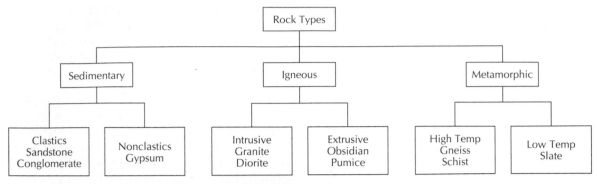

Figure 6.10 One way to structure content is to divide it from whole-to-part.

this model. Here is a chart I have prepared to help us as we work and play with rocks. Notice how. . . ."

SEQUENTIAL STRUCTURING Sequential structuring is organizing content and skills by ordering. Typically, the content or skills are presented from simplest to most complex. Sequential structuring is based on a hierarchical arrangement of science content or science skills. In a way, sequential structuring is an alternative to the whole-to-part organization. In the sequential structuring of science content or skills, students usually would be introduced first to prerequisite content or skills and then to content or skills dependent on the previously learned material or skill. For example, science skills or processes can be broken down into a number of simpler skills that can be mastered in sequence. Simpler or more basic process skills would be introduced first. Examples would include:

1. Observing
2. Using space/time relationships
3. Using numbers
4. Measuring
5. Classifying
6. Communicating
7. Predicting
8. Inferring

More complex science skills would be introduced later, after students had mastered the more simple or basic skills. Complex science skills often involve the integration of two or more process skills, and therefore are usually referred to as integrated process skills. Some include:

1. Formulating hypotheses
2. Controlling variables
3. Interpreting data

4. Defining operationally
5. Experimenting

Science content can similarly be arranged in a hierarchy. Scientists classify matter according to size and function. This classification leads to levels of organization. The levels of organization can be useful as a mechanism for sequence content. For example, to organize a unit of instruction on ecology, we could use the levels of organization of matter as the sequence of presentation of content from the microworld (which would contain nonlife, subatomic particles, atoms, protoplasm, and cells) to the supermacro world (consisting of stars, galaxies, and the universe). An alternative would be to organize the content in the reverse order.

COMBINATORIAL ORGANIZATION Science content can be presented by highlighting relationships among the various elements of content to be presented. One very effective means of doing this is to present the elements of the content in a cycle. There are many cycles in the various disciplines of science. In earth science, content could be organized by means of the rock cycle or the water cycle instead of teaching simply about rivers. In biology, the photosynthesis and the Krebs cycle could be presented in organizational cycles to show relationships and combinations.

Figure 6.11 shows a summary of the major components of an ecosystem and how they are interconnected through chemical and energy cycles. Nonliving chemicals, producers, macroconsumers, and microconsumers are presented in relationship to each other. The presentation of "new content" would include the relationships as well as the specific details of the elements (e.g., macroconsumers). The cycle itself is another powerful organizing element to help the student learn and understand the material being presented.

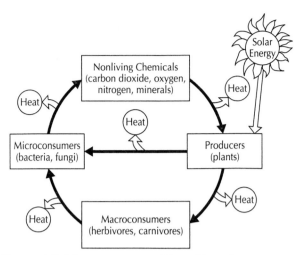

Figure 6.11 The ecosystem model can be used as a combinatorial organization to present science content. Content is organized not only around the key concepts, but also around the relationships among the concepts.

COMPARATIVE RELATIONSHIPS Another effective way to present content is by comparing categories of content to heighten similarities and differences. The example cited in Table 6.9 contrasts the similarities and differences among four types of drugs. The advantage of the comparative approach is that the organization

of the content into a chart is a useful learning device for the student, and individual elements (e.g., type of drug) are learned in relationship to others. Students can graphically compare, for instance, relative dependence and effects of the drugs.

From Structure to Interactivity

The four ways to structure science content are only one step in applying the DIT model. Students need to be active learners in the process of learning science. Science teachers often point out that they have a "lot of content to cover" and wonder how it is possible to engage the students while at the same time responding to the pressure to teach to the *Standards*. As we have learned, students construct knowledge, and most science educators would agree that an active learner is going to fare better than a passive one. There are ways of presenting information that encourage students take on an active role. Two steps are important:

1. Organize the content that students will learn using one of the four methods described in this section, or follow the organization in your text. However, make sure that you let students know what plan you are following, and provide each student with a "conceptual tool," such as a chart, a concept map, or a cycle showing how the content to be learned is organized.

Table 6.9 Structuring Content: Comparative Relationships—Drugs

Drug	Dependence Potential	Short-Term Effects	Long-Term Effects
Stimulants		Increased heart rate, increased blood pressure	Irregular heartbeat, high blood pressure, stomach disorders
• Caffeine	Probable		
• Amphetamines	High		
• Cocaine	High		
Depressants			
• Barbiturates	High	Drowsiness, decreased coordination	Depression, emotional instability, hallucinations, death
• Tranquilizers	High		
Psychoactive Drugs			
• Lysergic acid diethylamide (LSD)	Probable	Hallucinations	Psychosis
• *Cannabis sativa* (marijuana)	Probable	Short-term memory loss, disorientation	Lung damage, loss of motivation
Narcotics			
• Heroin	High	Drowsiness, respiratory depression, nausea, constricted pupils	Convulsions, coma, death
• Codeine	High		
• Morphine	High		

Source: Towle, Albert. *Modern Biology, Teacher's Edition*, p. 753. Austin: Holt, Rinehart, and Winston, 1989. Used with permission of the publisher.

2. As you present information in the form of a lecture, "lecturette," PowerPoint presentation, pre-lab, or post-lab experience, build in breaks, during which students are actively engaged with each other in pairs or small groups.

When you use the strategies described next, you do not have to reorganize your classroom. Students can turn toward each other to form pairs or groups of three. There is no need for them to get up and move around the room. Each strategy is a cooperative learning activity designed to help students process content. Practice using them, but keep in mind that these "breaks" are powerful reflective tools designed to have students discuss, solve problems, and answer questions among themselves.

PAIR AND COMPARE Students pair off with a student nearby to compare lecture notes or presentation information and fill in what they might have missed. Provide no more than two minutes for this activity.

PAIR, COMPARE, AND ASK Same as pair and compare, but the students also write questions based on the lecture or presentation content. You can then field questions that students cannot answer among themselves. Allow approximately three minutes with time for questions.

PERIODIC FREE-RECALL, WITH PAIR-AND-COMPARE OPTION Students put away their lecture notes and write the most important one, two, or three points of your lecture or presentation, as well as any questions they have. Use an overhead projector to outline the instructions the first time you implement this strategy. On later uses, you can provide verbal instructions. In this activity, students are asked to review and mentally process your lecture content. They can work individually, or in pairs or triads (in which case they can answer each others' questions). Allow two minutes, plus time to answer questions.

LISTEN, RECALL, AND ASK; THEN PAIR, COMPARE, AND ANSWER Students are allowed only to listen to your presentation—no note-taking is allowed—then open their notebooks and jot down all of the major ideas they can recall, as well as questions they have. A good technique is to have the students leave quite a bit of space between main points in their notebook. Then have students pair off and compare lecture notes, filling in what they missed and answering each other's questions. Again, this activity helps students

review and mentally process information. Allow three to four minutes for individual note writing, two to four minutes for pair fill-ins and question answering, plus time to answer any remaining questions.

SOLVE A PROBLEM Students solve a mathematical or word problem based on your presentation. You can use problems from your text for this activity. Students should work in pairs. Orally describe the problem or present in on an overhead or as a slide in a digital presentation. Allow one to three minutes, depending on the problem's complexity, plus one to three minutes to debrief and answer questions.

CASE STUDY Students debrief a short case study related to the content of the presentation. The case should be written out (overhead or digital slide) and should be based on a realistic application of the content of the presentation. Once the case is presented, have the students work in pairs or triads to debrief using the following questions: What are the problems? What are the solutions? How could these problems have been prevented? Allow three to eight minutes, depending on the length and complexity of the case, plus ten to fifteen minutes for class discussion and debate.

PAIR/GROUP AND DISCUSS AN OPEN-ENDED QUESTION Students pair off or get into small groups to discuss an open-ended question that asks them to apply, analyze, or evaluate material from your presentation. Open-ended questions should have multiple correct answers. Some suggestions for structuring the questions include the following: Ask comparative questions to compare and contrast different theories. Ask connective questions that challenge students to link facts, concepts, and theories. You can ask critical questions in which students examine or evaluate the validity of a particular argument or research claim. Or, you might ask a brainstorm question, instructing students to generate alternative responses to a question (e.g., What are some possible explanations for global warming?). Allow three to ten minutes, depending on the complexity of the question, plus five to fifteen minutes for class discussion.

PAIR/GROUP AND REVIEW Same as the previous activity, but with an essay question designed for pre-exam review. Students in selected groups present their answers to the class, while you provide feedback and explain your criteria for the feedback. Allow three to ten minutes, depending on the question's complexity, plus five to fifteen minutes for pair/group discussion.

PAIR/GROUP AND EXPERIENCE AN EEEP Students pair off or get into small groups. You present an EEEP that relates to the content. Students work in their groups to offer explanation. Provide each group with a white board or large sheet of paper, on which they diagram the EEEP phenomenon and use it to explain their ideas. Allow three to five minutes for the presentation and group discussion, plus four to eight minutes for random selection of team explanations and discussion.

Inquiry Models of Teaching

* A physics teacher asks students: Is it a good idea to continue to develop and build new nuclear power plants?
* An earth science teacher asks students to interpret a set of dinosaur footprints and generate several alternative hypotheses to explain the pattern of the prints.
* A biology teacher takes students on a field trip to collect leaves from different trees. Students are asked to create a classification system using the leaves.
* A chemistry teacher gives students an unknown substance and asks them to use scientific tests to determine the composition of the material.

In each of these scenarios, the science teacher has created a situation in the classroom in which students are asked to formulate their own ideas, state their opinion on an important issue, or to find things out for themselves. It is a radical departure from the DIT model, in which the teacher engages students to learn science information or skills. In each of the science teacher examples students were encouraged to ask questions, analyze specimens or data, draw conclusions, make inferences, or generate hypotheses. In short, the student is viewed as an inquirer—a seeker of information and a problem solver. This is the heart of the inquiry model of teaching.

What Is Inquiry?

J. Richard Suchman, the originator of an inquiry teaching program that was widely used throughout the United States, once said that "inquiry is the way people learn when they're left alone."[29] To Suchman, inquiry is a natural way that human beings learn about their environment. Think for moment about a very young child left in a play yard containing objects. The child, without any coaxing, will begin to explore the objects by throwing, touching, pulling, banging them, and trying to take them apart. The child learns about the objects and how they interact by exploring them, by developing his or her

own ideas about them—in short, learning about them by inquiry.

Many authors have discussed the nature of inquiry using such words as guided inquiry, open-ended inquiry, inductive thinking, creative thinking, discovery learning, the scientific method, and the like. To many authors, the essence of inquiry can be traced to John Dewey.

Dewey proposed that inquiry is the "active, persistent, and careful consideration of any belief or supposed form of knowledge in the light of the grounds that support it and the further conclusions to which it tends."[30] To Dewey, the grounding of "any belief" occurs through inquiry processes: reason, evidence, inference, and generalization. Recently, science educators have proposed various lists of inquiry processes. The *National Science Education Standards* and *Benchmarks for Scientific Literacy* include the following inquiry processes: observing, measuring, predicting, inferring, using numbers, using space-time relationships, defining operationally, formulating hypotheses, interpreting data, controlling variables, experimenting, and communicating.

The Practice of Inquiry

In the context of learning, students will engage in inquiry when faced with a "forked-road situation" or a problem that is perplexing and causes them some discomfort. In the model of inquiry presented in this chapter, the creation of forked-road situations or discomforting problems will be the essence of science inquiry activities.

Although research supports the inclusion of inquiry models of teaching in secondary science classrooms, there appears to be reluctance on the part of the science teachers to implement inquiry in the classroom. Several problems need to be recognized in order to overcome this reluctance.

Why is it that science teachers express the importance of inquiry yet pay little attention to it in the classroom? One reason may have to do with teacher education. It is possible that many teachers have not been exposed to inquiry teaching models in their preparation, and therefore lack the skills and strategies to implement inquiry. Some teachers report that inquiry teaching models are difficult to manage, and some report that they don't have the equipment and materials to implement inquiry teaching. Another concern expressed by teachers is that inquiry doesn't work for some students. These teachers claimed that inquiry was only effective with bright students and that it caused too many problems with lower-ability students.

Table 6.10 Inquiry Content Standards: Abilities and Understandings

Grades Levels	Inquiry Abilities	Inquiry Understandings
K–4	Ask a question about objects, organisms, and events in the environment.	Scientific investigations involve asking and answering a question and comparing the answer with what scientists already know about the world.
	Plan and conduct a simple investigation.	
	Communicate investigations and explanations.	Scientists review and ask questions about the results of other scientists' work.
5–8	Identify questions that can be answered through scientific investigations.	Different kinds of questions suggest different kinds of scientific investigations.
	Design and conduct a scientific investigation.	Current scientific knowledge and understanding guide scientific investigations.
	Communicate scientific procedures and explanations.	
9–12	Identify questions and concepts that guide scientific investigations.	Science advances through legitimate skepticism.
	Design and conduct scientific investigations.	Scientists usually inquire about how physical, living, or designed systems function.
	Communicate and defend a scientific argument.	Mathematics is essential in scientific inquiry.

Source: Based on the National Research Council. *Inquiry and the National Science Education Standards.* Washington, D.C.: National Academy Press, 2000, pp. 19–20.

In spite of these problems, the evidence supports inquiry models of teaching as viable approaches to teaching that should be part of the science teacher's repertoire. Science teachers have had a love affair with inquiry and many feel strongly that it should be a fundamental part of science teaching. Read about what teachers think about inquiry in the Science Teachers Talk section of the *Science Teacher Gazette* of this chapter. Note how the teachers interviewed link inquiry with discovery and indicate that the reason they were drawn to science was the excitement of finding out about things, probing, exploring—in short inquiring.

Inquiry and the Science Standards

The *Standards* (introduced earlier in the book) treat inquiry as both a learning goal and a teaching method. Specific inquiry content standards appear in the form of abilities and understandings and the essential features of classroom inquiry are outlined.

The inquiry content standards are spread across the K–12 science curriculum and recommend that students develop:

- Abilities necessary to do scientific inquiry
- Understandings about scientific inquiry

The inquiry abilities in the *Standards* are really "cognitive" abilities and engage the students in intellectual activity. For example, in the K–4 science class, students would learn to "ask a question about objects, organisms, and events in the environment"; at the grade

5–8 level, they would learn to "identify questions that can be answered through scientific investigations"; and at the grade 9–12 level, they would to "identify questions and concepts that guide scientific investigations." Table 6.10 summarizes some of the additional inquiry abilities and understandings. Consult the NSES to see the complete list of inquiry standards.

Features of an inquiry-oriented classroom are also outlined in the *Standards*. Table 6.11 summarizes the essential features of an inquiry classroom. Note that five features characterize inquiry teaching.

Some Questions about Inquiry

Anderson, Holland, and Palincsar point out that most of the reform documents have been heavily influenced

Table 6.11 Essential Features of an Inquiry Classroom

Learners are engaged by scientifically oriented questions.

Learners give priority to evidence, which allows them to develop and evaluate explanations that address scientifically oriented questions.

Learners formulate explanations from evidence to address scientifically oriented questions.

Learners evaluate their explanations in light of alternative explanations, particularly those reflecting scientific understanding.

Learners communicate and justify their proposed explanations.

Source: Based on the National Research Council. *Inquiry and the National Science Education Standards.* Washington, D.C.: National Academy Press, 2000, p. 25.

by a Western model of science and supported by conceptual-change research.[31] Their claim is that the *Standards* and other reports, such as the *Benchmarks for Scientific Literacy*, are based on the "scientific canon." According to Anderson and colleagues, the presently accepted view of reform is based on the following definition of scientific literacy: the accumulated knowledge, skills, and habits of mind of the scientific community. Thus, outlines of concepts and "inquiry abilities and understandings" are part of this accumulated wisdom of science. Anderson, Holland, and Palincsar also point out that science education research has supported this policy in the sense that research using the conceptual-change model has shown that student understanding can be improved using this constructivist model. Anderson and colleagues report that in traditional science classes only 5 percent to 20 percent of students achieve a functional understanding of the science content, whereas classes using the conceptual-change approaches often raised student understanding to the 50 percent level. In their analysis of the improvement, Anderson, Holland, and Palincsar raise this issue:

Yet the limitations of conceptual change research are as important as its accomplishments. Conceptual change researchers have consistently fallen well short of the goal of science for *all* Americans. Furthermore, the students who were most likely to be successful in classes influenced by conceptual change research were those who have traditionally been most successful in school: middle- and upper-class students, mostly of European or Asian origins. Poor children and children of color often did not achieve scientific understanding, even when conceptual change teaching methods were used.[32]

Science education research on this question has shifted toward a great degree of attention to sociocultural aspects of scientific literacy. In this view, scientific inquiry and the concepts that are presented in science class must be viewed in the sense that this knowledge and understanding are created by and shared among members of communities. Some researchers make the claim that a community shares its knowledge as a discourse, which includes ways of using language, thinking, and acting. Thus, according to Anderson, Holland, and Palincsar, "from a sociocultural perspective, acquiring functional scientific literacy is not simply a matter of mastering and using a canon. It requires appropriate scientific discourse—learning to use language, think and act in ways that identify one as a member of the community of scientifically literate people and enable one to participate fully in the activities of the community."[33] In

accordance with this view, the teacher is encouraged to create a community of practice within the science classroom, to engage students in collaboration and problem-solving activities, and to select problems and activities that will be of interest to a wide range of students.

Models of Inquiry

With the community view in mind, I will present four models of inquiry teaching: inductive inquiry, deductive inquiry, discovery learning (collaborative inquiry), and project-based inquiry.

INDUCTIVE INQUIRY Perhaps the best example of inductive inquiry is the inquiry development program developed a number of years ago by J. Richard Suchman.[34] Suchman produced a number of inquiry programs designed to help students find out about science phenomena through inquiry. Suchman's views on inquiry are quite applicable today, and this statement by him is worth pondering:

Inquiry is the active pursuit of meaning involving thought processes that change experience to bits of knowledge. When we see a strange object, for example, we may be puzzled about what it is, what it is made of, what it is used for, how it came into being, and so forth. *To find answers to questions* [emphasis mine] such as these we might examine the object closely, subject it to certain tests, compare it with other, more familiar objects, or ask people about it, and for a time our searching would be aimed at finding out whether any of these theories made sense. Or we might simply cast about for information that would suggest new theories for us to test. All these activities—observing, theorizing, experimenting, theory testing—are part of inquiry. The purpose of the activity is to gather enough information to put together theories that will make new experiences less strange and more meaningful.[35]

The key to the inquiry model proposed by Suchman is providing "problem-focus events." Suchman's program provided films of such events, but he also advocated demonstrations and developed a series of idea books for the purpose of helping students organize concepts. For the purposes of this book, the inquiry demonstrations will help you develop inquiry lessons.

The Inquiry Session As mentioned, the inquiry demonstration is a method to present a problem to your students. The demonstration is *not* designed to illustrate a concept or principle of science. Instead, it is designed to present a discrepancy or a problem for the students to explore. In fact, we refer to inquiry demonstrations

Table 6.13 Procedures for an Inquiry Session

Rule	Procedure
1: Questions	Student questions should be phrased in such a way that they can be answered yes or no. This shifts the burden of thinking onto the students.
2: Freedom to ask questions	A student may ask as many questions as desired. This encourages the student to use his or her previous questions to formulate new ones to pursue a reasonable theory.
3: Teacher response to statements of theory	When students suggest a theory, the teacher should refrain from evaluating it. The teacher might simply record the theory or ask a question about the theory.
4: Testing theories	Students should be allowed to test their theories at any time.
5: Cooperation	Students should be encouraged to work in teams to confer and discuss their theories.
6: Experimenting	The teacher should provide materials, texts, and reference books so that students can explore their ideas.

Source: Based on Suchman, J. R. *Developing Inquiry.* Chicago: Science Research Associates, 1966.

as discrepant events. An inquiry session is designed to engage the class in an exploration of a problem staged by means of the discrepant event. It should begin with the presentation of a problem through a demonstration (the discrepant event), a description of intriguing phenomena, or a problem posed by the use of prepared materials (see the inquiry box activity section).

Suchman proposed six rules or procedures that teachers have found helpful in conducting inquiry sessions (see Table 6.12). According to the inquiry model, students learn that in order to obtain information they must ask questions. Questioning becomes the students' initial method of gathering data. Thus the climate of the inquiry classroom must foster the axiom: "There are no dumb questions." Students must come to believe that you will accept their questions—no holds barred. For example, if you use the Wood Sinks and Floats activity, students will immediately be drawn to the discrepancy that one of the blocks of wood sinks. Once the event is presented, the teacher must be sure the students understand the real problem. Once the problem is established, the students engage in the inquiry session to construct a theory to account for the focus event. The major portion of the inquiry session is devoted to the students asking questions to gather data, which are then used to formulate one or more theories. You should refer to Table 6.12 before conducting your first inquiry session.

INQUIRY ACTIVITIES There are numerous sources of inquiry activities (including discrepant events). Following are some examples of inquiry activities and discrepant events.

The Inquiry Box Of all the approaches to help students learn about inquiry, the inquiry box might be considered the universal strategy. The inquiry box can be made

with a shoebox, and it should be painted black. For a classroom of students, you could prepare several inquiry boxes. Students are given the box and asked to determine what the inside of the box is like. An inquiry box contains a marble, which is the main probe that the student can use to determine the pattern that exists within the box. You can prepare different patterns by taping pieces of cardboard in interesting and perplexing patterns as shown in Figure 6.12. The inquiry activity consists of having teams of students explore each inquiry box. The students' theory consists of a diagram of the possible pattern in each box.

The Wood Sinks and Floats Discrepant Event The teacher shows two blocks of wood, one much larger than the other. The blocks are placed on an equal-arm

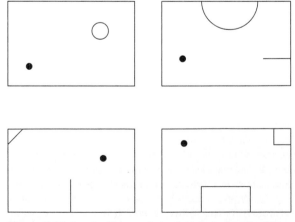

Figure 6.12 Inquiry Boxes. A shoebox is designed with an internal pattern requiring the student to use imagination and inquiry to probe its structure: a universal tool for focusing attention on inquiry and curiosity.

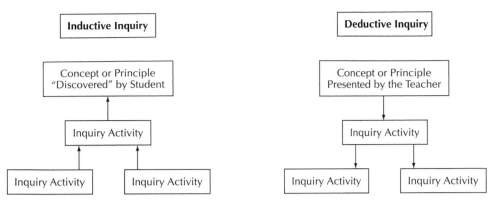

Figure 6.13 Comparison of Inductive and Deductive Inquiry.

balance demonstrating that the larger block is more massive than the smaller block. The blocks are then placed in container of water. The larger, more massive block floats, while the smaller and less massive one sinks. This discrepant event leads to an inquiry into the following questions: Why did the lighter block sink and the heavier one float? Why do objects sink and float? Science principles that emerge include displacement, Archimedes' principle, and pressure.

The Coin Drop and Throw The teacher places one coin (a quarter) on the edge of a table and holds another quarter in the air next to it. At the same instant he flicks the quarter on the table so that it flies horizontally off the table, and drops the other quarter straight down. Both coins strike the floor at the same time. An inquiry about why the coins strike the floor at the same time ensues. *Hint:* practice this demonstration before you perform it with a group of students. Science principles that will emerge from this inquiry include vectors, universal gravitation, and Newton's second law of motion.

The Double Pendulum The teacher places a long rod (meter stick) across the backs of two chairs. From the rod hang two simple pendulums of the same length. One of the pendulums is started swinging. The other is allowed to hang straight down. In a few minutes the stationary pendulum begins swinging as the arc of the swinging pendulum decreases. The inquiry focuses on these questions: Why does the second pendulum begin to swing? Why does the arc of the first pendulum decrease? The science principles in this inquiry include periodic motion and conservation of energy.

The Balloon in Water A balloon is partially inflated, tied shut, and tied to a heavy object. It is dropped into

the bottom of a tall cylinder filled almost to the top with water. A rubber sheet is placed over the top of the cylinder and sealed with a rubber band. The teacher pushes on the rubber cover, and the balloon becomes slightly smaller. When the rubber cover is released, the balloon returns to its original size. The inquiry focuses on why the balloon becomes smaller and then larger again. Principles of science in this inquiry include pressure, gases, liquids and solids, and Newton's first law of motion.

DEDUCTIVE INQUIRY Another form of inquiry teaching is deductive inquiry, which we can contrast with inductive inquiry (Figure 6.13). In this approach to inquiry, the teacher presents a generalization, principle, or concept, and then engages students in one or more inquiry activities to help understand the concept. For example, suppose the teacher's lesson plan calls for the introduction to the differences between physical and chemical weathering. The lesson begins with an explanation of physical weathering. Next the teacher discusses the attributes of chemical weathering. During the discussion of physical weathering the teacher would talk about various types of mechanical weathering, including frost action, drying, and cracking. Chemical weathering processes such as carbonation, oxidation, hydration, and leaching would be introduced.

After the development of the major concepts through presentation and questioning, the teacher engages the students in an inquiry activity in which they explore the concepts of physical and chemical weathering. One approach that has been successful with these concepts is as follows: The teacher places in individual trays examples of earth materials that have been affected by either physical or chemical weathering (e.g., rocks with cracks, soil, mud cracks, plants growing in cracks in

INQUIRY ACTIVITY 6.3

 ### Inductive versus Deductive Inquiry

In this activity you will examine some secondary science textbooks and make decisions about how inductive and deductive inquiry learning could be implemented.

Materials

- A secondary science textbook

Procedure

1. Examine the textbook and identify a chapter that interests you. Identify in the chapter the flow of concepts and how they are presented in the text.
2. Design the chapter inductively. That is, organize a series of lessons (describe them very briefly) in which the students will be introduced to the main concepts inductively.
3. Now design the chapter deductively. Organize a series of lessons in which the students will be introduced to the main concepts deductively.

Minds-On Strategies

1. What did you discover about inductive versus deductive teaching?
2. In which manner was the textbook organized, inductively or deductively?
3. Which model do you think is better for student learning? Why?

---

rocks, staining evident in the minerals of rocks). Working in teams, students study each tray and hypothesize what caused the changes they observe. After all teams have investigated each tray, students write their hypotheses on a large chart on the chalkboard. The teacher leads a post-activity discussion in which the students defend their hypotheses.

Most of the science textbooks written for middle and secondary science courses contain hands-on activities that reinforce the deductive inquiry approach. If the activities are used in the context of deductive inquiry they can be extremely helpful in aiding student understanding of the concepts in the course.

Discovery Learning

Discovery learning, a concept advocated by Jerome Bruner, is at the essence of how students learn concepts and ideas. Bruner talked about the "act of discovery" as if it were a performance on the part of the student. To Bruner, discovery "is in its essence a matter of re-arranging or transforming evidence in such a way that one

is enabled to go beyond the evidence so reassembled to new insights."[36] Bruner believed that discovery learning could only take place if the teacher and student worked together in a cooperative mode. He called this type of teaching "hypothetical teaching" and differentiated it from "expository teaching." Chapter 1 referred to these forms of teaching as "engagement" versus "delivery."

Discovery learning in the science classroom engages students in science activities designed to help then assimilate new concepts and principles. Discovery activities help guide students to assimilate new information. In such activities students will be engaged in observing, measuring, inferring, predicting, and classifying.

There are a number of practical suggestions that you can implement to foster discovery learning in the classroom:

1. *Encourage curiosity.* Because the student in discovery learning is the active agent in learning, the science teacher should foster an atmosphere of

curiosity. Discrepant events and inquiry activities are excellent ways to foster curiosity. Creating interesting and thought-provoking bulletin boards is another way to arouse curiosity.

2. *Help students understand the structure of the new information.* Bruner stressed that students should understand the structure of the information to be learned. He felt that teachers needed to organize the information in a way that would be most easily grasped by the student. Bruner suggested that knowledge could be structured by a set of actions, by means of graphics, or by means of symbols or logical statements. Demonstrating the behavior of objects is a more powerful way for some students to grasp Newton's laws of motion, rather than by the three classic verbal statements.

3. *Design inductive science labs or activities.* The use of inductive science activities is based on the assumption that the teacher is aware of the generalization, principle, or concept that the students are to discover. An inductive lab or activity is designed so that the student is actively engaged in observing, measuring, classifying, predicting, and inferring. Generally speaking, the teacher provides the specific cases, situations, or examples that students will investigate as they are guided to make conceptual discoveries. An example of an inductive science activity is the footprint puzzle (Figure 6.14), in which students are guided to make discoveries about the behavior and environment of dinosaurs. After the students have explored the footprint puzzle and have written at least three alternative hypotheses to explain the tracks, the teacher leads a discussion to help the students discover some concepts about the dinosaurs.

One of the points Bruner made about discovery was that it is the result of making things simpler for the student. In science, making the science concepts simpler through inductive activities is a far more powerful approach than presenting vast amounts of information about the concept.

4. *Encourage students to develop coding systems.* Coding systems help students make connections among objects and phenomena. Bruner felt that students could learn the method of discovery— the heuristics of discovery—if provided with many puzzling situations. For example, giving students a box of rocks and asking them to invent a classification system of their own would help them understand the principles of coding and

Figure 6.14 Dinosaur Footprint Activity. Give cooperative teams the footprint puzzle. Ask students to observe the footprint and then to generate at least three hypotheses to explain the events in the puzzle. *Source:* Earth Science Curriculum Project. *Investigating the Earth, Teachers Guide, Part II.* Boston, Mass.: Houghton-Mifflin Company, © 1967. American Geological Institute.

classification. The computer is a powerful learning tool in this regard. Programs are available to enable students to practice working with puzzling situations and develop expertise in coding.

5. *Design activities that are problem oriented.* Students need to be engaged in problem solving on a regular basis if they are to learn about the heuristics of discovery. Bruner said, "It is my hunch that it is only through the exercise of problem solving and the effort of discovery that one learns the working heuristics of discovery."[37] In short, he said that students need practice in problem solving or inquiry in order to understand

discovery. Activities that are problem oriented often have a simplistic ring to them. For example, here are some problems, any one of which could be a learning activity for students:

- Find a million of something and prove it.
- Go outside and find evidence for change.

6. *Foster intuitive thinking in the classroom.* To Bruner, intuitive thinking implied grasping the meaning, significance, or structure of a problem without explicit analytical evidence or action. Here is where Bruner thought that playfulness in learning was important. Students in a classroom whose teacher values intuition know that it is acceptable to play with all sorts of combinations, extrapolations, and guesses—and still be wrong. Including some science activities that encourage guessing and estimating will foster intuitive thinking. Qualitative activities in which students are not encouraged to find a specific answer to a problem will encourage intuitive thought.

Project-Based Science Inquiry

Project-based science as a method of inquiry can be used to teach problem-solving skills and engage students in the investigation of real problems. Don't be fooled by questions and problems that appear at the end of the chapters in science textbooks. For the most part, these "problems" are merely questions that require students to look up the answer in the text or plug in the numbers of a formula.

Project-based science in the context of inquiry engages students in problems that are real and relevant to them. The problems do not have to be ones that students generate (although this approach is probably more powerful). They can be problems that the teacher has presented to the students for investigation. Science, unfortunately, is often presented in textbooks as "problem-free." That is, the content of science is arranged in a very neat and tidy way. The truth of the matter is that science is often messy, cluttered, and full of problems.

Implementing project-based science inquiry will support a sociocultural approach to science teaching and increase the possibility that more students will be reached and find success in science class.

Other Models

We have presented three types of models based on behavioral, constructivist, and sociocultural learning theory. Next, several additional science teaching models are described to extend the previous three models.

Synectics

Synectics is a process in which metaphors are used to make the strange familiar and the familiar strange. Synectics can be used to help students understand concepts and solve problems. Synectics was developed by William J. J. Gordon for use in business and industry, but it has also been used an innovative model in education.

According to Gordon, "the basic tools of learning are analogies that serve as connectors between the new and the familiar. They enable students to connect facts and feelings of their experience with the facts that they are just learning." Gordon goes on to say, "good teaching traditionally makes ingenious use of analogies and metaphors to help students visualize content. For example, the subject of electricity typically is introduced through the analogue of the flow of water in pipes."[38] Synectics can be used in the concept introduction phase of the conceptual change teaching model.

The synectics procedure for developing students' connection-making skills goes beyond merely presenting helpful comparisons and actually evokes metaphors and analogies from the students themselves. Students learn how to learn by developing the skills to produce their own connective metaphors.

Gordon and colleagues, otherwise known as SES Associates, have developed texts and reference materials and provide training to help teachers implement synectics into the classroom.[39]

In the following synectics activity example, students learn to examine simple analogies and discuss how they relate to each other.

- Give students analogies and then ask them to explain how the content (the heart) and the analogue (water pump) are alike. Here are some examples:

    a. The heart and water pump
    b. Orbits of electrons and orbits of planets
    c. The nucleus of an atom and a billiard ball
    d. Location of electrons in an atom and droplets of water in a cloud
    e. Small blood vessels and river tributaries
    f. The human brain and a computer
    g. The human eye and a camera

- After students feel skillful linking the strange with the familiar, challenge them to create analogies for concepts they are studying.

Person-Centered Learning Model

The person-centered model of teaching focuses on the facilitation of learning and is based on the work of Carl

Rogers and other humanistic educators and psychologists.[40] The model is based on giving students freedom not only to choose the methods of learning, but to engage in the discussion of the content as well. In practical terms, the person-centered model can be implemented within limits. Rogers believed, as do other psychologists, that making choices is an integral aspect of being a human being, and is at the heart of learning. Rogers also advocated trusting the individual to make choices, believing that it was the only way to help people understand the consequences of their choices.

There are several aspects of the person-centered model that appeal to the science teacher: the role of the teacher in the learning process and the creation of a learning environment conducive to inquiry learning.

THE TEACHER AS A FACILITATOR To implement a person-centered approach, the teacher must take on the role of a facilitator of student learning rather than a dispenser of knowledge or information. Three elements seem to characterize the teacher who assumes the role of learning facilitator: realness, acceptance, and empathy. In the person-centered model, to show realness, a teacher must be genuine and willing to express feelings of all sorts—from anger and sadness to joy and exhilaration. In the person-centered model, the teacher acts as counselor, guide, and coach, and to be effective he or she must be real with the students.

Rogers also advocated and stressed the importance of accepting the other person—indeed prizing the person and acknowledging that he or she is trustworthy and can be held responsible for their behavior.

Finally, to Rogers at least, the most important element in this triad was empathy. Empathy is a form of understanding without judgment or evaluation. Empathy in the science classroom is especially important in developing positive attitudes and helping students who have been turned off to science to begin to move toward it.

Naturally, there are more than these three elements to being a learning facilitator. Technical aspects are involved as well, such as setting up a classroom environment conducive to learning, providing learning materials, and structuring lessons that encourage person-centered learning.

THE PERSON-CENTERED ENVIRONMENT AND INQUIRY In the person-centered classroom, students are encouraged to ask questions, choose content, decide on methods and resources, explore concepts and theories, and find out things on their own and in small teams. Clearly these are elements that foster inquiry.

Teachers who truly implement inquiry will find themselves fostering the attitude advocated by person-centered educators. Here is a checklist of elements that signal the existence of a person-centered environment:[41]

- A climate of trust is established in the classroom in which curiosity and the natural desire to learn can be nourished and enhanced.
- A participatory mode of decision making is applied to all aspects of learning and students, teachers, and administrators each have a part in it.
- Students are encouraged to prize themselves, to build their confidence and self-esteem.
- Excitement in intellectual and emotional discovery is fostered, which leads students to become lifelong learners.

Integrative Learning Model

Imagine for a moment a physics classroom. After the students have come in and seem ready to begin class, the teacher says that they are going to begin a new unit on mechanics. He begins the lesson by getting students (and himself) to stand in a circle and begin passing a tennis ball around. At first the teacher tells the students to pass the ball at a constant speed or velocity. Then he says, "Accelerate the ball!" Then, after a few moments, "Now, decelerate it!" The teacher now turns the activity into a game: Students may take turns calling out "constant velocity," "accelerate," and "decelerate." As simple and unusual as this activity is, this teacher has a reputation in the school for doing such activities in his physics class.

In another school, an earth science teacher is playing classical music while she reads a story to the class about how the giant continent of Pangaea broke up and drifted apart, creating new ocean basins, pushing rocks together to form huge mountain chains, and causing earthquakes and volcanoes. After the story, students get into small groups to collaborate and create a metaphor of the story (e.g., a drawing, a clay model, or a diagram).

The head of the biology department is seen taking her students outside (once again). This time, the teacher explains that the students are going on a "still hunt." The students are assigned to sit in an area of the school grounds (this school has a wooded area to which the teacher takes the class quite often). For five minutes the students sit in their assigned area watching for the presence of organisms—ants, spiders, earthworms, birds, mammals—anything that they can see. They are asked to observe and to record their observations in a naturalists notebook. The students are assembled at the edge of wood and report their findings from the still hunt. Then the teacher gives the students modeling clay, string, paper, yarn, buttons, cloth, toothpicks, and so on, and says, "Design an animal that will fit into this environment but will be difficult to be seen by other animals." When the creatures are completed, students place them in "their habitat." The teacher then has the whole class walk through the area looking for the creatures to find out how well they were designed to survive unnoticed in their environment.

Each of these teachers is implementing a model of learning that some refer to as integrative learning. It is a model of learning that suggests that all students can learn with a limitless capacity and that students can learn by interacting with their "environment freely, responding to any and all aspects of it without erecting barriers between them."[42]

The learning cycle used in the integrative learning model consists of three phases: input, synthesis, and output. Equal emphasis is placed on all three phases. The origin of integrative learning can be traced to Georgi Lozanov, of the University of Sophia (Bulgaria). Lozanov had discovered a method of learning that involved the use of music to help relax the learner, the creation of an atmosphere in which the mind is not limited, presentation of new material to be learned with what is called an "active concert," followed by a period of relaxation, and ending with a series of games and activities to apply the new material that was learned.[43] The Lozonov method made its way to the United States and can be found in such work as superlearning, accelerated learning, whole brain learning, and so forth. Peter Kline, developer of integrative learning, has stressed the importance of student synthesis and output in learning.[44] In the integrative classroom, the teacher encourages students to use their personal styles of learning,[45] and thus provides auditory, kinesthetic, visual, print-oriented, and interactive learning activities. Music, movement, color, mini-fieldtrip, painting, the use of clay, pair and small-group discussion are vital components of the integrated learning model.

Imagineering

Imagineering, a model of teaching developed by Alan J. McCormack, is designed to encourage visual/spatial thinking.[46] McCormack explains that imagineering is the result of fusing parts of the words "imagination" and "engineering." Imagineering is designed to apply existing scientific knowledge to visualizing solutions to challenging problems. McCormack, who is well known for his presentations at local, state, and national science teacher meetings, advocates the use of teacher demonstrations to set the stage for imagineering. He has

designed an array of imagineering activities that can be used in any science curriculum.[47]

SECTION 2: SCIENCE TEACHER GAZETTE

Volume 6: Models of Science Teaching

Think Pieces

1. Create a poster report that conveys the meaning of any one of the models of teaching presented in this chapter. Assume that you will present the poster at a local science teacher conference whose theme is: "Effective Models and Strategies of Science Teaching for the Twenty-First Century."

2. Design a graphic representation of your model of teaching. Don't be afraid to be inventive, and realize that creative thinking involves combining elements of other ideas. Present your model in class.

3. Which of the following models of teaching do you prefer?
   a. Direct/interactive teaching
   b. Inductive inquiry
   c. Cooperative learning
   d. Integrative learning
   e. Person-centered learning

4. Prepare a brief speech (three to five minutes) in which you identify the characteristics of your favorite model and explain why you prefer it to the other models. (And, of course, you can use visual aids if you are called on to give the speech!)

 Case Study: Hugging a Tree

The Case

David Brown is an undergraduate student who has been granted permission to student teach in his former high school because it is the type of school he in which he would like to teach.[48] The high school, however, is located 200 miles from David's university. His college supervisor, Dr. Ahrens, associate professor of biology, is not enthused about having to drive the distance to supervise David. Ahrens is under pressure to conduct research and publish the results, and he is having difficulty finding the time to do so. Furthermore, some of his younger colleagues are already full professors and are receiving federal grants for their research.

David was accepted with open arms at his "old" high school, and the department head assigned Bob Smith, one of David's favorite high school teachers, as his cooperating teacher. On his first biweekly visit to supervise David, Dr. Ahrens witnesses performance unlike anything he has ever witnessed in fifteen years of supervising student teachers. The lesson topic focused on trees. David had gotten up at daybreak and gone into a wooded area to collect leaves. But what Dr. Ahrens saw was much more than a leaf collection. David had brought tree limbs—dozens of them—and the classroom looked like an arboretum.

Dr. Ahrens entered through the door at the back of the room and quietly sat down. As usual, he prepared to take notes and complete an assessment form, and he quickly became so surprised by David's activities that he forgot to complete the form. David was running from one part of the room, to another, and then another, taking limbs and small trees with leaves and giving them to students to examine. First he had the students taste the sassafras leaves. Some comments about root beer were made. Then David took a double handful of sweet shrubs and crushed them. As he walked down each row of students, letting every student smell them, the students "oohed" and "aahed." Next, David gave each student a leaf from a cherry tree. He asked them to break the leaves in half and sniff them to see who could tell him the type of tree these leaves came from. Some students said that they smelled like a milkshake. Others said the smell reminded them of the chocolate-covered cherry candy that they get at Christmas. After a wisecrack guess that it was a Christmas tree, someone screamed, "cherry."

Next, David displayed some yellow roots. He asked the students to take a small hair of the root and taste it. They roots were as bitter as quinine and students gasped in exaggerated disapproval of the bitter taste; some ran to the door and spat outside. By the end of the period, every student was grappling with a piece of sugar cane, twisting it and swallowing the sweet juice. When the bell rang the students applauded and commented about the lesson. Some said that this is the way school ought to be—fun. David was pleased that the students received the lesson so well.

Dr. Ahrens realized that he had become so engaged with observing the activities and so bewildered and upset at having seen something that didn't even resemble a lesson that he failed to complete the rating instrument and was, therefore, unprepared for the assessment conference that was to follow. Nevertheless, he felt he must give David some badly needed feedback, however general. He would spare no words for this young maverick.

For Dr. Ahrens, the first step toward resolving the perceived disaster was to meet with Bob Smith, David's cooperating teacher. After sharing a few brief pleasantries, he fired the following questions at Mr. Smith:

"What do you think about this lesson?"

"The kids were really excited over it."

"Would you say that this was typical of David's lessons?"

"Yes, he always gets the students fired up."

"Do you think the lesson was well structured, well planned?"

"He obviously kept things moving at a good pace, and he didn't run out of material."

"Does David usually give you a well-prepared lesson plan when he teaches?"

"David has the type of personality that enables him to move through the lesson well without a written plan. I think lesson plans are good if you need them, but they can handicap a natural teacher. David knows that as long as his lessons work, I really don't insist on seeing a written lesson plan," Smith stated.

From this brief conversation, Dr. Ahrens concluded that he would get little help from this lackadaisical teacher. In fact, he assumed Mr. Smith was influencing David negatively by providing a loose, unstructured role model. Clearly, it was time to talk to David.

Dr. Ahrens began the session by asking David what he thought he was doing. He continued, "I drove 200 miles to watch you teach, and instead you provided a circus. My job is to help you raise the achievement scores in this class. From our pre–student-teaching seminar you learned that effective teachers give clear goals, hold high expectations, use direct instruction, and closely supervise all assignments. Instead of following this instructional model, you arranged for a disorganized, student-centered picnic, complete with refreshments. I am very disappointed. I will have to record these activities and place the report in your permanent records."

David was shocked. What could he do to salvage his student-teaching grade and his teaching career?

The Problem

Put yourself in David's place. What would you do?

REFLECTIVE TEACHING LESSON 6.1

 "Creatures"

All of these are Mellinarks.

None of these is a Mellinark.

Which of these are Mellinarks?

Description

You are one of several members of the class chosen to teach this short science lesson to a small group of your classmates. Plan to teach it in such a way that you believe both student learning and satisfaction will result.

Your Objective

Your goal is to get as many learners as possible to classify a set of "creatures" based on their similarities and differences

Materials

- The creatures (copy them from Figure 6.15)
- Learner satisfaction forms (see Figure 6.2)

Figure 6.15 Creatures. *Source:* From A. E. Lawson, M. R. Abraham, and J. W. Renner. *A Theory of Instruction.* Used with permission. Kansas State University Manhettan, K. S. National Association for Research in Science Teaching, 1989.

REFLECTIVE TEACHING LESSON 6.2

 Shark's Teeth

Description

You are one of several members of the class chosen to teach this short science lesson to a small group of your classmates. Plan to teach it in such a way that you believe both student learning and satisfaction will result.

Your Objective

Your goal is to get as many learners as possible to make observations and inferences about shark's teeth.

Materials

- Shark's teeth (if you cannot find any, use an interesting substitute)
- Learner satisfaction forms (see Figure 6.2)

Special Conditions

Learners can hold shark's teeth but cannot look at them during the lesson.

The Balloon Blower Upper

Description

You are one of several members of the class chosen to teach this short science lesson to a small group of your classmates. Plan to teach it in such a way that you believe both student learning and satisfaction will result.

Your Objective

Your goal is to get as many learners as possible to propose at least two hypotheses to explain the "balloon blower upper" phenomenon.

Materials

- Soda pop bottle
- Balloon
- Vinegar
- Baking soda
- Aluminum foil
- Learner satisfaction forms (see Figure 6.2)

Special Conditions

Make sure you have the demonstration set up so that the students cannot see the baking soda or that the liquid is vinegar. To make the demonstration work, wrap the bottle with foil. Fill the bottle about a quarter full with vinegar. Pour a small amount of baking soda in a balloon. Carefully cover the mouth of bottle with the balloon. The powder falls in and reacts with the vinegar, making the balloon blower upper work. Up goes the balloon! (See Figure 6.16.)

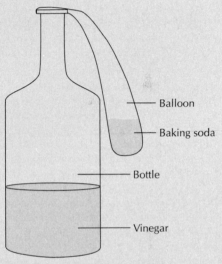

Figure 6.16 Balloon Blower Upper.

Mission to Mars

Description

You are one of several members of the class chosen to teach this short science lesson to a small group of your classmates. Plan to teach it in such a way that you believe both student learning and satisfaction will result.

Your Objective

Your goal is to get as many learners as possible to disagree with NASA's desire to jointly plan and execute a manned mission to the planet Mars in the early part of the 21st century.

Materials

- Learner satisfaction forms (see Figure 6.2), pre-test and post-test

Special Conditions

Discussions have been held among scientists and administrators from NASA and the Russian space program about the possibility of sending a joint mission to Mars. Although this seems like a beneficial scientific undertaking, your job is to get your learners to disagree with NASA and the Russians. You may want to consider the following: cost; there are problems on earth to solve first; the moon might be a better place to go; a station on the moon would be less expensive and more beneficial.

Test

Use Figure 6.17 as pre-test and post-test.

	Strongly Disagree	Disagree	Agree	Strongly Agree
1. The United States, China, Japan, Europe, and Russia should combine efforts and send a manned mission to Mars.				
2. The cost of the mission is well worth the potential benefits to humankind.				
3. Before such a mission takes place, we should resolve all problems facing us on earth.				

Figure 6.17 Mission to Mars Pre/Post Test.

CONSTRUCTIVISM AS A REFERENT FOR SCIENCE TEACHING

Anthony Lorsbach and Kenneth Tobin

Introduction

Why is it, in educational settings, we rarely talk about how students learn?[49] Why aren't teachers using how students learn as a guide to their teaching practices? These questions seem almost too absurd to ask; but think, when was the last time you spoke to colleagues about how students learn? Do you observe learning in your classroom? What does it look like? These are a few of the questions that we have begun to ask ourselves and our teaching colleagues.

One way to make sense of how students learn is through constructivism. Constructivism is a word used frequently by science educators lately. It is used increasingly as a theoretical rationale for research and teaching. Many current reform efforts also are associated with the notion of constructivism. But what exactly is constructivism and how can it be useful to the practicing teacher?

Constructivism is an epistemology, a theory of knowledge used to explain how we know what we know. We believe that a constructivist epistemology is useful to teachers if used as a referent; that is, as a way to make sense of what they see, think, and do. Our research indicates that teachers' beliefs about how people learn (their personal epistemology), whether verbalized or not, often help them make sense of, and guide, their practice.

The epistemology that is dominant in most educational settings today is similar to objectivism. That is to say, most researchers view knowledge as existing outside the bodies of cognizing beings, as beings separate from knowing and knowers. Knowledge is "out there," residing in books, independent of a thinking being. Science is then conceptualized as a search for truths, a means of discovering theories, laws, and principles associated with reality. Objectivity is a major component of the search for truths which underlie reality; learners are encouraged to view objects, events, and phenomenon with an objective mind, which is assumed to be separate from cognitive processes such as imagination, intuition, feelings, values, and beliefs. As a result, teachers implement a curriculum to ensure that students cover relevant science content and have opportunities to learn truths which usually are documented in bulging textbooks. The constructivist epistemology asserts that the only tools available to a knower are the senses. It is only through seeing, hearing, touching, smelling, and tasting that an individual interacts with the environment. With these messages from the senses, the individual builds a picture of the world.

Therefore, constructivism asserts that knowledge resides in individuals; that knowledge cannot be transferred intact from the head of a teacher to the heads of students. The student tries to make sense of what is taught by trying to fit it with his/her experience.

Consequently, words are not containers whose meanings are in the words itself, they are based on the constructions of individuals. We can communicate because individuals' meanings of words only have to be compatible with the meanings given by others. If a situation occurred in which your meaning of a word no longer sufficed, you could change the meaning of the word. Using constructivism as a referent, teachers often use problem solving as a learning strategy; where learning is defined as adaptations made to fit the world they experience. That is, to learn, a person's existing conceptions of the world must be unreliable, inviable. When one's conceptions

of the world are inviable one tries to make sense out of the situation based on what is already known (i.e., prior knowledge is used to make sense of data perceived by the senses). Other persons are part of our experiential world, thus, others are important for meaning making.

"Others" are so important for constructivists that cooperative learning is a primary teaching strategy. A cooperative learning strategy allows individuals to test the fit of their experiential world with a community of others. Others help to constrain our thinking. The interactions with others cause perturbations, and by resolving the perturbations individuals make adaptations to fit their new experiential world.

Experience involves an interaction of an individual with events, objects, or phenomenon in the universe; an interaction of the senses with things, a personal construction which fits some of the external reality but does not provide a match. The senses are not conduits to the external world through which truths are conducted into the body. Objectivity is not possible for thinking beings. Accordingly, knowledge is a construction of how the world works, one that is viable in the sense that it allows an individual to pursue particular goals.

Thus, from a constructivist perspective, science is not the search for truth. It is a process that assists us to make sense of our world. Using a constructivist perspective, teaching science becomes more like the science that scientists do it is an active, social process of making sense of experiences, as opposed to what we now call "school science." Indeed, actively engaging students in science (we have all heard the call for "hands-on, minds-on science") is the goal of most science education reform. It is an admirable goal, and using constructivism as a referent can possibly assist in reaching that goal.

Driver has used a constructivist epistemology as a referent in her research on children's conceptions of science.[50] Children's prior knowledge of phenomena from a scientific point of view differs from the interpretation children construct; children construct meanings that fit their experience and expectations. This can lead children to oftentimes construct meanings different from what was intended by a teacher. Teachers who make sense of teaching from an objectivist perspective fail to recognize that students solve this cognitive conflict by separating school science from their own life experiences. In other words, students distinguish between scientific explanations and their "real world" explanations (the often cited example that forces are needed to keep a ball in motion versus Newton's explanation is one such example). Children's conceptions are their constructions of reality, ones that are viable in the sense that they allow a child to make sense of his/her environment. By using a constructivist epistemology as a referent teachers can become more sensitive to children's prior knowledge and the processes by which they make sense of phenomena.

The teaching practices of two teachers at City Middle School may best illustrate how practice can be influenced by making sense of teaching and learning from constructivist- and objectivist-oriented perspective. To Bob, science was a body of knowledge to be learned. His job was to "give out" what he (and the textbook) knew about science to his students. Thus the learning environment Bob tried to maintain in his classroom facilitated this transfer of knowledge; the desks were neatly in rows facing Bob and the blackboard. Lectures and assignments from the text were given to students. Bob tried to keep students quiet and working all during the class period to ensure that all students could "absorb" the science knowledge efficiently. Another consequence of Bob's notion of teaching and learning was his belief that he had so much cover that he had no time for laboratory activities.

Let's look at an example that typifies Bob's teaching style. Bob's sixth grade students were to complete a worksheet that "covered" the concept of friction. After the students completed the worksheet, Bob went over the answers so the students could have the correct answers for the test later in the week. From a constructivist perspective, what opportunities did Bob's students have to relate the concept of friction to their own experiences? Were these opportunities in Bob's lesson plan to negotiate meanings and build a consensus of understanding? Bob spent one class period covering the concept of friction; is that sufficient time for students to learn a concept with understanding?

On the other hand, John made sense of teaching and learning from a constructivist perspective. John's classes were student centered and activity-based. Typically in his high school classes, John introduced students to different science topics with short lectures, textbook readings, and confirmatory laboratories. After the introduction John would ask students what interested them about the topic and encourage them to pursue and test these ideas. Students usually divided themselves into groups and then conducted a library research, formulated questions/problems, and procedures to test the questions/problems. In other words, the students were acting as scientists in the classroom. Like Bob, John taught a sixth grade class previously, and also taught students about friction. Included in John's lessons were activities to "get the students involved." Students rubbed their hands together with and without a lubricant so that they could see the purpose of motor oil in engines. The students conducted experiments with bricks to learn about different types of friction, and even watched *The Flintstones* in class to point out friction and what would really happen (e.g., Fred would burn his feet stopping the car, etc.). John spent two weeks teaching his unit on friction. Were John's students given opportunities to make sense of the concept of friction? Were they able to use personal experiences? Whose students do you think had a deeper understanding of friction?

Our research also indicates that as teachers made transitions from objectivist- to constructivist-oriented thoughts and behaviors their classroom practices changed radically.[51] It seemed as if many traditional practices no longer made sense to teachers. Specifically, teachers recognized that learning and making sense of what happens rests ultimately with the individual learners. Learners need time to experience, reflect on their experiences in relation to what they already know, and resolve any problems that arise. Accordingly, learners need time to clarify, elaborate, describe, compare, negotiate, and reach consensus on what specific experiences mean to them. This learning process must occur within the bodies of individuals, however, the inner voices of persons can be supplemented by discussion with others.

Therefore, an important part of a constructivist-oriented curriculum should be the negotiation of meaning. Students need to be given opportunities to make sense of what is learned by negotiating meaning; comparing what is known to new experiences, and resolving discrepancies between what is known to new experiences, and resolving discrepancies between what is known and what seems to be implied by new experience. The resolution of discrepancies enables an individual to reach equilibrium in the sense that there should be no remaining curiosity regarding an experience in relation to what is known. Negotiation also can occur between individuals in a classroom. The process involves discussion and attentive listening, making sense of the points of views of theories of peers. When a person understands how a peer is making sense of a point of view, it is then possible to discuss similarities and differences between the theories of peers within a group. Justifying one position over another and selecting those theories that are viable can lead to consensuses that are understood by those within a peer group.

The process of learning should not stop at what has been learned in the negotiation of a class consensus. This process can involve accessing other learning resources such as books, videotapes, and practicing scientists. The consensus negotiated within a class can be adapted by students as they make sense of the theories negotiated in other communities. By engaging in such a process students can realize that what is regarded as a viable theory depends on what is known at the time and the context in which the theory is to be applied. Also they can begin to understand how to select the best theoretical formulation for use in a particular set of circumstances.

For many years the conventional wisdom of teachers has been similar to Bob's teaching style: to control student behavior so that the class is quiet. Indeed research programs have been premised on this assumption. Accordingly, the research literature provides lists of teacher behavior and strategies that have been demonstrated to control students. If this assumption is abandoned there is little research to guide teachers in the selection of practices that are conducive to students constructing knowledge. Instead of managing to keep students quiet and attentive to the teacher, a classroom might be managed to enable students to talk with one another and utilize collaborative learning strategies. Instead of keeping students seated in rows throughout a lesson, a management system might be developed which permits students to move about the classroom and visit the library or a fieldwork station. Manage-

ment is still a priority, but it is subsumed below learning and the implementation of a curriculum that meets the needs of students.

Establishing and maintaining a learning environment that is conducive to learning is a priority for science teachers. However, this is not easy to do. To begin with, traditional teaching practices are sometimes difficult to discard. Teachers might commence a lesson with good intentions only to find that they forget to follow their game plan. We have learned from our research that sustained change can take a long time to establish. John, a third-year teacher, is committed to getting all of his students to accept his style of teaching. Many of his students have an image of teaching of which John's style does not fit. Therefore, students might also have difficulty adapting to an environment in which they are given the responsibility for making sense of science. They too have experienced traditional practices in which they are force-fed a diet of factual information to be rote learned. Many students expect to be controlled and filled up with knowledge. They believe teachers to be the experts whose role is to transfer the knowledge to students, much like one fills a bottle with liquid. If teachers do not fulfill their traditional roles students might be confused and have difficulty engaging as intended by the teacher. Just as teachers have to learn how to teach from a constructivist point of view, so too must students learn how to learn. Educating students to be effective learners is an important priority in establishing environments conducive to effective learning of science.

Reflect on your science teaching. Have you provided students with new knowledge to be memorized and repeated on a test without providing an opportunity for them to make sense of it? Or, have you provided students with an opportunity to use their prior knowledge and senses in making connections to the new concepts you introduced? If, like so many traditional science classrooms, the practices in your classroom are based on objectivism, you might like to commence the challenge of implementing change that accord with constructivism. If you would like to change your teaching practices (to whatever degree), then perhaps by reflecting on your practice from a constructivist point of view you can begin to construct a new vision of your classroom.

Science Teachers Talk

"Is the discovery or inquiry model of teaching important in your approach to teaching? Why?"

BEN BOZA (BOTSWANA): I find the inquiry model of teaching important indeed in my teachings and as an effective method of participatory learning whereby the learners perceive themselves as being responsible for the knowledge they unearth. Utilizing this model gives students the opportunity to discover things by themselves. Unraveling the mystery shrouding a certain new concept by themselves generates the "Eureka!" experience, which actually has a big impact on students. Learners identify with their new knowledge and can easily grasp the logic behind it and how it is applicable.

MICHAEL O'BRIEN: The inquiry model of learning is very important to my approach. I feel that students that explore and find for themselves the ideas and concepts about science are more engaged learners. Specifically, inquiry puts the learning where it belongs, which is with the student—not the teacher. With inquiry-based learning the students are not only engaged in the present but are discovering how to learn for the future.

GINNY ALMEDER: Because science is both a body of knowledge and a process, I value the inquiry learning approach. Knowledge of facts is necessary to develop scientific literacy but having opportunities to apply the knowledge in new contexts in order to develop problem-solving skills is essential. For the teacher, there is a delicate balance between presentation of factual information and the discovery process. However, with careful planning, both approaches can be successfully integrated. For example, after reading introductory material from the text or lab manual, students can be asked to describe the problem of a planned lab activity, devise hypotheses, and make predictions. During the post-lab session, students can discuss alternative hypotheses and experimental design as well as various interpretations of the data and suggestions for further experiments. Projects provide another vehicle for developing problem-solving skills. Individual students can present their proposals or projects and benefit from a class discussion of variables.

JOHN RICCIARDI: The essence of sciencing is discovery; the primary discovery of knowing oneself in relation to one's surrounding. For me, the inquiry learning model is the most important if our focus is first to know oneself—through the process of knowing the envelope of nature around us. As a teacher of astronomy and quantum physics, I must help focus my students' attention to aspects of physical reality that normally are not perceived by our primary senses. The size and distance extremes of an electron and a galaxy super cluster are awesome. We can only know these objects by "blindly touching them in the dark" with our instruments. One prime task in these sciences is to visualize, extrapolate, imagine, and wonder about these things we can't naturally see. This kind of thinking is a real, vital part of science; it unfolds and reveals nature by discovering our own "inner tools" and identity . . . our own potentiality.

JERRY PELLETIER: This learning model is the essence of my science teaching approach. In order for students to truly understand scientific ideas and concepts they must experience them for themselves and question what they observe, hear, and manipulate. Every one of my students is required to participate in a science fair exhibit at school. I feel that this is the most important project in their middle school science education. They are required to use all of the skills that have been developed in our science program: They must develop their own topic, form their own hypothesis, develop an experiment that tests their hypothesis, collect and analyze data, and draw a logical conclusion. This to me is learning. Students questioning, inquiring, observing, solving, and analyzing.

Problems and Extensions

1. Observe a video of a science teacher teaching a lesson. Make anecdotal comments on the chart presented in Figure 6.18, indicating examples of the various models of teaching observed during the lesson. What generalizations can you make about this teacher's approach to teaching? View a video of another teacher and compare the two teachers' approaches to teaching.

Model of Science Teaching	Anecdotal Comments: Examples of how the model was implemented; examples of teacher and student behavior
Direct/Interactive Teaching	
Inductive Inquiry	
Deductive Inquiry	
Discovery Learning	
Project-Based Learning	
Learning Cycle	
Cooperative/Collaborative Learning	
Synectics	
Person-Centered Learning	
Integrative Learning	
Imagineering	

Figure 6.18 Models of Teaching.

2. Present a discrepant event related to specific concepts drawn from earth science, life science, physical science, or environmental science. Your presentation should be brief and should be designed to engage the class in inquiry.

3. Present a five- to ten-minute lesson based on one of the following models of teaching. Write a one-page report on the strengths and weaknesses of the lesson and explain how you would change the lesson if you were to teach it again.

   a. Direct/interactive instruction
   b. Inductive inquiry
   c. Deductive inquiry
   d. Discovery learning
   e. Project-based learning
   f. Conceptual change teaching model
   g. Cooperative/collaborative learning

4. Create a chart in which you analyze at least five models of teaching. Your chart should provide insight into the purpose of the model, the essential characteristics of the model, and under what conditions the model should be used.

5. One criticism of inquiry and discovery methods of science teaching is that this approach takes too much time, and students can learn concepts and skills if presented more directly. Debate this criticism by first taking the side of inquiry and then the side of the criticism. In which were you more convincing? Is there a solution to this problem?

6. Is there a relationship between metaphors of teaching and the models of teaching presented in this chapter? Three metaphors for the nature of teaching are:

   a. *Entertainer:* Teaching is like acting; you're on a stage and you perform.
   b. *Captain of the Ship:* Teaching is like directing and being in charge.
   c. *Resource:* Teaching is making yourself available, assisting, facilitating.[52]

7. Either observe two teachers in their classrooms or observe videotapes of two teachers. Analyze their teaching in terms of the three metaphors. What relationship exists between the perceived metaphor and models of science teaching?

Notes

1. Modified from Bruce Joyce and Marsha Weil, *Models of Teaching* (Englewood Cliffs, N.J.: Prentice-Hall, 1995), p. 2.

2. Based on Richard A. Miller, "Descent from Innocence," in *The Intern Teacher Casebook*, ed. Judith H. Shulman and Joel A. Colbert (Eugene, Ore.: ERIC

Clearninghouse on Educational Management, University of Oregon, 1988), pp. 22–24.

3. Joyce and Weil, *Models of Teaching*. (Upper Saddle River, N.J.: Allyn & Bacon, Inc., 2003)

4. The concept of reflective teaching is based on *Reflective Teaching* (Bloomington, Ind.: Phi Delta Kappa, 1988).

5. There are many learning cycle models. For an excellent discussion of four different models, please refer to Roger Osborne and Peter Freyberg, *Learning in Science: The Implications of Children's Science* (Auckland: Heinemann, 1985), pp. 101–11.

6. Anton E. Lawson, Michael R. Abraham, and John W. Renner, *A Theory of Instruction: Using the Learning Cycle to Teach Science Concepts and Thinking Skills*, NARST Monograph, no. 1 (Manhattan, Kan.: National Association for Research in Science Teaching, 1989), p. 9.

7. Robert Karplus, "Science Teaching and the Development of Reasoning," *Journal of Research in Science Teaching*, 14, no. 2 (1977): 169–75.

8. Charles R. Barman, *An Expanded View of the Learning Cycle: New Ideas about an Effective Teaching Strategy* Monograph and Occasional Paper Series, no. 4 (Arlington, Va.: Council for Elementary Science International, 1990); Anton E. Lawson, Michael R. Abraham, and John W. Renner, *A Theory of Instruction: Using the Learning Cycle to Teach Science Concepts and Thinking Skills*, NARST Monograph, no. 1 (Manhattan, Kan.: National Association for Research in Science Teaching, 1989).

9. Based on Lawson, Abraham, and Renner, *A Theory of Instruction*, pp. 96–99.

10. J. A. Minstrell, "Teaching Science for Understanding," in *Toward the Thinking Curriculum: Current Cognitive Research*, ed. L. B. Resnick and L. E. Klopfer (Alexandria, Va.: Association for Supervision and Curriculum Development, 1989), pp. 129–49.

11. This teaching sequence was slightly modified from Minstrell, "Teaching Science for Understanding."

12. Osborne and Freyberg, *Learning in Science*.

13. The discussion that follows is based on Ibid., pp. 108–11.

14. James Bellanca and Robin Fogarty, *Blueprints for Thinking in the Cooperative Classroom* (Palatine, Ill.: Skylight Publishing, 1991), p. 241.

15. See David Johnson and Roger Johnson on cooperative learning: *Learning Together and Alone* (Englewood Cliffs N.J.: Prentice-Hall, 1976), and *Circles of Learning* (Alexandria, Va.: Association for Supervision and Curriculum Development, 1986).

16. Spencer Kagan, *Cooperative Learning* (San Clemente, Calif.: Kagan Cooperative Learning, 1999).

17. Jack Hassard, *Using Cooperative Learning to Enhance Your Science Instruction* (Bellevue, Wash.: Bureau of Education and Research, 1996), p. 123.

18. Robert Slavin, *Cooperative Learning: Theory, Research, and Practice* (Englewood Cliffs, N.J.: Prentice Hall, 1990).

19. Elizabeth Cohen, *Designing Groupwork: Strategies for the Heterogeneous Classroom* (New York: Teachers' College Press, 1994).

20. See Slavin, *Cooperative Learning*, or *Using Student Team Learning*, 3rd ed. (Baltimore, Md.: Center for Research on Elementary and Middle Schools, The Johns Hopkins University Press, 1986).

21. Eliot Aronson, *The Jigsaw Classroom* (Beverly Hills: Sage Publications, 1978).

22. Shlomo Sharan et al., *Cooperative Learning in the Classroom: Research in Desegregated Schools* (Hillsdale, N.J.: Lawrence Erlbaum Associates, 1984).

23. Spencer Kagan, *Cooperative Learning. Resources for Teachers* (Riverside, Calif.: University of California, 1985).

24. Jack Hassard, *Science Experiences: Cooperative Learning and the Teaching of Science* (Menlo Park, Calif.: Addison-Wesley, 1990).

25. Ibid., pp. 144–45. Used with permission of Addison-Wesley.

26. Clifford A. Hofwold, "Instructional Strategies in the Science Classroom," in *Research with Reach: Science Education*, ed. David Holdzkom and Pamela B. Lutz (Washington, D.C.: National Science Teachers Association, 1984), pp. 43–56.

27. B. Rosenshine, "Advances in Research on Instruction," *Journal of Educational Research*, 88, no. 5 (1995): 262–68.

28. Gary D. Birch, *Effective Teaching Methods* (Upper Saddle River, N.J.: Prentice Hall, 1999).

29. J. Richard Suchman, *Developing Inquiry* (Chicago: Science Research Associates, 1966).

30. John Dewey, *How We think: A Restatement of the Relation of Reflective Thinking to the Education Process* (Boston: D.C. Heath and Company, 1933), p. 9.

31. Charles W. Anderson, J. David Holland, and Annemarie S. Palincsar, "Canonical and Sociocultural Approaches to Research and Reform in Science Education: The Story of Juan and His Group," *The Elementary School Journal* 97, no. 4 (1997): 357–81.

32. Ibid., p. 363.

33. Ibid., pp. 363–64.

34. Suchman, *Developing Inquiry*. Also consult Suchman's *Inquiry Development Program in Physical Science* and *Developing Inquiry in Earth Science*, published by Science Research Associates, Inc.

35. J. Richard Suchman, *Developing Inquiry in Earth Science* (Chicago: Science Research Associates, Inc., 1968), p. 1.

36. Jerome Bruner, *Toward a Theory of Instruction* (Cambridge: Harvard University Press, 1973), p. 6.

37. Ibid., p. 8.

38. W. J. J. Gordon and Tony Poze, "SES Synectics and Gifted Education Today," *Gifted Child Quarterly*, 24, no. 4 (Fall 1980): 147–51.

39. For training and resource materials on synectics, contact: SES Associates, 121 Brattle Street, Cambridge, MA 02138.

40. Carl R. Rogers, *Freedom to Learn* (Columbus, Ohio: Charles E. Merrill Publishing Company, 1983).

41. Paul S. George, *Theory Z School: Beyond Effectiveness* (Columbus, Ohio: National Middle School Association, 1983).

42. Peter Kline, *The Everyday Genius* (Arlington, Va.: Great Ocean Publishers, 1988), p. 65.

43. Geogi Lozanov, *Suggestology and Outlines of Suggestopedy* (New York: Gorden and Breach, 1978).

44. Kline, *Everyday Genius*.

45. B. McCarthy, *About Teaching—4MAT in the Classroom* (Wauconda, Ill.: About Learning, Inc., 2000).

46. Alan J. McCormack, *Visual/Spatial Thinking: An Essential Element of Elementary School Science*, Monograph and Occasional Paper Series (Arlington, Va.: Council for Elementary Science International, 1988).

47. Alan J. McCormack, *Inventors Workshop* (Redding, Calif.: Fearon Teacher Aids, 1991).

48. Based on Theodore J. Kowalski, Roy A. Weaver, and Kenneth T. Henson, *Case Studies on Teaching* (New York: Longman, 1990), pp. 28–32. Used with permission of the publisher.

49. Anthony Lorsback and Kenneth Tobin, *Constructivism as a Referent for Science Teaching*, Research Matters . . . to the Science Teacher Monograph Series, no. 5, ed. F. Lawrenz, K. Cochran, J. Krajcik, and P. Simpson (Manhattan, Kan.: National Association for Research in Science Teaching, 1992). Used with permission.

50. R. Driver, "Changing Conceptions," in *Adolescent Development and School Science*, ed. P. Adey (London: Falmer Press, 1989).

51. See A. W. Lorsbach, K. Tobin, C. Briscoe, and S. U. LaMaster, "An Interpretation of Assessment Methods in Middle School Science," *International Journal of Science Education* (in press), and K. Tobin, "Conceptualizing Teaching Roles in Terms of Metaphors and Beliefs Sets" (paper presented at the annual meeting of the American Educational Research Association, 1990).

52. Based on Kenneth Tobin, Jane Butler Kahle, and Barry J. Fraser, *Windows into Science Classrooms* (London: Falmer Press, 1990), pp. 51–56.

Readings

Anderson, Charles W., Holland, J. David, and Palincsar, Annemarie S. "Canonical and Sociocultural Approaches to Research and Reform in Science Education: The Story of Juan and His Group." *The Elementary School Journal* 97, no. 4 (1997): 357–381.

Bellanca, James, and Robin Fogarty. *Blueprints for Thinking in the Cooperative Classroom*. Palatine, Ill.: Skylight Publishing, 1991.

Borich, Gary D. *Effective Teaching Methods*. Columbus, Ohio: Merrill, 1988.

Gilbert, Andrew, and Yerrick, Randy. "Same School, Separate Worlds: A Sociocultural Study of Identity, Resistance, and Negotiation in a Rural, Lower Track Science Classroom." *Journal of Research in Science Teaching* 38, no. 5 (2001): 574–98.

Hassard, Jack. *Science Experiences: Cooperative Learning and the Teaching of Science*. Menlo Park, Calif.: Addison-Wesley, 1990.

Joyce, Bruce, and Weil, Marsha. *Models of Teaching*. Englwood Cliffs, N.J.: Prentice-Hall, 2003.

Lemke, J. L. "Articulating Communities: Sociocultural Perspectives on Science Education." *Journal of Research in Science Teaching* 38, no. 3 (2001): 296–316.

Lord, Thomas R. "101 Reasons for Using Cooperative Learning in Biology Teaching." *American Biology Teacher* 63, no. 1 (2001): 30–38.

Nichols, Sharon E., and Tobin, Kenneth. "Discursive Practice among Teachers' Co-Learning During Field-Based Elementary Science Teacher Preparation." *Action in Teacher Education* 22, no. 2A (2000): 45–54.

Osborne, Roger, and Peter Freyberg. *Learning in Science: The Implications of Children's Science*. Auckland: Heinemann, 1985.

Polman, Joseph L. *Designing Project-Based Science: Connecting Learners Through Guided Inquiry*. New York: Teachers College Press, 2000.

Polman, Joseph L., and Pea, Roy D. "Transformative Communication As a Cultural Tool for Guiding Inquiry Science." *Science Education* 85, no. 3 (2001): 223–38.

Rogers, Carl. *Freedom to Learn for the 1980s*. Columbus, Ohio: Merrill, 1983.

Rowlands, Stuart. "Turning Vygotsky on His Head: Vygotsky's 'Scientifically Based Method' and the Socioculturalist's 'Social Other.'" *Science and Education* 9, no. 6 (November 2000): 537–75.

On the Web

Eisenhower National Clearinghouse: http://www.enc.org. This site provides a wealth of resources on science teaching, including lessons plans and project ideas.

Institute for Inquiry: http://www.exploratorium.edu/IFI/index.html. The Exploratorium Institute for Inquiry provides workshops, programs, online support, and an intellectual community of practice, which afford science reform educators a deep and rich experience of how inquiry learning looks and feels.

Science Links: http://www.sciencenetlinks.com/index.cfm. Providing a wealth of resources for K–12 science educators, Science NetLinks is your guide to meaningful standards-based Internet experiences for students.

Kathy Schrock's Guide for Educators: http://discoveryschool.com/schrockguide. This guide features a classified list of sites on the Internet found to be useful for enhancing curriculum and teacher professional growth. The site is updated daily and is searchable.

Cornell Theory Center Math Science Gateway: http://www.tc.cornell.edu/Edu/MathSciGateway/. This gateway provides links to resources in mathematics and science for educators and students in grades 9–12, although teachers of other levels also may find these materials helpful.

Designing Science Units and Courses of Study

It's the night before the first day of school, and the teacher can't sleep! First days are full of anxieties for teachers. What will the students be like? Will they like me? Am I ready for them? Do I have all my textbooks? Will I have the supplies I need? Why did the department head assign me four sections of survey biology and one section of survey earth science? Are my lesson plans written? One way to minimize these anxieties is to invest quality time in the preparation and development of teaching plans.

Question: What do the following concepts have in common?

- Concept planning maps
- Intended learning outcomes
- Working in cooperative planning teams
- Rationale
- Cognitions
- Cognitive skills
- Affects
- Psychomotor skills
- Brainstorming
- Performance assessments
- Portfolios

Answer: They are some of the elements that make up a dynamic and effective strategy that science teachers can use to design and assess learning materials for the science classroom.

Designing science units and courses of study is the focus of this chapter, which is organized to allow you to design science teaching plans as you work through the chapter. Planning and assessment are integral aspects of the process of teaching and you will find that the next chapter is devoted to assessment. You will need to look ahead to Chapter 8 when you work on the assessment strategy for you teaching plans.

How to Read This Chapter

This chapter has been organized to help you design a unit of science teaching, which will be called a miniunit. It is advisable that you work through this chapter from beginning to end. When you finish the chapter, you will have created the following products:

1. A rationale for a science unit, including general science education goals.
2. A list of objectives (we'll call them intended outcomes) for a science unit, grouped according to type of student learning.
3. A concept map showing the relationships among the central ideas in your unit.
4. An instructional plan (a set of lesson plans) describing the unit, including the intended learning objectives and the strategies you will employ to help students achieve them.
5. An assessment plan describing measures to assess the major objectives of the unit to provide feedback to the students and feedback for you on the effectiveness of your science unit.

SECTION 1: DESIGNING SCIENCE ACTIVITIES AND UNITS

Invitations to Inquiry

- What is pedagogical content knowledge? How is it different than content knowledge?
- What processes can be used to design an instructional plan?
- How should a teacher proceed to develop a miniunit of instruction?

- What are intended learning outcomes? How do cognitions, affects, cognitive skills, and psycho-motor skills differ?
- How can cognitive maps be utilized in the planning and development of teaching materials?
- What are the elements of the following types of lessons: direct/interactive, cooperative learning, constructivist, and inquiry/laboratory?
- What are the elements of a course of study?

Pedagogical Content Knowledge

In this chapter you will apply your knowledge of science to develop teaching materials to help students understand science. But you probably realize that being able to help students understand science is not a matter of giving them your content knowledge of science. There is a special kind of knowledge that you are developing as a science educator, called pedagogical content knowledge (PCK). PCK is a teacher's knowledge of how to help students understand specific subject matter. It also includes knowledge of how particular subject matter topics, problems, and issues can be organized, represented, and adapted for diverse interests and abilities of learners and then be presented for instruction. Effective science teachers know how to best design and guide learning experiences, under particular conditions and constraints, to help diverse groups of students develop scientific knowledge and understanding of scientific concepts.[1]

There are four key questions to keep in mind as you apply the principles of PCK:

1. What shall I do with my students to help them understand this science concept?
2. What materials are available to help me?
3. What are my students likely to already know and what will be difficult for them to learn?
4. How shall I best evaluate what my students have learned?

In this chapter I have devised a process that I hope will help you decide what to do with students to help them learn science content. The process is a creative one, and I want you to think about the process in the

Table 7.1 PCK and Science Curriculum Planning

PCK Component	What It's All About	Activity/Experience
Orientation toward science teaching	A way of thinking about science teaching. Types include direct/interactive, conceptual-change, discovery, project-based, inquiry, and so on.	Review Chapters 5 and 6 to become familiar with the models of science teaching, which are the same as "orientations" toward science teaching. You should be able to write a plan for any orientation.
Knowledge and beliefs about science curriculum	Being familiar with the goals for science teaching and examples of science curricula, including curriculum projects and text programs.	Link to the NSE *Standards* and the *Benchmarks for Scientific Literacy* to become familiar with science concepts. Participate in Inquiry Activity 7.1 to examine curriculum project materials on the Web.
Knowledge and beliefs about students' understanding of specific science concepts	Knowledge about what students bring to the class to learn new science content, and ability to identify areas of science that will probably give students great difficulty.	Building into teaching plans opportunities for students to reveal their prior knowledge. Also, researching what science educators know about areas that traditionally have given students difficulty. Use a search tool and find Web sites on student misconceptions, alternative frameworks, and prior knowledge.
Knowledge and beliefs about assessment in science	Being familiar with assessment standards at the local, state, and national levels. Knowing how to implement a variety of assessment procedures.	Chapter 8 will be a good resource on assessment. You should also refer to the NSE *Standards* on assessment. Assessment needs to be broad in scope to include written tests, laboratory practicals, journal writing, open-ended questions, performance assessments, and various artifacts such as drawings, multimedia documents, models, and posters.
Knowledge and beliefs about instructional strategies for teaching science	Being familiar with the various models presented in Chapter 6 as well as specific teaching models for specific content.	Writing out lesson plans using the four-stage constructivist sequence. Reviewing science curriculum projects, activity books, and texts to become familiar with key "activities" to teach specific content.

Source: Based on the ideas in Gess-Newsome, J. and Lederman, N. G. eds. *Examining Pedagogical Content Knowledge*. Dordrecht, The Netherlands: Kluwer Academic Publishers, 1999, pp. 95–132.

same way an artist thinks about creating a painting or a sculpture. Just as an artist uses physical and intellectual tools, this chapter presents you with tools to help you put together teaching plans that should be unique to you and your interpretation of science teaching.

According to research on science teaching, there are five components of PCK that should be helpful as you develop expertise in designing teaching materials. These include your orientation to science teaching, your knowledge and beliefs of science curriculum, knowledge about students' understanding of specific science concepts, knowledge of assessment, and knowledge and beliefs about specific teaching strategies. Table 7.1 outlines the five components and suggests implications for each.

INQUIRY ACTIVITY 7.1

 Developing Science PCK

In this activity you will become familiar with examples of goals of science teaching and curricular materials to develop your understanding of one of the components of PCK that will help you create an instructional miniunit.

Materials

- Access to the Web
- Samples of science curriculum materials

Procedures

1. Using Table 7.2, visit the Web sites listed to identify and evaluate concepts and science teaching materials. Although only two sites are identified for each component, you should feel free to supplement your search and access printed materials as well.

2. The science content *Standards* and the *Benchmarks* outline what students should know in each domain of science at different grade level groupings (K–4, 5–8, and 9–12). Visit either the *Standards* or *Benchmarks* site and select a domain of science (e.g., biology or life science). Within the domain, select a content area and then identify three to five concepts (ideas, principles). As you do this, consider how you would go about teaching these ideas. Prepare a chart identifying the concepts and listing three or four suggestions about how you would help students understand these ideas.

3. The two sites to help you review curriculum are at the Educational Development Center (in Massachusetts) and the Eisenhower National Clearinghouse (at the Ohio State University). You will find links at these two sites to various curriculum materials. Locate curriculum materials that relate to the domain you selected in the previous exercise and identify activities and projects that others have developed to help students understand the concepts and ideas that you selected. On the same chart, describe your findings so that others may benefit from your research.

4. Present your finding to others in small groups or to the whole class.

Table 7.2 Science Concepts and Curriculum Materials

Components	Resources
Science Concepts and Goals	*National Science Education Standards:* http://www.nap.edu/readingroom/books/nses/
	Benchmarks for Scientific Literacy: http://www.project2061.org/tools/benchol/bolframe.htm
Science Curriculum Materials	EDC K–12 Science Curriculum Dissemination Center: http://www2.edc.org/cse/work/k12dissem/materials.asp
	Eisenhower National Clearinghouse for Mathematics and Science Education: http://www.enc.org/

Minds-On Strategies

1. What orientation toward science teaching was evident in the curriculum materials that you examined? Explain how learning was presented in the materials.

2. How was learning assessed in the curriculum materials that you studied?

An Approach to Unit Design:
A Constructivist Approach

Designing teaching plans is an active, creative, and time-consuming process, yet it is one that is underrated by many teachers, and indeed taken for granted as well. As long as you are a teacher you will be involved in the design of teaching plans, even if you use the most current textbook or science curriculum project. Textbooks and curriculum projects need to be tailored to each group of students, and the person charged with this responsibility is you, the science teacher. Thus, it is advisable that you develop an approach to unit and course design that will enable you to modify existing teaching plans in textbooks and curriculum projects, as well as create original teaching units making use of the rich array of teaching materials available to science teachers.

Designing units and courses of study is a creative and artistic process that results in a product. The process of unit and course design is called instructional planning, and it will result in an instructional plan. The instructional plan that you will develop in this chapter will be a miniunit. It is important to experience the process of planning, and by scaling the product down, you will find it more manageable and will also have a better opportunity to field test your instructional plan with secondary students if it is relatively short.

Another concept that emerges from this discussion is curriculum. Curriculum is to be distinguished from instruction in the following way. Curriculum is not a process. It is a set of intended learning outcomes or goals. It is what science teachers hope students will learn. It focuses on the nature and organization of what science teachers want students to learn. Curriculum development, therefore, is a process in which the science teacher engages in the process of selecting and organizing learning objectives for a unit or course of study.

In this chapter you will be involved in curriculum development and instructional planning. We might summarize this by saying that the curriculum you develop consists of what is to be learned, the goals indicate why it is to be learned, and the instructional plan indicates how to facilitate this. Learning will only occur when you implement the instructional plan.

The general plan for designing units and courses of study is shown in Figure 7.1. In this curriculum and instruction design model, note that the boxes represent products and the lines show various processes in which you will be involved. Four questions will guide you through the process as you design a science miniunit, as well as complete science units and courses of study in the future.

1. *Why?* You need to consider why you are teaching the science unit, which leads to consideration of values and general science education goals and purposes.
2. *What?* Here you will consider the objectives of your unit and design a concept map to show the relationships among the major ideas of your miniunit.
3. *How?* The instructional plan for your miniunit—consisting of at least three lessons—will describe how you will engage students to achieve the stated learning objectives.
4. *What did the students learn?* Your evaluation plan will help you provide information about what the students learned and gague the success of your miniunit.

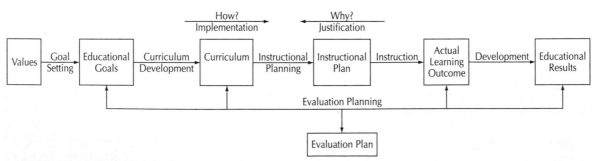

Figure 7.1 Curriculum and Instruction Design Model. The model integrates two design processes: curriculum development and instructional planning. *Source:* From Posner, J., and Rudnitsky, Alan N. *Course Design: A Guide to Curriculum Development for Teachers.* Copyright © 1986 by Longman Publishing Group. Reprinted with permission from the Longman Publishing Group.

INQUIRY ACTIVITY 7.2

Designing a Science Miniunit

In this activity you will proceed through the process of designing a science unit step by step.[2] The steps in the process are shown in Figure 7.2. You should take a moment to examine the figure before you continue. Note that the process is shown as a cycle rather than simply a linear process. The feedback you obtain from the evaluation component of the model will enable you to revise your teaching units.

One of the major emphases in this book and in the science education community is the use of cooperative learning. We have found that cooperative planning is an effective tool in helping beginning science teachers design teaching materials. Student interns can be organized in heterogeneous (different majors, sex, age, experience) dyads (teams of two) or triads (teams of three) for planning purposes. This will work especially well for designing teaching materials. Forming teams composed of different majors (e.g., an earth science major working with a biology major) will enable you to raise interdisciplinary questions for your teaching plans and allow you to play off each other's experience and knowledge. Although everyone will develop their own science miniunit, each will benefit from a cooperative team planning process. Now let's get on with the process of designing a science miniunit.

Materials

- Teaching unit progress checklist (Figure 7.3)
- Large sheets of newsprint
- Marking pens
- Secondary science textbooks in your field

Procedure

1. Your task is to design a miniunit in a content area of your choice. Discuss with members of your team the content area to work in. Be sure to agree on the course and the grade level of the students to help focus your work.

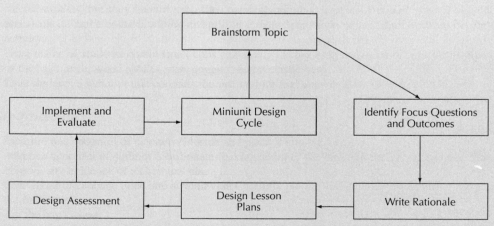

Figure 7.2 Design Cycle for Science Units.

Design Step	Progress Check	Notes
1. Brainstorming Ideas		
2. Naming Your Science Miniunit		
3. Identifying Intended Learning Outcomes		
4. Categorizing Intended Learning Outcomes		
6. Developing a Concept Map		
7. Writing a Rationale		
8. Categorizing Outcomes		
9. Listing Activities		
10. Developing Specific Lesson Plans		
11. Developing an Assessment Plan		
12. Implementing the Miniunit in a Classroom or in a Microteaching Format		
13. Feedback and Revision		

Figure 7.3 Miniunit Progress Checklist.

2. Develop a miniunit by following the teaching unit design steps in the next section. Use Figure 7.3 to keep track of your progress. Your goal is to create a four- to six-lesson miniunit that you will teach to a group of secondary students. Use the information in the section on teaching unit design steps as a reference manual during your work together as a team. The best way to use this material is to get in there and let the ideas flow.

3. Obviously, you will be unable to complete all your work in a team. There will times when you will have to work individually to write objectives, lesson plan details, and assessment items. However, you should take the time to explain to your design team what you have done in order to receive their feedback.

4. When the units are completed, you should report to the entire class by explaining the nature of the process and the details of the miniunit. The report to the class should include feedback data gathered during the implementation of the unit, either with peers or secondary students.

Minds-On Strategies

1. How effective was your miniunit in helping your students understand and develop positive attitudes toward science?

2. What were some problems you encountered in developing the miniunit?

3. How would you modify your unit planning process the next time you engage in the process? Do you think the process you used was effective? To what degree?

4. What do you think is the most important aspect of instructional planning?

The Teaching Unit Design Steps

Step 1: Brainstorm Ideas

This should be a fast, free-flowing listing of terms, words, and phrases that you have for your miniunit of instruction. It is and should be considered an initial list of ideas. It will definitely be revised and changed as you continue the process. Therefore, make no restrictions on yourself at this stage.

Here is an example of an initial topic brainstorming session for an earth science unit:

- Faults and cracking of the earth's crust
- Earthquakes
- P-waves, S-waves, L-waves
- How earthquake waves move
- Epicenter
- Drawing pictures of faults
- How to locate an epicenter
- Damage caused by earthquakes and other natural disasters
- Measuring the motion of the earth's crust
- Seismographs
- Field trip to a seismic station
- Using the computer to measure earthquake waves or to simulate earthquakes
- Plate tectonics
- The rock cycle
- Precautions people can take to lessen damage and save lives

Working in a dyad or triad, select a topic area and brainstorm a list of initial ideas for a potential teaching unit on the topic. Identify one member of the group as a recorder who will record the list on a large sheet of chart paper. (*TIP:* You might want to look at the *Benchmarks* or the content *Standards* prior to brainstorming. If you are interested in a unit on geology, then look at the earth science *Standards* or *Benchmarks* to get an idea of the kinds of concepts to teach.)

Step 2: Name Your Science Miniunit

Science units of instruction need focus, and naming them is a way to achieve this. Some teachers believe that science unit names are important because they can capture the importance or value of the unit as well as the content of the unit.

The name you give to your unit is also a way of making sure that your initial ideas are logically connected. As you can see from the following list of science miniunits produced by science interns, there is no shortage of ideas:[3]

- Touring the Tropical Forests
- Wet and Wild Wetlands
- Vision and Insight: The Structure and Function of the Eye
- Ecosystems
- Sensational Sediments
- Ocean Exploring
- The "Inevitable" Insect
- Mechanics in Our World
- A Hot Topic: Earth-Sun Relationships
- Light Goes Down Smooth
- What's Going on in That Cell?
- Are We Burning Up? Global Warming, Fact or Fiction?
- Mating Rituals of the Animal Kingdom
- What if You Had a Volcano in Your Backyard?

Miniunit titles can communicate the essential meaning of a unit. Here are some titles of minicourses from the high school science project ISIS: Packaging Passengers, Kitchen Chemistry, Using the Skies, Salt of the Earth, Seeing Colors, Cells and Cancer, Food and Microorganisms, Birth and Growth, and Sounds of Music.

Look over your initial list of ideas and name your science miniunit.

Step 3: Identify Focus Questions

Too often we don't consider what are the main points or questions for a science unit, especially when the ideas have been formulated for us as in a chapter of a textbook. Textbook chapters normally contain more information than students need to know. However, without focus or central questions it is difficult to help the students see the main point of the chapter, or in this case your science miniunit. Focus questions can also help students make a link with their prior knowledge, as well as establish a rationale for studying the science unit.

Which of the following questions would function as useful focus questions?

- What is an atom?
- How can knowledge about atoms affect the foods I eat?
- What can families do to prepare themselves for natural disasters such as tornadoes, floods, hurricanes, and earthquakes?
- How should people interact with the environment?
- When was the first atomic bomb detonated? Where? By whom?

Table 7.3 Focus Questions from Two Miniunits

The Process of Evolution by Jaime Delaney	Light Goes Down Smooth by Christopher Neill
How can the mechanisms of evolution be described through genetics?	What is light? Where does it come from?
What are some evolutionary agents and how do they work?	How do polarizing sunglasses help fishermen and divers?
Why is such variation found both within and among species?	Why does the sky appear red at dawn and dusk sometimes?
What role does chance/randomness play in evolution?	What is color and what causes it?
What role does selection play in evolution?	Why does refraction occur?
What forces act on individuals and what forces act on populations?	How do we correct bad vision?
How does selection lead to evolution and what is the difference between those two terms?	

Posner and Rudnitsky point out that focus questions should help you define the heart of your unit or course.[4] As you think about your unit, ask yourself these questions: Which of the questions you have identified really get at the heart of your unit? What kinds of questions are you asking? Are they mostly "where" or "when" questions? Have you considered "how" or "why" questions? To what extent do your questions relate to the students or to the relationship between the content of the unit and social issues?

Table 7.3 presents some additional focus questions taken from two science miniunits: The Process of Evolution: The How and Why of Population Change, by Jaime Delaney, and Light Goes Down Smooth, by Christopher Neill, graduates of Georgia State University.

Step 4: Identify Intended Learning Outcomes

Your initial list of ideas and your thinking about focus questions should help to create a list or set of intended learning outcomes or learning objectives. Intended learning outcomes are statements of what you want the students to learn. These statements can include skills, concepts, propositions, attitudes, feelings, and values.

The process of identifying learning objectives should begin with a consideration of your initial list of ideas from the brainstorming session. Learning objectives are skills, concepts, and values that you intend the students to learn. They are not activities or things the students will do. If you have a favorite activity or field trip, consider what the students will learn from the experience to derive an intended learning outcome. Dominant and recessive genes, chromosomes, blood vessel, hallucinogen, psychological dependence, Precambrian age, fossil, and cell wall are examples of science content that you might want students to learn. Computer keyboarding, focusing a microscope, how to measure temperature of the air, calculating averages, and graphing data are examples of skills you might want students learn. Your list of intended learning outcomes can also include attitudes and values, such as care for animals and plants, respect for the environment, and concern for the effects of research studies on the community.

Examine your initial list of ideas and decide which items are intended learning outcomes. Here is our original list. Items with a check mark represent, in our opinion, our classification of intended learning outcomes.

✓ Faults and cracking of the earth's crust
✓ Earthquakes
✓ P-waves, S-waves, L-waves
✓ How earthquake waves move
✓ Epicenter
  Drawing pictures of faults
✓ How to locate an epicenter
✓ Damage caused by earthquakes and other natural disasters
✓ Measuring the motion of the earth's crust
✓ Seismographs
  Field trip to a seismic station
  Using the computer to measure earthquake waves or to simulate earthquakes
✓ Plate tectonics
✓ The rock cycle
  Precautions people can take to lessen damage and save lives

The earthquake list above identifies words such as plate tectonics, earthquakes, and volcanoes. To give you an idea of how these initial ideas can be transformed into more robust intended learning outcomes, I've selected four learning outcomes from the *Benchmarks* and the *Standards* and listed them in Table 7.4. Notice how a context can be created and the potential for bigger ideas.

Use your initial list of intended learning outcomes to identify concepts and ideas in the *Benchmarks* and *Standards* related to your initial thinking.

Table 7.4 Sample Intended Outcomes from the *Benchmarks* and the *Standards*

- Some changes in the earth's surface are abrupt (such as earthquakes and volcanic eruptions) while other changes happen very slowly (such as uplift and wearing down of mountains). The earth's surface is shaped in part by the motion of water and wind over very long time periods, which act to level mountain ranges (*Benchmarks*, processes that shape the earth, 6–8).

- Earthquakes often occur along the boundaries between colliding plates, and molten rock from below creates pressure that is released by volcanic eruptions, helping to build up mountains (*Benchmarks*, processes that shape the earth, 6–8).

- Lithospheric plates on the scales of continents and oceans constantly move at rates of centimeters per year in response to movements in the mantle. Major geological events, such as earthquakes, volcanic eruptions, and mountain building result from these plate motions (*Standards*, earth and space science, 5–8).

- Landforms are the result of a combination of constructive and destructive forces. Constructive forces include crustal deformation, volcanic eruption, and deposition of sediment, while destructive forces include weathering and erosion (*Standards*, earth and space science, 5–8).

Step 5: Categorize Intended Learning Outcomes

The next step is grouping intended learning outcomes into skill and nonskill categories. A science skill is something that students are expected to be able to do at the end of the unit of teaching. Skills include physical abilities such as measuring the volume of water using a graduated cylinder, as well as mental abilities, including describing the physical properties of rocks, inferring past events from fossil evidence, solving mechanics problems, and writing chemical equations. Skills represent the behavioral outcomes of learning and can often be measured by having students do what was intended (e.g., write chemical equations and measure volumes).

There are nonskill outcomes that cognitive scientists and social psychologists claim are important in science courses. Nonskills are ideas (e.g., earthquakes, valence, momentum, force, uniformitarianism, dominance) and values (e.g., truth, openness, uncertainty) that are not necessarily directly observable outcomes, yet to many represent the heart of science courses. Posner and Rudnitsky put it is this way: "Generally speaking, non-skills comprise the knowledge and attitudes with which we think and feel. Skills comprise what we can do with this knowledge and how we can act on these feelings."[5]

Table 7.5 Environmental Problems in Our Community

Nonskill Outcomes	Skill Outcomes
Respects the environment	Ability to analyze a sample of water
Energy webs and food chains	
Pollution	Can measure the pH of liquids
Knows how acids affect river water	Can write equations for chemical processes
Understands biodegradable	

Categorize your intended learning outcomes into nonskill and skill categories. You might have to add skills and nonskills to your original list. You should end up with two lists of outcomes, as shown in Table 7.5.

Step 6: Develop a Concept Map

At this point, you should use the technique of concept mapping to analyze the important ideas and words that you hope students will understand in your miniunit. Novak and Gowin have advocated the use of concept mapping as a tool for planning, and it is introduced here in the instructional planning process. To develop a concept map, make a list of all the important concepts and terms that are related to the major concepts in your miniunit. The following steps should help you devise your concept map.[6]

1. Select the main concept from your list.
2. Add concepts to your list if needed.
3. Write the concepts on index cards.
4. Rank the concepts from the most inclusive to the most specific.
5. Group the concepts into clusters. Add more specific concepts (on cards) if necessary.
6. Arrange the concepts (cards) in a two-dimensional array.
7. Write the concepts on a sheet of paper as they appear in the two-dimensional array.
8. Link the concepts and label each link.

For example, here is a list of concepts and terms for a miniunit on the food chain, listed in order from most inclusive to least inclusive:

- consumers
- producers
- decomposers
- herbivores
- carnivores
- photosynthesizers

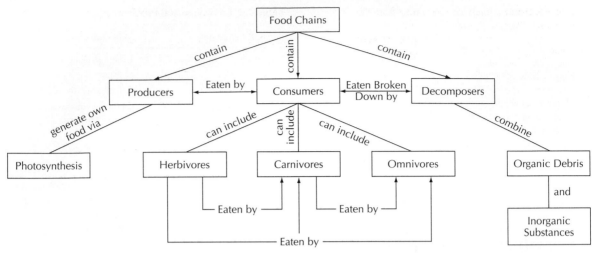

Figure 7.4 Concept Map on Food Chains.

- algae
- bryophytes
- tracheophytes
- organic debris

Figure 7.4 shows an arrangement of these concepts and terms for the miniunit on the food chain. Note the hierarchical nature of the map. The more inclusive concepts are located at the top of the map (e.g., food chains, producers), followed by less inclusive concepts (Herbivores, Carnivores) as you read down the map. Using this technique will help you analyze the nature of your miniunit at this stage. Does your concept map show inclusive concepts? Are there too many abstract concepts? What concrete concepts could you add to help students understand the abstract concepts?

There is a good chance that you are planning your miniunit using a secondary science textbook. If you are working with a single chapter (miniunits typically represent only a part of a chapter and on rare occasions a full chapter), make a list of the important concepts (no more than ten), and from this list create your concept map. You may discover that you will have to modify the map by adding concrete concepts that may have been "missing" from the textbook author's approach to the chapter or you may have to de-emphasize and eliminate some concepts.

Step 7: Write a Rationale

You're probably wondering why writing a rationale wasn't the first step in the curriculum development process. It should be clear, however, that you have invested some time thinking about the initial ideas of the miniunit, categorizing them as skill and nonskill, and analyzing the ideas in your unit by making a concept map. You are now in a much more powerful position to think about why you are teaching this miniunit and how you will communicate this rationale to your students.

In writing a statement describing the rationale for your miniunit you should consider these questions:

- How does the miniunit affect the future of the students as well as their individual needs and interests?
- How does the miniunit contribute to societal issues and help students deal responsibly with science-related issues?
- How does the miniunit reflect the spirit and character of scientific inquiry and the nature of the scientific enterprise?

Thus, a rationale statement will be determined by the values that influence your perception and conception of students (learners), society (science's relationship to society), and science (the subject matter).

Current trends and directions in science education can also influence course, unit, and miniunit rationales. In the last twenty years there has been a shift toward a more student-centered (hands-on) approach to the learner. A greater emphasis has and will continue to be placed on STS (science, technology, society; see Chapter 11). One of the challenges is to make the content of science relevant to your students. From a sociocultural perspective, the context created for students to achieve the intended learning outcomes may be as important as the selection of the outcomes. For example, the miniunit cited earlier with the title "What if you had a volcano in your backyard?" creates a context that students can relate to and it may help them see relevance as opposed to a miniunit entitled "Types of volcanoes."

Here is the rationale written by the author of "What if you had a volcano in your backyard?"

Science education in this modern world of high information availability must be an inquiry-based exercise. Science itself must be defined as a verb, an action, and a method of looking at the world. And when the world, with all of its uniqueness and exceptions to the "rules," is readily available through the Internet, simple memorization of facts can become useless. Students must use their brainpower for finding the threads that connect and relate all things. In this study of volcanoes, the Mt. St. Helen's example is used to show the power and the magnitude of a volcano; the devastation of all forms of life that occur following a blast. The lesson intent is to explore how a volcano affects more than just geology of the area. The example is used to show how life in a devastated area reforms and rejuvenates. The students are invited to put themselves into the vicinity of a modern-day active volcano and discover how their life and the world around them might change. Even though this is intended as an earth science unit, the interconnectedness of the threads that connect all things are woven together by teaching geography, geology, chemistry, biology, weather, history, and even social studies just by studying a volcano.[7]

Your miniunit rationale should also include a statement of science education goals (broad statements of intent) that reflect the integration of ideas concerning students, society, and the nature of science. For example, a rationale for a miniunit on the earth's past might contain a goal statement such as: This miniunit is designed to give middle school students an insight into and an appreciation of life as it existed in the past, and provoke ideas concerning how life evolved on earth.

A complete rationale should contain a goal statement, as well as how the miniunit attends to conceptions of the student, society, and the nature of science. A complete rationale for a unit on the environment follows. Notice that the rationale includes aspects of the student, society, and science, and specifies how each is addressed in the unit.

Rationale: Environmental Education Unit

To be truly educated, people need knowledge of, appreciation for, and skills relating to the world around them. Schools, largely responsible for educating individuals in our society, must equip people with the knowledge and ability necessary for them to preserve the environment for the physical, psychological, and aesthetic needs of future generations. A person educated in this way knows enough to exhibit intelligent and reasonable concern for his or her environment and can presumably direct this knowledge and concern toward the preservation and improvement of the environment. A person's actions affect the environment as they occur in the context of the environment.

It is important, from the standpoint of enhanced self-image, personal enjoyment, and a meaningful life, for people to know basic facts about the environment and their relationship to it. They should, as well, have the capability and inclination to act in a positive manner toward the environment.

In a technological society, which tends to insulate its members from the environment, this subject area is second to none in importance. Actual experience with the environment is necessary for the proper treatment of this subject. Technology in our society appears, at times, out of control, or at least controlled by factors not related to environmental quality. For the preservation of society and the enhancement of individual lives, people must interact with their world on a educated basis.[8]

Examine your list of intended learning outcomes and write a rationale for your miniunit. As you think about the rationale, consider the students you will teach and how the content will relate to them. Next, formulate the relationship between the content in your unit and potential social issues that it brings about. And, last, how will you approach the nature of science in this miniunit?

Step 8: Categorize Outcomes: Cognitions, Affects, and Skills

In this step of the instructional planning process, you will revise your initial learning outcomes, write these statements as objectives using a standard form, and categorize them into practical categories for teaching.

There are many ways to write learning objectives. You no doubt have learned how to do this in other educational experiences. Several samples of science objectives are provided next. Objectives should focus on what you want the student to learn, communicate clearly your intentions, and indicate how success can be achieved.

Table 7.6 Summary of Learning Outcomes

Category	Skill
Cognitions	Concepts and propositions
Affects	Attitudes and feelings
Cognitive skills	Cognitive abilities
Psychomotor skills	Motor and laboratory abilities

SAMPLE OBJECTIVES
- The student will solve seven out of ten stoichiometry problems.
- Given a box of ten rocks, the student will be able to sort the rocks into categories and subcategories based on physical appearance.
- Given a problem, the student can design an experiment to test a hypothesis.

We will return to stating objectives again as we examine the types of objectives that you will develop for teaching.

As you can tell from the title of this section, the categorization of objectives into nonskills and skills has emerged into four categories, as shown in Table 7.6. Cognitions and affects are nonskill learning objectives, while skill objectives are divided into the categories of cognitive skills and psychomotor skills.

Cognitions include the science concepts, principles, and generalizations (e.g., rock, mineral, force, matter, atom, erosion, photosynthesis) that form the substantive character of your miniunit and future units and courses of study. Affects are feelings and attitudes about the subject, inner feelings concerning the students' self-concept, or attitudes about ability to think scientifically or be successful in science courses. Cognitive skill objectives refer to students' ability to use intellectual abilities. Observing objects, inferring what happened from evidence, solving equations, and designing an experiment are examples of cognitive skill objectives. Psychomotor skill objectives include the obvious observable skills that students need to perform in science courses. Using a metric rule, massing objects with a balance, focusing a microscope, and preparing a slide are examples of psychomotor skill objectives.

Let's look at each of these categories and, while you read through these sections, revise and rewrite your initial list of learning outcomes to produce a final list that includes examples from each of the four categories.

COGNITIONS Science textbooks are full of cognitions. Take a moment and look at the glossary of a textbook (most science textbooks have one). Glossary entries represent the major cognitions that the textbook authors felt were the most important science ideas that students should learn. Cognitions can be concepts. They can be also propositions or generalizations. Here are some examples of cognitions that interns wrote for science miniunits:

- The students will know the cell theory.
- The students will understand the importance of a fossil.
- The students will know the characteristics of an earthworm.
- The students will know why chemical equations are used.

It is helpful to differentiate between two types of cognitions: concepts and propositions. A concept is a synthesis of objects, events, or actions into a single idea or representation. Concepts are classifications enabling students to comprehend the vast array of experiences in science. Grouping rocks into categories of igneous, metamorphic, and sedimentary is a powerful tool in learning about earth materials. Students can learn these categories through first-hand experience with rocks of each class. A learning objective for understanding rocks might look like this:

> The student should grasp the meaning of igneous (rocks formed from the crystallization of molten materials), sedimentary (rocks formed from the deposition of erosional material), and metamorphic (rocks that have changed by heat and/or pressure) rocks.

To further define this learning objective, you should also show a concept map indicating the relationship among the concepts (see the example shown in Figure 7.5). This approach to stating cognitions may seem familiar if you have had previous experience writing performance objectives. We will write performance objectives, but we will label them either cognitive skill objectives or psychomotor skill objectives.

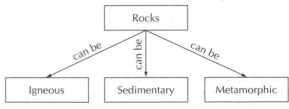

Figure 7.5 Concept Map on Rocks.

- The student will be able to describe how waves are created and how they transfer energy.
- The student will be able to distinguish between longitudinal and transverse waves.
- The student will be able to measure the approximate speed of sound in air.

Propositions are learning objectives in which concepts are linked together. Linking the concepts of mass and acceleration can give us the proposition of momentum. Or, the concepts of force and acceleration can be combined to give the following proposition: The acceleration of an object is directly related to the force exerted on it.

Propositions, like concepts, can be learned through actual experience with the concepts, but in a more indirect manner. Propositions by their very nature are abstractions and require the student to make associations and relationships among concepts. It is important to identify the concepts students will need to know in order to understand propositions.

At this point you should examine your list of outcomes and your concept map and rewrite your cognitions as either concrete concept objectives or propositional objectives. If you use the *Benchmarks* or the *Standards* as a reference, you can find statements that should help you generate cognitions. Table 7.7 lists some examples from these sources to help you in this task. I've selected cognitions from earth science, life

Table 7.7 Sample Cognitions from the *Benchmarks* and the *Standards*

- Students should know that the solid crust of the earth— including both the continents and the ocean basins—consists of separate plates that ride on a denser, hot, gradually deformable layer of the earth.
- Students should know that, within cells, many of the basic functions of organisms—such as extracting energy from food and getting rid of waste—are carried out. The way in which cells function is similar in all living organisms.
- Students should know that gravitational force is an attraction between masses. The strength of the force is proportional to the masses and weakens rapidly with increasing distance between them.
- Students should know that human activities also could induce hazards through resource acquisition, urban growth, land-use decisions, and waste disposal. Such activities can accelerate many natural changes.
- Students should know that natural environments might contain substances that are harmful to human beings (e.g., radon and lead). Maintaining environmental health involves establishing or monitoring quality standards related to use of soil, water, and air.

science, physical science, and science in personal and social perspectives.

AFFECTS Science courses of study should also include objectives that deal with feelings, values, and attitudes. Examples of such objectives include:

- The student should learn to expect and anticipate change.
- The student should have confidence in his or her ability to plan and carry out research investigations.
- The student should have respect for other living organisms.
- The student should learn that knowledge is tentative.
- The student is willing to listen to the opinions of others.
- The student is willing to reject scientific facts on the basis of new and valid information.

The *Benchmarks* and *Standards* address the topic of affects as well. Table 7.8 shows the attudes and values from the *Benchmarks* section "Habits of Mind" that students should learn by the end of grades 8 and 12.

Affects are often examined in terms of David Krathwohl's system of categorizing values. Affects need to be acted upon to be truly congruent with Krathwohl's highest category, characterization (the student acts on a set of internalized values, is generally predictable, and is willing to act individually and show self-reliance).[9] If you include affects in your miniunit (and you should), it is important to realize that students can learn affects at different levels.

Table 7.8 Affects in the *Benchmarks for Scientific Literacy*

Grade 8	Grade 12
- Students should know why it is important in science to keep honest, clear, and accurate records.	- Students should know why curiosity, honesty, openness, and skepticism are so highly regarded in science and how they are incorporated into the way science is carried out; exhibit those traits in their own lives and value them in others.
- Students should know that hypotheses are valuable, even if they turn out not to be true, if they lead to fruitful investigations.	
- Students should know that often different explanations can be given for the same evidence, and it is not always possible to tell which explanation is correct.	- Students should view science and technology thoughtfully, being neither categorically antagonistic nor uncritically positive.

Useful verbs to help you write affects include responds, choose, value, prize, trust, organize, inclined, like, and respect. Using the examples and suggestions, examine your initial list of outcomes and write at least one affect for your miniunit.

COGNITIVE SKILLS A cognitive skill is an objective that describes intellectual competencies that students will learn in the science course. No doubt your list of original learning objectives contained cognitive skill objectives. Cognitive skills can be recognized quite easily because they are normally stated in performance or behavioral terms. For example, look at this list of cognitive skill objectives:

- Students will be able to describe the characteristics of sound.
- Students will be able to distinguish between an atom and a molecule.
- Students will be able to predict the location of the moon in the daytime sky.
- Students will be able to calculate velocity, distance, or time given the other two.
- Students will be able to explain how satellites keep moving without their engines on.
- Students will be able to classify sedimentary rocks into limestones, conglomerates, sandstones, siltstones, and shales.

Cognitive skills are the most common form of objectives that teachers use to describe student learning. If you examine science textbooks, the objectives that are included in each chapter are generally cognitive skills.

When writing cognitive skills, you should consider the *action* words that you are using to describe the performance of the student. One convenient list of action words is the science processes that were discussed earlier. These include observe, classify, infer, measure, collect data, analyze data, predict, formulate hypotheses, design experiments, and test hypotheses. Other action words include write, state, select, point to, name, match, list, interpret, identify, describe, distinguish, contrast, and compare.

Cognitive skill objectives (as well as objectives for affects and psychomotor skills) should be written to include:

1. what the learner is expected to *do,*
2. what *conditions* are imposed when the student is asked to do it, and
3. how you will *recognize* the student's success in doing it.

Finally, when designing science units, you should consider the intellectual level of the cognitive skills by using Bloom's taxonomy as a planning tool.[10] Bloom's taxonomy organizes cognitive skills into a hierarchy of six levels (see Table 7.9). They are shown in the following list with representative performance or intellectual behaviors characteristic of each level.

- Level 1: Knowledge (name, match, state)
- Level 2: Comprehension (translate, interpret, write in your own words)
- Level 3: Application (apply, solve, generalize)
- Level 4: Analysis (trace, outline, break down)
- Level 5: Synthesis (combine, integrate, propose, plan, create)
- Level 6: Evaluation (judge, argue, validate)

Examine your list of intended learning outcomes and rewrite those that fall into the category of cognitive skills.

PSYCHOMOTOR SKILLS Science teaching should emphasize the learning of psychomotor skills, which certainly should include the work students do in the science laboratory as well as while engaged in the variety of hands-on activities that you will prepare for them. There are a number of categories of psychomotor skills, including moving, manipulating, communication, and creating. Trowbridge and Bybee explain these important psychomotor skills as shown in Table 7.10.[11]

Psychomotor skill objectives are most obvious in the science laboratory. Although there is not full agreement on what outcomes are derived in laboratory activities in science, the following represent the major categories:[12]

1. methodical procedure
2. experimental technique
3. manual dexterity
4. orderliness

From this list is obvious that laboratory science work involves cognitions and affects as well as psychomotor skills. Therefore, it is important to note that most psychomotor skill objectives that you write will involve cognitive thinking as well. For example, plotting a velocity-time graph with constant slope combines psychomotor skills of graphing and cognitive skills and understanding of velocity, time, and slope.

At this stage of your work, you should have a list of intended learning outcomes that include cognitions, affects, cognitive skills, and psychomotor skills. You are now ready to move to the next step—listing potential activities.

Table 7.9 Bloom's Taxonomy of Cognitive Skills

Category	Explanation	Illustrative Performance Behaviors and Learning Outcome
Level 1: Knowledge	Knowledge is defined as the remembering of previously learned specific facts to complete theories, but all that is required is the bringing to mind of the appropriate information. Knowledge represents the lower lever of learning outcomes in the cognitive domain.	*Performance behaviors:* Defines, describes, identifies, labels, lists, matches, names, reproduces, states. *Sample learning outcome:* The student will be able to *define* the following terms: solute, solution.
Level 2: Comprehension	Comprehension is defined as the ability to grasp the meaning of material. This may be shown by translating material from one form to another (words to numbers) and by interpreting material (explaining or summarizing). These learning outcomes go one step beyond the simple remembering of material, and represent the lowest level of understanding.	*Performance behaviors:* Converts, explains, extends, generalizes, gives examples, infers, paraphrases, rewrites, summarizes. *Sample learning outcome:* The student will be able to *summarize* the process of photosynthesis.
Level 3: Application	Application refers to the ability to use learned material in new and concrete situations. This may include the application of such things as rules, methods, concepts, principles, laws, and theories. Learning outcomes in this area require a higher level of understanding than those under comprehension.	*Performance behaviors:* Changes, computes, demonstrates, discovers, manipulates, operates, prepares, produces, relates, shows, solves, uses. *Sample learning outcome:* The student will be able to *compute* the area of a forest given the formula for area and a map of the targeted forest.
Level 4: Analysis	Analysis refers to the ability to break down material into its component parts so that its organizational structure may be understood. This may include the identification of the parts, analysis of the relationships between parts, and recognition of the organizational principles involved.	*Performance behaviors:* Breaks down, diagrams, differentiates, discriminates, distinguishes, outlines, points out, relates, selects, separates, subdivides. *Sample learning outcome:* The student will be able to *diagram* in the form of a concept map the concepts related to photosynthesis.
Level 5: Synthesis	Synthesis refers to the ability to put parts together to form a new whole. This may involve the production of a unique communication (theme of a report), a plan of operation (experimental design), or a set of abstract relations (scheme for classifying information). Learning outcomes in this area stress creative behaviors, with major emphasis on the formulation of new patterns or structures through combination.	*Performance behaviors:* Combines, compiles, composes, creates, devises, designs, generates, modifies, organizes, plans, rearranges, reconstructs, reorganizes, revises, rewrites, writes. *Sample learning outcome:* The student will be able to *plan* an experiment to test a hypothesis.
Level 6: Evaluation	Evaluation is concerned with the ability to judge the value of material (science article or newspaper report, research study) for a given purpose. The judgments are to be based on definite criteria. These may be internal criteria (organization) or external criteria (relevance to the purpose) and the student may determine the criteria or be given them. Learning outcomes in this category are highest in the cognitive skill hierarchy because they contain elements of all the other categories.	*Performance behaviors:* Compares, concludes, contrasts, criticizes, describes, discriminates, explains, justifies, interprets, rates, relates, summarizes. *Sample learning outcome:* After viewing videotaped speeches by environmental activists, the student will be able to *rate* the speeches in terms of content accuracy, persuasion, and tact.

Step 9: List Potential Activities

Potential activities should emerge from your list of learning outcomes. One way to look at the activities you select for your miniunit is to use the concept of "instructional foci." Instructional foci are the means with which you will enable students to attain the objectives you have created. For example, "understanding the nature of wave movement," is not an example of instructional foci. It's an objective. However, using a toy slinky to design experiments through which wave movement might be observed is an example of instructional foci. Instructional foci can be reading textbooks, field trips and experiences, case studies, debates, role-play/

Table 7.10 Psychomotor Skills

Moving	Manipulation	Communicating	Creating
The first level is referred to as gross body movements. It involves the coordination of physical actions or movements. In its most basic form, moving is a muscular response to sensory stimuli. Students in the science class will be involved in coordination and smooth movements.	Manipulating can include movements but adds fine body movements. In the science classroom, students will use manual dexterity to manipulate materials and equipment in order to observe, measure, classify, and analyze science experiences.	Communicating is activity that makes ideas and feelings known to other persons or, conversely, makes the need for information known. This level is based on movement or manipulation and extends these levels in that something is known, felt, or needed as a result of movement or manipulation and is communicated to others. At the most basic level there are signals involving nonverbal messages through facial expression, gestures, or body movements; speech, the verbal communication, starting with sounds and progressing to word-gesture coordination, and, finally, symbolic communication through the use of pantomime, writing, pictures, and other abstract forms. Science teachers are usually interested in learning results at this level.	Creating is the process and performance that results in new ideas. Creative products in science usually require some combination of moving, manipulating, and communicating in the generation of new and unique products. Here the cognitive, affective, and psychomotor are coordinated in efforts to solve problems and create new ones.

Table 7.11 Hands-On/Minds-On Instructional Foci

Miniunit: Human genetics	
Objectives	**Potential Instructional Foci**
1. The students will understand the patterns of inheritance for several genetic diseases. (*cognition*)	• Reading text, *Modern Biology*
	• *Brave New World* by Aldous Huxley
2. The students will be able to construct pedigrees and use them to determine inheritance patterns. (*cognitive skill*)	• Debate pro and con Huxley's book
	• Computer simulations of genetics
	• Lecture with visuals
3. The students will be inclined to express ethical and moral positions with regard to genetic diseases. (*affect*)	• Pedigree analysis worksheets
	• Field trip to a genetics research laboratory

simulations, cooperative group activities, hands-on experiences, and guest speakers. Each serves as a focal point for a type of classroom experience designed to facilitate learning of science objectives. Table 7.11 presents an example of instructional foci for a miniunit on human genetics. Each of these instructional foci in Table 7.11 has integrity of its own and can be used to achieve one or more different outcomes.

Another way to approach the listing of potential activities is to generate an outline of your miniunit, lesson by lesson, putting the emphasis on what kinds of activities students will be engaged in. Table 7.12 shows an outline of a unit on evolution. Notice the emphasis on "activities" for each lesson.

List potential instructional foci (activities) for the intended learning outcomes that you developed. Realize that some of the your instructional foci may score low on a feasibility scale (e.g., field trip); however, it is important to investigate all possibilities at this stage before you actually write your lesson plans. And that's the next step.

Step 10: Develop Specific Lesson Plans

Your miniunit should contain between four and six lesson plans. Draft a set of plans based on the curriculum that you have designed (i.e., the minicourse rationale and the set of learning objectives).

There are a number of formats that you can choose in designing lesson plans. Following are three models that you can use to write lessons for your miniunit. Lesson plan template I (Figure 7.6) is based on the constructivist learning cycle model introduced in Chapter 6. Lesson plan template II (Figure 7.7) uses an outline format. Lesson plan template III (Figure 7.8) uses an alternative of aligning the lesson outcomes, activities, materials, and student assessments.

Table 7.12 Key Activities and Instructional Foci for a Miniunit on Evolution Outline

I. Random Processes	II. Selective Processes
A. Lesson 1: River of Genes—Watch It Flow! (Gene Flow)	**A. Lesson 3: How to Attract the Chicks . . .** (Sexual Selection)
• Immigration/emigration and barriers activity to simulate gene flow	• Human mate selection activity
• Explanation and examples	• Case study activity
• Activity with bead model to simulate gene flow	• Introduce signaling
• Analysis of activity results	• Discuss female choice
• Discuss isolationism—Madagascar example	
	B. Lesson 4: Suit yourself . . . But Be Well Suited! (Adaptations)
B. Lesson 2: Drift on Over! (Genetic Drift)	• Galapagos introduction and activity
• Flying saucer activity to simulate genetic drift	• Build-a-beast activity
• Explanation and examples	• Introduce adaptation
• Activity with bead model to simulate genetic drift	• Talk about mutations
• Analysis of activity results	**C. Lesson 5: Cream of the Crop—Nature Selects Its Best** (Natural Selection)
• Causes and long-term effects	• Predator/prey interaction activity
	• Case study activity
	• Classify into three types
	• Discuss effects and evolution

Source: From the miniunit, "The Process of Evolution: The Why and How of Population Change" by Jaime Delaney, Falcon High School, Falcon, Colo. (http://www.delaneyweb.com/teems/index.html). Used with permission.

Lesson 1: Title of the Lesson
Overview
Materials
Invitation
Exploration
Explanation
Taking Action
Evaluation

Figure 7.6 Lesson Plan Template I.

Title of Lesson:
  A. Title of Lesson
  B. Grade Level
  C. Objectives
      1. Cognitive
          a. Cognitions
          b. Cognitive Skills
      2. Affects
      3. Psychomotor Skills
  D. Materials/Media
  E. Procedure
      1. Motivational Activity
      2. Development of Concepts
      3. Closure
  F. Evaluation/Assessment

Figure 7.7 Lesson Plan Template II.

Title_____		Grade Level_____	Course_____
Objectives	**Procedures**	**Materials/Media**	**Evaluation**

Figure 7.8 Lesson Plan Template III.

SAMPLE LESSON 7.1

Biological Attraction

Intended Outcomes

Nonskill Outcomes

Cognitions

- Know what sexual selection is
- Understand why sexual selection happens
- Understand what a signal is

Affects

- Expect other species to have complicated mating behavior and preferences

Skill Outcomes

Cognitive Skills

- Able to predict the outcome of sexual selection given certain conditions
- Able to infer what is driving sexual selection in certain conditions

Psychomotor Skills

- Able to create a drawing of a human model based on sexual selection

Invitation

Human Mate Selection Activity

- Ask students how they would feel about being randomly assigned a life partner from the people in the class.
- Should they say no, ask why.
- Collect pictures of "attractive mates" and ask the class to make generalizations about them. What superficial characteristics do humans look for in mates?
- Ask students if they know of any other species that has similar requirements of their mate.

Exploration

- Students will a complete case study activity in groups of three and answer questions related to it on a handout (see Web site listed at end of this lesson for the handout).

Explanation

- Groups summarize their ideas for the class.
- Clarify student conceptions and emphasize correct interpretations.
- Introduce the concept of signal and how it relates to sexual selection.
- Discuss why sexual selection leads to better offspring.
- Talk about types of species where sexual selection is strongest (female choice).

Take Action

- Assume humans act like bird populations, with one sex doing all the choosing and the other simply passing on as many genes as possible. For the sex that is chosen, draw what you think will be a typical human a long time from now, given that sexual selection is strong.
- Think about where sexual selection reaches a boundary and traits simply cannot become any more extreme. What factors might limit extreme growth of traits?

Evaluation

- Prepare your report from the Take Action section for homework and be ready to present in small groups during the next class.

Source: Jaime Delaney: www.delaneyweb.com/teems/miniunit/lesson3.html. Used with permission.

SAMPLE LESSON 7.2

 Drugs, Alcohol, and Tobacco

The following is a lesson developed by a teacher/intern during a summer institute. The lesson was the first of a four-lesson miniunit entitled Drugs, Alcohol, and Tobacco.[13] Note how the author includes a variety of objectives and involves the students in whole class, small team, and dyad activities.

A. Title: Drug Abuse

B. Grade 8

C. Objectives

- The students will understand drug abuse.
- The students will be able to describe the effects of drugs on the body.
- The students will be able to compare psychological and physical dependence.
- The students will develop confidence in expressing opinions about drug usage based on an understanding of the effects on the body.

D. Materials/Media

- Overhead projector
- Transparencies showing the lesson objectives
- Pretest sheet, one per student
- Variety of over-the-counter drugs: beer car, aspirin bottle, cold tablet package, cigarette pack, antacid sample, coffee can, tea bag
- Sample of generic drug
- Chart of commonly abused drugs, one per student
- 3×5 Notecards (for teacher use)

E. Procedure

1. Motivation

   a. Show students a variety of over-the-counter drugs: aspirin, cold   tablets, beer can, tea bag, coffee can, and cigarette package. Have them describe what they can see; ask how these groups can be categorized; and ask how each of the items can be used.
   b. Inform the students of the objectives by using the transparency.

2. Development

   a. Students will be administered a pretest to determine their current knowledge of drugs and drug abuse. (Test contains five questions asking them to identify a drug, the effects of the following on the body: alcohol, cigarettes, marijuana, crack.
   b. Students in small teams are asked to discuss and write a definition for each of these terms: counter drugs, generic drugs; to discuss what drugs can't be bought over the counter; and why some drugs require a doctor's prescription.
   c. Teacher asks students to compare the heroin/crack addict and the ten-cup per day coffee drinker.
   d. Teacher discusses the dangers of drug abuse, focusing on the following concepts: dependence, withdrawal, tolerance.
   e. Teacher presents drug abuse chart and asks students to work with a partner to answer a series of questions such as: What type of drug is crack? What effect does it have on the central nervous system? What drugs have severe withdrawal symptoms? Which type does not result in physical dependence when abused? Which type results in strong psychological dependence when used?

3. Closure

   a. Teacher asks each partner pair to write a short statement that defines drug abuse; compare psychological and physical dependence; and explain how this knowledge can be of benefit to people.
   b. Teacher calls on partner pairs at random and asks them to present their summary to the class.
   c. Teacher assigns homework: Find at least three advertisements in magazines in which drugs are being sold. Bring to class tomorrow.

F. Assessment

- Teacher observes groups and notes contributions of each member.
- Teacher collects and evaluates summaries written by partner pairs.

SAMPLE LESSON PLAN 7.3

Electricity—Make It Light!

Table 7.13 Lesson on Electricity

Title: **_Make It Light_**   *Grade Level:* **_Eight_**   *Course:* **_Physical Science_**

Objectives	Procedures	Materials/Media	Evaluation
1. The students will grasp the meaning of electric current, resistance, and potential difference.	*Motivation:* 1. The students will simulate an electric circuit. Each student will push a box around the room along a path defined by masking tape. Desks will be placed in the path of the students. 2. Teacher will introduce the purpose and objectives of the lesson.	Masking tape Shoe boxes Desks	
2. The students will be able to predict how the elements of a circuit should be connected.	*Development:* 1. The teacher will organize the students into teams of four. Each team will select a name from a list of electrical terms shown on the board: Ohm, resistance, wire, battery, and current. Each team will be asked to discuss and then to write "working definitions" of electric circuit, load, and source.	Chalkboard Chalk	
	2. Teacher will ask students to suggest examples of electric circuits they have encountered and identify the load and source in each.		Teacher monitors groups; records group behavior; asks questions.
	3. Teacher gives each group a bag containing a lightbulb, battery, and two pieces of wire. They will be asked to draw a picture of how they think the items should be connected to make the bulb light. Each group will connect the items to test their electric circuit. They will experiment to find the correct connection. Each group is asked to identify the source and the load.	Per team: Small lightbulb, Battery, One piece of wire	
3. The students will be able to assemble an electric circuit.	*Closure:* 1. Each group draws a picture of their circuit on a large sheet of chart paper. Pictures are assembled by the teacher, who asks each group to explain their results.	Chart paper Crayons	Teacher collects each group's chart and evaluates the work.
	2. Teacher assigns homework. Each team member is given part of the homework assignment (each does two problems from the text). Teacher explains that the whole team will turn in all problems tomorrow.		Teacher explains that homework will be graded such that a group grade is given for the homework assignment.

Source: Based on a lesson by Pamela Callahan Sandlin, teacher-intern, Georgia State University.

Step 11: Develop an Assessment Plan

Two elements of assessment are important at this stage in planning a miniunit. Assessment should serve two broad purposes:

1. To answer questions and provide feedback with regard to student learning
2. To provide data with respect to the effectiveness of instructional plans

Your miniunit should contain elements of both purposes in the assessment plan.

The most common or traditional approach to this step is to prepare a postevaluation instrument (a quiz or test) to be administered when the students complete the miniunit. The instrument can be used to assess student learning and provide feedback from the students about the effectiveness of the unit.

The assessment instrument should be designed to evaluate each type of learning outcome that you included in the unit. You should then develop measures to evaluate:

1. cognitions
2. cognitive skills
3. affects
4. psychomotor skills

Refer to Chapter 8 on assessment for specific suggestions for items, problems, questions, performance assessments, checklists, rubrics, and questionnaires that you could use to evaluate student learning.

You should also ask the students for feedback on how they reacted to the miniunit. One approach is to use the format you used in reflective teaching (see Chapter 6). Thus, you could include a separate form allowing students to complete these questions anonymously, as shown in Figure 7.9.

Assessment can also include other items and approaches. Informal and semiformal methods, as well as having students develop portfolios of their work, can be incorporated into an assessment plan.

Look ahead to Chapter 8 on assessment and prepare an assessment plan for your miniunit.

Step 12: Implement the Miniunit

If it is possible, make arrangements to teach your miniunit to a group of secondary students. This can be done with either a whole class or with a small group of

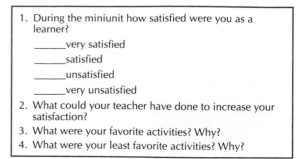

1. During the miniunit how satisfied were you as a learner?

_____very satisfied

_____satisfied

_____unsatisfied

_____very unsatisfied

2. What could your teacher have done to increase your satisfaction?
3. What were your favorite activities? Why?
4. What were your least favorite activities? Why?

Figure 7.9 Student Feedback Form.

students. If this is not possible, then try to arrange to teach one lesson from the miniunit to a group of peers. In either case, videotape one of your lessons to be used for reflection and feedback.

Step 13: Feedback and Reflection

Curriculum development and instructional planning are part of a large cycle. One of the most important parts of the cycle is a period of time devoted to gathering feedback on the unit and reflecting on its effectiveness. Questions to consider include:

1. To what extent did students attain the learning objectives of the unit?
2. In what way did the students respond to the activities, assignments, and content of the miniunit?
3. Were the goals and content of the miniunit appropriate for the students in this class?
4. What activities did students seem to enjoy? Did these contribute to their understanding of main cognitions of the unit?
5. What activities didn't students seem to enjoy? Do you think these activities are important? Do they contribute to the students' understanding of the main cognitions? How would you change these activities, if necessary?
6. Would you use this unit again in its present form? If not, how would you change it? What modifications would you make?

Models and Sample Lesson Plans

This section is designed to provide examples of lessons based on the models that were presented in Chapter 6.

Now that you have developed a miniunit, you might want to examine these lessons in more detail. Following you will find four types of lessons based on the models that were presented earlier:

1. Direct/interactive teaching lesson plan
2. Cooperative learning lesson plan
3. Inquiry/laboratory lesson plan
4. Constructivist lesson plan

Direct/Interactive Teaching Lesson Plan Guide

The elements of a lesson based on direct/interactive teaching follows. A sample lesson based on the model follows the guide.

LESSON PLAN GUIDE: DIRECT INSTRUCTION

1. Anticipatory Set

   - Focus students
   - State objectives
   - Establish purpose
   - Establish transfer

2. Instruction

   a. Provide information

   - Explain concept
   - State definitions
   - Provide examples
   - Model

   b. Check for understanding

   - Pose key questions
   - Ask students to explain concepts, definitions, attributes in their own words
   - Have students discriminate between examples and nonexamples
   - Encourage students to generate their own examples
   - Use participation

3. Guided Practice

   - Initiate practice activities under direct teacher supervision
   - Elicit overt responses from students that demonstrates behavior in objective(s)
   - Continue to check for understanding
   - Provide specific knowledge of results
   - Provide close monitoring

4. Closure

   - Make final assessment to determine if students have met objectives
   - Have each student perform behavior

5. Independent Practice

   - Have students continue to practice on their own
   - Provide knowledge of results

SAMPLE LESSON 7.4

 Direct Instruction

Natural/Processed Foods

1. Anticipatory Set

   a. Focus: Teacher holds up both a carrot and frosting filled cake. The teacher says, "You are what you eat."

   b. Objectives: Today you will learn to understand food. You will learn the difference between natural and processed foods.

   c. Purpose: This lesson will help you understand the foods you eat and perhaps influence the foods that you eat in the future.

2. Instruction
   a. Provide information
      * *Explanation:* Teacher gives a minilecture on relevant facts concerning vitamins, calories, minerals, preservatives, package labels.
      * *Model:* Teacher uses the school lunch menu and lists the foods into two categories on the chalkboard: natural foods and processed foods. Teacher explains why each is placed in the appropriate category.
   b. Check for understanding
      * *Key questions:* What is the difference between a natural food and a processed food? What is a preservative? What is an example of a natural food? What is an example of a processed food? What can you learn from the label on an item you buy in the store?
      * *Active participation:* Teacher holds up real food items. Students indicate whether item is natural or processed by means of finger signals or colored cards.

3. Guided Practice
   a. Activity: Students work in small teams. Each group is provided with a stack of pictures of food items. Students divide pictures into two categories: natural foods and processed foods. Teacher monitors, assists, and provides feedback.
   b. Feedback: Teacher moves from group to group and asks key questions to check for understanding. Also provides specific information as needed.

4. Closure
   * Teacher designates one side of the room as "natural food" side, the other as the "processed food" side. Both kinds of foods are written individually on 3 × 5 cards. Students draw a card and line up on the appropriate side of the room.

5. Independent Practice
   * Students assess food in refrigerator and/or cupboards at home. Students make list with two categories (natural and processed) based on food in refrigerator/cupboard. Lists are analyzed in small groups the next day.

Cooperative Learning Lesson Plan Guide

The following lesson plan guide should help you develop cooperative learning lessons. The sample lesson follows the guide.

COOPERATIVE LESSON PLAN GUIDE
1. Preliminary Information
   a. Course
   b. Grade level
   c. Lesson summary
   d. Objectives
   e. Materials
   f. Time required

2. Decisions
   a. Group size
   b. Assignment to groups
   c. Roles
3. Procedures
   a. Instructional task
   b. Positive interdependence
   c. Individual accountability
   d. Criteria for success
   e. Expected behaviors
4. Monitoring and Processing
   a. Monitoring
   b. Intervening
   c. Processing

SAMPLE LESSON 7.5

Mystery at the Ringgold Roadcut

1. Preliminary Information
   - Subject area: Earth science
   - Grade level: Middle school

   a. Lesson summary: Students are given samples of fossils (Crinoids). They work together to make observations and inferences about the fossils and then predict the nature of the environment at the time these now-fossilized organisms were alive.

   b. Objectives:
      - Students will observe and make inferences about a collection of fossil Crinoid stems.
      - Students will use their observations and inferences to predict the nature of the environment in which the Crinoids might have lived.

   c. Materials: Fossil Crinoid stems (put four to eight each in a small plastic bag), hand lens, metric ruler, geological time scale, copy of Team Data Organizer (Figure 7.10).

   d. Time required: Forty-five minutes.

	Student 1	Student 2	Student 3	Student 4
Observation 1				
Observation 2				
Inference				

Observation:

Inference:

Analysis Questions

1:

2:

3:

4:

Figure 7.10 Mystery at the Ringgold Roadcut Team Data Organizer.

2. Decisions
   a. Group Size: four
   b. Assignment: random (make four photocopies of as many different fossils as you have groups of four in your class. Shuffle the photographs and hand one to each student. Give them a few minutes to find other students in the class holding the same fossil to form their groups.
   c. Roles:
      * *Tracker:* Records observations and inferences on the team data organizer chart.
      * *Checker:* Keeps the group on the task by watching the time and helps the group understand the task.
      * *Encourager*: Makes certain each member is participating and invites any reluctant members in by asking them for their ideas.
      * *Materials Manager*: Picks up and returns equipment and materials for the lesson.

3. Procedures
   a. Instructional task: Teacher says: The materials manager of your group will pick up the materials, which contain objects that I collected in rocks in the North Georgia Mountains. Your team is to work together to make observations and inferences of these objects. Your group will be given a team data organizer, which the tracker will use to record your team's observations. Everyone should participate by making two observations and one interference about the objects.
   b. Positive interdependence: Teacher explains: I want one set of observations and inferences from the group. Your tracker will record your ideas on the team data organizer. Work together making sure that everyone contributes observations and inferences. To form the groups I am going to give each of you a picture of a fossil. Find other students in the class with the same picture. Sit at one of the tables as a team.
   c. Individual accountability: Each group member must be able to describe the objects using at least two observations and be able to name one inference. I will draw cards randomly from this deck of four and ask you to represent your group.
   d. Criteria for success: Groups that include two observations and one inference per team member will have achieved success in the activity.
   e. Expected behaviors: I expect to see each team member making observations and inferences and performing the role you were assigned.

4. Monitoring and Processing
   a. Monitoring: Teacher should circulate to see how the teams are doing and provide help when groups need assistance. Students may need help making inferences. Encourage reluctant learners to participate in the activity.
   b. Closing: Have a member of each team (select them randomly by drawing one of four numbered cards—have students number themselves off from 1–4 in each group) describe their objects. Then ask them to identify inferences. Ask the class what kinds of objects they think they are looking at. Do they think they once were alive? If they were alive, in what kind of an environment might they have lived in? For homework, have students draw pictures and diagrams of what they think the environment was like.
   c. Processing: Teacher provides feedback to the class on the work that groups did and asks groups to identify one thing that might make their work as a team more effective.

Inquiry/Laboratory Lesson Plan Guide

Inquiry activities and laboratory activities can be approached by employing a simple learning cycle consisting of

- prelaboratory (prelab)
- laboratory
- postlaboratory (postlab)

LESSON PLAN GUIDE

1. Prelab

    a. Objectives
    b. Overview of laboratory or inquiry

    c. Alternate demonstration/discrepant event/ inquiry session
    d. Safety precautions
    e. Group size
    f. Assignment to groups
    g. Roles

2. Lab

    a. Monitor
    b. Intervene

3. Postlab

    a. Whole class processing
    b. Application
    c. Clean up

SAMPLE LESSON 7.6

 Investigating Mass, Volume, and Density

1. Prelab

    a. Objectives: The student will devise methods to determine the density of an ice cube.
    b. Overview of laboratory or inquiry: Review with students the laboratory that was done previously in which they learned to determine the density of various objects and substances. Students determined the density of solid objects such as pebbles, marbles, and paper clips. Explain that today they are going to apply their knowledge of density to solve an inquiry problem.
    c. Discrepant event: Display two beakers containing equal amounts of clear liquids so all the students can see them. (One contains water and the other contains alcohol.) Do not tell the students what the liquids are or that they are different. Ask the students what would happen if you were to put ice cubes in each liquid. Then place an ice cube in each beaker and ask the students to explain the results. Students might remark that the ice must be strange or funny. Interchange the ice cubes. The students might comment that the water must be funny or strange. Lead the students to realize that one liquid supports the ice the way water does and the other does not. Students might guess that the first liquid is water and the second liquid, which does not support the ice, must be different than water. Ask the students to establish a relative density scale for the three materials: ice, water, and unknown liquid. (Answer: alcohol, ice, water) Now pose the problem: Find the density of the ice cube. Show the students where the materials are located that they can use to investigate the problem.
    d. Safety precautions: Warn the students not to taste the liquids or the ice cubes.
    e. Group size: three
    f. Assignment to groups: Random or high, low, average student per group
    g. Roles:

        - *Recorder:* Keeps a record of the methods that the group attempts. Records any results made by group.
        - *Principal Investigator:* Keeps the group on task by watching the time and not letting the group dwell on any one method.
        - *Materials Handler:* Responsible for obtaining materials and making sure they are returned at the end of the lab.

2. Lab

  a. Monitor: Circulate around the room from group to group. Remember that the most important part of this laboratory is for students to devise their own method of determining the density of an ice cube. Some groups will need encouragement. As you visit groups ask questions, but frame them so that students will think about the information they really need to determine density.

  b. Intervene: If you need to intervene in a group, ask the members to describe what they have done to determine the density of the ice cube, rather than tell them how.

3. Postlab

  a. Whole class processing: Ask each group to give a one-minute or less description of their method. You can expect the following methods:

  • Use a metric rule to calculate volume and balance to determine mass.
  • Push the ice cube into water in a graduated cylinder and then use balance to determine mass.
  • Ice placed in alcohol will sink. As water is added, and the mixture stirred, the ice will rise. When the density of the liquid is equal to the ice, the cube will be suspended. Density of liquid is determined by measuring volume and mass of a sample of the liquid.
  • Because ice sinks in alcohol, mass is determined on a balance, then volume is determined by using the displacement procedure in alcohol.

  Have the groups analyze their results for the density of the ice cube. How do their results vary? What is the average or central tendency of the groups' results? How does this compare with the known value of the density of ice?

  b. Application: Have each team select one of the following items and devise a method to determine its density: an elephant, a teenager, an automobile, a flea.

  c. Clean up: Materials handler should return materials to storage area.

Constructivist Lesson Plan

CONSTRUCTIVIST LESSON PLAN GUIDE Constructivist teaching employs another form of learning cycle. Four phases are included: invitation, exploration, concept explanatioin, and taking action.

1. Invitation Phase

  a. Ascertain student misconceptions
  b. Engage student interest through a motivating activity or experience

2. Exploration Phase

  a. Engage student interest through motivating activity/experience
  b. Facilitate discussion among students in small teams

  c. Pose open-ended questions
  d. Monitor and observe student groups

3. Explanation Phase

  a. Help students invent or discover concepts
  b. Give information
  c. Guide whole class discussion
  d. Provide explanations
  e. Define appropriate concepts and terms

4. Taking Action Phase

  a. Students take personal and/or social action on issues related to content
  b. Students interact and apply concepts in small teams (or individually)
  c. Facilitate discussion by means of open-ended questions
  d. Observe and monitor students in learning teams

SAMPLE LESSON 7.7

Electromagnetism

Students gain insight into the relationship between electricity and magnetism. Working in cooperative groups, they conduct a hands-on inquiry experiment in which they use basic laboratory equipment.

Materials

- Bags containing: 1.5-volt battery, wire, compass

Invitation

Students are divided into groups. Groups are challenged to write about a situation in which the needle of a compass would not point north. Groups should be given just a few minutes for this activity. Each group briefly shares its scenario. The teacher comments on the ideas and then mentions that another method (if not already mentioned) exits. This activity can be used to determine what students know about magnetism and what alternative ideas they bring with them into the lesson.

Exploration

Bags are distributed to the groups. Groups are challenged to find a way to alter the direction of the compass needle using the contents of the bag. Each group records with drawings each of its attempts and the results.

Explanation

After sufficient time, any group that discovered a means of altering the direction of the needle with the battery and wire presents its findings to the class. Teacher involvement at this stage consists of providing the class with accurate information (wrapping the wire around the compass), as needed. After the presentations, the remaining groups should be given a short time to test the correct setup.

Take Action

As an expansion activity, students could conduct research on electric cars. What are their benefits? Their drawbacks? Are there any in the United States? How much do they cost? Are they being used more extensively outside the United States? How do they benefit the environment? How do they work?

Designing a Science Course of Study

Designing a course of study involves the same principles that you employed to develop a miniunit. The difference is that for course design you will be clustering learning outcomes and sequencing the resulting units of instruction. Planning interesting courses of study starts with the consideration of goals and rationale for science teaching, just as it did when you planned a miniunit. The following discussion explores some of the elements that should be considered in designing a science course.

Elements of a Course of Study

I overheard some students make these remarks about one of their teachers while I was visiting their school: "I'm really looking forward to taking Mrs. D'Olivo's science course next year." "Yes, she plans interesting projects for the students, and her tests are not hard, but they are very interesting." Science courses can be interesting to students if they are carefully planned and if the needs of the students are taken into consideration.

Course planning involves the same processes that were used to develop a unit of teaching. In the section that follows, I have selected a high school science program entitled Global Science by John Christensen[14] to illustrate how to describe the elements of a course of study. There are several reasons that I have chosen this program. First, the program is based on a textbook, and the odds are good that most of your courses will be based on the use of a textbook. Second, Global Science is an example of an STS course and reflects an interdisciplinary approach. Five elements should be considered in the course planning process (listed next). These elements should be shared with students as part of a course syllabus and distributed to them at the beginning of the course. An abbreviated form of the elements should be prepared for the students' parents.

- Rationale/philosophy
- Learning outcomes
- Units of study
- Instructional strategies (foci)
- Evaluation

To make the elements of a course plan concrete, a sample course plan for Global Science follows (based on the curriculum written by John Christensen, a high school teacher in Englewood, Colorado).

Sample Course Plan: Global Science: Energy, Resources, Environment

RATIONALE/PHILOSOPHY The rationale for Global Science is described in a letter to the students and in a list of assumptions about secondary school science education. The letter, which you can use as a model for writing your own course rationales, follows:

Dear Student:

You are living at an exciting time. In the next several years extremely important decisions are going to be made, and you will play a role in making them. These decisions will affect the position of your country in the world of nations, your feeling of who you are and how you relate to other people around you, the standard of living you will have, and the amount of personal freedom you will enjoy. Many of these decisions are related to energy, resources, and the environment.

How well we make these decisions in large part depends upon how well we understand the issues. It is the purpose of this course to build a basic background for understanding energy/resource/ environmental problems. This is not just another science course. The problems we will be dealing with are in the here and now. You will find that the road your travel as you work through these pages can be an exciting journey—if you have the proper attitude.

Science is a tool at our disposal. It is a powerful tool, and it will play an important role at this turning point in our history. What is exponential growth? How bad is the energy/resource/environmental problem? Does the earth have a carrying capacity? Can we live better with less? What are our alternatives? How do we get there from here?

The study of this course won't provide all the answers, but you'll be much better prepared to face many issues because of your experiences with these materials.

In addition to this statement, Global Science is based on the following four assumptions about secondary school science education:

1. The study of science should be a meaningful endeavor for all students in a modern society.
2. Science is best learned by experimenting and analyzing data—not just by reading and doing problems. This is how basic science skills are gained.
3. Society is best served, and student interest held, when relevant material is emphasized.
4. If only one science course is required at the high school level, that course should emphasize the ecosystem concept and resource use.

INTENDED LEARNING OUTCOMES The following objectives constitute a sample of the intended learning outcomes for Global Science.

- Build a firm understanding of the ecosystem concept—the basic components of an ecosystem, how the living and nonliving interact, and the cyclic activities that take place. (*cognition*)
- Build an understanding of the concepts and laws that governs our use of energy and mineral resources. (*cognition*)
- Examine our present energy sources and consumption patterns and apply this knowledge as a component of future planning. (*cognitive skill*)
- Examine how humans relate to their economic environment and understand how economics affects social/scientific decision making. (*cognition*)
- Develop an awareness of the "spaceship earth" ethic and the interrelatedness of resources, economics, environment, food production, and population growth. (*affect*)

UNITS OF STUDY The approach to designing and sequencing the units of study in Global Science is based on the following themes:

1. The earth and its resources are finite.
2. Humans are partners with nature, *not* masters of nature.

INQUIRY ACTIVITY 7.3

Designing a Course of Study: The Course Syllabus

In this activity you identify and describe the major elements of a course of study for some area of middle or high school science. Your product will be course syllabus, which you would give to your students on the first day of class.

Materials

- Secondary science textbooks
- Newsprint
- Marking pens

Procedures

1. Select an area of science from the following list to develop a course of study for a one-semester or quarter course:

   - Introductory biology
   - Survey physical science
   - Advanced chemistry
   - Introductory chemistry
   - Geology
   - Introductory earth science
   - Unified science (seventh grade)

2. Design a course of study by preparing a course syllabus, which should contain the following elements:

   - Rationale/philosophy
   - Learning outcomes
   - List of the units of study
   - Instructional strategies
   - Evaluation

3. Work with a partner to brainstorm the content of the elements of the course of study. Use large sheets of newsprint to record your ideas from the brainstorming session. On your own, use the results of the brainstorming session to create the course syllabus.

Minds-On Strategies

1. Compare your product with those created by other students in your class. What problem areas were identified? How were they resolved?
2. How were the courses characterized? What philosophies guided the development of the courses?
3. Why are course syllabi important? Are they necessary?
4. What modifications in the plan presented here did you make?

The course is organized around ten units of study:

1. The Grand Oasis in Space
2. Basic Energy/Resource Concepts
3. Energy and Society
4. Growth, Population, and Food
5. Energy Supply and Demand
6. Energy for the Future
7. Mineral Resources
8. Making Peace with Our Environment
9. The Economics of Resources and Environment
10. Options for the Future

INSTRUCTIONAL STRATEGIES (FOCI) Global Science involves the students in a number of instructional strategies:

- *Global Science* (course text)
- Films (a detailed list is correlated by unit)
- Field trips

- Laboratory activities (every unit's development is focused around several laboratory, hands-on science activities)
- Discussion
- Problem-solving activities
- Debates
- Case studies

EVALUATION A comprehensive evaluation plan is employed in the Global Science course. Students are involved in a wide variety of learning activities, and the evaluation plan reflects this diversity. Evaluation is based on the following criteria:

1. *Course portfolio:* Each student maintains a portfolio of his or her work, including laboratory reports, a log in which the student makes weekly entries, copies of all homework, and reports.
2. *Tests and Quizzes:* Weekly quizzes and chapter tests (provided with the curriculum) are administered.
3. *Cooperative Team Investigation:* Each student works with a team to investigate a global problem and presents results to the whole class.
4. *Readings:* Students make concept maps of each chapter and write brief summaries of the main concepts of each map.
5. *Laboratory Activities:* Labs are conducted in small teams (although membership changes during the course). Students are evaluated on the basis of their cooperativeness and contribution to

the group's process, as well as on all activities. The principle of cooperative learning is employed in all laboratory activities.

SECTION 2: SCIENCE TEACHER GAZETTE

Volume 7: Models of Teaching

Think Pieces

1. What are the advantages and disadvantages of stating objectives in behavioral or performance terms?
2. How would the following theorists respond to question 1?
   a. Piaget
   b. Bruner
   c. Skinner
   d. Rogers
   e. Vygotsky
3. How is a cognition different than a cognitive skill? How does each notion relate to the other?
4. Explain why affects should be part of science instruction.
5. How do the following lesson plan models differ? Which one do you prefer? Why? Lesson plan models: direct/interactive teaching, cooperative learning, inquiry/laboratory, and constructivist teaching.

Science Teachers Talk

"What tips would you give beginning teachers in planning and preparing lessons?"

VIRGINIA CHEEK: Planning and preparation are not just helpful, they are mandatory. This next piece of advice may sound like heresy to professional "educators" but do not spin your wheels writing fancy "behavioral objectives" or even worry about the hierarchy's seven levels etc., etc. Do, however, decide what is worth spending an hour trying to get your students to know or do, then plan minute by minute how you will accomplish your goal. Prepare all the materials or equipment you will need well in advance of the day needed. Always plan more than

you can finish. This gives you options from which to choose, depending on how your kids respond to other parts of your lesson. Include frequent checks to see how you and your students are doing. Long-range outlines are also essential, but do not mandate strict adherence. Use your plans as a guide, but let your students' understanding dictate how closely you stick to it. Make sure that when you "cover" material that you don't just bury it!

BEN BOZA (BOTSWANA): Effective teaching takes careful planning and preparation and I cannot over-emphasize the importance of these steps. A teacher should always prepare a lesson guided by the syllabus. Time allocation should be calculated in such a manner that a lesson is introduced, discussed, and concluded all within the given period. Each lesson you carry out should have an objective and a goal to reach by the end of it. Therefore, the planning should focus around achieving it. A well-planned lesson should end by informing the students from whence the next lesson shall commence. In this way, you provide a flowing of the subject matter being taught. A lesson well planned is thorough, comprehensive, and easily understood.

When planning to carry out practical experiments and illustrations, go over them beforehand to ascertain that all works out well. It is important to be sure of intended results. In this way, as a teacher you portray mastery of the subject matter and this boosts the confidence of your students in you. Students perceive their teachers as perfectionists who should not get it wrong. There's nothing as unbalancing as to abandon an intended practical or illustration because it "backfires" on you as a teacher. By that I don't mean that occasional mishaps may not occur in the event of teaching, but they should not be a result of sketchy planning and preparation.

An important consideration to make during planning of the lesson should be the diverse capability of the students. Your planning should be accommodating enough to absorb the capacity of the weaker students and slow learners so that they are not left out in the progressive teachings. On the same note, plan how to have the fast learners occupied within the lesson to avoid them being distracted or becoming bored or edgy as you pull the weak ones along.

RACHEL ZGONC: At the beginning of the year I would spend hours planning lessons. While this planning helped me feel more comfortable getting up in front of the class, I think at times it hindered my creativity. In class, I would often concentrate so much on following what I had planned for that lesson that I missed some great opportunities for getting off track and talking about topics that the students wanted to focus on. The lesson I learned from these experiences is that flexibility is important. Just because your lesson plan says that the students should be at a certain point by the end of the period, this does not mean that the students have learned more or even as much as they might have if you had followed some of the unplanned avenues that presented themselves to you in class. After all, if the students are interested and involved, they will always learn more and remember it longer.

JERRY PELLETIER: The first tip I would give new teachers is that they must have good classroom management. Students must understand why they are in the class and what the teacher expects of them. When planning a lesson teachers must always keep in mind their audience. The lessons must be geared to the level and understanding of their students. Teachers should never assume that students have mastered a skill. For example, if students will be measuring distances with rulers a teacher should never assume that the students fully understand how a ruler should be used. These skills should always be integrated as part of the lesson. Reinforcement of key skills and concepts ought to be made part of any lesson. It is also important to have closure to summarize the main ideas developed during the lesson.

JOHN RICCIARDI: Be able. Be directed. Be diverse. Be clear and be yourself! Be able . . . by allowing yourself ample time to prepare daily lessons. Choose the time of day or night when you are most alert and rested. For me, the most ideal prep period occurs between 3:30 and 5:30 in the morning. Be directed . . . by identifying and being aware of your daily goals and objectives. Know exactly what you want your students to learn . . . before you begin constructing a lesson. Be attuned to the science content material that is least likely and most likely to be remembered and understood. Be diverse . . . by providing choices. Incorporate a variety of instructional mediums and multisensory activities. Make your lessons interdisciplinary by integrating art, drama, prose, and poetry into your science. Be clear . . . and your students will understand you and know what you expect from them. Assignment responsibilities should be in writing and easily accessible. Be yourself . . . and more real to students by weaving your personality and character into your lessons. Present and instruct in ways that feel right . . . rather than in ways that you *think* are right.

GINNY ALMEDER: In terms of planning and preparation for lessons, I would suggest the following:

- Be well informed about your subject. Read the text and relevant literature. Making reference to a recent magazine or newspaper article or television science program can make the material more relevant and directly involve students who may have been exposed to the same material.
- Write out your objectives and cross-reference them to your activities. This will enhance the clarity of your lessons and facilitate learning.

- Set up your labs in advance. Allow extra time to hunt for equipment or to make last-minute modifications.
- Have alternative plans in case your original one is not workable.

- Plan to incorporate some "real-life" applications into your presentations. This will help students appreciate the personal implications of science.

PLANNING ACTIVITY 7.1

Earth Science
Shake, Rattle, and Quake: Earthquake Waves

In this activity, students investigate the differences between primary and secondary earthquake waves by simulating waves with a toy called a Slinky. The activity can be done as a demonstration or as a small-group activity in which students work in pairs or groups of four.

Objectives

- Observe and differentiate earthquake waves.
- Understand the effects of earthquake waves.

Concepts

- Earthquake
- Waves (P and S)
- Energy

Materials

- Slinky (double length)

Procedures

1. To explore primary earthquake waves, with a partner, stretch a slinky to about 5 m in length. While holding one end, gather in about fifteen extra coils and let them go. Repeat several times while watching the coils. Draw a picture showing your observation.
2. To explore secondary earthquake waves, with a partner, stretch the slinky to about 5 m in length again. Quickly move your hand to one side and back again in a snapping motion. Repeat several times while watching the coils carefully. Draw a picture showing your observation.
3. To find out what happens when earthquake waves meet each other or bounce off objects, stretch the slinky to about 5 m again. Both you and your partner should quickly move your hands to one side and back again.

Applications to Science Teaching

1. Draw a concept map for earthquakes to describe the conceptual nature of a lesson or miniunit on earthquakes.
2. Rewrite the objectives of this activity to include a cognitive skill, psychomotor skill, and an affect.
3. Use this lesson as central instructional foci for a miniunit on earthquakes. What other instructional foci would you include?

PLANNING ACTIVITY 7.2

Earth Science
Don't Take It for Granite: Rock Classification

In this activity students use a simple dichotomous key (see Figure 7.11) to classify rocks as igneous, metamorphic, or sedimentary.

Objectives

- Identify the properties of rocks.
- Classify rocks according to their physical properties.

Concepts

- Rock
- Igneous
- Metamorphic
- Sedimentary
- Mineral
- Interlocking crystals (minerals)
- Noninterlocking crystals (minerals)

Materials

- Box of rocks: granite, obsidian, pumice, basalt, limestone, shale, sandstone, conglomerate, slate, schist, gneiss
- Small bottle dilute hydrochloric acid
- Hand lens

Procedure

1. Observing one rock at a time, use the classification key to determine whether the rock is igneous, metamorphic, or sedimentary.
2. Make a chart of your results including the rock sample, specific properties, and the class it belongs to.
3. Use reference books to determine the name of each of the rock specimens.

> 1a. If the rock is made up of minerals that you can see, go to 2a.
> 1b. If the rock is not made up of visible minerals, go to 5a.
> 2a. If the rock is made up of minerals that are interlocking ("melted together"), go to 3a.
> 2b. If the rock is made up of minerals that are noninterlocking ("glued together"), go to 6a.
> 3a. If the minerals in the sample are of the same kind, the rock is metamorphic.
> 3b. If the minerals in the sample are of two or more different types, go to 4a.
> 4a. If the minerals in the sample are distributed in a random pattern (not lined up), the rock is igneous.
> 4b. If the minerals in the sample are not distributed randomly but show a preferred arrangement or banding (lined up), the rock is metamorphic.
> 5a. If the rock is either glassy or frothy (has small holes), it is igneous.
> 5b. If the rock is made up of strong, flat sheets that look as though they will split off into slatelike pieces, it is metamorphic.
> 6a. If the rock is made of silt, sand, or pebbles cemented together (it may have fossils), it is sedimentary.
> 6b. If the rock is not made of silt, sand, or pebbles but contains a substance that fizzles when dilute hydrochloric acid is poured on it, it is sedimentary.

Figure 7.11 Rock Classification Key.

Applications to Science Teaching

1. Design a concept map that includes all the concepts listed. Make sure you show how the concepts are linked together. Use your map to answer this question: What prerequisite concepts do students need to know before they can do the rock classification activity? Add these concepts to the map.
2. What central or focus cognition will this activity help students understand?
3. What is the basis for the following statement? In this activity students will be involved in concept learning, not propositional learning.

PLANNING ACTIVITY 7.3

Life Science
Light On: Responses of Earthworms

In this activity students will explore the way earthworms respond to environmental changes.

Objectives

- Generate hypotheses regarding the interaction of earthworms and changing environmental conditions.
- Design safe experiments to find out how earthworms respond to environmental changes.
- Gather data to test hypotheses about earthworm behavior.

Concepts

- Environmental change
- Environmental factors (touch, smell, sound, gravity, temperature, light)

Materials

- Earthworms
- Pieces of paper
- Vinegar or household ammonia
- Damp sheet of newspaper
- Small box
- Flashlight
- Other materials as required by experiments

Procedure

1. Tap the head of an earthworm gently with a finger or a pencil eraser. How did the earthworm respond?
2. How do you think earthworms will respond if any of the following environmental factors are changed? (light, temperature, smell, gravity, sound)
3. Write one or more hypotheses that incorporate how you think earthworms will respond to various environmental conditions.
4. Design an experiment to test each hypothesis.
5. Conduct the experiment and use the data to "test" the hypotheses.
6. What do you conclude about earthworm behavior?

Applications to Science Teaching

1. This is an open inquiry science activity. Students will have to design experiments in order to test hypotheses. What cognitive skills are required to enable students to complete this activity?
2. Handling living things in the science classroom can be the medium to teach important attitudes and values about science. How would you ensure that these attitudes and values were indeed part of the activity and that the students were assessed on them as well? Describe your plan.

PLANNING ACTIVITY 7.4

Physical Science
Chemistry in the Bag

In this activity students will investigate a chemical reaction occurring in a plastic bag.[15]

Objectives

- Observe a chemical reaction.
- Describe the evidence indicating a chemical reaction has taken place.

Concepts

- Chemical
- Chemical change
- Heat
- Gas
- Indicator

Materials

- Calcium chloride
- Sodium bicarbonate (baking soda)
- Red cabbage juice (boil red cabbage for five minutes, pour off liquid) or phenol red indicator
- Plastic bags (quart size)
- Plastic spoon

Procedure

1. Ask students what they think is a chemical. Write their answers on the board.
2. Ask students what they think might happen if two chemicals are mixed together. Write their responses on the board.
3. Explain to students that they are going to explore chemicals and chemical reactions using relatively safe chemicals, but they should keep the chemicals off their clothes and skin, rinsing with water if chemicals do make contact, wiping up spills as they happen, and washing their hands at the end of the activity.
4. Have teams of students obtain small cups containing baking soda and calcium chloride, a small bottle of cabbage juice, wood splints, vial, goggles, and a plastic bag.
5. Give students a handout that contains the instructions and questions for investigation.

Inquiry Procedure

1. Measure one spoonful of calcium chloride and place it into the bag.
2. Add one spoonful of sodium bicarbonate (baking soda) to the bag. Zip the bag closed and shake it to observe any evidence of a chemical change.
3. Pour 10 ml of cabbage juice into a small vial. Carefully put the vial into the plastic bag without spilling the indicator.
4. Zip the bag closed.
5. Tip the vial of indicator.

Inquiry Questions

1. What happened when the indicator mixed with the baking soda and calcium chloride?
2. What are at least five observations?
3. Do you think a chemical reaction occurred?
4. How would you define a chemical reaction?

Application to Science Teaching

1. What safety precautions will you take during this activity? Can safety precautions be included as intended learning outcomes? How would you phrase a learning outcome that addressed safety in the science classroom?
2. Draw a concept map using the concepts listed. Be sure to include the linking phrases.
3. What are some additional activities that you could do with these chemicals to build on this initial activity? List ideas for at least three to five lessons.

PLANNING ACTIVITY 7.5

Physical Science
An Eggzact Experiment

In this activity, students observe a teacher demonstration (a discrepant event) and then theorize possible explanations for the event.

Objectives

- Describe the effects of air pressure on an object.
- Explain how an egg can be forced into a bottle.

Concepts

- Air pressure
- Molecules
- Heat
- Cooling

Materials

- Glass quart milk bottle
- Hard boiled egg with shell removed
- Match
- Crumpled-up piece of paper

Procedure

1. Tell the students that you are going to do a demonstration. You are going to try to put an egg (show it to them) into a bottle (show them) without touching or forcing the egg into the bottle. Ask them if they have any ideas about how this could be accomplished. Record their ideas.

2. Carefully drop a small wad of burning paper into the milk bottle. Just before the flame goes out, place the egg, smaller end down, in the opening of the bottle. Have the students watch the egg squeeze into the bottle.

3. Arrange the students in pairs to make a diagram and write explanations for what they think caused the egg to go into the bottle.

4. After ten minutes, have students explain their ideas to the whole class.

Applications to Science Teaching

1. Could this "activity" be used as a performance assessment? How would you set it up, and what criteria would you use to "evaluate" the students' performance?

2. What are some additional activities that you could use to help students understand air pressure or other properties of air?

3. What cognition does this activity help students understand?

Problems and Extensions

1. What is a performance assessment? Give one example for earth science, life science, physical science, and STS.

2. Write an objective for each of the levels in Bloom's taxonomy in one of the following content areas: rocks, electricity, and ecosystem.

3. Write an assessment item for each of the objectives you designed.

4. Select a chapter from a science book of your choice and create six assessment items using Bloom's taxonomy.

5. Prepare concept maps for one of the following:

   a. a chapter from a high school biology, chemistry, earth science, or physics text.

   b. a potential miniunit on electric circuits, physical and chemical changes, reproduction, erosion, ground water pollution.

Notes

1. Shirley Magnusson, Joseph Krajcik, and Hilda Borko, "Nature, Sources, and Development of Pedagogical Content Knowledge for Science Teaching." in *Examining Pedagogical Content Knowledge*, ed. J. Gess-Newsome and N. G. Lederman (Dordrecht, The Netherlands: Kluwer Academic Publishers, 1999), pp. 95–132.

2. The material in this section is based on the work of Dr. Charles Rathbone, University of Vermont; George J. Posner, and Alan N. Rudnitsky, *Course Design: A Guide to Curriculum Development for Teachers* (Menlo Park, Calif.: Addison-Wesley, 2000); and field-testing and feedback from graduate students in the TEEMS science teacher education program, Georgia State University, 1994–2002.

3. Miniunit titles developed by TEEMS graduate students, class of 2001, Georgia State University.

4. Posner and Rudnitsky, *Course Design*, p. 15.

5. Ibid., p. 20.

6. For additional information on developing concept maps, see Joseph D. Novak and D. Bob Gowin, *Learning How to Learn* (Cambridge, England: Cambridge University Press, 1984).

7. Excerpted from the unit "What if you had a volcano in your backyard?" by DeAnn Peterson, used with permission.

8. Posner and Rudnitsky, *Course Design*, p. 47.

9. David Krathwohl, Benjamin S. Bloom, and Bertram B. Masia, *Taxonomy of Educational Objectives, Book 2 Affective Domain* (Reading, Mass.: Addison-Wesley, 1999).

10. Benjamin Bloom, *Taxonomy of Educational Objectives, Handbook 1: Cognitive Domain* (Reading, Mass.: Addison-Wesley, 1984).

11. Leslie W. Trowbridge and Rodger W. Bybee, *Becoming a Secondary School Science Teacher* (Columbus, Ohio: Merrill, 1990), p. 150.

12. J. R. Eglen and R. F. Kempa, "Assessing Manipulative Skills in Practical Chemistry," *The School Science Review* 56 (1978): 261–73.

13. Written by Mr. Mal Wallace, intern at Georgia State University, currently teaching at the Cottage School, Roswell, Georgia. Used with permission.

14. John W. Christensen, *Global Science: Energy, Resources, Environment* (Dubuque, Iowa: Kendall Hunt), 1991.

15. This activity is an adaptation of one presented in Jacqueline Barber, *Chemical Reactions* (Berkeley, Calif: Lawrence Hall of Science, 1986); and Beth Baker et al., *CHEM-PACS*, (Denver, Colo.: Practical Activities with Common Substances, 1989).

Readings

Abruscato, Joe, and Hassard, Jack. *The Whole Cosmos Catalog of Science Activities for Kids of All Ages.* Glenview, Ill.: Scott Foresman, 1991.

Bosak, Susan V. *Science Is: A Sourcebook of Fascinating Facts, Projects, and Activities.* Washington, D.C.: National Science Teachers Association, 1998.

Cothron, Julia H., Giese, Ronald N., and Rezba, Richard J. *Science Experiments and Projects for Students.* Dubuque, Iowa: Kendall/Hunt Publishing Company, 2000.

Hassard, Jack. *Science As Inquiry.* Parsippany, N.J.: Goodyear Publishing Company, 2000.

National Research Council. *Inquiry and the National Science Education Standards.* Washington, D.C.: National Academy Press, 2000.

Rakow, Stephen J., ed. *NSTA Pathways to the Science Standards—Middle School Edition.* Washington, D.C.: National Science Teachers Association, 1998.

Texley, Juliana, and Wild, Ann. *NSTA Pathways to the Science Standards—High School Edition.* Washington, D.C.: National Science Teachers Association, 1998.

On the Web

Access Excellence: http://www.accessexcellence.org/. Access Excellence, launched in 1993, is a national educational program that provides high school biology and life science teachers access to their colleagues, scientists, and critical sources of new scientific information via the World Wide Web. The program was originally developed and launched by Genentech Inc., a leading biotechnology company that discovers, develops, manufactures, and markets human pharmaceuticals for significant unmet medical needs.

American Association for Physics Teachers: http://www.aapt.org/. The AAPT site contains resources for physical science teachers and an invitation to join the AAPT. One link on the site is the Physical Sciences Resource Center, which contains a wealth of resources, lesson plans, demonstrations, and activities.

American Chemical Society: http://www.acs.org/portal/ Chemistry. The ACS Web site contains resources for chemistry teachers, including access to current events, lesson plans, and projects.

American Geological Institute: http://www.agiweb.org/. The American Geological Institute is a nonprofit federation of forty geoscientific and professional associations that represent more than 100,000 geologists, geophysicists, and other earth scientists. Founded in 1948, AGI provides information services to geoscientists, serves as a voice of shared interests in the profession, plays a major role in strengthening geoscience education, and strives to increase public awareness of the vital role of geosciences in mankind's use of resources and interaction with the environment.

Benchmarks for Scientific Literacy: http://www.project2061.org/tools/benchol/bobintro.htm. The *Benchmarks* will help you define the scope of your teaching plans and provide you with examples of concepts that might be presente to your students.

Dynamic Earth: http://earth.leeds.ac.uk/dynamicearth. This site offers resources sponsored by the Leeds University U.K. on plate tectonics, volcanoes, earthquakes, and other earth science topics.

Forefront Curriculum: http://www.forefrontcurriculum.com/. Technology-based activities and resources are provided to help you develop powerful units of science teaching.

Matrix of Science Lessons, K–12: http://www.sciencenetlinks.com/. This site contains a collection of science lessons and activities maintained by the AAAS.

National Association of Biology Teachers: http://www.nabt.org/. NABT is the leader in life science education. To date, more than 9,000 educators have joined NABT to share experiences and expertise with colleagues from around the globe, keep up with trends and developments in the field, and grow professionally.

National Science Education Standards: http://books.nap.edu/html/nses/html/index.html. You will find Chapter 5 (Assessment Standards) and Chapter 6 (Content Standards) very helpful as you develop lesson plans and activities for you teaching units.

We will explore several aspects of assessment in this chapter. Through the assessment process, you will make judgments about the progress of your students and the effectiveness of your teaching plans. Assessment involves measurement and testing to gather data useful in making judgments. However, in the past several years new forms of assessment and evaluation have emerged from the emphasis on theory and research in cognitive and motivational psychology and cooperative learning.[1] This recent trend, which is incorporated in the discussion of assessment that follows, is characterized by the following elements:

1. Some of the new assessment strategies involve performance assessment. In this method students are required to actually perform the skills and strategies in the form of hands-on assessment questions.
2. Assessment strategies provide teachers with better knowledge of their students' strengths and weaknesses by giving teachers insights into students' process skill abilities.
3. Assessment strategies rely on cooperative learning. In this approach students actually work together on assessment problems.
4. Many assessment tasks are conceptual and therefore involve students in problem solving, higher-level reasoning, critical thinking, and creativity.
5. Evaluation should be authentic. Assessment is authentic if it is "congruent with the results needed from science education; that is, if it asks students to demonstrate knowledge and skills characteristic of a practicing scientist or of the scientifically literate citizen."[2] Authentic assessments involve the students in real experiences (e.g., doing science activities, solving problems,

thinking critically and creatively, and being involved in projects in their community).

We'll examine assessment from three contexts: the classroom context, assessment at the national level, and assessment at the international level. This approach will provide you with specific strategies to use to assess your own students, as well inform you about recent emphases on national and international comparisons of science progress. We'll start with a classroom case in which a teacher is being observed by a group of preservice teachers who wonder about the assessment strategy being used in the class.

 Case Study: Mrs. Cronin's Whirlybird Project: Assessment in Action?

The Case

Mrs. Cronin teaches ninth-grade physical science in a small urban high school. She has been teaching for twelve years and has a reputation for doing interesting projects with her students and using these projects to assess their work. On this particular day she has the students involved in an activity that she calls The Whirlybird Project. In it, teams of students build and fly paper whirlybirds, which are little rotor-copters made of a small strip of paper about 11 inches long and 2 inches wide. The students can manipulate the various parts of the whirlybird (e.g., changing the length of whirlybird wings, adding mass to change the weight, making the width wider, etc.). Several preservice teachers happen to be visiting and observing Mrs. Cronin today, and they are curious about why she is doing the activity and what the she hopes the students will get out of it. When she tells them that the activity is actually a test, some of the preservice teachers are quite surprised. A test? Doing a hands-on activity, and it's a test? Mrs. Cronin explains that it's a performance test. Each group in the class has been working together for the past six weeks on various projects and activities, and the whirlybird project is being used to assess their ability to work together to solve a problem. One of the preservice teachers asks, "What is the problem they are trying to solve?" Mrs. Cronin answers, "to try and build the whirlybird that will have the longest 'hang-time' when dropped from an eight-foot ladder." When the preservice teachers leave, they talk among themselves and can't understand how this activity could be used as a test, as an assessment.

The Problem

Do you think using the whirlybird project as a test is a valid way of assessing students in a science class? If you think it is, what criteria would you use to judge the students' performance? If you don't agree, what alternative ways would you suggest to assess student learning?

How to Read This Chapter

Assessment is presented from three contexts: the classroom level, the national level, and the international level. If you are looking for specific assessment strategies, then you'll want to focus on the first part of the chapter. If you are interested in national and international assessments then the sections on these reports will be of interest. You will want to come back to this chapter from time to time to find examples of assessment strategies that you can integrate into your teaching plans.

SECTION 1: ASSESSING ACTIVE LEARNING

Invitations to Inquiry

- What are some trends in the development of assessment strategies?
- What are the components of a comprehensive assessment strategy for student learning and instruction?
- How can inquiry-based learning be assessed?

- What methods of assessment are effective in understanding student learning?
- How can assessment items be classified?
- What are the trends in the national assessment of science progress?
- What are the trends in the international assessment of science achievement?

Assessing Classroom Learning

In this book, I have emphasized an active approach to learning in the science classroom. Assessment must be a part of the active learning philosophy that is not only supported by documents such as the *Standards* and the *Benchmarks*, but by science education research. Assessment might be considered the centerpiece for instruction because it is the process by which teachers make judgments about what their students have learned. As you know from your own experience as a student, the most common assessment method that teachers (at all levels of instruction) use is the paper-and-pencil test. Yet there is discontent among science educators that paper-and-pencil tests do not tell the whole story when it comes to knowing what students are learning in our classes. In an exercise that I conduct with practicing teachers as part of full-day seminar on science teaching, I ask them to think about their own classrooms, turn to someone sitting nearby, and tell that person what they look for as evidence that their students are really understanding what they are teaching. I've done this with several thousand experienced teachers and here is a summary of their indicators that students are really learning in their class:

- when students can teach another student
- when students ask questions about the content we are studying
- if a student can apply what they have learned to another situation
- when the student's eyes light up—like a light went on
- when the students say that they really enjoy coming to this class

Notice that a score on a test does not appear on the list. It wasn't that the teachers didn't think tests were important, but instead that, as professional teachers, they realized the importance of other pieces of evidence over test scores to indicate what students were really learning in their classrooms.

Reform efforts have challenged teachers to devise alternative ways to assess their students. Hein and Price

Table 8.1 Changing Emphases on Assessment Practices

Less Emphasis On	More Emphasis On
Assessing what is easily measured	Assessing what is most highly valued
Assessing discrete knowledge	Assessing rich, well-structured knowledge
Assessing scientific knowledge	Assessing scientific understanding and reasoning
Assessing to learn what students do not know	Assessing to learn what students do understand
Assessing only achievement	Assessing achievement and opportunity to learn
End-of-term assessments by teachers	Students engaged in ongoing assessment of their work and that of others
Development of external assessments by experts alone	Teachers involved in the development of external assessments

Source: National Research Council, *National Science Education Standards* (Washington, D.C.: National Academy Press, 1995), p. 100.

point out that current views of how students learn and how they express their learning have opened the window to new ways to thinking of assessment.[3] As I have pointed out in this book, constructivism and socio-cultural perspectives on learning (especially collaborative learning) now play a dominant role in shaping classroom instruction. Assessments that support this role need to take on an active character. In fact, these approaches to learning theory have defined some changing emphases on assessment practices over the past decade (Table 8.1). We will find that assessment activities that have relevance to classroom instruction will center on authentic, active, and performance assessment strategies.

INQUIRY ACTIVITY 8.1

Designing an Assessment Plan

In this inquiry activity you will design an evaluation plan for the miniunit you developed earlier in the last chapter. The evaluation plan should include informal, semiformal and formal methods, as well as a description of a student portfolio for the miniunit.

Materials

- Rough draft plans of a miniunit

Procedures

1. Design a preassessment to help you identify students' views of the major cognitions of your miniunit. The preassessment can be a series of survey questions, an activity the student performs and has to write about, a demonstration you perform followed by student response in writing, or small-group discussion.
2. Design a performance assessment activity for your miniunit based on a cognition or a big idea.
3. Design assessment items for each intended learning outcome in your miniunit. You should develop assessment measures for cognitions, cognitive skills, affects, and psychomotor skills.
4. Describe the elements of the student portfolio. The portfolio should include a list of the documents and materials that you will require students to collect in their portfolio. Describe the criteria you will use to evaluate the student portfolios.
5. What informal and semiformal methods of assessment will you use? Describe any observation instruments and specific strategies you will employ.

Minds-On Strategies

1. The following is an evaluation plan that was included in a ninth-grade physical science course.

   Grading Scale and Criteria

25%	Quizzes	92–100	A
20%	Tests	83–91	B
10%	Final Exam	74–82	C
45%	Lab/Class/Vocabulary	70–73	D
	Activities	0–69	F

   What is your evaluation of this assessment plan? How does it compare with the plan you have developed?

2. The evaluation plan described in question 1 is a typical approach used in secondary science classrooms. What are the strengths of this plan? What are the weaknesses? What changes would you recommend this teacher make in the assessment plan?

A Model for Assessment in the Classroom

It's useful to think about a rationale or a model for your approach to assessment in the classroom. Assessment needs to be envisioned in a context of the goals for science education. Each school district and state, as well as nation, has expectations for school science. In the United States the expectations are defined in the *Standards* and the *Benchmarks*. To different degrees, states and local districts have adapted or adopted these national expectations and, indeed, these are the basis for individual classroom assessments. Thus the vision for science teaching is as follows.

The *National Science Education Standards* present a vision of a scientifically literate populace. The *Standards* outline what students need to know, understand, and be able to do to be scientifically literate at different grade levels. In the ideal *Standards* educational system, all students demonstrate high levels of performance, teachers are empowered to make the decisions essential for effective learning, interlocking communities of teachers and students are focused on learning science, and supportive educational programs and systems nurture achievement.[4]

Atkin, Black, and Coffey, citing Black and Wiliam, report that ongoing assessments by teachers, combined with appropriate feedback to students, can have powerful, positive effects on student learning and achievement.[5] They also point out that, although using a variety of teacher-designed assessment methods can result in increased student understanding, these practices are not widely implemented in school science.

In their report, Atkin, Black, and Coffey take into account an approach to assessment within the context of learning theories, which include social and collaborative methods, constructivist thinking, and meta-cognitive strategies.[6] With these ideas in mind, Atkin and colleagues propose a model of assessment that is driven by three guiding questions:

1. *Where are you trying to go?* (Identify and communicate the learning and performance goals)
2. *Where are you now?* (Assess, or help the student to self-assess, current levels of understanding)
3. *How can you get there?* (Help the student with strategies and skills to reach the goal)

Assessment becomes a process in which we identify goals, help students assess where they are in the learning process, and use strategies to help the students reach the goals.

For question one, the key notion is clearly knowing what goals are being used with students and to articulate those goals so there is clarity of direction. The *Standards* and the *Benchmarks* provide a framework for thinking about science education goals.

For question two, the new emphasis on active learning implies that a single approach to assessment simply will not do the job. A variety of assessment strategies needs to be used to help students understand *where they are*. Focusing on student artifacts (e.g., papers, project posters, drawings, graphs, portfolios) enables the teacher to delve more deeply into what students are thinking about and provide students with feedback that is more concrete and relevant to instruction.

For question three, teachers of science need to engage in ongoing assessment of their teaching and of student learning. According to the *Standards*, in doing this, teachers

- use multiple methods and systematically gather data about student understanding and ability;
- analyze assessment data to guide teaching;
- guide students in self-assessment;
- use student data, observations of teaching, and interactions with colleagues to reflect on and improve teaching practice; and
- use student data, observations of teaching, and interactions with colleagues to report student achievement and opportunities to learn to students, teachers, parents, policy makers, and the general public.[7]

To enact an assessment system in the science classroom based on this model, I present a three-level approach to assessment in the classroom, including informal methods of assessment, semiformal methods, and formal methods. Together they present a multiple approach to classroom assessment.

Multiple Methods of Classroom Assessment

Informal Methods of Assessment

It's unfortunate, but many teachers do not make use of informal evaluation methods to give students feedback or to measure their own effectiveness. Informal methods involve the direct interaction of the teacher with the students, sometimes during class time, but also at prearranged times for an informal session, such as a conference with a student. Let's examine a few informal techniques you can use in the science classroom to assess student learning.

OBSERVING STUDENTS David Berliner points out that it is not always obvious from student nonverbal behavior (e.g., frowns, puzzled looks, shaking head) whether the student understands.[8] However, observation of social behavior is an effective tool to determine the level of involvement of students in groups. Because it is important to involve students in small-group activities, paying attention to their behavior, verbal as well as nonverbal, is a helpful way to gain insight into their learning. One useful device is to create an observation form that efficiently enables the teacher to watch student behavior during cooperative learning activities and to record instances of social/interpersonal skills that are being encouraged. For example, interpersonal skills such as active listening, staying on task, asking questions, and everyone contributing, can be observed by using an observation chart as shown in Figure 8.1. The teacher records the names of the students in each group, spends a few minutes watching each group individually, and then records instances of the interpersonal skill. Later the teacher returns to the group and provides specific feedback about interpersonal skill development.

Using questioning strategies and listening carefully to student questions can enhance observing student behavior and interaction. Let's look at these two informal methods of assessing learning.

ASKING QUESTIONS Asking classroom questions can be employed to informally assess student learning. Let's examine how.

One of the most powerful uses of classroom questions as an assessment tool is when students are engaged in cooperative learning activities or laboratory activities. The role of the teacher during small-group and laboratory activities takes on a monitoring function. During

Group Members				
Interpersonal Skill	**Group 1**	**Group 2**	**Group 3**	**Group 4**
Active Listening				
Staying on Task				
Asking Questions				
Contributing Ideas				

Figure 8.1 Interpersonal Skill Observation Form.

this time, the teacher can visit individual groups to explore the content and methods that students are using in their investigations and small-group work.

The following techniques are useful in assessing student understanding:

- *Use a variety of questions.* Try to strike a balance between low-order (recall) and high-order (application, synthesis, evaluation) questions. The use of high-order questions has been shown to be motivational, whereas low-order questioning is useful for a probing strategy.
- *Use wait time.* Mary Budd Rowe found that most teachers wait less than a second for answers after asking a question. Science teachers who practice waiting at least three seconds can create a classroom atmosphere beneficial to students' cognitive as well as affective learning. Rowe found that as the length of student response increases, failures to respond decrease, confidence increases, speculative responses increase, student questions increase, and variety of student responses increases.[9]
- *Ask probing questions.* If a student, after the teacher asks a question and waits at least three seconds, gives an incorrect answer, then the teacher should probe the student answer with other questions. Probing provides a second opportunity for the student and gives the student a chance to express his or her understanding. Berliner explains that probing to help students clarify and improve answers is more effective than probing to get an answer in increasing student achievement.[10]
- *Redirecting.* If you are working with a cooperative group, redirecting the same question is a useful assessment tool for the group. Suppose you ask one student in the group a question, and this student is unable to answer or gives an incorrect answer. You then could redirect by asking another student in the group the same question.

STUDENT QUESTIONS You will have many experiences saying to your students, "Any questions?" This is usually followed by silence. For student questions to be useful tools for assessing student learning, an environment must exist whereby students will be willing to ask questions.

The kinds of questions that students ask can inform teachers directly about student understanding of what has been taught. In general students do not ask very many questions unless the teacher encourages this to happen in the classroom. One of the skills that should be taught in small-group learning is asking questions.

Asking questions is not only a way to learn, but also a tool for the teacher to gauge student understanding. Some researchers have found that the level (using Bloom's taxonomy, see Chapter 7) of student questions can be increased by creating a more favorable or positive climate through the use of positive reinforcement.[11]

One technique science teachers can use to increase the chance that students will ask questions is to use a lot of silence. The use of wait time to induce students to ask questions can work if you are willing to "wait out the silence." Eventually, after some period of discomfort, the students might ask a question. Listening to kinds and levels of questioning is another informal assessment tool.

CONFERENCING Meeting with students individually or in small teams is a powerful informal method of assessment. I have found, as have many other teachers, that the student who appears shy and reticent in class is open and talkative in a private meeting and is willing to answer questions and share information. One of the things students appreciate about conferences is how special they feel that they have your undivided attention, even for a brief period of time.

Conferences should be used to build rapport between the teacher and the student. It's a wonderful time to strengthen a bond between you and the student and at the same time to "clear the air" over a problem that might persist if not attended to.

Conferences can be used as a time to review a student's portfolio (see later sections of this chapter). The portfolio can become the "agenda" for the conference and serve as an opportunity for the teacher and student to ask questions.

Semiformal Methods of Assessment

Semiformal methods of assessment, although similar to informal methods, require more thoughtfulness than informal methods. We will look at two semiformal methods that you could use to gather assessment information and evidence about student learning: monitoring classroom practice and homework.

MONITORING CLASSROOM PRACTICE The type of science classroom advocated in this book suggests that students should be actively involved in learning activities. In some activities students work in small teams tutoring each other, discussing concepts and the results of laboratory activities, reviewing for a quiz, as well as completing activities and worksheets. In all of these cases the teacher should be actively involved in

Students/Groups	Observing	Classifying	Inferring	Data Analysis	Hypothesizing

Figure 8.2 Anecdotal Assessment Chart.

monitoring the students as they interact with each other or work individually.

Structuring classroom activities for diagnostic purposes and as a way to check student understanding is an important aspect of student learning. Involving students as active learners is a way of perceiving and observing student abilities. Recent research has criticized the traditional approach to assessment as being overly static (e.g., relying on end-of-the-week quizzes or unit tests). A more viable approach is to observe students at work as learners, and use this experience as a valid measure of student learning.

For instance, the Russian psychologist Lev Vygotsky advocated the creation of an atmosphere (zone of influence) in which students could act on what they learned. Instead of asking children to describe a picture, the teacher instructed them to act it out. In these cases, students were able to show that they had a grasp of concepts and relationships, even at a very young age.[12] Using static quizzes and tests may not provide a legitimate opportunity to assess what students know. This is one of the main reasons for the movement toward dynamic evaluation and performance testing.

One technique that can be employed here is to have a section in a student portfolio (see ahead) devoted to classroom practice. That is, students can be instructed to collect and file samples of their classroom experience as viable evidence of their learning, not simply as a chore to be carried out. If value is placed on this aspect of student performance, then the student will value it.

Anecdotal comments and observations of individual students and teams of students is another technique

that you can use to assess student performance in class. Teachers can use matrix charts in which specific behaviors and evidences of competence are noted. For instance, suppose you want to assess students' process abilities. A chart such as the one shown in Figure 8.2 can be used by the teacher as a monitoring device to note evidence of student process skills.

HOMEWORK In general, the reason for homework is to give the student an opportunity to practice what has been presented or started in class, or perhaps to prepare for the next class. Homework can also be used as an assessment device. Berliner points out that by assigning homework that is not evaluated (or perceived as being evaluated), or is seen as busywork by the student, the teacher misses an opportunity to assess student competence and enhance student learning.[13]

Formal Methods of Assessment

- On a weekly quiz, students are asked to answer ten questions, each similar to the following question: What bearing does the fossil record have on Darwin's theory of evolution?

  a. It shows that the theory has serious defects.
  b. It provides conclusive proof that the theory is correct.
  c. It provides supporting evidence for the theory.
  d. It neither supports nor conflicts with the theory.

- A team of students is asked to design and conduct an experiment to calculate the distance that hot wheels car can jump between ramps when

Table 8.2 Sample T-Chart

What Have We Heard about Ozone?	What Questions Do We Have about Ozone?
It makes us burn up.	What causes ozone?
It's smog and is harmful to us.	How can we tell if there is ozone in the air?
Makes the earth heat up.	Is it different in the center of a city compared to the suburbs?
Air pollution can cause ozone.	What effect does ozone have on humans?
It's caused by chemicals in the air.	Do cars cause it?
It can be dangerous to people with breathing problems.	What will happen if the ozone in the air is all gone?
There is good ozone and there is bad ozone.	

released from a given height on an inclined plane.[14]

- Students are given the results of five students who perform in three athletic events (i.e., Frisbee toss, weight lift, and 50-yard dash). They are asked to evaluate and decide which of the five students would be the all-around winner. Students need to devise their own approaches to reviewing and interpreting the data, applying it, and explaining why they selected a particular winner.[15]

Formal assessment methods historically meant that students would be evaluated using a formal test. As you have already read in this chapter, a single approach will not work and, for many of the goals that students are working toward, a traditional paper-and-pencil test might not be the method of choice.

Formal assessment has been undergoing a transformation. The trend is toward using a variety of methods, including performance assessments, questions that look more like activities, and having students develop portfolios of their work. In the following sections you will find a variety of assessment strategies that you should consider as you develop an assessment plan for your instructional plans.

PREASSESSMENT STRATEGIES Finding out or making visible students' prior knowledge on a topic is helpful not only to us as teachers but to students because it gives them an opportunity to think about where they are now on the concepts and ideas they are learning about. Uncovering students' prior knowledge can be achieved in a variety of ways. Least effective is giving the students a paper-and-pencil pretest. Most effective is engaging students in an activity, discussion, interview, or conference where they can express their ideas verbally, visually, or kinesthetically. Here are some possibilities.

T-Charts The T-chart is a strategy in which teams of students work together to answer two questions about the new topic you are about to teach. The questions are:

1. What have you heard about . . . ozone (or dinosaur extinction, or the Big Bang theory, or the laws of motion)?
2. What questions do you have about this topic?

Table 8.2 shows a T-chart created by a group of seventh graders. As you read the listings under the "What we have heard about ozone?" column, note that some of the ideas may not be considered "correct" using the referent of the scientist. From the standpoint of the students, these ideas seem acceptable, but teachers might consider them naive theories or alternative frameworks (some use the term misconceptions). When you use a T-chart, you do not have to "correct" these ideas, but return to them later in the unit and have the students reflect. To conduct a T-chart session, give each team a large sheet of chart paper and marking pens and have them set up the T-chart to look like Table 8.2. Give the students between six and ten minutes to complete the chart. Students can then present their findings to the class. Hang the T-charts in the classroom and, as students study the topic further, have them evaluate their ideas, crossing off those they can refute and discussing questions they posed.

Pictorials and Drawing Having students make drawings of their ideas and work with diagrams is another way to help them bring their prior knowledge into the classroom dialog. For example, suppose you give the students a picture showing the earth and two of layers of the atmosphere (troposphere and stratosphere). The picture shows a satellite in orbit above the stratosphere, and the sun is shown in the background. Say this to the students: "In the next minutes you and your teammates should work together, and discuss what you know

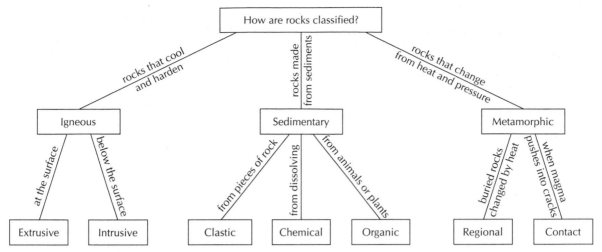

Figure 8.3 Concept Map Connecting Concepts Associated with Rocks.

about ozone. Use the picture as a starting point to draw and explain what your team knows. In your drawing and explanations, please try to use the following ideas as well as others that you know: ozone, smog, car emissions, ultraviolet light, people, and plants." The drawings can then be presented to the class or a member of each team can rotate to another group in the class and present their drawing.

Concept Mapping Having students link ideas one to another is another way to find out about their prior knowledge. One strategy that many teachers use is the concept map, which is a drawing of the connections that we make among ideas. It is a powerful tool for assessing prior knowledge. Figure 8.3 shows a concept map that depicts connections among concepts associated with rocks. Notice that the concepts are connected with "linking terms" that define how the concepts are connected.

TRADITIONAL PAPER-AND-PENCIL TESTS Most assessment is carried out using traditional paper-and-pencil tests such as multiple choice, true or false, fill-in-the-blank, and short answer. Typically, assessment using this method engages the students in the recall or recognition of information and oftentimes the information is discrete and unrelated. An interesting strategy to raise the cognitive level being assessed is to use an "alternative" multiple-choice model. This strategy makes use of the traditional multiple-choice format, but the students are asked to write the reasons for the choice they made. For example, a multiple-choice question about birds might be as follows:

1. Which of the birds listed below probably lives around ponds and eats snails and small fish?

A. Herron
B. Sparrow
C. Hawk
D. Swallow

What are the reasons for your choice?

_____

_____

The strategy can also be used with other formats such as true or false. If you are planning to administer a multiple-choice or true-or-false test containing twenty to twenty-five questions, you might select five of them and add the question "What are your reasons for your choice?"

TRADITIONAL SHORT ANSWER Short-answer questions can be useful to help students organize their ideas about the concepts they are learning about. Short-answer questions can be useful for assessing higher-level thinking.

STUDENT WRITING Student writing in science class can assess higher levels of thinking. However, more than 70 percent of the writing in science classes is of two types: copying dictated notes or teacher talk, and answering worksheets, test, and exam questions. How can writing move from these formats to formats that might challenge students to think at higher levels and more critically?

Open-Ended Questions One strategy that you might consider is the open-ended question. For example, suppose you have just completed a biology unit on plant growth and development with a group of seventh graders. You ask this question: "How would you explain photosynthesis to a small group of fourth graders?" Notice that this question provides a context for the student to write in and also challenges the student to use language that would be understandable to someone younger. Open-ended questions generally do not have a single answer and, in some cases, no answer is considered wrong. Key words such as describe, explain, compare, tell, analyze, show, demonstrate, sketch, explore, illustrate, contrast, prove, model, or predict can help create the context for an open-ended question. Examples might be:

* How would you explain . . . ?
* Analyze the variables and . . .
* How would you test the model you developed?

Content-Specific Tasks Hein and Price suggest that having students respond to content specific tasks using activity sheets (see Figure 8.4). For example, they describe an activity in which the students observe what happens when they place an acrylic bead in salt water and then in fresh water. The students are asked to draw what they saw happening and then answer this question: "What are at least two reasons you can think of for what you observed?"[16]

Activity Sheet

Name: _____ Date: _____

What did you see happening?

What are at least two reasons you can think of for what you observed?

1.

2.

3.

Figure 8.4 Activity Sheet for Assessing Student Understanding.

Science Journals Journaling is a process of reflection and is therefore a powerful way to help students develop their knowledge, understanding, and appreciation of science. Students can record reflections on science class several days a week and report the results of investigations, including the procedures they used as well as other aspects of the investigation. They should be encouraged to expand their journal by including their own drawings of science phenomena and concepts, concept maps, and other pictorial representations. They can also paste pictures, diagrams, charts, and results of experiments in their journal.

Written Reports, Video, or Multimedia Presentations Technology enables students to create artifacts that demonstrate their knowledge of science and it also allows them to present their products to others to teach what they learned and gain feedback on their work. Written reports can be converted to Web-based documents and can be shared on a Web site. The use of video and multimedia tools enables students to creatively depict their knowledge.

Performance-Based Assessment

Performance assessments typically involve students, either individually or in small teams, in the act of solving a problem or thinking critically about a problem, data, or observation. Performance assessments also involve assessing students' ability to use science skills such as sorting and classifying, observing and formulating hypotheses, interpreting data, and designing and conducting an experiment. Table 8.3 includes some examples of performance assessment items used in a recent test. Notice that each item is a task requiring the student to "do science," reflecting the hands-on/minds-on approach advocated by science educators.

Performance assessments are creative approaches that you can employ in an assessment plan. They are creative because the emphasis is on the methods as well as the ideas that students generate. They place the student in situations that are in accordance with what science instruction should look like. There is a high correlation between performance assessment and a hands-on, conceptual approach to science teaching. Following are some characteristics of performance assessments:[17]

* Typically involve students in real-world contexts.
* Involve students in sustained work, sometimes over several days.
* Focus on the "big ideas" and major concepts, rather than isolated facts and definitions.

Table 8.3 Examples of Performance Assessment Items

1. *Observing:* Students watch a demonstration of centrifugal force and then respond to written questions about what occurred during the demonstration. Students need to make careful observations about what happens as the teacher puts the steel balls in different holes on the Whirlybird arms and then infer the relationship between the position of the steel balls and the speed at which the arm rotates.

2. *Formulating Hypotheses:* Students describe what occurs when a drop of water is placed on each of seven different types of building materials (equally sized pieces of plastic, painted wood, brick, metal, roof shingles, glass). Then the students are asked to predict what will happen to a drop of water placed on the surface of an unknown material (piece of porous cinderblock), which is sealed in a plastic bag so they can examine it, but not actually test it.

3. *Classifying:* Students are asked to sort a collection of small-animal vertebrae into three groups and to explain how the bones in the groupings are alike. To complete the task, students need to make careful observations about the similarities and differences among the bones and choose their categories according to sets of common characteristics.

Source: Based on *Learning by Doing: A Manual for Teaching and Assessing High-Order Thinking in Science and Mathematics.* Princeton, N.J.: Educational Testing Service, 1987.

- Are broad in scope, usually involving several principles of science.
- Involve the students in using science processes, the use of scientific methods, and manipulation of science tools.
- Present students with open-ended problems.
- Encourage students to collaborate and brainstorm.
- Stimulate students to make connections among important concepts and ideas.
- Based on scoring criteria related to content, process, group skills, and communication skills.

Performance assessment often resembles science activities. An example of an assessment is the "paper tower project." In this assessment, the teacher is interested in finding out how well teams can work together to solve a problem and explain what they have built and the rationale for their design. Each team is given a sheet of paper measuring 8.5 × 11 inches, scissors, and 50 cm of masking tape. The students are told that the task is to build the tallest freestanding tower using one sheet of paper. They will be given thirty minutes to complete the task. The masking tape can only be used to connect pieces of paper; it cannot be used to fasten the tower to

---

INQUIRY ACTIVITY 8.2

 Designing Performance Assessment Tasks and Rubrics

In this inquiry you are going to design a performance task that would assess student understanding of a big idea or concept in science.

Materials

- Table 8.5, which contains several big ideas or concepts from the *Standards* and the *Benchmarks* that you could use to develop your performance assessment
- Access to concepts or ideas related to a specific area of science (you can access the *National Science Education Standards* or the *Benchmarks for Scientific Literacy* online, or use the big ideas/concepts from your own teaching plans or miniunit

Procedure

1. Select a content area from Table 8.5 and use the Big Idea/Science Concept from the table to develop a performance assessment (or use your own selection from your miniunit, the *Standards*, or the *Benchmarks.*
2. Consider the following criteria as you work through the development of the performance assessment:
   a. It should involve the students in real-world contexts.
   b. Focus on the big idea, rather than isolated facts.

Table 8.5 Big Ideas and Concepts in Science

Content Area	Grade Level	Big Idea/Science Concept
Science as Inquiry	9–12	Investigations are conducted for different reasons, including exploring new phenomena, to check on previous results, to test how well a theory predicts, and to compare different theories. (*Benchmarks*)
Physical Science	5–8	The motion of an object can be described by its position, direction of motion, and speed. That motion can be measured and represented on a graph. (*Standards*)
Life Science	9–12	Plant cells contain chloroplasts, the site of photosynthesis. Plants and many microorganisms use solar energy to combine molecules of carbon dioxide and water into complex, energy-rich organic compounds and release oxygen into the environment. This process of photosynthesis provides a vital connection between the sun and the energy needs of living systems. (*Standards*)
Earth and Space Science	6–8	Some changes in the earth's surface are abrupt (such as earthquakes and volcanic eruptions), while other changes happen very slowly (such as uplift and wearing down of mountains). The earth's surface is shaped in part by the motion of water and wind over very long times, which act to level mountain ranges. (*Benchmarks*)
Science and Technology	3–5	Technology has been part of life on the earth since the advent of the human species. Like language, ritual, commerce, and the arts, technology is an intrinsic part of human culture, and it both shapes society and is shaped by it. The technology available to people greatly influences what their lives are like. (*Benchmarks*)
Science in Personal and Social Perspectives	9–12	Humans have a major effect on other species. For example, the influence of humans on other organisms occurs through land use—which decreases space available to other species—and pollution—which changes the chemical composition of air, soil, and water. (*Standards*)
History and Nature of Science	K–4	Many people choose science as a career and devote their entire lives to studying it. Many people derive great pleasure from doing science. (*Standards*)
Unifying Concepts and Processes	K–12	Models are tentative schemes or structures that correspond to real objects, events, or classes of events, and that have explanatory power. Models help scientists and engineers understand how things work. Models take many forms, including physical objects, plans, mental constructs, mathematical equations, and computer simulations. (*Standards*)

    c. It should engage the students (individually or in small teams) in using science processes, scientific methods, and the use of equipment and tools.

    d. Encourage students to collaborate and brainstorm.

    e. Stimulate students to make connections among concepts and ideas.

3. Prepare a draft of the performance task, and present it to another group of peers for feedback. Make revisions based on this feedback.

4. Outline the elements of a scoring rubric based on the nature of the task. The rubric should be easy to use (by both you and the students) to assess performance on the task.

Minds-On Strategies

1. What cognitive strategies do performance assessments help teachers evaluate?

2. To what extent do you think performance assessments are reliable and valid testing methods?

Table 8.4 The Paper Tower Scoring Rubric

Assessment	Criteria	Rating
Outstanding	Worked together well; clear explanation of plan and scientific concepts; tower built at least 11 inches tall.	4
Competent	Meets criteria for 4, but slightly lacking in one or more areas.	3
Satisfactory	Worked together well; tower was built but explanation was lacking.	2
Unsatisfactory	Attempt was made, but poor cooperation or tower didn't stand; weak explanation.	1
No Attempt	Tower not constructed.	0

a desk or some other structure. When the towers are built, each team must present its tower to the class and explain the rationale for the structure design. The other groups of students are given a rubric (Table 8.4), which they will use to assess the presenting team. The teacher also completes a rubric.

Portfolios

An assessment strategy that I have used for many years is to have students collect and file their coursework in a loose-leaf notebook or a folder. This collection of student work is called a portfolio. In recent years, educators have been advocating that school science assessments include portfolios of students' work. Portfolios have at least three characteristics:[18]

1. *They contain real documents.* Portfolios contain authentic representations of students' work, such as homework, laboratory data sheets, and journal entries.
2. *They contain a range of material.* The science portfolio contains a full range of student work to demonstrate a range of performance and ability.
3. *They demonstrate growth over time.* The portfolio should include samples of work over time. For example, the daily journal entries will provide insight into the students' experience over time.

Using portfolios as part of an assessment strategy enables students to be evaluated on a broad set of competencies, skills, performances, and products, and may, in some educators' opinions, be closer to an authentic assessment of student performance than traditional methods. Portfolios will contain student work that can be evaluated and graded with checklists and test scores,

as well as work that lends itself to oral and conference evaluation. Portfolios encourage a dynamic approach to assessment in which teacher notes, samples of students' work—lab reports, logs, worksheets, videotapes, as well as quiz and test papers—are included.

Susan Holt, a science teacher in Williamsville East High School (East Amherst, New York), reported that she found using portfolios to be an effective strategy with high school students. She used portfolios because they promoted the kind of learning that was being incorporated into traditional assessment techniques. Holt found that students could be trusted to work in a more open situation, which is promoted by the portfolio concept. She found that students were using resources (such as college texts) that they probably never would have used, and they used them without really thinking the resources were "above their level." Students reported to Holt that keeping a portfolio was fun, yet they also said was almost too much work. They liked the idea of choosing some of the elements of the portfolio and the fact that biology was being related to their own lives and community. Yet other students reported they struggled trying to figure out what to choose and what step to take next. Holt found that short-term portfolios (a unit of teaching) were more effective than full-semester portfolios.

An example of a portfolio is shown Table 8.6. The sample portfolio, developed by Michael Dias and Sarah Bexell, was used for the assessment of a zoology unit within a biology course. In this example, students put together a notebook containing eleven elements.

Assessing Science Learning at the National Level

The National Assessment of Education Progress (NAEP) is a federally mandated organization that administers assessments to measure educational progress in science as well as other subject areas, including mathematics, reading, social studies, and writing. Two types of assessments are made by NAEP: long-term, and national and state assessments. The long-term trend assessments use multiple-choice questions and test students ages 9, 13, and 17. The national assessment tests students in grades 4, 8, and 12 and is based on a matrix developed in 1996. Test questions include performance measures, open-ended questions, and multiple-choice items. State-by-state assessments have been made in mathematics and science in grades 4 and 8.

Long-Term Trend Assessments

Since 1969, the NAEP has conducted a series (now about every three years) of assessments involving

Table 8.6 Zoology Portfolio

Overview

For the zoology unit you will be required to develop a portfolio. This portfolio is a collection of your work that shows what you have learned during this unit on animal biology. The portfolio allows you to demonstrate your maturity as an independent learner who is willing and able to pursue some personal learning interests. It will also provide a format in which you will organize some lab and activity work, which we do during class time. Your portfolio should be organized in either a small three-ring binder or a three-clasp folder with divided sections.

Assessment

Some time will be given throughout the animal biology unit for you to build your portfolio. You will show your completed portfolio to some of your peers. The portfolio will be turned in and graded according to the following scale. Realize that this portfolio will count as a test grade or evaluation for this unit. We expect great things of you!

Element	Score	Description of Element
1. Creative Writing: "Any Animal for a Day"	5	If you could be any nonhuman animal for day, which one would it be? Explain why you chose that particular animal. Describe the typical day in the life of that animal. What would you eat? Where would you live? What would you do all day? What would be your overall role or job in the web of life? What new things could you do as this animal? How would the structure and function of your body be different as that particular animal?
2. Bio/Student Biography	5	In this writing piece, we'd like for you to tell us a little bit about your own history, personality, and interests. The better your instructors know you, the better they can serve you, so don't be shy about telling all about yourself. Start with a paragraph on your general timeline (places lived, family information, schools attended, etc.). Then go on in the next paragraph to discuss hobbies, interests, and any academic curiosities that you would like to develop. A final aspect to consider is the intersection between your life and biology. What aspects of life science most interest you? What do you know and think of some of the big issues of modern biology, such as environmental problems, genetic engineering, cloning, or biotechnology; DNA forensics; medical technology; epidemiology; animal rights; genetic disorders; cancer research; AIDS research. (Pick one or two of the above areas).
3. Taxonomy Notes and Dichotomous Key Activity	5	These are done in class. Make sure these items are neat and complete.
4. Alpha-Animal Sort and Chart of Nine Major Phyla	5	A set of animal types is given as an alphabetical list spanning the nine major phyla. You are to cut them out and then sort them according to some grouping system that makes sense to you. It will be interesting to compare your prior knowledge of animal taxonomy to the traditional groupings we will learn. We will discuss the nine major phyla of animalia and record a simple table in our learning log. I'd like you to construct a more elaborate chart of the nine major phyla, including the nickname, general characteristics, relative diversity, and several examples with illustrations.
5. Lab: Survey of Lower Invertebrates	10	This and the following lab will be done in class. The lower invertebrates include Porifera, Cnidaria, Platyhelminthes, and Nematoda. The higher invertebrates include the Mollusca, Annelida, Arthropoda, and Echinodermata. Do your best to make good observations at each station. Work with your classmates to organize the information and answer the questions on the lab sheet.
6. Lab: Survey of Higher Invertebrates	10	Lab
7. Research Report of Invertebrate Group	10	There is so much cool stuff to learn about animals that we will divide and conquer the wealth of knowledge that is out there. In groups of two or three, you are to go to the literature (library, Internet, texts) and dig up some interesting details from one of the phyla of invertebrates. This is particularly appropriate at this point in your academic career, since most animals are invertebrates and most people tend to know relatively little about them. To present your research, the class will be divided in half such that each group contains at least one expert on each animal group. Brief presentations will be made within these groups of about a dozen students. You should have a handout for your classmates to follow your presentation. Some points you may pursue are: amazing facts about some members of the group, fulfillment of basic life functions (respiration, circulation, nutrition, excretion, reproduction), ecological significance or role, and connection to human beings.

Table 8.6 (*continued*)

Element	Score	Description of Element
8. Group Teaching on Vertebrate Class	10	In a larger group of three or four, you are to develop a "hands-on learning station" for one of the classes of vertebrates. Some materials and ideas will be provided for each group. Your job is to study your vertebrate class in detail and collaborate with your group to design a learning station. We'll turn the lab into a "Museum of the Vertebrates" and spend the entire period learning about the six classes of vertebrates. Each student will split time as learner and facilitator.
9. Option 1	15	Pick any two of the following options (worth 30 percent of the portfolio). (Items with two asterisks may be extended to count as both options.)
		Give a book talk on some animal book you've read or are reading.
		Make an instructional poster on an endangered animal species.
		Evaluate the zoological accuracy of animal depictions on television and comic strip cartoons.
		Produce an illustrated collection of specimens from your favorite animal groups.
		Write a comparative anatomy study that traces one organ system through the animal kingdom.
		Interview a zoology teacher at this school and tell us what you learned about this elective.
		Interview a professional from a local zoo regarding his or her work and find out about volunteer opportunities.
		Evaluate several Internet sites for one animal phylum.
		Identify one area of current research in zoology and summarize some recent related discoveries.
10. Option 2	15	**Organize an illustrated report on one group of animals native to our state.
		**Conduct an animal behavior study at a local zoo.
		**Conduct an animal behavior experiment and present the results to the class.
		**Zoological College and Career interest inquiry.
		** Zoological Fine Art: compose instructional poems, music, cartoons, paintings, and sketches.
		Design your own option, with teacher approval.
11. Overall Reflection	10	To wrap up the zoology portfolio, we'd like you to reflect or think back over the entire unit. What have you learned? What did you like and dislike about the entire unit? How do you feel about all the work you've done? (That is, did all of these portfolio assignments really teach you a lot about animal behavior?) How closely does this collection of work represent your best work? What area of zoology would you like to learn more about?

Source: Portfolio developed by Dr. Michael Dias and Dr. Sara Bexell. At the time Michael was Sarah's mentor while she was completing her high school internship as part of the TEEMS science education program at Georgia State University. Dias is now a professor at the University of Georgia, and Bexell is a zoologist at Zoo-Atlanta.

nationally representative samples of students ages 9, 13, and 17.[19] From 1983, NAEP has also included assessments of students ages 9, 13, and 17.[20] These studies provided information about trends in science learning among American students (assessments are also made of mathematics, reading, and writing). I will examine very briefly some of the results of these studies in order to address the question: What is the status of student learning in science? Before we delve into this discussion, you should keep in mind that all test procedures have limitations. A test cannot measure in precise terms what a

The NAEP investigated a number of areas of student learning, including *achievement* in science, *attitudes* toward science, and *experiences* in science. I'll touch on each of these. Before we delve into this discussion, you should keep in mind that all test procedures have limitations. A test cannot measure in precise terms what a

group of students know. For example, some of the results that we will discuss were based a multiple-choice format. The earlier versions of the NAEP assessments did not include performance testing; that is, students were not asked to make observations of real objects, develop inferences based on actual data collection procedures, or design and carry out an experiment. The recent NAEP assessments included formats that evaluated student performance, including performance tasks in which students manipulated physical objects and drew scientific understandings from the materials, open-ended questions that encouraged higher-level thinking and communication, collections of students' work (such as portfolios), and higher-order multiple-choice items.

Let's start with a question about learning. Do you think that most seventeen-year-old high school students could answer the following question?[21]

Which of the following is the best indication of an approaching storm?

1. a seismogram that is a straight line
2. a decrease in barometric pressure
3. a clearing sky after a cold front passes
4. a sudden drop in the humidity

According to the results of the most recent NAEP study, the odds are that only 41 percent of the seventeen-year-olds would answer this question correctly (correct response: b). Does this surprise you? Let's examine how the NAEP reported its findings and what the results were.

Long-Term Proficiency Levels

To report long-term achievement results, the NAEP created five levels of proficiency and used these as a mechanism to examine trends and compare various groups of students. The five areas were defined as follows:

- Level 150: Knows Everyday Science Facts
- Level 200: Understands Simple Scientific Principles
- Level 250: Applies Basic Scientific Information
- Level 300: Analyzes Scientific Procedures and Data
- Level 350: Integrates Specialized Scientific Information

These levels were computed as the weighted composite of proficiency on five content-area subscales: nature of science, life science, chemistry, physics, and earth and space science. What follows is a description of the nature of each level, including sample items from the NAEP science test.[22]

LEVEL 150: KNOWS EVERYDAY SCIENCE FACTS Students at this level know some general scientific facts of the type that could be learned from everyday experiences. They can read graphs, match the distinguishing characteristics of animals, and predict the operation of familiar apparatus that work according to mechanical principles.

Question: Which of the following living things in the pond system uses the energy from sunlight to make its own food?

1. insect
2. frog
3. water Lily
4. small fish

LEVEL 200: UNDERSTANDS SIMPLE SCIENTIFIC PRINCIPLES Students at this level are developing some understanding of simple scientific principles, particularly in the life sciences. For example, they exhibit some rudimentary knowledge of the structure and function of plants and animals.

Question: Why may you become ill after visiting a friend who is sick with the flu?

1. The room your friend was in was too warm.
2. You ate the same kind of food your friend ate.
3. You did not dress properly.
4. The virus that causes the flu entered your body.

LEVEL 250: APPLIES BASIC SCIENTIFIC INFORMATION Students at this level can interpret data from simple tables and make inferences about the outcomes of experimental procedures. They exhibit knowledge and understanding of the life sciences, including a familiarity with some aspects of animal behavior and of ecological relationships. These students also demonstrate some knowledge of basic information from the physical sciences.

Question: Blocks A, B, and C are the same size. Blocks B and C float on water. Block A sinks to the bottom. Which one of the following do you know is true?

1. Block A weighs more than block B.
2. Block B weighs more than block C.
3. Block C weighs more than block A.
4. Block B weighs more than block A.
5. I don't know.

LEVEL 300: ANALYZES SCIENTIFIC PROCEDURES AND DATA Students at this level can evaluate the appropriateness of the design of an experiment. They have more detailed scientific knowledge and the skill to apply their knowledge in interpreting information from text graphs. These students also exhibit a growing understanding of principles from the physical sciences (see Figure 8.5).

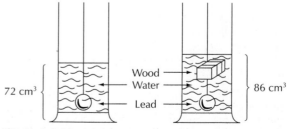

Figure 8.5 Block of Wood Test Item.

Question: The volume of a block of wood can be found by suspending it in water, as the diagrams above show. What is the volume of the block?

1. $(86 - 72)$ cm^3
2. 86 cm^3
3. $(72 - 86)$ cm^3
4. $(72 + 86)$ cm^3

LEVEL 350: INTEGRATES SPECIALIZED SCIENTIFIC INFORMATION Students at this level can infer relationships and draw conclusions using detailed scientific knowledge from the physical sciences, particularly chemistry. They also can apply basic principles of genetics and interpret the societal implications of research in this field (see Figure 8.6).

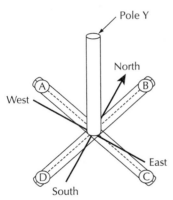

Figure 8.6 Drawing of Shadows Cast by Pole.

In the central United States at 8:00 A.M. on September 23 it is sunny, and the vertical pole shown in the diagram above casts a shadow. Which shaded area best approximates the position of the shadow?

1. A
2. B
3. C
4. D

Long-Term Trends in Science Achievement

If we compare student results since 1969 (see Figure 8.7), it is evident that overall student proficiency and achievement on the test decrease at first, but then show a slight increase to 1999. Although scores increased over this period, the level of performance still remains below the 1969 levels.

TRENDS BY AGE The trends in science are characterized by slight declines in the 1970s followed by increases during the 1980s and early 1990s. Performance has been stable since then. After declining between 1969 and 1982, average scores for seventeen-year-olds increased until 1992. Although the average score in 1999 was higher than scores from 1977 through 1990, it remained lower than the average score in 1969. For thirteen-year-olds, after declining between 1970 and 1977, average scores increased until 1992. A slight decline since 1992, however, resulted in an average score in 1999 that was similar to that in 1970. At the elementary grade level, after declining between 1970 and 1973, average scores for nine-year-olds remained relatively stable until 1982. Increases between 1982 and

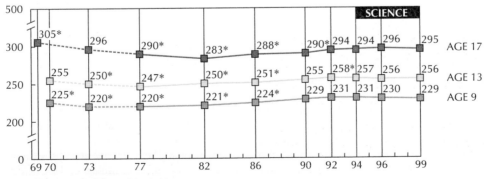

* Significantly different from 1999.
Note: Dashed lines represent extrapolated data.

Figure 8.7 National Trends in Science Learning. NAEP 1999 Trends in Academic Progress. *Source:* National Center for Education Statistics, *National Assessment of Educational Progress* (NAEP), 1999 Long-Term Trend Assessment.

1990, followed by relatively stable performance in the 1990s, resulted in an average score in 1999 that was higher than scores in 1970.

TRENDS BY RACE/ETHNICITY Among white and black students, overall gains in science are evident for nine-year-olds and thirteen-year-olds. Hispanic students at each age show overall gains across the assessment years. In 1999, white students had higher average science scores than their black and Hispanic peers. The gap between white and black students in science has generally narrowed since 1970 for nine- and thirteen-year-olds, but not for seventeen-year-olds. The gap between white and Hispanic students at any age in 1999 was not significantly different from 1977. It has widened somewhat among thirteen-year-olds since 1992.

THE GENDER GAP? Looking at male and female scores, declines seen in the 1970s and early 1980s have reversed, and scores generally increased during the 1980s and early 1990s for each group. However, the 1999 scores were lower than the scores in 1969. Female nine-year-olds scored higher in the 1999 assessment than in 1970. In the 1999 assessment, thirteen- and seventeen-year-old males outperformed females, but the average nine-year-old male score was not significantly higher. For seventeen-year-olds, the gap between scores has narrowed since 1969.

PARENTAL EDUCATIONAL LEVEL What was the relationship between parental level and education and science achievement? Students in the long-term trend assessments were asked to identify the highest level of education attained by each of their parents. The highest education level of either parent, as reported by students, was used in these analyses.

Science scores increased since 1982 for thirteen- and seventeen-year-old students who had at least one parent graduating from college. For students whose parental highest level of education was some education after high school, scores increased since 1982 for seventeen-year-olds. For students whose parents did not go beyond high school graduation, scores have increased since 1982. Among students whose parents did not go beyond high school graduation, scores have increased for seventeen-year-olds since 1982; however, the apparent difference for thirteen- and seventeen-year-olds between 1977 and 1999 was not statistically significant. Among students whose parents did not finish high school, 1999 and 1977 scores were similar at seventeen, and the apparent increase at thirteen was not statistically significant.

TRENDS IN ACHIEVEMENT BY TYPE OF SCHOOL Public school students showed overall gains in science for nine-, thirteen- and seventeen-year-olds since 1977. However, among non-public-school students, the slight increase between 1977 and 1999 at each age level was not statistically significant.

TRENDS IN SCIENCE CURRICULUM At the middle school level a greater percentage of students in 1999 than in 1986 indicated that their science curriculum was general, rather than focused on a content area (earth, physical, or life science). Science courses taken by seventeen-year-olds increased between 1986 and 1999 in all content areas: general science, biology, chemistry, and physics. And among male and female seventeen-year-olds, a greater percentage had taken biology and chemistry in 1999 than in 1986. Among white seventeen-year-olds, the percentage of science being taken at all levels of science had increased between 1986 and 1999. Among black and Hispanic seventeen-year-olds taking chemistry increased, and the percentage of blacks taking biology had increased.[23]

Mullis and Jenkins, the authors of NAEP report *The Science Report Card*, summarize the results by making these points:

- Although recent progress has been made, most has occurred at the lower end of the proficiency scale.
- Not only is it necessary to increase the average science proficiency of all students in our country, but it is also essential that the percentages of students reaching the higher ranges of proficiency increase substantially.
- Students' knowledge of science and their ability to use what they know appear remarkably limited.
- Although progress has been made by black and Hispanic students and those living in the southeastern region of the country, vast performance gaps remain across racial/ethnic groups and essentially no progress has been made in closing the performance gap between males and females.

Trends in Student Attitudes toward Science

The NAEP studies have also investigated students' perceptions of science. As we will see later in this chapter, some theorists believe that student attitudes play an important role in determining science achievement. In fact, NAEP researchers found that a positive relationship appears to exist between attitudes toward science and proficiency in the subject, especially among eleventh-grade students.[24]

Students have many views on the utility and value of science. For example, when students were asked if they would use science as an adult, only 51 percent of the seventh graders and 46 percent of the eleventh graders responded "yes." And less than 43 percent of both groups said that knowing science would help them earn a living or be important in their life's work.[25]

Another measure of students' attitude toward science is how they believe science can be applied to help resolve particular global problems, such as world starvation, diseases, overpopulation, and birth defects, and such environmental problems as depletion of natural resources, air and water pollution, and destruction of the ozone layer. An interesting finding by the NAEP was that students who perceived numerous applications of science tended to have higher science proficiency.[26]

In 1977 and 1986, eleventh graders were more likely than seventh graders to believe that science could help alleviate national and global problems. Students were more likely in 1986 than 1977 to agree that science knowledge could help preserve natural resources, reduce air and water pollution, and prevent birth defects. However, students were not as likely to agree that science could solve the world starvation problem.[27]

INQUIRY ACTIVITY 8.3

 Surveying Students' Knowledge and Attitudes about Science

In this activity, you will use a survey instrument to find out about student knowledge and attitudes toward science. The instrument will by no means enable you to make conclusive statements about student knowledge and attitudes about science, but it will give you a sampling of their performance and attitude.

Materials

* Science survey instrument (Figure 8.8). (For the questions listed in Part I, see pp. 314–15.)

Part I

1. Pond system question
2. Flu question
3. Blocks question
4. Wood question
5. Shadow question

Part II

6. Knowing science will help me to earn a living.
   Strongly agree
   Agree
   Neutral
   Disagree
   Strongly Disagree
7. I will use science in many ways when I am an adult.
   Strongly agree
   Agree
   Neutral
   Disagree
   Strongly Disagree

8. Science will be important to me in my life's work.
   Strongly agree
   Agree
   Neutral
   Disagree
   Strongly Disagree
9. When you have science in school, do you like it?
   Yes
   No
10. When you have science in school, does it make you feel interested?
   Yes
   No
11. Are there things you learn in science useful to you when you are not in school?
   Yes
   No

Figure 8.8 Science Survey Instrument.

Procedure

1. The survey instrument has two parts: science content and attitudes about science. The science content will consist of the five questions (samples from the NAEP test).
2. The attitude part will consist of six attitudinal questions. You might want to have the students explain their response to the attitudinal questions.
3. Seek the permission of the school, the teacher, and the students to whom you will administer the survey instrument. Remember your responsibilities for the human rights of the students you will test. You should explain the nature of the survey to the contact person in the school and then follow the procedures set forth by the school.
4. Administer the instrument to a sample of students in one of the following ways:

   a. Ten students at the sixth or seventh grade and the eleventh grade
   b. An equal number of boys and girls at any grade level
   c. A small sample of students enrolled in a biology, chemistry, and physics course.

5. After administering the instrument, tabulate the results in such a way that you can compare the obvious groups in your study (e.g., sixth graders versus eleventh graders, boys versus girls).

Minds-On Strategies

1. How did students perform at each proficiency level?
2. What differences in proficiency existed in the groups you compared?
3. How do students perceive science? Are you surprised?
4. How do the results compare to the NAEP results?

National NAEP Assessments

The two recent NAEP assessments in science were constructed using the framework shown as a matrix in Figure 8.9. The science framework is organized along two major dimensions: the three fields of science (earth, physical, and life sciences) and the three elements of knowing and doing science (conceptual understanding, scientific investigation, and practical reasoning). Each question in the assessment is categorized as measuring one of the fields of knowing and doing within one of the fields of science.

Student performance for the NAEP national assessments is reported as (1) average scale scores and (2) achievement levels. Student performance, which is reported as a scale score, and can range from 0 to 300, reflects the overall science performance of a particular group of students. The scales were developed independently for each grade level; therefore, scores across grades cannot be compared. Student performance can also be reported as one of three achievement levels:

basic, proficient, and advanced. Basic achievement denotes partial mastery of prerequisite knowledge and skills. Proficient represents solid academic performance by demonstrating competency over challenging subject matter. Advanced achievement signifies superior performance.

NATIONAL RESULTS The overall results for national NAEP assessments from 1996 to 2000 are shown in Figure 8.10.[28] This science assessment was first administered to nationally representative sample of fourth-, eighth-, and twelfth-grade students in 1996. It should be noted that the scores remained essentially the same, except at the grade 12 level, where there was a three-point drop between 1996 and 2000.

If we look at the results of the national assessments using achievement levels (basic, proficient, advanced), very few changes are evident (Figure 8.11). At grade 4 there was no change among the achievement levels between 1996 and 2000. At grade 8, there was an increased in the number of students reaching the

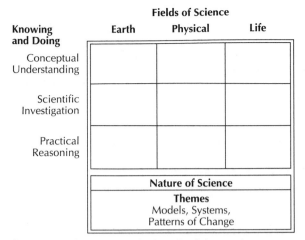

Fields of Science

Knowing and Doing	Earth	Physical	Life
Conceptual Understanding			
Scientific Investigation			
Practical Reasoning			

Nature of Science

Themes
Models, Systems, Patterns of Change

Figure 8.9 Matrix of the NAEP Science Assessment Framework. *Source:* National Center for Education Statistics. *The Nation's Report Card: Science Highlights 2000.* Washington, D.C.: U.S. Department of Education, Office of Educational Research and Improvement, 2001, pp. 2002–452.

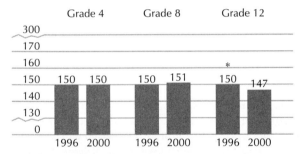

* Significantly different from 2000.
Note: Results are based on administration procedures that did not permit accommodations.

Figure 8.10 National Average Science Scale Score Results, Grades 4, 8, and 12 (Public and Nonpublic Schools Combined): 1996 and 2000. *Source:* National Center for Education Statistics, National Assessment of Educational Progress (NAEP), 1996 and 2000 Science Assessments.

proficient level between 1996 and 2000. At grade 12, there was a decrease in the percentage of students at or above basic between 1996 and 2000.

STATE-BY-STATE RESULTS In addition to national results, the NAEP also collected data for fourth- and eighth-grade students in forty states and five other

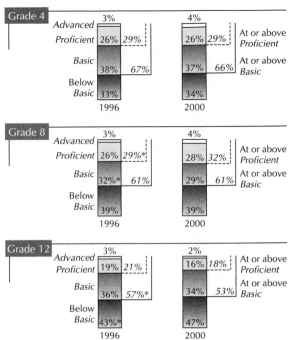

HOW TO READ THESE FIGURES:

- The italicized percentages to the right of the shaded bars represent the percentages of students at or above *Basic* and *Proficient*.
- The percentages in the shaded bars represent the percentages of students within each achievemendt level.

* Significantly different from 2000.
Note: Percentages within each science achievement-level range may not add to 100, or to the exact percentages at or above achievement levels, due to rounding.

Figure 8.11 Achievement Levels 1996 and 2000. *Source:* National Center for Education Statistics, *National Assessment of Educational Progress* (NAEP), 1996 and 2000 Science Assessments.

jurisdictions. For example at the, eighth-grade level, of the forty-two states and jurisdictions that participated in the 2000 study, eighteen had scores that were higher than the national average, eleven had scores that did not differ from the national average, and thirteen had scores that were below the national average (Table 8.7). One state and two jurisdictions showed significant gains science 1996 (Missouri and the domestic and overseas Department of Defense Schools).

SUBGROUP RESULTS NAEP also looked at the performance of various subgroups. For example, the average scores for five major racial/ethnic subgroups: white, black, Hispanic, Asian/Pacific Islander, and American

Table 8.7 State Scores 1996 and 2000

	1996	2000		1996	2000		1996	2000
Nation: public schools	148	149						
Alabama	139	141	Maine	163	160	South Carolina	139	142
Alaska	153	—	Maryland	145	149	Tennessee	143	146
Arizona	145	146	Massachusetts	157	161	Texas	145	144
Arkansas	144	143	Michigan	153	156	Utah	156	155
California	138	132	Minnesota	159	160	Vermont	157	161
Colorado	155	—	Mississippi	133	134	Virginia	149	152
Connecticut	155	154	Missouri	151	156	Washington	150	—
Delaware	142	—	Montana	162	165	West Virginia	147	150
Florida	142	—	Nebraska	157	157	Wisconsin	160	—
Georgia	142	144	Nevada	—	143	Wyoming	158	158
Hawaii	135	132	New Mexico	141	140			
Idaho	—	159	New York	146	149	Other		
Illinois	—	150	North Carolina	147	147	Jurisdictions		
Indiana	153	156	North Dakota	161	161	American	—	72
Iowa	158	—	Ohio	—	161	Samoa District of Columbia	113	—
Kentucky	147	152	Oklahoma	—	149	DoDEA/DDESS	153	159
Louisiana	132	136	Oregon	155	154	DoDEA/DoDDs	155	159
			Rhode Island	140	150	Guam	120	114
						Virgin Islands	—	—

Source: National Center for Education Statistics, National Assessment of Educational Progress (NAEP), 1996 and 2000 Science Assessments.

Indian are shown in Figure 8.12. The data show that there has been little change in the achievement of racial/ethnic subgroups between 1996 and 2000. However, average scores of two subgroups have declined. American Indian students in grade 8 and white students at grade 12 had lower scores in 2000 than in 1996.

Figure 8.13 shows average scores for males and females in 1996 and 2000. At grade 8, males' scores were higher than females', while in grade 12, males' scores declined in 2000. When scores of males and females are compared, males outscored females in 2000 at grades 4 and 8. The difference at the grade 12 levels was not significant.

Assessing Science at the International Level

Since the 1960s, the International Association for the Evaluation of Educational Achievement (IEA) has conducted international comparative studies of mathematics and science. In 1995, the Trends in International Mathematics and Science Study (TIMSS) collected data in forty-one nations at the fourth grade, eighth grade, and final year of high school. The data included achieve-

ment test results, schools, curricula, instruction, lessons, textbooks, policy issues, and background information on teachers. In 1999, TIMSS-R collected data in thirty-eight countries at the eighth-grade level to provide information about change in the mathematics and science achievement of our students compared to those in other nations over the last four years.

TIMSS Results

According to the National Center for Education Statistics, more a half-million students worldwide, including 33,000 U.S. students and 500 public and private schools, participated in TIMSS. At the fourth-grade level, U.S. students were above the international average in science and mathematics. In the eighth grade, U.S. students scored above the average in science and below in mathematics. At the end of secondary education, U.S. students' performance was among the lowest in both science and mathematics.

Table 8.8 compares the national averages among the forty-one nations in eighth grade science achievement. The nations are grouped into three clusters, those significantly above the U.S. average, those not significantly

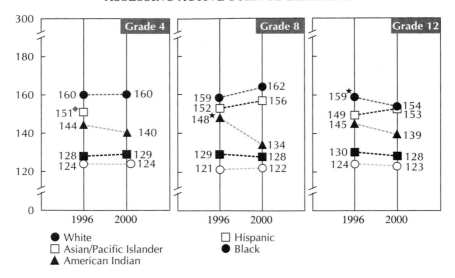

Figure 8.12 Average Science Scores by Race/Ethnicity, Grades 4, 8, and 12: 1996–2000. *Source:* National Center for Education Statistics, *National Assessment of Educational Progress* (NAEP), 1996 and 2000 Science Assessments.

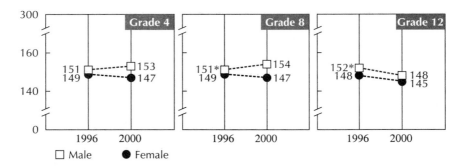

Figure 8.13 Average Science Scores by Gender, Grades 4, 8, 12: 1996–2000. *Source:* National Center for Education Statistics, *National Assessment of Educational Progress* (NAEP), 1996 and 2000 Science Assessments.

different than the U.S. average, and those significantly lower than the U.S. average. Table 8.8 also shows that the United States scored above the international average. TIMSS also revealed that the U.S. eighth grade science curriculum was similar to the science curriculum in other nations.

There were also differences at the last grade level of secondary education among the nations in TIMSS. According to TIMSS, fewer students in the last year of school in the United States were taking science (53 percent) than in other nations (67 percent). U.S. twelfth graders scored below the international average and outperformed only South Africa and Cyrus.

TIMSS-R Results

Thirty-eight nations participated in the TIMSS-R, enabling the collection of data on a number of attributes of science education, including achievement, curriculum, and schools. Data were collected at the grade 8 levels. Table 8.9 compares eighth-grade science achievement across the nations participating in the study. U.S. eighth-graders exceeded the international average among the thirty-eight nations participating in the study. However, their scores did not change significantly, while scores in Latvia, Lithuania, Canada, Hungary, and Hong Kong did improve significantly since 1995.

Table 8.8 Average Science Performance, Grade 8: United States versus Other Nations, TIMSS 1995

Cluster Relation to U.S. Score	Nation	Average
Significantly Higher than U.S. Average	Singapore	607
	Czech Republic	574
	Japan	571
	Korea	565
	Bulgaria	565
	Netherlands	560
	Slovenia	560
	Austria	558
	Hungary	554
Not Significantly Different than U.S. Average	England	552
	Belgium-Flemish	550
	Australia	545
	Slovak Republic	544
	Russian Federation	538
	Ireland	538
	Sweden	535
	United States	534
	Germany	531
	Canada	531
	Norway	527
	New Zealand	525
	Thailand	525
	Israel	524
	Hong Kong	522
	Switzerland	522
	Scotland	517
Significantly Lower than U.S. Average	Spain	517
	France	498
	Greece	497
	Iceland	494
	Romania	486
	Latvia	485
	Portugal	480
	Denmark	478
	Lithuania	476
	Belgium-French	471
	Iran, Islamic Republic	470
	Cyprus	463
	Kuwait	430
	Colombia	411
	South Africa	326

International Average = 513

Source: National Center for Education Statistics. *Pursuing Excellence: A Study of U.S. Eighth-Grade Mathematics and Science Teaching, Learning, Curriculum and in International Context.* Washington, D.C. NCES, 1996.

Table 8.9 Comparisons of Eighth-Grade Science Achievement, by Nation: 1995 and 1999

Nation	1995 Average	1999 Average	1995–1999 Difference
Latvia	476	503	27*
Lithuania	464	488	25*
Canada	514	533	19*
Hungary	537	552	16*
Hong Kong	510	530	20**
Australia	527	540	14**
Cyprus	452	460	8**
Russian Federation	523	529	7**
England	533	538	5**
Netherlands	541	545	3**
Slovak Republic	532	535	3**
Korea	546	549	3**
United States	513	515	2**
Belgium-Flemish	533	535	2**
Romania	471	472	1**
Italy	497	498	1**
New Zealand	511	510	−1**
Japan	554	550	−5**
Slovenia	541	533	−8**
Singapore	580	568	−12**
Iran	463	448	−15**
Czech Republic	555	539	−16**
Bulgaria	545	518	−27†
International Average (23 Nations)	518	521	3**

* The 1999 average is significantly higher than the 1995 average
** The 1999 average does not differ significantly from the 1995 average
† The 1999 average is significantly lower than the 1995 average.

Source: National Center for Education Statistics. U.S. Department of Education, 2000.

SECTION 2: SCIENCE TEACHER GAZETTE

Volume 8: Assessing Active Science Learning

Think Pieces

1. What are the elements of a model of assessment that you would implement with middle or high school students?
2. What is a performance assessment and how does it differ from traditional paper-and-pencil tests?
3. What do you think is the fairest way to assess students in a heterogeneous chemistry class? What is the basis for your thinking?

4. Are the results of national assessments of science achievement valid in making comparisons from one state to another state or region of the country? What do you think?

5. How can international assessments of science be helpful to educators?

 Case Study: The False Crisis in Science Education

The Case

At a two-day conference for science teachers, the featured speaker on the first day, Alexis Soledad, a well-known education reporter for a major east coast newspaper, started her talk with this quote: "Despite the doom and gloom rhetoric popular among science educators, what scant data there are indicate that Americans are getting better at science, not worse." Soledad went on to say that there has been a long history of national professional groups announcing the newest crisis in education. She said in her talk that, even with the infusion of billions of dollars of cash into education with accompanying reform, little has changed in terms of what and how students learn. Soledad also pointed out that generally there has been no statistical data to support the "bottom falling out syndrome" and, indeed, she displayed graphs showing that the average adult actually knows more than young adults did decades ago. And the third reason to doubt a crisis is that, with all the rhetoric on increasing science achievement scores, science education researchers and teachers are not convinced that what is being tested (higher levels of content knowledge) is of value to citizens. They point out, Soledad said, that what schools ought to be doing is producing scientifically literate citizens, not candidates for the scientific elite. In the audience is a representative from the National Assessment of Science. During the question-and-answer session, he tells Soledad that there is a crisis in education and that international and national tests show it.

The Problem

Is there really a crisis in science education? How would you have reacted to Ms. Soledad's speech? (*Note*: You might want to read the online article "The False Crisis in Science Education," by searching for online at Scientific American Online http://www.sciam.com).

[handwritten: can't access without membership]

RESEARCH MATTERS

SCIENCE LITERACY: LESSONS FROM THE FIRST GENERATION

Marlene M. Hurley *State University of New York at Albany*

Introduction

As secondary science teachers or elementary teachers implementing science, we are constantly barraged with concepts intended to reform education and to improve the level of student learning.[29] Yet, we often don't have access to the research that supports the concepts or adequate information to assess the legitimacy of the research claims. We do know that science literacy has been proclaimed the major concern in science education for a number of years and by a great many sources (for example, the National Science Teacher's Association, NSTA). This paper will attempt to provide a brief overview of the concept of science literacy through its conceptual lineage and current research endeavors.

First-Generation Literacy

All of the currently hotly discussed literacies (e.g., science, mathematics, computer) in education stem from the original term for the basic abilities to read, write, listen, and speak. Both the term *literacy* and the skills inherent in its meaning have changed throughout history and have varied through the context in which they were used. The terms *basic* or *functional literacy* have been used by Venezky, who attempted to illuminate the complexities of definition through the existence of both various types and levels of literacy.[30] *Functional literacy* is also the term used by the Literacy Volunteers of America (LVA), a group dedicated to eradicating illiteracy in the United States one adult at a time.[31] LVA defines functional literacy as the ability of an individual to use reading, speaking, writing, and computational skills in everyday life situations. Eradicating adult illiteracy is a large job if one considers the statistics used by LVA (the National Adult Literacy Survey, conducted by the U.S. Department of Education in 1993): 21 to 23 percent of the adult population (40 to

44 million people) in the United States are at the functionally illiterate level; another 25 to 28 perent of the adult population are considered to be barely functioning.

Both Venezky and the LVA were concerned with adult literacy, not the literacy of children or students. This is because literacy is considered in terms of abilities needed to function independently in society; for example, voting, applying for jobs, reading a map, signing one's name. The ability to make informed societal and personal decisions is an implication of functional literacy. Literacy for societal reasons requires an assessment that occurs during the years after schooling has ended, when the adult attempts to take his or her place in society. In light of the fact that volunteer efforts by groups (such as the LVA and public libraries) to thwart functional illiteracy are reaching fewer than 10 percent of the population in need (from a survey by the Office of Technology Assessment in 1993)—coupled with the fact that the population is growing—the actual number of people needing literacy education continues to increase.

Whether these adults have forgotten what they learned in school or whether they never actually received the instruction necessary to sustain them through life—whatever the reason—the results are identical: We have not been meeting the needs of individuals or society in our current system and methods of education.

Second-Generation Literacy

It is reasonable to assume that the "functionally illiterate" population is also not literate in science; in fact, it is estimated that 90 percent of the population is not science literate.[32] Science literacy, also known as scientific literacy or, in the United Kingdom, the "public understanding of science," has been used as a term since the 1950s and is often credited to Paul Hurd, who declared a crisis in education due to a "great discontinuity in scientific and social development" and a science curriculum "spread so thin over so many topics that students acquire only dribbles and dabbles of assorted information."[33] Domain literacies, such as science, could be considered as second generation literacies . . . the offspring of adult functional literacy.

Hurd's early definition of scientific literacy had emphasized "science and society," as opposed to many definitions of the day that emphasized the so-called scientific method. Others saw scientific literacy only as the ability to be able to read and understand the science of popular media. The science and society theme continued to gain momentum until it became a part of the science-technology-society (STS) movement of the 1970s and 1980s. STS proponents advocated science education that was humanistic, value-laden, and relevant to personal, societal, and environmental concerns. The STS movement eventually evolved into advocacy of science education through a societal framework.[34]

Throughout the recent period of science education, no definitions for science literacy have been agreed upon; thus, no generally accepted basis for establishing policy, research, curriculum, and teaching exist. Graff stated three tasks required for the study and interpretation of literacy: (1) A consistent definition that serves over time and across space; (2) A set of techniques for communications and for decoding and reproducing written or printed materials; (3) the use of precise, historically specific materials and cultural contexts.[35] The second task implies that literacy is a skill acquired over time and (conversely) forgotten over time. The third task in part reiterates the first; that is, time and geographic location make the definition contextual, even though a "consistent" definition would imply generality rather than specificity.

For example, meeting a national goal becomes dependent upon a single, consistent definition. The *National Science Education Standards* now serve as national goals for science teaching in the United States. The *Standards* support the concept of science literacy and have defined it as the "knowledge and understanding of scientific concepts and processes required for personal decision making, participation in civic and cultural affairs, and economic productivity."[36] Definition of specific abilities can be found in the "content standards." While considered a general definition, the NRC definition also became a limiting definition—limited because it did not consider the needs of the whole person and because it was dependent upon specific abilities that were not conceived from a science literacy perspective. "Despite the attention given to science literacy in the United States national standards for science education, the documents leave unanswered many of the questions for which teachers and curriculum developers must have answers."[37]

On the other hand, a definition designed for the global issue of science literacy—adapted from an earlier definition by Champagne and Lovitts[38]—defined scientific literacy as "a desired level of depth and breadth of scientific understanding appropriate to the interests and needs of the person being taught, set within the context of the developmental, educational, economic, and political needs and interests of a country at a given point in time."[39] This definition generalized the science content, recognized the contextual factors, and provided for the needs of the entire person; thus, developing a definition that serves across time and space. However, like the *Standards*, it leaves teachers with questions: What is the desired level? What is the appropriate understanding? While a general definition must withstand the test of time, teachers need to have more specific knowledge for their more practical concerns.

There is research underway currently that will help teachers to implement effective science literacy instruction and assessment into the classrooms. One example is Project Life at Louisiana Tech University, where teachers are being trained to teach reform-based science with highly positive results.[40] Project Life's model of professional development for teachers reads like a checklist for good science literacy instruction.[41] Another example is the Project on Mathematical and Science Literacy at the National Center on English Learning and Achievement (NCELA) at the University at Albany, State University of New York. NCELA approaches a definition for science literacy from an English education perspective through the design of assessment tasks that are aligned with national standards and that specify science literate responses to the tasks. NCELA's working definition for science literacy is based upon a general, functional literacy definition of reading, writing, listening, and speaking, plus reasoning (an adaptation for science and mathematics derived from the ability to think and make decisions). Research groups such as NCELA will be instrumental in paving the way for administrators to plan policy and for science teachers and curriculum specialists to design, implement, and assess science literacy in the schools using authentic, real-world tasks.

Implications

Science illiteracy has been shown to be related to functional illiteracy, a major problem in society. The reasons for adult functional illiteracy are stated to be school dropout, physical or emotional disability, ineffective teachers, lack of reading readiness, parents who couldn't read or didn't know the English language, and so on.[42] While LVA realizes that these problems begin in the home, it is difficult to look at this list of reasons for illiteracy and deny that schools are innocent of any blame. Conversely, at the level of domain literacy, it is also difficult to blame the lack of science literacy on the home; although it is certainly a factor. Functional illiteracy or scientific illiteracy . . . first generation or second . . . as science educators, we must seek out the knowledge that research is trying to create for us and prepare future generations of students (and ultimately adults) for life in their time and space.

Problems and Extensions

1. What are examples of performance assessments in life science? Can you give examples from physical, earth, and STS?
2. Select a chapter from a middle or high school science text and create an assessment.
3. Write a rationale for teaching a miniunit on any one of the following topics to a group of either middle or high school students.
   a. Risk factors of cancer
   b. Potential hazards associated with earthquake country
   c. Floods and their effect on the local community
   d. Radiation: Benefits and harmful effects
4. Find out how students in any one of the countries featured in Chapter 4 (Australia, Chile, China, Ghana, Russia) did on the latest international comparison of science achievement.

Notes

1. For an in-depth examination of this trend, see Sandra K. Enger and Robert E. Yager, *Assessing student understanding in science: A Standards-Based K–12 Handbook*, (Thousand Oaks, Calif.: Corwin Press, 2000).

2. Barbara E. Lovitts and Audrey B. Champagne, "Assessment and Instruction: Two Sides of the Same Coin," in *Assessment in the Service of Instruction*, ed. Audrey B. Champagne, Barbara E. Lovitts, and Betty J. Calinger (Washington, D.C.: American Association for the Advancement of Science, 1990), p. 6.

3. George E. Hein and Sabra Price, *Active Assessment for Active Science: A Guide for Elementary Science* (Portsmouth, N.H.: Heinemann, 1994).

4. Lovitts and Champagne, "Assessment and Instruction," p. 3.

5. J. Atkin, Paul Myron Black, and Janet, Coffey, eds., *Classroom Assessment and the National Science Education Standards* (Washington, D.C.: National Academy Press, 2001).

6. Ibid.

7. National Research Council, *The National Science Education Standards* (Washington, D.C.: National Academy Press, 1995).

8. David C. Berliner, "But Do They Understand?" in *Educators' Handbook: A Research Perpective*, ed. Virginia Richardson-Koehler (New York: Longman, 1987).

9. Mary Budd Rower, "Science, Silence and Sections," Science and Children 1966: 36: 22–25.

10. Berliner, "But Do They Understand?" p. 270.

11. Ibid., p. 271.

12. Mikhail Yaroshevsky, *Lev Vygotsky* (Moscow: Progress Publishers, 1989), p. 267.

13. Berliner, "But Do They Understand?"

14. Joan Boykoff Baron, "Performance Assessment: Blurring the Edges among Assessment, Curriculum, and Instruction," in Champagne, Lovitts, and Calinger, *Assessment in the Service of Instruction*, p. 127.

15. *Learning by Doing: A Manual for Teaching and Assessing High-Order Thinking in Science and Mathematics* (Princeton, N.J.: Educational Testing Service, 1987), pp. 20–21.

16. George E. Hein and Sabra Price, *Active Assessment for Active Science: A Guide for Elementary School* (Portsmouth, N.H.: Heinemann, 1994).

17. Baron, "Performance Assessment," pp. 133–34.

18. Angelo Collins, "Portfolios for Assessing Student Learning in Science: A New Name for a Familiar Idea?" in Champagne, Lovitts, and Calinger, *Assessment in the Service of Instruction*, pp. 157–66.

19. I. V. S. Mullis and L. B. Jenkins, *The Science Report Card* (Princeton, N.J.: Educational Testing Service, 1988).

20. See NAEP Science Consensus Project, *Science Framework for the 1996 and 2000 National Assessment of Educational Progress* (Washington, D.C.: National Assessment Governing Board, 2001). This report outlines the framework upon which the national assessments in science are based.

21. Mullis and Jenkins, *The Science Report Card*, p. 49.

22. Ibid., pp. 4–54. These items were selected from representative samples of the items used on the NAEP test. Used with permission of the Educational Testing Service.

23. Ibid.

24. Ibid., p. 123.

25. Ibid., p. 128.

26. Ibid., pp. 128–29.

27. Ibid., pp. 129–30.

28. National Center for Education Statistics, *The Nation's Report Card: Science Highlights 2000* (Washington, D.C.: U.S. Department of Education, Office of Educational Research and Improvement, 2001), 2002–452.

29. Marlene M. Hurley, *Science Literacy: Lessons from the First Generation*, Research Matters . . . to the Science Teacher Monograph Series (National Association for Research in Science Teaching). Used with permission.

30. R. L. Venezky, "Definitions of Literacy," in *Toward Defining Literacy*, ed. R. L. Venezky, D. A. Wagner, and B. S. Ciliberti (Newark, Del.: International Reading Association, 1990).

31. Literacy Volunteers of America, *History of Literacy Volunteers in America*.

32. W. C. Kyle, Jr., "Science Literacy: Where Do We Go from Here?," *Science Education* 32, no. 10 (1995): 1007–9.

33. Paul Hurd, "Science Literacy: Its Meaning for American Schools," *Educational Leadership*, 16, no. 1 (1958): 13–16, 52.

34. G. E. DeBoer, *A History of Ideas in Science Education: Implications for Practice* (New York: Teachers College Press, 1991).

35. H. J. Graff, *The Legacies of Literacy: Continuities and Contradictions in Western Culture and Society* (Bloomington: Indiana University Press, 1987), pp. 3–4.

36. National Research Council, *National Science Education Standards* (Washington, D.C.: National Academy Press, 1996), p. 22.

37. A. B. Champagne and V. L. Kouba, "Science Literacy: A Cognitive Perspective" (paper presented at the

International Conference on Science Education, Korea, May 1997).

38. A. B. Champagne and B. E. Lovitts, "Scientific Literacy: A Concept in Search of Definition," in *This Year in School Science: Scientific Literacy*, ed. A. B. Champagne, B. E. Lovitts, and B. J. Callinger (Washington, D.C.: Amercian Association for the Advancement of Science, 1989), pp. 1–14.

39. R. C. Laugksch, "Development of a Test for Scientific Literacy and Its Application in Assessing the Scientific Literacy of Matriculants Entering Universities and Technikons in the Western Cape, South Africa" (Ph.D. diss., University of Cape Town, 1996).

40. D. L. Radford, "Transferring Theory in Practice: A Mocel for Professional Development for Science Education Reform," *Journal of Research in Science Teaching*, 35, no. 1 (1998): 73–88.

41. Ibid., p. 86.

42. Literacy Volunteers of America, *History of Literacy Volunteers in America*.

Readings

Atkin, J. Myron, and Coffey, Janet, eds. *Classroom Assessment and the National Science Education Standards*. Washington, D.C.: National Academy Press, 2001.

Beatty, Alexandra, ed. *Learning from TIMSS: Results of the Third International Mathematics and Science Study*. Summary of a Symposium. Washington, D.C.: National Academy Press, 1997.

Beatty, Alexandra, ed. *Taking Stock: What Have We Learned about Making Education Standards Internationally Competitive?* Washington, D.C.: National Academy Press, 1997.

Beatty, Alexandra et al., eds. *Next Step for TIMSS*. Washington, D.C.: National Academy Press, 1999.

Doran, Rodney, Chan, Fred, Pinchas, Tamir, and Lenhardt, Carol., *Science Educator's Laboratory Guide to Assessment*. Washington, D.C.: National Science Teachers Association, 2002.

Hein, George E., and Price, Sabra. *Active Assessment for Active Science: A Guide for Elementary School*. Portsmouth, N.H.: Heinemann, 1994.

Pellegrinao, James W., et al., eds. *Grading the Nation's Report Card: Evaluating NAEP and Transforming the Assessment of Educational Progress*. Washington, D.C.: National Academy Press, 1999.

On the Web

Assessment and Evaluation: http://www.mcli.dist.maricopa.edu/ae0. This site provides balanced information concerning educational assessment, evaluation, and research methodology. It also provides resources to encourage the responsible use of educational data.

The Nation's Report Card: http://nces.ed.gov/nationsreportcard/. Here you find the results of the National Assessment of Educational Progress (NAEP). NAEP, also known as "the Nation's Report Card," is the only nationally representative and continuing assessment of what America's students know and can do in various subject areas.

Third International Mathematics and Science Study (TIMSS): http://nces.ed.gov/timss/. The site provides details concerning the largest international study of mathematics and science education in the world.

Science Framework for the 1996 and 2000 National Assessment of Educational Progress: http://www.nagb.org/pubs/96-2000science/toc.html. This site describes in detail the framework used for the assessing science at the national level.

PART 4

STRATEGIES OF SCIENCE TEACHING

CHAPTER 9

Strategies Fostering Thinking in the Science Classroom

Would anyone believe that thinking is not a central part of the science classroom? Who would not emphasize thinking in the science classroom? Unfortunately, research studies indicate that the predominant strategy used in science classes is recitation, with the teacher in control. What impact will this strategy have on student thinking? In most cases this form of teaching will reinforce memorization and rote learning.

In this chapter we will explore teaching strategies in the context of how they influence and facilitate student thinking. Some teachers refer to these as "active learning strategies" because of their determination on high levels of student involvement. We will explore the first set of strategies in terms of their impact on students' ability to think critically and creatively.

We'll develop some teaching strategies in the context of "microteaching" environments that will enable you to focus on specific abilities, such as using advanced organizers, questioning, and creating a stimulating environment.

We'll investigate "intelligent" strategies, which refer to the notion that teachers create learning environments full of a spectrum of intelligences. This implies that the strategies we use can foster many kinds of intelligences in the science classroom.

Language plays a critical role in helping students learn and think in the context of the science classroom. We'll explore powerful ideas to help students talk, read, and write science.

We will also explore strategies that will foster independent and collaborative thinking among secondary students. How can students be empowered to be thinkers in their own right? We'll examine science process skills more carefully, as well as the nature of problem solving, and make some connections to science projects and science fairs.

Finally, we'll consider how the computer can be instrumental in enhancing student thinking in the science classroom. We'll examine the computer as a medium to enhance students' scientific skills, along with its power to help students write, communicate, and conduct research.

 Case Study: The Learning Log

The Case

Harold Wells was in his second year of teaching and was very excited about implementing a writing-to-learn project in his eighth grade science class. He had attended a summer institute that focused on how language activities could enhance students' understanding of science as well as increase students' interest in science. In the institute, Harold worked with other teachers and researchers on ways of helping students express their ideas freely using their own language. One of the approaches was the use of a structured learning log that involved a combination of open-ended writing as well as structured writing experiences related to science activities and projects. Jason Douglass, one of Harold's colleagues, thought the idea of a learning log was a waste of time because most kids couldn't write sentences of more than five words. How would writing help them enhance their understanding of science? Furthermore, wasn't science about hands-on learning and doing experiments? Harold was surprised at Jason's attitude.

The Problem

Should writing play a prominent role in science teaching? If you were Jason, what would convince you that writing might enhance student understanding? What can Harold do to show his colleague how writing could be beneficial?

How to Read This Chapter

Three major ideas are developed in this chapter: strategies for interactive teaching, strategies for establishing a culture of learning, and strategies for fostering independent and collaborative thinking. You will be able to implement many of these strategies into the classroom and consequently you will want to return to this chapter from time to time. If you are interested in improving interactivity among you and your students, then you'll find the first part of the chapter very appealing. This chapter also includes a section on language and learning science, with specific strategies on talking about, reading, and writing about science. The last section explores the importance of problem solving in the context of independent and collaborative thinking.

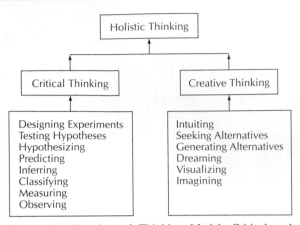

Figure 9.1 Drawing of Thinking Model. Critical and creative thinking can be integrated to form a holistic model of thinking.

SECTION 1: THINKING IN THE SCIENCE CLASSROOM

Invitations to Inquiry

- What teaching strategies can be used to foster critical and creative thinking among students?
- How does the idea of multiple intelligences expand the way we think of human potential?
- How does research on language—in particular the work on talking, reading, and writing science—contribute to the development of a constructivist classroom?
- What strategies aid student independent and collaborative thinking?
- How can projects be used to enhance thinking in science?

Strategies Fostering Critical and Creative Thinking

Critical and creative thinking are counterparts of a holistic view of student thinking. They are not opposite; they are indeed complimentary (Figure 9.1). Critical thinking is "reasonable, reflective thinking that is focused on deciding what to believe or do." Critical thinkers in a science class have learned how to look at phenomena aware of their own biases and approach the situation objectively and logically.[1] Creative thinking, on the other hand, is the ability to form new combinations of ideas to fulfill a need.[2] Examples of creative thinking in science classes are brainstorming, creating alternative hypotheses, synthesizing information, and thinking laterally.

Critical thinking and creative thinking can be contrasted (Figure 9.1) to indicate the differences in these forms of thinking. Look over the following list of science teaching tasks and decide which are examples of critical thinking and which are examples of creative thinking:

- summarizing the main ideas in a chapter on forces and momentum
- building models of atoms using clay and toothpicks
- inventing a system that will measure the mass of an elephant
- writing review questions based on specific pages in the science textbook
- observing an event and then writing at least three alternative explanations
- estimating the volume of a science classroom
- listing as many observations as possible of a burning candle during a five-minute observation session

There are many strategies to foster creative and critical thinking in the science classroom. Three assertions will guide our approach to these strategies that foster this development. Critical and creative thinking are fostered in classrooms that:

- focus on active learning
- integrate personal and social perspectives of learning
- encourage talk, reading, and writing as a means to understanding science
- bring students in contact with real-world problem solving

Interactive Teaching Strategies

Critical and creative thinking require that students be actively engaged in learning science, as opposed to the more traditional, yet typical, approach in which the student is on the receiving end of a lecture. The interactive classroom is one in which communication patterns involve students to teacher, teacher to students, and students to students. The interactive classroom is a stimulating place in which students have been motivated to learn and are given the freedom to explore, discover, and inquire. In the interactive classroom you will find teacher-centered as well as student-centered activities. Regardless of the type of activity that the teacher selects, there appear to be at least six specific strategies that teachers use to create an interactive science classroom.

Interactive teachers:

1. use advance organizers to establish interest and instructional goals
2. create a stimulating classroom environment
3. understand the art of questioning
4. use examples to help students understand concepts
5. create a positive learning environment
6. use closure and transitional skills

Lets look at each of these strategies in some detail.

Advance Organizers

Wouldn't you agree that helping students make meaningful connections between what they know and what is to be learned would facilitate learning new ideas? An advance organizer is a device that teachers use to help students make these connections. Advance organizers are frameworks for helping students understand what is to be learned.

An advance organizer is not an overview, but rather a presentation of information (either verbal or visual) structured as "umbrellas" for the new material to be learned. Psychologist David Ausubel proposed the concept of advance organizer. To Ausubel, effective advance organizers are presented by teachers at a "higher level of abstraction, generality, and incisiveness" than the science material that is to follow.[3]

Advance organizers can be useful devices at the start of a unit, before a discussion, before a question-and-answer period, before giving a homework assignment, before student reports, before a video, before students read from their science textbook, before a hands-on activity, and before a discussion of science concepts based on students' laboratory experiences.

Look at some examples of advance organizers and then consider designing your own:

- A teacher shows a picture of Mendeleyev in his laboratory in Leningrad and discusses his contribution to the development of the periodic table before introducing any details about the table of the elements.
- A teacher has students bring in pictures that show the destruction caused by earthquakes before introducing earthquake waves and how they are measured.
- A teacher asks students how they think life on earth originated before introducing a unit on evolution.
- A teacher shows a poster depicting many forms of energy and asks students to discuss and identify the examples of energy before introducing a new unit on heat energy.

Advance organizers help students organize the conceptual knowledge they are to learn. The teacher can refer back to the organizer and use it to link a sequence of lessons. For example, the science textbook can provide clues and examples of advance organizers. Look at a secondary science textbook and identify advance organizers for one chapter. Discuss the advance organizers with a peer in your class. Do they meet the criteria of being "at a higher level of abstraction, generality, and inclusiveness" than the materials in the chapter?

Creating a Stimulating Classroom Environment

Imagine walking down the hall of a school and being able to peer through the doors to compare classroom environments of a variety of teachers. One teacher is sitting on the desk talking with students; a half hour later you pass by the classroom again and the teacher is still sitting. In another classroom, you have to strain your head to find the teacher, who is in a corner of the room pointing to an aquarium during a discussion. In a third classroom, you notice the hand and body movements of the teacher, who is explaining what the students are to do in lab. In the fourth class, you observe the teacher walking among six groups of students who appear to be wrapped up in intense discussions.

There are a number of specific teaching skills that impinge on creating a stimulating environment in the classroom, which will have positive effects on critical and creative thinking of students. The use of movement, gestures, focusing, different interaction styles, and multiple sensory channels (Table 9.1) appear to affect the environment that the teacher establishes in the classroom.

Table 9.1 Interactive Teaching Skills

Classroom Teaching Skill	Teacher Actions
Movement	Moving throughout the classroom and not hovering at the front of the classroom, especially behind the demonstration desk, is desirable.
Gestures	Complimenting verbal messages with body language is an important aspect of communication. Teachers should use hand, head, and body gestures to convey meaning.
Focusing	Teachers who focus students use verbal statements (e.g., "Look at this chart of vertebrates") and use gestures (pointing to a fault line on a map projected on the overhead), or a combination of both.
Interaction Styles	Stimulating environments occur where there are a variety of interaction styles between teacher and students. Whole class, small-group, and individual interaction styles should be utilized.
Multiple Sensory Channels	Research on student learning styles suggests benefits of the creation of multiple sensory classrooms. Teachers should provide verbal, tactile, and kinesthetic experiences for students.

The Art of Questioning

Of all the skills discussed in this section, questioning, according to many science educators, is one of the most important. Teachers sometimes ask over a hundred questions in a class session to encourage student thinking. Questions are a very powerful way to find out about student leaning. However, quite often the teacher ends up answering his or her own question for fear of waiting too long for student responses. This then results in teachers asking questions that solicit short answers and a consequence is that students really don't think much about anything. How can teachers' questions facilitate critical and creative thinking? Are some questioning strategies more effective than others? Let's examine some aspects of the art of questioning, including types of questions, wait time, and strategies that will result in thoughtful and more in-depth student responses.

CATEGORIES OF QUESTIONS Examine the following list of questions. Can you assign each question to one of two categories? Identify the criteria you used to name the categories.

1. Are all the fruit flies alike for each feature?
2. What is weathering?
3. What do you predict will happen if a jar is put over a candle?
4. Using evidence that you choose, do you think scientists should be limited in the areas they want to research?
5. Which element in the periodic table do you think is the most important to living things? Why do you think so?

Table 9.2 Categories of Questions

Category 1	Category 2
Factual	Higher Cognitive
Closed	Open
Convergent	Divergent
Lower Level	Higher Level
Low Order	High Order
Low Inquiry	High Inquiry

6. Which planet is largest: Mars, Venus, or Mercury?

There are many systems that teachers use to classify questions. Upon close observation, in most systems questions are typically classified into two categories. Various terms are used to describe these two categories (Table 9.2). The binary approach is useful because two categories are more manageable for a beginning teacher to implement than the typical approach of using systems with six categories.

What kinds of questions do teachers ask in the classroom? Gall reports that 60 percent of teachers' questions require students to recall facts, about 20 percent require students to use higher cognitive processes, and the remaining 20 percent are procedural.[4] If teachers want to foster critical and creative thinking in the classroom, then this pattern of questioning should be changed. Let's examine more closely how questioning strategies might be used to enhance critical and creative thinking.

One way to classify questions is to determine whether they are low inquiry (closed or convergent) or high inquiry (open or divergent).

Low-Inquiry Questions These questions focus on previously learned knowledge in order to answer questions posed by the teacher that require students to perform *one* of the following tasks:

1. elicit the meaning of a term
2. represent something by a word or a phrase
3. supply an example of something
4. make statements of issues, steps in a procedure, rules, conclusions, ideas, and beliefs that have previously been made
5. supply a summary or a review that was previously said or provided
6. provide a specific, predictable answer to a question

High-Inquiry Questions These questions focus on previously learned knowledge in order to answer questions posed by the teacher that require the students to perform *one* of the following tasks:

1. perform an abstract operation, usually of a mathematical nature, such as multiplying, substituting, or simplifying
2. rate some entity as to its value, dependability, importance, or sufficiency, with a defense of the rating
3. find similarities or differences in the qualities of two or more entities utilizing criteria defined by the student

4. make a prediction that is the result of some stated condition, state, operation, object, or substance
5. make inferences to account for the occurrence of something (how or why it occurred)

Low-inquiry questions tend to reinforce "correct" answers or focus on specific acceptable answers, whereas high-inquiry questions stimulate a broader range of responses and tend to stimulate high levels of thinking. There is evidence to support the use of both types of questions. Low-inquiry questions will help sharpen students' ability to recall experiences and events of science teaching. Low-inquiry questions are useful if you are interested in having students focus on the details of the content of a chapter in their textbook or a laboratory experiment. High-inquiry questions encourage a range of responses from students and tend to stimulate divergent thinking. Table 9.3 summarizes the differences between low- and high-inquiry questions.

WAIT TIME Knowledge of the types of questions and their predicted effects on student thinking is important. However, researchers have found that there are other factors associated with questioning that can enhance critical and creative thinking. One of the purposes of questioning is to enhance and increase verbal behavior of students in the science classroom. Mary Budd Rowe has discovered that the following factors affect student verbal behavior:[5]

1. Increasing the period of time that a teacher waits for students to construct a response to a question.

Table 9.3 Differences between Low-Inquiry and High-Inquiry Questions

Type of Question	Student Responses	Type of Response	Examples
Low inquiry (convergent)	• Recall, memorize • Describe in own words • Summarize • Classify on basis of known criteria • Give an example of something	Closed	How many . . . ? Define . . . In your own words . . . state similarities and differences . . . What is the evidence . . . ? What is an example . . . ?
High inquiry (divergent)	• Create unique or original design, report, inference, prediction • Judge scientific credibility • Give an opinion or state an attitude • Make value judgments about issues	Open	Design an experiment . . . What do you predict . . . ? What do you think about . . . ? Design a plan that would solve . . . What evidence can you cite to support . . . ?

2. Increasing the amount of time that a teacher waits before replying to a student response.
3. Decreasing the pattern of reward and punishment delivered to students.

Rowe has found that, if teachers increase the time they wait after asking a question to five seconds or longer, then the length of responses increases. In the science classroom, where the teacher is trying to encourage inquiry thinking, wait time becomes an important skill as well as a symbol of the teacher's attitude toward student thinking. Teachers who are willing to wait recognize that inquiry thinking requires thoughtful consideration on the part of the students. Rowe points out that teachers who extend their wait times to five seconds or longer increase "speculative" thinking. The use of silence in the classroom can become a powerful tool to enhance critical and creative thinking.

Rowe also believes that teacher sanctions (positive and negative rewards), if used indiscriminately, can reduce student inquiry. At first glance, this doesn't make sense. However, Rowe has found that when rewards are high, students tend to stop experimenting sooner than if rewards are low. When students begin attending to rewards rather than the task, the spirit of inquiry tends to decrease.

Another factor related to questioning is the attitude of the teacher. Have you ever been in a class situation in which you wanted to ask a question but feared the teacher's reaction (that it might be a dumb question)? One important classroom rule is "there are no dumb questions." A corollary to this rule is "there are no dumb answers." Students need to believe that the teacher will accept their responses; anything short of this will tend to reduce the probability of student participation.

Waiting three to five seconds for student responses often does not evoke the kind of answers that you are striving for. How can you integrate knowledge of question types and wait time to increase the likelihood that student responses are thoughtful and high level? Here are some suggestions:[6]

- After you ask a question, have the students pair off or form small groups to discuss the question. Then ask one member of each team to respond for the others.
- Using a multiple-choice format, ask the students to vote on the choices and then ask some of the students to justify their vote.
- Ask all of the students to write down a response and call on individuals to read out their answers.

If your class is engaged in microteaching you might want to focus your lessons on questioning. Prepare a lesson and use the evaluation form in Figure 9.2 to analyze your effectiveness.

Teacher_____   Topic_____

Observer/Coach_____

First Lesson_____

Second Lesson_____

	Low						**High**
A. *Increasing Probability for Student Response:* At various times during the lesson the teacher paused after asking questions and called on both volunteers and nonvolunteers.	1	2	3	4	5	6	7
B. *Decreasing Teacher Verbal Participation:* The teacher was observed redirecting the same question to several students and asked more high-inquiry questions than low-inquiry questions.	1	2	3	4	5	6	7
C. *Probing:* The teacher prompted students and asked them to clarify their responses.	1	2	3	4	5	6	7
D. *Reducing Interference:* The teacher made an attempt not to repeat or answer his or her own questions and not to answer student questions.	1	2	3	4	5	6	7

Figure 9.2 Asking Questions Evaluation Form.

Using Examples to Help Students Understand Science Concepts

The word *example* comes from the word *sample*, which means a portion of the whole that shows the quality and character of the whole. The use of examples is fundamental to helping students understand science concepts. The teacher who identifies examples of concepts or asks students to cite examples of concepts is acknowledging that learning must be tied to students' prior knowledge. Using examples is a way to tie science teaching to the students' world.

Examples should be exciting and should be recognizable as everyday phenomena. We use the acronym EEEP to mean "exciting examples of everyday phenomena." EEEPs should be used to help students understand science concepts and can exist in the form of an object (e.g., a rubber door wedge to represent an inclined plane), an artifact (e.g., a piece of pottery to help students understand soil), a machine, photograph, a piece of technology, or a toy.

One way to help you think about examples is to examine a list of categories and use it as a stimulus for connecting these categories with science concepts. What kinds of examples can you generate from the following list?

- Detergents
- Household chemicals
- Fertilizer
- Nails
- Muddy water
- Vegetables
- Flowers
- Building materials (bricks, mortar, wood)
- Paper products
- Beach stones
- Playground rocks
- Food items
- Slinkies
- Dishware
- Eyeglasses and lenses
- Recycled newspaper
- Biodegradable plastic bags
- Balloons
- Oil and other viscous fluids
- Toy cars

Examples can be used deductively or inductively to help students understand concepts. However, it is important to keep in mind what we have discussed about the learning cycle and the generative model of learning.

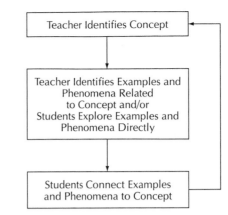

Figure 9.3 Deductive Use of Examples Teaching Process.

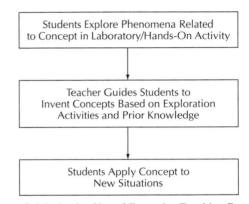

Figure 9.4 Inductive Use of Examples Teaching Process.

As you recall, cognitive psychologists theorize that students construct their knowledge (of concepts) and must do so through their interaction with ideas, phenomena, and people. In the deductive approach of using examples, learning begins with the idea, principle, or concept and is then followed by an exploration of examples and phenomena. The process culminates in relating the concept to the examples (Figure 9.3).

In the inductive approach, which is closer to the constructivist notion of how students learn concepts, students begin with an exploration of ideas and phenomena, followed by a teacher-directed activity to facilitate the "invention" of the science concepts (see Figure 9.4).

In either approach, it is important to start with the simplest examples and ones that are relevant to your students' experience and knowledge. Examples can be thought of as metaphors and analogies of the science concepts in the curriculum. The more familiar the examples are to the students' experience, the greater the probability of hooking their understanding of the concept.

Research by Treagust and colleagues has shown that examples, especially those in the form of analogies, are rarely used to help students understand science concepts.[7] Typically, the teacher introduces the new science concept by defining it or using an example that is not too familiar to the students. An interesting finding by Treagust and colleagues was that teachers who were not familiar with the content being taught typically used definitions to explain concepts; teachers well versed in the content used definitions the least.

Positive Learning Environment

Psychologist Carl Rogers has shown that student attitudes (toward themselves, their peers, their teachers, and subject) are an integral aspect of student learning.[8] Rogers has suggested that a climate of inquiry, which is essential for critical and creative thinking, is fostered when students perceive the learning environment in terms of realness or genuiness, acceptance, and empathy. Throughout this book we have emphasized the importance of inquiry learning and have substantiated the claims of cognitive psychologists that students must explore, invent, and apply their knowledge in real situations to develop and construct science concepts. The science teacher must foster a classroom climate that projects and supports this cognitive perspective. Such an environment is characterized as follows:[9]

- The teacher projects an image to the students that tells them "I am here to help you build your character and your intellect."
- The teacher conveys the notion that each and every student is unique and he or she is interested in them as a unique individuals.
- The teacher conveys the idea that all students can accomplish work, can learn, and are competent.
- The teacher expects high standards of values, competence, and problem-solving ability.
- The teacher conveys, through his or her own behavior, a character of authenticity.
- The teacher conveys high ethical standards by establishing a high degree of private or semi-private communication with students.

Rogers claims that the most important aspect of the teacher-facilitator role is that of empathy. In the context of science education, this makes perfectly good sense.

The student who has "science anxiety" can only be helped in an environment in which the teacher empathizes with this state. Too often, the student who was interested in science in the early grades gets turned off to science in the middle grades. Perhaps one of the reasons for this low interest in science is the lack of an empathic classroom climate.

Closure and Making Transitions

Closure is the complement of advance organizers. Closure acts as a cognitive link between past knowledge and the new knowledge (experiences). Closure can also function to help give the students a feeling of accomplishment or achievement.

Closure is not limited to the end of a lesson. There are many instances in a lesson in which you will help the students make a transition; for example a transition from a prelab session to the laboratory activity itself functions as a transition from one activity to another.

There are a number of ways to integrate closure and transitions into your lesson plans. Three are identified next:

1. *Draw attention to the completion of a lesson or a part of the lesson.* The teacher can provide a consolidation of concepts and elements that were covered before moving to a subsequent activity. It is extremely helpful to relate the lesson back to the original organizing principle (advance organizer). Some teachers review (preferably with the students) the main ideas of the lesson by means of an outline or a concept map. Another closure technique is to stop throughout a teacher-directed lesson and ask student pairs to explain the ideas that were developed.
2. *Make connections between previous knowledge and the new science concepts.* Teachers find it helpful to review the sequence that has followed in moving from previous knowledge to the new ideas. The learning cycle or generative model emphasizes this general sequence. Using EEEPs can facilitate student transition from a misconception state to one of understanding the concept.
3. *Allow students the opportunity to demonstrate what they have learned.* It is a much more powerful technique if students can suggest ways that demonstrate closure. One technique that researchers and teachers have found effective is concept mapping. A concept map drawn after a lesson, chapter, or unit of study is a visual mechanism in which students describe their understanding.

INQUIRY ACTIVITY 9.1

Microteaching: Practicing Science Teaching Skills

In this section we discussed several teaching strategies (advance organizers, interactive teaching skills, questioning, using examples, creating a positive learning environment, and closure) that are related to the establishment of an interactive classroom. In this inquiry activity, you will prepare a brief lesson, teach it to a group of peers, view a video of the lesson during a reflective teaching conference, and then reteach the lesson incorporating changes suggested by your reflective teaching coach. Figure 9.5 provides an illustration of a microteaching setup.

Materials

- VCR
- Camera
- Videotape
- Microteaching Evaluation Form (Figure 9.6)

Procedures

1. Prepare a five-minute lesson on a science topic of your choice. Prepare the lesson in such a way that you focus on the teaching skills listed in Table 9.1. Please note that in five minutes you will not be able to teach a "complete" lesson.
2. Meet with your observer-coach (a peer) prior to the lesson to explain your objectives and the skills you plan to focus on.
3. Teach the lesson to four to six peers. The lesson should be videotaped.
4. The observer-coach should complete the microteaching evaluation form (Figure 9.6) and use the results in a reflective teaching conference.

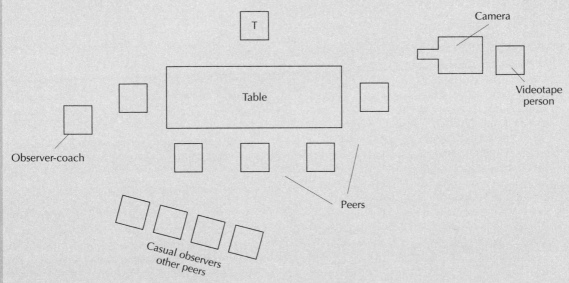

Figure 9.5 Microteaching Class Arrangement.

Teacher_____ Topic_____

Observer/Coach_____

First Lesson_____

Second Lesson_____

Interactive Teaching Skills

	Low						High
Teacher Movements: At various times during the lesson, the teacher was noted in various parts of the teaching space.	1	2	3	4	5	6	7
Teacher Gestures: The teacher used gestures (hand, body, etc.) to help convey extra meaning in the presentation of the lesson.	1	2	3	4	5	6	7
Focusing: When the teacher wanted to emphasize a point, it was clearly stressed through the use of gestures or through the use of verbal expressions ("Listen closely," "Watch this," etc.) or combining gestures and verbal acts.	1	2	3	4	5	6	7
Interacting: The teacher varied the kind of participation required of the students. That is, students could be directly called on, group questions were asked, student–student interchange could occur. Students could role-play, go to computer centers, to the board, etc.	1	2	3	4	5	6	7
Pausing: The teacher gave the students time to think or get ready for new ideas by using wait time.	1	2	3	4	5	6	7
Oral-Visual Switching: The teacher used visual material (words on a whiteboard, projector, objects, pictures, etc.) in such a way that the student must look to get information.	1	2	3	4	5	6	7

Comments:_____

Figure 9.6 Microteaching Evaluation Form. *Source:* Based on Allen, Dwight, and Ryan, Kevin, *Microteaching* (Reading, Mass.: Addison-Wesley, 1969), pp. 15–18.

5. The observer-coach should conduct a reflective teaching conference immediately following the five-minute lesson, during which the video should be viewed and suggestions should be made on how the lesson might be changed for the reteaching session.

6. Reteach the lesson to another group of peers. Following the lesson, view the video with your coach and evaluate the effectiveness of the changes that you tried to incorporate into the second lesson.

Minds-On Strategies

1. How successful were you in integrating the skills into the five-minute lessons?

2. Use the microteaching format to practice other critical and creative thinking teaching strategies. Your five-minute lessons can focus on the following:

   a. using advance organizers in science teaching.

   b. using low- and high-inquiry questions in science lessons.

   c. using examples to help students understand science concepts.

Establishing a Culture of Learning:
Language and Vygotsky

Picture this: The bell is ringing and the teacher shouts, "For tonight's homework, read Chapter 8 and do problems 1 through 11 on page 243!" Secretly, the teacher knows that very few of the students will "read" the chapter, and maybe half of them will turn in the answers to the questions. In another classroom, the teacher is explaining an assignment in which the students are to identify the main ideas in the first half of a chapter in their text and then write supporting details that explain, prove, or tell something about the main idea. In a third classroom, a teacher has prepared on large sheets of paper the main terms in the current biology unit. The words are written in English and Spanish, and the teacher has pictures pasted next to each word. The teacher is reviewing the words with the class.

To a growing number of science educators, focusing on language should be an integral aspect of science teaching. The three examples cited here are only the tip of the iceberg with regard how language is used in the science classroom. To some, the teaching of language or study skills is seen as remedial action necessary for students with low reading scores or abilities. For these students, this is beneficial if they do indeed have teachers that provide "special" instruction to help them comprehend their science textbook or give them pointers for writing reports.

However, there is more powerful argument. Jones points out that language is a tool used for the expression of information and ideas.[10] In the science classroom, bringing a variety of language (or linguistic) modes is fundamental to helping students construct ideas: listening and talking; reading and writing; discussing and arguing; narrating and describing; using actions, images, and symbols.

Russian psychologist Lev Vygotsky promoted the idea that all higher-level learning (e.g., learning science concepts and ideas) took place on the "social plane."[11] Listening and talking, reading and writing, are essential. To Vygotsky and his proponents, the social context and language are the essence of learning. Teachers embodying this view would integrate personal and social perspectives on learning and emphasize the role of language in helping students construct science knowledge.

Vygotsky distinguished between two different forms of experience that give rise to two interrelated concepts: the "scientific" and the "spontaneous." According to Vygotsky scientific concepts develop in highly structured and specialized activity in school classrooms. Spontaneous concepts, on the other hand, originate from the student's own reflections on everyday experience. Vygotsky emphasized the development of scientific concepts in the school environment and neglected the spontaneous concepts that the student brought to school.

Nevertheless, Vygotsky studied concept formation in school settings, which led to a major finding; namely, the dialogical character of learning. Vygotsky saw that schooling provided the environment for a dialog between the student's spontaneous concepts (which in present-day language can be described as naive or misconceptions) and the logic of scientific concepts. Vygotsky argued that the development of scientific concepts could be achieved in cooperation with adult interaction and indeed with others (peers and other adults). Vygotsky coined the term "zo-ped," which referred to the "zone of proximal development," meaning the place where the student's rich experiential knowledge (spontaneous concepts) meets the systematic and logical thinking of the adult world (of teaching and learning). Central to the "zo-ped" would be dialog and language that would enable the student to develop "upwardly" the spontaneous concept meeting the abstract scientific concepts in their "downward" development toward concreteness.

Thus, this section of the *Art of Teaching Science* focuses on language and its role in the development of students' ideas and concepts in science. We'll explore the importance of:

* talking science
* reading science
* writing science

Talking Science

Students need to talk about their ideas in the science classroom. However, teachers do most of the talking. Jones cites Lemke's analysis that the most common communication pattern in the classroom is triadic dialogue: The teacher asks a question; a student answers the question; the teacher evaluates the answer. The dialog ends.[12] But more significantly, thinking ends. The student is not encouraged to reflect and work out relationships between the spontaneous concepts brought into class with the scientific concepts and ideas that permeate the classroom.

Earlier in the book, the concept of students' prior knowledge was introduced in connection with the constructivist theory of learning and the models of teaching that emerged. Researchers, such as Jones and Lempke and others, are finding that students' prior knowledge (call it spontaneous concepts, unscientific concepts, naive ideas, everyday explanations, children's ideas, misconceptions) are undervalued and underappreciated.

William Cobern terms these ideas, which include cultural and social factors, as worldviews.[13] Each student comes to class with a worldview, or picture of the everyday. Hills puts it this way:

> It seems evident that children come to school already equipped with a more or less sophisticated understanding of how the world works. Common-sense, then, is the range of concepts, beliefs and values that people share, which provides a basic view of the world, of their position in the world and of how they ought to act. It is more properly viewed as a system of shared beliefs or concepts which provides the basis for day-to-day activity within a culture.[14]

The concept of worldview challenges the positivist notion that the scientific explanation for the world is more important than "nonscientific" views. When we help students "uncover" their preexisting ideas about the phenomena that are presented in science courses, their views (even after instruction) may not change. McCoy asserts that not every culture has the same worldview and, indeed, students from a culture may not hold the same views as other members of that culture. McCoy investigated the worldviews (on selected biology concepts) of high school students prior to entering biology class. For instance, after interviewing students individually (the interviews involved asking students to respond to scenarios about several biological concepts like classification, DNA, and so forth) and bringing them together for a focus group discussion, McCoy found that the students held implicit theories of the world that were as much based on personal feelings as on thinking:

> Each student explained nature based on their own personal experience, which included experience as a science student, but also as a religious person, as a person who cares about animals and other people, as a moralist, as a conservationist, and as a potential influential and powerful adult.[15]

Talking about science in the classroom is fundamental to helping students deal with their preexisting concepts in the context of the science curriculum. Some researchers have suggested that the science class should be used to "induct" the students into a new way of talking, science talk. For this to happen, teachers need to structure activities carefully so that students have opportunities to talk among themselves and to interact with the teacher.

There are several strategies that teachers can employ to provide opportunities for students to talk about their ideas and how these ideas relate to the science concepts and theories that they are learning.

STRUCTURED CONTROVERSIES A strategy that appears to encourage science talk is to involve students in the exploration of science controversies—a kind of academic conflict that arises when one student's opinions and ideas are incompatible with those of another student. Johnson and Johnson have experimented and field tested a series of environmental issues structured for controversies in the science classroom.[16] The recent emphasis on STS (science, technology, society) (see Chapter 11) provides the science teacher with a wide range of topics for a structured controversy strategy. Some potential topics include:

- Global Warming: Is the Earth Really Heating Up?
- A Hungry Earth: Can the Earth Feed Its Human Population?
- Crisis in the Ocean: How Polluted Is the Ocean?
- The Garbage Problem: What Is the Best Way to Manage Waste?
- Chemicals on the Highways: How Can Hazardous Waste Be Managed?
- Extinction: How Endangered Is Life on the Planet?

The strategy of structured controversies consists of four procedures: selecting a topic, preparing learning materials, structuring the controversy, and conducting the controversy in the classroom.

Selecting a Topic Teacher and student interest are critical in the selection of a topic. It is important that two positions on the issue can be identified and that students are able to deal with the content of the topic. The teacher can either present the class with the topic or have the students choose from a list of topics.

Preparing Learning Materials According to the developers of this strategy, the following materials are needed for each position on the issue:

- a description of the group's task
- a description of the phases of the process (see conducting the controversy that follows)
- a definition of the position to be advocated
- resource materials, including a bibliography, pamphlets, magazines, newspaper articles, and a list of Web sites

Structuring the Controversy The controversy should be investigated in a cooperative learning context. Students should be grouped into teams of four heterogeneously; pairs of students will work together on one side of the issue. (Refer to section on cooperative learning models in Chapter 7.)

Conducting the Controversy in the Classroom To manage the process in the classroom, students should be led through a series of phases as follows:

- *Learning position:* Each partner team should become thoroughly familiar with its position on the issue by reading the materials and preparing a persuasive presentation. Additional reading may be required to master the position.
- *Presenting positions:* Each partner team presents its position to the other team in the group. It is important to listen carefully as well as ask questions to clarify points on the issue.
- *Discussing the issue:* During this phase each team should argue its position forcefully by presenting facts to support points on the issue. Students should be encouraged to ask their opposing teammates to support their arguments with information and facts.
- *Reversing positions:* In this phase each pair presents the opposing pair's position in as a sincere and forceful manner as possible.
- *Reaching a decision:* In this final phase each team must prepare a report on the issue that summarizes and synthesizes the best arguments for both points of view. However, as a team, the students must reach consensus on a position that is supported by the evidence. Each team should prepare a single report and be prepared to engage in a large-group discussion.

Throughout the process, students should be held accountable by acknowledging a set of discussion rules for academic controversies:[17]

1. I am critical of ideas, not people.
2. I focus on making the best decision possible, not on "winning."
3. I encourage everyone to participate and master all the relevant information.
4. I listen to everyone's ideas, even if I do not agree.
5. I restate (paraphrase) what someone has said if it is not clear.
6. I first bring out *all* the ideas and facts supporting both sides and then try to put them together in a way that makes sense.

7. I try to understand both sides of the issue.
8. I change my mind when the evidence clearly indicates that I should do so.

Throughout the process, critical thinking emerges as students analyze points of view and search for evidence to support their arguments. Facts and information are analyzed in terms of a position or argument. Creative thinking manifests itself in a number of ways. Students have to reverse positions on the issue, requiring them to move from one side of the issue to the other. This encourages flexibility in thinking, an important component of creative thinking. Using this strategy to encourage science talk is powerful.

OPEN-ENDED QUESTIONS This strategy employs the techniques discussed earlier in the art of questioning section. Asking open-ended (high-level inquiry) questions gives the students the freedom to express their ideas, first in a small-group format and within the whole class context. Open-ended questions typically have many acceptable responses and provide students with opportunities to connect their preexisting ideas with science concepts and reflect on the meaning of this type of talk. Examples of open-ended questions might be:

- What is your favorite animal? Why?
- If you could be any rock, which rock would you be, and why would you want to be that rock?
- In the experiment we just completed, what are some additional methods that we could have used to try and answer the research question?
- How do you think living things evolved on the earth?

Some teachers would present any one of these questions to the class and facilitate a discussion among all of the members of the class. A more successful method is to present the question to the class, then have the students pair off or form small groups and discuss the question. Usually two to five minutes is enough time for the students to talk among themselves. At this point, a good strategy is to select a student from some of the groups randomly or by asking for volunteers.

THINK-ALOUD PAIR PROBLEM SOLVING This strategy structures science talk such that one person in the pair talks out loud, trying to solve a problem. The other student in the pair acts as a coach or facilitator, encouraging the "talker" to go on and try and solve the problem.

SCIENCE TALKS This strategy acknowledges a special time when the focus is to talk out loud about a question that the teacher or a student poses that is related to a central idea or concept in the science curriculum. Some teachers like to rearrange the room so that students are sitting in a circle. Gallas suggests that teachers need to set the stage for this kind of talk so that it is inclusive and everyone in the class is admitted.[18] Students may offer their own theories on the question for discussion, and in these sessions, ideas need to be heard. The teachers' role is that of moderator and, as such, he or she should use questions and encouragement to involve as many students as possible in the "science talk." Open-ended questions also should be used, such as "Why do some animals migrate?" or "Why do leaves change color?"

USING SCIENCE STORIES This is not actually a strategy as much as it is a message that you can use with students to inform them that the science they read and hear about on the news appears to be very logical and precise. However, an idea that might be logically described in a book might have been developed in a complex and disorderly way. Telling stories about scientific discoveries is extremely informative in validating the students' worldview and preexisting ideas.

Reading Science

First, let's start with the notion that reading is as important to scientific activity as observing, classifying, measuring, and hypothesizing. If we want science to be more accessible to our students, then we must recognize reading as a new science process skill. Leslie Bulman, in *Teaching Language and Study Skills in Secondary Science*, writes:

> If pupils can read about science it makes it potentially more accessible both in terms of present understanding and, even more important, of future interest. Most learning, after the exposition of school and lecture hall is over, is via books . . . Reading is more important as a scientific technique than many practical skills. It is clear from the aims of science education . . . that they cannot be achieved with advanced reading skills.[19]

The most recent edition of *Modern Biology*, the most widely used science textbook in the United States, has over 800 pages of text and lists over 1,100 entries in the glossary.[20] Tackling that text is quite a formidable task for a fourteen-year-old student to undertake! Regardless of the students' intellectual development, student success in science courses could be enhanced if they were

taught in a manner that we might call *learning how to learn*. Recent research in metacognition supports efforts in which students are taught strategies of learning that will enable them to learn science, but also understand their own thinking processes.

Jones reports that one of the dangers in using science texts for reading is "passive reading."[21] When students passively read, they do not process anything. What researchers suggest is that science texts need to be read for a specific purpose to engage the interests of the students. Using the science text to help students learn science requires an active reading approach. These researchers suggested a number of direct activities called DARTs (direct activities related to text):[22]

* *Reconstruction activities:* require students to reassemble text, such as with scrambled segments of a text.
* *Completion activities:* activities in which students fill in a word or complete a diagram or a table related to the text.
* *Analysis activities:* activities that can involve underlining, providing headings for text segments, or making diagrams or maps.
* *Text extension:* activities in which students generate questions about the text

With this idea in mind, we shall explore several strategies that will enhance students' reading abilities.

LISTENING Teachers talk about two thirds of the time in an average classroom; therefore, listening is an important survival skill that students need to develop. Good listeners are active listeners in that they concentrate and participate in the process of communication. Listening is half of the act of communication; however, in the classroom students do not always have the opportunity to respond and interact directly with the speaker. The listener must develop skills to "communicate" alone and the teacher must implement strategies that provide students (in pairs or small groups) the opportunity to interact.

Listening Skill Activity 1 In this activity students practice being an active listener by concentrating and participating. Tell the students that you are going to read a passage to them and that they should participate in the following ways:

1. When you listen, ask yourself questions about what you are hearing: answer the questions if you can.

2. Try to connect what you hear with what you already know.
3. Try to "picture" in your mind what is being said and draw a picture if it is appropriate.
4. When the passage has been read write the main idea in your notebook.

Passage to be read:

In this science class you will be doing a number of activities in the laboratory and it is important to use the right tools and instruments. You wouldn't use a thermometer to measure the height of a building. You wouldn't use a microscope to observe the moon. You wouldn't collect rocks in a glass beaker. You would choose the equipment that best fits the task you are doing. In this course, you will be measuring and observing objects, living things, and phenomena and you will learn what tools and instruments you should use.

Listening Skill Activity 2 Another active listening device is taking notes. In this activity we will focus on note taking during the listening process; more strategies for note taking are found ahead in the section on mapping. In this activity, students listen to a passage and actively participate in the process by taking notes. Instruct your students as follows:

1. Do not write down everything. Instead, listen for words that seem key or important. Listen for speaker's clues, such as emphasis or repetition.
2. As you listen, jot down all the key words or phrases.
3. When the speaker is finished, go back and write a phrase or sentence for each key word.
4. Describe the main idea by writing a sentence or two.
5. Share your main idea with a partner, listening to your partner's ideas as well. Compare the results and make necessary modifications.

Passage to read:

Evolution—the theory that species change over time—is the unifying theme of biology. The theory of evolution helps explain how all the kinds of organisms came into existence. It helps us understand why organisms look the way they do and how organisms of the past are related to organisms alive today. It also helps explain relationships among various groups of living organisms. Scientists suggest that evolution occurs by a process called natural selection. According to the theory of evolution by natural selection, organisms that have certain inheritable traits are better able to survive in specific environments than organisms that lack those traits. Such favorable traits are called adaptations.[23]

Listening Skill Activity 3 This activity is a modification of the "think-aloud-pair strategy, in which students are presented with some information, a problem, or a question, and are asked to think about their response or comprehension and then share their idea with a partner. In the science classroom this technique is very powerful, especially if it is repeated over the course of the year. Present information to students in the form of a minilecture. At a convenient point in the presentation stop and either ask a question or ask the students to identify the main ideas or concepts presented. Give the students a minute to think about their response and then have them share their thinking with their partner. The process enables all students in the class to become active listeners, and participants in small-group interaction.

COMING TO TERMS—THE VOCABULARY PROBLEM
Thelen suggests that science teachers not preteach new vocabulary words.[24] If, indeed, the words are new, then students should be engaged in learning activities to construct knowledge about these new words, most of which are science concepts. Instead, Thelen suggests that science teachers should reduce the number of vocabulary words that students need to learn and use vocabulary reinforcement activities to help enhance vocabulary development.

One technique that science teachers can use to reduce vocabulary is to use a structured overview—a sort of visual overview showing the relationship among science concepts. In this approach the teacher would identify the vocabulary of the learning activity, chapter, or unit, and arrange the words in a scheme that depicts the relationships among the concepts. The structured overview is then presented to the students and used to find out what they already know about the concepts and terms. The structured overview or organizer can be used as students explore the topic (see Figure 9.7).

Most science textbooks identify by means of bold print, underlining, or italics the key vocabulary words in a chapter. Students need to learn how to interpret meanings by reading about the concepts and focusing on context clues. Context clues are the sentences and phrases in the text surrounding the vocabulary word. Reading guides might suggest an activity after the student has read a passage in a text or might ask the student to read a passage and then write the meaning of several vocabulary words.

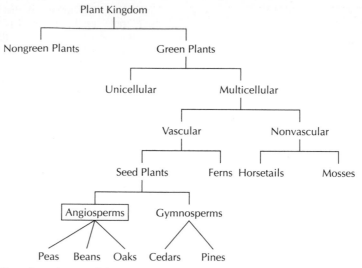

Figure 9.7 Structured Overview. A map of the concepts is shown as an overview of what students will learn.

For example, you might have the students read a passage such as the one shown below and then write the meaning of selected words from the passage. The meaning of the words will be based on the student's prior knowledge as well as the contextual clues in the passage.

All organisms are composed of and develop from cells. Some organisms are composed of only one cell. These organisms are called *unicellular* organisms. Most of the living things you see around you are composed of more than one cell. Such organisms are called multicellular organisms. *Multicellular* organisms usually arise from a zygote. The process by which a zygote becomes a mature individual is called *development*.[25]

Based on emphasis indicators (italics) in the passage, you could ask students to define: unicellular, multicellular, and development.

A number of types of vocabulary activities can be used to reinforce and extend students' vocabulary development. These include categorizing, word puzzles, matching, magic squares, crossword puzzles, and various writing forms (see ahead in the section on science writing). Here are some examples:

Word Categories

There are five words in each section below. Cross-out the two words in each you feel are not related to the others. Explain the relationship by titling each group.

1. _____
2. _____

amino acids	waste
energy	storage
water	food
enzyme	pocket
protein	contractile

Word Puzzles

Using the clue list, complete the spelling of each word.

1. _ _ _ _ _ S _
2. _ _ _ _ _ O _ _ _ _
3. _ _ _ U _ _ _ _ _
4. _ R _ _ _ _ _ _ _ _
5. _ _ _ _ C _ _ _ _ _ _ _
6. _ _ _ _ _ _ _ _ E _ _ _ _ _ _ _ _ _ _ _ _
7. _ _ _ _ _ S _ _ _

Clues:

1. Source of chemical energy in all animal cells
2. Plant energy source
3. Reaction involving gain of electrons
4. Conversion of organic acid
5. One place where reaction for liberation of energy takes place
6. Key substance that occurs in every living organism and cell
7. ADP

K: What we know	W: What we want to find out	L: What we learned and still need to learn

Figure 9.8 K-W-L Strategy Sheet.

READING FOR MEANING AND UNDERSTANDING
How can textbooks be used so that students will read them for meaning and understanding? A partial answer to this question lies in how we think students learn. In this book we are asserting that students construct knowledge through the interaction with the environment at the personal and social levels, and learning of science in school settings must be connected to their prior knowledge and their worldview. If the textbook is to be one of the "environments" in which the learner will interact, then we must find a way that involves the student actively with the textbook. Simply telling students to read pages 20–30 for homework will not be effective.

Although textbooks have become more visual, there is still the problem that "few users of textbooks, instructors and students alike, are literate enough to derive full value from the textbook's illustrations."[26]

For students to read for meaning and understanding, teachers must employ strategies that actively engage students in comparing what they already know with the new material, as well as involve students in processes such as predicting, inferring, hypothesizing, summarizing, drawing conclusions, and discussing.

K-W-L According to Donna Ogle, the originator of K-W-L, prior knowledge is an integral aspect of how we interpret what is read and what students will learn from reading.[27] Unfortunately, most science teachers fail to make use of what their students bring to a topic. The K-W-L procedure supports the main assertion of cognitive

psychology that student preconceptions of science need to be determined prior to learning new concepts. The procedure comprises three cognitive steps: assessing what I **k**now, determining what I **w**ant to learn, and recalling what I did **l**earn. Ogle has developed a K-W-L strategy sheet (Figure 9.8) that students can use as they "read" a section of the science textbook. Briefly, the next sections describe the essential characteristics of each step in the K-W-L procedure, followed by an example of a lesson plan on earthquakes.

Step K—(What I know) is a brainstorming session in which students express what they know about the topic. This knowledge can be written on the chalkboard or on chart paper by students working in small groups. The focus at this stage should be specific. If the students are going to read a section in their text on earthquakes, ask, "What do you know about earthquakes?" Do not ask "What do you know about natural disasters?" or "Have you ever been to San Francisco?" Focusing on the content will help bring out the cognitive structures of the students' prior knowledge.

A second part of the K step is to have the students categorize the information they generated during the brainstorming session. For example, in the lesson plan on earthquakes, the teacher might suggest that students group their information in the following categories: causes of earthquakes, how earthquakes are measured, and damages caused by earthquakes.

Step W (What do I want to learn?) helps students anticipate the reading that is to come and helps them focus on what they want to learn from the reading. This step should be done as a group activity. The teacher should ask the students to write down on the K-W-L worksheet questions that they are most interested in having answered as a result of the prior discussion and brainstorming session. Once the questions are written, the teacher might have the students share their questions in small groups prior to actually reading.

Step L (What I learned) occurs when students write what they learned on the K-W-L strategy sheet. They can also check to see if their questions were answered and whether some of their prior knowledge was confirmed. Students should work in small groups and discuss their questions to determine if they were answered.

SAMPLE LESSON 8.1

Earthquakes

Objectives

1. Describe how earthquakes are caused
2. Predict the effects of an earthquake

Reading

You can use the chapter on earthquakes from any middle school earth science text

K: What Do Students Already Know about Earthquakes?

1. Pairs of students brainstorm and record what they know about earthquakes.
2. Pairs of pairs (groups of four) share lists and prepare a composite list.
3. Groups of four share with the whole class by taping lists on the walls of the classroom. The teacher focuses on the lists and asks groups of four to categorize the information: topics include at least: causes of earthquakes, damage caused by earthquakes, earthquake waves, and how earthquakes are measured.
4. The teacher asks students how they got their information about earthquakes. This last procedure personalizes student knowledge and acknowledges the sources of students' prior knowledge.

W: What Do Students Want to Know about the Topic?

1. Each group of four develops four questions about the topic.
2. The teacher records these questions on the board. The teacher can elaborate on the questions, perhaps selecting two or more that seem interesting to the students.

L: What Did Students Learn about the Topic?

1. Each group circles information on the master list that the text confirmed.
2. Information is crossed off that text refuted.
3. Students contribute to new list: What we learned!
4. The teacher goes around the class and asks each student to indicate, by thumbs up or thumbs down, if their question(s) were answered.
5. The teacher asks each group to make a map of the main ideas and supporting secondary categories of what they learned from the reading.

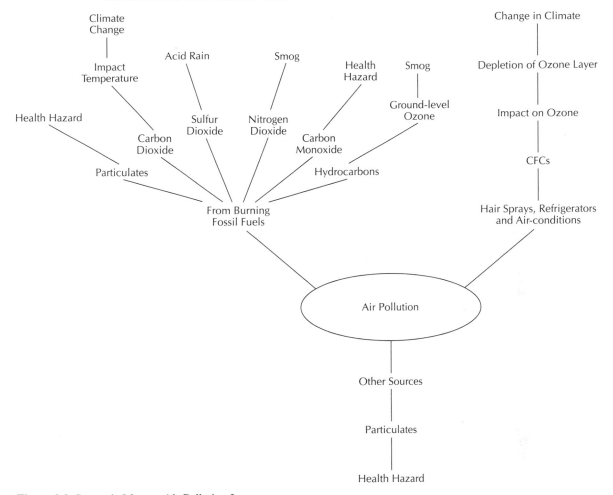

Figure 9.9 Semantic Map on Air Pollution Impacts.

SEMANTIC MAPPING Although mapping was used in both of the reading process procedures described earlier, the concept of mapping deserves additional discussion. Semantic mapping is the structuring of information in graphic form. It is not a new process, and it has been known as concept mapping, webbing, networking, and plot maps.[28] Semantic mapping is a tool that teachers can use to help students connect prior knowledge with new science concepts to be learned in terms of a schemata or a holistic conceptual system. In many cases, new science words are often introduced and defined in isolation from a more general system of idea.

As Heimlich and Pittelman point out, semantic maps are diagrams that help students see how words or concepts are related to one another.[29] In most cases semantic mapping begins with a brainstorming session in which students are encouraged to make associations to the main topic or concept presented. Students are actively engaged in using their prior knowledge, as well new science concepts and experiences that the teacher has provided, to develop a semantic map. Semantic maps can be accomplished individually, in small cooperative groups, or with the whole class.

Semantic maps (Figure 9.9) can be used in many different contexts in the science classroom, including:

1. as a science vocabulary (concept) building strategy
2. as a pre- and postreading strategy
3. as a science study skill strategy

Heimlich and Pittelman have developed a basic strategy for developing semantic maps; this strategy can be used in any of the three purposes just listed. The following is an adaptation of their strategy:[30]

1. Choose a science concept related to the chapter or unit students are studying.
2. List the concept on large chart paper or on the chalkboard.
3. Encourage the students to think of as many words or concepts as they can that are related to the main concept (see the example in Figure 9.9) and list them in categories on the paper or board. This step of the process can be done individually, in a small team, or with the whole class. Encouraging interaction among the students is an important part of the process and, therefore, most teachers choose to do this as a small group or whole class activity.
4. Students can share their results with each other.
5. Students should discuss by comparing and contrasting their semantic maps to develop deeper understanding of science concepts.

Writing Science

Some researchers support the notion that students should be taught how to write scientifically because this kind of writing "trains the mind" to think scientifically. In a sense, this kind of writing helps the student understand the nature of science writing and scientific knowledge and thereby might entice students to make a career of science (or writing). On the other hand, some researchers suggest that students should be allowed to express their ideas freely using their own language. They argue that trying to teach students the "language" of science writing may neglect the content and that scientific writing may turn some students away from science. Nevertheless, most researchers would agree that writing brings thought to consciousness and thus helps the student reconstruct knowledge and ideas.[31] Writing is important and should be an integral part of science lessons.

WRITING TO LEARN Consider the science-writing lesson in a middle school earth science course presented in Sample Lesson 8.2.[32] Students are asked to collect data on a set of rocks. Their data consist of written observations of the rocks, using all of the senses. From the observations, students construct a poem using their written observations. This lesson, which enables students to make connections between science process skills and writing, is not the typical way in which students write in science classrooms.

SAMPLE LESSON 8.2

 Crusty (Rock) Writing

Objectives

1. collect data on rocks using observational skills
2. record notes about a natural object, a rock
3. reconstruct notes in poetry form

Description

As part of a science unit on local geology, students select a rock that they observe carefully, using all five senses. They then write words and phrases based on their observations. After reading and thinking about their notes, they write an ode to their individual rock, beginning, "Oh, rock . . ."

Procedures

Have students gather rocks as part of field trip or bring in enough rocks from the local scene so that each student will have one to observe.

1. Stimulus: All students have a rock on their desk. Discuss what the students can observe about a rock based on each of the senses. Have a student recorder write key words on the board or on chart paper, such as:

   - Sight: size, shape, and color
   - Hearing: rattle, scraping
   - Taste: mineral content, dirt
   - Touch: shape, roughness, smoothness, unevenness, bumps
   - Smell: sweet fragrance, earthiness

   Have students fold a sheet of composition paper in thirds, labeling one section for each sense, and the sixth one entitled "Other Ideas." Ask students to observe their rocks and to jot down notes about what they observe.

2. Activity: After students have had time to observe and write notes, tell them that they can use their observation to write an ode to their rocks. Tell them that an ode is a song that begins, "Oh . . ." and usually praises a person. Students can begin their poem with "Oh rock . . ." and speak to their rock as a person, using personification.

3. Follow-up: After students have written for a while, have them read their poems to a partner. Partners can assist each other in adding ideas or revising the poem, as needed. Their poems might be something like this:

   Oh, wonderful little gray rock,
   Bumpety, lumpety, and tough.
   You have tumbled down from the high mountain,
   You have survived the trampling of many rough feet,
   The crush of an automobile's wheels.
   I will give you an easier life now
   Perched on my bedroom windowsill.

4. Evaluation: Circulate around the room to observe student participation as the class observes, writes, and shares. Have students determine criteria (scientific and poetic) for an especially good poem after they have shared and have them answer the question: What made some poems stand out as especially effective? Students can revise their poems based on the established criteria. Have students display the rock writing with rocks laid on a table or shelf.

Unfortunately, creative writing, which can help students become successful science learners, is low on the priority list of "science writing assignments." Bulman reports that students spend between 11 percent and 20 percent of their time in science classrooms involved in writing activities. However, Bulman also reports that over half of the writing time is devoted to copying or taking dictated notes (Table 9.4).[33]

What is the purpose of writing in the science curriculum? To improve the writing abilities of students in all subjects, many school districts have implemented a concept known as "writing across the curriculum" in which subject matter teachers are given training and teaching materials to integrate writing into their subject. Any approach to integrating writing into the science classroom must take into consideration the goals of student writing in science. Bulman has suggested four goals:[34]

1. Help the growth of understanding of science concepts
2. Provide a record of concepts and activities that can be used for revision later
3. Provide feedback to the teacher on the growth of the students
4. Develop students' ability to communicate

How can these goals be achieved? In general, writing should be viewed as an integral part of the learning cycle that was presented in Chapter 5. Students need the

Table 9.4 Types of Writing in High School Science Classes

Types of Writing	Percent of Time Spent	
	First Year	**Fourth Year**
1. Copying: copying or dictated note taking	46	56
2. Reference: making notes from printed material	0	19
3. Personal: essay writing, writing in own way, diary, some project work, reports of experiments	29	8
4. Answering: answering worksheets, exercises, answering test and exam questions	25	17

Source: Based on Bulman, Lesley. *Teaching Language and Study Skills in Secondary Science.* London: Heinemann, 1985, p. 54.

opportunity to reflect on their thinking, and writing about their observations, inferences, hypotheses, and conclusions is a powerful strategy. The strategies suggested next are designed to help students clarify and extend their thinking by having them write in a variety of forms.

- Web writing
- science logs
- letter writing
- science newspapers
- story writing

WEB WRITING Writing projects and activities on the Web can help students reflect on their ideas and express them in a variety of ways. There are many forms that can be used in this medium that will attract a wide range of students. You will find more details on these activities in Chapter 12, which focuses on the Web.

- *E-mail Projects*: Using e-mail in the context of collaborative science projects enables students to describe what they have done, report the results of their observations and experiments, analyze their results, and use other's results to draw conclusions. E-mail writing can also be informal in the sense that students are able to talk about their community and themselves to share with others who they are.
- *Bulletin Board Discourse*: Discourse on an Internet bulletin board can enable students to use the same process as in e-mail projects, but in this context their writing is placed on a public and/or community bulletin board. One way to approach the use of this form is to have students respond to open-ended questions that you pose. For example, you might ask high school biology students to

write on the topic: Do you think animals should have rights? Should they be the same as the rights that humans have? In this context, students are given several days to post a response to the teacher's question and are also asked to respond to at least two other students' responses to encourage a conversation in writing.

- *Web Pages*: The writing associated with Web pages can be of interest to many students. In some cases, teachers have students develop a Web page in the same way they would write up a science laboratory activity. This enables the students to reflect on the laboratory activity and then share the results with others. Web pages are also used to describe participation in Internet collaborative projects.

SCIENCE LOGS — VISUAL AND VERBAL JOURNALS OF STUDENTS' IDEAS Writing is a way of expressing ideas and concepts that are within us. These concepts and ideas are based on prior experiences, imagination, and the willingness to let these ideas emerge. We have already shown that talking, reading, and writing are integrated processes. In real-life experiences of talking, reading, and writing, this is known to be true. For example, if you ask a writer what is essential to writing, the answer invariably is talk and read, talk and read, talk and read. Talking, writing, and reading are inseparable processes and in the science classroom the teacher can help students by providing integrated language experiences.

The science log is one such experience. It can become a place—a creative space—in which students organize their ideas from their reading of the science text, from science experiments and activities, and the day-to-day activities that are part of your teaching process. Here are some specific suggestions for using the science log:

1. *As a note taking device.* Students should follow the K-W-L procedure and use the log as the place to record their results.
2. *As a record of experiments and activities.* Visual and verbal thinking should be encouraged as students record the results of experiments and hands-on activities.
3. *To prepare a daily log.* Some teachers have students use their logs as a post-lesson review. However, students are asked to make a map of the lesson by writing the main idea in the center of a page in the log and then identifying the supporting ideas and concepts by connecting them to the main idea.
4. *As a learning tool.* Iris McClellan Tiedt suggests that the science log be conceptualized as a learning log.[35] Students express their findings or their questions, and can use the log to clarify concepts, ask questions of the teacher, or set goals for learning. Logs can be kept in spiral-bound notebooks, loose-leaf notebooks, in a folder, or on the computer. As we have outlined, logs should help students summarize and clarify what they learned in a class session, a laboratory exercise, a class discussion, or a reading. Teachers should read logs to evaluate the effectiveness of lessons, as well as a way to identify students who need specific help. Sample Lesson 8.3 should give you an idea of how to make the science log a learning tool.

In Sample Lesson 8.3 the log is used in an active way. Students not only write in their own logs, but also exchange logs with other students in the class and have an opportunity to write in their classmate's logs. Logs are also viewed as feedback mechanisms for the teacher. Logs can be an integral part of the science curriculum and can foster critical and creative thinking.

Now let's examine some other types of writing formats appropriate for the science classroom.

SAMPLE LESSON 8.3

 Using the Learning Log with a Hands-On Activity

Objectives

1. Write in order to clarify what they observed in a hands-on activity
2. Ask questions immediately after the hands-on activity
3. Write in science class

Description

This lesson shows how the science log can and should be used immediately following a hands-on activity. It provides an opportunity for you to have the students express what they have learned from the activity.

Procedures

1. Stimulus: Have students observe a discrepant event or inquiry demonstration. Students should be involved in the activity, not simply passive observers of the event.
2. Activity: Following the discrepant event activity, the students record their findings in their science logs. Encourage the students to connect new learning with old, express discoveries, ask questions of the teacher, and express any frustration related to the activity.
3. Follow-up: Have students exchange logs with their partner, or read the logs yourself.
4. Evaluation: Have the partner respond to the log in writing to the individual. A brief comment is all that is needed. Peers can answer questions and comment on the log.

LETTER WRITING There are at least two aspects of the letter writing format that have been shown to be effective: writing to others for information and writing "letters to the editor." Letters can be the beginnings of potential research, especially of the survey type. For instance, students might want to write to various organizations related to a topic they are studying. The Sierra Club, Audubon Society, National Aeronautics and Space Administration, National Transportation Board, Environmental Protection Agency, and the United Nations are good sources of information. Letters to the editor are especially significant if students are working on an STS project or debating an issue that has personal and societal implications.

Students can be given a format to follow to write letters of inquiry and letters to the editor, and can use the computer to prepare the documents.

SCIENCE NEWSPAPERS Students in your class might be interested in applying desktop publishing to produce a science newspaper that could be distributed to other students in the school as well as to citizens in the community. There are number of software packages available that will allow students to design newspapers in a quality that compares with commercially produced newspapers. The newspaper activity is especially useful in that it provides a creative mode for students to write about famous scientists, discoveries made by scientists, ecological and environmental concerns, as well as science and society issues.

STORYWRITING: SCIENCE FICTION Imagination is as important to science as it is to art forms such as pottery, painting, and writing novels. Reading as well as writing science fiction can be a powerful medium for many students in your science class. Books by Robert Heinlein, Carl Sagan, Isaac Asimov, and Ray Bradbury can provide the stimulus needed for students to write their own science fiction. I recommend that you read passages from your favorite authors as a vehicle for brainstorming about imagination and science.

Writing science fiction brings students into the world of invention and creativity. Students can explore the limits of their own creativity by writing imaginative stories about the future or the past by attempting to integrate science concepts into the story line. Imagine what kind of thinking might be activated if students were to write stories that involved:

- Black holes
- The Big Bang
- Anti-matter
- Speeds approach that of light
- Life on Io and other moons of Jupiter

Strategies That Foster Independent and Collaborative Thinking

School science needs to help students become independent thinkers. School science also needs to show students how to think collaboratively. In Project 2061: Science for All Americans, researchers pointed out that science teaching related to scientific literacy needs to be consistent with the spirit and character of scientific inquiry and with scientific values. Students must be engaged actively "in the use of hypotheses, the collection and use of evidence, and the design of investigations and processes, and placing a premium on the students' curiosity and creativity."[36] The authors of the report refer to this kind of thinking as the "scientific habit of mind," and view its implementation as an important goal:

> Scientific habits of mind can help people in every walk of life to deal sensibly with problems that often involve evidence, quantitative considerations, logical arguments, and uncertainty; without the ability to think critically and independently, citizens are easy prey to dogmatists, flimflam artists, and purveyors of simple solutions to complex problems.[37]

The habit of mind that is being suggested here is problem solving, and as Stanley L. Helgeson points out, "problem solving has been a concern of science education for at least three quarters of a century."[38] Helgeson goes on to point out whether we use terms such as scientific method, scientific thinking, critical thinking, inquiry skills, and science processes, these are in essence expressions of a more general concept: problem solving.

In this section, we will explore problem solving and pay particular attention to strategies that secondary science teachers can use to emphasize problem solving in their curriculum. We will begin with the notion of problem solving and will move on to conclude this section by relating problem solving to school science fair projects and research investigations.

Problem Solving

One of the problems with problem solving is the wide variety of ways to define it. Some define problem solving in terms of the skills needed to solve problems; for example, testing hypotheses, analyzing data. Others define problem solving as a series of steps that people use to find a solution or answer to a question.

Helgeson reports that in the literature of science education there is a strong linkage between problem solving and science process skills. That is, many science teachers teach students science process skills in the context of a subject—earth science, biology, chemistry, physics—because they accept the notion that these process skills are indeed the elements of problem solving. There are two aspects of this notion that should be questioned: What are the generally accepted steps in problem solving? What are the science processes associated with problem solving?

SCIENTIFIC THINKING SKILLS AND PROBLEM SOLVING Curriculum development efforts in the past have placed emphasis on problem solving, and the organization of the curriculum centered around a series of problem-solving skills (Table 9.5), which became known as the processes of science. They are sometimes

Table 9.5 Scientific Thinking Skills

Basic Science Thinking Skills	Integrated Science Thinking Skills
Observing	**Controlling Variables**
Using the senses to gather information about an object or an event.	Being able to identify variables that can affect an experimental outcome, keeping most constant while manipulating only the independent variable.
Example: Describing a mineral as red.	*Example:* Controlling the type of soil or sand and the angle of incline when testing to find out what affect the amount of flow (water) has on the depositional rate of a model river in a stream table.
Inferring	**Defining Operationally**
Making an "educated guess" about an object or event based on previously gathered data or information.	Stating how to measure a variable in an experiment.
Example: Saying that a landform was once underwater because of the presence of brachiopod and trilobite fossils in the rocks.	*Example:* Stating that depositional rate will be measured in grams of sand deposited in the stream table's "ocean."
Measuring	**Formulating Hypotheses**
Using both standard and nonstandard measures or estimates to describe the dimensions of an object or event.	Stating the expected outcome of an experiment.
Example: Using an equal-arm balance to measure the mass of an object.	*Example:* The greater the amount of flow in a river, the greater the depositional rate.
Communicating	**Interpreting Data**
Using words or graphic symbols to describe an action, object, or event.	Organizing data and drawing conclusions from it.
Example: Describing the change in temperature over a month in writing or through a bar graph.	*Example:* Recording information about weather changes in a data table and forming a conclusion that relates trends in the data to variables (such as temperature, pressure, cloud cover, precipitation).
Classifying	**Experimenting**
Grouping or ordering objects or events into categories based on properties or criteria.	Being able to conduct an experiment, including asking an appropriate question, stating a hypothesis, identifying and controlling variables, operationally defining those variables, designing a "fair" experiment, conducting the experiment, and interpreting the results of the experiment.
Example: Placing all minerals having a certain hardness into one group.	*Example:* Describing and carrying out a process to find out the effect of stream flow on depositional rates in rivers.
Predicting	**Formulating models**
Stating the outcome of a future event based on a pattern of evidence.	Creating a mental or physical model of a process or event.
Example: Predicting the position of the moon in the sky based on a graph of its position during the previous two hours.	*Example:* The model of how the processes of erosion, deposition, metamorphism, and igneous activity interrelate in the rock cycle.

Source: Based on Padilla, Michael J. *The Science Process Skills.* Research Matters . . . to the Science Teacher Monograph Series. National Association for Research in Science Teaching.

called the skills of science. Today, these skills are referred to as scientific thinking skills. It is important to note that problem solving as perceived in science classrooms is intimately related to these thinking skills.

The thinking skills of science are conceptualized as belonging to two distinct groups: basic thinking skills and integrated thinking skills. As you examine different science curriculum project materials, you will find some variation in the "lists" of skills, but in general:

- Basic thinking skills, such as observing, emphasize the foundations of science learning. The basic thinking skills are seen as a prerequisite for the integrated thinking skills.
- Integrated thinking skills are related more directly to problem solving and are seen as the higher-order intellectual skills that problem solvers use.

Focusing on science thinking skills in the science curriculum is clearly one way of helping students become independent thinkers and problem solvers. How should secondary science teachers plan science courses to achieve this goal? Three approaches seem apparent. The first is a behavioral approach. In this approach the thinking skills of science are taught as separate skills or behaviors (e.g., observing, classifying, inferring, hypothesizing). A second approach—a cognitive or constructivist approach—that is favored by most science educators is to integrate the thinking skills of science with the content or concepts of science. In this plan, science thinking skills would be taught in the context of learning biology, chemistry, earth science, and physics concepts. A third approach is called the research or science project approach. In this plan, students would engage in a science research project using the thinking skills of science to inquire about natural phenomena.

Most secondary science programs are not organized around a thinking skills approach; that is, texts and courses are organized around units or chapters of content. However, on closer inspection, one discovers that middle school/junior and high school science programs include a series of "skill" activities spread throughout the textbook. In this approach, a skills approach becomes a strand in the science course. For example, in one science textbook the following skills are taught in separate lessons throughout the text:

- Observations and inferences
- Determining variables and controls
- Constructing models
- Determining length, area, and volume
- Performing investigations
- Constructing graphs
- Making a map
- Using laboratory equipment
- Using a globe
- Comparing and contrasting
- Making scale drawings
- Using star charts
- Reading a weather map
- Limiting the number of variables
- Forming hypotheses
- Interpreting a glacial map
- Classifying minerals
- Classifying rocks
- Using tables and charts
- Graphing data
- Interpreting data
- Sequencing events
- Designing an experiment
- Predicting outcomes

These twenty-four lessons constitute a behavioral approach to teaching the skills of science in the context of an earth science course. From time to time students engage in a hands-on lesson specifically designed to teach a particular process of science.

Another approach used to teach the process of science is to include a separate chapter at the beginning of the course on science process skills. Usually the chapter is titled "Problem Solving in Science," "The Nature of Science," or "How Scientists Think."

Lessons that focus on the processes or skills of science are evident by the stated objectives or by a question that is asked. For example, in a lesson, students are asked to find out how observations differ from inferences. Students are asked to drop sheets of paper folded different amounts and record observations and inferences. There is no mention in the lesson of forces, gravity, and air resistance—any one of which could have been the conceptual organization of the lesson. In the skill approach, the emphasis is on the process of science, not the concepts of science.

COGNITIVE/CONSTRUCTIVIST APPROACH: INTEGRATING PROCESS AND CONTENT A second approach to dealing with the scientific skills of thinking is the cognitive or constructivist approach. In this method, science thinking skills are integrated with the learning of concepts. Joseph Novak, a leading proponent of this idea, points out that:

It should be evident . . . that there should no longer be a debate about the extent of emphasis on teaching the content of science vs. teaching the processes of science. If a constructivist perspective guides our work, and especially if we use compatible meta-cognitive tools, there is no reasonable way to teach the processes of science without simultaneously teaching its concepts and principles.[39]

In this approach scientific thinking skills are *learning strategies* that enable students to interact with the environment. If students are learning about theories of rock formation, they should observe and make inferences about rocks. If they are to learn about the structure of the atom, they might construct models and test hypotheses with regard to different theories. In this view, the processes of science are an integral part of the learning cycle proposed by cognitive science educators. That is, when the teacher engages students in the "exploration" stage of the learning cycle to encounter a new science concept, his or her intent is to have the students utilize the processes of science to explore objects, phenomena, and events. Thus students would be involved in making observations and measurements, collecting and interpreting data, and making conclusions for the purpose of investigating a scientific object, event, or phenomena. In other cases, students might design experiments to test the efficacy of a particular scientific theory.

The processes of science become tools to help students *understand* the concepts of science. In the cognitive perspective, science processes are the learning strategies for students to learn science concepts. In the initial stage of the constructivist's model of learning, the student gathers information about new science concepts. Typically, students make observations, collect data, interpret data, and draw conclusions in light of the main concept.

Problem Solving in Practice: Project-Based Teaching and Science Fairs

High-level thinking can be fostered by involving students in activities that involve the solving of problems in the context of science projects, research investigations, and science fairs. Although individual students have in the past carried out activities of this sort, many more students will benefit from these problem-solving activities if teachers organize them as group projects. Bringing into the mainstream of the science curriculum emphasis on science projects and research investigations expands students' concept of science and enables them to be immersed in problem solving. Let's take a closer look at how to implement science projects, and science fairs in the school setting.

PROJECT-BASED TEACHING A ninth grade physical science teacher, during the first semester of a two-semester course, organizes the students into four-member teams to investigate a problem, question, or topic. The teams have several weeks to complete their research and prepare for a class and a school presentation. Typical questions or topics that students investigate in this introductory physical science course include:

- Which metals conduct heat best?
- Do magnetic fields affect the growth of beans?
- Do plants grow better with tap water or distilled water?
- How are earthquakes predicted?
- Which toothpaste is most abrasive?
- What is the acidity of rain and how has it affected the environment in selected sites in North America? How does this compare to other continents?
- How can the global warming trend be changed?
- How do the laws of reflection apply to driving an automobile?
- What are optical illusions, and are they really?
- How can mirrors be used as communication devices?
- How are the laws of reflection applied in everyday life?

Project-based science teaching provides a context for involving a wide range of students in collaborative work. For some teachers, using a project-based approach represents a paradigm shift from a more traditional role in which knowledge is transmitted through lectures and demonstrations to a role in which knowledge is acquired making use of prior knowledge in the context of classroom experiences. Project-based teaching moves students away from working individually to working in a community of practice. In this context, the textbook-oriented approach gives way to learning in authentic situations.

In *Designing Project-Based Science*, Polman describes what it was like when a teacher turned his science curriculum into a totally project-based approach.[40] Polman notes that project-based teaching supports the social constructivist tradition, but many students have been ingrained in the cultural transmission model and find it very difficult to accept the role teachers must assume in a project-based tradition.

Most teachers use a project as an activity within a unit of teaching. Projects become one aspect of the pedagogy the teacher uses to interest the students in the content. However, teachers have the potential of creating an environment that could reach a very wide range of students who come to school with a diversity of interests, cultures, motivations, and abilities.

There are a number of projects that you can use to get started with project-based science teaching. The collection that follows includes projects that can be done in a single lesson and others that might take a week or more.

Life Science Projects

The Biodrama Project Students write a play about the parts of a cell and the life process of a cell. The director selects a cast of students, who rehearse and then present their play to other groups in the school. Students might want to explore topics related to cells, such as cancer, sickle cell anemia, or cell division.

The Dirty Water Project In this project teams are challenged to design a method to clean up dirty water. You will need to provide students with small samples of materials that will be used to make a large container of water dirty. Give pairs of students a small amount of the following materials: wood chips, sand, grass, shells, potting soil, baking soda, vinegar, pieces of newspaper, Styrofoam. Have student teams place their material in a large container of tap water. After all material has been put into the water, challenge the students to devise a method to clean up the water. Tell them they can use any of the following materials to design a water treatment system: small plastic cups, beakers, sand, activated charcoal, cotton balls, and filter paper. The students may add other materials with your approval. Students should design a system that will clean the water and they should document their work by recording ideas in a journal.

The Insect Project Student teams should select an insect that they will investigate. After selecting an insect to study, the students should search for information about the insect, including its characteristics, habitat, beneficial and harmful traits, and literature about the insect. Students should then create a model of their insect using any materials they wish. The model can be scaled up in size, but the various parts of the insect must be proportional. Students should present the results of their research to the class or another group.

The Design-an-Organism Project Students use any materials they wish to design an organism that they think will be able to survive in a specified environment. You should specify an actual environment, such as a forest or wooded area near your school, a meadow, a city park, or a playground. Tell the students that they should also be prepared to explain why they think their organism will survive. What characteristics does it have to protect it from predators?

Project Birdwatch Backyard or schoolyard birding provides a powerful environment for students to investigate the behavior and characteristics of birds in their region. Students can build a bird feeder by consulting references on professional feeder designs and then set the feeder in area that is convenient for observation and study. Students should use observation skills to study the characteristics and behavior of birds and the environmental factors that may affect them. Students can then design research questions to investigate aspects of bird behavior as well as the types of birds that they observe at their feeder. Students might consult an online project called Classroom Feeder Watch (http://teaparty.terc.edu/comweb/cfw/cfw.html/), which involves students in monitoring and data analysis of birds in North America.

Physical Science Projects

The Paper Tower In this project collaborative teams are challenged to construct the tallest possible structure using one sheet of paper (8.5 × 11 inches) and 50 cm of cellophane tape. Each team will also need a pair of scissors. The project can be accomplished in one or two days. If assigned as a one-day project, give the students about twenty minutes to experiment with various designs, testing them as they talk aloud. Then provide fresh materials and give the students thirty minutes to build the paper tower. If assigned as a two-day project, use day one for talking aloud and testing designs and day two for the challenge contest.

Clay Boats The challenge in this project is to design a boat that will float in water and hold the most number of paper clips (or any other weight you decide upon). Give students a measured amount of clay (50 grams), a container of water, and paper clips. Give students thirty minutes to work with the clay and test their designs. Tell the students to record their ideas and designs in their logs and to be ready to recreate their design tomorrow. Allow ten minutes to build the boat and then have students demonstrate in front of the class the number of "weights" the boat can hold. Awards can be given for a variety of criteria: longest boat, most innovative, and so on. Alternative materials: You can substitute the clay with aluminum foil. Give each team an equal amount of foil.

Spaghetti Cars Students build cars out of spaghetti and small marshmallows and then calculate how fast the car rolls down an incline. Students will need six pasta wheels, twenty-five spaghetti strands, and ten marshmallows. Students must build a car that rolls and can hold one large marshmallow. Set up a "downhill track" and have students test and measure how fast their cars roll.

Earth Science Projects

The Mars Egg Drop The challenge of this project is to design a cargo system to safely protect an egg dropped from a high place. A drop from 3 to 10 meters is recommended. Provide a variety of materials such as aluminum foil, string, Styrofoam packing peanuts, cereal boxes, cups, tape, cardboard, and paper. Students should be encouraged to provide additional materials. Eggs: you can choose to use either raw eggs or hard-boiled. Students should record their ideas in a journal or log. They should make drawings of their designs and, as they test them out, record the results and explanations of the results. Establish a time period for the construction of the containers, as well as a day for the competition. Students can relate this project to NASA's Mars Pathfinder mission. Sojourner, NASA's Mars rover, withstood a crash landing into Mars. Packed inside a protective shield of balloons, the vehicle bounced about fifteen times after a freefall landing on the planet. Even after this landing, Sojourner was able to navigate the surface for several months, transmitting data and images of Mars. Have students visit NASA's Mars Web site at http://www.jpl.nasa.gov/mars.

Eratosthenes Project This project is named for the Greek astronomer who accurately estimated the circumference of earth. It is described in *LabNet: Toward a Community of Practice* as a telecommunications project among several science classes.[41] By measuring the length of an object's shadow and comparing this to the actual length of the object, students can determine the angle at which the sun's rays strike earth in their area at a given time of the year. Data collected in places that are at least 10° latitude from one another may then be used to calculate the circumference of earth. By contacting teachers using the Internet, science classes can collaborate to try and solve this problem. In the original experiment conducted by Eratosthenes, he assumed that earth was round and that the sun's rays were parallel. He set up a stick in Alexandria and measured the angle of the sun's shadow when a well at Syene (a city many miles away from Alexandria) was completely sunlit. He knew from geometry that this angle represented the angle of the earth's center between Alexandria and Syene. He also knew the distance between the two cities was a distance of 5,000 stadia (1 stadium = about 200 meters). From the distance and the angle he measured, Eratosthenes calculated the earth's circumference to be 250,000 stadia, which is equal to about 46,250 kilometers (the actual circumference is about 40,000 kilometers).

Shadows Another interesting telecommunications-type project is to have classes from different locations measure the length of the shadow cast by a meter stick on specified days of the year. For a long-term project, students might measure shadow lengths at noon on September 21, December 21, March 21, and June 21. Since the Internet has no boundaries, Northern Hemisphere schools can collaborate with Southern Hemisphere schools to compare results.

Lunar Settlement Student design a lunar settlement out of cardboard, pipe cleaners, cotton, sand, construction paper, plastic, tape, and paint. Students need to consider the environment of the moon and what alterations need to be made to sustain a human colony on the moon.

Planetary Travel Brochure Using both fact and fantasy, students design a travel brochure about one of the planets of our solar system. Students also design a transportation system used to shuttle people back and forth between the destination planet and earth.

National Park Project Students design a national park to demonstrate their knowledge of the environmental impact of national parks. Designs should also include a topographic map of the park and information about how the park affects the environment in and around the park. Students should also design a brochure about the park describing its operation.

SCIENCE FAIRS Teachers who involve students in science fair projects commit themselves to many months of planning for an event that typically takes place during two or three days during the spring of each year. Yet, the rewards of science fairs for teachers and students far exceed the required effort.

Science fairs can be the stimulus that is needed to motivate some students who otherwise might be turned off to science. Science fairs not only encourage critical and creative thinking, but they encourage students with a wide range of learning styles to become involved in a science fair project. Science fair projects also involve the community and the parents in science education. Parental involvement, which sometimes is seen as intrusive, can actually be a positive aspect of the science fair. School science must extend beyond the walls of the school; the science fair is the perfect event to bring science to the community.

Some school districts arrange with a shopping mall to use its space to display and conduct the judging of the science fair. Other school districts set up the fair in one school. Atlanta Public Schools conducts its science fair (The Atlanta Science Congress) in a district school, but involves hundreds of community agencies, universities, and businesses by soliciting prizes for various categories and asking local professionals to participate as judges.

Teachers can integrate the science fair concept into the ongoing science curriculum by encouraging science projects and by helping students learn how to carry out research studies. Too often, students are not given enough guidance, and lack experience in conducting a research study or in preparing for one of a variety of science fair projects.

Science fairs have the potential to encourage the habit of mind that the authors of Project 2061 so aptly put forward. As they point out, students can end up with richer insights and deeper understanding (by participating in an in-depth study) than they could hope to gain from a superficial exposure to more topics than they can assimilate.[42]

SECTION 2: SCIENCE TEACHER GAZETTE

Volume 9: Strategies Fostering Thinking in the Science Classroom

Think Pieces

1. Make a list of strategies you think will enhance critical thinking in science classrooms. Then make a separate list of strategies you think will enhance creative thinking. What criteria did you use to generate each list? How do the criteria compare?
2. Construct an essay (no more than two pages) on the efficacy of using structured controversies in the science classroom to enhance critical and creative thinking.
3. Find an article in the literature on the K-W-L reading strategy and write a brief report for the class.
4. Prepare a think piece that defends the integration of reading and writing skills in the science curriculum *or* argue against the integration of these skills in science teaching.
5. What habits of mind do you think are enhanced by encouraging students to participate in either science projects or science fairs?

Case Study: Questioning: Inquiry or the Inquisition?

The Case

Joe Ellis, a high school biology teacher, was conducting a review session one day before the midterm examination. During the first four weeks of the course, he had covered the first three units in the text on biological principles, cells and genetics. Joe was in his fourth year of teaching and had a reputation among the students as "fair but tough." During the review period, Joe asked questions based on the material in the text and what was covered during the labs. One of the questions he asked was "What is cell theory?" He waited about a second and then called on Jack McKenna, a student who was struggling in the course and was not doing well in his math and history courses either. Jack started to say something, but Joe interrupted and said, "If you can't answer this question, then there isn't much hope for you on the test." He moved quickly to another student who answered the question easily. On two other occasions Jack tried to answer questions but was ignored by his teacher.

The Problem

Should students who don't know the answer be called on in class? If a student doesn't know the answer, how should the teacher respond? What feedback would you give Joe Ellis?

Science Teachers Talk

"What strategy of instruction do you find to be the most effective with your students?"

TOM BROWN: My teaching strategies focus on the establishment and maintenance of a relaxed and encouraging learning environment. I try to establish early on that this classroom is going to be a support-ive, nonthreatening, and engaging place to be. Regarding the subject matter, the students quickly see that I love science and that I am passionate in communicating what I consider the core concepts needed to build their understanding. They also see how hard I work to set up the numerous demonstrations and labs that we do and so it seems inherently fair to them that they would work in a similar manner to facilitate their own growth. As part of this process, we do a great deal of small-group work and discussion, as I have found through experience that kids benefit greatly by discussing difficult concepts with each other. It is my hope that kids feel comfortable and confident enough in my class to openly share their ideas, questions, and confusions.

RACHEL ZGONC: I find discussion to be most effective with my students. Discussion can take many different forms and I use if very differently in my junior high classes versus my high school classes. In the junior high, I find that the discussion needs to be much more structured. I act as the leader of the discussion and the students discuss, comment, or ask questions about concepts and ideas I put out there for them. In the high school, the discussion essentially starts off in this same manner, but I become less of a focus once the discussion gets underway. In the junior high it is usually (although it depends on the individual class) imperative that the students raise their hands. In the high school, I find the discussion method to be effective is the students can speak freely and I am simply there to monitor and direct the discussion.

JOHN RICCIARDI: Be honorable. Be equitable. Be open. When I can adhere to it, this basic strategy works well for me. Honoring your students is respecting their diversity and wholeness . . . their individuality and integrity. Honor their being always . . . whatever particular mental phase they may be in. Be equitable with your students. Rules must be fair and equal for all. No favoritism, belittlement, or force. Free choice should be the bedrock upon which all activities are constructed. Be open . . . and real to your limitations and weaknesses. If you do, your students will be open, too, and grow with you. Be open to trust by believing in them. Be open . . . and aware of a learning that may be taking place in them that you don't fully perceive.

MARY WILDE: I have always had positive results with small-group learning; however, I have really been able to enhance this teaching strategy by incorporating the cooperative learning format. There are many different cooperative learning models; however, the one I find most successful is where each student within a group learns different material. Then each student is required to teach the others in the group what has been learned. The group is responsible for each member, for I often give individual tests and average them together to determine a group grade. I also like to organize small groups by assigning each member of a team a different task in order to achieve a single goal. For example, when we studied shoreline erosion, each group was responsible for building a papier-mâché model, painting and labeling depositional and erosional shoreline features, reading an article entitled "America Is Washing Away," and writing an abstract or review of the article. Tasks were divided among the students and each had a responsibility to the group. One group grade was given for the entire project.

I really feel that small-group work helps develop responsibility and commitment. Also, more can be accomplished and learned in small groups where a variety of skills and abilities are pulled together. The learner becomes active, not passive, and greater achievement results can be obtained.

RESEARCH MATTERS

USING QUESTIONS IN SCIENCE CLASSROOMS

Patricia E. Blosser

One objective of science teaching is the development of higher-level thinking processes in students.[43] To achieve this objective, teachers need to facilitate communication with and among students. One of the methods for encouraging students to communicate is to ask them questions. Teacher questions can serve a variety of purposes:

- To manage the classroom ("Have you finished the titration?" "How many have completed problem 17?")
- To reinforce a fact or concept ("The food making process in green plants is called photosynthesis, right?")
- To stimulate thinking ("What would happen if . . . ?")
- To arouse interest
- To help students develop a mindset

Any teacher can create his/her own list of additional functions questions can serve.

Science teachers are concerned about helping students to become critical thinkers, problem solvers, and scientifically literate citizens. If we want students to function as independent thinkers, we need to provide opportunities in our science classes that allow for greater student involvement and initiative and less teacher domination of the learning process. This means a shift in teacher role from that of information giver to that of a facilitator and guide of the learning process.

Central to this shift in teacher role are the types of questions that teachers ask. Questions that require students to recall data or facts have a different impact on pupils than questions, which encourage pupils to process and interpret data in a variety of ways.

The differential effects of various types of teacher questions seem obvious, but what goes on in classrooms? In one review of observational studies of teacher questioning, spanning 1893–1963, it was reported that the central focus of all teacher questioning activity appeared to be the textbook. Teachers appeared to consider their job to be to see that students have studied the text. Similar findings have been reported from observational studies of teachers' questioning styles in science classrooms. Science teachers appear to function primarily at the "recall" level in the questions they ask, whether the science lessons are being taught to elementary students or secondary school pupils.

Why doesn't questioning behavior match educational objectives? One hypothesis is that teachers are not aware of their customary questioning patterns. One way to test this hypothesis is to use a question analysis system. One commonly used system is that of Bloom's taxonomy of educational objectives, ranging from knowledge to evaluation. Other systems categorize questions as higher-order or lower-order. Lower-order questions are those of cognitive-memory thinking and higher-order questions involve convergent thinking, divergent thinking, or evaluative thinking.

Blosser developed a category system for questions used in science lessons. In this system, questions are initially classified as:

- Closed . . . limited number of acceptable responses

- Open . . . greater number of acceptable responses
- Managerial . . . facilitate classroom operations
- Rhetorical . . . re-emphasize, reinforce a point

Questions that are classified as being either open or closed can be further classified relative to the type of thinking stimulated: cognitive memory or convergent for closed questions and divergent or evaluative thinking for open questions. This system has been used successfully with both pre-service and in-service science teachers to help them analyze their questioning behavior.

Investigations have been conducted to see if pre-service teachers could improve their questioning behavior through question analysis. From these studies, it has been concluded that the use of models (audio, video) is helpful, that skill in the use of science processes appears to be related to the complexity of questions asked, that the use of a question category system can be learned, and that the number of divergent and evaluative questions asked in lessons can be increased.

Research involving in-service teachers has produced mixed results. When in-service teachers learned to use questions at different levels of complexity, their students achieved at a higher level than did pupils of teachers who experienced instructional modules designed to improve their questioning skills asked a wider variety of questions. However, some teachers found it difficult to allocate time to working with the modules provided.

Teachers who want to improve their questioning behavior (e.g., ask a wider variety of questions) can do several things. They need to locate a question category system they can use comfortably and then apply it, during lesson planning and in postlesson analysis. Because of the variety of things that go on during a lesson, a postlesson analysis is best accomplished by taperecording the lesson or at least those parts of the lesson containing the most teacher questions. Start with the class in which the lesson and activities seem to flow most smoothly. After getting accustomed to hearing yourself and analyzing the questions you ask, tape your problem class(es). Are the kinds of questions you ask and the context in which you ask them different in these classes? Are some patterns of teacher–student interaction more effective (than others) for you?

Don't forget about the value of written questions as well as oral ones. If a teacher's oral questioning behavior involves using a variety of question types and promotes different levels of thinking, so should quiz and test questions. Students quickly determine what teachers value by the type of questions used to formulate their grade.

The kinds of questions science teachers ask, the interaction strategies they use, and the students of whom they ask questions have not been the focus of many science education studies. The cognitive aspects of questions have been researched more than have the affective aspects. More collaborative (school-university) research needs to be done on the impact of questions on students' attitudes toward science and science classes. The following questions are worthy of consideration. Do science teachers customarily direct higher-level questions to their more able students? Do they distribute the opportunity to respond equally among students of different ability levels, and of different social and cultural backgrounds, and between male and female students? Do teachers react differently to similar responses from different students? Are some communication strategies more effective than others for promoting student participation and thinking? What kinds of questions do students ask?

RESEARCH MATTERS

WHEN ARE SCIENCE PROJECTS LEARNING OPPORTUNITIES?

Marcia C. Linn and Helen C. Clark[44]

Introduction

Science projects have played a central role in schools at least since turn of the twentieth century, when they were championed by John Dewey.[45] How can we ensure that projects are efficient, effective learning experiences that promote knowledge integration and lifelong science learning? For answers we draw on more than a decade of research by the Computer as Learning Partner project, and specifically on dissertation research by Clark.[46]

Why include science projects in the classroom? Science projects can engage students in *authentic* science experiences—essentially the work of experts. Projects can encourage sustained reasoning, connect classroom to personal problems, make science relevant to everyday life, and prepare students for lifelong learning. Projects give students a window into the complexities and uncertainties of science. Professional scientists engage in projects in a supportive community of mentors, peers, and skilled technicians. They benefit from shared methodologies, standards, and criteria for success. They follow sanctioned critiquing practices in reviewing each other's work and in participating in scientific meetings. How can we make these supports a part of classroom science? Our research in designing middle school science projects in the Computer as Learning Partner project results in four recommendations.

Recommendation 1: Start with Small, Accessible Projects

First, start small. Experts-in-training (such as graduate students) often replicate the work of others or apply established procedures before designing their own projects. In the Computer as Learning Partner eighth grade classroom, students start with projects that are slightly more complicated than the most demanding class assignment. These projects, nevertheless, require the sustained reasoning necessary to link and connect ideas, reflect on progress, and incorporate feedback.

We found three types of projects that succeed most of the time. In a *critique* project students evaluate an experiment or conclusion reached by another student or an account of a scientific result reported in the media. A *design* project engages students in building a solution to a project, such as designing a house for the desert. An *explain* project asks students to use science principles to account for an observation such as the "dog dish" project, where students explain why the water in the dog dish gets warmer than the water in the swimming pool. These three types of projects allow students to generate several different ideas about the scientific question, distinguish among their ideas using evidence from class or other experiences, and draw conclusions.

Projects succeed when students can connect class experiences to their project questions.[47] This requires the alignment of class scientific principles with both class projects and student prior knowledge. Instruction can then promote knowledge integration across all problems.

Recommendation 2: Develop Class Criteria for Projects

Second, help students develop shared standards and criteria for the intellectual work of carrying out a project. We designed "composite" projects based on several students' work and engaged the class in critiquing them: encouraging students to identify improvements and describe weak or contradictory links among ideas or between explanations and evidence. Often students' intuitive criteria reflected superficial, schoolish standards like neatness and grammar. As a group, students developed criteria such as "back up assertions with evidence from class experiments or personal observations" and "identify confusing observations and seek additional information." These group criteria were posted and used regularly in class and individual discussions.

Recommendation 3: Provide Support and Coaching

Third, provide support and coaching to encourage linking and connecting of ideas and use of shared criteria. Experts carry out projects with extensive support and guidance from mentors, peers, and experts in other fields. They revise their plans based on this support. Citizens need to learn how to locate dependable coaches or experts, ways to make sense of the views of others, and strategies for incorporating useful views into revisions of their projects. To emulate this process in the science classroom, we used peer coaching, trained graduate student coaches, and teacher coaches.

We found that coaching helps students learn to monitor their progress and to make improvements to their projects. When students revise their projects, they add connections using scientific ideas, personal experience, and conclusions they have drawn. Fairly specific coaching comments, such as "what happens to light when it hits water?" or "describe a class experiment that supports your view" were more effective than general encouragement to think about related information, such as "what other variables might be influencing how warm the water gets?" Students tended to add links and resolve inconsistencies in response to specific coaching comments.

In the Computer as Learning Partner classroom we synthesized the best individual coaching comments into a cybercoaching system.[48] Once a project had been coached, we identified frequent student responses and we selected the most useful coaching comments for the system. The "cybercoach" allows coaches to match frequent student responses with appropriate coaching statements and to send a message to the student. Cybercoaching took 90 percent less time and was almost as effective as individual coaching.

We also designed prompts based on coaching experience. These prompts raise issues, ask students to analyze their own work, and encourage them to reflect on their own progress. Using our Computer as Learning Partner software, students could access these hints or prompts for some projects. Examples of the kinds of prompts that have proven successful in our research include, "what do you need to know to carry out this project?" "what is still confusing about your results?" and "connect your conclusions to a class experiment."

Recommendation 4: Make Project Assessment Part of Learning

Fourth, make project assessment both efficient and a part of the learning process. To help students develop shared criteria for arguments and learn to critique the work of others, we structure oral project presentations. We require each student or group to *prepare* a project report and to *write* a question in response to each project presentation. We randomly select groups to present their projects and individuals to ask questions so that each student participates at least once in the project discourse. In addition, we grade the written questions and written reports using a straightforward holistic system that rewards knowledge integration.

We also assess student learning from projects through written, in-class tests of knowledge integration. In these tests, students critique, design, or explain a novel event and give the main reasons for their choice. We score responses using the same holistic criteria that follows.

Example 1 of a CLP project

On a hot summer day Shawn's little sister notices that the water in the dogs' dish, which is sitting in the sun, feels fairly hot but the water in the swimming pool is still very cool. If you were Shawn what would you say to your little sister to help her understand her observations?

Dog Dish versus Swimming pool: Holistic Scoring for Projects and Classroom Knowledge Integration Test Items

Score Criteria

1. No science principle mentioned—descriptive only (bowl is smaller).
2. Mentions principle but inaccurate or incomplete (small things get hotter).
3. Accurately restates principle without elaboration or connections (if same heat is added than smaller object reaches higher temperature).
4. Clear and accurate understanding of single principle and adds elaboration and or context (e.g., if same heat added to two objects then the smaller object has less space, so heat is denser like in the lab where we heated the small and large beaker . . . so it reaches a higher temperature).
5. Clear and accurate understanding of principle and also ties in one or more additional principles from the same or related topic area (e.g., the light from the sun hits the water and changes to heat energy, which warms both the bowl and the pool, but since the pool has more water and surface area it doesn't reach as warm a temperature).

Example 2: Classroom Knowledge Integration Test Items

It is a hot summer day and Mac has invited some friends over. Mac takes two identical pitchers of lemonade out of the refrigerator and puts one on the counter in the 20°C air-conditioned kitchen and one on the picnic table outside on the covered porch where the temperature is 40°C.

1. Which lemonade will warm at a faster rate? (Check one)

   __ The lemonade on the kitchen counter
   __ The lemonade on the picnic table
   __ Both lemonades will warm at the same rate

2. Fill in the blank to make a principle that applies to these pitchers:

   Heat energy flows _____ when the temperature faster/slower/at the same rate difference between an object and its environment is greater.

3. Give the main reasons for your answer.

In general, projects give students a chance to be creative in science class. Most students become engaged and carry their projects to completion, providing authentic examples of their thinking for teachers. The satisfaction of finishing a project is sufficient reward for some. Since students vary in resources for completing projects, we place more course evaluation emphasis on knowledge integration tests, oral presentations, and written questions than on the completed project.

In conclusion, classroom projects can prepare students to carry out future personally relevant science projects. Projects succeed when they build on what students know, starting small. Furthermore, projects are most successful when students have developed shared criteria for scientific arguments that they can apply to their own and others' work. In addition, instruction that includes coaching to stimulate reflection and revision results in more sophisticated projects. Finally, instructors can best evaluate students using projects and multiple forms of assessment. Under these circumstances, projects can engage students in sustained scientific thinking, prepare them to seek and use feedback from peers or experts, and help them systematically analyze experiments and claims they encounter in their lives.

Problems and Extensions

1. Present a demonstration, teaching tool, simple lab activity, creative homework assignment, or strategy or technique related to one of the following areas of science teaching: earth science, life science, physical science, or STS.

2. Create an EEEP for at least one concept from the fields of science identified in the previous problem and extension. Remember that an EEEP should help make the unfamiliar familiar. Prepare your EEEP and present it to the class, or videotape your EEEP describing how you would use the EEEP in a science lesson. Present the video to the class.

3. Prepare a microteaching lesson that focuses on one of the following teaching strategies and present it to your peers or a small group of secondary students. Videotape the lesson, review it, and write a brief report outlining the success you had in presenting the teaching strategy and specifying how you might change the lesson for a future presentation. Select from these teaching strategies:

   a. using advance organizers
   b. elements of a stimulating classroom environment
   c. questioning
   d. using examples
   e. closure
   f. creating a positive learning environment

4. Select a chapter from a secondary science textbook and analyze the questions posed in the chapter. You can use the system presented in the chapter (low inquiry versus high inquiry), or some other system that you prefer. What is the ratio of low- to high-inquiry questions? To what extent is high-level thinking encouraged in the chapter?

5. View videotapes of science teaching and analyze the lessons in terms of the teachers' use of questions. Use the coding system shown in Figure 9.10.

6. Using the process outlined in this chapter on the use of structured controversies, prepare the necessary teaching materials to conduct a structured controversy either in your method's course, or in a secondary science classroom. Evaluate the results of the strategy by administering a student feedback form. You might use the form on page 280 (Figure 7.9).

7. Select a chapter from a secondary science textbook and develop a science reading guide for the chapter using the example on page 344 as a guide. The reading guide should be interesting and can include experiential "activities," such as a hands-on activity.

8. Use the K-W-L reading strategy and design a series of lesson plans to help students comprehend the ideas in a chapter from a secondary science textbook or one of the chapters in this book. Have your plans checked by a peer in your class. Test out your secondary science plans by field testing the lessons with your peers or a group of secondary students; if you choose this book, try them out on your peers and then send the results to me!

9. Choose a partner in your class. Select a chapter from a secondary science textbook and draw a semantic map of the chapter. You and your partner should do this separately at first. Share maps with each other, and then create a cooperative semantic map. How do the individual and cooperative maps compare?

10. Select one of the writing strategies presented in the chapter as the basis of a science lesson. Plan the lesson and then present it to a group of peers or students. How effective was the lesson in enhancing the student's writing skills?

11. Draw a map of a classroom showing how you would set it up to include a computer center. How would you enable students to gain access to the computer when you have twenty-eight students in each of your five classes?

Question Category	Lesson: Subject Grade	Lesson: Subject Grade	Lesson: Subject Grade
Closed Questions (Low Inquiry)			
Open Questions (High Inquiry)			
Summary			

Figure 9.10 Question Categories

Notes

1. Robert J. Marzano et al., *Dimensions of Thinking: A Framework for Curriculum and Instruction* (Alexandria, Va.: Association for Supervision and Curriculum Development, 1988), p. 146.

2. Ibid.

3. David Ausubel, *Educational Psychology: A Cognitive View* (New York: Holt, Rinehart and Winston, 1968), p. 149.

4. Meredith Gall, "Synthesis of Research on Teachers' Questioning," *Educational Leadership* 42 (November 1984): 40–47.

5. Mary Budd Rowe, "Wait Time and Rewards As Instructional Variables, Their Influence on Language, Logic, and Fate Control: Part One—Wait-Time," *Journal of Research in Science Teaching* 40 (2003): S19–S32. (Originally published in 11, no. 2 (1974): 81–94.)

6. See Paul Black and Chris Harrison, "Formative Assessment," in *Good Practice in Science Teaching: What Research Has to Say*, ed. Martin Mond and Jonathan Osborne (Buckingham, U.K.: Open University Press, 2000), pp. 25–40.

7. David F. Treagust et al., "Science Teachers' Use and Understanding of Analogies As Part of Their Regular Instruction" (paper presented at the annual meeting of the National Association for Research in Science Teaching, Atlanta, April 1990).

8. C. Rogers and H. J. Freiberg, *Freedom to Learn*, 3rd ed. (New York: Merrill, 1993).

9. Nancy Battista, *Effective Management for Positive Achievement in the Classroom* (Phoenix, Ariz.: Universal Dimensions, Inc., 1984), p. 26.

10. Carys Jones, "The Role of Language in the Learning and Teaching of Science," in *Good Practice in Science Teaching: What Research Has to Say*, ed. Martin Monk and Jonathan Osborne (Buckingham, U.K.: Open University Press, 2000), pp. 88–103.

11. Lev Vygotsky, *Thought and Language* (Cambridge, Mass.: MIT Press, 1986).

12. Jones, "The Role of Language."

13. William W. Cobern, *World View Theory and Science Education Research* (Manhattan, Kans.: National Association for Research in Science Teaching, 1991).

14. G. L. C. Hills, "Students' Untutored Beliefs about Natural Phenomena: Primitive Science or Commonsense?" *Science Education* 73, (1989): 155–86, as cited in ibid., p. 6.

15. Wes McCoy, "Student World View as a Framework for Learning Genetics and Evolution in High School Biology" (Ph.D. diss., Georgia State University, 2002), p. 166.

16. David W. Johnson and Roger T. Johnson, "Critical Thinking Through Structured Controversy," *Educational Leadership* 45 (May 1988): 58–64.

17. Ibid.

18. K. Gallas, *Talking Their Way into Science* (New York: Teachers College Press, 1995).

19. Leslie Bulman, *Teaching Language and Study Skills in Secondary Science* (London: Heinemann, 1985), p. 20.

20. Albert Towle, *Modern Biology* (Austin, Tex.: Holt, Rinehart and Winston, 2000).

21. Jones, "The Role of Language," p. 97.

22. Ibid., p. 98.

23. Towle, *Modern Biology*, p. 6.

24. Judith N. Thelen, *Improving Reading in Science* (Newark, Del.: International Reading Association, 1984).

25. Towle, *Modern Biology*, p. 7.

26. Robert V. Blystone and Beverly C. Dettling, "Visual Literacy in Science Textbooks," in *What Research Says to the Science Teacher: The Process of Knowing*, vol. 6, ed. Mary Budd Rowe (Washington, D.C.: National Science Teachers Association, 1990), p. 19.

27. Donna M. Ogle, "K-W-L: A Teaching Model That Develops Active Reading of Expository Text," *The Reading Teacher* (February 1986): 564–70.

28. Joan E. Heimlich and Susan D. Pittelman, *Semantic Mapping: Classroom Applications* (Newark, Del.: International Reading Association, 1986), pp. 1–3.

29. Ibid.

30. Ibid.

31. Jones, "The Role of Language," pp. 99–100.

32. Iris McClellan Tiedt et al., *Reading/Thinking/Writing* (Needham Heights, Mass.: Allyn and Bacon, 1989), pp. 21–22.

33. Lesley Bulman, *Teaching Language and Study Skills in Secondary Science* (London: Heinemann, 1985).

34. Ibid.

35. Tiedt, *Reading/Thinking/Writing*, pp. 248–51.

36 *Project 2061: Science for All Americans* (Washington, D.C.: American Association for the Advancement of Science, 1989), p. 5.

37. Ibid., p. 13.

38. Stanley L. Helgeson, "Problem Solving in Middle Level Science," in *What Research Says to the Science Teacher: Problem Solving*, ed. Dorothy Gabel (Washington, D.C.: National Science Teachers Association, 1989), p. 13.

39. Joseph D. Novak, "The Role of Content and Process in the Education of Science Teachers," in *Gifted Young in Science*, ed. Paul F. Brandwein et al. (Washington, D.C.: National Science Teachers Association, 1988), pp. 316–17.

40. Joseph L. Polman, *Designing Project-Based Science* (New York: Teachers College Press, 2000).

41. Richard Raupp, *LabNet: Toward a Community of Practice*, (Mahwah, N.J.: Lawrence Erlbaum Associates, 1994).

42. *Project 2061*, p. 21.

43. Patricia E. Blosser, "Using Questions in the Science Classroom," Research Matters to the Science Teacher Monograph Series (National Association for Research in Science Teaching). Used with permission of the National Association for Research in Science Teaching.

44. Marcia C. Linn and Helen C. Clark, "When Are Science Projects Learning Opportunities," Research Matters to the Science Teacher Monograph Series (National Association for Research in Science Teaching). Used with permission of the National Association for Research in Science Teaching.

45. John Dewey, *Psychology and Social Practice: Contributions to Education* (Chicago: University of Chicago Press, 1901).

46. M. C. Linn and N. B. Songer, "Teaching Thermodynamics to Middle School Students: What Are Appropriate Cognitive Demands?" *Journal of Research in Science Teaching*, 28, no. 10 (1991): 885–918; M. C. Linn, N. B. Songer, and B. S. Eylon, "Shifts and Convergences in Science Learning and Instruction," in *Handbook of Educational Psychology*, ed. R. Calfee and D. Berliner (Riverside, N.J.: Macmillan, 1996), pp. 438–90; and H. C. Clark, "Design of Performance-Based Assessments as Contributors to Student Knowledge Integration" (Ph.D. diss., University of California at Berkeley, May 1996).

47. M. C. Linn and L. Muilenburg, "Creating Lifelong Science Learners: What Models Form a Firm Foundation?" *Educational Researcher*, 25, no. 5 (1996): 18–24.

48. Clark, "Design of Performance-Based Assessments."

Readings

Abad, Ernesto A. "Field Trip Preparation." *The Science Teacher* 70, no. 2 (2003): 44–47.

Chin, Christine. "Success with Investigations: Strategies for Facilitating Student Science Investigations." *The Science Teacher* 70, no. 2 (2003): 34–40.

Fitzgerald, Mary Ann, and Byer, Al. "A Rubric for Selecting Inquiry-Based Activities." *Science Scope* 25, no. 9 (2002): 31–36.

Laposata, Mathew M., Howick, Thomas, and Dias, Michael. "Current Events and Technology: Video and Audio on the Internet." *Science Scope* 25, no. 3 (2002): 21–24.

Mond, Martin, and Osborne, Jonathan, eds. *Good Practice in Science Teaching: What Research Has to Say*. Buckingham, U.K.: Open University Press, 2000.

Vondracek, Mark. "Chapterless Science: Taking a New Approach to Presenting Science Material." *The Science Teacher* 69, no. 9 (2002): 44–47.

On the Web

Creative Writing for Teens: http://teenwriting.about.com/. Visit this site for resources that focus on the process of writing.

DiscoverySchool.com: http://www.discovery.com. This outstanding site (for teachers, students, and parents) will bring you in touch with activities, projects, and resources for teaching.

Learning to Read: http://www.toread.com. Links to developments in literacy, professional materials, research, and critical issues in the area of reading are available at this site.

Lev Vygotsky Page: http://www.massey.ac.nz/~alock/virtual/project2.htm. Papers, articles and biographical information about Vygotsky are presented at this site.

National Science Teachers Association: http://www.nsta.org. At NSTA's site you can access the key science teaching journals (*Science Scope* for middle school and *The Science Teacher* for high school) that contain articles by teachers describing outstanding teaching strategies. You can also brose the NSTA bookstore and find excellent sourcebooks for science teaching strategies.

Science Fair Central: http://school.discovery.com/sciencefaircentral/. At this site, which is within the DiscoverySchool.com site, you will find a rich collection of resources about science fairs, including project ideas, how to organize fairs, and key resources for your students.

Facilitating Learning in the Science Classroom

- "Jim, put your history book away and help Alice with the assignment."
- "Class, you have ten minutes to complete the activity."
- "Material handlers, be sure everyone has a pair of goggles before going into the lab."
- Speaking quietly to a cooperative team, a teacher says, "Your team should be proud of the way you reported the results of yesterday's lab—nice work!"
- "Today we'll be organized into six groups; count off by four in each group; the ones will take the role of facilitator; twos material handler; threes recorders; and fours reporters."
- "Stop the action! There's one more piece of equipment each group needs. Here it is. Send your material handler to get it."
- "When you finish working with the mice today, be sure to put them carefully in their cages."

These samples of teacher statements focus on the role of the teacher in the science classroom. If you reread the statements you will note that in each case the teacher is directing the students in some aspect of classroom behavior or performance. These are management behaviors that all teachers engage in during every science lesson. Knowing how to manage science classrooms is the focus of this chapter.

Effective classroom management incorporates teacher behaviors that result in high levels of student involvement in classroom activities and minimize student disruptions and other behaviors that interfere with student involvement in science learning. The classroom manager can also be viewed as a facilitator of learning. Facilitators help others learn by creating a classroom environment that is conducive to learning. Facilitators take into consideration the individual needs of students and at the same time realize that they are working with groups of students and therefore must be focused on group dynamics and social behavior. Group management behaviors that result in effective learning environments will be explored and related to science teaching.

Effective classroom management requires that teachers get off to a good start each year, or whenever a new course begins. We will explore effective science teaching behaviors for the beginning of the year and examine sample lessons that effective science teachers use to begin the year.

We will also examine the physical dimensions of classroom management by focusing on room design and materials in the science classroom, and we will consider some of the issues related to safety in the science classroom.

 Case Study: Ecosystem Study

As part of a biology project in which students are studying the ecosystem of a sandy creek, the teacher wishes to collect tadpoles and put them in a classroom aquarium so that students can observe them before they metamorphose. The teacher then plans to use some of the frogs for the dissection unit that follows.

The Problem

You are a member of a school-wide review board and you are at a meeting convened by the chair of the committee to review this and other proposals. Is the proposal permissible, in your view? What permission do you think is required? What are the ethical issues in the proposal? What other concerns do you and the committee have about the teacher's proposal?

How to Read This Chapter

This chapter focuses on the role of the teacher in facilitating learning in the science classroom. Four aspects of facilitation and management are presented in the chapter, and you can explore them in any order. These aspects include the facilitative role of the teacher, getting off to good start at the beginning of the year, managing science materials and facilities, and safety in the classroom. One of the key ideas of this chapter is the concept of leadership in the social process of the classroom. Several inquiry activities have been designed to aid in the development of leadership abilities: You will observe and interview teachers and colleagues (The Effective Leader Project); establish a classroom management plan; plan classroom activities for an extended period of time; prepare an equipment order; and design a hands-on science tool kit.

SECTION 1: FACILITATING LEARNING IN THE CLASSROOM

Invitations to Inquiry

- What are effective management behaviors?
- What are some effective methods of facilitating laboratory and small group work?
- How can teachers facilitate high-level thinking tasks?

- What are effective management procedures for the beginning of the school year?
- What are the elements of an effective classroom plan?
- What principles should guide the management of science materials and facilities?
- What considerations should be made to ensure a safe classroom-learning environment?
- What do teachers need to know about handling and using living things in the classroom?

Leadership in the Science Classroom

Leadership is a social influence process; in the classroom, the teacher-as-leader focuses on working with the students in the class to collectively achieve an end or a set of goals. This implies that all members of the class need to be part of the process and know what goals the "leader" has in mind. One model of leadership is advocated by Harry and Rosemary Wong. In their book, *The First Days of School*, the Wongs outline the key attributes of effective classroom leadership (Table 10.1). One of their underlying ideas about teaching is that the first few days of school are crucial and will determine one's success or failure for the rest of the year. The Wongs have created a model that includes three key attributes of the effective leader in the classroom in which the teacher: exhibits positive expectations for student success, is an outstanding classroom manager, and knows how to design lesson for student success and learning.[1]

INQUIRY ACTIVITY 10.1

 The Effective Leader Project

In this activity you are going to interview a teacher to find how he or she manages the classroom with the goal of helping students achieve success in science class. You can do this project individually or as part of small-team effort. One way that we have found this inquiry to be very effective is for it to be an activity you carry out as part of an internship or student-teaching experience. In this context you will be able to work alongside a teacher or team of teachers over an extended period time, thereby making your conclusions more realistic and valid.

Materials

- *The First Days of School* by Harry and Rosemary Wong
- Digital camera

Procedures

1. Obtain permission from the teacher or team of teachers you are working with to inquire into classroom leadership and management practices. Explain that you are trying to find out about leadership practices used in the classroom.
2. Over an extended period of time (between four and eight weeks), observe, assist, co-teach, and talk with the teacher and use these experiences to gather information to help you answer any one of the questions shown below:
   a. How are positive expectations communicated and demonstrated in the teacher's classroom?
   b. What is the evidence that effective techniques are utilized to create a well-managed classroom?
   c. What strategies does the teacher use to design lessons that help students achieve success in science?
3. Collect "data," such as interviews (if you audiotape these, get the teacher's permission), digital pictures, sketches, and samples of work to help answer your project questions.
4. Prepare a report in the form of multimedia slide show, a Web page, or a three-panel "low-tech" report, and present it to your teacher and then to a group of your peers.

Minds-On Strategies

1. How do you communicate positive expectations to students?
2. What do you do to create a well-managed classroom?
3. What strategies do you build into your lessons to help students achieve success?

Table 10.1 The Wongs' Effective Attributes of Classroom Leadership

Key Attribute of the Leader	Wongs' Concept	Deeper Understanding
Has positive expectations for student success	The teacher believes in the learner and that the learner can learn. Research base on this concept is very powerful and supportive.	School is a place where all students can learn. Let students know that you expect all of them to do well. Invite students to learn. Teacher exhibits sincere caring and warmth toward students.
Is an outstanding classroom manager	Management of the classroom environment consists of practices and procedures to maintain a well-ordered environment. The Wongs assert that discipline has little to do with classroom management.	According to the Wongs, effective teachers manage their classrooms; ineffective teachers discipline in their classrooms. Students are deeply involved. Students know what is expected of them. Relatively little time is wasted. Climate is work oriented but relaxed and friendly.
Knows how to design lessons for student mastery and learning	Once the classroom is characterized with high expectations and is well ordered then the environment is ready. The blueprints for success are knowing how to design lessons in which students will learn and knowing how to evaluate learning to provide the feedback students need for success.	An effective assignment has structure and is precise. Assignments tell students what they will accomplish. Assessment needs to be related to goals and objectives. Cooperative learning is showing students how to cooperate to learn.

Source: This table is based on material in Wong, Harry K. and T. Wong, Rosemary. *The First Days of School.* Mountain View, Calif: Harry K. Wong Publications, Inc., 2001. Used with permission.

The Facilitative Science Teacher

The facilitative science teacher is a leader who knows how to work with groups of students to produce high levels of involvement. There is a wide body of research and a number of programs that indicate the importance of issues related to classroom management. When we ask our beginning science interns what their number-one concern is about teaching, invariably they respond: "How do I deal with discipline problems?" No one would deny that discipline problems could create havoc for the beginning teacher. Instead of dealing with discipline problems as the issue, our approach here will be to examine management behaviors that contribute to increasing levels of learning and involvement in the classroom. Putting out the fires of discipline might seem at first appearance to be an effective method of "controlling" student behavior. The research on classroom behavior shows this not to be true.

Researcher Jacob Kounin identified a cluster of proactive teacher behaviors that distinguished effective classroom leaders from ineffective ones.[2] The way he discovered this is worth reporting. Initially, Kounin was interested in how teachers handled misbehavior. That is, he wanted to know what effect the teachers' action to stop the misbehavior (called a desist) had on other students in the class. Some of the questions he considered included: Does a desist serve as an example and restrain behavior in other students? Does a desist cause other students to behave better, or pay more attention? Which students are affected by desist actions—off-task students or on-task students?

Kounin found that the manner in which teachers handled misbehavior made no difference in how the students reacted. The only exception he found was that punitive desists tended to create emotional discomfort among other students in the class. Kounin's research did not imply that teachers' desists were not effective. For example, he reported that one teacher used the technique of flicking the lights on and off as a signal for the students to stop talking. For this the teacher, the technique worked. However, he also reported that for another teacher in the same school the same technique didn't work. Kounin realized that some other aspect of teacher behavior was influencing students rather than the teacher's desist techniques.

Kounin discovered by studying videotapes of over eighty teachers that certain group management strategies created a class environment characterized by high levels of student involvement. And as we pointed out when discussing the Wongs' approach to leadership, a high level of student involvement is the key to effective learning. Proactive behaviors on the part of the teacher, taken as a whole, created a class climate that prevented or discouraged behavior problems *before* they started. Let's take a look at Kounin's strategies and relate them to leadership in the science classroom. Then we'll turn our attention to management strategies appropriate for small-group work and, finally, we'll look at some recent suggestions for managing science classrooms that attempt to engage students in high-level tasks.

Effective Management Behaviors

To be an effective facilitator of learning requires that you understand effective group management behaviors. We will explore six group management behaviors that effective teachers appear to incorporate into their style of teaching.[3] These six behaviors, which are summarized in Table 10.2, are qualities that have been connected with student involvement in learning activities. The behaviors are evident in classrooms of teachers who have few student misbehaviors (or, if there are student misbehaviors, teachers eliminate them swiftly and fairly).

WITH-IT-NESS With-it-ness is the teacher's ability to communicate to students that he or she knows what they are doing in the classroom at all times. With-it-ness is a monitoring behavior, not only during small-group work, but when you are making a presentation or if students are working individually.

Teachers who are successful in observing students appear to have "eyes in the back of their head." They are able to spot misbehavior via a sixth sense—almost as if they are able to see every student all of the time. To communicate with-it-ness to students, teachers must indicate this perception through some action indicating an awareness of student behavior. The easiest way to exhibit this is to stop misbehavior in a timely and appropriate manner. This means nipping behavior problems in the bud—before they manifest themselves and spread to other students like a virus.

Eye contact, asking questions, physically moving toward impending misbehaving students, and redirecting students to prevent misbehavior are some individual teacher behaviors that will convey to students the teacher's sense of with-it-ness.

OVERLAPPING In the real world of the classroom, multiple events occur simultaneously, and the effective manager is able to deal with them. In this management practice, the science teacher does not get totally immersed in one event (e.g., helping a team with their titration apparatus) at the expense of other pending situations. Throughout the day, there is a very high

Table 10.2 Effective Group Leadership Practices

Practice	Explanation	Key Questions
With-it-ness	Teacher's ability to communicate to students what they are doing in the classroom at all times. It involves nipping problems in the bud before they escalate.	Do you have eyes in the back of your head?
Overlapping	The teacher's ability to effectively handle two classroom events at the same time as opposed to becoming so totally glued to one event that other is neglected.	Can you deal with working with a small group, while at the same time a student returns from the counselor, another student drops a cup containing a mixture of water and sand, and the teacher across the hall sends a student in with a message for you?
Smoothness	Teacher's ability to make smooth transitions between learning activities.	Do you ensure that activities have clear endings before moving on to new ones?
Momentum	Teacher's ability to maintain a steady sense of movement or progress throughout a lesson.	Are your activities conducted: A. At a brisk pace? B. In logical steps? C. Without lengthy directions?
Group Focus and Accountability	Teacher's ability to: • Keep the whole class involved in learning so all students are actively participating. • Hold students accountable for their work. • Create suspense or high interest.	Would students in your class say they were kept on their toes?

chance of interruptions from students entering your class from the outside or from announcements over the P.A. system. The effective leader is able to maintain the flow of instruction by holding the entire class accountable for continuing, while at the same time dealing with the intrusion.

SMOOTHNESS This management practice refers to the teacher's ability to make smooth transitions between learning activities. Kounin identified a number of classroom behaviors that tended to impede smoothness. Here, in summary, are some behaviors to be on the lookout to reduce:

1. Bursting in on a group or the whole class with new information or instructions when the students are really not ready for it. For example, suppose the teacher told the class that groups had ten minutes to complete an activity in which they were classifying vertebrate bones. With four minutes of the students' time left, the teacher bursts in with these instructions: "In addition to what you are doing, now I want each group to name the bones and to report their finding to the whole class." It might have been better if the teacher said this as part of the original instructions, or waited until the ten-minute period was up before

announcing the new instructional procedures and then allowed necessary time for completion.

2. Some teachers have a tendency to start an activity and then leave it dangling by beginning another activity. For example, a physical science teacher begins the lesson by going over the homework and asks three students to go to the board to write the answers to the first three problems. While the students are on the way to the board, the teacher asks the class if it is ready to review yesterday's laboratory activity. Many students raise their hands and start talking about the lab. Meanwhile, one student at the board is having difficulty with one of the homework problems. The teacher's attention is now drawn to the class talking about the lab.

3. Sometimes activities are never completed. The activity is truncated. As in the case above, there is a chance that the teacher might not finish going over the homework assignment.

4. Sometimes teachers call attention to a problem in the middle of an activity, instead of waiting to deal with it later. The interruption stops the flow of instruction. Examples of this are minor misbehaviors, such as a student in chemistry class looking over an English term paper. Simply walking to the student and pointing or touching the paper

can handle an incident like this. The paper is put away with no incident. A problem occurs when the teacher goes up the student and asks why he or she is reading an English paper in chemistry class and gets into a discussion. By this time the whole class is interrupted.

MOMENTUM Effective teachers move their lessons at a brisk pace and appear to have very few slowdowns in the flow of activities. Maintaining momentum or a steady sense of movement throughout the lesson helps engage the learners in activities. Slowdowns and time not well utilized between activities tend to cause students to lose interest.

Teachers generally cause slowdowns by dwelling on a task and fragmenting activities into trivial steps when it might have been better to organize the process as a single activity. Overdwelling can kill a good activity. Teachers who spend too much time giving detailed instructions on a laboratory activity can reduce students' initial interest. Writing out the instructions or reconceptualizing the activity can eliminate overdwelling. Another practice to be aware of is lecturing for too long a period of time. Unless there is brisk movement during the lecture, it can be a turnoff to student interest. Lecturing students about misbehavior can also impede the flow of instruction.

According to Kounin's work, momentum appeared to be the most important management behavior for promoting active involvement among students and reducing misbehaviors.

GROUP FOCUS AND ACCOUNTABILITY We might have called this practice group focus and "individual" accountability. As a teacher you will always be involved with a large group of students, and at the same time you must hold each student accountable for learning. Maintaining group focus—keeping students on their toes—as well as holding each student in class responsible for learning are key leadership practices.

One of the key behaviors in this practice is the format that you choose for student involvement. Which of the following formats do you think will result in greater student involvement?

- teacher-led large-class format
- individual seatwork
- small-group format

Reports show that teacher-led large-class and small-group work were more effective in promoting focus and involvement.[4] Individual seatwork appears to be less motivating than the pace set by the teacher with the whole class or work established for small cooperative teams.

Keeping students "on their toes" also can achieve group focus. Here are some strategies to achieve this goal:[5]

1. Attracting students' attention by asking a question before calling on a student to respond.
2. Holding attention by pausing to look around the group to bring the students in before calling on someone to respond or recite, by asking for a show of hands before selecting someone, or by using other high-interest cues such as, "be ready, this might fool you."
3. Keeping students in suspense as to who will be called upon next by avoiding a predictable pattern for selecting students.
4. Calling on different students with sufficient frequency so that students don't tune out because the same group is always called upon.
5. Interspersing individual responses with mass unison responses.
6. Alerting nonperforming students in a group that they may be called upon in connection with the performer's response or to recall something the performer recited.
7. Using a random number technique (having students in each group number off) to call on students in the class.

Group focus is also dependent on conveying to students that they are each accountable for their academic and social behavior. If you convey to the class that you expect each person to be ready to respond or to complete assignments, then the chances are good that they will remain academically involved. Some ways to maintain accountability in a group format include:[6]

1. Teacher checks students' answers or other performances by asking them to hold up answers or some prop indicating an answer.
2. Teacher requires group to recite in unison while actively listening for individual responses.
3. Teacher checks for understanding of a larger number of students by asking some students to comment on whether another student's answer or performance was correct.
4. Teacher circulates around the group and checks the answers or performance of students at their seats while another student is asked to perform aloud or at the board.

5. Teacher asks for the raised hands of students who are prepared to demonstrate a skill or problem and then requires some of them to do so.

The management practices presented here are reflected in classrooms of teachers who have high rates of student engagement and low rates of misbehavior. These practices appear to be essential in the variety of tasks that teachers plan to involve students in during science activities. However, I would like to highlight two special aspects of science teaching and examine the important management or facilitative skills and behaviors. First we will examine management of laboratory and cooperative learning activities and then move on to investigate facilitative skills important to teaching high-level tasks.

Facilitating Laboratory and Small-Group Work

Most laboratory work is planned for small teams of students. It is therefore important to keep in mind the management strategies that researchers on cooperative learning have found to be essential and effective in maintaining student involvement. As discussed in Chapter 6, Johnson, Johnson, and Holubec have identified five management practices that teachers should employ in cooperative learning experiences.[7] These include positive interdependence, individual accountability, face-to-face communication, interpersonal skills, and processing. Briefly, here is a review of these behaviors.

POSITIVE INTERDEPENDENCE Students need to value the performance of each member of the group as well as their own. Agreeing on a goal; dividing the workload or materials, resources, or information;

differentiating roles; and providing joint rewards helps establish a sense of mutual dependence. Each of these activities creates contributes to creating an environment of positive interdependence. Specific management strategies that will help create positive interdependence during small-group or laboratory activities are shown in Table 10.3.[8]

INDIVIDUAL ACCOUNTABILITY There is always the fear that group work will result in one or two students doing all the work, while the rest get a free ride. The structure of cooperative learning is dependent also on each student's mastery of the material being learned and sense of responsibility for sharing in the attainment of the group's goal. Individual testing, grading, and feedback are part of the cooperative learning approach. Table 10.4 presents some additional management strategies that can be used to structure individual accountability into cooperative learning and laboratory activities.[9]

FACE-TO-FACE COMMUNICATION Students need to be put in situations where they interact with each other face to face. Learning in small groups is dependent on students talking with each other. Paying attention to room arrangement is crucial here. You may have to take the time to rearrange the furniture of your room so that small groups of students can sit facing each other.

INTERPERSONAL SKILLS Just as students need to learn the skills of doing science, you will discover that students, if placed in cooperative learning groups, will need to learn some communication skills. One effective strategy is to teach students the interpersonal skills that they will be using in small-group activities. A technique that is effective is the use of an interpersonal T-chart

Table 10.3 Establishing a Sense of Interdependence Within Groups

Establishing Common Goals	Structuring Joint Rewards	Structuring the Task
• Each group completes and turns in single product (worksheet, report, project, data sheet) • Structuring group discussion resulting in agreement or consensus	• Single group reward given to individual groups, such as grade, score, or tangible reward (e.g., privilege, treat) • Group gets extra reward for individual efforts of its members (e.g., bonus points, improvement scores)	• Roles for each group member (facilitator, materials handler, encourager, recorder/reporter) • Turn taking as part of the activity • Use of Experts—division of labor (e.g., dividing content so each team member becomes an expert: igneous, metamorphic, sedimentary) • Dividing resources or information (limiting materials or access to information) • Structuring intergroup competitions (e.g., games, tournaments)

Table 10.4 Establishing a Sense of Individual Accountability

Focusing on the Contribution of Individuals	Focusing on Individual Outcomes
• Using roles (chief scientist, materials handler, praiser, recorder/reporter)	• Individual tests, quizzes
• Dividing the task (minitopics, subdivision of text, part of assignment)	• Individual homework assignments
• Using experts/resource individuals	• Individual reports, data, essays
• Coding individual contributions (markers, individual papers)	• Group rewards for individual behavior (each person receives bonus points for every person who turns in homework)
• Feedback on individual student behavior	
• Group/individual reflection	

Table 10.5 Interpersonal Skills T-Chart: Active Listening

Sounds Like	Looks Like
• Say "uh-huh" as speaker talks.	• Nod
• Use open-ended questions to keep the speaker talking.	• Eye contact
• Paraphrase what the speaker says.	• Lean forward
• Use encouragement to keep the speaker talking.	• Smile
• Accept what the speaker says rather than giving your opinion.	• Relaxed postures
• Summarize the speaker's comments.	• Hands unclenched
	• Arms not crossed

Source: Based on Lundgren, Linda. *Cooperative Learning with Biology: The Dynamics of Life.* Columbus, Ohio: Merrill, 1991, p. 13.

(Table 10.5). T-charts are created by a teacher-led discussion of the interpersonal skill that will be utilized in the small-group activity or laboratory activity. Students are asked to brainstorm what the skill "sounds like" by coming up with phrases they would use while working in the group to encourage "active listening" (or other identified skills, everyone contributes, questioning, staying on task). Then students are asked to brainstorm what the skill "looks like." The results are written as a large poster, which is mounted in a place where all students can see it. During the cooperative activity or lab, students "practice" using the skill.

PROCESSING Providing time for groups to process their work is important management strategy. Too often students work together but never have the opportunity to reflect on their work, make suggestions for improvement, or give each other feedback. The effective manager of small groups provides each team with a few minutes to process. The teacher organizes this by presenting to the groups one or more problems or questions

to discuss after the activity has been completed. For example, a science teacher might give the groups any one of the following questions to discuss:

1. Write positive statements about how each member contributed ideas in the activity. Share these statements with the other group members.
2. What skills did you effectively use? Which need to be worked on?
3. What behaviors contributed to learning in your group?
4. In what ways did your group encourage contributions of all members?
5. How did you feel about participating in this task?
6. What did you learn from this activity?
7. How would you do this activity differently?
8. Did you participate fully in the activity?

In addition to knowing these five management strategies, it is important to put them together in a smooth flowing plan or series of phases. The next section describes a series of phases that constitute a management plan for small-group and laboratory activity.

Management Plan for Small-Group or Laboratory Work

The following phases should be used when implementing small-group or laboratory activities.[10] The phases enable the science teacher to integrate positive management strategies with the elements of lesson planning developed in Chapter 7.

PHASE I: PREPARATION A number of management decisions have to be made in advance if cooperative group work and laboratory work are to be effective. You should decide upon the goals for the activity. Once goals have been established and you have chosen the activity, task, or laboratory exercise or problem in which students will be engaged, you will need to make the following decisions:

1. Decide upon the size of each group and determine how students will be assigned to them. Generally, keep groups from between two and four students. Student teams should be heterogeneous by ability, sex, and ethnicity. You can use a random method as well.
2. Identify roles for each member of the team. Examples include facilitator or team leader (principal investigator), recorder, reporter, materials handler.
3. Obtain all the materials needed for the activity. Organize them either at stations around the room or in the laboratory, or put them in containers that can easily be distributed to individual teams.

PHASE II: PREACTIVITY DISCUSSION Effective facilitators of small-group work prepare students to work in small teams and in the laboratory. Students need to have a clear understanding of the task, whether it is a problem to investigate, a phenomenon to observe and analyze, or a small-group activity that is accomplished sitting together around tables pushed together. The teacher's ability in establishing group focus is important at this stage. Here are some of the management procedures that should be accomplished during this phase:

1. Explain the task, pointing out the goal and purpose of the activity.
2. Explain how students will work together to achieve positive interdependence and how each group member is individually accountable.
3. Identify the interpersonal skill(s) that will be emphasized in the activity.
4. Explain time constraints and when students should be finished with their work.

After students are in their assigned teams and arranged as small groups at their workstations (around desks, in the lab), take time to explain the equipment needs of the activity. A materials handler should pick up equipment for each group (this student also is responsible for clean-up and return of the equipment at the end of the period). If equipment is already set up at workstations in the classroom or at laboratory tables, someone from each group should be designated as being responsible for the equipment.

You need to anticipate any safety problems associated with the equipment and materials that students will be handling. At all times, students should wear safety goggles when handling materials in a science activity. One principle to keep in mind is to weigh an activity's science educational value against it hazards. School liability experts recommend that if a potentially hazardous activity cannot be changed or altered to reduce the risk, then it should be eliminated. Take the time to demonstrate the proper use of materials or equipment before the students begin the activity. Discovering how to use equipment and materials is not one of the goals of the science laboratory.

PHASE III: ACTIVITY MONITORING Effective science teachers actively monitor the work of students in cooperative activities and laboratory work. Active monitoring involves observing the groups as they work on the problem or task. Some teachers make notes on each group's performance, especially noting progress on interpersonal skills. The teacher should intervene by asking students, from time to time, to explain what they are doing or to answer questions. An important role in monitoring is to exhibit with-it-ness by preventing misbehavior before it begins. Laboratory work, especially if students are standing in a laboratory environment, can "facilitate" misbehavior among students. Your careful monitoring will head off most of these problems.

PHASE IV: POSTACTIVITY PROCESSING The facilitator role of the teacher is maximized during postactivity processing. There are two crucial aspects to postactivity facilitating. On the one hand, the teacher is responsible for helping the students understand the concepts or the results of the experiment carried out in the laboratory. The teacher should be center stage in order to facilitate verbal communication among the entire class. Reports (by the reporter) from each group can be given. The teacher can ask high-level questions to extend the reasoning ability of students. The teacher might arrange for the results from each group to be posted for all to observe. This dimension of the postactivity processing should focus on the cognitive and affective outcomes associated with the activity.

On the other hand, postactivity processing should also be an opportunity for the cooperative groups to process their work as a team. This is an opportunity for the team to reflect on how well they worked as a team and consider what steps they need to take to improve the team's ability to function. The teacher can suggest a question or two for the team to think about and discuss (e.g., What skills did the group use effectively? What are some areas that need to be worked on?).

Facilitating High-Level Thinking Tasks

In their book *Windows into Science Classrooms*, Tobin, Kahle, and Fraser address a problem that is associated with attempts by science teachers to create higher-level cognitive learning environments.[11] Many of the issues discussed in their work focus on the classroom management behaviors exhibited by science teachers. These authors, who take a strong stand in favor of constructivism (students build or construct their own knowledge structures), point out that in the two classrooms that they studied, the level of cognitive thinking tended to hover near the bottom of Bloom's taxonomy in the cognitive domain.

What can teachers do and, specifically, what management strategies might they employ to raise the cognitive thinking level of students? Let's explore this a bit. Floyd H. Nordland, a contributor to *Windows into Science Classrooms*, describes how teacher behavior can influence the cognitive level of learning activities. Norland describes the following scene in one teacher's classroom: Peter (a high school biology teacher) is positioned in front of the demonstration desk expounding on the human respiratory system. The students are seated behind long horizontal benches. They are quiet and attentive to Peter's lecture presentation and many of them are taking notes.

PETER: The nervous system has the most critical oxygen requirements of any tissue of the body. In fact, brain tissue deprived of an oxygen supply for as short a time as one or two minutes will produce irreparable brain damage.
[At the front bench to Peter's right, Jeffrey's hand shoots up. Peter continues lecturing, either unaware of Jeffrey's insistent hand waving or studiously avoiding it.]

PETER: Are there any questions?
[Peter carefully scrutinizes the entire class before somewhat reluctantly calling on Jeffrey.]

JEFFREY: I was watching *Sixty Minutes* on the television recently and they talked about an American kid who was under water for a long time. I think that it was about fifteen or twenty minutes. When they pulled him out, they were able to revive him and apparently there was very little brain damage. How can you explain this?

PETER: Well, I don't know anything about that, as I don't watch *Sixty Minutes*.
[Peter continues with some disparaging comments about the negative aspects of watching too much television and Jeffrey's excellent question is never acknowledged intellectually. Thus, an opportunity to teach and learn at the application, synthesis or analysis level is lost and the instruction continues at the lowest possible cognitive level.[12]]

A simple management decision could have resulted in a high-level cognitive discussion and exploration of the case that Jeffrey described. Unfortunately this opportunity was lost. What are some management decisions science teachers can make to improve or raise the cognitive level of thinking in their classrooms?

In a study to investigate the management of comprehension and other higher-level cognitive tasks, Julie P. Sanford found a number of management strategies that appear to foster higher-level thinking in the science classroom.[13] Sanford found that, in order for teachers to successfully engage students in comprehension-level tasks, teachers should:

- create an aura of accountability around the task to force students to attempt it
- provide a variety of safety-net devices to keep students from failing at the task

Sanford reported that, in order to make students accountable, "teachers raised the price of noncompliance," by making the following types of management decisions: making the task count more toward a final grade and sending messages home to parents indicating little or no progress on research reports.

Sanford's safety nets are interesting management devices to encourage students to take risks while attempting higher-level cognitive tasks. In general, Sanford explained that these safety nets were designed to reduce the individual's risk of failure, thereby increasing the chance that students would attempt the tasks. Here are some management strategies that were found to be effective:

1. *Small-group work:* Team learning in which the individual student's work was pooled was more effective than individual students turning in their own "lab reports."
2. *Peer assistance:* Allowing students to help each other.
3. *Test procedures:* One technique was to balance difficult material with very familiar or easy material on the test. Another technique was to count the higher-level questions on test *less* than the easy questions so that lack of success on high-level questions did not result in failure.

INQUIRY ACTIVITY 10.2

Windows into Science Classrooms

In this activity, you will either observe teachers in action in their classrooms or observe science teaching videotapes. In either case, you will be looking into classrooms to find out about how teachers manage the classroom and apply the principles of group management behavior.

Materials

- Videotape of science teacher
- Visit to a science classroom
- Windows observation form (Figure 10.1)

Procedure

1. Secure permission from a science teacher to visit his or her classroom. Explain that you are interested in observing the way he or she manages the classroom. Tell the teacher that you will be using a form to look for certain examples of classroom behavior.
2. Observe the science teacher for at least one complete lesson. Keep a narrative record of the verbal behavior of the teacher (i.e., keep a running record of what the teacher does and says). This will help you discuss the management behavior of the teacher and enable you to ask better questions.
3. Use the windows observation form (Figure 10.1) to record examples of the management behaviors.

Minds-On Strategies

1. To what extent did the teacher show evidence of each management behavior? What was the teacher's strength in management?
2. How did the teacher handle small-group activities?
3. How did the teacher handle laboratory activities?
4. Did the students show evidence of being engaged in high-level thinking tasks? How did the teacher encourage and manage high-level thinking tasks?
5. How did the teacher manage misbehaviors?

Management Behavior	What the Teacher Did or Said	How the Students Responded
With-it-ness		
Overlapping		
Smoothness		
Momentum		
Group Focus and Accountability		

Figure 10.1 Windows Observation Form.

4. *Revision option:* Giving students the option of revising papers and products before final grades are determined.
5. *Teacher assistance:* Making time to answer student questions and help resolve difficulties.
6. *Extra credit assignments.*
7. *Models:* Providing models of successful products for students to examine.
8. *No-risk pop quizzes:* students receive extra credit for perfect papers or for each correct answer; no penalty for incorrect ones.
9. *Review sessions.*
10. *Flexible grading system:* Allows the teacher to reduce the value of assignments on which the whole class did poorly.[14]

Effective Teaching for the Beginning of the Year

To many teachers, the first day of a course is ground zero: the day that sets the tone for the year and the first opportunity to let the students know how interesting science can be and how they can relate to the course.

In this section, I want to not only deal with management practices on the first day of school, but for the extended period of time we will call the "beginning of the year." We will examine several aspects of classroom management that will help get the year off to a good start, including effective room arrangements, establishment of rules and procedures, first-day lesson plans, and plans for the first two weeks of school.

Room Arrangements

Although teachers typically have no control over the size or shape of the classroom, and in some cases the movement of furniture, there are quite a number of things that can be done to arrange the classroom for effective science teaching. There are a number of management considerations to guide the way you arrange the classroom. Research by Evertson, Emmer, and Anderson has indicated that effective managers of classrooms had good room arrangement, which helped eliminate potential distractions for students and opportunities for inappropriate behavior and permitted easy monitoring of students at all times.[15]

In these cases furniture is arranged to facilitate easy flowing traffic patterns, avoiding congestion in areas such as the pencil sharpener, trashcan, laboratory stations, demonstration table, and work areas. Desk arrangement will depend on the instructional goals and needs of the students. Some arrangements allow for relatively easy transitions, simplifying the process of stopping the action and having the students move their desks together for cooperative learning activities. (Incidentally, this can work even if the students have slanted desks.) Effective teachers, according to Evertson and colleagues, take stock or control of their room and create an environment conducive to learning.

Establishing Rules and Procedures

Good management begins with a set of classroom rules and procedures, which are clearly articulated and taught to the students. The effective set of rules and procedures tends to be general, which requires thinking and interpreting on the part of the students. Naturally, there might be exceptions to this, such as, "You may not work in the laboratory without safety goggles" or "Only one person speaks at a time." Let's take a look at some of the dimensions of establishing rules and procedures.

RULES FOR THE SCIENCE CLASSROOM Here are some of the findings from research with regard to the establishment of classroom rules and procedures.[16]

- Effective teachers created rules and procedures to guide students' behavior with respect to appropriateness of student talk; movement within and outside the classroom; getting the teacher's attention; storing personal belongings; use of equipment (computer); work during laboratory.
- Effective teachers also created strategies to positively reinforce good student behavior or sanction misbehavior.
- Effective managers taught the rules and procedures just as they would teach any concept or idea.
- Effective teachers presented their rules over a period of days or weeks, and retaught the rules on a regular basis.
- Teachers also integrated rules and procedures into the ongoing classroom instruction by teaching rules appropriate to an instructional activity (e.g., handling acids, using a microscope, using dissecting equipment).
- Rules tended to be stated positively, rather than negatively.

What rules and procedures, and how many, should science teachers establish in their classroom? First, a rule is statement that describes a general expectation of behavior, whereas a procedure typically applies to a specific activity.[17] Typically, teachers should try to keep the number of rules between four and seven. For example, one set of rules that I have seen in a number of beginning teachers' classroom is this simple list of 4Ps:

- prepared
- prompt
- productive
- polite

These rules lend themselves to discussion and interpretation and they encourage students to think about classroom behavior. Other teachers prefer rules to be spelled out in more detail. Here is a list of rules that effective teachers put into practice:

1. Bring all needed materials to class.
2. Be in your seat and ready to work when the bell rings.
3. Respect and be polite to all people.
4. Do not talk or leave your desk when someone else is talking.
5. Respect other people's property.
6. Obey all school rules.

Many teachers see rules as an opportunity to teach students responsibility and try to involve students in the development of rules. To do this, some teachers suggest stating rules in terms of students' rights (e.g., to learn respect for other people and property). This has the added advantage of giving students an opportunity to feel ownership of rules. In the science classroom attempting to foster inquiry and high-level cognitive thinking, this aspect of democracy seems rather important.

On the first day of class, time should be devoted to teaching the rules and involving the students in a discussion of the interpretation of the rules. Some would argue, "Why do you allow interpretation, why not be specific and eliminate any argument?" The problem with this approach is too many rules would have to be stated and student misbehavior would tend to increase given the lengthy list of rules.

Consequences ought to be used to teach responsibility. If used properly, consequences are not punishments. For example, a consequence of not cleaning up the lab table is to be told to clean it up. A punishment would be to apologize to the teacher in front of the whole class. This approach to positive discipline accepts the notion that dealing with student misbehavior is part of the teaching role, that students should be treated with dignity, and that discipline works best when it is integrated with effective teaching and management practices.[18]

Rules, consequences, and rewards should be included as part of the course syllabus, and each student should get a copy. The system should also be posted in a prominent place in the classroom.

BEGINNING AND END OF CLASS Communicating clearly your expectations regarding the beginning and ending of class is an important aspect of classroom management. Effective teachers communicate what is expected of students when class begins. Some teachers begin class by taking attendance using a seating chart (especially at the beginning of the year). This is done quickly and routinely. At the beginning of the year, teachers prefer to call names from the roll in order to learn the names of students and use it as an alternative attendance device throughout the year. You will also have to establish a routine to deal with students absent the previous day—some teachers have a folder or bin containing handouts and assignments from previous lessons so that students who were absent simply obtain their work from this place. Whatever routine is established, it should be the student's responsibility to find out what was missed on the absent days.

The beginning of the class period for many teachers is when homework is collected. If you are going to go over the homework, then hold off collecting it until you have dealt with it in the lesson. Once the routines have been established, you can formally begin the lesson. Some teachers have a routine for this—walking into the center of the room, standing in front of the chalkboard or wall containing a planning schedule for the lesson. Other teachers begin the lesson with a stimulating inquiry demonstration. Letting students know that it's "show time" establishes a businesslike, yet friendly atmosphere of learning.

Routines are needed to end a class and you should establish from day one a concluding procedure. If during the class period the students were involved in a lab or hands-on activity, then you need to establish a clean-up routine. Normally, the assignment of materials handlers can facilitate this routine. However, you need to build in time at the end of the lesson—two or three minutes—for this to happen. Let students know how you want them to be dismissed. Most teachers prefer to dismiss the students directly, rather than letting them dash out the door on the bell signal.

HANDLING MATERIALS AND EQUIPMENT In activities that require the use of materials, you should appoint materials handlers for each team. This person should be given responsibility for picking up the materials for the group, distributing them within the group, coordinating the clean-up of the group, and returning the materials to a designated area.

INQUIRY ACTIVITY 10.3

Developing a Classroom Management Plan

In this activity, you will think ahead and design a classroom management plan suitable for a middle or high school science classroom Your plan should include classroom rules, rewards, and consequences.

Materials

- Poster board
- Marking pens
- Ruler

Procedure

1. List the rules that you would use in a science class. The rules should be based on the principles discussed in this chapter.
2. Identify the consequences for breaking the rules.
3. List a series of rewards and explanation of how students can earn points to achieve the rewards.
4. Design a large classroom management poster that could easily be read by all students in a class.
5. Present your classroom management plan to the class.

Minds-On Strategies

1. What general principles guide the management of student behavior?
2. How effective, in your judgment, are your plans?
3. Show your plans to a practicing science teacher for feedback. What suggestions did the teacher make?

Special equipment use, such as microscopes, probes, electronic balances, and computers, should be preceded by a procedural minilesson. Post procedures and rules for the use of computers and access to the Internet.

If you have plants, terraria, aquaria, or animals in your classroom, you should plan to teach lessons on the use, care, and observation of living things. The use of living things in the classroom, especially animals, is a controversial issue in science education. The procedures that you develop concerning living things in the science classroom can be used to teach cognitive as well as affective outcomes of learning.

How should the science teacher begin the year? How should lesson plans during the beginning of the year be structured? We now turn our attention to the first day and beyond, and examine the management strategies that will promote high levels of involvement among students.

The First Day

The first day's lesson should be planned to spark interest in the course but, perhaps more importantly, to include activities that will help you initiate contact with the students and establish you as the leader of the class. One way to begin is to greet students at the door, hand them a one- or two-page syllabus of the course, and tell them that today they can sit anywhere they wish. If you were going to do a small-group activity on day one, you could give each student a color-coded card, which would be used later to form groups. This procedure helps to establish the teacher as being in charge as soon as the students pass through the door.

Contact with the students is an important aspect of day one. As soon as the students are seated and the bell has rung, effective teachers begin with attendance and then introduce students to the room. Some teachers take a few minutes to allow students to introduce themselves to each other.

What should be included in the lesson structure for day one? Effective teachers prepare first-day lessons that:

- establish the teacher as the leader of the class
- provide as much opportunity as possible for teacher-student contact
- present the class rules, consequences, and reward system
- involve the students in an interesting activity
- establish appropriate opening and closing lesson routines

Let's look a couple of first-day science lessons and then examine a two-week schedule put into place at the beginning of the year.

First Lessons

Getting off to a good start requires careful planning, not only of the first lesson, but of the first two or three weeks of school. In this section, we present several first-day lessons.[19] Notice the management practices that are included in each lesson, and pay attention to how the teachers establish themselves as classroom leaders, engage the students, and have the students leave the class knowing that their teacher is with it!

PHYSICAL SCIENCE: DAY ONE This lesson could serve as an example for either an eighth grade physical science class or first-year chemistry or physics class.

Greeting Students As students enter the classroom, Mrs. McKay greets them at the door, tells them to take a seat near the front of the room, and answers their questions.

Introduction (1 Minute) When the bell rings, Mrs. McKay moves to the front of the demonstration table and sprays a mist on a piece of newsprint. The words *Chemistry I* appear in a vivid orange color. She tells the class that this is first-year chemistry and to check their schedules to make sure they are in the right room. She extends a warm welcome to the class and tells them that she hopes they will like chemistry.

Roll Call (3 Minutes) Mrs. McKay explains that when she calls a name, she wants the student to raise his or her hand and tell the class the name he or she wished to be called. After roll call, she records the names of the two students not present.

Course Syllabus and Overview (6 Minutes) Mrs. McKay distributes copies of the course syllabus, which contains the title of the course, rationale, a few course objectives, and the topics for the quarter. She directs student attention to her demonstration table, which displays about eight household items (e.g., baking soda, bleach, mineral water). Mrs. McKay says that chemistry is all around them and that in this course she hopes the students will come to appreciate the world of chemistry. She uses an overhead transparency that lists the first two topics they will be study: how chemists find out about the world, and atoms, building blocks of the world. Mrs. McKay goes over the syllabus and answers a few questions.

Presentation of Class Rules and Procedures (12 Minutes) Mrs. McKay distributes a photocopied sheet that summarizes the rules and requirements for Chemistry I. The sheet lists five rules, a section on the method of grading and evaluation, and information on keeping all work in a three-ring notebook, which Mrs. McKay calls a portfolio. She tells students to put their name and the date on this sheet and to place it as the first page (behind the cover sheet) of their portfolio. Mrs. McKay explains that the classroom rules are very important, especially because the students are in Chemistry I and will be doing experiments that require safety precautions. She emphasizes the importance of having their cooperation at all times. Mrs. McKay then describes the grading system and shows the class an example of a completed portfolio.

The teacher then takes a few minutes to go back over the rules and the consequences for not following the rules. She asks the students if they have any questions about the rules. One student asks about rule 1: Bring all needed materials to class. He asks, "What materials are needed?" Mrs. McKay smiles and says to the class, "let's make a list of the things that are needed." The class makes this list: textbook, notebook, and pencil. Mrs. McKay explains that there will be additional procedures, especially when they start doing activities. She will teach these procedures when they are needed. She also tells the students that she will review the rules again and again.

Activity: Burning Candle (20 Minutes) Mrs. McKay presents a very large candle to the class (it is about 15 inches tall). She walks around the room so that the students can observe it closely. She distributes paper and asks the students to write their name, date, and period on the top of the paper. She then instructs the class to write at least ten things about the candle. To enable all students to observe the candle more easily, Mrs. McKay mounts it on the demonstration table. After two minutes, she tells the class to stop writing. Next, she lights the candle and asks the students to observe it and to write five more observations, this time of the burning candle. After two minutes, Mrs. McKay tells the students to stop writing and she blows out the candle. She then goes to the board and asks for a student volunteer to provide at least three observations. A student raises her hand, and Mrs. McKay calls on her. This process continues with different students until she has written about twenty-five observations of the candle on the board. Mrs. McKay explains to the class that this chemistry activity is important because chemistry begins with observing things in the natural world. She collects the papers and tells the students that they will do a variety of activities during the course.

End of Class (4 Minutes) After collecting the papers, Mrs. McKay tells the students that she would like them to find pictures of examples of chemicals in magazines and newspapers and bring at least one to class tomorrow. She also explains that students should write ten observations of the "chemical" that they find. Mrs. McKay explains that it is her procedure to dismiss the students and they are not to leave until she does so, even if the bell rings. She tells them that, before they leave, she expects the lab (if they used it) and desks (if they did a hands-on activity there) to be clean before dismissal. She compliments the students on their behavior and says she looks forward to seeing them tomorrow.

LIFE SCIENCE: DAY ONE This day-one activity could be used in a middle school life science class or in first-year biology.

Greeting Students Mr. Rose greets the students standing outside the door of his life science classroom. The students are coming from across the hall where they have been in math class. He smiles and says hello to the students as they enter the classroom.

Introduction (4 Minutes) Mr. Rose introduces himself at the front of the room. He says that he enjoys teaching life science and was greatly influenced by where he grew up—in the Colorado Rockies—and has always loved the outdoors. He tells the students that this course is called Life Science and they should be sure they are in the correct room.

Routines (6 Minutes) Mr. Rose tells the students to raise their hands when he calls out their name during attendance and to tell him if they prefer to be called by a different name. He then passes out 4×6 cards to the student seated at the head of each row. He tells the students to take one card and pass the rest back. He asks the students to fill out the card as shown on the screen, which displays a sample card with this information: name, address, telephone number, pets, how many brothers/sisters, and favorite animal and plant.

Presentation of Rules and Course Requirements (20 Minutes) Mr. Rose has four rules—be prompt, polite, productive, and prepared—and they are listed on a sheet of paper that he gives to each student. Some examples of behaviors for each rule are included and Mr. Rose uses these examples to help the students understand the rules. He encourages questions and a few students ask him about the rules. Mr. Rose points out the plants, aquaria, and terraria in the room. He explains that these are there for the students' enjoyment, but also to help them learn about life science. He tells the students that they will be using computers during this class, but he will explain the rules for computer use in three days, when they begin work in that area. Mr. Rose explains that the students should obtain a three-ring notebook, like the one he shows them, and instructs them to bring it to class tomorrow. He also points out that they should purchase a set of dividers (which he shows them) for the notebook. He explains that they will be keeping their work in these notebooks. He distributes a handout describing the objectives and activities for the first unit of the course (Ecology) and goes over the handout with the class. Mr. Rose then collects the student information cards.

Activity (12 Minutes) Mr. Rose gives each student a small brown paper bag containing one object (e.g., pencils, erasers, marbles, rocks, leaves, pinecones). He also gives each student a sheet of paper, and tells them to put their name, date, and period on the paper. He tells the students to lift the bag and move it about, but not to look in the bag. Mr. Rose asks the students to write at least three things about the unseen object in the bag. Next, he tells the students to open the bag and look inside, but not to touch the object. Without naming the object, Mr. Rose tells the class to write three more things about the object. Finally, he tells the students to take the object out of the bag and write three more observations of it. Mr. Rose tells the students to compare their observations with the person sitting near them with the *same* object. Finally, Mr. Rose tells the students to put the objects back in the bag and to place them on the desks. Mr. Rose asks for student volunteers to describe some of their observations. He makes the point that learning about life science begins with careful observations. He asks one student in each row to collect the bags and bring them to the demonstration table.

End of Class Mr. Rose gives each student a handout containing pictures of animals and plants. He explains that he wants the students to look around their environment, on the way home and at home, and check off each animal or plant that they can observe. They should put their name and date on the paper and bring it to class tomorrow. Finally, the bell rings, and Mr. Rose dismisses the class.

Beyond Day One

If we assume that the "beginning of the year" includes the first two or three weeks, or perhaps even a month, of the course, then it is important that you carefully plan these weeks to establish routines that will help your classes run smoothly. In the first-day cases, both Mrs. McKay and Mr. Rose established a routine, but, more importantly, established themselves as the leader in charge of the class. The teachers also involved the students in an interesting learning activity and extended it by assigning "activity"-oriented homework to continue the approach. Here is what each teacher did on day two.

Mrs. McKay started class by taking roll. She then used the pictures the students brought from home to discuss chemistry in the environment. She distributed the textbooks and spent some time showing the students the sections of the book, the glossary, and giving them tips on using the book. She introduced a two-day activity (chemical observations) and assigned a homework reading and problems for each student to complete.

Mr. Rose began day two by reviewing the rules, then proceeded with an activity in which students in pairs observed seashells. They measured the shells and drew diagrams showing the shapes and the environment in which the shells live. Mr. Rose then distributed the textbooks and had the students look over the first chapter: "Life in the Sea." Mr. Rose read (rather dramatically) the first section of the book and then asked the students to study the first chapter and come to class the next day with three questions about the first chapter, each written on a card.

For the next two weeks, both teachers set in place the character of their course that would continue throughout the semester. Table 10.6 shows highlights of the activities and procedures of the first two weeks of Mrs. McKay's chemistry class. Notice that she introduced the students to different aspects of her chemistry course (lab, small-group work, use of the computer, the textbook) over the two-week period of time. Mrs. McKay took the time to teach and reteach the rules and routines in a proactive approach to class management.

Table 10.6 The First Two Weeks of Chemistry Class

Monday	Tuesday	Wednesday	Thursday	Friday
Introduction Rules Burning candle	Go over homework Chemical Observation Activity I Textbook: *ChemCom*	Chemical Activity Part II	Introduce Chapter 1: "Quality of Water" Role-play of water emergency in Riverwood	Prelab procedures Lab: Foul water Postlab discussion
Monday	**Tuesday**	**Wednesday**	**Thursday**	**Friday**
Cooperative learning activity (rules for groupwork) Students in teams study Chapter 1 and answer worksheet problems	Introduce survey activity: "Water use in your home" Presentation on earth's water: the water cycle	No-risk pop quiz Prelab Lab: Classifying mixtures	Postlab (mixtures) Introduction to using symbols and formulas: student practice in teams	Introduction to use of computer center in class: students will use program on symbols and formulas. Each team will have ten minutes today in center.

INQUIRY ACTIVITY 10.4

 Planning for Three Weeks

In this inquiry you will make brief plans for three weeks of teaching. Although your plan does not have to show what you would do at the beginning of the year, you should keep day one in mind as you complete this activity.

Materials

- Three-week planning guide (Figure 10.2)

Procedures

1. If you are doing an internship, complete this inquiry as part of your activity at the school. Using the text and the teacher's syllabus, plan three weeks of instruction.
2. Each box in the "three-week planning guide" should include the topic for the lesson and summarize how the students will be involved with the topic.
3. Complete the three-week planning guide and then code how you are involving the students by categorizing the "activities" using these groupings: (1) hands-on activity, (2) laboratory activity, (3) lecture/discussion, (4) class work, (5) assessment activity, (6) homework review. Create additional categories to complete your analysis.
4. Collaborate with your mentor if you are doing the planning as part of an internship or with your peers if the activity is not part of an internship. Present your results to a group of peers.

Minds-On Strategies

1. How coherent were your plans?
2. If you were to plan three additional weeks of instruction, what would you do differently?

Day-by-Day Topic and Student Activities				
Monday	**Tuesday**	**Wednesday**	**Thursday**	**Friday**

Figure 10.2 Three-Week Planning Guide.

Managing Science Classroom Materials and Facilities

As a science teacher you will be responsible for the materials that you will need to teach science—from textbooks, to string, to microscopes and rock samples. Where are materials for the science classroom obtained and how should they be organized in the classroom facility?

Materials for Science Teaching

If you ever have gone to a national science conference, or even a state science conference, you probably came away knowing that there is an enormous supply of materials—textbooks, hands-on materials, and equipment—available for science teaching. One place to visit on the Web is the National Science Teachers Association Web site at http://www.nsta.org. Here you will find links to science supply houses as well as links to sites dealing with issues related to safety, the use of animals in the science teaching, and chemicals in the science classroom.

INVENTORYING SCIENCE MATERIALS It is important to a have broad view of the nature of science materials and equipment. As a science teacher you will use textbooks, supplemental books, computers, audio-tutorial materials, day-to-day teaching supplies, equipment, and various technological projectors. Two aspects of science materials and equipment are considered here. First, you should evaluate the nature of equipment and materials and then take inventory of existing equipment and materials to ensure accurate accounting.

Evaluating the teaching/learning equipment and material needs of a science department requires collaboration among department members. As a student intern or student teacher, you will have the opportunity to gain some insight into equipment and material needs by discussing the organization and arrangement of science equipment and materials with a member of a science department.

Keeping up with equipment and materials needs to be a cooperative effort among members of the department. In middle schools in which teachers are not organized into content departments, the science teachers across teams need to collaborate to evaluate the equipment and materials and then move to the next step, keeping an accurate inventory so that orders can be made for each year.

The budgets for purchasing science equipment and materials are typically very limited. Textbooks for science are often purchased on a rotating basis every four to six years. These funds are provided by the state government in half of the states in the United States and by the local schools in the remaining states. The purchase of teaching materials for laboratory work is cited as a problem in many schools, although this varies considerably from one district to the other. Equipment and material needed can be evaluated more effectively if an inventory is made and kept current. A paper-and-pencil inventory can keep up with existing materials and can be used to make decisions when ordering time rolls around. Some science departments use one of several computer programs to inventory science materials.

INQUIRY ACTIVITY 10.5

 Preparing a Science Equipment Order

You should be familiar with sources of science teaching materials. This activity is designed to acquaint you with one or more major science suppliers by using their catalogs to prepare an order.

Materials

- Two or more science supply catalogs (refer to Science Education Suppliers, National Science Teachers Association, at http://suppliers.nsta.org/listings.asp)

Procedure

1. Collaborate with at least one other person, but preferably with a small team of peers who collectively represent either all the science teachers of the same grade level in a middle school or the faculty of a high school science department.
2. Your team is limited to spending $1,000 on science materials for the entire school year.
3. Brainstorm needs for the science program and then prioritize the items that are needed. Consider the following categories: equipment and supplies, computer software, media (e.g., videos), and trade books (e.g., science activities).
4. Consult at least two suppliers of the items that you need in order to make wise decisions about price and quantity.
5. Fill out a sample order form, which you will be able to access at the supplier's Web site.

Minds-On Strategies

1. Were your needs satisfied? Did you have adequate budget to fulfill the needs of the team?
2. What other sources of funding for science materials could you explore to meet the needs of the department?
3. Are there funding sources that teachers can apply for to implement innovative programs and thereby fund science teaching materials? What programs exist in your state?
4. Are there free and inexpensive sources of materials that might be utilized to complete the order? What are they?

OBTAINING SCIENCE SUPPLIES Science equipment and materials can be obtained locally or from textbook companies, computers suppliers, and science suppliers. A worthwhile activity for you is to write to a few supply companies and request their current catalog.

It is important to know which companies are reliable before you purchase science teaching materials. Other teachers can, of course, help, but it is worthwhile to investigate this on your own. Visiting a company's Web site and then writing and requesting a catalog is one way to begin. To see a comprehensive listing of suppliers visit the NSTA supplier site listed in Inquiry Activity 10.5. This listing provides detailed information about each company and links to their Web sites. Visiting vendors at science conferences is another way to learn about suppliers. For instance, if you are a biology teacher and you want to order live organisms, you will want to be sure that the company will deliver when they promise. Establishing a relationship with the company, either via e-mail or through a sales representative, is one way to ensure good service.

SCIENCE KITS Science teaching materials can be purchased as individual items and also are available as kits. A number of science suppliers have designed science kits around single topic areas such as weather, mechanics, magnetism, electricity, sound, aeronautics, plant growth, energy alternatives, human body, and ecology. The kits contain the hands-on materials that you can use to design inquiry activities, experiments, and demonstrations. Most kits are supplemented with a teacher's guide or resource book describing suggested activities and experiments.

Microchemistry kits are a recent innovation of kit makers, and they have provided chemistry teachers an opportunity to plan chemistry activities in a safety-enhanced environment. For instance, kits focus on concepts and principles such as acids, bases and salts, rates of reaction, electrochemistry, and organic chemistry. There are several advantages to using microscience kits. For one, the quantities of chemicals are minimal yet the chemistry remains the same as if larger quantities were used. Lab setup time is reduced because the teacher does not need to prepare as much material. The activities also lend themselves to desktop lab experiences and in some cases movement into the lab is unnecessary.

Science kits can be ordered from a number of science suppliers. The companies in the following list provide kits that can be used in middle school and high school.

- Carolina Biological Supply Co. (2700 York Rd., Burlington, NC 27215, 1-800-334-5551)
- Fisher Scientific-EMD (4901 W. LeMoyne Street, Chicago, IL 60651, 1-800-621-4769)
- Frey Scientific (P.O. Box 8101, Mansfield, OH 44901, 1-800-225-FREY)
- Science Kit & Boreal Laboratories (Tonawanda, NY 14150, 1-800-828-7777)

Science kits provide the science teacher with a unit approach to ordering teaching materials and they support the hands-on/minds-on philosophy developed in this book. Most kits contain a generic supply of teaching materials for a topic, so the science teacher can be creative and innovative when planning lessons. For example, a kit on "kitchen chemistry" would contain materials enabling you to design lessons on mixtures, compounds, solutions, crystals, acids, bases, electrolysis, and chromatography. Instead of having to order items separately, the innovative teacher can order a kit and then tailor it to the kinds of experiences deemed appropriate for his or her students.

Science kits can also be an organizational structure for storing and maintaining science materials. Once you have purchased several kits, you can then begin to design and develop your kits based on your own teaching units.

Science teachers have taken the concept of science kits and adapted it to create what commonly are called "shoe-box" science learning kits. These learning kits have the same characteristics as commercial science kits: They contain smaller quantities of science materials and they focus on science concepts and principles. Shoebox kits can be easily stored and facilitate the management of the science teaching environment.

INQUIRY ACTIVITY 10.6

 ### Designing a Science Tool Kit

In this inquiry you will develop a science kit, called a "science tool kit." It should contain a lesson plan and all the equipment needed for a class of twenty-five students.

Materials

- A container such as a shoebox
- Hands-on equipment gathered for the tool kit

Procedures

1. Select a middle school or high school science concept or topic and use it as the focus for your science tool kit design. The ideas for your tool kit should be contained in a lesson plan, which also should be part of the kit. If you design a data table, charts, or graphs, or specialized laboratory procedures, be sure to include them in the kit.
2. Develop a lesson plan for your tool kit that contains the following elements:
   a. title of the science tool kit
   b. Goals
   c. Materials
   d. Procedures: You may want to use the constructivist sequence that was introduced in Chapters 6 and 7. The four phases include invitation, exploration, explanation, and take action.
3. Field-test your science tool kit with a group of students or, if that is not possible, present it to your peers.

Minds-On Strategies

1. How can this approach to curriculum design be useful as you begin your teaching career?
2. Examine one or more "commercial" kits (see Table 10.7) and think about the kinds of activities you could develop with the materials contained in the kits.

Table 10.7 Science Tool Kits

Elements of the Science Tool Kit	Astronomy Tool Kit: Comet in a Box, by Anne Gunn	Biology Tool Kit: Create a Life Form, by Lissa Blankenship
Goal	This lesson gives students an understanding of comets and an idea of what landforms are created when objects collide with a planet's surface.	To gain an understanding of adaptation. To analyze a planet and create a life form that could live on that planet. Evaluate how well a life form would live in certain conditions.
Materials	Aluminum tray Styrofoam balls Flour Beads Cocoa Dice Marbles Recording chart	Lots of Styrofoam packing peanuts Cottonballs Toothpicks Craft (Popsicle) sticks Pipe cleaners Styrofoam egg trays, cut out each egg cup Craft eyes Construction paper, cut in 3-inch squares Bottles of glue and glue sticks Markers Crayons Planet cards from NASA (may need copies) Note cards with planet assignments written on them Plastic bags Assembly: Place six to eight Styrofoam peanuts, two cottonballs, six toothpicks, three craft sticks, one pipe cleaner, one egg cup, two craft eyes, and four squares of different colors of construction paper in a plastic bag and repeat for each pair of students you have. Write the name of one planet on each note card (except earth) and the details of the pair's assignment (create life form, write a "natural history", and describe planet's environment), three sets of eight planets (or however many you need). Place the note card in each bag.
Synopsis of Lesson	The students will then create their own "surface of Jupiter" by layering the cocoa and flour in their aluminum trays (in groups of three or four). They will experiment by dropping the different weighted and sized objects onto the surface and recording their observations in their chart.	Students have the class period to create the life form, write the "natural history" of this life form, and describe their planet's environment. The "natural history" should include what it eats, where on the planet it resides, and describe the habitat and how the life form's body allows it to live on the planet. In addition, the students should describe the planet's environment, including the surface, atmosphere, magnetic field, surface pressure, geologic formations, temperature differences, seasonal changes, and weather patterns. The students will present their life form, "natural history," and their planet's environment to the class.

Source: Anne Gunn and Lissa Blankenship, graduates of the TEEMS Program, Georgia State University.

Facilities for Science Teaching

The facilities used in science teaching should reflect purposes, goals, and trends in science education. The principle recommendations made by the most prestigious groups influencing science education today (the National Science Teachers Association and the American Association for the Advancement of Science) suggest an approach to science teaching in which students:

- are given opportunities to inquire into science phenomena.
- are actively engaged in collecting, sorting, observing, interviewing, graphing, experimenting.
- solve problems of relevance to themselves and the world around them.
- should work together to solve problems and using a team approach.

These recommendations have implications for the nature and philosophy upon which decisions about science facilities should be made and what the resulting science classrooms should look like.

Undergirding the conditions for good science teaching are the *National Science Education Standards* and the *Benchmarks for Scientific Literacy*. You might want to visit the Web site of the National Science Education Leadership Association (http://www.nsela.org/index.htm) for ideas regarding the kinds of conditions that should characterize science teaching as well as recommendations made by this organization.

SPACES FOR LEARNING: GUIDELINES FOR SCIENCE FACILITIES AND CLASSROOMS We have already discussed room arrangements (see page 380). In this section, we will explore some guidelines that you should keep in mind as you think about and then take over responsibly for your own science teaching environment. We'll approach the subject from an inquiry view; that is, you will investigate the science facilities of a local school and use some guidelines to assess the facilities, and then, based on your experiences, try your hand at designing a science classroom facility.

The National Science Teachers Association has recommended a number of principles that should guide decision makers with regard to science spaces and the furnishings within them. Science educators must take into account:

- the great diversity of students who will use the spaces.
- the nature of present-day science and technology.
- current trends and approaches to science teaching.
- safety of the students.
- flexibility, for adaptation to future uses.

DESIGNS FOR ENGAGEMENT Science classrooms can be designed to engage students as well as provide a teaching space conducive to a variety of teaching models (e.g., direct instruction, inquiry, and cooperative learning). Figure 10.3 shows a high school science classroom that meets these requirements. Naturally, the physical and life sciences have different requirements in terms of specialized equipment. For instance, the life science classroom will include options for living things, such as greenhouses, terraria, and aquaria.

Note that in Figure 10.3, the science classroom shown is a combination laboratory/classroom. Specific modifications can be made for biology, chemistry, earth science, and physics. The peripheral laboratory provides an excellent design because the teacher has good visibility in either a lab or whole-class mode, the flow of traffic is good, and the room lends itself to rearrangement quite easily, especially for small-group learning. Desks can be moved to attain this goal.

Safety in the Science Classroom

A hands-on/minds-on science program might run the risks associated with potential accidents while students are handling chemicals, working with glass, or heating things with open flame burners. However, Gerlovic and Downs investigated school-related accidents and found that "science environments are generally among the safest places in schools."[20] For example, they reported that of 1,042 Iowa school accidents reported during a two-year period, only 9 percent were science related. Science teachers appear to provide relatively safe places for students to work. However, in a more recent study, Gerlovich and Parsa found that very few teachers were aware of safety obligations within their own science Classrooms.[21]

One thing you'll want to become familiar with is the Laboratory Safety Institute, located in Natick, Massachusetts. The purpose of the institute is to help science teachers become informed about safety issues and to make safety an integral aspect of science education.[22] In this section, we will explore some of the principles and practices that you should consider as you plan science lessons for science classroom environments.

A Safe Science Environment

A safe classroom environment begins at the start of the school year and should be one of the aspects of planning

Figure 10.3 A Science Classroom. Note that in the design of the science classroom shown is a combination laboratory/classroom. How is this design supportive of an inquiry approach to science teaching? *Source:* Photodisc.

and preparation for the opening of school. Here are some aspects of the environment that you should use as a checklist to determine the "safety-worthiness" of the science classroom. Not all science rooms contain labs, so you will find that when a teacher is about to do a lab activity, he or she will make arrangements to use the lab. Therefore, when considering safety, the teacher will need to include all rooms he or she uses for science instruction.

- The school has an automatic sprinkler system.
- Each lab has two unobstructed exits.
- Each lab is provided with adequate ventilation, fume hoods, and heat removal systems.
- Safety-glass screens or shields are available at each demonstration table.
- Labs are equipped with a readily accessible fire blanket and fire extinguishers.
- Labs are equipped with a readily accessible shower and an eyewash fountain.

- Each lab has a readily accessible, properly equipped first-aid cabinet.
- Safety goggles are available for each student and teacher for hands-on/lab activities.
- Laboratory coats or aprons are provided for each student and teacher.
- All possibly hazardous materials (i.e., chemical reagent bottles) are labeled with safety precautions and are used only under direct supervision.
- Printed, easily accessible instruction for handling laboratory accidents is available and known by the teacher.
- Printed, easily readable safety precautions are posted in each laboratory.[23]

A safe science learning environment occurs when the teacher assumes leadership for the general safety regulations that must be put into place in the classroom. Signs should be posted listing safety precautions and the rules of behavior while doing science lab activities.

The teacher should describe safety issues related to the activity (e.g., handling of glass, chemicals, or biological materials).

The first time that a hands-on activity or a laboratory experiment is conducted, the teacher should point out and show students how the following safety equipment should be properly used.

- First aid kit
- Fire blanket
- Eyewash facilities
- Safety goggles
- Laboratory gloves
- Laboratory aprons

General classroom safety can be accomplished by integrating safety rules into your lesson plans. If, for example, you are dissecting fruit, reinforce the safety rule that no items in the science classroom can be tasted. Here are some general safety rules that you might post on a large sign placed where students can easily read it:

1. Wear safety goggles when doing hands-on laboratory activities.
2. Wash hands thoroughly at the end of each laboratory period.
3. Clean up work areas after each activity or laboratory period.
4. Do not eat, drink, or engage in boisterous play in the classroom.
5. Lab activities can only be done under the supervision of the teacher.
6. Do not touch face, mouth, or eyes when working with plants, rocks, soil, or chemicals.

Chemical Safety

The use of chemicals in the science classroom requires knowledge of the potential danger associated with any chemical. The Occupational Safety and Health Administration (OSHA) and the Environmental Protection Agency (EPA) have produced guidelines and recommended lists of chemicals that should not be used in middle and high school science classrooms. In this section we will consider two aspects of chemical safety: rules for chemical usage and assessment and storage of chemicals.

RULES FOR CHEMICAL USAGE Regardless of the chemical, it should be treated as potentially hazardous and the teacher should always alert students to this notion. Students should be instructed to handle all chemicals with care. The following rules, suggested in the use of *ChemCom*, a high school chemistry program, outline an approach to chemical safety:

1. Perform lab work only when your teacher is present.
2. Always read and think about each laboratory procedure before starting.
3. Know the locations of all safety equipment (e.g., safety shower, eyewash, first aid kit, fire extinguisher, and blanket).
4. Wear a lab coat or apron and protective glasses or goggles for all lab work. Wear shoes (rather than sandals) and tie back loose hair.
5. Keep the lab table clear of all materials not essential to the lab activity.
6. Check chemical labels twice to make sure you have the correct substance.
7. Do not return excess material to its original container unless authorized by the teacher.
8. Avoid unnecessary movement and talk in the lab.
9. Never taste laboratory materials. If you are instructed to smell something, do so by fanning some of the vapor toward your nose. Do not place your nose near the opening of the container.
10. Never look directly down into a test tube; view the contents from the side. Never point the open end of the test tube toward yourself or your neighbor.
11. Any lab accident should immediately be reported to the teacher.
12. In case of a chemical spill on your skin or clothing, rinse the affected area with plenty of water. If the eyes are affected, water-washing must begin immediately for ten to fifteen minutes or until professional assistance is obtained.
13. When discarding used chemicals, carefully follow the instruction provided.
14. Return equipment, chemicals, aprons, and protective glasses to their designated locations.
15. Before leaving the laboratory, ensure that gas lines and water faucets are shut off.
16. If in doubt, ask![24]

Audio-visual programs are available from some suppliers in the form of filmstrips and videos that demonstrate and discuss safety issues in the science class. Such materials can be used to teach specific lessons on safety (also refer to the Laboratory Safety Institute).[25]

ASSESSMENT AND STORAGE OF CHEMICALS Chemical safety is dependent upon the teacher's

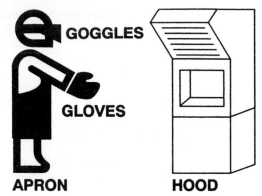

Figure 10.4 Safety Codes. *Source:* Fisher Scientific.

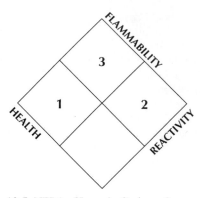

Figure 10.5 NFPA Hazard Codes. *Source:* Fisher Scientific.

knowledge of the chemicals used in lab activities. Suppliers of chemicals have devised various systems to inform purchasers of chemicals about the nature of the chemicals and how to store them. For example, Fisher Scientific has devised a chemical safety and alert system that includes

- safety symbols (which can be used with the students)
- chemical storage codes
- National Fire Protection Association (NFPA) diamond hazard code.

For each chemical, information is provided that immediately informs the teacher about the hazards associated with the item, how and where it should be stored, and what precautions should be taken when using the chemical.

The safety codes (Figure 10.4) identify the equipment and gear that need to be worn when handling a specific chemical. The teacher is informed and warned whether goggles, gloves, an apron, or a hood are needed with each chemical.

The NFPA hazard codes rate hazards numerically inside a diamond on a scale of 0–4 (Figure 10.5). In practice, the diamond shows a red segment (flammability), a blue segment (health; i.e., toxicity), and a yellow one (reactivity). The fourth segment is left blank and is reserved for special warnings, such as radioactivity or hazardous when in contact with moisture.

The numerical ratings are:

4: extreme hazard
3: severe hazard
2: moderate hazard
1: slight hazard
0: according to present data: none

A rating of 4 (most severe hazard) indicates that goggles, gloves, protective clothing, and fume hood should be used. A rating of 0 (no special hazard) may safely be handled and used in the lab with no special protection required other than safety glasses.

Storage of chemicals should not be organized alphabetically (as in some schools). Chemicals should be organized according to a classification system designated the U.S. Department of Transportation (D.O.T.). Materials are rated as:

- *Flammable:* Store in areas segregated for flammable reagents.
- *Reactive and oxidizing:* May react violently with air, water, or other substances. Store away from flammable and combustible materials.
- *Health hazard:* Toxic if inhaled, ingested, or absorbed through skin. Store in secure area.
- *No more than moderate hazard:* May store in general chemical category.
- *Exceptions:* Some reagents may be incompatible with other reagents of same category and must be stored separately.

These ratings can be used to organize a storage plan for the chemical stockroom and for organizing a school's storage room. Oxidizers must be isolated from flammables, and all flammables should be stored in a dedicated flammable storage cabinet. If highly toxic chemicals or poisons are part of the inventory, they should receive special security. In general, chemicals should not be stored on the floor or above eye level. Finally, the chemical storage room always should be locked.

Living Organisms in the Classroom

Living organisms should be part of life science programs at the middle and high school levels. The inclusion of living organisms also results in a number of safety and humane issues that the science teacher needs to address.

The National Science Teachers Association has published a set of guidelines on the responsible use of organisms in the precollege classroom. The guidelines provide a framework for the professional use of organisms in the classroom. Visit the Web site (http://www.nsta.org/486/) and note how your experience as a student of science supports the guidelines.

If live animals, such as rabbits, guinea pigs, hamsters, gerbils, mice, and rats are used in the classroom they should be handled carefully with gloves. Teachers should not bring wild animals into the classroom because the likelihood of zoonotic diseases is high.

It is of the utmost concern that all animals in the classroom be treated in the most humane manner possible. In general, animals should be used for behavioral studies, not for invasive studies. For such other studies, bacteria, protozoans, and insects can be used to achieve the objectives.

Animal dissection should be done with the utmost care and only after careful consideration of goals and objectives. Care must be taken when students perform dissections. Only clean and sterilized instruments should be used, and the students should be warned about cutting themselves using the equipment. Students should thoroughly wash their hands after dissections.

Teachers should be aware of the regulations of the state in which they teach with regard to the use of animals in the classroom. The teacher needs to protect the students from potential diseases while protecting himself or herself from violating state regulations.

SECTION 2: SCIENCE TEACHER GAZETTE

Volume 10: Facilitating Learning in the Science Classroom

Think Pieces

1. Do some research on the following issue: Should dissection be used in middle and high school science classrooms? Find at least two sources in science education journals that discuss the issue. What are arguments for the use of dissection? What are arguments against the use of dissection?

2. The following descriptors are considered to be important classroom management behaviors: with-it-ness, overlapping, smoothness, momentum, group focus, and accountability. Which one do you think is the most important? Why? How do these behaviors relate to each other?

3. What special safety precautions should be taken given each of the following situations?
   a. Middle school life science course
   b. High school physics course
   c. High school chemistry course
   d. Middle school earth science course

 Case Study: Misbehavior in the Lab

The Case

Mrs. Jones, a first-year teacher, is conducting one of the first laboratory exercises of the year. One of her students, John, throws rubbing alcohol into a burning Bunsen burner. Brad, the student working next to John, gets burned on his hand.

The Problem

How would you handle this situation? How could this incident have been prevented? What safety violations do you think might be part of this case?

 Case Study: The Smiths Come to School

The Case

Doreen Smith is a student in Jeff Murdock's first-period Biology I course. Doreen has visited Mr. Murdock quite often for detention after school. Doreen has, since the first week of school, been breaking the rules. After eight weeks, Mr. Murdock has decided it's time for a parent-teacher conference. The meeting has been set for before school (because it is more convenient for the Smiths). On the day of the conference, the Smiths arrive and, as soon as they come into Mr. Murdock's class, they accuse him of picking on their daughter and treating her differently than the other students in the class.

The Problem

How would you proceed from here? What would you say to the Smiths? How would you resolve this dilemma?

Science Teachers Talk

"How do you manage your classroom and what is the most important piece of advice you would give a prospective teacher concerning classroom management?"

CAROL MYRONUK (CANADA): Initially, I gather and give out lab equipment, materials, and supplies to demonstrate an efficient distribution system. As soon as possible, students assume the facilitator role to design and take responsibility for organizing lab distribution, collection and cleaning of equipment, recycling and disposal of materials, and general inventory. "Mean what you say and say what you mean."

BEN BOZA (BOTSWANA): My classroom management is always based on striking a rapport with the students that makes them relaxed, attentive, and thus receptive to instructions. I act as their mentor, from whom they can seek guidance and direction in their quest to succeed. I establish authority by earning the students' respect rather than through intimidation. I have found it much easier to maintain such authority when it is achieved in this way and it goes a long way in avoiding confrontational management.

For prospective teachers, it is important to understand that effective class management involves being in control and having full authority over the class. Teachers should strive to ensure that they not undermined and their authority is not challenged by students. At the same time, students should experience an accommodative atmosphere that stimulates discussions and arguments that relate to subject matter being taught. Authority that stifles expression and debates by students is counterproductive. Participatory teaching is easily achieved by establishing discipline and responsibility from both students and teacher. On occasions where misbehavior arises, a teacher should promptly and sternly take remedial action, including punishment, in order to maintain control. Whenever this is done, it should be perceived as a correctional rather than a retributive measure.

JERRY PELLETIER: I would say that I am always in charge. I try to create an atmosphere in which students can question, move about, and converse with each other within a *structured environment*. Students understand that if they work well within this environment there will be rewards throughout the year.

The reward for eighth graders is a trip to Great America for Physics Day. The most important piece of advice I would give to teachers regarding classroom management is that they must be consistent. Students must understand the goals of the classroom and the consequences of not attaining these goals.

GINNY ALMEDER: I am most comfortable in a relaxed but structured classroom. I try to give the students as much freedom and responsibility as they can manage. Seating is open. I am fairly flexible and try to remain open to student input. Short class discussions are held to deal with classroom procedures. I typically follow a set of rules consistent with school policy.

If behavioral problems occur, I deal with them immediately and directly in class. If the behavior persists, I speak with the individual after class and describe the situation as a mutual problem that both of us need to solve. I ask for suggestions and offer suggestions, and we arrange a strategy to deal with the situation. If the problem persists, I will use a seating change, parent conference, or, rarely, an afterschool detention for further dialogue.

JOHN RICCIARDI: I sense a classroom of students as being a unified, but independent entity unto itself —an awesome ecosystem of thought and feeling—a kind of greater being of multibody mind and spirit. If a classroom is perceived as such a creature, *then its management can be like maintaining the healthful life of an organism* [emphasis added].

Here are three helpful "care and feeding" hints for the classroom:

1. The classroom organism must be comfortable in its physical environment—changing and using a variety of lighting levels, furniture positions, wall decorations, and background music are important to maintaining a stimulating "mind space" for the creature to grow in.
2. The classroom organism must not be harnessed and controlled. Learn instead to coax and nurture it with reflexive input and response. Distractions and disruptive "order imbalances" are normal and natural. Know that the creature, by itself, will quickly find its equilibrium again.
3. The classroom organism must be treated humanely—with dignity and respect at all times. The integrity of all individuals must be equally honored within the wholeness of their own identity and unity.

Problems and Extensions

1. Make a list of the classroom rules and identify the disciplinary consequences for students who break each rule.

2. Consider the following classroom routines: attendance, passing out materials, taking care of living organisms, clean up. Select one or two from the list or pick a routine of your choice and try to think of ways in which these routines could be used to provide academic experience for your students.

3. How should a class begin? What routines or transitions will facilitate students coming to your class and being ready to begin?

4. What are some "activities" or "events" that could prevent a class from starting on time?

5. What are some routines you could use at the beginning of each class or while students are entering that could help to ready students to focus their attention while you take care of necessary administrative tasks or prepare to begin? (*Hint:* journal/log writing, picking up materials.)

6. Brainstorm some potential strategies you can employ at the end of a class if the activities you planned don't take you to the end of the period. What are some successful ways of utilizing this end-of-class time?

7. Prepare a lesson plan for the first day of one of the following classes: earth science, biology, chemistry, physics, and physical science. Your lesson plan should detail and account for each minute in the lesson

8. Design a set of "safety person says" signs for a secondary science classroom. Some ideas include: danger—flammable materials, danger—acid, danger—poisons, eyewash, wear your goggles.

Notes

1. Harry K. Wong and Rosemary T. Wong, *The First Days of School* (Mountain View, Calif.: Harry K. Wong Publications, Inc., 2001).

2. Jacob Kounin, *Discipline and Group Management in Classrooms* (Huntington, N.Y.: Robert E. Kreiger Publishing, 1970).

3. This section is based on "Research on Effective Group Management Practices," in *Educational Research and Dissemination Program*, ed. Lovely Billups (Washington, D.C.: American Federation of Teachers, 1998).

4. Edmumd T. Emmer and Carolyn M. Evertson, and Murray E. Worsham. *Classroom Management for Secondary Teachers* (Boston: Allya and Bacon, 2003), pp. 110–17.

5. "Research on Effective Group Management Practices," p. 14.

6. Ibid., pp. 14–15.

7. R. T. Johnson, D. W. Johnson, and E. J. Holubec, *The New Circles of Learning: Cooperation in the Classroom and School* (Alexandria, Va.: Association for Supervision and Curriculum Development, 1994).

8. Jack Hassard, *Science as Inquiry* (Parsipanny, N.J.: Good Year Books, 2000), pp. 10–11.

9. Ibid., p. 11.

10. Based on Johanna Strange and Stephen A. Henderson, "Classroom Management," *Science and Children* 8 (November/December 1981): 46–47.

11. Kenneth Tobin, Jane Butler Kahle, and Barry J. Fraser, eds., *Windows into Science Classrooms* (London: The Falmer Press, 1990).

12. Floyd H. Nordland, "The Cognitive Level of Curriculum and Instruction: Teaching for the Four Rs," in Tobin, Kahle, and Fraser, *Windows into Science Classrooms*, p. 135.

13. Julie P. Sanford, "Management of Science Classroom Tasks and Effects on Students' Learning Opportunities," *Journal of Research in Science Teaching* 24, no. 3 (1987): 249–65.

14. Ibid.

15. Edmund T. Emmer, Carolyn M. Evertson, and Murray E. Worsham. *Classroom Management for Secondary Teachers* (Boston: Allyn & Bacon, 2003), pp. 1–3.

16. "Research on Effective Group Management Practices."

17. Edmud T. Emmer, Carolyn M. Evertson, and Murray Worsham, p. 17.

18. Richard L. Curwin and Allen N. Mendler, *Discipline with Dignity* (Alexandria, Va.: Association for Supervision and Curriculum Development, 1988).

19. These first-day lessons are modeled after ones Emmer, Evertson, and Worsham, *Classroom Management for Secondary Teachers*, pp. 70–85.

20. J. A. Gerlovic and G. E. Downs, *Better Science Through Safety* (Ames: Iowa State University Press, 1981).

21. J. Gerlovich and R. Parsa, "Surveying Science Safety: NSTA Analyzes Safety in the Classroom," *The Science Teacher* 69, no. 7 (2002): 52–55.

22. You can find out more about the Laboratory Safety Institute by visiting its Web site (http://www.labsafety.org/) The Laboratory Safety Institute: 192 Worcester Road, Natick, MA 01760; Phone: 508-647-1900; Fax: 508-647-0062; Email: labsafe@aol.com.

23. For further information, see the Laboratory Safety Institute online at http://www.labsafety.org/.

24. *ChemCom: Chemistry in the Community*, Teacher's Guide (Dubuque, Iowa: Kendall/Hunt, 1988), pp. xi–xii.

25. See Frey Scientific, 905 Hickory Lane, P.O. Box 8101, Mansfield, OH 44901 (1-800-589-1900). Audio-visual material includes: Safety in the Science Lab Videotape, Science Safety Program (filmstrip or video), Science Safety for Elementary (appropriate for middle schools), as well as a lab safety sign set and handbooks on safety.

Readings

Doran, Rodney, et al. *Science Educator's Guide to Laboratory Assessment*. Arlington, Va.: National Science Teachers Association, 2002.

Emmer, Edmund J., Evertson, Carolyn M., and Worsham, Murray E. *Classroom Management for Secondary Teachers*. Boston: Allyn & Bacon, 2003.

Davidon, Anne. "Contracting for Safety." *The Science Teacher* 23 (September 1999): 36–39.

Gerking, Janet. "Science in a Safe Learning Environment." *The Science Teacher* 69, no. 11 (2002): 8.

Gerlovich, Jack A., and Parsa, Rahul. "Surveying Science Safety." *The Science Teacher* 26 (October 2002): 52–55.

Kwan, Terry, and Texley, Juliana. *Exploring Safely: A Guide for Elementary Teachers*. Arlington, Va.: National Science Teachers Association, 2002.

Wong, Harry K., and Wong, Rosemary T. *The First Days of School*. Mountain View, Calif.: Harry K. Wong Publications, Inc., 2001.

On the Web

Teachers Gazette: http://teachers.net/gazette. At this site you will find articles and resources dealing with classroom management and a collection of articles by Harry Wong.

The American Society for the Prevention of Cruelty to Animals: http://www.aspca.org. ASPCA exists to promote humane principles, prevent cruelty, and alleviate fear, pain, and suffering in animals. The site provides links to the humane use of animals in the classroom, as well as lesson plans and activities.

The Laboratory Safety Institute: http://www.labsafety.org/. The Laboratory Safety Institute is a nonprofit national center for health, safety, and environmental affairs. The institute's mission is to make health and safety integral and important parts of science education, our work, and our lives.

Articles on Safety and Science Teaching: http://www.ase.org.uk/safety/safety0.html. From the U.K.'s Association for Science Education, this site contains a collection of articles written by science teachers about safety issues and examples.

Occupational Safety and Health Administration: http://www.osha.gov/. The mission of OSHA is to save lives, prevent injuries, and protect the health of America's workers. To accomplish this, federal and state governments must work in partnership with the more than 100 million working men and women and the 6.5 million employers who are covered by the Occupational Safety and Health Act of 1970.

Science, Technology, and Society in the Science Classroom

Imagine secondary students inspecting bags of garbage, counting bottles and cans that their family uses in a week, or collecting the exhaust gases from the school principal's car. Odd activities for a science class? Not exactly. In fact, a growing number of science teachers are designing lessons similar to the following:

- Organizing a recycling campaign in the school in which all cans, bottles, paper, plastic containers and bags, and newspapers are separated and recycled.
- Debating issues such as: In an environmentally sustainable global economy should most people ride bicycles (or use some energy efficient and environmentally safe form of transportation) rather than driving cars?
- Participating in an electronic international conference by linking classrooms around the globe with computers to discuss and exchange ideas with fellow students in other nations about environmental problems such as global warming, ozone depletion, acid rain, or rainforest degradation.
- Engaging in a brainstorming session to identify environmental problems and issues that impinge on their lives. Teams of students will be organized to select one of the problems, and then plan a project in order to take action to solve the problem.

These and other activities similar to them enable secondary students to explore real issues in the classroom. The activities give a context for science learning—the local community, the school grounds, the water system in a school, an automobile, a local pond or lake, the local atmosphere. Although not limited to local environments, acting locally on problems that have relevance to students increases the chances for participation and taking action. In the past fifteen years thousands of students from around the world have been involved in a

global reach dealing with problems such as these. These activities, and indeed, this approach to science teaching have been called the science-technology-society (STS) approach and represent a major trend in science education. You will find other terms or approaches that are either offshoots or similar to STS, including environmental education, social responsibility, public understanding of science, and citizen science. This chapter will be devoted to exploring STS not only from a theoretical point of view but also, more importantly, from the practical aspect of implementing STS in the classroom.

 Case Study: A Controversial Student Project

The Case

In your first-year biology class, you have decided to integrate STS into your course by having teams of students do a project. The results of the project will be presented to the whole class. Project teams must do three projects throughout the year. The projects must be related to one of the nine biology units that make up your course. One of the teams decides to do an STS project related to the unit on human reproduction. They submit their proposal (as all teams must do). The student project is entitled: Birth Control Centers on the High School Campus. In their proposal, the students write, "it is evident that teenage pregnancy is a problem at our high school. Last month, twelve girls had to leave school because of pregnancy. We plan to investigate this problem and make recommendations for action to the school administration. One idea that we have in mind is to recommend a birth control information center on our campus. We will, however, investigate many alternatives and recommend what we find to the most effective in reducing pregnancies among high school students." As with all your projects, the student team has two weeks to do their research and prepare for their presentation to the class. During the two-week research period, the principal of the school finds out about this team's research. The principal puts a note in your mailbox, demanding a meeting with you to discuss the students' project.

The Problem

How will you prepare for the conference? What evidence will you present to the principal to defend the work that the students are doing? What will you say to your principal?

How to Read This Chapter

STS represents a departure from "traditional" science education, as it tends to see curriculum in an interdisciplinary context and in the context of personal and social perspectives. As you work with this chapter, reflect on your views of science as they relate to your science discipline (biology, chemistry, geology, physics) and ask yourself how these disciplines interact with technology and society. There are many interesting strategies of teaching presented in this chapter, and you might want to focus on them. Also, you will find a couple of case studies of curriculum projects that are based on STS (Education for a Sustainable Future and Science Education for Public Understanding Program). You might also want to visit the Web sites of these two projects, as well as some of the other projects indentified in the chapter.

SECTION 1: STS IN THE SCIENCE CLASSROOM

Invitations to Inquiry

- What are the characteristics of environmental education and STS programs?
- What strategies do science teachers use to present STS lessons in the classroom?
- What are some of the significant STS themes, and how do teachers present them in the classroom?
- What are some STS curriculum examples used in today's secondary science classrooms?
- How are STS modules evaluated? Are there criteria that science teachers agree on?

The Nature of STS

The central premise of STS teaching is to help students develop the knowledge, skills, and effective qualities in order to take responsible citizenship action on science and technologically oriented issues.[1] This was not a goal that was prevalent in science education prior to 1980. According to Aikenhead, STS emerged from social realities that affected "some" educators' views of schooling, including "World War II, the Pugwash movement (science for social responsibility), the environmental movement, women's movement, the post-Sputnik science curriculum reforms (and the 1970s critical reaction to that reform movement), research into science instruction and student learning, decreasing enrolment in physical science, and a nagging persistence, by a minority of science educators, to present science to students in a more humanistic way (rather than elitist preprofessional science training)."[2] Worldwide, the STS movement has had individuals who questioned the current status of science education: in the United States, it was Paul deHart Hurd and Robert Yager; in Australia, Peter Fensham and Roger Cross; in Canada, Glen Aikenhead; and in England, Joan Soloman. As I will show later in this chapter, much of the work of STS was spearheaded by environmental educators, who continue to this day to lead the field of STS.

One of the earliest groups to support and outline goals of STS was the National Science Teachers Association (NSTA). In 1981, Norris Harms and Robert Yager outlined the following as characteristics of STS programs:[3]

- STS programs should prepare students to utilize science for improving their own lives and coping with an increasingly technological world.
- STS programs should prepare students to utilize science to deal responsibly with science and technology oriented issues.
- STS programs should identify fundamental knowledge in science and technology so that students can deal with STS issues.
- STS programs should provide the student the appropriate expertise and experience to make decisions and take advantage of career options in science and technology.

In a 1990 position paper, the NSTA suggests "STS requires that we rethink, restructure, reorganize, rewrite, and revise current materials (e.g., curriculum, texts, audiovisuals) used to teach science. STS will require a realignment of goals and objectives and a reallocation of resources. STS will require re-education on all levels from policy makers to teachers to parents. Such reform of science education is essential."[4] The NSTA also stated that students should be involved in experiences and issues that directly affect their lives. This enables students to develop abilities to become active, responsible citizens throughout their lives.

Some of the goals identified by the NSTA position paper suggest that students:

- use concepts of science and of technology as well as an informed reflection of ethical values in solving everyday problems and making responsible decisions in everyday life, including work and leisure
- engage in responsible personal and civic actions after weighing the possible consequences of alternative options
- defend decisions and actions using rational arguments based on evidence
- engage in science and technology for the excitement and the explanations they provide

STS goals and concepts are part of the *National Science Education Standards* and AAAS's *Benchmarks for Scientific Literacy*. However, some STS educators point out these documents dealt with STS marginally.[5] Nevertheless, in the *Standards*, two areas outline the emphasis on STS: (1) science and technology and (2) science in personal and social perspectives. In the *Benchmarks*, STS goals are included in subthemes of the designed world, human society, and the nature of technology.

According to the *Standards*, STS concepts within the science in personal and social perspectives are differentiated at the middle and high school levels (Table 11.1).

According to the *Standards*, the organizing principles for this standard do not identify specific personal and societal challenges; rather they form a set of conceptual organizers, fundamental understandings, and implied actions for most contemporary issues. The organizing principles apply to local as well as global phenomena and represent challenges that occur on scales that vary from quite short (e.g., natural hazards) to very long (e.g., the potential result of global changes). For example, if we look at two of the organizing principles for grades 9–12, environmental quality and science and technology in local, national, and global challenges, we can identify specific concepts and goals that could be used to create STS teaching materials (Table 11.2).

The authors of the *Standards* claim that "many high school students hold the view that science should

Table 11.1 STS Understandings in the *National Science Education Standards*

Grades 5–8: Students should develop an understanding of	Grades 9–12: Students should develop an understanding of
• Personal health • Populations, resources, and environments • Natural hazards • Risks and benefits • Science and technology in society	• Personal and community health • Population growth • Natural resources • Environmental quality • Natural and human-induced hazards • Science and technology in local, national, and global challenges

Source: Based on National Research Council. *National Science Education Standards.* Washington, D.C.: National Academy Press, 1995.

inform society about various issues and society should set policy about what research is important. In general, students have rather simple and naive ideas about the interactions between science and society. There is some research supporting the idea that STS (science, technology, and society) curriculum helps improve student understanding of various aspects of science- and technology-related societal challenges."[6]

According to a number of science educators, much can be learned about how to develop successful STS lessons, modules, and courses by examining a closely related movement, the environmental education (EE) movement. Environmental educators, motivated by the first Earth day celebration in April 1970, recognized the need for educational programs that would develop an awareness and appreciation for the environment. Furthermore, these educators, who represented a large and growing number of scientists, teachers, and ordinary citizens around the world, were concerned about the serious deterioration of the atmosphere, water resources, biosphere, and other earth systems. Environmental educators began to focus on teaching materials that enabled students to explore the local environment and develop skills and abilities that would enable them to do so. In general, EE involved the following characteristics:[7]

- Programs are typically oriented toward a problem.
- Focus on realistic situations.
- Helps students develop alternatives for situations and the skill of choosing between them.
- Empowers students to take action on issues and problems.

Table 11.2 Environmental Quality and Technology Concepts and Big Ideas in the *Standards*, Grades 9–12

Environmental Quality	Technology in Local, National, and Global Challenges
• Natural ecosystems provide an array of basic processes that affect humans. Those processes include maintenance of the quality of the atmosphere, generation of soils, control of the hydrologic cycle, disposal of wastes, and recycling of nutrients. Humans are changing many of these basic processes, and the changes may be detrimental to humans.	• Science and technology are essential social enterprises, but alone they can only indicate what can happen, not what should happen. The latter involves human decisions about the use of knowledge.
• Materials from human societies affect both physical and chemical cycles of the earth.	• Understanding basic concepts and principles of science and technology should precede active debate about the economics, policies, politics, and ethics of various science- and technology-related challenges. However, understanding science alone will not resolve local, national, or global challenges.
• Many factors influence environmental quality. Factors that students might investigate include population growth; resource use; population distribution; overconsumption; the capacity of technology to solve problems; poverty; the role of economic, political, and religious views; and different ways humans view the earth.	• Social issues and challenges can affect progress in science and technology. Funding priorities for specific health problems serve as examples of ways that social issues influence science and technology.
	• Individuals and society must decide on proposals involving new research and the introduction of new technologies into society. Decisions involve assessment of alternatives, risks, costs, and benefits and consideration of who benefits and who suffers; who pays and gains; and what the risks are and who bears them. Students should understand the appropriateness and value of basic questions: "What can happen?" "What are the odds?" and "How do scientists and engineers know what will happen?"
	• Humans have a major effect on other species. For example, the influence of humans on other organisms occurs through land use—which decreases space available to other species—and pollution—which changes the chemical composition of air, soil, and water.

Source: Based on National Research Council. *National Science Education Standards.* Washington, D.C.: National Academy Press, 1995.

• Uses the real environment of the school and its surroundings as a context.
• Involves the clarification of values.
• Aspires to increase the ability of students to improve their own environmental situation.

Programs such as Project Wild, Project Learning Tree, Global Lab, EnviroNet, and the GLOBE program are examples of EE curriculum projects. They are in use in today's schools and serve as a model for EE and STS in the classroom.

STS programs parallel the goals of EE programs and, indeed, are often difficult to differentiate. Historically, STS was given impetus for inclusion in science education curricula through the efforts of Project Synthesis. Project Synthesis outlined the following goals as characteristics of STS programs:[8]

• Prepare students to utilize science for improving their own lives and coping with an increasingly technological world.
• Prepare students to utilize science to deal responsibly with science- and technology-oriented issues.
• Identify fundamental knowledge in science and technology so that students can deal with STS issues.

• Provide the student the appropriate expertise/experience to make decisions and take advantage of career options in science and technology.

STS and EE programs are oriented in the same direction and place a great deal of emphasis on problem solving, empowering students to take action, the application of science knowledge to real issues and problems, and an awareness of careers.

For purposes of discussion in this chapter, and the remainder of the book, I am going to let the concept of STS subsume EE programs and when I make reference to STS, it is understood that EE is included as well. Whether it is an STS or an EE program, there are at least five elements that characterize these programs: problem oriented, interdisciplinary, relating science to society, global awareness, and relevance.

Some Characteristics of STS and EE Programs

PROBLEM AND ISSUE ORIENTED STS and EE teaching is problem and issue oriented. Students often choose the problem or issue they will investigate, which is contrary to most of the schooling process. Problem- and issue-oriented teaching involves two important dimensions of learning that characterize STS and EE teaching:

1. Anticipation
2. Participation

Anticipation in STS and EE teaching implies that students will develop the capacity to face new situations. Anticipation is the ability to deal with the future, predict coming events, and understand the consequences of current and future actions. Anticipation also implies "inventing" future scenarios and developing the philosophy that humans, especially ordinary citizens, can influence future events.

Participation, on the other hand, is the complementary side of anticipation. Students must participate directly in learning. As we pointed out in Chapter 5, cognitive psychologists have developed powerful ideas that suggest that knowledge is constructed by the learner, not transmitted from teacher to student. STS and EE programs underscore participation by designing activities and strategies that involve students' process or a series of stages, beginning with problem identification and ending with action on the problem or issue. In *Thinking Constructively about Science, Technology, and Society Education*, Cheek links constructivism to STS learning and reviews the research supporting this view.[9]

During the 1990s, which was called by some "the environmental education decade," educators around the world began to focus attention on STS and EE teaching, but from a global perspective.[10] Students found that the problems and issues they tackle locally were not only similar to problems and issues people encounter elsewhere, but the local problems had global consequences. James Botkin, Mahdi Elmandjra, and Mircea Malitza, in their report *No Limits to Learning*, make the point very clearly:

> Participation in relation to global issues necessarily implies several simultaneous levels. On the one hand, the battleground of global issues is local. It is in the rice fields and irrigation ditches, in the shortages and overabundances of food, in the school on the corner and the initiation rites to adulthood. It is in the totality of personal and social life-patterns. Thus participation is necessarily anchored in the local setting. Yet it cannot be confined to localities. Preservation of the ecological and cultural heritage of humanity, resolution of energy and food problems, and national and international decisions about other great world issues all necessitate an understanding of the behavior of large system whose complexity requires far greater competence than we now possess. The need to develop greater competence and to take new initiatives is pressing. For example, during times of danger or after a natural catastrophe, nearly everyone participates. Can we not learn to participate constructively when animated by a vision of the common good rather than a vision of common danger?[11]

INTERDISCIPLINARY THINKING As we will discuss later in this chapter, a number of individuals as well as groups have proposed a lists of topics upon which STS and EE programs should be based. Among others, these topics include health, food and agriculture, energy, land, water and mineral resources, industry and technology, the environment, information transfer, and ethics and social responsibility.[12] These topics fall outside the traditional disciplines of biology, chemistry, physics, and earth science, and instead require an interdisciplinary view.

Students working on any one of the topic areas listed (Figure 11.1) will be required to gather information from several disciplines, thereby bringing the student into interdisciplinary study. The content of biology will be seen as relevant to chemistry if students investigate health problems. Yet, as they look at the problems, students will not be confined to the disciplines of science. Philosophy and psychology (especially since most of the STS and EE problems and issues involve ethics, values, and decision making) will be important to students, as will geography, history, and sociology.

CONNECTING SCIENCE TO SOCIETY Peter Fensham made an important statement when he pointed out "most of the great reforms in science curriculum looked inwards to science and scientific research for their inspiration." On the other hand, STS and EE curricula "look outwards from science to society to see how science is, or could be, applied" (see Figure 11.2).[13]

There is the conception that the views of the citizenry are important, and that making these views a part of the process of education could lead to a more pragmatic scientific literacy. For example, Law, Fensham, Li, and Wei suggest the importance of asking and listening to adult needs for scientific literacy in terms of the societal contexts that make up life in societies.[14] Their model (which could serve as another way of looking at STS), labeled the sociopragmatic approach, will result in different content for the school science curriculum (Figure 11.3). In their research, Law and colleagues interviewed adults in Hong Kong to explore two contextual categories, everyday coping and participating in social decisions. Using the results of interviews, the researchers conclude that the science content relevant to issues and problems that citizens identify could provide the basis for STS curriculum.

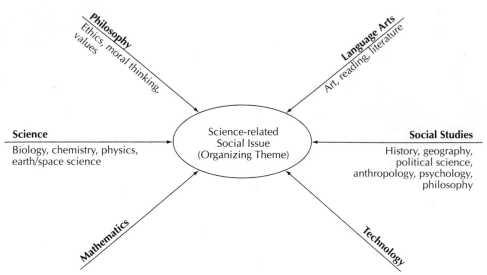

Figure 11.1 Interdisciplinary Thinking Model.

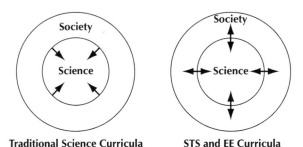

Figure 11.2 Traditional versus STS Curricula. STS curricula interact with society in such a way that the content of science is relevant to the views of citizens and to science-related social issues.

The STS and EE teacher or curriculum developer needs to consider the views of the citizenry as well important social issues (where all the garbage will go, earthquake preparedness, human diseases, pesticides and home gardens, to name a few). Using this data could be the basis for "appropriate" science content that is relevant to the social issue or problem. In this sense, science content is not seen in isolation (as it is typically presented in textbooks and by teachers), but rather in a real context that is related to their community or personal lives.

GLOBAL THINKING AND THE GAIA HYPOTHESIS
Global thinking was surely manifested when the first pictures were sent back earth by Apollo astronauts giving the single-celled picture of earth. Yet global thinking is more than a visual picture of the earth, it implies something more powerful. Global thinking implies that all things are connected, that the nature of the atmosphere over Toledo can affect trees in Boston, that removing trees from the forests of Brazil could change the temperature of Moscow, and that recycling newspapers could reduce the chances of oil spills. The environmental motto "act locally, think globally" has relevance here.

And just as the space age has given us new visual images of earth, it has led to new questions and theories. James Lovelock was one of the scientists to work on the Martian project that looked for signs of life on the "red planet." Lovelock and his colleagues on the Martian project devised a number of "life-detection" experiments. One of their suggestions was that a planet bearing life might have an unexpected mix of gases in its atmosphere if life's chemistry was at work. Dr. Norman Myers, editor of *GAIA: An Atlas of Planetary Management*, described Lovelock's breakthrough this way:

> When they looked at Earth in this light [having an unexpected mix of gases], their predictions were borne out with a vengeance. Earth's mix of gases, and temperature, were hugely different from what they predicted for a "nonliving" Earth, as well as from neighboring planets. The fact that these conditions appeared to have arisen and persisted alongside life led to the Gaia hypothesis—the proposal that the biosphere, like a living organism, operates its own "life-support" systems through natural mechanisms.[15]

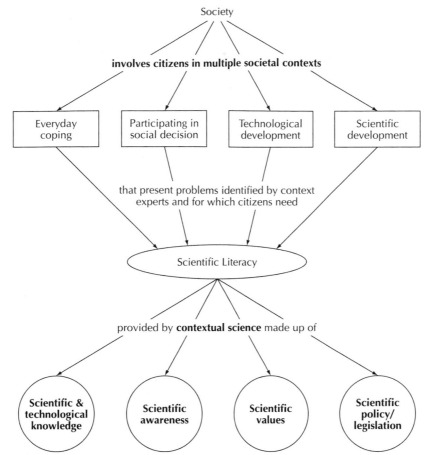

Figure 11.3 Sociopragmatic Approach to the Content of a School Science Curriculum for Scientific Literacy. The "flow" of decisions about science content is from societal contexts, not the disciplines of science. *Source:* Law, Nancy, Fensham, Peter J., Li, Steven, and Wei, Bing. "Public Understanding of Science as Basic Literacy." In *Science and the Citizen*, edited by Roger T. Cross, and Peter J., Fensham, p. 150. Melbourne: Arena Publications, 2000. Used with permission of the publisher.

What Lovelock and microbiologist Lynn Margolis, co-author of the Gaia hypothesis, suggested was that the earth's atmosphere was not simply a product of the biosphere, but was "a biological construction—like a cat's fur, or a bird's feathers; an extension of a living system, designed to maintain a chosen environment."[16]

The Gaia hypothesis is a useful tool to help students think about the interrelationship of earth's basic resources—energy, water, air, and climate (Figure 11.4). According to the Gaia hypothesis, these elemental resources can be radically affected by changes in any one of them. Many of the STS themes that are identified later in this chapter are evident in one of these elemental resources. Students will discover that management of these elemental resources is what many environmental action groups advocate.

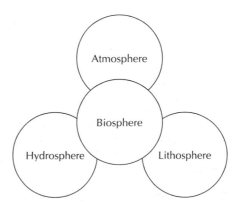

Figure 11.4 Interacting/Interdependent Elements of GAIA.

Global awareness and the philosophy of the Gaia hypothesis lead to a new way of reasoning about the earth, its environment, and inhabitants; namely, global thinking. Global thinking is systemic thinking in which whole systems are perceived as well as the consequences of changes on any aspect of the system. Global thinking is not a foreign concept to students. Here are remarks made by middle school students about global thinking in response to the question, "What, in your opinion, is the meaning of global thinking?"[17]

- "Global thinking is thinking how our actions and reactions affect the entire world."
- "Thinking globally means the world must come together and solve the problems of today so that the world of tomorrow can be a better place."
- "To me, global thinking means being in tune with the different cultures of the world, and everybody having the worlds' environmental problems and social issues strongly at heart."
- "Thinking of the world as a whole with differences but not divided."

During the past decade a number of curriculum projects emerged that were based on the interrelatedness of the earth's resources and on systemic thinking. The Internet made it possible for students and teachers separated by huge distances and cultures to work together on "global problems." Later in this chapter you will be introduced to some of these projects, including the Global Thinking Project, Global Lab, Kids Net, and GLOBE.

RELEVANCE A useful way to understand STS is to contrast STS programs with traditional or standard science education programs (Table 11.3). STS programs tend to be problem oriented, whereas traditional science programs are based on concepts found in the textbook or curriculum guide. STS programs depend on a facilitative teacher who organizes the learning environment so that students engage in identifying problems, seeking resources and information to learn about the problem, and developing action plans to solve the problem. STS teaching deals squarely with the problem of relevance by involving the student in problems that relate to the student's world.

Table 11.3 Traditional versus STS Science Programs

Traditional or Standard Science Programs	STS Programs
Survey of major concepts found in standard textbooks	Identification of problems with local interest/impact
Use of labs and activities suggested in textbook and accompanying lab manual	Use of local resources (human and material) to locate information that can be used in problem resolution
Passive involvement of students assimilating information provided by teacher and textbook	Active involvement of students in seeking information that can be used
Science being contained in the science classroom for a series of periods over the school year	Science teaching going beyond a given series of class sessions, meeting room, or educational structure
A focus on information proclaimed important for students to master	A focus on personal impact that makes use of students' own natural curiosity and concerns
A view that science is the information included and explained in textbooks and teacher lectures	A view that science content is not something that merely exists for student mastery simply because it is recorded in print
Practice of basic process skills—but little attention to them in terms of evaluation	A deemphasis of process skills that can be seen as the glamorized tools of practicing scientists
No attention to career awareness, other than an occasional reference to a scientist and his/her discoveries (most of whom are dead)	A focus on career awareness—emphasizing careers in science and technology that students might expect to pursue, especially those in areas other than scientific research, medicine, and engineering
Students concentrating on problems provided by teachers and text	Students becoming aware of their responsibilities as citizens as they attempt to resolve issues they have identified
Science occurring only in the science classroom as a part of the school's science department	Students learning what role science can play in a given institution and in a specific community
Science as a study of information where teachers discern the degree to which students acquire it	Science as an experience students are encouraged to enjoy
Science focusing on current explanations and understandings; little or no concern for the use of information beyond classroom and test performance	Science with a focus on the future and what it may be like

Source: Yager, Robert E. "STS: Thinking over the Years." *The Science Teacher* (March 1990): 52–55.

Cheek reports that some researchers distinguish between two approaches to the relevance; namely, the social issues approach and social aspects of science. The social issues approach, to which most K–12 STS is modeled, focuses on contemporary issues. Cheek suggests that focusing on social aspects of science approach is broader and more durable. Social issues change, whereas the social aspects of science represent a more stable approach to STS curriculum.[18]

INQUIRY ACTIVITY 11.1

 ### Getting Involved in STS

To appreciate the nature of STS and EE, there is nothing like getting directly involved, just as we want secondary students to participate. Following are several STS and EE activities. Choose one of the actions and carry it out with a partner or a small team, or create your own project.

Materials

- The materials you need will depend on the action you choose

Procedure

Choose an action and carry it out. If you wish, create your own action by considering some of the social aspects of science and how they affect your own community. Prepare a poster report on you activity, and be prepared to report to the entire class.

Actions

1. Science-in-the-News: Select a topic, such as water and health, conserving resources, drugs and toxins in the human body, and create a "Science-in-the-News" bulletin board, poster, or Web page. Assemble from local, regional, and national newspapers or magazines, articles, editorials, or cartoons that relate to the topic. Use colored highlighters to identify: (a) the problem or issue; (b) relevant science facts; (c) proposed solutions; and (d) political/economical implications.
2. Bicycles-to-Autos Ratio: Look at the list of countries shown next. Which country do you think has the highest bicycle-to-auto ratio, and which do you think has the lowest ratio? Rank the other countries that fall between the two extremes. Check your results.[19] What do these results imply?

   The countries:

   a. Australia   e. Mexico
   b. China   f. Netherlands
   c. Egypt   g. South Korea
   d. India   h. United States

3. Conservation: Collaborate with a small group of your peers and make a list of environmental actions you have been involved with or currently are participating in that are considered a conservation activity. Categorize the actions and suggest how you could use this data and category system to teach high school students one concept about STS.

Minds-On Strategies

1. How can these STS actions be turned into science lessons?
2. Should STS be conceptualized as a separate course, or should it be integrated into existing science courses? What is your opinion?

Strategies for Teaching STS in the Classroom

An important aspect of the STS movement is that science teaching must go beyond teaching information and help students clarify their values, develop the skills to take action on issues, and learn how to discuss the moral and ethical implications of science. Typically, teachers are interested not only in helping students learn about STS interactions, but also in teaching them to take action through responsible social action and to integrate new learnings into their intellectual and ethical schema. Cheek presents an STS cycle developed by Waks, which can be used an organizer for any STS lesson, activity, or project (Figure 11.5).

STS teaching strategies are grounded in moral education, group discussion and cooperative learning, and problem solving and critical thinking skills. The discussion and sample activities that follow provide ideas for the development of an STS approach in the classroom.

Clarifying Values

- Chemicals are harmful to humans.
- Nuclear power plants should be banned.
- Fast foods are not nutritious and should be avoided.
- Smoking should be banned in public settings.

STS teaching creates an environment where students are confronted with situations in which they must clarify their values on a variety of issues. The nature of today's value-laden issues and problems is contrary to the neutral or value-free connotation of science. How can students be helped to clarify their values about science issues?

The question that always arises in discussions of values teaching is what values should be taught, if they should be taught at all. In a class discussion of abortion, what is the role of the teacher, and whose value beliefs should guide the direction of a decision? Most educators would claim that class activities of value-laden issues should involve a process of valuing as opposed to a particular value direction.

A process model of values clarification developed by Raths, Harmin, and Simon is known as the values clarification approach. Raths and colleagues define a value in terms of three key valuing processes: choosing, prizing, and acting (Figure 11.6).[20]

According to Raths, Harmin, and Simon, the valuing process, whether the subject is abortion, drugs, birth control, health, population control, or the social responsibility of scientists, collectively involves seven criteria. In the spirit of science, Raths, Harmin, and Simon claim that these criteria must emerge in a climate of

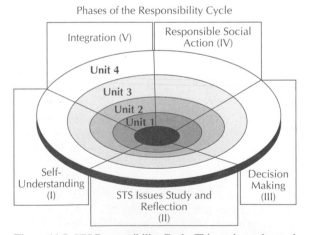

Phases of the Responsibility Cycle

Figure 11.5 STS Responsibility Cycle. This cycle can be used by teachers to enact STS activities, lessons, and projects. *Source:* Based on Waks, Leonard J. "The Responsibility Cycle." In *National STS Network—STS Leadership Resources,* as it appeared in Cheek, Dennis W. *Thinking Constructively about Science, Technology, and Society Education.* Albany, N.Y.: State University of New York Press, 1992, p. 43. Used with permission.

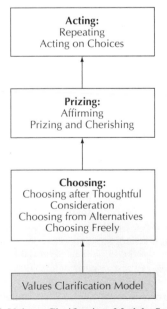

Figure 11.6 Values Clarification Model. *Source:* After Raths, L. E., Harmin, M. and Simon, S. B. *Values and Teaching.* Columbus, Ohio: C.E. Merrill, 1978.

Table 11.4 The Values Clarification Process

Key Valuing Process	Student Actions	Criteria	Key Teacher Questions
Acting	Repeating	At this level, the action will reappear a number of times	• How did you decide which had priority?
	Acting on choices	Demonstrating choices by integrating the choice in our life	• How has it already affected your life?
Prizing	Affirming	Willing to affirm the choice publicly	• Would you explain to others how you feel about this?
	Prizing and cherishing	The individual esteems, respects, and holds the value dear	• Are you glad you feel that way?
Choosing	Thoughtful consideration	Reflective thought based on research and investigation	• What is the basis for your choice?
	Choosing from alternatives	Examining alternatives and then making a choice	• What ideas did you reject before making this choice?
	Choosing freely	Choosing without coercion	• Where did the idea for your choice come from?

free inquiry independent of authoritarian persuasion. Table 11.4 outlines the major aspects of the valuing process as it relates to science teaching.

One of the keys to implementing values clarification in the science classroom is the utilization of methods that enable students to choose, prize, and act on STS issues. Five methods are designed to help students develop clearer values about STS issues: value dilemma sheet, STS action dramas, action voting, case studies, and STS action projects.

STS VALUE DILEMMA SHEET The STS value dilemma sheet consists of a provocative statement (or illustration) and series of questions. The purpose of the provocative statement (or illustration) is to raise an STS issue that has value implications for students. The questions are designed to take the student through the value clarifying process (choosing, prizing, acting). The STS value dilemma sheet should be used individually with students. They should be given the chance to reflect on the dilemma, write their responses, and then perhaps participate in a small-group discussion. Large-group discussions do not necessarily help students clarify their values. An example follows.

STS Value Dilemma Sheet: Nuclear Reactors In the spring of 1979, a reactor at the Three Mile Island nuclear power plant in Pennsylvania suffered a partial core meltdown, releasing radioactive material into the surrounding environment. Thousands of people in the vicinity claim to suffer from cancer or thyroid damage as a result of the accident. Thus far cleanup has cost close to $1 billion, not including the cost of the reactor itself (about $2 billion) or the more than 2,500 lawsuits filed by nearby residents. Consult the American Experience at the PBS site for more information on the Three Mile Island meltdown: http://www.pbs.org/wgbh/amex/three/.

On April 26, 1986, in what was the world's largest nuclear disaster ever, a reactor at the Chernobyl nuclear power plant in the Soviet Union exploded, releasing vast quantities of radioactive material into the atmosphere. Clouds of fallout covered large areas of Europe, contaminating food supplies and increasing the rate of cancer in human beings. The ongoing cleanup has cost $14 billion so far, and over 250 people have died. Consult this site for further information: http://www.nucleartourist.com/events/chernobl.htm.

Following the Chernobyl disaster, one National Research Council (NRC) member estimated the chance of an accident in the United States as big or bigger occurring by 2005 to be as high as 45 percent. In 1989, citizens of Sacramento, California, voted to shut down the publicly owned Rancho Seco nuclear power plant because it was unsafe and uneconomical.

There are 560 commercial nuclear power plants in operation worldwide, 112 of which are in the United States.

Dilemma Questions
1. Is there justification for building new nuclear power plants?
2. Do you think nuclear power plants should continue to be part of the world's energy sources?

3. Some people think that nuclear power plants are unsafe not because an accident might happen, but because the nuclear industry has not figured out a safe method for discarding the radioactive waste products produced by nuclear plants. Discuss your feelings on this matter.

4. Would you buy a house or take a job that was within a mile of a nuclear power plant?

5. What would you do to show your position on this issue?

STS ACTION DRAMAS STS action dramas (or role-playing, sociodramas, or dramatic improvisation, as they are variously called) give students the opportunity to get out of their role and into a new one to explore an STS issue. STS action dramas do not have to be elaborately directed. They work best if students are left to devise their own approaches. The important element is for the teacher to establish a condition in which the students can temporarily take on a new character, express ideas, and then reflect (with the whole class participating).

Sources of ideas for STS action dramas include newspapers (especially papers that regularly feature debates), congressional decisions, actions and new laws, environmental incidents (accidents), and STS issues featured in textbooks.

No More Bikes! The city council has decided to ban bicycles on main roads from 7 A.M. to 9 A.M. and 3 P.M. to 6 P.M. on weekdays because of the number of bicycle-related accidents. Students at the city's only middle school have protested and will present their petition and arguments at the next council meeting.

ACTION VOTING Voting is a form of survey research in which students are asked to vote on questions related to a particular topic. Voting is an action that citizens can take regarding issues, and their vote affirms the choice they have made on an issue.

To use the voting method in the classroom, prepare a ballot similar to the one shown next. Have each student complete the ballot independently, and then summarize the results on chart paper or on the chalkboard.

Voting Ballot: Birth Control[21] Put a check mark (✓) if you agree with the statement. Put a double check (✓✓) if you agree emphatically. Put a cross (✗) is you disagree with the statement.

___ Birth control is a legitimate health measure.
___ Birth control is necessary for women who must help earn a living.
___ The practice of birth control may be injurious physically, mentally, or morally.
___ We simply must have birth control.
___ The practice of birth control is equivalent to murder.
___ Birth control has both advantages and disadvantages.
___ Only a fool can oppose birth control.

CASE STUDIES The case study is a popular teaching strategy to help students learn STS principles by analyzing an STS issue. Agne points out that the case study can be used to study science-technology interactions, can be used quite readily throughout the year, and requires simply the identification of a relevant case for student analysis.[22] Case studies are readily available in most contemporary science textbooks. Most textbooks contain one or more case studies for each instructional unit in the course. The following list identifies the case studies found in a contemporary middle school physical science text.[23]

- Do the benefits of industrial robots outweigh their disadvantages?
- Should all forest fires in national parks be extinguished?
- Is information stored in computers a threat to people's privacy?
- How useful are instant replays in helping football officials judge plays?
- How can people be protected from lead in the environment?
- To protect the ozone layer, should chlorofluorocarbons be banned?
- What can be done about the buildup of greenhouse gases in the atmosphere?
- Should highly radioactive waste be stored in Yucca Mountain?

At the National Center for Case Study Teaching in Science at the State University of New York at Buffalo, you will find a collection of cases that you could use directly, or modify with your students. Some examples include:

- Is a Mars sample return mission too risky?
- Should dinosaurs be "cloned" from ancient DNA?
- Selecting the perfect baby: Prenatal genetic diagnosis
- Morgan: A case of diabetes
- The Tokaimura accident: Nuclear energy and reactor safety

ONLINE DILEMMA DISCUSSIONS In this strategy the teacher makes use of the online environment to enable students in a single class to participate in an ongoing discussion of an STS dilemma. For example, Tom Brown has used the strategy in his biology class to infuse the class with STS discussions. Using a bulletin board on the Web, he asks the students to post and reply to the problem that is posed. The strategy focuses around a dilemma that students can discuss online. The teacher posts the dilemma and asks the students to post at least one reply to the dilemma as well as several replies to other students. Depending on student access to the Web, the teacher gives them three to five days to conduct their "online discussion." When the online part of the strategy is complete, a fifteen- to twenty-minute class discussion is held. Some teachers prefer to do this first in small groups, giving each group ten minutes for discussion, followed by one-minute reports from each group to the whole class.

In one dilemma that he put up on the bulletin board, Dr. Brown raised this question: "Do animals deserve their own rights and, if so, what does this mean?" Students in his class were asked to respond to the initial question and also to respond to other students as they posted replies on the bulletin board.

In another example, Dr. Brown asked "Do you think that humans should have the right to clone themselves if they desire to do so? Support your answer. Be thoughtful." Examples follow of ninth grade students responses to Dr. Brown's query:

Alexander

I believe that humans should not clone themselves. I think that we should clone human organs for transplant usage. I feel that God has meant for us not to create other people, but I believe that he would want us to create organs to help prolong the life of humans needing a transplant.

Corwin

Since I am not going to be doing any of the cloning, I don't care what else is done in cloning humans. I don't think it is ethical, but I can't do anything to stop science from growing.

George

Hey Corwin, this is George. I'm supposed to reply to your statement. I don't think cloning humans is right either, but I do believe that it could have great effects in livestock and helping bring back extinct/near-extinct animals.

Helen

I don't know you guys, why not clone humans? I agree with Alexander, in that we should clone organs, but what harm can come from cloning humans? If we do clone humans, it will be as if the two are twins. However, we would be trying to play the role of God, so maybe it isn't a good idea. I think that I am neutral on the whole situation. Someone will eventually try to clone a human anyway, so how would we stop that person? What would you do if someone went public right now and said that they were going to clone a human? Would you stop them? I probably would not do much except watch the progress on TV; however, I would not be the one to do the cloning. I guess, if you really think about it, it is pretty unethical, but I really believe that it is more like growing a baby from a test tube. No one really goes against that and it is almost the same thing.

THINK PIECES You will note that I've included think pieces in the *Science Teacher Gazette* of each chapter. Think pieces are a powerful tool to get your students to "think" and to write about scenarios, interesting situations, or questions that might pique their curiosity. Think pieces can be used to find out what students' initial conceptions are on an STS issue or as a way to stimulate class discussion. Students could write alone on the think piece or you could pair students off and have each pair construct a response. A think piece example follows.

Think Piece: Two Views of the Earth, Which Do You Support?

View 1 Basically, this view (the cornucopian view) sees the world as a horn of plenty, primarily for human use and ingenuity, and maintains that if our economic system is left unfettered, it will always find new energy and resources to replenish the supplies coming out of that horn.

View 2 This view, called the deep ecology view, sees the earth as a finite vessel of diverse life and believes that the human species must learn how to curb its appetites and work for a sustainable earth society on behalf of all the creatures that share the vessel they inhabit.

Activity Read each view and give it some thought. What are some of your first impressions and ideas? Write these in your journal. Interview other people in your school and community. What do they think? Record their ideas. How do they compare to your ideas? Come back to this think piece later in your study of this unit. Have your ideas changed?

ACTION PROJECTS Action projects are designed to get small teams of students involved in researching and investigating a local STS or environmental issue. Issues students might investigate are limitless and could include:

- Waste disposal
- Pollution problems and control
- Recycling efforts and conservation
- Zoning of land
- Energy issues
- Environmental protection
- Local endangered wildlife concerns

Action projects begin with the identification of a local problem and result in taking some action on the problem. The following six-step procedure is designed to help students carry out a project.[24]

1. *Problem Identification:* Students brainstorm possible problems or situations to improve the local community.
2. *Fact-Finding:* Students find out information to understand why the problem exists. They are informed that they can obtain information from: (1) community resources, (2) national and international organizations, (3) opinionnaires, (4) resource people, and (5) independent and group study.
3. *Problem Selection and Definition:* Students choose one or two problems that, if solved, could make the biggest difference. They must decide if they have the tools and resources available to successfully solve the problem.
4. *Brainstorming Solutions:* Students generate as many solutions to the problem as possible.
5. *Evaluating Solutions:* Students rank-order the effectiveness of their solutions and choose the top two to three ideas. They list criteria to help them decide what might be the best solution. Criteria include: Will the solution make a long-term difference? Are there adequate resources to help them in acting on their solution?
6. *Taking Action:* In this step, students decide the different ways to carry out their solution. They decide which strategies will be most effective. They create a time line and plot a course of action.

The STS Module

Except for the action project, most of the values clarification strategies are single-lesson approaches to teaching STS. An alternative strategy is to develop an STS or EE module that would be taught as part of an existing science course. This approach seems to be more powerful. Rather than adding a day on acid rain, global warming, or endangered species, the module approach advocates that teachers identify a significant science-based social issue and use the learners' interest in the topic as basis for a two- to four-week module within the existing science program.[25]

Although there are many commercially available STS modules on the market, the purpose of this section is outline criteria that you might use to develop your own STS module. According to Wiesenmayer and Rubba, environmental educators developed a model of instruction in which students develop the ability and desire to take responsible environmental actions.[26] Harold Hungerford and colleagues at the University of Southern Illinois developed a model to investigate and evaluate environmental issues and actions skill development.[27] The model went well beyond the environmental awareness level and achieved success in getting students involved in action taking. Details of the model are described in the STS Curriculum Examples section of this chapter. Wiesenmayer and Rubba adapted the environmental model to STS and proposed four levels or stages of activities in developing an STS module. The goal of any STS module would be to "aid citizens in developing the knowledge, skills, and effective qualities needed to make responsible decisions on STS issues, and to take actions on those decisions toward issue resolution."[28] The levels of activities are as follows: Level I: STS Foundations; Level II: STS Issue Awareness; Level III: STS Issue Investigation; and Level IV: STS Action Skills Development (see Figure 11.7).

The starting point for an STS module is a list of possible social issues or social aspects of science that might interest students. Here are some suggestions:

- Space-flight and science fiction
- Evolution and human population
- How can we be sure? (*nature of science*)
- Technology, invention, and industry
- Health, food, and population
- Energy; the power to work
- Ground-level ozone and respiratory illness
- Skin cancer
- Acid rain
- Exposure to ionizing radiation
- AIDS
- Solid waste disposal
- Biological terrorism
- Drinking water
- Tornado preparedness

Goals of STS Module

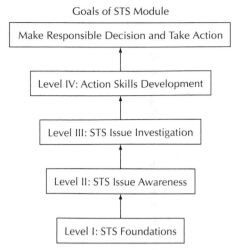

Figure 11.7 STS Action Model. Instructional sequence follows this linear process, progressing to action taking. *Source:* After Hungerford, Harold R. *Investigating and Evaluating Environmental Issues and Actions Skill Development Modules.* Champaign, Ill.: Stipes, 1988.

An STS module on any one of these topics should normally take between three and four weeks. The time spent on the unit should be divided among the four levels of instruction. To help you in planning an STS module, brief sections about each level follow.[29]

STS FOUNDATIONS At the foundation level, you must identify the concepts that are related to the issue in question (e.g., acid rain, oil spill, AIDS). However, in the STS approach the concepts that should be identified are those that cut across the traditional disciplines of earth, life, and physical science. Candidates for this would include unifying themes such as change, field, interaction, model, system, or energy transfer, evolution, stability, patterns of change, systems and interaction, and scale and structure. For example, in a module on oil spills, STS foundation concepts might include system, change, energy, and interaction. If students were investigating the an oil spill they might explore the interaction effects of oil on the ocean-beach system.

Selecting unifying concepts and themes leads students to new ways of thinking. Students learn to connect ideas —to think holistically. Facts and concepts are not taught in a linear fashion (concept 1, concept 2, concept 3), but are taught in the context of an issue (Figure 11.8). In this light, concepts are seen as being interdependent and interdisciplinary. Finally, students are engaged in

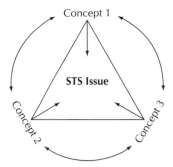

Figure 11.8 Concepts in Relationship to an STS Issue.

exploring major ideas not for their own sake, but as useful constructs in helping them solve relevant social and global problems. The foundation level should also show the students how science and technology interact and demonstrak their interdependence.

STS ISSUE AWARENESS A series of lessons should be planned to help students realize how STS interactions result in controversy surrounding an issue. The lessons would help students examine (a) all sides of the issue, (b) beliefs and attitudes affecting the issue, and (c) alternative solutions to the issue. For example, in module on risk from smoking, students might explore:

- the negative physiological effects of cigarette smoking
- the nature of addiction and the difficulty experienced by many smokers who attempt to quit but can't
- the efforts made by the cigarette industry to attract young people between the ages of twelve and eighteen years to smoking
- the attempts of the cigarette industry to keep important information about the health hazards of smoking secret

Values clarification and awareness activities such as value dilemma sheets, STS action dramas, case studies, think pieces, online discussions, and voting are useful tools at this level.

ISSUES INVESTIGATION The issues investigation level is similar to the action project discussed in the values clarification section. At this level, students are taught how to investigate an issue through training with problem identification skills, including problem identification and statement, use of secondary sources, data collection via primary sources, data analysis, and drawing conclusions. Students then apply these newly acquired skills to an investigation of a real local issue.

ACTION SKILL DEVELOPMENT Taking action on an issue involves an understanding of new skills that many students are unfamiliar with. Wiesenmayer and Rubba suggest that lessons be designed to help students with consumerism, legal action, persuasion, physical action, and political action. They also point out that students should have the opportunity to apply these skills. Wiesenmayer and Rubba found, in a study of seventh graders, that an STS module that employed all four levels promoted greater understanding of STS and responsible action on an STS issue (trash disposal).[30]

STS Themes and How to Teach Them

The content of STS lessons, modules, and courses of study is derived from students and teachers constructing problems and investigations from real-world issues and concerns. In this section I explore a number of issues and concerns, which I refer to as STS themes. A number of individuals and groups have identified themes that ought to be addressed in STS lessons, modules, and courses (Table 11.5). Project Synthesis identified eight areas of concern and admitted that these may not be the "most significant" but that they exemplified the kinds of issues that students should explore. At the international conference on Science and Technology Education and Future Human Needs, held at Bangalore, India, in 1985, the conference coordinators identified eight issues that they referred to as interdisciplinary topics. They made the point that STS requires teachers and students to work outside the normal boundaries of science. The third set of topics listed in Table 11.5 is one that was proposed by Rodger Bybee. Bybee referred to these as global problems, and surveyed scientists and engineers to find out how they would rank these global problems.

INQUIRY ACTIVITY 11.2

 STS Issues in Science Textbooks

In this inquiry activity you are going to find out what issues are emphasized in secondary science textbooks. To do this, you will analyze one middle school/junior high or high school science textbook using a classification system of STS issues.

Materials

- A secondary science textbook

Procedure

1. Look over the categories of STS issues in Figure 11.9. The categories represent a comprehensive listing of STS issues. Analyze the text by identifying all the STS issues that are presented by studying the table of contents and the pages of the text. Indicate the number of pages devoted to the issue when identified. Illustrations count, just as the verbal text does. Estimate the amount of space devoted to the issue on each page and record as 1 page, 1/2 page or 1/4 page.

Minds-On Strategies

1. In Rosenthal's study, the social system of science and evolution were the most commonly presented STS issues in biology textbooks. How do your results compare with Rosenthal's? You might want to read her study and compare her results with yours.[31]
2. What categories are least presented in secondary science textbooks? You'll need to collaborate with others in your class to make this conclusion.
3. In examining biology, physical science, and earth science texts, what differences in the relative emphases of STS issues did you find?

STS Issue Category	STS Issue in Textbook (*Use key words to identify the issue*)	Number of Pages Devoted to Topic	Percentage of Total Pages in the Book. Total Pages in Book: _____
Nature of Science: definitions, assumptions, aims of science			
Social System of Science: history, lives of scientists, science and government, industry, public			
Human Behavior: genetic, environmental factors, human intelligence, behavior modification, theories of development, ethical issues related to control of behavior			
Population: growth, overpopulation, problems in developing countries, control, projections, population ethics			
Food Supply and Agriculture: history, food production, scarcity, crops, economics of food, ethics of food			
Human Reproduction: aspects of human reproduction, sex education, venereal diseases, reproductive control and engineering, fetal rights			
Human Genetics: traits and disorders, mutations, genetic diagnosis, counseling and interventions, ethical issues			
Human Health: health and disease, causes of disease, health care, aging, death and dying, health habits, world health problems			
Evolution: origin of life, evidence for evolution, theories of, application to social theories, evolution versus creationism, population genetics, human evolution			
Energy Resources: sources, energy conservation, new sources, economics of, energy policies, quality of life, international politics and energy			
Environment: human view of nature, effect of human activities on biosphere, natural resources, pollution, endangered species, biological and nuclear weapons			
Space Research/Exploration: extraterrestrial life, space stations, colonization, planetary exploration, militarization of space, effect of space exploration on view of human species and the planet			
Totals			

Figure 11.9 Textbook Analysis Chart of STS Issues. *Source:* These categories are based on a study reported by Rosenthal, Dorothy B. "Social Issues in High School Biology Textbooks: 1963–1983." *Journal of Research in Science Teaching* 21, no. 8 (1984): 819–31.

Table 11.5 Lists of STS Themes

List 1. Project Synthesis: Areas of Concern*	List 2. Bangalore, India Conference: Interdisciplinary Topics**	List 3. Global Problems Proposed by Bybee†
• Energy	• Health	• Population growth
• Population	• Food and agriculture	• War technology
• Human engineering	• Energy resources	• World hunger and food resources
• Environmental quality	• Use of land, water, and mineral resources	• Air quality and atmosphere
• Utilization of natural resources	• Environment	• Water resources
• National defense and space	• Industry and technology	• Land use
• Sociology of science	• Information transfer and technology	• Energy shortages
• Effects of technological development	• Ethics and social responsibility	• Hazardous substances
		• Human health and disease
		• Extinction of plants and animals
		• Mineral resources
		• Nuclear reactors

* See recommendations made by Piel, E. Joseph. "Interaction of Science, Technology, and Society in Secondary Schools." In *What Research Says to the Science Teacher*, Vol. 3, pp. 94–112, edited by Norris C. Harms and Robert E. Yager. Washington, D.C.: National Science Teachers Association, 1981.
** See Lewis, J. L. and Kelly, P. J. *Science and Technology Education and Future Human Needs*. Oxford: Pergamon Press, 1987.
† Bybee, Rodger. "Global Problems and Science Education Policy." In *Redesigning Science and Technology Education*, pp. 40–75, edited by Bybee, Rodger W., Carlson, Janet, and McCormack, Alan J. Washington, D.C.: National Science Teachers Association, 1984.

The order presented in Table 11.5 reflects the ranking reported in Bybee's study.

The purpose of this section is to examine some potential STS themes and make suggestions for actions (classroom activities) that you might take with students. Inquiry Activity 11.3 will involve you in the design of an STS module based on an STS issue. The information and ideas proposed here could be the seeds for the lessons in the modules that you develop. The following STS themes will be presented:

- Population growth
- Air quality and atmosphere
- Energy
- Effects of technological development
- Hazardous substances
- Water resources
- Utilization of natural resources
- Environment

Population Growth

The size of the human population affects virtually every environmental condition facing our planet. As our population grows, demands for resources increase, leading to pollution and waste. More energy is used, escalating the problems of global warming, acid rain, oil spills, and nuclear waste. More land is required for agriculture, contributing to deforestation and soil erosion. More homes, factories, and roads must be built, occupying habitat lost by other species that share the planet, often leading to their extinction. Simply put, the more people inhabiting our finite planet, the greater the stress on its resources.

WHY IS POPULATION GROWTH AN ENVIRONMENTAL AND STS ISSUE? It took from the beginning of time to about the year 1810 for the human population to reach 1 billion people.[32] Just more than 100 years passed before the next billion people were added, and the population doubled again to 4 billion people by 1974. By 1987, earth was home to 5 billion human beings and this number is growing. We started the twenty-first century with 6 billion people.

A society is not sustainable when it consumes renewable resources faster than they can be replenished. In other words, an overpopulated society clears forests and uses water supplies faster than they are renewed, or pollutes faster than the environment can adapt to sustain life. By these measures, the United States and most other nations of the world are overpopulated.

Contrary to some people's impression, the population explosion has not stopped. In 1990 another 95 million people were added to the earth, more than in any previous year. At this rate, the world's population would easily surpass 10 billion and could exceed 14 billion people late in the next century. No realizable amount of improvement in agriculture, pollution control, energy efficiency, or other areas would be able to keep up with this pace of growth. Some would say today's 6 billion humans is already more than our planet can handle.

The major consumers of the earth's resources are the developed countries, such as the United States. While these countries contain less than 20 percent of the world's people, they consume 80 percent of its resources. Although the United States is home to just 5 percent of the human population, we use one quarter of the total energy. The current population of the United States is about 300 million people. At the current rate of growth, we are expected to add 60 million more people in the next fifty years—110 times as many people as now live in Boston!

Vast areas of land in the United States have been cleared to support our population. Over 3 billion tons of topsoil is lost annually as a result of intensive farming and overgrazing. Large stretches of forest have been cut to provide wood and paper, leaving only 5 percent of our ancient (uncut) forests standing. In water-poor areas, high rates of growth are leading to water diversion and depleted groundwater reserves. As urban areas expand, air and water pollution are amplified.

STS ACTIONS

- Visit the Population Connection Web site (formerly Zero Population Growth), and find one resource on population education that you could share with your peers (http://www.population connection.org/).
- Ask students to identify which graph in Figure 11.10 describes the growth pattern of the human population over the past 2,000 years. Then ask them to identify the impact of the human population growth pattern on:

a. Earth's atmosphere
b. Availability of mineral resources
c. Water resources
d. Trees
e. Temperature of earth

Use the results of this exercise to identify student misconceptions.

- Get students involved in writing elected officials to support legislation to fund family planning, develop better contraceptives, promote equality for women, and break the cycle of poverty.
- Have students do research on the size of families in the United States and other "developed countries," and compare the results with family sizes in "underdeveloped countries." Create a values dilemma sheet based on this idea: We should encourage small families by example and by educating others about the need to make environmentally responsible reproductive choices.
- Have students find out what efforts are being made in their own community to limit the impact of growth on the environment.
- Have students make graphs showing how the population has changed in the last twenty years in their school, community, and state.

Air Quality and Atmosphere

The quality of earth's atmosphere is a significant social issue, not only in the United States, but also in every industrialized nation on the planet. One issue that has captured the attention of governments and ordinary citizens is the effects of ground-level ozone on the environment. Ground-level ozone has also been the topic of several Internet-based projects, including the Global Laboratory, GLOBE, and the Global Thinking Project.

ACID RAIN ISSUE Acid rain, more accurately called acid precipitation, is rain, snow, or fog that contains a

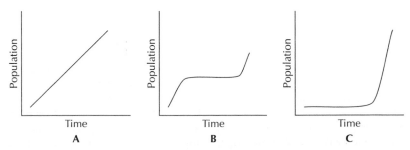

Figure 11.10 Population Graphs. Which describes the growth of the human population over the past 2,000 years?

significant amount of sulfuric acid or nitric acid.[33] The primary cause of acid rain is the combustion of coal and oil, processes in which large quantities of sulfur dioxide and nitrogen oxide are released into the atmosphere. Once in the atmosphere, sulfates and nitrates combine with moisture to form sulfuric acid and nitric acid. A small percentage of acid precipitation results from natural causes, such as volcanic activity.

THE EFFECTS OF ACID RAIN Acid rain is harmful to human health, increasing the rate of infant mortality and reducing proper lung functioning in many Americans. Research has implicated airborne sulfates in at least 50,000 premature deaths each year—as many lives as are lost in automobile accidents. For people with asthma, even low levels of sulfur pollution can cause serious lung damage in a matter of minutes.

Acid rain also causes acidification of rivers and lakes, a process disruptive to aquatic ecosystems. When acidity levels become too high, fish can no longer reproduce and soon die out. High acidity levels leach heavy metals, such as mercury and lead, from lakes and riverbeds. These metals often end up in the tissues of fish, making them toxic to human consumption. Acid levels in rivers and lakes are highest in the spring when snow packs melt and release high concentrations of pollutants. Unfortunately, this happens at a crucial time in fish spawning season.

Damage to tree foliage and degraded soil quality are other effects of acid rain. About half of West Germany's forests show signs of damage caused by high levels of acidity in rain and fog. In Canada and northern New England acid rain has been linked to large-scale damage to maple trees, threatening the maple syrup industry. Because factories are often equipped with tall smokestacks that send sulfur dioxide and nitrogen oxides high into the atmosphere, wind streams may carry them for hundreds of miles. Thus, one country will often receive another's acid rain. Half of Canada's acid rain originates in the United States.

Numerous buildings and construction materials are also subject to damage caused by acid rain, making the problem directly economic as well as environmental. A draft EPA study estimated the damage to building materials in seventeen northeastern and midwestern states to run as high as $6 billion annually. Not even our cultural history is safe, as thousands of statues and monuments are crumbling and corroding—some of the hardest hit include the Statue of Liberty and the Gettysburg Battlefield. For further information on Acid Rain, visit the EPA acid rain page: http://www.epa.gov/airmarkets/acidrain/index.html.

STS ACTIONS

- Ask students to make a diagram showing how they think acid rain is formed and how it affects the environment. Give the students the following list of terms to use in the creation of the diagram: coal, power plant, smokestacks, water vapor, rain, acid, combustion products, trees, rivers. Use the results to identify student misconceptions.
- Collect rain samples over a sustainable period and determine the pH using cabbage juice (boil four or five red cabbage leaves in two quarts of water) as an indicator. The purple juice turns pink in acid solutions and green in basic solutions. Students can also collaborate with peers in other schools to gather data on acid rain over a larger area.
- Participate in the National Geographic KidsNet System, which enables students in different states share acid rain data. (Write: National Geographic Society, 1145 17th Street NW, Washington, D.C. 20036.)

Energy

RECYCLING ISSUE Recycling saves energy, natural resources, and landfill space. In 2000, Americans threw away over 1 million tons of aluminum cans and foil, more than 11 million tons of glass bottles and jars, over 4.5 million tons of office paper, and nearly 10 million tons of newspaper. Almost all of this material could be recycled, cutting down on the environmental damage caused by mining, logging, and manufacturing raw materials, while decreasing the amount of garbage being dumped. The average American generates 3.5 pounds of garbage every day for a national total of over 150 million tons per year. Over 70 percent of this waste could be recycled using existing technologies.

ENERGY USAGE Global warming, acid rain, and oil spills are problems directly related to our extravagant use of energy. Three percent of our nation's energy is used to produce packaging materials, such as bottles and cans. By recycling aluminum it is possible to save 95 percent of the energy that it would take to manufacture new products from raw materials. In other words, recycling an aluminum can saves as much energy as if the can were half full of gasoline. Americans throw away about 35 billion aluminum cans every year— enough to rebuild our entire commercial air fleet four times over. If all these cans were recycled, we would save an amount of energy equal to 150 Exxon Valdez oil spills every year. In 1988, Americans set an all-time high by recycling 42.5 billion cans—54.6 percent of the total produced. This alone saved enough energy to supply power for the city of Boston for one full year.

For every ton of paper that is manufactured from recycled pulp, seventeen trees are saved and 3 cubic yards of landfill space avoid fill. With paper making up over 40 percent of our municipal waste stream, recycling could extend the lives of our existing dumps considerably. For recycling to work, however, it is important that there is a market for the new product. The United States uses about 40 percent of the world's newsprint supply; yet only 14 percent of this paper is made from recycled fiber. Recycled paper uses 64 percent less energy to manufacture than virgin paper and produces only a quarter the air pollution.

At present, more newspapers are recycled than recycled newsprint bought, causing a glut in the market for recycled newsprint. Barriers to increased recycling include federal subsidies to the timber industry that make the price of virgin paper artificially low. A tax credit for those manufacturers who use recycled materials could offset this perverse incentive for using virgin materials. A worldwide paper shortage is creating opportunities for community economic development through small-scale paper manufacturing plants located near the source of supply for waste paper. For every million Americans who recycle, some 1,500 manufacturing jobs are created.

STS ACTIONS
- Ask students to:

  a. Make a list of the advantages of recycling paper, aluminum, steel, and plastics.
  b. Describe how recycling saves energy.
  c. Discuss what would happen if nothing was recycled.

  Use the results to identify misconceptions, and as a starters for the early lessons in a recycling module.

- Tell the students that the United States produces about a third of the world's newsprint supply (about 13 million tons per year), yet only 14 percent is made from recycled fiber. According to some estimates, for every ton of recycled newsprint that is used instead of virgin paper:

  a. 17 trees are saved
  b. 3 cubic yards of land avoid being filled
  c. About 25 percent less energy is used
  d. 74 percent less air pollution is produced
  e. 58 percent less water is used

- Have the student do some "if-then" thinking. What would happen to the forest population of trees if the amount of recycled paper produced doubled from its present value? How would this affect landfill space? What impact would it have on energy usage?

- Have students investigate the environmental impact of the production of their local newspaper. They should call the newspaper and ask the following questions: How many tons of newsprint does your paper use per year? (A) _____ tons per year. What percentage of the paper is recycled fiber? (B) _____ percent recycled fiber. Now they can make the following calculations to determine how many trees-worth of newsprint are used, effect on landfills, and energy usage.

  a. To find out how many tons of recycled newsprint your paper company uses, multiply (A) by (B) and divide by 100.

  (A) _____ × (B) _____ /100 = (C) _____ tons of recycled newsprint.

  b. To calculate how many tons of newsprint are made from virgin paper, subtract (C) from (A).

  (A) _____ − (C) _____ = (D) _____ tons of virgin newsprint.

  c. To find out how many trees-worth of newsprint the newspaper company uses in one year, multiply (D) by 17 trees.

  (D) _____ × 17 = (E) _____ trees.

  d. To figure out how much waste paper could avoid landfill if the newspaper used all recycled fiber, multiply (D) by 3 cubic yards.

  (D) _____ × 3 = (F) _____.

Effects of Technological Development

NUCLEAR ENERGY ISSUE Created only sixty years ago, the first nuclear reactors were used only to produce plutonium for nuclear weapons.[34] Most reactors today make primary use of the heat energy from the nuclear reaction to produce electricity, propel Navy ships, or power space satellites. To create power, radioactive uranium atoms within the nuclear reactor are split, shooting particles in every direction with great force. The particles slam into other atoms, shearing off their electrons or, in the case of a direct hit, splitting their nuclei. The process releases tremendous amounts of heat, which is used to convert water to steam. The steam spins a large turbine, producing electricity. There are 560 commercial nuclear power plants in operation worldwide, 112 of which are in the United States.

PROBLEMS WITH NUCLEAR ENERGY All nuclear reactors produce plutonium and a variety of other radioactive wastes. Radiation changes the way cells divide, causing mutations that prevent organs from functioning properly. Even a small dose of radiation can cause cancer in living organisms, so radioactive waste must be kept out of the biosphere for tens of thousands of years. There are currently 18,000 tons of high-level radioactive waste in the United States alone, yet there is no permanent waste site for this material.

In the process of producing electricity, radiation permeates machinery, equipment, and the entire reactor building. After about twenty years, materials and equipment become so degraded that the plant must shut down. More than half of all U.S. reactors will have to be decommissioned by 2010, at an estimated cost of $400 million to $3 billion each. Dismantling one nuclear power plant would yield enough low-level radioactive waste to cover a football field 13 feet deep. Decommissioning all U.S. reactors would yield a wall of radioactive material 3 feet wide and 10 feet high stretching from Washington, D.C., to New York City.

Three Mile Island In the spring of 1979, a reactor at the Three Mile Island nuclear power plant in Pennsylvania suffered a partial core meltdown, releasing radioactive material into the surrounding environment. Thousands of people in the vicinity claim to suffer from cancer or thyroid damage as a result of the accident. Thus far cleanup has cost close to $1 billion, not including the cost of the reactor itself (about $2 billion) or the more than 2,500 lawsuits filed by nearby residents.

Before the three mile Island meltdown, the Nuclear Regulatory Commission (NRC) estimated the chance of an accident of that type to be one in a billion. The odds did not hold. Now, the Sandia National Laboratory predicts that an accident at the Indian Point nuclear plant in New York State could cost more than $400 billion and cause over a hundred thousand deaths. However, the Price-Anderson Act, first passed by Congress in 1957, limits the responsibility of utilities in the event of an accident to about $7 billion.

Chernobyl On April 26, 1986, in what was the world's largest nuclear disaster ever, a reactor at the Chernobyl nuclear power plant in Ukraine exploded, releasing vast quantities of radioactive material into the atmosphere. Clouds of fallout covered large areas of Europe, contaminating food supplies and increasing the rate of cancer in human beings. The ongoing clean up has cost $14 billion so far, and over 250 people have died. Hundreds of thousands of others will die prematurely, because radiation concentrates in body tissues, where it decays slowly.

More than 6 million people in Ukraine were directly affected by the Chernobyl disaster. Cross, Zatesepin, and Gavrilenko report that it resulted in numerous disorders and decline of health status. People reported chronic uncertainty and anxiety about their health and the future of their children, which has caused many psychological problems among the population. Cross and colleagues also suggest that in Ukraine, more than 3.5 million people were exposed to radiation and that the incidence of cancer of the thyroid among adolescents has risen tenfold.[35]

Following the Chernobyl disaster, one NRC member estimated the chance of an accident in the United States as big or bigger occurring to be as high as 45 percent. In 1989, citizens of Sacramento, California, voted to shut down the publicly owned Rancho Seco nuclear power plant because it was unsafe and uneconomical to operate.

Nuclear advocates are mounting a $40 million-a-year campaign to promote nuclear power as a solution to the greenhouse effect. However, the Rocky Mountain Institute estimates that to reduce the emissions that cause global warming 20 to 30 percent by the middle of the twenty-first century (substituting nuclear power for coal power) would mean building one new plant every three days for the next forty years at a cost of $9 trillion.

STS ACTIONS
- Give students a drawing of a building that contains a nuclear power plant. Have the students explain how they think a nuclear power plant produces electricity. Tell them to illustrate their ideas on the drawing of the plant. Use the results to identify student misconceptions.
- Have students investigate power-generating plants that use nonrenewable energy sources (coal, oil, nuclear material) and renewable energy sources (wind, water, volcanic steam).
- Organize a debate on the issue: Should nuclear power be eliminated from power companies' future construction plans?
- Have students visit the American Nuclear Society's Web site at http://www.ans.org/links/. They can use the site to search online sites dealing with topics including nuclear energy, nuclear power, radiation, radioactive wastes, and radioisotopes.
- For further information on issues related to nuclear energy, consult these sites:
  a. U.S. Nuclear Regulatory Commission: http://www.nrc.gov/.

b. Student and Teacher Site at the NRC: http://www.nrc.gov/reading-rm/basic-ref/ students.html.

c. Nuclear Threat Initiative: http://www.nti.org. This is a charitable organization working to reduce the risk of use and prevent the spread of weapons of mass destruction.

Hazardous Substances

PESTICIDES ISSUE Pesticides, which include insecticides, herbicides and fungicides, are a group of poisons used for killing or repelling unwanted organisms.[36] Each year, more than 4 billion pounds of pesticides are used worldwide. Although law requires that all new pesticides undergo a series of tests before being marketed, the National Academy of Sciences has reported that very few of all pesticides have ever been tested for long-term health effects. Less than 1 percent of the U.S. food supply is tested for pesticides.

According to the EPA, pesticides are substances used to prevent, destroy, repel, or mitigate any pest, ranging from insects, animals, and weeds to micro-organisms such as fungi, molds, bacteria, and viruses. EPA licenses or registers pesticides for use in strict accordance with label directions, based on review of scientific studies on the pesticide to determine that it will not pose unreasonable risks to human health or the environment. EPA is reviewing older pesticides to ensure that they meet current safety standards and is taking action to reduce risks where needed. For pesticides used on food, EPA sets limits on how much of a pesticide residue may remain in or on foods. EPA also sets standards to protect workers who may be exposed to pesticides on the job. EPA works to promote a safer means of pest control through research, public education, and public-private partnerships.

Many pesticides can be indiscriminate in what they kill and often harm nontargeted animals that may be beneficial to crops. In areas of heavy pesticide use, poisoning of birds, mammals, and fish are common. Some of the more persistent pesticides may remain dangerous for up to twenty years, slowly leaching into underground water supplies. In the United States, pesticides have been found in groundwater supplies in twenty-six states. Nearly half of all Americans rely on groundwater for home use.

Every year up to 2 million people suffer from pesticide poisoning worldwide, resulting in about 40,000 deaths. In the United States, 50,000 cases of pesticide poisoning are recorded annually. Pesticide exposure can cause cancer, birth defects, and damage to a number of body organs. Children often receive greater pesticide exposure because of their greater consumption of food and air, pound per pound, than adults. One study found that in households where pesticides are used, children are much more likely to suffer from leukemia.

Over the years, many insect species have become resistant to insecticides, necessitating higher doses and increased applications of more dangerous pesticides. Over the last forty years, pesticide use has increased tenfold, yet crop loss has almost doubled, from 7 to 13 percent.

U.S. law currently allows any pesticide to be exported as long as the importing country is notified of its regulatory status. As a result, many pesticides that are banned or restricted in the United States because of their danger to health and the environment are exported to developing countries. In many cases pesticides are applied by farm workers who are unable to read instructions or warnings on product labels (which are frequently written in English). These laborers are often inadequately protected and are exposed to heavy doses of dangerous pesticides. Ironically, 70 percent of the pesticides exported to developing countries are used in the production of food imported by the United States. Recently, 6 percent of all agricultural imports to the United States carried unacceptably high levels of pesticides.

STS ACTIONS

- Have students make lists of the advantages and disadvantages of using pesticides. You might want to tell the students that a pesticide is a general word for poisons that control or kill insects, fungi, weeds, and rodents. Use the lists as way to identify student misconceptions.
- Have the students investigate pheromones, which are natural sex attractants, as a safe, biological alternative to chemical pesticides.
- Have students find out what effect the following actions have on chemical pesticides:

  1. Wash fruits and produce.
  2. Buy domestically grown produce in season.
  3. Buy organically grown produce.
  4. Grow your own food.
  5. Tend the lawn without chemicals.

- Have students find out about organic gardening.
- For further information on pesticides consult:

  1. The EPA Office of Pesticide Programs: http://www.epa.gov/pesticides/.
  2. Beyond Pesticides—National Coalition against the Misuse of Pesticides: http://www.beyond pesticides.org/main.html.

Water Resources

WATER CONSERVATION ISSUE Conserving water saves energy and money and preserves fresh water habitat.[37] Much energy goes into transporting water to your residence and then more is used to heat water for bathroom and kitchen uses. By conserving water it is possible to prevent some of the pollution caused by excessive energy use, such as global warming and acid rain.

Many of the problems relating to water use can be attributed to development in areas where there is an insufficient water supply. For example, although the Southwest has only 6 percent of the country's fresh water, 31 percent of our water is used to meet the demands of heavy farming and urbanization in this area. As a result, increasing amounts of water are diverted from the Colorado River, and now only a limited amount of water, heavy with pesticides and fertilizers, reaches the sea.

Water diversion often leads to the destruction of wildlife. When rivers shrink, fish can no longer follow their normal paths of migration to spawn and may fail to reproduce. Diverting water also has a heavy impact on our diminishing wetlands, destroying animal habitat. In California, huge amounts of water are being diverted from Mono Lake's tributaries to be used in Los Angeles County. Mono Lake's water is naturally very salty, but as increased amounts of fresh water are diverted, the salt content has risen. Soon levels may be too high for brine shrimp to survive. If this happens, the food supply for the millions of birds that use Mono Lake as a stopover in their migration routes will be destroyed.

Much of the water we consume comes from underground reserves. If this water is used faster than it is replenished, it can cause land to sink, a process called subsidence. In Florida a few years ago, houses and cars were swallowed by sinkholes. Once subsidence occurs, the underground aquifers where water was stored cannot be reformed. According to the U.S. Geological Survey, thirty-five states are pumping groundwater faster than it is being replenished.

STS ACTIONS
- Show students a glass of water. Ask them to draw a diagram showing where the water originated in their community, what happened to it along the way until it was drawn from the tap. Use the students' ideas to identify misconceptions about water.
- Have students find out the source of drinking water in their community. Have them contact the water department to find out how their drinking water is purified. Students should prepare maps to show the sources of water in their community and charts to describe how water is purified.
- Take the students to a waste treatment or water purifying plant. Students can investigate the physical, biological, and chemical processes used to purify the water.
- Have students investigate how water is used (conserved) in their school. Have them inspect faucets, toilets, and water usage in the kitchen. Have them draw up a list of recommendations for the school to carry out a water conservation program. Challenge them to come up with an implementation plan.
- For further information consult:

  1. Rocky Mountain Institute: http://www.rmi.org/. The institute fosters the efficient and restorative use of resources to create a more secure, prosperous, and life-sustaining world. In addition to research on water resources, you will find information on energy, buildings and land, communities, climate, transportation, and other issues such as forestry, biotechnology, and global security.
  2. EPA Water Homepage: http://www.epa.gov/OW/index.html. At this site you'll find resources on groundwater, water science, wastewater management, wetlands, oceans, and watersheds, as well links to pages containing classroom activities.

Utilization of Natural Resources

TROPICAL RAINFORESTS ISSUE Tropical rainforests are broad-leafed evergreen woodlands that receive at least 100 inches of rain annually.[38] Rainforests once covered about 5 billion acres in the tropics. As a result of human interference, only half of the original rainforests exist today. Nevertheless, they are home to at least 5 to 10 million species of plants and animals approximately half of earth's life-forms. Remaining rainforests are disappearing at a rate of 100 acres per minute—an area the size of Kansas—every year.

Many natural resources and much of our food come from tropical rainforests. Rainforests serve as a genetic pool for many fruits and vegetables, and new varieties continue to be discovered. Only 1 percent of the tropical rainforest plants that have been identified have been scientifically analyzed, yet they are the source of more than a quarter of the medical compounds sold on the market today.

Nearly the entire acreage of tropical rainforests lies within the borders of developing countries. Often the governments of these countries are encouraged to exploit the resources of their forests to pay off foreign loans. External financial pressures have forced them to sacrifice long-term sustainability to service short-term national debt. Population growth and inequitable distribution of land have further contributed to the problem.

Each year millions of acres of tropical rainforests are burned to make way for agriculture, much of it for export. The nutrients of the rainforest are stored in its multilayered canopy. When forests are burned, these nutrients mix with the barren topsoil, where they are quickly eroded by rain. When the land is depleted of nutrients, the farmer moves on and clears more rainforest.

In Central America the primary motive for clearing rainforest is to make way for cattle ranching. Most of the beef, however, is produced for export to developed countries to be used by fast food restaurants. Over 120 million pounds of beef are imported by the United States from Central America annually.

According to the World Bank and the United Nations Development Programme, at least 12.5 million acres of tropical rainforest are logged every year. Much of this lumber is exported for use in furniture and other hardwood products. Teak, mahogany, rosewood, purpleheart, and ramin are some of the more common tropical hardwoods imported by developed countries. The United States imports about 15 percent of the world's hardwood products.

Many acres of rainforest are flooded each year as a result of large hydroelectric projects built to provide energy for large metropolitan areas and for multinational industrial projects. As a result of these hydroelectric projects, great numbers of indigenous peoples who have relied upon the sustenance of the rainforests for thousands of years have been relocated and their cultures destroyed.

Clearing tropical rainforests means destruction of habitat for the millions of species of plants and animals that live in these regions. Furthermore, forests act as a natural sink for carbon dioxide, the major "greenhouse" gas responsible for global warming. As rainforests are destroyed, carbon dioxide is released into the atmosphere, leading to higher global temperatures. Scientists predict that as global temperatures rise we will face an increase in crop failure, oceans will rise and flood coastal areas, and many species of plants and animals will become extinct.

Two thirds of the world's fresh water, excluding that which is locked in the polar ice caps, is cycled within tropical rainforest systems. Rainforests absorb this large amount of water, releasing it slowly and evenly through the process of evapotranspiration. But, as rainforests are cleared, soils become exposed to heavy rain, leading to flooding and erosion. It is often impossible to reestablish a rainforest once it has been cleared.

STS ACTIONS

* Provide students with a map of the world and ask them to identify the location of at least one tropical rainforest. Tell them that about 50 acres of rainforest are destroyed each minute (almost 27 million acres per year, equal in size to the state of Pennsylvania). What impact could this deforestation have on the following?

  a. Earth's temperature
  b. Animal and plant extinction
  c. Amount of carbon dioxide in the atmosphere
  d. Quality of life for people in the tropics

* For further information consult:

  a. The Rainforest Action Network: http://www. ran.org/. Rainforest Action Network works to protect the earth's rainforests and support the rights of their inhabitants through education, grassroots organizing, and nonviolent direct action.
  b. The Gander Academy Rainforest Page: http:// www.stemnet.nf.ca/CITE/rforest.htm. This school-based site contains a full spectrum of resources on rainforests, including lesson plans and activities.
  c. Global Rivers Environmental Education Network: http://www.green.org/. GREEN provides youth the educational opportunities to understand, improve, and sustain the water resources in their communities.

Environment

The burning of coal, oil, and natural gas, according to some scientists, is changing the earth into a planetary hothouse, changing climates worldwide. Coupled with the destruction of huge areas of tropical rainforests, the amount of carbon dioxide and other heat-trapping gases, the earth is experiencing a change in its average temperature. This phenomenon is better known as global warming, and represents one of the major environmental issues of the century.

GLOBAL WARMING ISSUE Over the past century, the human species has turned the earth into one huge unplanned experiment.[39] By releasing unprecedented

INQUIRY ACTIVITY 11.3

STS Module Design

What are the elements of an STS module? In this inquiry activity you will use the four instructional levels of STS modules to sketch the elements of an STS module.

Materials

* None

Procedure

1. Select an STS issue or a social aspect of science (ethics, truthfulness, communication) that you think would be interesting and suitable for secondary students. You might want to refer to the previous section in this chapter for some suggestions of STS themes, including issues such as tropical rainforests, water conservation, global warming, pesticides, nuclear energy, recycling, population growth, and acid rain. You might also want to visit one or more of the STS project Web sites in this chapter's On The Web section.
2. Create a concept map for the STS module that you have decided upon. The concept map should identify the main concepts (unifying themes) related to the STS issue. Work with someone else while you develop the concept map.
3. Using the following instructional levels, briefly describe one or two lessons for each category in the STS module. The descriptions should identify the purpose of the lesson and what the students would do. Prepare your plans in the form of a chart as shown in Figure 11.11.

    STS Levels:

    * Level I: STS Foundations
    * Level II: STS Issue Awareness
    * Level III: Issues Investigation
    * Level IV: STS Action Skill Development

4. Identify an evaluation plan for the STS module. How are you going to find out what the students have learned?

Minds-On Strategies

1. What unifying concepts did you identify? How did these unifying concepts compare with those identified by other students in your class?
2. What social action (of the part of the students) did you suggest in your module?

STS Level	Major Concept/Idea	Student Activities
Level I: STS Foundations		
Level II: STS Issue Awareness		
Level III: Issues Investigation		
Level IV: STS Action Skill Development		

Figure 11.11 Outline of STS Lessons.

amounts of greenhouse gases (carbon dioxide, methane, chlorofluorocarbons, nitrous oxide, and gases that create tropospheric ozone) into the atmosphere, we have in effect turned up the global thermostat. Greenhouse gases act in a fashion similar to the windshield of a car parked in the sun, allowing light-energy to pass through, but then trapping the reemitted heat. The greenhouse effect occurs naturally and without it the earth would be ice-covered and uninhabitable. However, over the past century, human practices have led to an increased buildup of greenhouse gases.

Scientists already have detected a 1 degree F temperature rise, which may be due to the greenhouse effect. They predict a further increase of between 4 and 9 degrees F by the middle of the next century if greenhouse gas emissions grow at expected rates. The 6 warmest years of the century have been in the last ten years, with 2000 and 2001 being the hottest on record. As world population and fossil fuel use grow, greater quantities of greenhouse gases will be released into the atmosphere. Although the United States has only 5 percent of the world's population, we are responsible for 25 percent of the carbon dioxide that is released from burning fossil fuels.

Carbon dioxide (which accounts for approximately half of the global warming trend), nitrous oxide, and tropospheric ozone are byproducts of burning fossil fuels (coal, oil, and gas) and wood. It is important to note that burning natural gas releases 70 percent as much carbon dioxide per unit of energy as oil, and half that of coal. Forests and oceans are natural sinks for carbon dioxide, but are unable to absorb the quantities currently being emitted. Deforestation releases large quantities of carbon dioxide as well as methane, carbon monoxide, ozone, and nitrous oxide. Swamps, cattle, rice paddies, landfills, termites, swamps, and fossil fuels also produce methane, which accounts for 18 percent of the greenhouse effects. Chlorofluorocarbons (CFCs), used in refrigerators and air conditioners, as foam blowers, as circuit board cleaners, and as aerosol propellants, account for 17 percent of the greenhouse effect.

Scientists predict that as global temperatures rise, life on earth will face a series of potentially disastrous threats. Precipitation will decline in some areas, leading to crop failure and expanding deserts. Elsewhere, rainfall will increase, causing flooding and erosion. Changes in habitat could lead to mass extinctions of plants and animals that are unable to migrate to more compatible climates. And sea levels will rise, flooding coastal areas and causing salt-water intrusion into coastal aquifers.

STS ACTIONS

- Ask students to make a diagram showing how they think the following contribute to create the "greenhouse effect": sun, earth's surface, burning of fossil fuels, atmosphere, carbon dioxide. Use the results to identify student misconceptions.
- Ask students to predict how the following human activities would influence the "greenhouse effect":
  a. Using transportation systems such as high-gas-mileage cars, public transportation, and bicycles.
  b. Constructing buildings with super-insulated material, smaller windows, and automated controls for thermostats and lighting.
  c. Using fluorescent lights.
  d. Buying efficient appliances.
  e. Advocating renewable energy such as wind power, small-scale hydro, geothermal, and solar.
- Climate researchers have predicted natural disasters would increase as a result of global warming. In the early 1980s they predicted the following phenomena:[40]
  a. Drought in midcontinent areas
  b. More frequent and severe forest fires
  c. Flooding in India and Bangladesh
  d. Extended heatwaves over large areas
  e. Super hurricanes
- For further information consult:
  a. EPA Global Warming Site: http://www.epa.gov/globalwarming/. This EPA site presents information on the very broad issue of climate change and global warming in a way that is accessible and meaningful to all parts of society—communities, individuals, business, public officials, and governments.
  b. Intergovernmental Panel on Climate Change: http://www.ipcc.ch/. This site was established by the World Meteorological Organization and the United Nations Environment Programme to assess research relevant to human-induced climate change.

STS Curriculum Examples

STS curriculum materials are not a prominent feature in the science curriculum landscape, but since the early 1990s, a number of projects devoted to developing STS curriculum materials have appeared. We examine some of these STS curriculum materials in this section.

Aikenhead has proposed a scheme that describes a spectrum of meanings found in STS courses and program (Table 11.6). The spectrum describes the relative

Table 11.6 Categories of STS in School Science

1. Motivation by STS content
2. Casual infusion of STS content
3. Purposeful infusion of STS content
4. Singular discipline through STS content
5. Science through STS content
6. Science along with STS content
7. Infusion of science into STS content
8. STS content

Source: Based on Aikenhead, Glenn. "STS: A Rose by Any Name." In *Crusader for Science Education: Celebrating and Critiquing the Vision of Peter J. Fensham*, edited by Roger T. Cross. Melbourne: Routledge Press, 2002.

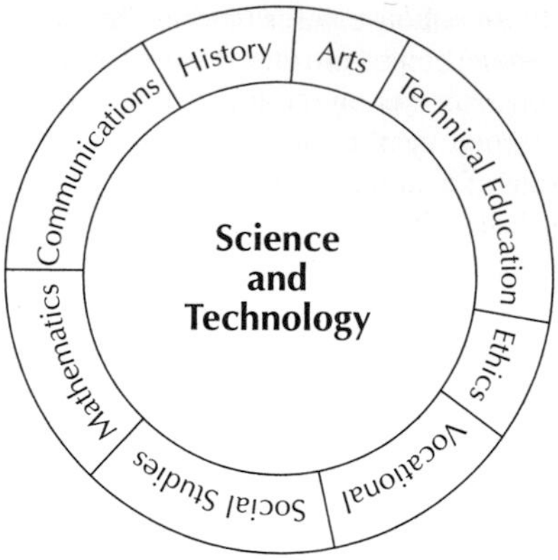

Figure 11.12 STS Connection Diagram. Based on Catalogue of STS Instructional Materials.

importance given to STS content, according to two factors: (1) content structure (the proportion of STS content versus canonical (normal) science content, and the way the two are integrated) and (2) student assessment (the relative emphasis on STS content versus canonical science content).[41] In Aikenhead's scheme, category 1 represents the lowest priority for STS content, whereas category 8 is the highest. Categories 3 and 4 represent the shift from discipline-based STS to a course that is defined by the social or technological issue. According to Aikenhead, interdisciplinary science begins at category 5 (science through STS content).[42]

STS Evaluation Criteria

The curriculum materials presented here have a number of characteristics in common. These characteristics are the criteria for evaluating STS materials established by a task force of the S-STS (Science through Science Technology Society). According to the SSTS task force, the following criteria constitute the characteristics of STS modules and courses of study:

1. *Societal Relevance:* The relations of technological or scientific developments to societally relevant issues are made clearly to capture attention.
2. *Relate STS:* The influence and effect of technology, science and society on each other are presented.
3. *Self and Society:* The material develops learners' understanding of themselves as interdependent members of society and society as a responsible agent within the ecosystem of nature.
4. *Balance of Views:* A balanced treatment of differing viewpoints about the issues is presented without author bias.
5. *Broadens Interest:* The material helps students go beyond specific subject matter to broaden considerations of STS, which include a treatment of personal and societal values/ethics.
6. *Decision-Skills:* The material engages students in problem solving and decision-making skills.
7. *Suggested Action:* The material encourages learners to become involved in a societal or personal course of action.
8. *Introduces Some Science or Qualification:* The STS material helps students develop understanding in at least one area of science and learn to use qualification as a basis for making judgments.

STS materials should help students make connection or linkages with other disciplines, as shown in the STS connection diagram (Figure 11.12). The STS connection diagram can be used to help you highlight linkages as you examine curriculum materials, and as you develop your own modules.

✶ *Education for a Sustainable Future (ESF)*

Education for a Sustainable Future (http://csf.concord.org/esf/) is a collaborative curriculum development project between the Center for a Sustainable Future (http://csf.concord.org), a division of the Concord Consortium (www.concord.org) and the Cobb County School District, Marietta, Georgia. ESF is an example of a sustainable education program that reflects the underlying goal of STS education.[43]

Sustainable development involves complex, interdisciplinary issues and the ESF project-integrated technology in all aspects of its development, field testing, and implementation. Thus technology-based tools were used to assist planning, modeling, communication, collaboration, and decision making. According to the project, these tools were essential for the study of sustainable development, for involving teachers and students in participating in activities, as well as fostering career education.

The foundation for classroom learning in ESF is student inquiry. In the teacher-developed units of the projects, students have access to a mix of existing software tools and three tools designed specifically for ESF. These technology tools enable students to visualize and explore possible futures. The ESF-specific technology tools (Table 11.7) include the What-If Building, the Community Planner, and the Ecological Footprint

Calculator. These tools enable students to building tree-branching futures (What-If Builder), design communities that can be visualized and studied (Community Planner), and finding out what their "ecological footprint" is and thus visualize their ecological impact.[44]

The ESF curriculum is organized around five themes, including designing sustainable communities, global issues, stewardship of resources, sustainable economics, and thinking about and affecting the future (Table 11.8). Using the themes and related STS content, curriculum units were developed by teams of teachers and then field tested at the target grade levels. Units were created for students in grades K–12. Table 11.8 outlines examples of units across the grade levels for each of the theme areas. A team of teachers residing in a single school typically developed each unit. The units were evaluated using the ESF rubric, which included three broad categories: Curriculum—High Expectations, Instruction—Opportunity to Learn and Time-on-Task, and Assessment—Frequent Monitoring. An examination of the instructional category includes the following attributes for assessing the unit: rigor, relevance, driving questions, degree of inquiry, use of technology, sequence and content process, benchmark lessons, systems thinking, grouping strategies. Each attribute was rated on a 3-point scale (low being 1), and units to be included in the ESF project had to attain scores of 3. Similar attributes were designed for evaluating the curriculum and assessment of the units. The project is being evaluated independently by Karen C. Cohen and Associates, and the evaluations for each year can be read at the ESF Web site. Using a qualitative methodology, the project evaluators have reported that the most successful outcomes were:[45]

Table 11.7 ESF Technology Supporting Sustainable Education

Technology Tool	Educational Use
What-If Builder	This scenario-building tool allows creation of branching stories. With it, students can create decision-tree models, also known as Action Mazes, tree literature, plot branching, or choose their own adventure.
Community Planner	Using this spatial modeling and visualization tool for community design and evaluation, students can create a map of their neighborhood, town, or community and analyze it based on indicators.
Ecological Footprint Calculator	This tool measures our use of nature by calculating how much land is required to produce all of the resources we consume and absorb all of the waste we produce.

Source: Based on The Concord Consortium. *Education for a Sustainable Future.* Online: http://csf.concord.org/esf/Software.cfm, 2003.

Table 11.8 ESF Curriculum Topic Areas and Examples of Curriculum Units

Topic Area	K–2	3–5	6–8	9–12
Designing Sustainable Communities	What Would You Include in an Earth-Friendly, Sustainable Community?	Are We Growing Like Weeds or Cultivating a Garden?	People, People Everywhere—Get Off the Roads!	S.E.L.F. (Sustaining Environments for Livable Futures)
Global Issues			Is Hunger a Global Problem?	
Stewardship of Resources	Reduce, Reuse, Recycle, Rethink, Relearn		Saving Energy	Energy Sources for a Sustainable World
Sustainable Economics	Building a Sustainable Economy	USA Today and Tomorrow	Brazil—Yesterday, Today, and Tomorrow	Economics, Resources, and the Future
Thinking about and Affecting the Future	Our Forest, Our Community	Time for Technoloogy	Stayin' Alive in 2025	Physics in the Future

Source: Based on The Concord Consortium. *Education for a Sustainable Future, Curriculum by ESF Topic.* Online: http://csf.concord.org/esf/, 2003.

- Student understanding and use of technology
- Student understanding and implementation of sustainability concepts
- The impact of the technology/technologies used in developing knowledge and understanding of the topic of sustainability for teachers
- The impact of the units on the teachers' role—teachers became facilitators and co-learners with their students
- Change in the classroom environment—students worked in teams or groups most often
- Collaboration in some instances helped "slow learners" become engaged and involved

Areas that were challenges included finding the time to master the concepts, create, and develop the units and master the technology. Additional but less frequently mentioned problems were to make the units fit school schedules, state mandated curriculum requirements, and project expectations with newly developing software and a technological infrastructure that was being deployed but not, in all instances, functioning. However, the researchers noted that the vision of equipping teachers throughout the nation with the knowledge, tools, and vision to engage their students in contributing to a sustainable, information-rich future is succeeding.

✸ *Science Education for Public Understanding Program (SEPUP)*

SEPUP (http://www.lhs.berkeley.edu/sepup/) is a project that has developed STS modules for middle school/junior and high school students and yearlong courses of study. The SEPUP materials are designed to promote scientific literacy and enhance the role of students in science and society.

The goals of SEPUP are as follows:[46]

- Develop learner-centered instructional materials that enhance the role of students as independent thinkers and active participants in science.
- Design a model for upper elementary and secondary school science reform that is flexible and responsive to local school needs and appropriate for students of all ethnic, cultural, and socioeconomic backgrounds, especially students at risk.
- Provide educational experiences focusing on science and technology and their interaction with people and the environment.
- Promote the use of scientific principles, processes, and evidence in public decision making.
- Build and expand existing SEPUP partnerships with industry and the public sector for the financial

and intellectual support of the development and use of issue-oriented science materials and programs in the schools.
- Enhance the role of teachers as facilitators of student learning and as educational leaders within their communities by having them share in the development, implementation, and assessment of issue-oriented science materials and programs.

The SEPUP courses include Science and Life Issues (grades 7 and 8); Issues, Evidence, and You (grades 8 and 9); and Science and Sustainability (grade 10). The courses highlight concrete and experience-based issues that affect not only students' personal lives but also their local communities.

The SEPUP modules (formerly know as CEPUP) series, focuses on an issue such as toxic waste, groundwater, risk comparison, solutions, and pollution. The module consists of a teacher's manual and modular kits, which contain equipment and teaching materials. The teacher's manual provides an overview of the activities, conceptual overview, description of the six to eight activities for each SEPUP module, evaluation items, and a glossary of terms. The activities include traditional science experiments, as well STS-type activities. For example, in the module Investigating Groundwater: The Fruitvale Story, students role-play different members of Fruitvale at a town meeting. In another unit, Determining Threshold Limits, students investigate threshold by determining the threshold of taste for salt in a solution. In the Risk Comparison module, students are introduced to chance and probability by flipping coins and rolling dice. The case study is introduced in this module. Students read and react to a story of smallpox inoculation and immunization and, in another activity, they investigate John Snow's research on cholera. Here is a full listing of the SEPUP modules:

- Chemical Survey and Solutions and Pollution
- Risk Comparison
- Determining Threshold Limits
- Investigating Groundwater: The Fruitvale Story
- Toxic Waste: A Teaching Simulation
- Plastics in Our Lives
- Investigating Chemical Processes: Your Island Factory
- Experiencing Scientific Research: An Air Pollution Study
- Chemicals in Foods: Additives
- The Waste Hierarchy
- Investigating Hazardous Materials

* Household Chemicals
* Investigating Environmental Health Risks

SEPUP also has fifteen Chem-2 units that are issue oriented and relate to a specific societal issue. The units include Everyday Chemicals, Build a Community, Energy to Go, Hazardous Home, and Smoking and My Health.[47]

✷ ChemCom (Chemistry in the Community)

This one-year chemistry course, developed by the American Chemical Society (ACS) with support from NSF and other sources, was designed for students who intend to pursue nonscience careers.

ChemCom is designed to help students:[48]

* realize the important role that chemistry will play in their personal and professional lives
* use principles of chemistry to think more intelligently about current issues they will encounter that involve science and technology
* develop a lifelong awareness of the potential and limitations of science and technology

The ChemCom curriculum consists of eight units, each of which focuses on a chemistry-related technological issue now confronting society and the world. The issue is the vehicle used to introduce the chemistry needed to understand and analyze it. Each topic is set in a community. Communities include the school, the town or city in which the students reside, or the whole earth.

This highly structured, yet unique chemistry curriculum involves the students in real issues facing society. Students are engaged in hands-on laboratory activities, as well as reading about environmental problems, solving problems, and answering questions.

The units in the ChemCom curriculum include:

* Supplying Our Water Needs
* Conserving Chemical Resources
* Petroleum: To Build or to Burn?
* Understanding Food
* Nuclear Chemistry in Our World
* Chemistry, Air, and Climate
* Chemistry and Health
* The Chemical Industry: Promise and Challenge

The curriculum involves the students in a variety of decision-making activities. For example, "Chem Quandary" is designed to get the students to think about chemical applications and society issues, which are often open ended. These activities usually generate additional questions beyond specific answers.[49]

✷ Project Learning Tree (PLT)

PLT is an environmental education project sponsored by the American Forest Foundation.[50] The curriculum consists of two teacher's activity guides, one for Pre-K–8 and one for Secondary (9–12).[51] The Pre-K Environmental Education Activity Guide contains ninety-six hands-on, interdisciplinary activities that cover a vast array of topics, such as water and air quality, ecology, forests, wildlife, urban environments, trees and plants, recycling, biodiversity, and land use. The secondary program contains separate modules on a variety of topics. Modules include: Exploring Environmental Issues—Focus on Risk, Exploring Environmental Issues—Focus on Forests, The Changing Forest —Forest Ecology, and Exploring Environmental Issues —Municipal Solid Waste.

The PLT curriculum is based upon five themes as follows:

* *Theme I: Diversity.* Throughout the world, there is a great diversity of habitats, organisms, societies, technologies, and cultures.
* *Theme II: Interrelationships.* The ecological, technological, and sociocultural systems are interactive and interdependent.
* *Theme III: Systems.* Environmental, technological, and social systems are interconnected and interacting.
* *Theme IV: Structure and Scale.* Technologies, societal institutions, and components of natural and human-built environments vary in structure and scale.
* *Theme V: Patterns of Change.* Structure and systems change over various periods of time.

The activities in PLT are interdisciplinary and, as a result, they can be used in a variety of curricula areas. This makes them especially valuable to the middle schools that are planning to develop interdisciplinary units for their students. PLT involves students in an assortment of indoor and outdoor activities. The curriculum consists of ready-made lessons on trees and forest ecology that can be used to supplement existing curricula.[52]

Other STS Materials

✷ BSCS MODULES Separate modules on STS, including Genes and Surroundings; Making Healthy Decisions; The Commons: An Environmental Dilemma; The Human Genome Project: Biology, Computers, and Privacy; and Genes, Environment, and Human Behavior Biological Science Curriculum Study (BSCS).[53]

INQUIRY ACTIVITY 11.4

 Evaluating an STS Module or Project

The purpose of this inquiry activity is for you or a team of peers to evaluate an STS module using criteria established by the STS task force. You can use the STS curriculum projects that were reviewed in the previous section and make use of the project's Web site to conduct your research.

Materials

- An STS module or project of your choice, including the equipment for the module if necessary

Procedure

1. Examine the STS module in light of the following criteria. Complete the chart shown in Figure 11.13 for each criteria.
2. Determine the curriculum linkages for the module and shade the appropriate STS connections in the STS Connections Diagram (Figure 11.12).

Minds-On Strategies

1. Would you recommend this STS module for use in the science classroom? In what contexts?
2. What evaluation materials were provided?

STS Criteria	Excellent	Good	Fair	Poor
Societal Relevance of the Issue				
Relate STS				
Self and Society				
Balance of Views				
Broadens Interest				
Decision-Skills				
Suggested Action				
Introduces Some Science or Quantification				

Figure 11.13 STS Evaluation Chart.

ECO-CONNECTIONS This Web-based environmental education project was developed by an international team of teachers and science educators from Georgia, U.S.A, and St. Petersburg, Russia. The curriculum consists of a series of Web-based modules on topics such as acid rain, air pollution, soil and agriculture, solid waste, water pollution, weather and living things, and watershed.[54]

★ PROJECT WILD This interdisciplinary, supplementary environmental, and conservation education program emphasizes wildlife and is published in two guides: the Project WILD K–12 Curriculum and Activity Guide and the Project WILD Aquatic K–12 Curriculum and Activity Guide.[55]

SUSTAINABILITY EDUCATION PROJECT This project works to balance human population, economic development, and resource consumption within the limits of nature to benefit current and future generations. The Izaak Walton League of America sponsors the project.[56]

SECTION 2: SCIENCE TEACHER GAZETTE

Volume 11: Science, Technology, and Society in the Science Classroom

Think Pieces

1. Why should STS be part of all science courses?
2. In your opinion, what are the ten most significant global STS issues facing the planet today? How are they related to each other?
3. What is global thinking?
4. What qualities should be included in STS modules?

When heroes of mine, such as David Suzuki, point out that there is such a glut of scientific knowledge now available that we cannot expose students to all of it with any realistic expectation of retention, then it does seem to indicate that there must be a change in what we're doing. Many of my colleagues would argue that the content is not really being taught for content's sake alone, but used as a vehicle to develop a number of extremely important tools including process skills and, believe it or not, to actually develop discussion skills the students have and to make them aware of the impact of science on our society. There seems to be a real concern that students are able to discuss the interface between science and society and be able to look at societal problems in a scientific manner. While I think this is good and certainly should be a part of courses, to dedicate the entire program to it is, I feel, highly questionable. Where do students get the knowledge base to discuss these at anything other than an emotional or gut level if they don't have some content that they can fall back on? I also think when you get into an area such as the values aspect of science, that you're starting to place teachers, who have been trained in a completely different manner, in a position that's a little suspect.[57]

The Problem

How would you react to this teacher? Is it highly questionable to base the science program on STS? Will students only react on an emotional or gut level without formal instruction in science content? And, by the way, who is David Suzuki?

Case Study: STS as the Entire Science Program: Some Questions

The Case

At a seminar to examine the future directions of the science curriculum, a high school chemistry teacher who has been a proponent of environmental chemistry, makes a brief presentation regarding her views on STS and the curriculum. The focus of her presentation follows:

Case: Biased Teaching?

The Case

You are teaching chemistry to college-bound students in a suburban community. Since this is your second year of teaching, you've decided to get students involved in some "environmental chemistry" activities. During the first semester you intend to have students read high-interest articles that you have copied (after securing permission, of course) from popular magazines such as *Time, Newsweek, Natural History,* and *National Geographic.* Your plan is to give the students one article every other week, followed by small- and large-group discussions. The first article you have selected is entitled: "Nuclear Energy: Its Time Has Passed." In order to conserve paper, each small team of four students gets one article, which they must share among themselves. The day after you distribute the article, you receive a phone call from one of your student's parents. He explains that he is quite concerned that students are reading such a highly biased article on nuclear energy. He accuses you of indoctrinating

the students with environmental sentimentality and says that if you continue having students read these "outside" articles, he will complain to the school board.

The Problem

What do you do in this situation? Did you expect to get this kind of reaction from any of your students' parents? What information can you provide the parent that might remove his objection that your teaching is indoctrination? Who would you see before responding to the parent, and what would you say?

Science Teachers Talk

"How do you deal with STS issues in the classroom?"

JERRY PELLETIER: It is not my style to hide from STS issues, so these issues are part of my curriculum. This year we dealt with the problem of nuclear energy. In order to make the students more aware of this issue we read *Hiroshima* by John Hershey and discussed the ramifications of the release of radioactive particles within the earth's atmosphere. We analyze the effects of that event with nuclear accidents such as Three Mile Island and Chernobyl. I handled the issue of evolution in the same manner. We read the play *Inherit the Wind* and discussed the controversy that is still brewing today between creationists and evolutionists. I find that by reading and sharing in the same literary experience student find it easier to discuss and understand various STS issues.

DALE ROSENE: There are a number of guidelines that I follow when dealing with STS issues. These include: (1) Be open—allow all students to voice their opinions and views. Encourage them to examine the basis for these views. (2) Try to provide balance when appropriate. (3) Invite experts into the classroom to provide their point of view. (4) Use writing exercises, because these cause the students to more carefully examine their beliefs. (5) Role-playing activities provide an excellent forum for STS issues. (6) Don't try to infuse your views on the class—unless appropriate. (7) Involve community

groups when integrating new curricula such as sex education.

JOHN RICCIARDI: My curriculum content is full of controversy and speculation. The entire knowledge base of "quantum" and "astro" phenomena is built on human subjectivity. To object, dispute, and oppose is also to be thinking scientifically. There are many "pictures," perceptions and schools of thought concerning "what is." Science's controversy is science's excitement, strength, and vitality.

In my classes, popular STS issues, such as creationism versus evolution and high-tech mechanical/biological creationism versus environmental preservation, are presented. However, within the context of the entire curriculum, their significance becomes deaccentuated. It seems that the issues are realized for what they are—only small pieces to the whole of nature's puzzle—only a "fuzziness" of parts to a grander, unseen clearness of "what is."

GINNY ALMEDER: An important goal of education is to develop the students' ability to deal with societal issues. Many of these issues result from theoretical research and scientific technology and are controversial by their very nature. STS issues such as creation science, AIDS, in vitro fertilization, genetic testing, and environmental hazards should not be ignored. Students need opportunities to develop critical thinking skills and well-informed opinions.

In our biology classes, we deal with such topics as creation science and evolution, the ethical and legal implications of genetic counseling, animals in research, the use of steroids, and environmental issues such as the "greenhouse effect" and ozone depletion. The students are encouraged to discuss their political and ethical positions regarding the various topics. With this approach, we are able to have nonthreatening discussions that promote both an increased understanding of the issues and a greater acceptance of other viewpoints. For example, a discussion of creation science and evolution provides a fertile setting for distinguishing between a scientific theory and a religious belief. If students are able to understand the difference, they are more likely to appreciate that science and religion are not mutually exclusive. In addition, such a discussion can be used to develop arguments and counterarguments for various issues and thus improve critical thinking skills as well as an appreciation for the differences of opinion that characterize our pluralistic society.

SCIENCE-TEACHING LITERATURE

EDUCATION FOR ENVIRONMENTAL SUSTAINABILITY[58]

David L. Haury

Early in the final decade of the twentieth century, the largest group of world leaders ever to assemble defined what may be education's greatest challenge and responsibility: to help citizens of the world prepare for a future of sustainable development.[59] Sustainable development has been defined over the years in a variety of ways, but Jacobs has suggested that all definitions have a core meaning characterized by three elements: (a) consideration of environmental issues and objectives interdependently with economic issues and objectives; (b) a commitment to social equity and the fair distribution of environmental benefits and costs, both geographically and across human generations; and (c) an enlarged view of "development" that extends beyond simple measures of "growth" to include qualitative improvements in daily life.[60]

The educational challenges for sustainable societies are great for several reasons: (a) the global sustainability challenge is unprecedented in both magnitude and complexity, (b) there is no history of societies willingly and deliberately taking steps to institutionalize restraints and change individual and collective behaviors to achieve greater sustainability, and (c) a constructive educational response must include a comprehensive, coordinated attempt to redefine the human role in nature and reexamine many assumptions, values, and actions we have long taken for granted.[61] We must "prepare each student to lead a sustainable lifestyle" and "place ecosystems concepts at the intellectual center of all disciplines."[62]

In the United States, the president has responded to the challenge by creating the President's Council on Sustainable Development (online at http://clinton2.nara.gov/PCSD/). The Council, in turn, convened a National Forum on Partnerships Supporting Education about the Environment and produced a report, *Education for Sustainability: An Agenda for Action*.[63] In outlining an array of strategic actions and initiatives promoting education for sustainability, the report focuses on six themes:

1. Lifelong learning within both formal and nonformal educational settings.
2. Interdisciplinary approaches that provide themes to integrate content and issues across disciplines and curricula.
3. Systems thinking as a context for developing skills in problem solving, conflict resolution, consensus building, information management, interpersonal expression, and critical and creative thinking.
4. Partnerships between educational institutions and the broader community.
5. Multicultural perspectives of sustainability and approaches to problem solving.
6. Empowerment of individuals and groups for responsible action as citizens and communities.

These themes reflect an acknowledgment that education about the environment and sustainability is interdisciplinary in nature, must allow for multiple perspectives, depends on collaboration across agencies and groups, and presumes a lifelong path of learning that extends through all levels of formal education into a variety of nonformal settings. The task, simply put, is to transform prevailing mindsets to recognize the long-term limits that nature imposes and the need to "nurture, rather than jeopardize, the ecological systems" that support our activities.[64]

What Is to Be Learned?

Just as there is a wide range of definitions for sustainable development, there is great diversity in the characterizations of education for sustainability. One starting place in considering the content of education for sustainability is to examine the relationship with environmental education. The North American Association for Environmental Education (NAAEE) has developed a set of guidelines for environmental education, *Excellence in Environmental Education Guidelines for Learning (K–12)*.[65] The guidelines provide a conceptual framework for environmental education, and they are organized around themes that are well aligned with the ideas shaping education for sustainability. Indeed, some have suggested that education for sustainability has become the new focus and justification for environmental education.[66]

The organizing themes for the NAAEE guidelines are as follows:

- Questioning and analysis skills.
- Knowledge of environmental processes and systems.
- Skills for understanding and addressing environmental issues.
- Personal and civic responsibility.

These themes clearly complement the six themes of Education for Sustainability, and they reflect a connectedness among natural systems, human actions, and the need for individuals and groups to analyze issues, make decisions, and take actions that support sustainable ecosystems. It is also clear from these two sets of themes that teaching for sustainability cannot be relegated to a single course or subject area; the themes of education for sustainability must come to permeate all subject areas at all educational levels.[67]

Neal has suggested a four-component framework for teaching about sustainable development:

(a) people, (b) environment, (c) economics, and (d) technology.[68] The component focusing on people would consider such matters as human populations, health care, literacy, equity, and urbanization. The environment component would foster awareness of issues related to water supplies, waste disposal, energy use and pollution, farming practices, and habitat preservation. Matters related to trade, expenditures on defense, wasteful consumption, poverty, and access to resources would be considered in the economics component, and the technology component would focus on control of emissions, fossil fuels, transportation, and industrial processes.

Rather than prescribe the content for sustainability education, Tilbury has suggested combining approaches that build on past practices but lead to an outcomes-oriented futures perspective.[69] She characterizes traditional environmental education as being "about" the environment; students gain awareness, knowledge, and understanding of human-environment interactions, usually within the context of a science, social studies, or geography class. Another common approach is education "in" the environment where experiential learning fosters both awareness and concern for the environment. To these components, Tilbury would add education "for" the environment that would promote "a sense of responsibility and active pupil participation" in resolving environmental problems."[70]

As Sitarz has suggested, education for sustainability is not a new course of study or new content, but rather "it involves an understanding of how each subject relates to environmental, economic, and social issues."[71] Developing the content of this new educational dimension will require "educators at all levels [to] reach beyond school walls to involve parents, industry, communities, and government in the educational process."[72]

One way to begin the process is to create environmentally safe and healthy school buildings and grounds where daily routines and facilities reflect attention to environmentally sound practices. *The Blueprint for a Green School* is a comprehensive guidebook that provides background information, activities, and resources for creating environmentally sound learning environments.[73]

Challenge to Communities

Though sustainable development is a national and international issue, it becomes locally defined through actions and decisions within cities, neighborhoods, and communities. It is clear from the nature and magnitude of the challenge that providing education for sustainability will require communities to view schools as components within the educational system, not the sole agents responsible for education. Indeed, education for sustainability will not be sustained unless communities embrace the concept and systematically build sustainable patterns of living where the local economy, policies, services, resource consumption, and land-use regulations meet the needs of residents while preserving the environment's ability to support the desired standards of living into the future. Roseland has developed a practical handbook for communities ready to take the challenge, and the Izaak Walton League of America has produced several community-oriented workshop guides on sustainability, including, *Monitoring Community Sustainability*.[74] This and other curriculum materials associated with the League's Sustainability Education Project are described online [see http://www.iwla.org/sep/]. One possible community education strategy would be to involve school students in the collection and reporting of data related to environmental indicators. *Community Sustainability*, a mini-curriculum produced by the Izaak Walton League for grades 9–12, includes guidelines for conducting a community sustainability-monitoring project.[75]

Another curriculum guide produced by Zero Population Growth for middle school students includes activities that lead to development of a "Quality of Life Index."[76] Developing an index with ten community indicators is one of the culminating activities after students have examined general principles relating to population dynamics, use of natural resources, and global issues.

The supplementary curriculum materials described here represent modest moves toward engaging students in local actions that promote community sustainability. The long-term goals of education for sustainability will be realized, however, only when communities build on these efforts and involve schools in comprehensive plans to create sustainable communities. More resources supporting such efforts are available through the following World Wide Web sites:

- Second Nature: Education for Sustainability: http://www.2nature.org
- President's Council on Sustainable Development: http://clinton2.nara.gov/PCSD/
- Envirolink: The Online Environmental Community: http://www.envirolink.org/

Problems and Extensions

1. What research skills will students need to develop in order to carry out STS action projects?
2. Select an area of science (earth science, physical science, life science) and develop a list of STS issues that could be integrated into a one-year course in the field.
3. Cartoons (especially those found in the editorial pages of newspapers) could be used as value dilemmas for STS activities. Collect at least five, identify the STS issue that each reflects, and explain how you would use them in the science classroom.
4. Design either a case study, a voting activity, or a value dilemma for any one of the following STS issue areas: health care, prolongation of life, euthanasia, artificial organs, genetic counseling, abortion, human experimentation, suicide, biological weapons. Field test your activity with a group of peers, friends, or secondary students.
5. Do a survey of a group of secondary students to find out how much emphasis is given to STS teaching in their science courses. Here are a few questions that you can use to find out.[77] To begin, ask the students: "In your opinion, how much emphasis has been given in the science classes you have taken until now to the following ideas?" (You could give them a sheet of paper with this list, and the direction to check (1) a lot, (2) some, or (3) not much for each.)

   a. Society controls science and technology.
   b. Science and technology influence society.
   c. Science and technology have limitations.
   d. Science and technology are useful in advancing human welfare.
   e. There is a difference between scientific knowledge and personal opinion.

f. People must make careful decisions about the use of technology.

g. There are many good, reliable sources of scientific information that a person can find and use in making decisions.

Notes

1. See Randall L. Wiesenmayer and Peter A. Rubba, "The Effects of STS Issue Investigation and Action Instruction and Traditional Life Science Instruction on Seventh Grade Students' Citizenship Behaviors" (paper presented at the National Association for Research in Science Teaching meeting, Atlanta, Ga., April 1990).

2. Glen Aikenhead, "STS Education: A Rose by Any Other Name," in *Crusader for Science Education: Celebrating and critiquing the Vision of Peter J. Fensham*, ed. Roger T. Cross (Melbourne: Routledge Press, 2002).

3. Norrris Harms and Robert Yager, What Research Says to the Science Teacher, vol. 3 (Washington, D.C.: National Science Teachers Association, 1981), pp. 94–112.

4. National Science Teachers Association, 1990. Position Statement: Science/Technology, Society, You can read this at http://www.nsta.org/159&psid=34.

5. Aikenhead, "STS Education."

6. National Research Council, *National Science Education Standards* (Washington, D.C.: National Academy Press, 1995), p. 197.

7. Based on P. J. Fensham, "Changing to a Science, Society and Technology Approach," in *Science and Technology Education and Future Human Needs*, ed. J. L. Lewis and P. J. Kelly (Oxford: Pergamon Press, 1987), p. 72.

8. E. Joseph Piel, "Interaction of Science, Technology, and Society in Secondary Schools," in *What Research Says to the Science Teacher*, vol. 3, ed. Norris C. Harms and Robert E. Yager (Washington, D.C.: National Science Teachers Association, 1981), pp. 94–112.

9. Dennis W. Cheek, *Thinking Constructively about Science, Technology, and Society* (Albany, N.Y.: State University of New York Press, 1992).

10. See Victor J. Mayer, "Teaching from a Global Point of View," *Science Teacher* (January 1990): 47–51.

11. James W. Botkin, Mahdi Elmandjra, and Mircea Malitza, *No Limits to Learning* (Oxford: Pergamon Press, 1979), p. 31.

12. Suggested by the Bangaore Conference on Science and Technology Education and Future Human Needs, Banagore, India, 1985. See Lewis and Kelly, *Science and Technology Education.*

13. Fensham, "Changing to a Science, Society and Technology Approach," p. 69.

14. Nancy Law, Peter J. Fensham, Steven Li, and Bing Wei, "Public Understanding of Science as Basic Literacy," in *Science and the Citizen*, ed. Roger T. Cross and Peter J. Fensham (Melbourne: Arena Publications, 2000), pp. 145–55.

15. Norman Myers, ed. *GAIA: An Atlas of Planet Management* (Garden City, N.Y.: Anchor/Press/Doubleday and Company, 1984), p. 13.

16. James E. Lovelock. "Elements," in Meyers, Gaia, p. 100.

17. These student comments were provided by Dr. Phil Gang, The Institute for Educational Studies, Atlanta, Ga. The comments were made by junior high students in a workshop on global thinking conducted by Dr. Gang.

18. Cheek, *Thinking Constructively*, p. 42.

19. Answers: China: 25.0; India: 3.0; South Korea: 2.0; Egypt: 3.0; Mexico: 3; Netherlands: 2.2; Australia: 1.0. *Source: USA Today*, 20 April 1990, p. 15E.

20. L. E. Raths, M. Harmin, S. B. Simon, *Values and Teaching* (Columbus, Ohio: C.E. Merrill Publishing Company, 1978).

21. *Human Reproduction: Social and Technological Aspects.* © BSCS. (Dubuque, Iowa: Kendall/Hunt, 1984), p. 57.

22. R. M. Agne, "Teaching Strategies for Presenting Ethical Dilemmas," in *Ethics and Social Responsibility in Science Education*, ed. M. J. Frazer and A. Kornhauser (Oxford: Pergamon Press, 1986), pp. 165–74.

23. Mark A. Carle, Mickey Sarquis, and Louise Mary Nolan, *Physical Science: The Challenge of Discovery* (Lexington, Mass.: D. C. Heath, 1991).

24. Excerpted from Micki McKisson and Linda MacRae-Campbell, *No Time to Waste! The Greenpeace East-West Educational Project, Teacher Guide* (Washington, D.C.: Greenpeace International, 1989), p. 23.

25. See Herbert D. Their, "The Science Curriculum in the Future: Some Suggestions for Experience-Centered Instruction in the Fifth through Ninth Grades," in *Redesigning Science and technology Education*, ed. Rodger W. Bybee, Janet Carlson, and Alan J. McCormack (Washington, D.C.: National Science Teachers Association, 1984), pp. 162–69.

26. Wiesenmayer and Rubba, "The Effects of STS Issue Investigation."

27. Harold R. Hungerford et al., *Investigating and Evaluating Environmental Issues and Actions Skill Development Modules* (Champaign, Ill.: Stipes, 1988).

28. Wiesenmayer and Rubba, "The Effects of STS Issue Investigation," p. 4.

29. Ibid., pp. 5–11.

30. Ibid.

31. Dorothy B. Rosenthal, "Social Issues in High School Biology Textbooks: 1963–1983," *Journal of Research in Science Teaching* 21, no. 8 (1984): 819–31.

32. This section on population growth is modified from Ron Anastasia and Susan Weber, "Population Growth Fact Sheet," *EarthNet* (a forum on the Connect Business Telecommunications System).

33. This section on acid rain is modified from Ron Anastasia and Michael Fischer, "Acid Rain Fact Sheet," *EarthNet* (a forum on the Connect Business Telecommunications System).

34. This section on nuclear energy modified from Ron Anastasia and Joan Claybrook, "Nuclear Energy Fact Sheet," *EarthNet* (a forum on the Connect Business Telecommunications System).

35. Roger Cross, Veniamin Zatesepin, and Ivan Gavrilenko, "Preparing Future Citizens for Post 'Chernobyl' Ukraine: A National Calamity Brings about Reform of Science Education," in Cross and Fensham, *Science and the Citizen*, pp. 179–87.

36. Ron Anastasia and John Adams, "Pesticides Fact Sheet," *EarthNet* (a forum on the Connect Business Telecommunications System).

37. The section on water conservation is modified from Ron Anastasia and Amory Lovins, "Water Conservation Fact Sheet," *EarthNet* (a forum on the Connect Business Telecommunications System).

38. The section on tropical rainforests is modified from Ron Anastasia and Randy Hayes, "Tropical Rainforests Fact Sheet," *EarthNet* (a forum on the Connect Business Telecommunications System).

39. The section on global warming is modified from Ron Anastasia and Gus Speth, "Global Warming Fact Sheet," *EarthNet* (a forum on the Connect Business Telecommunications System).

40. H. Patricia Hynes, *Earth Right* (Rocklin, Calif.: Prima Publishing & Communications, 1990), p. 177.

41. Glenn. Aikenhead, "STS: A Rose by Any Name," in *Crusader for Science Education: Celebrating and Critiquing the Vision of Peter J. Fensham*, ed. Roger T. Cross (Melbourne: Routledge Press, 2002).

42. This discussion based on Aikenhead, "STS, A Rose by Any Name."

43. See The Concord Consortium, *Education for a Sustainable Future* (Online: http://csf.concord.org/esf/, 2003).

44. Ibid., http://csf.concord.org/esf.

45. Cohen, Karen, et al., *External Evaluation Report, Year III: Education for a Sustainable Future.* (Concord Consortium Online: http://csf.concord.org/esf/Eval00/index.htm, 2003).

46. Based on SEPUP Web site: http://www.sepuplhs.org/approach.html.

47. SEPUP is available from Lawrence Hall of Science, University of California, Berkeley, CA 94720, or you can visit the SEPUP Web site: http://www.sepuplhs.org/.

48. American Chemical Society, *ChemCom: Chemistry in the Community* (Dubuque, Iowa: Kendall/Hunt, 1988), p. ix.

49. ChemCom is available from Kendall/Hunt Publishing Company, 2460 Kerper Blvd., P.O. Box 539, Dubuque, IA 52001. Visit the ChemCom Teacher's Resource site: http://www.lapeer.org/ChemCom/Index.html.

50. *Project Learning Tree Workshop Handbook* (Washington, D.C.: American Forest Institute, 1984).

51. *Project Learning Tree Activity Guide K–11* and *Project Learning Tree Activity Guide 7–12* (Washington, D.C.: American Forest Institute, 1988).

52. PLT is available from American Forest Foundation, 1111 19th Street, N.W., Suite 780, Washington, DC 20036, 1-888-889-4466, or http://www.plt.org/.

53. BSCS modules are available from 5415 Mark Dabling Blvd., Colorado Springs, CO 80918-3842, 719-531-5550, http://www.bscs.org.

54. Eco-Connections is available from Walker County Science Center, 409 Pond Springs Road, Chickamauga, GA 30707, http://www.eco-connections.org/.

55. Project Wild is available from Project Wild National Office, 5555 Morningside Drive, Suite 212, Houston, TX 77005, or http://www.projectwild.org/.

56. The Sustainability Education Project is available from the Izaak Walton League of America, 707 Conservation Lane, Gaithersburg, MD 20878, or http://www.iwla.org/sep/.

57. Excerpted from Douglas A. Roberts, "What Counts as Science Education?" in *Development and Dilemmas in Science Education*, ed. Peter Fensham (London: The Falmer Press, 1988), p. 41.

58. David L. Haury, "Education for Environmental Sustainability," Columbus: Clearinghouse for Science, Mathematics, and Environmental Education, 2002. ERIC SE 061 972. This digest is in the public domain and may be freely reproduced. This digest was funded by the Office of Educational Research and Improvement, U.S. Department of Education under contract no. RI-93002013. Opinions expressed in this digest do not necessarily reflect the positions or policies of OERI or the Department of Education.

59. D. Sitarz, ed., *Agenda 21: The Earth Summit Strategy to Save Our Planet.* (Boulder, Colo.: EarthPress, 1993).

60. M. Jacobs, *The Green Economy: Environment, Sustainable Development, and the Politics of the Future* (Vancouver: University of British Columbia Press, 1993).

61. David W. Orr, *Ecological Literacy: Education and the Transition to a Postmodern World* (Albany: State University of New York Press, 1992). [ED 377 036]

62. J. Disinger, "Education," in *From Rio to the Capitols: State Strategies for Sustainable Development*, ed. Rebecca Stutsman (Louisville: Commonwealth of Kentucky, 1993).

63. President's Council on Sustainable Development, *Education for Sustainability: An Agenda for Action* (Washington, D.C.: U.S. Government Printing Office, 1996) (available online at http://www.gcrio.org/edu/pcsd/toc/html). [ED 403 158]

64. G. A. Smith, *Education and the Environment: Learning to Live with Limits* (Albany: SUNY Press, 1992), p. 90. [ED 356 554]

65. North American Association for Environmental Education, *Excellence in Environmental Education Guidelines for Learning (K–12)* (Washington, D.C.: Author, 1998).

66. D. Tilbury, "Environmental Education for Sustainability: Defining the New Focus of Environmental Education in the 1990's," *Environmental Education Research*, 1, no. 2 (1995): 195–212 [EJ 509 039], and "Environmental Education for Sustainability in Europe: Philosophy into Practice," *Environmental Education and Information*, 16, no. 2 (1997): 123–40. [549 703]

67 K. G. Munson, "Barriers to Ecology and Sustainability Education in the U.S. Public Schools." *Contemporary Education*, 18, no. 3 (1997): 174–76. [EJ 553 049]

68. P. Neal, "Teaching Sustainable Development," *Environmental Education*, 50 (Autumn 1995): 8–9. [EJ 546 445]

69. Tilbury, "Environmental Education for Sustainability."

70. Ibid., p. 207.

71. Sitarz, *Agenda* 21, p. 202.

72. Ibid., p. 200.

73. J. Chase, *Blueprint for a Green School* (New York: Scholastic, 1995).

74. Mark Roseland, *Toward Sustainable Communities: Resources for Citizens and Their Governments* (Stony Creek, Conn.: New Society Publishers, 1998).

75. B. J. Hren and D. M. Hren, *Community Sustainability* (Gaithersburg, Md.: Izaak Walton League, 1996).

76. P. Wasserman, ed., *People and the Planet: Lessons for a Sustainable Future.* (Washington, D.C.: Zero Population Growth, 1996).

77. Excerpted from Faith Hickman, "An Instrument for Assessing STS Courses," *Global Science: Energy, Resources, Environment Newsletter* 2, no. 1 (Fall, 1987): 3.

Readings

Bloomfield, Molly. "Assessing Air Quality," *The Science Teacher* 67, no. 9 (2000): 40–44.

Bodzin, Alex M., and Mamlok, Rachel. "STS Simulations." *The Science Teacher* 67, no. 11 (2000). 36–39.

Botkin, Daniel B., et al. *Changing the Global Environment.* Boston: Academic Press, 1989.

Cheek, Dennis W. *Thinking Constructively about Science, Technology, and Society Education.* Albany: State University of New York Press, 1992.

Cross, R. *Fallout: Hedley Marston and the British Bomb Tests in Australia.* Kent Town, South Australia: Wakefield Press, 2001.

Cross, R. T., and Fensham, P. J., eds. *Science and the Citizen.* Melbourne: Arena Publications, 2000.

Friday, Gerald. "Conservation Presentation." *The Science Teacher* 68, no. 5 (2001): 44–45.

Hassard, J., and Weisberg, J. *Environmental Science on the Net.* Parsippany, N.J.: Goodyear Books, 1999.

Lucidi, Louis, and Mecca, Peter M. "Researching Radon." *The Science Teacher* 68, no. 5 (2001): 40–41.

Walter, Eric, et al. "Environmental Activism." *The Science Teacher* 65, no. 5 (1999): 48.

Welch, Peggy, and Harrison, Jerry. "School Energy Audit." *The Science Teacher* 66, no. 5 (1999): 44.

On the Web

EarthComm: http://www.agiweb.org/earthcomm/. An NSF-supported project developed by the American Geological Institute, Earthcom teaches students the principles and practices of earth science and demonstrates the relevance of earth science to their life and environment.

Environmental Health: http://www.cdc.gov/health/environm.htm. Located at the Centers for Disease Control Web site, this page focuses on environmental health concerns.

STS Links Page: http://www.ncsu.edu/chass/mds/stslinks.html. This site provides a comprehensive set of links to STS sites, including activists, environmental and ecology, genetics and biotechnology, ethics in STS, and women and minorities in STS.

Center for Democracy and Technology: http://www.cdt.org/index.html. The Center for Democracy and Technology works to promote democratic values and constitutional liberties in the digital age. With expertise in law, technology, and policy, CDT seeks practical solutions to enhance free expression and privacy in global communications technologies.

Educators for Social Responsibility: http://www.esrnational.org/. ESR's mission is to make teaching social responsibility a core practice in education so that young people develop the convictions and skills needed to shape a safe, sustainable, democratic, and just world.

The EE-Link: http://eelink.net/. EE-Link is a participant in the Environmental Education and Training Partnership (EETAP) of the North American Association for Environmental Education (NAAEE). The site provides links to professional resources, class resources, organizations and projects, and grants and jobs.

Education Realms: http://www.stemworks.org/. Resources on science, mathematics and environmental education.

Contains many of the materials originally produced by the ERIC Clearinghouse.

National Center for Case Study Teaching in Science: http://ublib.buffalo.edu/libraries/projects/cases/ubcase.htm. This site contains a large collection of cases including the environment, medicine, nutrition, health, and engineering.

Shallow Footprints Links: http://www.iwla.org/sep/links_footprint.html. The links at this site can help you learn more about our individual and cumulative effects on the earth. The concept of ecological footprint is referenced here, as well as a link to the ecological footprints calculator.

The Internet: Moving toward Web-Based Learning Environments

The science classroom can be a special place. It can be one in which students work together in learning teams to answer questions, inquire, pose questions, and learn new ideas about the world. It can be a place in which critical and creative thinking are fostered. In this book we have emphasized the importance—based especially on the work of Piaget and Vygotsky resulting in a theory of constructivist-based teaching—that should be attached to the notion that student knowledge about the world develops as a result of interaction with physical objects, events and phenomena, and people. We have emphasized the importance of involving students in the process of learning as described by the learning cycle.

Recently, the computer and now the Internet have made their way into the educational scene. Can the Internet and related technology enhance the goal of involving students in the learning process, of encouraging inquiry and problem solving, and fostering critical and creative thinking? Or are we simply witnessing another educational innovation that will have little effect on classroom learning?

A recent report on the Internet and its potential for learning stated "the Internet is perhaps the most transformative technology in history, reshaping business, media, entertainment, and society in astonishing ways. But for all its power, it is just now being tapped to transform education."[1] The report indicated that the Internet is moving us closer to making learning of all kinds and at any level a practical reality for all people. However, there is still the problem of access limitations and lack of knowledge of how to make use of the Internet as a learning tool.

The Internet and related technologies represent new ways of thinking about how computers can be used in schools. Instead of using computers to "teach" what is currently in the science curriculum, these applications suggest rethinking what can be taught in the science curriculum and how teachers and students might be involved. This chapter explores the potential of the Internet as a tool for learning. The Internet has already become an important aspect of science education, and its impact on learning and the management of instruction will be presented here.

Case Study: Web-Based Teaching, Just Another Progressive Education Fad?

The Case

Jerry Squire, a twenty-year veteran science teacher in a midwestern urban high school, was sitting in the audience at a staff development conference listening to a speaker from a science education research and development center present ideas about the benefits of online or Web-based teaching and learning. The speaker, a very well-known science educator, indicated that the Web was one of the keys to reforming science education and that schools needed to move toward creating more online opportunities for students. In the question-and-answer session following the presentation, Jerry stood and addressed the speaker: "For the past twenty years we have tried to integrate computers into the classroom, and with little effect. We've used them in our science department with mixed success. Why do you think Web-based teaching and the use of online resources are going to be any different than our experiences using technology in the past? The record is dismal. Please show me how it can be better."

The Problem

What do you think about the potential of the Web in science teaching? Is Jerry relying too much on his own experience and thereby not listening to the results of this science educator's experience with the Web? What are the issues to be on the lookout for when we start thinking about technology, online learning, and science teaching?

How to Read This Chapter

I have organized the chapter around several themes: student experiences using the Internet (a collection of activity structures describing different ways the Internet can be used in the classroom), telecommunications projects and student inquiry (case studies and examples of Internet-based projects that involve students in authentic inquiry and social action), and Internet-based science activities (the nuts and bolts of designing Web-based science activities). You can start your exploration at any one of these three points. If you are interested in finding out how you can use the Web creatively, you might want to start with the section on student experiences. On the other hand, if you are interested in involving students in collaborative inquiry projects, look at the section on telecommunications. If you are interested in designing online learning experiences, you might want to start with the last section of the chapter.

SECTION 1: WEB-BASED LEARNING ENVIRONMENTS

Invitations to Inquiry

- What is the nature of an online classroom?
- What kinds of student experiences using the Internet will lead to the active construction of science knowledge?
- How can the Internet be used to foster student inquiry, creative activity, and problem solving?
- How can collaboration and research investigations lead to socially responsible actions at the local and the global levels?
- What principles from research should affect the use of the Internet and related technology resources in the science classroom?
- What design elements foster the integration of the Internet resources in classroom instruction?
- How would you design or select Internet-based science activities for the science classroom?

Creating a Web-Based Classroom

Tim Berners-Lee, the inventor of the World Wide Web, had a dream for the Web: "When I proposed the Web in 1989, the driving force I had in mind was communication through shared knowledge, and the driving 'market' for it was collaboration among people at work and at home."[2] His dream of the Web was to link people "mind to mind," a powerful mantra for how the Web could be used in the classroom.

Web-based classrooms afford teachers and students the potential to think differently about their interactions with science and society. In Web-based classrooms students have ready access to the resources and people connected to the Internet. For many teachers, however, access is a serious challenge that can curtail the dream that Berners-Lee envisioned. Access not only means having easy technical connections to the Internet, but also knowing how to use the resources of the Net in ways that put the student in the center of the learning process.

Several trends are important to observe with regard to Internet access and usage. Households with Internet access have increased from 26.2 percent in 1998 to 50.5 percent in 2001. According to the Web-Based Education Commission report, about a third of the total U.S. population uses the Internet at home, while only 16.1 percent of Hispanics and 18.9 percent of blacks do.[3] Unfortunately, the gap in Internet access between black households and the national average grew from 15 percent to 18 percent; for Hispanic households the gap grew from 14 percent to 18 percent. Furthermore, wealthy classroom access nearly doubled that of poor classrooms. Currently, for wealthy schools the ratio is seven students per computer, while the national average is nine to one. Poor schools lag behind these averages.[4]

Another aspect of access is the preparation and competence of teachers. Many teachers (nearly two thirds) do not feel adequately prepared to use technology in their teaching. And, for many teachers, the introduction of a computer into their classroom has represented their first use of the machine.[5] One of the goals of this chapter is to provide learning tools to help you learn how to integrate the Internet into your instructional planning and teaching in ways that support inquiry-based learning and constructivism. My goal here is to increase your access to the Internet by showing you how it can be used in your classroom to support student learning and how it can be used to support your own professional development. The Web-based classroom can be a hub for learning, connecting you and your students to world.

INQUIRY ACTIVITY 12.1

 Designing Web-Based Science Activities

In this inquiry activity your task will be to explore the Web-based tools that follow and use one or more of them to design an Internet activity that you would use with a group of students.

Materials

- Access to the Internet
- Chart paper
- Making pens

Procedures

1. Identify an STS goal, a science inquiry goal, or science concept goal in a content area of your choice (astronomy, biology, chemistry, earth science, environmental science, physics). As you do this, think about how the Internet will enhance student understanding and attainment of the goal.
2. Review the Web-based tools in Table 12.1, using them as a guide for the type of Internet activity you will design. Note that you can make use of one or more Web-based tools in your activity.
3. Go online and preview some of the Web-based resources identified in the discussions of each Web-based tool.

Table 12.1 Web-Based Tools

Categories	Web-Based Tool	Student Experiences and Activities
Interpersonal Exchange Activity Structures	Key Pals in the context of the Global Classroom	Like pen pals, this structure links individuals or groups of students with each other to collaborate. Working with teachers who collaborate with other classrooms, students can use e-mail and Web sites to work together locally and globally.
	Online Discussions and Chats	Using bulletin boards and chat rooms, these interactions involve students in discussing issues and solving problems. These work very powerfully within a single classroom structure.
	Telementoring (Experts and Question-and-Answer Services)	This structure makes use of experts and people in the community to answer student inquiries and provide mentoring support. Useful for teachers too!
Information Collections and Resources	Pooled Data Analysis (Network Science)	In this structure, two or more classrooms at different sites coordinate the collection and pooling of data and information on some phenomena (acid rain, migration) or science-related social issue (bioterrorism, effects of drugs and alcohol).
	Tele-Field (Virtual) Trips	Tele-field trips enable you to plan online "field-trip" experiences using Web sites or planned projects (e.g., JASON Project).
Problem Solving and Social Action Activities	Net Publishing	Student experiences include integrating multimedia to create Web-based products.
	Social Action Projects	These activities involve students in taking action on an important social aspect of science or a science-related social issue.
	Virtual Classroom	A classroom offering or participating in an online course or experience using Web-based methods.

4. Design the Internet activity, basing it on one or more of the Web-based tools with specific goals, tasks, and outcomes.
5. Set a specific timeline for the students, with beginning and ending deadlines for the activity.
6. Present your ideas to your peers. You can do so by sketching your activity on a sheet of chart paper or presenting it as a Web page (which they can view from a projection or on computers). Use feedback from your presentation to make modifications in your activity.
7. Field-test your activity with a group of students (or peers). Evaluate your activity by designing a rubric that you can have the students use to give you feedback on the efficacy of the activity.

Minds-On Strategies

1. What role did technology play in your activity? Could you do the activity without technology? Would you want to?
2. What role did group learning play in your activity? How important was it for students to work together in teams, and was the success of the activity based on group collaboration?

First, we'll explore some important ways that the Internet can be used. You'll be introduced to eight powerful structures, each of which leads to a different pathway of experiences on the Internet for you and your students. Second, we'll explore some Web-based curriculum projects that focus on inquiry learning and social action, and provide models of how to use the Internet to get your students involved in local and global activity. Third, you'll find out how to design Internet activities and be introduced to wealth of resources to help you on your quest to achieve the dream of Berners-Lee.

Web-Based Tools

In this section you will be introduced to a collection of Web-based tools (see Table 12.1), any one of which will direct you and your students to a different set of resources on the Internet and therefore to different types of Internet activities. Note that I have divided the eight Web-based tools into three broad categories: interpersonal exchange activities, information collections and analysis activities, and problem-solving activities. There is no hierarchy implied here. Use your own preferences to explore and use them.

Interpersonal Exchange

Communicating with peers is a powerful use of the Internet for students and teachers. Interpersonal exchange activity structures use the Web to bring people together for sharing, asking questions, discussions, and problem solving.

KEY PALS AND GLOBAL CLASSROOMS The electronic equivalent of pen pals, key pals enables students to interact with others over the Internet. In the context of collaboration among two or more classrooms (locally, statewide, nationally, or globally), key pals is a method of structuring "talk" over the Net. In many instances teachers organize students into key pals groups, and thus use the group as the unit of collaboration. Each group can send e-mail directly to another group, or send their e-mail to a list. If many schools (more than five) are participating in collaboration, then it is advisable to use a list to send e-mail among the project participants. Otherwise, school-to-school collaboration can be effective. The following example shows an introductory e-mail letter from a group of Russian students to the Global Thinking Project list. The students were introducing themselves as part of the early stage of the project.

Hello!
We are the group of Russian students, which entered Global Thinking Project this Year. We go to Experimental Secondary School of Pushchino (the school number 2: we have 3 schools in Pushchino). Our school is the best one in Serpukhov district (that is true!), we have brilliant teachers and bright students.
We have fifteen students in our group, aged 12–14. Well, we actually are: Kulikov Dmitri, eighth

grade; Brykovskaya Nastya, eighth grade; Gayazova Daria, Stepanova Yulia, Mironenko Basil (the author of this text), Montrel Mikhail, Lantsov Andrei, Osmanov Buba, Tchernova Ekaterina, tenth grade; Zaplatin Aleksei, Goryatchev Dmitri, Ezhokina L., Krukov F., Trushkina M. ninth grade and Egorova M. eighth grade. Everybody likes to read (especially fantastic novels), watch TV (the greatest ivention through the ages!), play PC games. Many of us go to music school, some guys and girls are sports fans. There are history, biology, English, maths, and geography among our favorite subjects.

Our teachers, connected with GTP, are Bukina Tatyana Vasilievna, English teacher, and Martynova Elena Borisovna, biology teacher.

That is all I've got for this time. Good luck!

An example of a key pal activity is the environmental travel brochure. In this example students work on a project in which their team's task is to produce an ecologically oriented travel brochure to a distant location. To gather interesting and relevant information, students contact peers in the destination country and interview them to find out about the local environment. Another example is the equinox and solstice project, in which students measure the length of a shadow cast by a meter stick at noon local time. Students share their data (shadow length, latitude, and longitude). Done over the period of a school year, students can use the data to try and explain the varying lengths of shadows not only at their own location but also among the locations. A third example is a social issues activity, in which students exchange e-mail letters regarding their opinions on an important issue.

Key pal and global classroom resources you might want to explore include:

- *E-Pals Classroom Exchange* (http://www.epals. com/) brings educators together to participate in cross-cultural activities. The site is presented in eight languages.
- *The Global Schoolhouse* (http://www.gsn.org/) is one of the oldest sites dedicated to bringing students and teachers together worldwide to foster problem solving and social action.
- *Yahoo Groups* (http://groups.yahoo.com/) allows you to set up your own list or e-group that you can use for students in your classes, or you can invite others to join your online group. The list enables you to create an online community among your students.

ONLINE DISCUSSIONS AND CHATS Similar to key pals in the sense that students are encouraged to use writing to participate jointly in online activities, online discussions, and chats through Web-based bulletin boards and chat rooms. The bulletin board discussion is more practical because the discussions can take place asynchronously, whereas chat rooms require participants meet at a particular time in a chat room.

Bulletin boards can be used in a variety of ways to foster reflective writing, sharing of information, and as a means to cross cultural boundaries. For example, you can set up a bulletin board for your class and have students use it to participate in "within-class" discussions. In Chapter 11, I introduced the idea of conducting "online dilemma discussions" using a bulletin board. In this activity, the teacher proposes a science dilemma to the students and requests that they post initial responses to the dilemma and then reply to classmates online as they make their responses to the problem. In these online discussions the only participants are students in your class. The activity gives each student an opportunity to reflect upon an issue and then express ideas in writing that can be read publicly. Teachers who use this method have a follow-up discussion in class after giving students time to participate in an online discussion for at least a week.

Chat rooms, although more difficult to manage because of the requirement that participants meet at the same time, can be effective. Some teachers use chat sessions as "help sessions" for questions and answers or to discuss an assignment or topic.

TELEMENTORING—EXPERTS AND QUESTION-AND-ANSWER SERVICES Telementoring is a way to bring students in contact with people who can serve as mentors, provide expertise, and answer student questions. One way of making use of this Web tool is to create a task in which a group of students in your class interviews a person you have identified to serve as a mentor or an expert for your students. For example, if you are teaching a biology class, the assignment might be to find out how this person uses biology in his or her "line of work." After you have identified a list of experts and assigned them to respective groups in your class, each group needs to make contact via e-mail with its "expert" and conduct research through a series of e-mail interviews (no more than three). The information the students obtain from their expert can be used in a presentation to the entire class. (Refer to the "Ask an Expert" site listed later to access hundreds of experts on the net.)

Experts may be closer to your classroom than you think. Starting with the local community is a good way to bring your students in contact with human resources close to their homes. For example, you could do the "expert" activity by exclusively lining up people in your community. A more specific example is the college-students-as-mentors project. In this activity, a professor of geology wanted students in her undergraduate earth science class to mentor students in the middle school that was close to campus. After contacting the science department head at the middle school and collaborating with the earth science teachers at the school, the geology professor assigned each of her college students to a group of about four middle school students. The college student was used as an online mentor to help the students with a major earth science project. After using e-mail for the semester, the college professor arranged a "real" field trip to the middle school, enabling the middle schools students to meet their mentors.

Telementoring resources you might want to explore include:

- *Ask an Expert* (http://www.askanexpert.com/) provides access to hundreds of "experts" who have volunteered their time to answer questions.
- *Scientific American Ask the Experts* (http://www.sciam.com/askexpert/) provides access to current questions and answers as well an archive of previous questions in astronomy, biology, chemistry, computers, environment, geology, mathematics, medicine, and physics.

Information Collections and Resource Web Tools

These Web tools allow you to create two types of activities. In the first type (pooled data analysis), students collect and exchange information with other classrooms on topics organized by the teacher or on special projects or topics related to the ongoing curriculum. "Virtual" field trip activities are designed by collecting and organizing Web resources (Web pages, video, sound, music, images).

POOLED DATA ANALYSIS (NETWORK SCIENCE)
Pooled data analysis activities on the Internet have a long history, dating back to the 1980s. In this approach, students focus on real problems that are relevant to them and their community by asking questions and seeking answers by collecting real data. Through the process of inquiry and being connected to the Internet, students participate in a pooled data analysis project, oftentimes at a global level. Some teachers and researchers refer to

this kind of activity as "network science," implying that a community of practice in which students research, share, and analyze data is established over the network of the Internet. The pioneers of this approach saw network science as a valuable way to get students involved in STS projects, to articulate social constructivism in the context of real problems and issues, and to witness the application of new technologies to science education.[6]

Network science projects typically involve the following processes: A phenomenon is identified by either a project entity or agreed upon by collaborating schools. Phenomena could include the investigation of acid rain, amount of cloud coverage, bird migrations, ground-level ozone, road kills, native plants, stream or river investigations, daily minimum/maximum air temperatures, and so forth.

1. A *schedule of observations* and data sharing are established.
2. *Data is shared* either by e-mail or by means of Web forms that can be used to post data in a way that is accessible to all participating in the project. Web forms are the most typical way that pooled data analysis projects share data, especially when many schools are participating in the project.
3. Teachers at the local level work with students to *analyze the data* on the network. This typically involves printing the data (usually in the form of a data table), providing small groups of students with the data table, and then suggesting that students make graphs or charts to summarize the data.
4. The final step is for students to *take action* on their analyses. At one level, students can "publish" their findings and conclusions by posting them on a bulletin board, sending out e-mail to each collaborating school, or making a Web page available to project collaborators. At another level, students take action locally by sharing their findings and conclusions with the community by means of a conference, a presentation or fair at a local mall, or by sharing their findings with a local school.

Many teachers involve students in inquiry-based science teaching through pooled data analysis projects. These projects also can involve students in social action (STS) projects in which students investigate the impact of a science phenomenon (e.g., ground-level ozone) on society at the local level, but comparing their research among schools over the network.

Network science resources you might want to explore include:

- *TERC* (http://www.terc.edu/) provides access to the group that first developed network science activities. You will find examples of many network science projects.
- *Global Laboratory* (http://globallab.terc.edu/) introduces students to science as inquiry, engaging them in collaborative scientific investigations. It was one of the first network science projects and is described more fully in the next section of this chapter.
- *Project Pigeon Watch* (http://birds.cornell.edu/ppw/) is an international research project that involves people of all ages and locations in a real scientific endeavor. People participate by counting pigeons and recording courtship behaviors observed in their neighborhood pigeon flocks. Data is sent to the Cornell Lab of Ornithology by citizens from all over the world to find out why city pigeons exist in so many colors and what color mates choose pigeons.

VIRTUAL FIELD TRIPS Virtual field trips enable teachers to involve their students in experiences normally not available, by visiting museums or participating in field trips sponsored by a project or a notable scientist.

One approach is to design a project in which teams of students are assigned a science museum Web site to research and then create a multimedia or low-tech (three-panel poster board) presentation. Students are given a set of inquiry question that they use to guide their research and construct their presentation.

1. What is name and location of the museum visited?
2. What is the central focus of the museum? What is its mission? What are its goals? What kinds of virtual and real-time programs does it sponsor?
3. How does the museum contribute to the public's understanding of science and technology?
4. What is one exhibit that stood out, and how does it contribute to the public's understanding of science?
5. What are some of the most interesting resources at this site?
6. What is the best aspect of this site? Why do you think so?
7. How would rate this site? (World class, excellent, okay, needs improvements.)

Another type of virtual field trip is one in which students participate in a "live" virtual field trip, often sponsored by an organization, that might involve the research of scientists in the field or participation in observation studies, such as the tracking of migratory species.

Virtual field resources you might want to explore include:

- *Journey North* (http://www.learner.org/jnorth/) is a virtual field trip in which students and teachers track the journeys of a dozen migratory species.
- *The JASON Project* (http://www.jasonproject.org/) involves a yearlong curriculum that comes to life during an annual expedition. Each year, Dr. Ballard leads a team of scientists, students, and teachers on a two-week journey to explore and study in research locations featured in the curriculum. Satellite and Internet technologies bring students in classrooms around the world into direct, real-time contact with scientists and researchers as the expedition is happening. JASON expeditions have ventured to the Mediterranean Sea, the Great Lakes, the Galapagos Islands, the Sea of Cortez, Belize, Hawaii, the coral reefs of Florida's Keys, Yellowstone National Park, Iceland, Bermuda, Monterey Bay, the Peruvian rainforest, and NASA's Johnson Space Center in Houston, Texas.

Problem-Solving Web Tools

NET PUBLISHING Publishing on the Web is an important part of Web-based teaching. Now that it is easy to create Web pages and put them on the Web, students can publish the results of their work and teachers can use the Web pages to communicate with students and parents.

For teachers, having a Web site can provide a Web tool for organization of instruction, communication among students and parents, and publishing opportunities for students. More and more students already have their own Web site, and teachers can capitalize of their students' expertise to teach other students. Using the Web's publishing capacities is way for students to share their work in projects and activities, do reflective writing, design pages, write up experiments, publish digital collections (e.g., of rocks, minerals, and insects), and publish the results of research projects.

SOCIAL ACTION PROJECTS One powerful use of the Web is to involve students in STS projects. Social aspects of science and science-related social issues provide the basis for such activities. Social action projects can involve students in environmental issues related to endangered species; air, water, and soil pollution; population growth and sustainable development; and food, nutrition, poverty, and hunger.

Among the social action project resources you might want to explore include:

- *IEARN* (http://www.iearn.org), International Education and Resource Network, enables teachers and youth from around the world to use the Web to carry out projects in which "youth make a difference in the world." Teachers from South American countries, Africa, and Europe originate many of the projects.

THE VIRTUAL OR ONLINE CLASSROOM The virtual classroom can be used to teach courses entirely online or in hybrid form. Over the past several years, a number of local school districts, consortiums, and states have created their own virtual schools by offering courses through Internet or Web-based methods enabling them to teach courses entirely online.[7] According to one study, an estimated 40,000 to 50,000 students were enrolled in a virtual school course in the year 2002.[8] Virtual courses allow for interactive learning for any student at any time. Virtual courses have been developed for elementary, middle, and high school students. You might want to visit Virtual High School (http://www. govhs.org/website.nsf), one of the first virtual school projects, developed in collaboration between Hudson Public Schools, Massachusetts, and the Concord Consortium (http://www.concord.org).

For the individual teacher, however, the hybrid approach is a practical alternative in which the teacher combines online and face-to-face activities.[9] Thousands of teachers are using this approach by creating a Web site with aspects of the course syllabus, activities, projects, and evaluation, or by using one of several course management systems, such as Blackboard, Nicenet, or WebCT. Course mangement systems have built-in tools that create an interactive online component. Indeed, the course that you are taking might be organized as a hybrid course, with online and face-to-face activities. During your fieldwork experience, or if you are currently teaching, you might want to consider using a course management system to organize a unit of teaching or even an entire course.

Teachers use several methods in creating a hybrid course. One place to begin is to build a Web page with links to your syllabus, a bulletin board, and a calendar of assignments, activities, and student products. By building a Web site or using a course management system, you can use the resources of the Web as an assistant in your approach to teaching. This enables you to implement Web-based teaching strategies in a seamless manner. Your Web site becomes a hub that organizes the work of your course for your students. Many teachers make use of Web sites such as discoveryschool.com (http://school.discovery.com) that support online quiz systems to help students assess their progress. Table 12.2 presents a checklist you might use to begin building an online course.

Virtual classroom resources you might want to explore include:

- *Blackboard* (http://www.blackboard.com) is a robust course management system that allows you to place course materials on the Web.
- *Nicenet* (http://www.nicenet.org) is a free, very easy to use course management system. Nicenet includes such tools as conferencing (bulletin board), link sharing, documents, class schedule, and class members.
- *WebCT* (http://www.webct.com/) is course management system typically used at the university level.
- *Virtual High School* (http://www.govhs.org/ website.nsf) is a collaboration of participating high schools; for every semester, a participating school offers a VHS NetCourse and can enroll up to twenty students in VHS courses. Courses in many areas of the curriculum are offered online.
- *Quia* (http://www.quia.com/) provides tools to create educational games, activities, quizzes, surveys, and Web pages.
- *DiscoverySchool.com* (http://school.discovery. com/) offers tools to create and store online activities and includes links for teachers, students, and parents.

Telecommunications Projects and Science Inquiry

Telecommunications (network science) has had a profound impact on nearly all aspects of human communication, including the desire of educators to create environments in which school science can be presented in a global context. Yet schools have been slow to incorporate the Internet and, indeed, other technologies as integral aspects of classroom instruction. Recent research on the potential effects of telecommunications

Table 12.2 Checklist for Developing an Online Course

Content Area	Explanation
Basic Information	Course title, instructor's name, and semester information; include last revised date.
Contact Information	Course instructor's contact information.
Course Description	Description of the course as it would appear in a printed list of courses, but with more details.
Objectives	Make a list of course outcomes (i.e., what you expect the students to learn). Consult Chapter 6 for more details on writing objectives.
Texts and Materials	Include any books you are using in the course, as well as related texts, journals, and software.
Grading	Details of the grading criteria and components of the entire grade; list all quizzes, tests, homework, science log, lab experiments, projects, and so forth. You should also include the criteria for your grading procedures.
Organization of the Course	An explanation of how students are to use the Web site as an integral part of the course. Explain how the online component works and how it will help them with their progress in the class.
Schedule	You can be as detailed as you wish with the schedule, which should be organized week by week. Create a table that includes the science topics, assignments, readings, Web sites, quizzes, activities, and Web resources.
Policies	Any relevant school policies or ways you wish the students to make use of the Web.

on classroom learning has been mixed. For example, Dunkerly-Kolb and Hassard, Hassard, and Hassard and Weisberg found that environmental projects involving students from Russia and the United States affect students' and teachers' attitudes about the environment and result in authentic projects designed by students with teacher assistance. These researchers also reported that telecommunications (e-mail, e-mail mailing lists, bulletin boards, and Web sites) are powerful tools to augment student and teacher research.[10] Yet Fabos and Young, in a review of telecommunications projects in the classroom, argue that much of the current research of telecommunications exchanges is contradictory, inconclusive, and possibly misleading. They point out that technology-based projects are problematic in light of the larger, exceedingly complex role of technology in society.[11] In this section, we'll examine network science and see how it can be used in the science classroom.

Network Science Projects

In a major study of network science, Feldman, Konold and Coulter reported, "Our thinking has evolved during the four years of research leading to this volume. We are less convinced today that the Internet will provide an easy route to improved learning; we have come to believe that people-to-people connections and especially face-to-face communication play a central role in learning."[12] Despite their conclusion, the study provides important information regarding the nature of network

science projects and how they can contribute to some of the most important goals of science teaching. Furthermore, Feldman and colleagues offer suggestions for making network science projects more effective in the science classroom. We'll first take a look at the nature of network science projects, then examine the Global Lab: An Integrated Science Program, and, finally, we will find out how to use network science projects more effectively.

ATTRIBUTES OF NETWORK SCIENCE PROJECTS According to Feldman, Konold, and Coulter, network science emerged in the late 1980s and early 1990s, when the availability of desktop computers merged with the networked environment of the Internet. Feldman and colleagues attribute inquiry-based teaching and learning, the STS movement, U.S. reports urging reform, and the emerging thinking about the role of technology in education as the impetus for network science. Inquiry-based teaching and learning promoted the role of "student-as-scientist," but others realized that network science also involved students in social action or STS work, and soon the terms citizen-scientist and science and the citizen emerged.[13] The early development of network science projects, including KidsNet, Global Lab, and the Global Thinking Project, explored ways of using networked technologies that brought together students and teachers from schools in different parts of the world. These projects also based their

Table 12.3 Attributes of Network Science Projects

Network Science Attribute	Contribution of Attribute to Science Teaching
Investigation of "Real Science" and Science-Related Social Issues	Earlier network science projects had students focus on real and compelling problems that were relevant to their lives. More recent projects have incorporated STS approaches.
Students-as-Scientists	Students investigate problems not yet studied by scientists.
	Students learn scientific processes: framing investigative questions, conducting experiments, analyzing data, and sharing results.
Students-as-Citizen-Scientists	Students learn how to participate as "citizen scientists," people who not only know and study, but who care and take action on environmental issues.
The Role of Data Is Critical	Investigations require substantial data and the efforts of many investigators.
	Students learn to frame empirical questions related to the problems they studied and use the project data to answer them.
Constructivist Learning	A departure from traditional learning models; here students learn by constructing their own understandings.
Societal Implications of Science	Students explore the ways that science and society interact.
	Students advocate actions on the basis of what they learn.
Global Learning Community	Students learn about different cultures and different environments through telecommunications and collaboration with peers.
Cross-Cultural Understanding	Experience in these projects deepens students' understanding and empathy for people from different cultures.
Pedagogical Shifts	Because answers are not always known, teachers must give more attention to becoming the expert on how-to-know, rather the content expert.
	Teachers are active members of the community of practice, facilitating student learning and coaching them as they participate in the project.
Collaborative/Cooperative Learning	Investigations promote the idea that science learning is a cooperative venture and reflects communities of practice outside the school, such as what scientists do.
The Role of Technology	Critical to a successful project.
	Promotes collaboration and data sharing.
	Provides access to up-to-date information.
	Expansion of the classroom into the global community decreases isolation.

Source: Based on Feldman, A., Konold, C., and Coulter, B. *Network Science a Decade Later: The Internet and Classroom Learning.* Mahwah, N.J.: Lawrence Erlbaum Associates, 2000, pp. 6–7. Also see Hassard, J., and Weisberg, J. "The Emergence of Global Thinking among American and Russian Youth as a Contribution to Public Understanding." *International Journal of Science Education* 21, no. 7 (1999): 1–13.

pedagogical approaches on constructivism and designed curriculum materials that provided opportunities for students to make meaning out of their work locally and with their peers in distant locations.

Network science brought meaning to the concept of a community of learners and, because of the network, these communities were global in scope. It was this construct that created such high interest among teachers and students who were involved. The idea of communicating with students thousands of miles away motivated students and created intense interest with the school.[14]

Network science projects involve students in real problems, including the study of soil erosion, chemical and biological pollution of streams, acid rain, and ground-level ozone. Often, these problems have societal implications, and students take action based on their research. Network science is characterized by a number of attributes (Table 12.3) that make it a compelling approach to science teaching. Look over the list of attributes in Table 12.3 and determine how each contributes to students' participation and understanding of science. To provide deeper understanding of network science, read the following case study of the Global Laboratory Program, one of the first network science projects, as well as brief descriptions of other projects you may want to investigate.

Case Study: Global Lab

Global Lab (http://globallab.terc.edu/) was developed by TERC, a firm devoted to the development of mathematics, science, and technology programs for K–12 schools.[15] Global Lab was developed to reform science education through the implementation of experiential, student-based collaborative inquiry. The focus of the project was to promote the use of telecommunications, affordable scientific tools, and innovative curricula to create a *global* community of student researchers engaged in real world, hands-on investigation of *global* environments.[16]

Global Lab was designed as a secondary science project intended to achieve the following:

1. Use the tools of technology to enable students around the world to participate in global studies.
2. Use environmental studies as the theme to organize the content of Global Lab.
3. Develop students' research skills by encouraging them to work as real scientists.
4. Worldwide collaboration among students to design and conduct experiments, exchange data from their own experiments, and analyze the full set of data to answer questions of current scientific interest.

The curriculum of Global Lab consists of five units of teaching:

- Unit I: Becoming a Global Community
- Unit II: Investigating Our Earth: Land
- Unit III: Investigating Our Earth: Water
- Unit IV: Investigating Our Earth: Air
- Unit V: Extended Investigations

To provide a better sense of the content, let's look at one of the units of teaching. Unit II, Investigating Our Earth: Land, focuses on geological, physical and chemical, and biological characteristics of the student's terrestrial environment. Students conduct fieldwork at their study site and experiment with a biological model. The content is organized into four investigation areas: Investigation One—Investigating Continents (a global picture of earth's major land masses), Investigation Two—From Rocks to Soil (exploring the substances of earth, including rocks, minerals, and soil), Investigation Three—Soil Fertility (impact

of agriculture on human society by looking at soils, plant metabolism, and the carbon cycle), and Investigation Four—Energy at Your Study Site (examination of heat energy at the study site by exploring relationships between light and heat and between sun angle and light intensity).

Each unit is divided into a series of investigations. Some of the investigations take place in the classroom, but many involve student fieldwork at a "study site." Study sites may be an urban park, a green space, pond stream, or marsh near a school. In any event, the study site becomes the focus for students as they conduct their investigations. Data collected at the study site is shared with other schools in the project.

The Web tools developed for Global Lab allow students and teachers to easily generate and edit Web pages, enabling classes to publish, share, and peer review their findings—just like professional scientific communities. The Global Lab search engine and Listserv help students find other students with common interests (supporting collaborative work), as well as communicate with the entire Global Lab community. The online workspace permits students to upload their own data and download data collected by other Global Lab schools, allowing classes to place their local findings into global perspective. Table 12.4 summarizes the main features of the Global Lab program.

IMPLICATIONS FOR SCIENCE TEACHING Projects such as Global Lab have contributed to an understanding of how network science learning can be more fully understood and used in the classroom. In their study of three network science projects (in addition to Global Lab, they also reported on National Geographic Kids Network and Journey North), Feldman, Konold, and Coulter identified several key principles for utilizing the benefits of network science:[17]

1. The Internet should be used to broaden the context of locally grounded inquiry.
2. The classroom, not the online community, should be the primary learning environment.
3. Teachers and students should have multiple entry points for using the technology and the curriculum.
4. Students should be helped to find productive Internet resources.
5. The data the project produces should be used to deepen student inquiries.

Table 12.4 Main Features of the Global Lab Program

Attribute	Global Lab
Grade Level	8–12
Availability	Published by Kendall/Hunt
	Web site: http://globallab.terc.edu/
Project Structure	Full-year course with five units
	Curriculum begins with Becoming a Global Community and culminates with Extended Investigations (the conduct of authentic research)
Content	Interdisciplinary science with an environmental theme. Covers four science disciplines: biology, chemistry, earth science, and physics.
	Five units focus on learning (1) how to participate in a global community and do scientific research, (2) about the terrestrial environment, (3) about the relationship between water and the earth's biotic environments, (4) about the characteristics of air and the atmosphere, and (5) how to conduct authentic research.
Data Sharing	Data are submitted on the Internet using Web-based forms. Data are posted of the project Web site for retrieval by other classes.
Data Analysis Tools	Teachers choose software locally, such as a spreadsheet program.
Internet Use	Students' projects use Web resources to extend inquiry.
	Extensive use of Web-based collaboration, online publishing, and e-mail.

INQUIRY ACTIVITY 12.2

 Network Science—Exploring Online Projects

In this inquiry activity you are going to visit the Web sites of four network science projects to determine and evaluate their attributes. This activity can be done individually or as a group project.

Materials

- Access to the Web sites of the Global Thinking Project (http://www.gsu.edu/~www.gtp), GLOBE (http://www.globe.gov), Hands-On Universe (http://www.handsonuniverse.gov), and Journey North (http://www.learner.org/jnorth/)

Procedures

1. Use the chart in Figure 12.1 to determine the attributes of one or more of the four network science projects posted in the chart. You should visit the Web site and use any of the resources at the site to complete the chart and evaluate the project.
2. Share your findings with other members of your team or the class.

Minds-On Strategies

1. How do these projects contribute to the public's understanding of science?
2. In what ways do these projects make use of the science-as-inquiry theme and constructivism in their structure?
3. What is the role of technology in these projects? Could they be successful without technology? Why do you think so?

Attribute	Global Thinking Project	Globe	Hands-On Universe	Journey North
Grade Level				
Availability				
Structure				
Content				
Data Sharing				
Data Analysis Tools				
Internet Use				
Rating on a Scale of 1–5 (5 being outstanding)				

Figure 12.1 Network Science Analysis Chart. *Source:* The template for the chart is based on Feldman, A., Konold, C., and Coulter, B. *Network Science a Decade Later: The Internet and Classroom Learning.* Mahwah, N.J.: Lawrence Erlbaum Associates, 2000, pp. 28–29.

These principles are significant in that they focus on the local level, in which students work with their teachers to explore a topic relevant to them and their community. The principles also anchor the teacher in his or her classroom and lessen dependency on the online community for the success of the students' work. Explore some of the projects identified next and participate in Inquiry Activity 12.2.

OTHER NETWORK SCIENCE PROJECTS In this section, we present a selection other network science projects that you might want to investigate by visiting the program Web sites.

Global Thinking Project The GTP is a "hands across the globe" environmental education project that provides a paradigm for students and teachers to participate in environmental study and use new technology tools with peers around the world. The project, formed in 1989, emerged from collaboration among science educators from Georgia (U.S.A.) and Russia. GTP has sponsored teacher exchanges among six countries

(Australia, Czech Republic, Spain, Russia, and the United States) and student exchanges for more than 600 American and Russian youth. The project also supports an active program of educational research.

Hands-On Universe Hands-On Universe, located at the Lawrence Hall of Science, University of California at Berkeley, is an educational program than enables students to investigate the universe while applying tools and concepts from science, mathematics, and technology. Using the Internet, participants around the world request observations from an automated telescope, download images from a large image archive, and analyze them with the aid of user-friendly image processing software.

GLOBE GLOBE is a network of K–12 students, teachers, and scientists from around the world working together to help us learn about the environment. By participating in GLOBE, teachers guide their students through daily, weekly, and seasonal environmental observations, such as air temperature and precipitation. Using the Internet, students send their data to the Globe Student Data Archive. Scientists and other students use this data for their research.

Web-Based Science Activities for the Online Classroom

This section is designed to help to establish an online classroom by showing the elements you need to build one and demonstrating how to design individual and group online activities.

Establishing an Online Classroom

To create an online classroom you need to put your work (activities, resources, quizzes, and other supporting resources) online. Refer to Table 12.2 for a summary of the basic principles of an online class home page. These categories of activities and experiences could be used whether you were teaching the course entirely online or as a hybrid course, where you are also meeting with the students face to face. The online course home page will contain those elements that you think will facilitate learning in your classroom. As you develop your online class home page, include the following elements as links to start: course syllabus, course agenda, calendar of assignments, grading procedures, quizzes/tests, course hotlist, projects, and activities. You might also want to have a chat room, a place to link to student Web pages, and a collection of your lecture notes developed as interesting Web pages with links and graphics. If you use a course management system, such as Blackboard or Nicenet, it will have links and places for you place the elements of your site (such as your syllabus, bulletin board, activities, and so forth).

In the section that follows you will find tips on the development of activities for the online class. You will find further resources at the end of this chapter for developing your approach to using the online environment in science teaching.

Activities for the Web

USING WEB RESOURCES The Web contains an enormous collection of resources that can expand the quality of your course and bring students in contact with multimedia learning opportunities. One issue that teachers have reported is the lack of time available for students to actually work online. Thus it is important to streamline students' access to the Web and eliminate the need for students to search for resources (unless that is the purpose of the activity). It is advisable that you visit the sites you wish students to use and organize them so that students have easy access and know what is expected when they use the sites. Here are four suggestions for assembling resources for your students: develop a hotlist or a scrapbook, as well as design hunts and sampler activities. Table 12.5 outlines the elements of each of these approaches and shows how they can be used to facilitate student learning. Many teachers start by developing a hotlist, and have it prominently placed on their Web site. The list can be used as an open-ended resource for students and also as the basis for the development of activities using these resources.

There are a number of ways you can begin your work using these resources. In one middle school earth

Table 12.5 Strategies for Using Web Resources

	Hotlist	Scrapbook	Hunt	Sampler
Purpose	A collection of links related to your online course.	A collection of Internet sites organized around specific categories, such as photographs, maps, stories, facts, quotations, sound clips, videos, virtual reality tours.	To help students construct knowledge based on several inquiry questions and related sites.	Designed to affect the attitudes of students on a science topic.
Structure	The links should be organized into subcategories based on the content of your course.	Students make use of the collection to use the scraps to create a newsletter, a Web page, or a digital presentation.	The hunt is organized into inquiry questions, Web resources (pages, images, sounds), and the Big Question. The Big Question is designed to have students summarize what they learned into three to five statements.	Four or five Web sites are identified. For each site, two or three inquiry questions guide the students to explore the site. Students are asked to write a brief summary of what they learned.

Source: This structure is based on Filamentality, online at http://www.kn.pacbell.com/wired/fil/.

science class, the teacher organized the first hotlist of the year into different ways that earth science phenomena affect people and their communities, including earthquakes, hurricanes, floods, tornadoes, meteors, volcanoes, and tsunamis. For each topic she had located three sites. The teacher assigned each phenomenon to a group of four students and asked them to find out how the phenomenon affected communities and what people could do if they were faced with such a disaster. She also asked that each group find two additional Web sites that could be added to the hotlist and provide a one- or two-sentence description of the site. Activities like this add to the richness of the class and help students make meaning by structuring the way they investigate the Web.

WEBQUESTS WebQuests are inquiry-based activities in which most of the resources are located on the Internet. According to Dodge, WebQuests should focus on knowledge acquisition and integration, thus supporting a constructivist approach to learning.[18] WebQuests typically are designed around six organizational categories, including an introduction, a description of the task, a listing of the informational resources needed by the students, the process of how to accomplish the task, guidance, and a conclusion. At the WebQuest site, you will find training materials to help you construct WebQuests.

CONSTRUCTIVIST WEB-BASED ACTIVITIES One strategy that many teachers have found effective is to design Web-based activities using the constructivist theory of learning as a referent. Although there are many ways to go about this, the constructivist approach that has been used by many teachers.[19] The constructivist approach to using the Web encourages students to make meaning and synthesize ideas and construct their own knowledge, but within the context of a group. In this section we'll outline a specific process that you can use to design lessons that are correlated to your own curriculum, and supply Web site information for making use of the work of other teachers.

The "template" for a constructivist Web-based lesson has six components: introduction, invitation, exploration, explanation, take action, and conclusion. Table 12.6 outlines the components of a constructivist Web-based lesson. Sample Lesson 12.1 is an example of a constructivist Web-based lesson.

Table 12.6 Elements of a Constructivist Web-Based Lesson

Element	Function of Element	Potential Activities
Introduction	Short paragraph introducing the activity Setting the stage for further activity	You should include: Objectives Materials
Invitation	Finding out about students' prior knowledge about the concepts in the Web-based lesson	Provocative questions Demonstrations Brainstorm session Fuzzy situation
Exploration	An activity that will assist students in exploring the key concepts in the lesson	Data collection in connection with a pooled data analysis or network science project Internet information search Tele-field trip Groups explore a set of Web sites linked to inquiry questions Construct models based on Web site information
Explanation	Students work together to discuss new findings and explain their ideas to each other	Writing reports and posting them on a bulletin board Constructing a model and presenting to the class, or publishing on a Web site Designing an Internet activity based on initial research Participating in debates on the various theories and topics in the lesson
Take Action	An activity that will assist students in furthering their understanding; taking personal and/or social action on issues related to the content of the lesson	Finding and reporting on Web sites that demonstrate the key concepts in the lesson Presenting findings to another group in the community Publishing a Web site that outlines their work, and shows how social action can be taken on issues related to the content
Conclusion	A brief review of what you hoped the students would learn as a result of participating in the activity	Further questions to extend students' thinking A few additional Web sites that students could visit to extend their interest

SAMPLE LESSON 12.1

Mission to the BLUE PLANET: A Terrafirma Inquiry

Introduction

You are part of a team of planetary scientists and explorers contracted by a firm representing the OTHERWORLD, a planetary system from the star Alpha Centuri. Your team's task is to investigate various PHENOMENA that interest the Prime Scientific Society (PSS) of the OTHERWORLD. Your team should use Terrrafirma databases available on the World Wide Web. Your team will have to provide a written report to be submitted to the Prime Scientific Society Bulletin Board. You will also have to make presentation to a representative of the Prime Scientific Society.

Invitation

Imagine swooping into the solar system in a spaceship traveling at warp speed, headed toward what your astronomers have called the BLUE PLANET. They are very interested in having your team study the planet remotely. Your team is also required not to do any harm to the Blue Planet and its inhabitants and to be sure that you are not observed by the "intelligent" species inhabiting the planet. To ensure this, you have been traveling in the "Stealth" Spaceship X-38, the first known Stealth ship in the UNIVERSE. As you orbit the BLUE PLANET, look "down" on its surface and discuss your first impressions with your team. In a sentence or two, write a journal entry in your Stealth Log, numbered entry 777230915.

Exploration

Your team is going to remotely investigate impact craters and one of the other phenomena that you have contracted to study for the Prime Scientific Society (Table 12.7):

- impact craters
- quakes and cracks in the planet's surface
- radical temperature changes in the BIG OCEAN
- volcanoes
- cyclones (tornadoes or hurricanes)

1. You will find the materials to set up an impact crater research site in your spaceship. Use the materials and instructions located there to find how these features are formed on the BLUE PLANET and its major satellite, THE MOON. (*Materials include:* a small tray, flower, and small rocks.) Do this research first. Make sure that you make at least one digital photograph of your investigation and load it onto your workstation computer. Seek help if you are not sure how to do this, or how to copy images from the Internet.
2. Select one other phenomenon from the list to investigate after completing your impact crater research. Use the resources and database to provide the answers to the questions that the Prime Scientific Society wants answered.
3. You should file a brief report by sending it to the Prime Scientific Society on their Internet bulletin board.
4. Prepare a digital/low-technology report that will be presented to the other researchers and the Prime Scientific Society's representative. This means your team must download onto your "disk" one or more images to be used to answer the research questions.

Table 12.7 BLUE PLANET Phenomena Chart

Phenomenon	Task	Questions and Resources	BLUE PLANET Databases
Impact Craters	Find out what impact craters are how they form, and key features of such sites.	How do craters form? What are bolides? How does the mass of bolides affect the size and other features of impact craters?	Terrestrial Crater: http://www.solarviews.com/eng/tercrate.htm
Quakes and Cracks	Study the pattern of earthquakes on the BLUE PLANET and provide *visual data* explaining the extent of quaking on the planet.	What is the pattern of earthquakes on the BLUE PLANET? What is the extent of the database of earthquakes established by the intelligent life on the BLUE PLANET? How can the point of an earthquake be located? What can you say about the energy released by earthquakes?	Earthquake Information: Center: http://neic.usgs.gov Earthquake Search Catalog: http://guatergeo.borkeley.edu/cnss/catalog-search.html
Radical Temperature Changes in the BIG OCEAN	Compare and contrast these phenomena and report on the predicted affects of the BLUE PLANET's weather patterns.	What are these radical temperature changes? How do they appear to affect the weather on the BLUE PLANET? "Intelligent life" refers to these phenomena as El Niño and La Niña. Tell us how these are different. What seems to cause these differences? Provide a map view of each phenomenon.	La Niña Phenomenon: http://www.elnino.noaa.gov/lanina.html El Niño Phenomenon: http://www.elnino.noaa.gov
Volcanoes	Identify specific volcanoes and report on their activity, history, and implications for the planet. See a volcano erupting.	What is a volcano? Where are volcanoes located on the BLUE PLANET? What are the shape and structure of volcanoes? What impact do volcanic eruptions have on the environment of the BLUE PLANET? Provide maps and images of these phenomena.	Volcano World: http://volcano.und.nodak.edu Volcanoes Currently Erupting: http://volcano.und.nodak.edu/vwdocs/current_volcs/current.html
Hurricanes and Tornadoes	Find out how hurricanes and tornadoes form, their patterns, and potential impact on the BLUE PLANET.	What do these phenomena look like from your spaceship? What patterns seem to describe the behavior of hurricanes? Are these the same kind of phenomena as tornadoes? What can you tell us?	Hurricane Database: http://ww2010.atmos.uiuc.edu/guides/mtr/hurr/home.rxml Tornado Information Database: http://www.usatoday.com/weather/wtwisto.htm

Explanation

Discuss your findings among members of your subteam. What did you learn about the phenomena that you investigated? What does this tell you about the BLUE PLANET? Summarize your findings and prepare for a digital and poster report. Your poster report should be set up in the format shown in Figure 12.2.

Taking Action

How do your findings compare to other planets that your research team has investigated or knows about? What are some important things that you could tell the "intelligent" species on the BLUE PLANET about this phenomenon and how your knowledge could be used to improve the quality of life on the planet?

Task: Summary of Your Team's Task	
Key Questions	**Findings**

Figure 12.2 Phenomenon Analysis Chart.

Conclusion

It is my hope that you have learned some new things about the BLUE PLANET. You might continue your research by checking databases gathered by an earlier team that visited the BLUE PLANET and actually landed in Roswell, New Mexico. You might also tune into one of the BLUE PLANET's favorite TV shows, the *X-Files*. Do you recognize anyone in the show?

GUEST "SPEAKERS" The Web enables teachers to bring "speakers" into the classroom to interact with their students. You can do this through a question-and-answer format or through the use of online chat. If you use the question-and-answer format, one very effective way to do so is to set up a bulletin board linked to your Web site. The speaker can then open a discussion forum on the bulletin board. The speaker could post information in the form of text, or perhaps ask the students to look at some material on the Web (streaming video, a Web page, or a "speech"), and then engage the students in an asynchronous class discussion. The chat room format can also be an effective way to bring a guest speaker into your classroom. For example, if your students have been working on an environmental network science project studying the stream that runs through the school campus, you might want to invite an environmental scientist from the state environmental protection division for a chat-style question-and-answer session. You could also carry this out using video conferencing.

CROSS-CULTURAL EXCHANGES Students have a natural desire to find out about their peers, especially if they are from another country. Your participation in global projects offers the possibility of using the Web to foster communication among your students and a group of students from another country. If you do this, I recommend that you work with a teacher that you have "met" through your collaborative work in a network science project. You should work with the students to help them learn about the culture of the students with whom they will "exchange." Set up a collection of links on the country and have students find out about the geography of the country, the political system, the religions, customs, and interests of the people. You can use one of several formats, including e-mail exchange, a bulletin board, chat room, or video conferencing. The bulletin board is perhaps the most efficient in that is asynchronous and the postings are easily available to each cultural group.

Resources for designing online activities that you may want to explore include:

* *Filimentality* (http://www.kn.pacbell.com/wired/fil/) provides resources and templates to help you design hotlists, scrapbooks, hunts, and WebQuests.
* *The WebQuest Page* (http://webquest.sdsu.edu/webquest.html) provides the knowledge to develop WebQuests as well as access to more than a hundred WebQuests developed by teachers, K–12.

INQUIRY ACTIVITY 12.3

 Designing a Web-Based Science Activity

In this activity you will develop a Web-based activity using the stages shown in Table 12.6 and share your work by posting it on a Web site.

Materials

- Access to the Web
- Science texts
- Links to state standards and the *National Standards*

Procedures

1. Working with a small team of peers, identify goals from a science curriculum, science text, or from state or national standards to form the basis of a Web-based lesson.
2. Using the constructivist Web-based lesson plan format shown in Table 12.6, develop the activities for each of the stages. Use a chart like the one in Figure 12.3 to outline your thinking.
3. Present your Web-based lesson to a group of peers, or ask your peers to access lesson online to submit their evaluation and feedback.

Minds-On Strategies

1. What goals was your lesson based on? Was the Web essential in helping students achieve these goals?
2. What other technologies did your lesson use to help students achieve the goals of the plan?

Stage	Activity	Related Web Links
Introduction		
Invitation		
Exploration		
Explanation		
Take Action		
Conclusion		

Figure 12.3 Constructing a Web-based Lesson.

SECTION 2: SCIENCE TEACHER GAZETTE

Volume 12: The Internet: Moving toward Web-Based Learning Environments

Think Pieces

1. What are the fundamental differences between interpersonal exchange activities and information collections and analyses as ways of using the Internet?
2. What would be your rationale for using an electronic bulletin board in your classroom with middle school students?
3. Make a list of the benefits and drawbacks of moving toward an online teaching environment. Where do you stand with regard to the value of online learning for the secondary science classroom?
4. How can the Web and related technology support student inquiry? Is the effort required justified?
5. What can be done to overcome the gap in technology usage that exists between students from poor families and students from wealthy families?
6. What do you think is the value of network science projects?
7. How would you use the concept of an online classroom to enhance your beliefs about science teaching and learning?

Science Teachers Talk

"How do you use technology (including the Internet) in your science lessons? Why do you, and what do you see as the benefits for your students?"

RACHEL ZGONC: I am fortunate to have had the opportunity this year to teach both high school and junior high students. At the beginning of the school year, I spent quite a bit of time considering how I could incorporate technology into my high school classroom, but neglected my junior high classrooms on the technology front. I am not sure if I thought that the junior high students were not ready for technology or if I thought it would be too much of a challenge my first year, but whatever my reasoning, I was wrong. The one technology-based project that I did with my junior high students this year was a PowerPoint presentation on an extinct species. Each student was required to research their species using the Internet, create a PowerPoint presentation on their species, and present their findings to the class. The students absolutely loved this project! It took such little effort on my part and they got so much out of it. In order to introduce them to PowerPoint, I had one of the computer teachers give them a brief introduction and that is all they needed. They were off and running. Needless to say, many of the students did not even need that introduction and some of the students were way ahead of me techno-

logically. I often have to remind myself that these students have been using computers since they were babies. While I may not be completely comfortable with technology yet, most of them are and I need to take advantage of their aptitude and learn from them. The presentations turned out beautifully. The students presented their findings on a Smart Board Interactive White Board, which was a new piece of technology for all of them. The project was such a success that I will never hesitate to incorporate technology into my junior high classroom again. As for my high school class, I have incorporated technology into the classroom in several ways, but not nearly as much as I could have in an A.P. environmental science classroom. This is one of my main goals for next year. This year, we sampled Nancy Creek, which runs through our campus, using dissolved oxygen and pH probes. It is my opinion that when students use technology for this purpose, they should also be required to learn how to collect these measurements using traditional means. I believe that technology can sometimes hinder learning when used independently of traditional methods. For example, whenever I ask my students to graph something, they immediately whip out their TI-80 graphing calculators. While I do not discourage the use of such tools (because I do think they are invaluable tools that can enable students to do much more than they could do by hand), I do require that they demonstrate their graphing skills and not rely solely on this technology for the answer. Technology can be an amazing tool. It can allow teachers, especially science teaches, to do more than they could ever dream of doing without technology. However, one of my university professors once pointed out a philosophy that I try to always follow: Technology is only an invaluable tool if used when appropriate. I believe this should be the cardinal rule in the classroom when deciding how and when to use technology.

BEN BOZA (BOTSWANA): The use of technology in the teaching of science in my school has become more prominent than just a few years ago. The rapid developments taking place in diverse areas of technology generally, and more specifically in the digital front, have made available new ways of incorporating some of the appropriate technology in the teaching of science. The most significant utilization has come from Internet technology, through which a collaborative approach to teaching and learning that facilitates both research and reference has been made more convenient.

In using the Internet, I allow students the opportunity to sample scientific works of relevant lessons we deal in, access chat boards that discuss scientific topics that we cover in our syllabi, and, most importantly, have them be part of the wider scientific body outside our school enclosure. This process has enabled students to carve an identity for themselves and cultivate a sense of belonging to the scientific community. Not only do they benefit from the resourcefulness of this technology, but it also triggers inquisitiveness in them, which is vital in an inquiry approach to teaching.

The other area of technology that I frequently make use of in teaching is the utilization of CD materials on computers. With their multimedia capability, CDROMs provide for textual, audio, and visual presentation to students. At their own pace, students are able to learn and understand scientific concepts in a manageable way. I also make use of projected videos on the big screen to allow for illustrative and visual presentation on selected topics as well as use of projected transparencies.

One interesting use of technological utilization that I began using recently is to collaborate with a local TV station together with five other local schools for a unique teaching setup whereby lessons, conducted by respected scientists, are beamed into science classrooms from the neighboring country (South Africa) through a cable-like TV feed at arranged times. Students are able to participate in the lessons through use of a call-in line to ask questions and make comments pertaining to the day's lessons. This approach has generated a high level of interest in students, thus capturing their attention and creating more interest in science subjects. With such a positive attitude toward science subjects, it has become easier for students to become receptive of the new scientific knowledge offered in the classroom.

Generally, the utilization of technology in the teaching of sciences has had a significant impact on improving the effectiveness of the teaching process. This has occured through, stimulating student interest in science subjects. In a society like ours, whereby most students have traditionally perceived science subjects as difficult and boring, the new approach has become successful in making students realize that learning science can be exciting and fun. This new way of thinking among my students has resulted in improvement in their academic performances in science. The quality of the learning process has been raised tangibly and the my objectives of incorporating technology into science lessons are being met.

ANNA MORTON: I find technology, especially the Internet, to be an exceptional educational tool. I use the Internet to establish a classroom climate of research. My students often engage in projects that require them to research a particular topic, such as endangered species or genetics. Students have access to vast library from prominent research institutions. Some of these sites are interactive and allow students to test what they have learned. Some of my students find dissecting a horrible experience; therefore, using the Internet dampens that horror and students experience dissection through visual imaging. The virtual frog dissection has proven to be a rewarding experience for my students. The Internet also increases the desire to learn and motivates my students. Because the multimedia nature of the Internet engages my students, which results in their becoming more interested in the topic, this leads to students asking more questions and engaging in intense class discussions.

Technology is not limited to the use of the Internet. My students often construct brochures and PowerPoint presentations to demonstrate their understanding of the content. My students also write letters using word processing programs to express themselves to their families and friends about what they are learning. The use of laboratory equipment, which is also technology (i.e., microscopes and oscilloscopes), affords students the opportunity to begin to develop some of the behaviors of scientists. Students begin to think as scientists, in their pursuit of knowledge and understanding, through the use of technology.

CAROL MYRONUK (CANADA): Technology and science lessons consist of a mix of components, including optical (hand lens, microscopes, overhead projector, SLR and digital cameras), audio (tape recorder, CDs), multimedia (videos, verbal-visual displays, CD ROMs), computer (CAI, templates, key visuals, databases, spreadsheets, data analysis displays), and the Internet (Web site searches, real-time communication, virtual labs/explorations/museums). These technologies allow our students to develop practical skills in using tools of science, data management, and communication systems during the process of inquiry. Acquiring skills builds students' confidence in their problem-solving abilities and nurtures social responsibility in ethical research and practice as global citizens contributing to the world's scientific knowledge.

BARRY PLANT (AUSTRALIA): I use what we call ICT (information and communication technologies) extensively in the science classroom. A student in my class will research ideas and information using an electronic-based resource such as the Internet, plan experiments using simulation programs, record experimental results using data loggers, analyze data using a spreadsheet program or a graphical calculator, and report using word processing or electronic presentations.

I have found the use of simulation programs to be an excellent way of allowing students to explore ideas and experiment without some of the dangers or ethical concerns associated with more typical laboratory activities. Students can test an electronic circuit using a computer-based simulation program before connecting one using real materials.

Ready access to the Internet through a cluster of computers attached to the rear of my main teaching room has provided my students with extra dimensions to the learning process. We can visit locations, explore information collections, research social concerns, communicate with others, and the list goes on.

MICHAEL O'BRIEN: Since 60 to 65 percent of my classroom activities are labs, and most of them use computer interfaces to function, I am using technology every day. I also construct Internet-based lessons. In using the computer-based labs, the students gain time for exploring concepts and ideas because a lot of the data capture is automated. Most of my students are computer literate, so they often find creative and effective ways to manipulate data for presentation purposes. In other words, technology gives students more time to be creative in presenting their results without the extra time required to use manual manipulation techniques.

The students use the Internet for research on projects I assign during the year. They find this useful, but I also require them to use materials other than the Internet for their projects. Internet-based lessons are useful in a number of ways. They are easily constructed and easily edited. The students enjoy doing the lessons, either as a group or individually.

TOM BROWN: We use technology in our classroom for a variety of purposes. First of all, we have class Web site that provides a vehicle for communicating with students and parents in an efficient and engaging manner. Among other things, the Web site includes an overview of the class, various Web-based lessons, a bulletin board for students to voice their opinions, and a list of useful science links.

The Web-based lessons provide opportunities for small groups of students to explore topics such as cloning, ecological footprints, and ozone problems in Atlanta. The bulletin board (www.nicenet.org) provides an opportunity for each student to voice his or her opinions about these (and other) issues in a nonthreatening manner. I have found that many students who are reluctant to share their ideas verbally will write thoughtful and compelling exposes outlining their perspectives. Through this online conversation and discussion with their peers, students express, critique, and listen to each other in ways that facilitate their growth as responsible members of our society.

Problems and Extensions

1. Prepare a Web-based lesson using one of the following Web-based tools: key pals, online discussions, chat, telementoring, pooled data analysis, virtual field trip or social action project. Include the goals for the lesson and how students would be active learners in the lesson.
2. Discuss the implications of using the Web to make your teaching environment a "global classroom." What do you think will be the outcomes and benefits for your students and colleagues?
3. Locate a science museum on the Web and design a virtual field trip using the museum as the basis for your project.
4. Design a pooled data analysis project for a group of middle or high school students in any content area of science. Visit some of the examples of pooled data analysis projects identified in the chapter. After studying these projects, outline a new project by working with a group of peers. Share the project by putting it on the Web and presenting it to a group of peers.
5. Discuss the implications (pro and con) of involving students in online social action projects. How can social action projects contribute to students' understanding of science?
6. Sketch out on newsprint the elements you would include on an online course Web site. Assume you would use this site with the students you are currently teaching or with a group that you would teach in an internship environment.

Notes

1. Web-Based Education Commission, *The Power of the Internet for Learning: Moving from Promise to Practice* (Washington, D.C.: Web-Based Education Commission, 2000).

2. T. Berners-Lee, *Weaving the Web: The Past, Present, and Future of the World Wide Web by Its Inventor* (London: Orion Business Books, 1999).

3. Web-Based Education Commission, *The Power of the Internet*, p. 25.

4. Ibid., p. 27.

5. Ibid., p. 39.

6. For a full analysis of Network Science, see A. Feldman, C. Konold and B. Coulter, *Network Science a Decade Later: The Internet and Classroom Learning* (Mahwah, N.J.: Lawrence Erlbaum Associates, 2000).

7. T. Clark, *Virtual Schools: Trends and Issues— A Study of Virtual Schools in the United States* (Macomb, Ill.: WestEd, 2001).

8. Ibid.

9. S. Ko and S. Rossen, *Teaching Online: A Practical Guide* (Boston: Houghton Mifflin, 2001), p. 10.

10. See S. Dunkerly-Kolb and J. Hassard, "Citizen Scientists: Student Experiences in the GTP—Georgia/ Russia Exchange Project," *Journal of Science Education and Technology* 6, no. 4 (1997): 315–21; J. Hassard, "Teaching Students to Think Globally," *Journal of Humanistic Psychology* 37, no. 1 (1997): 24–63; and J. Hassard and J. Weisberg, "The Emergence of Global Thinking among American and Russian Youth As a Contribution to Public Understanding," *International Journal of Science Education* 21, no. 7 (1999): 1–13.

11. B. Fabos and M. D. Young, "Telecommunications in the Classroom: Rhetoric versus Reality," *Review of Educational Research* 69, no. 3 (1999): 217–59.

12. Feldman, Konold and Coulter, *Network Science a Decade Later*, p. 132.

13. See Dunkerly-Kolb and Hassard, "Citizen Scientists"; and R. T. Cross and P. J. Fensham, *Science and the Citizen* (Fitzroy, Australia: Arena Publications, 2000).

14. J. W. Robinson, "The Effects of the Global Thinking Project on Middle School Students' Attitudes Toward the Environment" (Ph.D. diss., Georgia State University, Atlanta, 1996).

15. Kendall/Hunt Publishing Company publishes Global Lab. You find additional information on Global Lab at the Kendall/Hunt Web site: http://www.kendallhunt.com. At the site, click on K–12, then Middle School, and you will find a link to Global Lab.

16. Boris Berenfeld, "Technology and the New Model of Science Education: The Global Lab Experience," *Machine-Mediated Learning* 4, no. 2–3 (1994): 203–27.

17. Feldman, Konold, and Coulter, *Network Science a Decade Later*.

18. B. Dodge developed the concept of a WebQuest. See the WebQuest site at http://webquest.sdsu.edu/webquest.html.

19. Jack Hassard, *Using the Internet As an Effective Science Teaching Tool* (Bellevue, Wash.: The Bureau of Education and Research, 2000), pp. 205–10.

Readings

Berners-Lee, T. *Weaving the Web: The Past, Present, and Future of the World Wide Web by Its Inventor*. London: Orion Business Books, 1999.

Bodzin, Alec M., and Cates, Ward Mitchell. "Inquiry Dot Com: Web-Based Activities Promote Scientific Inquiry Learning." *The Science Teacher* 69, no. 9 (2002): 48–52.

Bombaugh, Ruth, Sparrow, Elena, and Mal, Tarun. "Using GLOBE's Plant Phenology to Monitor the Growing Season." *Science Scope* (March 2003): 20–23.

Brooks, David. *Web-Teaching: A Guide to Designing Interactive Teaching for the World Wide Web.* New York: Plenum Press, 1997.

Cohen, Karen C. *Internet Links for Science Education: Student-Scientist Partnerships.* New York: Plenum Press, 1997.

Dodge, B. *Some Thoughts about Webquests.* Online: http://edweb.sdsu.edu/courses/edtec596/about_webquests.html

Feldman, A., Konold, C., and Coulter, B. *Network Science a Decade Later: The Internet and Classroom Learning.* Mahwah, N.J.: Lawrence Erlbaum Associates, 2000.

Harrell, John, Christmann, Edwin, and Lehman, Jeffrey. "Technology-Based Planetary Exploration," *Science Scope* (January 2002): 8–11.

Lucking, Robert A., and Christmann, Edwin P. "Science Research on the Internet." *Science Scope* (February 2003): 48–52.

Marcum-Dietrich, and Ford, Danielle. "The Tools of Science." *The Science Teacher* 70, no. 2 (2003): 48–51.

Munson, Bruce H., et al. "Field Trips Online." *The Science Teacher* 70, no. 1 (2003): 44–49.

Sterling, Donna R., "Science on the Web: Exploring Hurricane Data." *Science Scope* (March 2002): 86–90.

Sumrall, William J., Chessin, Debby, and Schillinger, Don, "Investigating Science Careers Online." *The Science Teacher* 70, no. 9 (2001): 74–78.

Tapscott, Don. *Growing Up Digital: The Rise of the Net Generation.* New York: McGraw Hill, 1998.

On the Web

CERES Astronomy Education: http://btc.montana.edu/ceres/. This Web site contains a collection of astronomy activities, as well a library of online and interactive science teaching materials.

Education Week on the Web: http://www.edweek.org/. This site will help you keep up to date on education and educational technology and Internet issues.

Explorer: http://explorer.scrtec.org/explorer/. This is a collection of resources, including software, lab activities, lesson plans, and teaching materials for K–12 math and science education.

Microsoft Anytime, Anywhere Learning: http://www.microsoft.com/education/aal/default.asp. This site provides a comprehensive approach to software and hardware solutions.

National Science Teachers Association: http://www.nsta.org/. This link shows an extensive collection of resources for many science topics, K–12.

Visionlearning: http://www.visionlearning.com/. Visionlearning provides free, award-winning instructional lessons in modular form. This allows instructors to link together the lessons of their choice with personal Web pages, such as a course home page or syllabus page.

Science Curriculum Developers

Activities Integrating Math and Science (AIMS)
Education Foundation
1595 S. Chestnut Avenue
Fresno, CA 93702
http://www.aimsedu.org

Biological Science Curriculum Study
Pikes Peak Research Park
5415 Mark Dabling Blvd.
Colorado Springs, CO 80918
http://www.bscs.org

Concord Consortium
10 Concord Crossing, Suite 300
Concord, MA 01742
http://www.concord.org

Educational Development Center, Inc.
55 Chapel Street
Newton, MA 02158
http://www.edc.org

Lawrence Hall of Science
University of California
Centennial Drive
Berkeley, CA 94720
http://www.lhs.berkeley.edu

TERC
2067 Massachusetts Avenue
Cambridge, MA 02140
http://www.terc.edu

Professional Societies and Organizations

Accelerated Schools Project
Stanford University
CERAS 109
Stanford, CA 94309
http://www.acceleratedschools.net/

American Association of Physics Teachers
One Physics Ellipse
College Park, MD 20740
http://www.aapt.org

American Chemical Society
1155 16th Street, N.W.
Washington, DC 20036
http://www.acs.org

American Geological Institute
4220 King Street
Alexandria, VA 22302
http://www.agiweb.org

American Indian Science and Engineering Society
5661 Airport Blvd.
Boulder, CO 80301
http://www.aises.org

The Coalition of Essential Schools
Box 1969
Brown University
Providence, RI 02912
http://www.essentialschools.org

Comer School Development Program
53 College Street
New Haven, CT 06510
http://info.med.yale.edu/comer/

Council for Exceptional Children
1920 Association Drive
Reston, VA 22091
http://www.cec.sped.org/

Council of Great City Schools
1301 Pennsylvania Avenue, N.W., Suite 702
Washington, DC 20004
http://www.cgcs.org

Dwight D. Eisenhower Mathematics and Science
Education Program
U.S. Department of Education
55 New Jersey Avenue, N.W.
Washington, DC 20208
http://www.enc.org

International Technology Education Association
1914 Association Drive
Reston, VA 22091
http://www.iteawww.org

National Academy of Sciences
2101 Constitution Avenue, N.W.
Washington, DC 20418
http://www.nas.edu

National Action Council for Minorities in Engineering
3 West 35th Street
New York, NY 10001
http://www.nacme.org

National Assessment of Educational Progress
P.O. Box 6710
Princeton, NJ 08541
http://www.ccsso.org/projects/National_Assessment_of_
Educational_Progress/

National Association of Biology Teachers
11250 Roger Bacon Drive, No. 19
Reston, VA 22090
http://www.nabt.org

National Association of Geology Teachers
Department of Geology
Western Washington University
Bellingham, WA 98225
http://oldsci.eiu.edu/geology/NAGT/NAGT.html

National Association for Research in Science Teaching
http://www2.edu.sfu.ca/narstsite/

National Center for Improving Science Education
2000 L Street, N.W., Suite 603
Washington, DC 20036
http://www.wested.org/

National Earth Science Teachers Association
American Geophysical Union
2000 Florida Avenue, N.W.
Washington, DC 20009
http://www.nestanet.org

National Science Resources Center
Smithsonian Institution
MRC 50–2
Washington, DC 20560
http://www.si.edu/nsrc

National Science Teachers Association
1840 Wilson Blvd.
Arlington, VA 22201
http://www.nsta.org

Office of Science and Technology Policy
Old Executive Office Building
17th and Pennsylvania Avenue, N.W.
Washington, DC 20500
http://www.ostp.gov

Triangle Coalition for Science and Technology
Education
5112 Berwyn Road
College Park, MD 20740
http://www.triangle-coalition.org

Science Equipment and Computer Software Suppliers

Apple Computer, Inc.
20525 Mariani Avenue
Cupertino, CA 95014
http://www.apple.com

Carolina Biological Supply Co.
2700 York Road
Burlington, NC 27215
http://www.carolina.com/

Delta Education, Inc.
80 Northwest Blvd.
P.O. Box 3000
Hudson, NH 03061
http://www.delta-education.com/

Fisher Scientific
4901 W. LeMoyne Street
Chicago, IL 60651
https://www.fisherscientific.com

Flinn Scientific, Inc.
131 Flinn Street
P.O. Box 219
Batavia, Il 65010
http://www.flinnsci.com/

Forestry Suppliers
205 West Rankin Street
P.O. Box 8397
Jackson, MS 39284
http://www.forestry-suppliers.com/

IBM
Department CF1
101 Paragon Drive
Montvale, NJ 07645
http://www.ibm.com

Science Kit and Boreal Laboratories
777 East Park Drive
Tonawanda, NY 14150
http://www.sciencekit.com/

Sunburst Communications
101 Castleton Street
Suite 201
Pleasantville, NY 10570
http://www.sunburst.com/

Wards National Science Establishment, Inc.
5100 West Henrietta Rd.
P.O. Box 92912
Rochester, NY 14692
http://www.wardsci.com/

INDEX